ACCA

STUDY TEXT

FINANCIAL REPORTING (FR)

FOR EXAMS IN SEPTEMBER 2018, DECEMBER 2018, MARCH 2019 AND JUNE 2019

BPP
LEARNING MEDIA

First edition 2007
Eleventh edition January 2018

ISBN 9781 5097 1678 4
(Previous ISBN 9781 5097 0853 6)

e-ISBN 9781 5097 1708 8

British Library Cataloguing-in-Publication Data

A catalogue record for this book
is available from the British Library

Published by

BPP Learning Media Ltd
BPP House, Aldine Place
142-144 Uxbridge Road
London W12 8AA

www.bpp.com/learningmedia

Printed in the United Kingdom

Your learning materials, published by BPP Learning Media
Ltd, are printed on paper obtained from traceable sustainable
sources.

We are grateful to the Association of Chartered Certified
Accountants for permission to reproduce past examination
questions. The suggested solutions in the practice answer bank
have been prepared by BPP Learning Media Ltd, unless
otherwise stated.

BPP Learning Media is grateful to the IASB for permission to
reproduce extracts from the International Financial Reporting
Standards including all International Accounting Standards, SIC
and IFRIC Interpretations (the Standards). The Standards
together with their accompanying documents are issued by:

The International Accounting Standards Board (IASB) 30
Cannon Street, London, EC4M 6XH, United Kingdom. Email:
info@ifrs.org Web: www.ifrs.org

Disclaimer: The IASB, the International Financial Reporting
Standards (IFRS) Foundation, the authors and the publishers do
not accept responsibility for any loss caused by acting or
refraining from acting in reliance on the material in this
publication, whether such loss is caused by negligence or
otherwise to the maximum extent permitted by law.

Contents

Helping you to pass

As an ACCA **Approved Content Provider**, BPP Learning Media gives you the **opportunity** to use study materials reviewed by the ACCA examining team. By incorporating the examining team's comments and suggestions regarding the depth and breadth of syllabus coverage, the BPP Learning Media Study Text provides excellent, **ACCA-approved** support for your studies.

These materials are reviewed by the ACCA examining team. The objective of the review is to ensure that the material properly covers the syllabus and study guide outcomes, used by the examining team in setting the exams, in the appropriate breadth and depth. The review does not ensure that every eventuality, combination or application of examinable topics is addressed by the ACCA Approved Content. Nor does the review comprise a detailed technical check of the content as the Approved Content Provider has its own quality assurance processes in place in this respect.

The PER alert

Before you can qualify as an ACCA member, you not only have to pass all your exams but also fulfil a three year **practical experience requirement** (PER). To help you to recognise areas of the syllabus that you might be able to apply in the workplace to achieve different performance objectives, we have introduced the 'PER alert' feature. You will find this feature throughout the Study Text to remind you that what you are **learning to pass** your ACCA exams is **equally useful to the fulfilment of the PER requirement**.

Your achievement of the PER should now be recorded in your online *My Experience* record.

Tackling studying

Studying can be a daunting prospect, particularly when you have lots of other commitments. The **different features** of the Study Text, the **purposes** of which are explained fully on the **Chapter features** page, will help you whilst studying and improve your chances of **exam success**.

Developing exam awareness

Our Study Texts are completely **focused** on helping you pass your exam.

Our advice on **Studying Financial Reporting (FR)** outlines the **content** of the paper, the **necessary skills** you are expected to be able to demonstrate and any **brought forward knowledge** you are expected to have.

Exam focus points are included within the chapters to highlight when and how specific topics were examined, or how they might be examined in the future.

Exam references are provided to the September 2016 and December 2016 full exams. Subsequently, only a selection of constructed response questions (CRQ) were released by ACCA. Exam references post December 2016 do represent a full exam; the reference should be taken as a guide. BPP Learning Media and ACCA do not advocate question spotting.

Testing what you can do

Testing yourself helps you develop the skills you need to pass the exam and also confirms that you can recall what you have learnt.

We include **Questions** – lots of them – both within chapters and in the **Practice Question Bank**, as well as **Quick Quizzes** at the end of each chapter to test your knowledge of the chapter content.

Chapter features

Each chapter contains a number of helpful features to guide you through each topic.

Topic list

Topic list	Syllabus reference

Tells you what you will be studying in this chapter and the relevant section numbers, together with ACCA syllabus references.

Introduction

Puts the chapter content in the context of the syllabus as a whole.

Study Guide

Links the chapter content with ACCA guidance.

Exam Guide

Highlights how examinable the chapter content is likely to be and the ways in which it could be examined.

 FAST FORWARD

Summarises the content of main chapter headings, allowing you to preview and review each section easily.

Examples

Demonstrate how to apply key knowledge and techniques.

Key terms

Definitions of important concepts that can often earn you easy marks in exams.

Exam focus points

Tell you when and how specific topics were examined, or how they may be examined in the future.

Formula to learn

Formulae that are not given in the exam but which have to be learnt.

 PER alert

Gives you a useful indication of syllabus areas that closely relate to performance objectives in your Practical Experience Requirement (PER).

 Question

Give you essential practice of techniques covered in the chapter.

Chapter Roundup

A full list of the Fast Forwards included in the chapter, providing an easy source of review.

Quick Quiz

A quick test of your knowledge of the main topics in the chapter.

Practice Question Bank

Found at the back of the Study Text with more comprehensive chapter questions. Cross referenced for easy navigation.

1 Studying FR

Financial Reporting (FR) is a demanding paper covering all the fundamentals of financial reporting. It has five main sections:

1   The conceptual framework of accounting
2   The regulatory framework
3   Preparation of financial statements which conform with IFRS
4   Preparation of consolidated financial statements
5   Analysis and interpretation of financial statements

All of these areas will be tested to some degree at each sitting. Sections 3, 4 and 5 are the main areas of application and you must be able to analyse and produce financial statements of both single entities and groups in your exam.

Some of this material you will have covered at lower level papers. You should already be familiar with accounting for inventories and non-current assets and preparing simple statements of profit or loss, statements of financial position and statements of cash flows. You should know the basic ratios.

Financial Reporting advances your Financial Accounting knowledge and skills. New Financial Reporting topics include the analysis of consolidated financial statements, contracts where performance obligations are satisfied over a period of time, biological assets, financial instruments, leases and foreign currency. There is also coverage of creative accounting and the limitations of financial statements and ratios. The new leasing standard, IFRS 16, is examinable from the September 2017 sitting.

If you had exemptions from lower level papers or feel that your knowledge of lower level financial reporting is not good enough, you may want to get a copy of the Study Text for *Financial Accounting (FA)* and read through it, or at least have it to refer to. You have a lot of new material to learn for Financial Reporting and basic financial accounting will be assumed knowledge.

The way to pass Financial Reporting is by practising lots of exam-level questions, which you will do when you get onto revision. Only by practising questions do you get a feel for what you will have to do in the exam. Also, topics which you find hard to understand in the Study Text will be much easier to grasp when you have encountered them in a few questions. So don't get bogged down in any area of the Study Text. Just keep going and a lot of things you find difficult will make more sense when you see how they appear in an exam question.

2 The exam paper

Computer-based exams

ACCA have commenced the launch of computer-based exams (CBEs) for this exam. They have been piloting computer-based exams in limited markets since September 2016 with the aim of rolling out into all markets internationally over a five-year period. Paper-based examinations will be run in parallel while the CBEs are phased in and BPP materials have been designed to support you, whichever exam option you choose.

Exam duration

The syllabus is assessed in both computer-based (CBE) and paper-based (PBE) exam formats. PBE exams are 3 hours 15 minutes in duration to reflect the manual effort required to write up your solutions. CBE exams are 3 hours and 20 minutes to reflect the 10 extra marks for seeded questions included in the CBE exams.

At each sitting, there is only one version of the paper-based exams, however, as of March 2017, CBE questions will be extracted from a bank of questions, meaning for CBEs you may not necessarily be sitting the same exam as your neighbour. To ensure that the exams remain fair and equivalent, ACCA has included 10 additional marks of seeded questions. You will not be able to determine which question is the seeded content and all questions are quality assured and set to the same standard as the rest of the exam. Having seeded content feeds into the rigorous processes that ACCA have been working with worldwide experts to ensure all students can be confident that the new CBEs will be fair and equivalent for all.

For more information on these changes and when they will be implemented, please visit the ACCA website. www.accaglobal.com/uk/en/student/exam-support-resources/fundamentals-exams-study-resources/f1/technical-articles/201617-changes.html

Format of the exam

The exam format is the same irrespective of the mode of delivery and will comprise three exam sections:

Section	Style of question type	Description	Proportion of exam, %
A	Objective test (OT)	15 questions × 2 marks	30
B	Objective test (OT) case	3 questions × 10 marks Each question will contain 5 sub-parts each worth 2 marks	30
C	Constructed Response (Long questions)	2 questions × 20 marks	40
Total			100

Section A and B questions will be selected from the entire syllabus. The paper version of these objective test questions contain multiple choice only and the computer-based version will contain a variety. The responses to each question or sub-part in the case of OT cases are marked automatically as either correct or incorrect by computer.

Section B questions will mainly focus on the following syllabus areas but a minority of marks can be drawn from any other area of the syllabus:

- Analysing and interpreting the financial statements of single entities and groups (syllabus area C)
- Preparation of financial statements (syllabus area D)

The responses to these questions are human marked.

Syllabus and study guide

The complete Financial Reporting (FR) syllabus and study guide can be found by visiting the exam resource finder on the ACCA website: www.accaglobal.com/uk/en/student/exam-support-resources.html

1

The conceptual framework

Topic list	Syllabus reference
1 Conceptual framework and GAAP	A1
2 The IASB's *Conceptual Framework*	A1
3 The objective of general purpose financial reporting	A1
4 Underlying assumption	A1
5 Qualitative characteristics of useful financial information	A1
6 The elements of financial statements	A2
7 Recognition of the elements of financial statements	A2
8 Measurement of the elements of financial statements	A2
9 Fair presentation and compliance with IFRS	A2

Introduction

A conceptual framework for financial reporting can be defined as an attempt to codify existing **generally accepted accounting practice (GAAP)** in order to reappraise current accounting standards and to produce new standards.

Under IFRS we have the IASB *Conceptual Framework*.

Study guide

		Intellectual level
A1	**The need for a conceptual framework and the characteristics of useful information**	
(a)	Describe what is meant by a conceptual framework of accounting	2
(b)	Discuss whether a conceptual framework is necessary and what an alternative system might be	2
(c)	Discuss what is meant by relevance and faithful representation and describe the qualities that enhance these characteristics	2
(d)	Discuss whether faithful representation constitutes more than compliance with accounting standards	1
(e)	Discuss what is meant by understandability and verifiability in relation to the provision of financial information	2
(f)	Discuss the importance of comparability and timeliness to users of financial statements	2
A2	**Recognition and measurement**	
(a)	Define what is meant by 'recognition' in financial statements and discuss the recognition criteria	2
(b)	Apply the recognition criteria to:	2
	(i) Assets and liabilities	
	(ii) Income and expenses	
(c)	Explain and compute amounts using the following measures:	2
	(i) Historical cost	
	(ii) Current cost	
	(iii) Net realisable value	
	(iv) Present value of future cash flows	
	(v) Fair value	

1 Conceptual framework and GAAP

FAST FORWARD

There are advantages and disadvantages to having a conceptual framework.

1.1 The search for a conceptual framework

A **conceptual framework**, in the field we are concerned with, is a statement of generally accepted theoretical principles which form the frame of reference for financial reporting.

These theoretical principles provide the basis for the development of new accounting standards and the evaluation of those already in existence. The financial reporting process is concerned with providing information that is useful in the business and economic decision-making process. Therefore a conceptual framework will form the **theoretical basis** for determining which events should be accounted for, how they should be measured and how they should be communicated to the user. Although it is theoretical in nature, a conceptual framework for financial reporting has highly practical final aims.

The **danger of not having a conceptual framework** is demonstrated in the way some countries' standards have developed over recent years; standards tend to be produced in a haphazard and fire-fighting approach. Where an agreed framework exists, the standard-setting body act as an architect or designer, rather than a fire-fighter, building accounting rules on the foundation of sound, agreed basic principles.

The lack of a conceptual framework also means that fundamental principles are tackled more than once in different standards, thereby producing **contradictions and inconsistencies** in basic concepts, such as those of prudence and matching. This leads to ambiguity and it affects the true and fair concept of financial reporting.

Another problem with the lack of a conceptual framework has become apparent in the USA. The large number of **highly detailed standards** produced by the Financial Accounting Standards Board (FASB) has created a financial reporting environment governed by specific rules rather than general principles. This would be avoided if a cohesive set of principles were in place.

A conceptual framework can also bolster standard setters **against political pressure** from various 'lobby groups' and interested parties. Such pressure would only prevail if it was acceptable under the conceptual framework.

1.2 Advantages and disadvantages of a conceptual framework

Advantages

(a) The situation is avoided whereby standards are developed on a patchwork basis, where a particular accounting problem is recognised as having emerged, and resources were then channelled into **standardising accounting practice** in that area, without regard to whether that particular issue was necessarily the most important issue remaining at that time without standardisation.

(b) As stated above, the development of certain standards (particularly national standards) has been subject to considerable **political interference** from interested parties. Where there is a conflict of interest between user groups on which policies to choose, policies deriving from a conceptual framework will be **less open to criticism** that the standard-setter buckled to external pressure.

(c) Without a conceptual framework, some standards may concentrate on **profit or loss** whereas some may concentrate on the **valuation of net assets** (statement of financial position).

Disadvantages

(a) Financial statements are intended for a **variety of users**, and it is not certain that a single conceptual framework can be devised which will suit all users.

(b) Given the diversity of user requirements, there may be a need for a variety of accounting standards, each produced for a **different purpose** (and with different concepts as a basis).

(c) It is not clear that a conceptual framework makes the task of **preparing and then implementing** standards any easier than without a framework.

Before we look at the IASB's attempt to produce a conceptual framework, we need to consider another term of importance to this debate: generally accepted accounting practice, or GAAP.

1.3 Generally Accepted Accounting Practice (GAAP)

GAAP signifies all the rules, from whatever source, which govern accounting.

In individual countries this is seen primarily as a **combination** of:

- National company law
- National accounting standards
- Local stock exchange requirements

Although those sources are the basis for the GAAP of individual countries, the concept also includes the effects of **non-mandatory sources** such as:

- International accounting standards
- Statutory requirements in other countries

In many countries, like the UK, GAAP does not have any statutory or regulatory authority or definition, unlike other countries, such as the US. The term is mentioned rarely in legislation, and only then in fairly limited terms.

There are different views of GAAP in different countries. The UK position can be explained in the following extracts from *UK GAAP* (Davies, Paterson & Wilson, Ernst & Young, 1997).

'Our view is that GAAP is a dynamic concept which requires constant review, adaptation and reaction to changing circumstances. We believe that use of the term 'principle' gives GAAP an unjustified and inappropriate degree of permanence. GAAP changes in response to changing business and economic needs and developments. As circumstances alter, accounting practices are modified or developed accordingly ... We believe that GAAP goes far beyond mere rules and principles, and encompasses contemporary permissible accounting **practice**.

It is often argued that the term 'generally accepted' implies that there must exist a high degree of practical application of a particular accounting practice. However, this interpretation raises certain practical difficulties. For example, what about new areas of accounting which have not, as yet, been generally applied? What about different accounting treatments for similar items – are they all generally accepted?

'It is our view that 'generally accepted' does **not** mean 'generally adopted or used'. We believe that, in the UK context, GAAP refers to accounting practices which are regarded as permissible by the accounting profession. The extent to which a particular practice has been adopted is, in our opinion, not the overriding consideration. Any accounting practice which is legitimate in the circumstances under which it has been applied should be regarded as GAAP. The decision as to whether or not a particular practice is permissible or legitimate would depend on one or more of the following factors:

- Is the practice addressed either in the accounting standards, statute or other official pronouncements?
- If the practice is not addressed in UK accounting standards, is it dealt with in International Accounting Standards, or the standards of other countries such as the US?
- Is the practice consistent with the needs of users and the objectives of financial reporting?
- Does the practice have authoritative support in the accounting literature?
- Is the practice being applied by other companies in similar situations?
- Is the practice consistent with the fundamental concept of 'true and fair'?'

This view is not held in all countries, however. In the US particularly, generally accepted accounting principles are defined as those principles which have 'substantial authoritative support'. Therefore accounts prepared in accordance with accounting principles for which there is not substantial authoritative support are presumed to be misleading or inaccurate.

The effect here is that 'new' or 'different' accounting principles are not acceptable unless they have been adopted by the mainstream accounting profession, usually the standard-setting bodies and/or professional accountancy bodies. This is much more rigid than the UK view expressed above.

A **conceptual framework** for financial reporting can be defined as an attempt to codify existing GAAP in order to reappraise current accounting standards and to produce new standards.

2 The IASB's *Conceptual Framework*

FAST FORWARD

The 1989 *Framework for the Preparation and Presentation of Financial Statements* was replaced in 2010 by the *Conceptual Framework for Financial Reporting* (IASB). This is the result of a joint project with the FASB.

The IASB *Framework for the Preparation and Presentation of Financial Statements* was produced in 1989 and is gradually being replaced by the new *Conceptual Framework for Financial Reporting* (IASB). This is being carried out in phases. The first phase, comprising Chapters 1 and 3, was published in September 2010. Chapter 2 entitled 'The reporting entity' has not yet been published. The current version of the *Conceptual Framework* includes the remaining chapters of the 1989 Framework as Chapter 4.

In September 2017, it was announced that the IASB expected to publish a revised Conceptual Framework in early 2018 following feedback from the Exposure Draft: *The Conceptual Framework for Financial Reporting*. The ED proposes comprehensive changes to the Conceptual Framework, notably:

- Revisions to the **definitions of elements** in the financial statements
- Guidance on **derecognition**
- Discussions on **measurement bases**
- Principles for including items in **other comprehensive income**

2.1 Introduction

The Introduction to the *Conceptual Framework* points out the fundamental reason why financial statements are produced worldwide, ie to **satisfy the requirements of external users**, but that practice varies due to the individual pressures in each country. These pressures may be social, political, economic or legal, but they result in variations in practice from country to country, including the form of statements, the definition of their component parts (assets, liabilities etc), the criteria for recognition of items and both the scope and disclosure of financial statements.

It is these differences which the IASB wishes to narrow by **harmonising** all aspects of financial statements, including the regulations governing their accounting standards and their preparation and presentation.

The preface emphasises the way **financial statements are used to make economic decisions** and thus financial statements should be prepared to this end. The types of economic decisions for which financial statements are likely to be used include the following.

- Decisions to buy, hold or sell equity investments
- Assessment of management stewardship and accountability
- Assessment of the entity's ability to pay employees
- Assessment of the security of amounts lent to the entity
- Determination of taxation policies
- Determination of distributable profits and dividends
- Inclusion in national income statistics
- Regulations of the activities of entities

Any additional requirements imposed by **national governments** for their own purposes should not affect financial statements produced for the benefit of other users.

The *Conceptual Framework* recognises that financial statements can be prepared using a **variety of models**. Although the most common is based on historical cost and a nominal unit of currency (ie pound sterling, US dollar etc), the *Conceptual Framework* can be applied to financial statements prepared under a range of models.
(IASB, *Conceptual Framework*: Introduction)

2.2 Purpose and status

The introduction gives a list of the purposes of the *Conceptual Framework*:

(a) To assist the Board in the **development of future IFRSs** and in its review of existing IFRSs

(b) To assist the Board in **promoting harmonisation** of regulations, accounting standards and procedures relating to the presentation of financial statements by providing a basis for reducing the number of alternative accounting treatments permitted by IFRSs

(c) To assist **national standard-setting bodies** in developing national standards

(d) To assist **preparers of financial statements** in applying IFRSs and in dealing with topics that have yet to form the subject of an IFRS

(e) To assist **auditors** in forming an opinion as to whether financial statements comply with IFRSs

(f) To assist **users of financial statements** in interpreting the information contained in financial statements prepared in compliance with IFRSs

(g) To provide those who are interested in the work of the IASB with **information** about its approach to the formulation of IFRSs

The *Conceptual Framework* is not an IFRS and so does not overrule any individual IFRS. In the (rare) case of conflict between an IFRS and the *Conceptual Framework*, the **IFRS will prevail**.

(IASB, *Conceptual Framework*: Purpose and Status)

2.2.1 Scope

The *Conceptual Framework* deals with:

(a) The **objective** of financial statements

(b) The **qualitative characteristics** that determine the usefulness of information in financial statements

(c) The **definition, recognition and measurement** of the elements from which financial statements are constructed

(d) Concepts of **capital and capital maintenance**

(IASB, *Conceptual Framework*: Scope)

2.2.2 Users and their information needs

Users of accounting information consist of investors, lenders and creditors, customers. You should be able to remember enough to do the following exercise.

Question	Users of financial information

Consider the information needs of the users of financial information listed above.

Answer

(a) **Investors** are the providers of risk capital,

  (i) Information is required to help make a decision about buying or selling shares, taking up a rights issue and voting.

  (ii) Investors must have information about the level of dividend, past, present and future and any changes in share price.

  (iii) Investors will also need to know whether the management has been running the company efficiently.

  (iv) As well as the position indicated by the statement of profit or loss and other comprehensive income, statement of financial position and earnings per share (EPS), investors will want to know about the liquidity position of the company, the company's future prospects, and how the company's shares compare with those of its competitors.

(b) **Lenders** need information to help them decide whether to lend to a company. They will also need to check that the value of any security remains adequate, that the interest repayments are secure, that the cash is available for redemption at the appropriate time and that any financial restrictions (such as maximum debt/equity ratios) have not been breached.

3 The objective of general purpose financial reporting

FAST FORWARD

The *Conceptual Framework* states that:

'The objective of general purpose financial reporting is to provide information about the reporting entity that is useful to existing and potential investors, lenders and other creditors in making decisions about providing resources to the entity.' (IASB: OB2)

These users need information about:

- The **economic resources of the entity**
- The **claims against the entity**
- Changes in the entity's **economic resources and claims**

Information about the entity's **economic resources and the claims against it** helps users to assess the entity's liquidity and solvency and its likely needs for additional financing.

Information about a reporting entity's financial performance (the **changes in its economic resources and claims**) helps users to understand the return that the entity has produced on its economic resources. This is an indicator of how efficiently and effectively management has used the resources of the entity and is helpful in predicting future returns.

The *Conceptual Framework* makes it clear that this information should be prepared on an **accruals basis**.

Key term

> **Accruals basis.** The effects of transactions and other events are recognised when they occur (and not as cash or its equivalent is received or paid) and they are recorded in the accounting records and reported in the financial statements of the periods to which they relate.

Financial statements prepared under the accruals basis show users past transactions involving cash and also obligations to pay cash in the future and resources which represent cash to be received in the future.

Information about a reporting entity's cash flows during a period also helps users assess the entity's **ability to generate future net cash inflows** and gives users a better understanding of its operations.

(IASB, *Conceptual Framework*: OB2–11)

4 Underlying assumption

FAST FORWARD

Going concern is the underlying assumption in preparing financial statements.

4.1 Going concern

Key term

> **Going concern.** The entity is normally viewed as a going concern, that is, as continuing in operation for the foreseeable future. It is assumed that the entity has neither the intention nor the necessity of liquidation or of curtailing materially the scale of its operations. (IASB, *Conceptual Framework*: para. 4.1)

It is assumed that the entity has no intention to liquidate or curtail major operations. If it did, then the financial statements would be prepared on a **different (disclosed) basis**.

5 Qualitative characteristics of useful financial information

FAST FORWARD

The *Conceptual Framework* states that qualitative characteristics are the attributes that make financial information useful to users.

Chapter 3 of the *Conceptual Framework* distinguishes between **fundamental** and **enhancing** qualitative characteristics, for analysis purposes. Fundamental qualitative characteristics distinguish useful financial reporting information from information that is not useful or misleading. Enhancing qualitative characteristics distinguish more useful information from less useful information.

The two fundamental qualitative characteristics are **relevance** and **faithful representation**.

(IASB, *Conceptual Framework*: QC5)

5.1 Relevance

Key term

> **Relevance.** Relevant information is capable of making a difference in the decisions made by users. It is capable of making a difference in decisions if it has **predictive value**, **confirmatory value** or both.
>
> (IASB, *Conceptual Framework*: QC6)

The relevance of information is affected by its **nature** and its **materiality**.

Key term

> **Materiality.** Information is material if omitting it or misstating it could influence decisions that users make on the basis of financial information about a specific reporting entity.
>
> (IASB, *Conceptual Framework*: QC11)

5.2 Faithful representation

Key term

> **Faithful representation.** Financial reports represent **economic phenomena** in words and numbers. To be useful, financial information must not only represent relevant phenomena but must **faithfully represent** the phenomena that it purports to represent. (IASB, *Conceptual Framework*: QC12)

To be a faithful representation information must be **complete, neutral** and **free from error**.

A **complete** depiction includes all information necessary for a user to understand the phenomenon being depicted, including all necessary descriptions and explanations.

A **neutral** depiction is without bias in the selection or presentation of financial information. This means that information must not be manipulated in any way in order to influence the decisions of users.

Free from error means there are no errors or omissions in the description of the phenomenon and no errors made in the process by which the financial information was produced. It does not mean that no inaccuracies can arise, particularly where estimates have to be made.

5.2.1 Substance over form Leasing

This is **not a separate qualitative characteristic** under the *Conceptual Framework*. The IASB says that to do so would be redundant because it is **implied in faithful representation**. Faithful representation of a transaction is only possible if it is accounted for according to its **substance and economic reality**.

5.3 Enhancing qualitative characteristics

5.3.1 Comparability

Key term

> **Comparability.** Comparability is the qualitative characteristic that enables users to identify and understand similarities in, and differences among, items. Information about a reporting entity is more useful if it can be compared with similar information about other entities and with similar information about the same entity for another period or date. (IASB, *Conceptual Framework*: QC21)

Consistency, although related to comparability, **is not the same**. It refers to the use of the same methods for the same items (ie consistency of treatment) either from period to period within a reporting entity or in a single period across entities.

The **disclosure of accounting policies** is particularly important here. Users must be able to distinguish between different accounting policies in order to be able to make a valid comparison of similar items in the accounts of different entities.

When an entity **changes an accounting policy**, the change is applied retrospectively so that the results from one period to the next can still be usefully compared.

Comparability is **not the same as uniformity**. Entities should change accounting policies if those policies become inappropriate.

Corresponding information for preceding periods should be shown to enable comparison over time.

(IASB, *Conceptual Framework*: QC22–25)

5.3.2 Verifiability *Verify whats in the acc - contact banks, attend stock take*

> **Verifiability.** Verifiability helps assure users that information faithfully represents the economic phenomena it purports to represent. It means that different knowledgeable and independent observers could reach consensus that a particular depiction is a faithful representation.
> (IASB, *Conceptual Framework*: QC26)

Information that can be independently verified is generally more decision-useful than information that cannot.

5.3.3 Timeliness *Accuracy v timing.*

> **Timeliness.** Timeliness means having information available to decision-makers in time to be capable of influencing their decisions. Generally, the older information is the less useful it is.
> (IASB, *Conceptual Framework*: QC29)

Information may become less useful if there is a delay in reporting it. There is a **balance between timeliness and the provision of reliable information**.

If information is reported on a timely basis when not all aspects of the transaction are known, it may not be complete or free from error.

Conversely, if every detail of a transaction is known, it may be too late to publish the information because it has become irrelevant. The overriding consideration is how best to satisfy the economic decision-making needs of the users.

5.3.4 Understandability

> **Understandability.** Classifying, characterising and presenting information clearly and concisely makes it understandable. (IASB, *Conceptual Framework*: QC30)

Financial reports are prepared for users who have a **reasonable knowledge of business and economic activities** and who review and analyse the information diligently. Some phenomena are inherently complex and cannot be made easy to understand. Excluding information on those phenomena might make the information easier to understand, but without it those reports would be incomplete and therefore misleading. Therefore matters should not be left out of financial statements simply due to their difficulty as even well-informed and diligent users may sometimes need the aid of an advisor to understand information about complex economic phenomena.

The cost constraint on useful financial reporting

This is a pervasive constraint, not a qualitative characteristic. When information is provided, its benefits must exceed the costs of obtaining and presenting it. This is a **subjective area** and there are other difficulties: others, not the intended users, may gain a benefit; also the cost may be paid by someone other than the users. It is therefore difficult to apply a cost-benefit analysis, but preparers and users should be aware of the constraint. (IASB, *Conceptual Framework*: QC35)

PYC - prior year comparative.

6 The elements of financial statements

Transactions and other events are grouped together in broad **classes** and in this way their financial effects are shown in the financial statements. These broad classes are the **elements** of financial statements.

(IASB, *Conceptual Framework*: para 4.2)

The *Conceptual Framework* (IASB: paras. 4.2–4.35) lays out these elements as follows.

Elements of financial statements

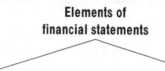

Measurement of financial position in Statement of financial position

- Assets
- Liabilities
- Equity

Measurement of performance in Statement of profit or loss and other comprehensive income

- Income
- Expenses

A process of **sub-classification** then takes place for presentation in the financial statements, eg assets are classified by their nature or function in the business to show information in the best way for users to take economic decisions.

6.1 Financial position

We need to define the three terms listed under this heading above.

Key terms

> - **Asset.** A resource controlled by an entity as a result of past events and from which future economic benefits are expected to flow to the entity.
>
> - **Liability.** A present obligation of the entity arising from past events, the settlement of which is expected to result in an outflow from the entity of resources embodying economic benefits.
>
> - **Equity.** The residual interest in the assets of the entity after deducting all its liabilities.
>
> (IASB, *Conceptual Framework*: para. 4)

These definitions are important, but they do not cover the **criteria for recognition** of any of these items, which are discussed in the next section of this chapter. This means that the definitions may include items which would not actually be recognised in the statement of financial position because they fail to satisfy recognition criteria particularly the **probable flow of any economic benefit** to or from the business.

Whether an item satisfies any of the definitions above will depend on the **substance and economic reality** of the transaction, not merely its legal form.

6.2 Assets

We can look in more detail at the components of the definitions given above.

Key term

> **Future economic benefit.** The potential to contribute, directly or indirectly, to the flow of cash and cash equivalents to the entity. The potential may be a productive one that is part of the operating activities of the entity. It may also take the form of convertibility into cash or cash equivalents or a capability to reduce cash outflows, such as when an alternative manufacturing process lowers the cost of production.
>
> (IASB, *Conceptual Framework*: para. 4.8)

Assets are usually employed to produce goods or services for customers; customers will then pay for these. **Cash itself** renders a service to the entity due to its command over other resources.

The existence of an asset, particularly in terms of **control**, is not reliant on:

(a) **Physical form** (hence patents and copyrights); **nor**

(b) **Legal rights**

Transactions or events **in the past** give rise to assets; those expected to occur in the future do not in themselves give rise to assets. For example, an intention to purchase a non-current asset does not, in itself, meet the definition of an asset. (IASB, *Conceptual Framework*: para. 4.13)

6.3 Liabilities

Again we can look more closely at some aspects of the definition. An essential characteristic of a liability is that the entity has a **present obligation**.

Key term

> **Obligation.** A duty or responsibility to act or perform in a certain way. Obligations may be legally enforceable as a consequence of a binding contract or statutory requirement. Obligations also arise, however, from normal business practice, custom and a desire to maintain good business relations or act in an equitable manner. (IASB, *Conceptual Framework*: para. 4.15)

It is important to distinguish between a present obligation and a **future commitment**. A management decision to purchase assets in the future does not, in itself, give rise to a present obligation.

Settlement of a present obligation will involve the entity giving up resources embodying economic benefits in order to satisfy the claim of the other party. This may be done in various ways, not just by payment of cash.

Liabilities must arise from **past transactions or events**. In the case of, say, recognition of future rebates to customers based on annual purchases, the sale of goods in the past is the transaction that gives rise to the liability. (IASB, *Conceptual Framework*: para. 4.18)

6.3.1 Provisions

Is a provision a liability?

Key term

> **Provision.** A present obligation which satisfies the rest of the definition of a liability, even if the amount of the obligation has to be estimated. (IASB, *Conceptual Framework*: para. 4.19)

Question

Assets and liabilities

Consider the following situations. In each case, do we have an asset or liability within the definitions given by the *Conceptual Framework*? Give reasons for your answer.

(a) Pat Co has purchased a patent for $20,000. The patent gives the company sole use of a particular manufacturing process which will save $3,000 a year for the next five years.

(b) Baldwin Co paid Don Brennan $10,000 to set up a car repair shop, on condition that priority treatment is given to cars from the company's fleet.

(c) Deals on Wheels Co provides a warranty with every car sold.

Answer

(a) This is an asset, albeit an intangible one. There is a past event, control and future economic benefit (through cost savings).

(b)	This cannot be classified as an asset. Baldwin Co has no control over the car repair shop and it is difficult to argue that there are 'future economic benefits'.

(c)	The warranty claims in total constitute a liability; the business has taken on an obligation. It would be recognised when the warranty is issued rather than when a claim is made.

6.4 Equity

Equity is defined above as a **residual**, but it may be sub-classified in the statement of financial position. This will indicate legal or other restrictions on the ability of the entity to distribute or otherwise apply its equity. Some reserves are required by statute or other law, eg for the future protection of creditors. The amount shown for equity depends on the **measurement of assets and liabilities**. It has nothing to do with the market value of the entity's shares.	(IASB, *Conceptual Framework:* para. 4.20)

6.5 Performance

Profit is used as a **measure of performance**, or as a basis for other measures (eg earnings per share). It depends directly on the measurement of income and expenses, which in turn depend (in part) on the concepts of capital and capital maintenance adopted.	(IASB, *Conceptual Framework:* para. 4.24)

The elements of income and expense are therefore defined.

Key terms

> - **Income.** Increases in economic benefits during the accounting period in the form of inflows or enhancements of assets or decreases of liabilities that result in increases in equity, other than those relating to contributions from equity participants.
>
> - **Expenses.** Decreases in economic benefits during the accounting period in the form of outflows or depletions of assets or incurrences of liabilities that result in decreases in equity, other than those relating to distributions to equity participants.	(IASB, *Conceptual Framework:* paras. 4.29–35)

Income and expenses can be **presented in different ways** in the statement of profit or loss and other comprehensive income, to provide information relevant for economic decision-making. For example, income and expenses which relate to continuing operations are distinguished from the results of discontinued operations.

6.6 Income

Both **revenue** and **gains** are included in the definition of income. **Revenue** arises in the course of ordinary activities of an entity.

Key term

> **Gains.** Increases in economic benefits. As such they are no different in nature from revenue.
> 	(IASB, *Conceptual Framework:* para. 4.30)

Gains include those arising on the disposal of non-current assets. The definition of income also includes **unrealised gains**, eg on revaluation of marketable securities.

6.7 Expenses

As with income, the definition of expenses includes losses as well as those expenses that arise in the course of ordinary activities of an entity.

Key term

> **Losses.** Decreases in economic benefits. As such they are no different in nature from other expenses.
> 	(IASB, *Conceptual Framework:* para. 4.34)

Losses will include those arising on the disposal of non-current assets. The definition of expenses will also include **unrealised losses**, eg the fall in value of an investment.

6.8 Section summary

Make sure you learn the important definitions.

- Financial position:
  - – Assets
  - – Liabilities
  - – Equity

- Financial performance:
  - – Income
  - – Expenses

7 Recognition of the elements of financial statements

FAST FORWARD

Items which meet the definition of assets or liabilities may still not be recognised in financial statements because they must also meet certain **recognition criteria**.

Key term

Recognition. The process of incorporating in the statement of financial position or statement of profit or loss and other comprehensive income an item that meets the definition of an element and satisfies the following criteria for recognition:

(a) It is probable that any future economic benefit associated with the item will flow to or from the entity

(b) The item has a cost or value that can be measured with reliability. Regard must be given to **materiality** (see Section 5 above).

(IASB, *Conceptual Framework*: para. 4.37)

7.1 Probability of future economic benefits

Probability here means the **degree of uncertainty** that the future economic benefits associated with an item will flow to or from the entity. This must be judged on the basis of the **characteristics of the entity's environment** and the **evidence available** when the financial statements are prepared.

(IASB, *Conceptual Framework*: para. 4.40)

7.2 Reliability of measurement

The cost or value of an item, in many cases, **must be estimated**. The *Conceptual Framework* states, however, that the use of reasonable estimates is an essential part of the preparation of financial statements and does not undermine their reliability. Where no reasonable estimate can be made, the item should not be recognised, although its existence should be disclosed in the notes, or other explanatory material.

Items may still qualify for recognition **at a later date** due to changes in circumstances or subsequent events.

(IASB, *Conceptual Framework*: paras. 4.41–3)

7.3 Assets which cannot be recognised

The recognition criteria do not cover items which many businesses may regard as assets. A skilled workforce is an undoubted asset but workers can leave at any time so there can be no certainty about the probability of future economic benefits. A company may have come up with a new name for its product which is greatly increasing sales but, as it did not buy the name, the name does not have a cost or value that can be reliably measured, so it is not recognised. (IASB, *Conceptual Framework*: para. 4.43)

7.4 Recognition of items

We can summarise the recognition criteria for assets, liabilities, income and expenses, based on the definition of recognition given above.

Item	Recognised in	When
Asset	The statement of financial position	It is probable that the future economic benefits will flow to the entity and the asset has a cost or value that can be measured reliably.
Liability	The statement of financial position	It is probable that an outflow of resources embodying economic benefits will result from the settlement of a present obligation and the amount at which the settlement will take place can be measured reliably.
Income	The statement of profit or loss and other comprehensive income	An increase in future economic benefits related to an increase in an asset or a decrease of a liability has arisen that can be measured reliably.
Expenses	The statement of profit or loss and other comprehensive income	A decrease in future economic benefits related to a decrease in an asset or an increase of a liability has arisen that can be measured reliably.

8 Measurement of the elements of financial statements

Where are the numbers coming from.

FAST FORWARD

A number of different measurement bases are used in financial statements. They include:

- Historical cost
- Current cost
- Realisable (settlement) value
- Present value of future cash flows

Measurement is defined as follows.

Key term

Measurement. The process of determining the monetary amounts at which the elements of the financial statements are to be recognised and carried in the statement of financial position and statement of profit or loss and other comprehensive income.   (IASB, *Conceptual Framework*: para. 4.54)

This involves the selection of a particular **basis of measurement**. A number of these are used to different degrees and in varying combinations in financial statements. They include the following.

Key terms

Historical cost. Assets are recorded at the amount of cash or cash equivalents paid or the fair value of the consideration given to acquire them at the time of their acquisition. Liabilities are recorded at the amount of proceeds received in exchange for the obligation, or in some circumstances (for example, income taxes), at the amounts of cash or cash equivalents expected to be paid to satisfy the liability in the normal course of business. *used alot*

Current cost. Assets are carried at the amount of cash or cash equivalents that would have to be paid if the same or an equivalent asset was acquired currently.

Liabilities are carried at the undiscounted amount of cash or cash equivalents that would be required to settle the obligation currently.

Realisable (settlement) value.

- **Realisable value.** The amount of cash or cash equivalents that could currently be obtained by selling an asset in an orderly disposal. *Assets used alot*

- **Settlement value.** The undiscounted amounts of cash or cash equivalents expected to be paid to satisfy the liabilities in the normal course of business. *Liabilities Not discounted for the time value of money*

Present value. A current estimate of the present discounted value of the future net cash flows in the normal course of business. *of future cash flows* (IASB, *Conceptual Framework*: para. 4.55)

Historical cost is the most commonly adopted measurement basis, but this is usually combined with other bases, eg inventory is carried at the lower of cost and net realisable value.

(IASB, *Conceptual Framework*: para. 4.56)

Recent standards use the concept of **fair value**, which is defined by IFRS 13 as 'the price that would be received to sell an asset or paid to transfer a liability in an orderly transaction between market participants at the measurement date' (para. 9). *used alot market value at the measurement date.*

Example

NB

A machine was purchased on 1 January 20X8 for $3m. That was its original cost. It has a useful life of 10 years and under the **historical cost convention** it will be carried at **original cost less accumulated depreciation**. So in the financial statements at 31 December 20X9 it will be carried at:

$3m − (0.3 × 2) = $2.4m

The current cost of the machine, which will probably also be its fair value, will be fairly easy to ascertain if it is not too specialised. For instance, two year old machines like this one may currently be changing hands for $2.5m, so that will be an appropriate fair value.

The **net realisable value** of the machine will be the amount that could be obtained from selling it, less any costs involved in making the sale. If the machine had to be dismantled and transported to the buyer's premises at a cost of $200,000, the NRV would be $2.3m.

The **replacement cost** of the machine will be the cost of a new model less two year's depreciation. The cost of a new machine may now be $3.5m. Assuming a ten-year life, the replacement cost will therefore be $2.8m.

The **present value** of the machine will be the discounted value of the future cash flows that it is expected to generate. If the machine is expected to generate $500,000 per annum for the remaining eight years of its life and if the company's cost of capital is 10%, present value will be calculated as:

$500,000 × 5.335* = $2,667,500

* Cumulative present of $1 per annum for eight years discounted at 10%

9 Fair presentation and compliance with IFRS

internatational financial Reporting Standards

Most importantly, financial statements should **present fairly** the financial position, financial performance and cash flows of an entity. **Compliance with IFRS** is presumed to result in financial statements that achieve a fair presentation.

(IAS 1: para. 15)

International Accounting standards.

IAS 1 stipulates that financial statements shall present fairly the financial position, financial performance and cash flows of an entity. Fair presentation requires the faithful representation of the effects of transactions, other events and conditions in accordance with the definitions and recognition criteria for assets, liabilities, income and expenses set out in the *Conceptual Framework*.

The following points made by IAS 1 expand on this principle.

(a) **Compliance with IFRS** should be disclosed

(b) **All relevant IFRS** must be followed if compliance with IFRS is disclosed

(c) Use of an **inappropriate accounting treatment** cannot be rectified either by disclosure of accounting policies or notes/explanatory material

IAS 1 states what is required for a fair presentation.

(a) Selection and application of **accounting policies**

(b) **Presentation of information** in a manner which provides relevant, reliable, comparable and understandable information

(c) **Additional disclosures** where required

(IAS 1: para. 17)

Chapter Roundup

- There are advantages and disadvantages to having a conceptual framework.

- The 1989 *Framework for the Preparation and Presentation of Financial Statements* was replaced in 2010 by the *Conceptual Framework for Financial Reporting* (IASB). This is the result of a joint project with the FASB.

- The *Conceptual Framework* states that:

  'The objective of general purpose financial reporting is to provide information about the reporting entity that is useful to existing and potential investors, lenders and other creditors in making decisions about providing resources to the entity.' (IASB, para: OB2)

- **Going concern** is the underlying assumption in preparing financial statements.

- The *Conceptual Framework* states that qualitative characteristics are the attributes that make financial information useful to users.

- Transactions and other events are grouped together in broad **classes** and in this way their financial effects are shown in the financial statements. These broad classes are the **elements** of financial statements. (IASB, *Conceptual Framework*: para 4.2)

- Items which meet the definition of assets or liabilities may still not be recognised in financial statements because they must also meet certain **recognition criteria**.

- A number of different measurement bases are used in financial statements. They include:

  - Historical cost
  - Current cost
  - Realisable (settlement) value
  - Present value of future cash flows

Quick Quiz

1 Define a 'conceptual framework'.
2 What are the advantages and disadvantages of developing a conceptual framework?
3 The needs of which category of user are paramount when preparing financial statements?
4 Define 'relevance'.
5 In which two ways should users be able to compare an entity's financial statements?
6 A provision can be a liability.

   True ☐
   False ☐

7 Define 'recognition'.
8 The cost or value of items in the financial statements is never estimated.

   True ☐
   False ☐

9 What is the most common basis of measurement used in financial statements?

Answers to Quick Quiz

1   This is a statement of generally accepted theoretical principles, which form the frame of reference for financial reporting.

2   *Advantages*

    - Standardised accounting practice

    - Less open to criticism

    - Concentrate on statement of profit or loss and other comprehensive income or statement of financial position, as appropriate

    Disadvantages

    - Variety of users, so not all will be satisfied
    - Variety of standards for different purposes
    - Preparing and implementing standards not necessarily any easier

3   Needs of investors

4   Information has relevance when it influences the economic decisions of users by helping them evaluate past, present or future events or confirming (or correcting) their past evaluations.

5   - Through time to identify trends
    - With other entities' statements

6   True. It satisfies the definition of a liability but the amount may need to be estimated.

7   See Key Term Section 7.

8   False. Monetary values are often estimated.

9   Historical cost

Now try the Section C questions below from the Practice Question Bank

Number	Level	Marks	Time
1		10	20 mins

The regulatory framework

2

Topic list	Syllabus reference
1 The need for a regulatory framework	A3
2 Setting of International Financial Reporting Standards	A3

Introduction

We have already discussed the IASB and IFRSs to some extent. Here we are concerned with the IASB's relationship with other bodies, and with the way the IASB operates and how IFRSs are produced.

Later in this text we look at some of the theory behind what appears in the accounts. The most important document in this area is the IASB's *Conceptual Framework for Financial Reporting*.

Study guide

		Intellectual level
A3	**Regulatory framework**	
(a)	Explain why a regulatory framework is needed, including the advantages and disadvantages of IFRS over a national regulatory framework	2
(b)	Explain why accounting standards on their own are not a complete regulatory framework	2
(c)	Distinguish between a principles based and a rules based framework and discuss whether they can be complementary	1
(d)	Describe the IASB's Standard setting process including revisions to and interpretations of Standards	2
(e)	Explain the relationship of national standard setters to the IASB in respect of the standard setting process	2

Exam guide

You may be asked about these topics as part of a longer question.

1 The need for a regulatory framework

1.1 Introduction

The regulatory framework is the most important element in ensuring relevant and faithfully presented financial information and thus meeting the needs of shareholders and other users.

Without a single body overall responsible for producing financial reporting standards (the IASB) and a framework of general principles within which they can be produced (the *Conceptual Framework*), there would be no means of enforcing compliance with GAAP. Also, GAAP would be unable to evolve in any structured way in response to changes in economic conditions.

1.2 Principles-based versus rules-based systems

FAST FORWARD

> A principles-based system works within a set of laid down principles. A rules-based system regulates for issues as they arise. Both of these have advantages and disadvantages.

The *Conceptual Framework* provides the background of principles within which standards can be developed. This system is intended to ensure that standards are not produced which are in conflict with each other and also that any departure from a standard can be judged on the basis of whether or not it is in keeping with the principles set out in the *Conceptual Framework*. This is a **principles-based** system.

In the absence of a reporting framework, a more **rules-based** approach has to be adopted. This leads to a large mass of regulation designed to cover every eventuality, as in the US. As we have seen over the past few years, a large volume of regulatory measures does not always detect or prevent financial irregularity. One presumed advantage of rules-based systems is that the exercise of judgement is minimised. Auditors who fear litigation tend to prefer rules-based systems. It could be that a rules-based approach is appropriate for controversial areas in accounting.

1.3 IFRS: advantages and disadvantages

The advantages and disadvantages of adopting IFRS have to be considered by each adopting country and are being widely debated in the US at the moment.

The main advantages are seen to be:

(a)   A business can present its financial statements on the same basis as its foreign competitors, making comparison easier

(b)   Cross-border listing will be facilitated, making it easier to raise capital abroad

(c)   Companies with foreign subsidiaries will have a common, company-wide accounting language

(d)   Foreign companies which are targets for takeovers or mergers can be more easily appraised

The disadvantages are perceived to be:

- The cost of implementing IFRS
- The lower level of detail in IFRS

Countries which have national standards which are very prescriptive are worried about the principles-based standards in IFRS which require the application of judgement. This is particularly so in the US. US accountants are subject to a high degree of litigation and their defence in court is usually that they complied with the relevant sub-section of one of the hundreds of detailed standards which make up US GAAP. They fear that adoption of IFRS will remove this defence.

Question   Harmonisation

In accounting terms what do you think are:

(a)   The advantages to international harmonisation?
(b)   The barriers to international harmonisation?

Answer

(a)   *Advantages of global harmonisation*

    The advantages of harmonisation will be based on the benefits to users and preparers of accounts, as follows.

    (i)   Investors, both individual and corporate, would like to be able to compare the financial results of different companies internationally as well as nationally in making investment decisions.

    (ii)   Multinational companies would benefit from harmonisation for many reasons including the following.

        (1)   Better access would be gained to foreign investor funds.

        (2)   Management control would be improved, because harmonisation would aid internal communication of financial information.

        (3)   Appraisal of foreign entities for take-overs and mergers would be more straightforward.

        (4)   It would be easier to comply with the reporting requirements of overseas stock exchanges.

        (5)   Preparation of group accounts would be easier.

        (6)   A reduction in audit costs might be achieved.

        (7)   Transfer of accounting staff across national borders would be easier.

    (iii)   Governments of developing countries would save time and money if they could adopt international standards and, if these were used internally, governments of developing countries could attempt to control the activities of foreign multinational companies in their own country. These companies could not 'hide' behind foreign accounting practices which are difficult to understand.

    (iv)   Tax authorities. It will be easier to calculate the tax liability of investors, including multinationals who receive income from overseas sources.

(v) Regional economic groups usually promote trade within a specific geographical region. This would be aided by common accounting practices within the region.

(vi) Large international accounting firms would benefit as accounting and auditing would be much easier if similar accounting practices existed throughout the world.

(b) *Barriers to harmonisation*

(i) Different purposes of financial reporting. In some countries the purpose is solely for tax assessment, while in others it is for investor decision-making.

(ii) Different legal systems. These prevent the development of certain accounting practices and restrict the options available.

(iii) Different user groups. Countries have different ideas about who the relevant user groups are and their respective importance. In the USA investor and creditor groups are given prominence, while in Europe employees enjoy a higher profile.

(iv) Needs of developing countries. Developing countries are obviously behind in the standard setting process and they need to develop the basic standards and principles already in place in most developed countries.

(v) Nationalism is demonstrated in an unwillingness to accept another country's standard.

(vi) Cultural differences result in objectives for accounting systems differing from country to country.

(vii) Unique circumstances. Some countries may be experiencing unusual circumstances which affect all aspects of everyday life and impinge on the ability of companies to produce proper reports, for example hyperinflation, civil war, currency restriction and so on.

(viii) The lack of strong accountancy bodies. Many countries do not have strong independent accountancy or business bodies which would press for better standards and greater harmonisation.

1.4 The IASB and current accounting standards

The IASB's predecessor body, the IASC, had issued 41 International Accounting Standards (IASs) and on 1 April 2001 the IASB adopted all of these standards and now issues its own International Financial Reporting Standards (IFRSs). So far 17 new IFRSs have been issued.

1.5 European Commission and IFRSs

All listed entities in member states have been required to use IFRSs in their consolidated financial statements since 2005.

To this end the IASB undertook **improvements projects**, dealing with **revisions to IFRS**, for example in the area of materiality, presentation, related parties and earnings per share.

The aim of the European Commission is to build a fully-integrated, globally competitive market. As part of this it aims to harmonise company law across the member states and to establish a level playing field for financial reporting.

1.6 UK GAAP and IFRSs

The convergence process between UK GAAP and IFRS began in 2003 but was subsequently paused. During that time, UK standards did not keep pace with business changes, particularly with regard to financial instruments. The FRC decided that the optimum solution was a transition to an IFRS-based framework and over the course of 2012 and 2013 it issued three new standards:

- FRS 100 *Application of financial reporting requirements*

- FRS 101 *Reduced disclosure framework*

- FRS 102 *The Financial Reporting Standard Applicable in the United Kingdom and Republic of Ireland*

FRS 102 replaces the majority of UK accounting standards, adopts an IFRS-based framework and improves accounting for financial instruments. It is based on the *IFRS for Small and Medium-sized Entities*, amended to comply with UK company law. It is intended for all UK entities other than listed companies preparing group financial statements who are already required to report under full IFRS. Small or medium sized companies who used to report under the FRSSE now either report under Section 1A of the FRS 102 for a small entity, or under FRS 105 *The Financial Reporting Standard for Micro-entities Regime* (issued July 2015).

This represents a very high level of convergence between UK GAAP and IFRS.

2 Setting of International Financial Reporting Standards

FAST FORWARD

IFRSs are developed through a formal system of due process and broad international consultation involving accountants, financial analysts and other users and regulatory bodies from around the world.

2.1 Due process

The overall agenda of the IASB will initially be set by discussion with the IFRS Advisory Council. The process for developing an individual standard would involve the following steps.

Step 1   During the early stages of a project, the IASB may establish an **Advisory Committee** to give advice on issues arising in the project. Consultation with the Advisory Committee and the IFRS Advisory Council occurs throughout the project.

Step 2   IASB may develop and publish **Discussion Papers** for public comment.

Step 3   Following the receipt and review of comments, the IASB would develop and publish an **Exposure Draft** for public comment.

Step 4   Following the receipt and review of comments, the IASB would issue a final **International Financial Reporting Standard**.

The period of exposure for public comment is normally 120 days. However, in exceptional circumstances, proposals may be issued with a comment period of not less than 30 days. Draft IFRS Interpretations are exposed for a 60 day comment period.

(IFRS Foundation *Due Process Handbook:* para.6.7)

2.2 Co-ordination with national standard setters

Close co-ordination between IASB due process and due process of national standard setters is important to the success of the IASB's mandate.

The IASB is exploring ways in which to integrate its due process more closely with national due process. Such integration may grow as the relationship between the IASB and national standard setters evolves. In particular, the IASB is exploring the following procedure for projects that have international implications.

(a)   IASB and national standard setters would co-ordinate their work plans so that when the IASB starts a project, national standard setters would also add it to their own work plans so that they can play a full part in developing international consensus. Similarly, where national standard setters start projects, the IASB would consider whether it needs to develop a new standard or review its existing standards. Over a reasonable period, the IASB and national standard setters should aim to review all standards where significant differences currently exist, giving priority to the areas where the differences are greatest.

(b)   National standards setters would not be required to vote for the IASB's preferred solution in their national standards, since each country remains free to adopt IASB standards with amendments or to adopt other standards. However, the existence of an international consensus is clearly one factor that members of national standard setters would consider when they decide how to vote on national standards.

(c)   The IASB would continue to publish its own Exposure Drafts and other documents for public comment.

(d) National standard setters would publish their own exposure document at approximately the same time as IASB Exposure Drafts and would seek specific comments on any significant divergences between the two exposure documents. In some instances, national standard setters may include in their exposure documents specific comments on issues of particular relevance to their country or include more detailed guidance than is included in the corresponding IASB document.

(e) National standard setters would follow their own full due process, which they would ideally choose to integrate with the IASB's due process. This integration would avoid unnecessary delays in completing standards and would also minimise the likelihood of unnecessary differences between the standards that result.

2.3 IASB liaison members

Seven of the full-time members of the IASB have formal liaison responsibilities with national standard setters in order to promote the convergence of national accounting standards and International Financial Reporting Standards. The IASB envisages a partnership between the IASB and these national standard setters as they work together to achieve convergence of accounting standards worldwide.

In addition all IASB members have contact responsibility with national standard setters not having liaison members and many countries are also represented on the IFRS Advisory Council.

Exam focus point

This topic could be examined as an MCQ.

2.4 Current IFRSs/IASs

The current list is as follows.

International Accounting Standards		Date of issue/revision
IAS 1 (revised)	Presentation of financial statements	Sep 2007
IAS 2	Inventories	Dec 2003
IAS 7	Statements of cash flows	Dec 1992
IAS 8	Accounting policies, changes in accounting estimates and errors	Dec 2003
IAS 10	Events after the reporting period	Dec 2003
IAS 12	Income taxes	Nov 2000
IAS 16	Property, plant and equipment	Dec 2003
IAS 19*	Employee benefits	Dec 2004
IAS 20	Government grants and disclosure of government assistance	Jan 1995
IAS 21*	The effects of changes in foreign exchange rates	Dec 2003
IAS 23 (revised)	Borrowing costs	Jan 2008
IAS 24*	Related party disclosures	Dec 2003
IAS 26*	Accounting and reporting by retirement benefit plans	Jan 1995
IAS 27 (revised)	Separate financial statements	May 2011
IAS 28	Investments in associates and joint ventures**	Dec 2003
IAS 29*	Financial reporting in hyperinflationary economies	Jan 1995
IAS 30*	Disclosure in the financial statements of banks and similar financial institutions (not examinable)	Jan 1995
IAS 32	Financial instruments: presentation	Dec 2003
IAS 33	Earnings per share	Dec 2003
IAS 34*	Interim financial reporting	Feb 1998

International Accounting Standards		Date of issue/revision
IAS 36	Impairment of assets	Mar 2004
IAS 37	Provisions, contingent liabilities and contingent assets	Sept 1998
IAS 38	Intangible assets	Mar 2004
IAS 40	Investment property	Dec 2003
IAS 41	Agriculture	Feb 2001
IFRS 1*	First time adoption of International Financial Reporting Standards	June 2003
IFRS 2*	Share-based payment	Feb 2004
IFRS 3 (revised)	Business combinations	Jan 2008
IFRS 4*	Insurance contracts	Mar 2004
IFRS 5	Non-current assets held for sale and discontinued operations	Mar 2004
IFRS 6*	Exploration for and evaluation of mineral resources	Dec 2004
IFRS 7	Financial instruments: disclosures	Aug 2005
IFRS 8*	Operating segments	Nov 2006
IFRS 9	Financial Instruments	Jul 2014
IFRS 10	Consolidated financial statements	May 2011
IFRS 11*	Joint arrangements	May 2011
IFRS 12*	Disclosures of interests in other entities	May 2011
IFRS 13	Fair value measurement	May 2011
IFRS 14*	Regulatory deferral accounts	Jan 2014
IFRS 15	Revenue from contracts with customers	May 2014
IFRS 16	Leases	Jan 2016
IFRS 17*	Insurance contracts	May 2017

* These standards are not examinable at Financial Reporting.

** Associates are examinable at Financial Reporting; joint ventures are not.

2.5 Alternative treatments

Many of the old IASs permitted two accounting treatments for like transactions or events. One treatment was designated as the **benchmark treatment** (effectively the **preferred treatment**) and the other was known as the **alternative treatment**. This is no longer the case. The last standard to have a benchmark alternative was IAS 23 which was revised to remove the benchmark treatment. Under the revised standard allowable borrowing costs **must** be capitalised (para. 8). However, some standards do still allow more than one policy – for instance IAS 16 allows property, plant and equipment to be carried at cost or revalued amount (para. 29).

2.6 Interpretation of IFRSs

The IASB has developed a procedure for issuing interpretations of its standards. In September 1996, the IASC Board approved the formation of a **Standards Interpretations Committee (SIC)** for this task. This has been renamed under the IASB as the **IFRS Interpretations Committee** . The duties of the IFRS Interpretations Committee are:

(a)   To **interpret the application** of International Financial Reporting Standards and provide timely guidance on financial reporting issues not specifically addressed in IFRSs or IASs.

(b)   To have regard to the Board's objective of working actively with **national standard setters** to bring about convergence of national accounting standards and IFRSs to high quality solutions.

(c)   To review on a timely basis, any **newly identified financial reporting issues** not already addressed in existing IFRSs.

In developing interpretations, the IFRS Interpretations Committee will work closely with **similar national committees**. If no more than three of its members vote against an interpretation, the IFRS Interpretations Committee will ask the Board to approve the interpretation for issue. Interpretations will be formally published after approval by the Board.

The IFRS Interpretations Committee adopts a principles based approach, using the IASB *Conceptual Framework* basis. The Committee then informs the IASB where discrepancies or inadequacies lie and develops interpretations through public consultation (Draft Interpretations).

2.7 Scope and application of IFRSs

2.7.1 Scope

Any limitation of the applicability of a specific IFRS is made clear within that standard. IFRSs are **not intended to be applied to immaterial items, nor are they retrospective**. Each individual IFRS lays out its scope at the beginning of the standard.

2.7.2 Application

Within each individual country **local regulations** govern, to a greater or lesser degree, the issue of financial statements. These local regulations include accounting standards issued by the national regulatory bodies and/or professional accountancy bodies in the country concerned.

The IASB **concentrated on essentials** when producing IFRSs. They tried not to make IFRSs too complex, because otherwise they would be impossible to apply on a worldwide basis.

(Preface to IFRSs: para. 7)

2.8 Worldwide effect of IFRSs and the IASB

The IASB, and before it the IASC, has now been in existence for more than 30 years, and it is worth looking at the effect it has had in that time.

As far as **Europe** is concerned, the consolidated financial statements of many of Europe's top multinationals are now prepared in conformity with national requirements, EC directives and IFRSs. Furthermore, IFRSs are having a growing influence on national accounting requirements and practices. Many of these developments have been given added impetus by the internationalisation of capital markets. As mentioned previously, IFRSs have been implemented in the EU for listed companies since 2005.

In **Japan**, the influence of the IASC had, until recently, been negligible. This was mainly because of links in Japan between tax rules and financial reporting. The Japanese Ministry of Finance set up a working committee to consider whether to bring national requirements into line with IFRSs. The Tokyo Stock Exchange has announced that it will accept financial statements from foreign issuers that conform with home country standards, which would include IFRS.

This was widely seen as an attempt to attract foreign issuers, in particular companies from Hong Kong and Singapore. As these countries base their accounting on international standards, this action is therefore implicit acknowledgement by the Japanese Ministry of Finance of IFRS requirements.

In **America**, the Securities and Exchange Commission (SEC) agreed in 1993 to permit but not require foreign issuers (of shares, etc) to follow IFRS treatments on certain issues, including cash flow statements under IAS 7. The overall effect is that, where an IFRS treatment differs from US GAAP, these treatments are now acceptable. Domestic issuers are required to apply US GAAP. The SEC is now supporting the IASB because it wants to attract foreign listings. In October 2002, under the Norwalk Agreement the FASB and the IASB formally agreed that they would work towards convergence between US GAAP and IFRS and in February 2006 they released a 'roadmap' setting out the convergence projects.

The pace of convergence has slowed over the past few years, however 2014 saw the publication of IFRS 15 *Revenue from contracts with customers*, which is the result of an IASB/FASB collaboration, followed in 2016 by IFRS 16 *Leases*.

Other **worldwide** countries have mandatory application of IFRS for domestic listed companies, including Australia, Georgia, Jamaica, Jordan, Kenya, Malawi, Nepal, Peru, Serbia, South Africa and Trinidad and Tobago (this list is not exhaustive).

2.9 Criticisms of the IASB

You need to be able to understand the problems that can arise.

We will begin by looking at some of the general problems created by **accounting standards**.

2.9.1 Accounting standards and choice

It is sometimes argued that companies should be given a choice in matters of financial reporting on the grounds that accounting standards are detrimental to the quality of such reporting. There are arguments on both sides.

In favour of accounting standards (both national and international), the following points can be made.

- They reduce or eliminate confusing variations in the methods used to prepare accounts.

- They provide a focal point for debate and discussions about accounting practice.

- They oblige companies to disclose the accounting policies used in the preparation of accounts.

- They are a less rigid alternative to enforcing conformity by means of legislation.

- They have obliged companies to **disclose more accounting information** than they would otherwise have done if accounting standards did not exist, for example IAS 33 *Earnings per share*.

Many companies are reluctant to disclose information which is not required by national legislation. However, the following arguments may be put forward **against standardisation** and **in favour of choice**.

- A set of rules which give backing to one method of preparing accounts might be **inappropriate in some circumstances**. For example, IAS 16 on depreciation is inappropriate for investment properties (properties not occupied by the entity but held solely for investment), which are covered by IAS 40 on investment property.

- Standards may be subject to **lobbying or government pressure** (in the case of national standards). For example, in the US, the accounting standard FAS 19 on the accounts of oil and gas companies led to a powerful lobby of oil companies, which persuaded the SEC (Securities and Exchange Commission) to step in. FAS 19 was then suspended.

- Many national standards are not based on a **conceptual framework of accounting**, although IFRSs are.

- There may be a **trend towards rigidity**, and away from flexibility in applying the rules.

2.9.2 Political problems

Any international body, whatever its purpose or activity, faces enormous political difficulties in attempting to gain **international consensus** and the IASB is no exception to this. How can the IASB reconcile the financial reporting situation between economies as diverse as developing countries and sophisticated first-world industrial powers?

Developing countries are suspicious of the IASB, believing it to be dominated by the **US**. This arises because acceptance by the US listing authority, the Securities and Exchange Commission (SEC), of IASs is seen as a major hurdle to be overcome. For all practical purposes it is the US market which must be persuaded to accept IFRSs.

Developing countries are being catered for to some extent by the issue of a standard on **agriculture**, which is generally of much more relevance to such countries.

There are also tensions between the **UK/US model** of financial reporting and the **European model**. The UK/US model is based around investor reporting, whereas the European model is mainly concerned with tax rules, so shareholder reporting has a much lower priority.

The break-up of the former USSR and the move in many **Eastern European countries** to free-market economies has also created difficulties. It is likely that these countries will have to 'catch up' to international standards as their economies stabilise.

You must keep up to date with the IASB's progress and the problems it encounters in the financial press. You should also be able to discuss:

- **Due process** of the IASB
- **Use and application** of IFRSs
- **Future work** of the IASB
- **Criticisms** of the IASB

One of the competences you require to fulfil Performance Objective 7 of the PER is the ability to prepare drafts or review primary financial statements in accordance with relevant accounting standards and policies and legislation. The information in this chapter will give you knowledge to help you demonstrate this competence.

Chapter Roundup

- A principles-based system works within a set of laid down principles. A rules-based system regulates for issues as they arise. Both of these have advantages and disadvantages.

- IFRSs are developed through a formal system of due process and broad international consultation involving accountants, financial analysis and other users and regulatory bodies from around the world.

Quick Quiz

1   What recent decisions will have a beneficial effect on global harmonisation of accounting?

2   One objective of the IASB is to promote the preparation of financial statements using the Euro.

   True   ☐

   False   ☐

3   A conceptual framework is:

   A   A theoretical expression of accounting standards
   B   A list of key terms used by the IASB
   C   A statement of theoretical principles which form the frame of reference for financial reporting
   D   The proforma financial statements

4   What development at the IASB aided users' interpretation of IFRSs?

5   Which of the following arguments is not in favour of accounting standards, but is in favour of accounting choice?

   A   They reduce variations in methods used to produce accounts
   B   They oblige companies to disclose their accounting policies
   C   They are a less rigid alternative to legislation
   D   They may tend towards rigidity in applying the rules

Answers to Quick Quiz

1   The IOSCO endorsement, and the EC requirement that listed companies should use IFRS from 2005.
2   False
3   C
4   The formation of the IFRS Interpretations Committee
5   D – The other arguments are all in favour of accounting standards.

Now try the Section C questions below from the Practice Question Bank

Number	Level	Marks	Time
2		10	20 mins
3(a)		5	10 mins

Tangible non-current assets

Topic list	Syllabus reference
1 IAS 16 *Property, plant and equipment* – Cost accounting	B1
2 IAS 16 *Property, plant and equipment* – Depreciation accounting	B1
3 IAS 40 *Investment property*	B1
4 IAS 23 *Borrowing costs*	B1

Introduction

IAS 16 should be familiar to you from your earlier studies, as should the mechanics of accounting for depreciation, revaluations of non-current assets and disposals of non-current assets. Some questions are given here for revision purposes.

IAS 40 deals with investment properties, which can be treated differently from other property under IAS 16.

IAS 23 deals with borrowing costs, which will form part of the cost of a qualifying asset.

Study guide

		Intellectual level
B1	**Tangible non-current assets**	
(a)	Define and compute the initial measurement of a non-current asset (including borrowing costs and an asset that has been self-constructed)	2
(b)	Identify subsequent expenditure that may be capitalised, distinguishing between capital and revenue items	2
(c)	Discuss the requirements of relevant accounting standards in relation to the revaluation of non-current assets	2
(d)	Account for revaluation and disposal gains and losses for non-current assets	2
(e)	Compute depreciation based on the cost and revaluation models and on assets that have two or more significant parts (complex assets)	2
(f)	Discuss why the treatment of investment properties should differ from other properties	2
(g)	Apply the requirements of relevant accounting standards to an investment property	2

1 IAS 16 *Property, plant and equipment* – Cost accounting

FAST FORWARD

IAS 16 covers all aspects of accounting for property, plant and equipment. This represents the bulk of items which are **'tangible' non-current assets**.

1.1 Scope

IAS 16 should be followed when accounting for property, plant and equipment *unless* another international accounting standard requires a **different treatment**.

IAS 16 **does not apply** to the following.

(a)   Biological assets related to agricultural activity, apart from bearer biological assets (see below)
(b)   Mineral rights and mineral reserves, such as oil, gas and other non-regenerative resources

However, the standard applies to property, plant and equipment used to develop these assets.

(IAS 16: paras. 2–3)

1.1.1 Bearer biological assets

Following an amendment to IAS 41, bearer biological assets, especially plantation trees such as grape vines, rubber trees and oil palms, are now classified under IAS 16. This amendment applies to plants which are solely used to grow produce over several periods and are not themselves consumed, being usually scrapped when no longer productive. They are measured at **accumulated cost** until maturity and then become subject to depreciation and impairment charges. (IASB, *Agriculture: Bearer Plants (Amendments to IAS 16 and IAS 41)*)

1.2 Definitions

The standard gives a large number of definitions.

Key terms

- **Property, plant and equipment** are tangible assets that:
  - Are held for use in the production or supply of goods or services, for rental to others, or for administrative purposes
  - Are expected to be used during more than one period
- **Cost** is the amount of cash or cash equivalents paid or the fair value of the other consideration given to acquire an asset at the time of its acquisition or construction.
- **Residual value** is the net amount which the entity expects to obtain for an asset at the end of its useful life after deducting the expected costs of disposal.
- **Entity specific value** is the present value of the cash flows an entity expects to arise from the continuing use of an asset and from its disposal at the end of its useful life, or expects to incur when settling a liability.

  (IAS 16: para. 6)
- **Fair value** is the price that would be received to sell an asset or paid to transfer a liability in an orderly transaction between market participants at the measurement date. (IFRS 13)
- **Carrying amount** is the amount at which an asset is recognised in the statement of financial position after deducting any accumulated depreciation and accumulated impairment losses.

  (IAS 16: para. 6)
- An **impairment loss** is the amount by which the carrying amount of an asset exceeds its recoverable amount.

  (IAS 16: para. 6)

Note that the definition of fair value has now been changed by IFRS 13.

1.3 Recognition

In this context, recognition simply means incorporation of the item in the business's accounts, in this case as a non-current asset. The recognition of property, plant and equipment depends on two criteria:

(a)   It is probable that **future economic benefits** associated with the asset will flow to the entity

(b)   The cost of the asset to the entity can be **measured reliably**

These recognition criteria apply to **subsequent expenditure** as well as costs incurred initially. There are no separate criteria for recognising subsequent expenditure.

Property, plant and equipment can amount to **substantial amounts** in financial statements, affecting the presentation of the company's financial position and the profitability of the entity, through depreciation and also if an asset is wrongly classified as an expense and taken to profit or loss.   (IAS 16: para. 7)

1.3.1 First criterion: future economic benefits

The **degree of certainty** attached to the flow of future economic benefits must be assessed. This should be based on the evidence available at the date of initial recognition (usually the date of purchase). The entity should be assured that it will receive the rewards attached to the asset and it will incur the associated risks, which will only generally be the case when the rewards and risks have actually passed to the entity. Until then, the asset should not be recognised.

1.3.2 Second criterion: cost measured reliably

It is generally easy to measure the cost of an asset as the **transfer amount on purchase**, ie what was paid for it. **Self-constructed assets** can also be measured easily by adding together the purchase price of all the constituent parts (labour, material etc) paid to external parties.   (IAS 16: para. 10)

1.4 Separate items

Most of the time assets will be identified individually, but this will not be the case for **smaller items**, such as tools, dies and moulds, which are sometimes classified as inventory and written off as an expense.

Major components or spare parts, however, should be recognised as property, plant and equipment.

(IAS 16: para. 8)

[handwritten: Exam question]

For very **large and specialised items**, an apparently single asset should be broken down into its composite parts. This occurs where the different parts have different useful lives and different depreciation rates are applied to each part, eg an aircraft, where the body and engines are separated as they have different useful lives.

(IAS 16: para. 13)

1.5 Safety and environmental equipment

These items may be necessary for the entity to **obtain future economic benefits** from its other assets. For this reason they are recognised as assets. However the original assets plus the safety equipment should be reviewed for impairment.

(IAS 16: para. 11)

1.6 Initial measurement

Once an item of property, plant and equipment qualifies for recognition as an asset, it will initially be **measured at cost**.

(IAS 16: para. 15)

1.6.1 Components of cost

[handwritten: Settlement Discount isn't deducted. A Trade discount is.]

The standard lists the components of the cost of an item of property, plant and equipment.

- **Purchase price**, less any trade discount or rebate
- **Import duties** and non-refundable purchase taxes
- **Directly attributable costs** of bringing the asset to working condition for its intended use, eg:
    - The cost of site preparation
    - Initial delivery and handling costs
    - Installation costs
    - Testing
    - Professional fees (architects, engineers)
- **Initial estimate** of the unavoidable cost of dismantling and removing the asset and restoring the site on which it is located

(IAS 16: paras. 16–18)

The revised IAS 16 provides **additional guidance on directly attributable** costs included in the cost of an item of property, plant and equipment.

(a) These costs bring the asset to the location and working conditions necessary for it to be capable of operating in the manner intended by management, including those costs to test whether the asset is functioning properly. *[handwritten: Refers to testing.]*

(b) They are determined after deducting the net proceeds from selling any items produced when bringing the asset to its location and condition.

(IAS 16: para. 16)

The revised standard also states that income and related expenses of operations that are **incidental** to the construction or development of an item of property, plant and equipment should be **recognised** in profit or loss.

The following costs **will not be part of the cost** of property, plant or equipment unless they can be attributed directly to the asset's acquisition, or bringing it into its working condition.

- Administration and other general overhead costs
- Start-up and similar pre-production costs
- Initial operating losses before the asset reaches planned performance

All of these will be recognised as an **expense** rather than an asset.

(IAS 16: para. 11)

In the case of **self-constructed assets**, the same principles are applied as for acquired assets. If the entity makes similar assets during the normal course of business for sale externally, then the cost of the asset will be the cost of its production. This also means that abnormal costs (wasted material, labour or other resources) are excluded from the cost of the asset. An example of a self-constructed asset is when a building company builds its own head office. (IAS 16: para. 22)

1.6.2 Subsequent expenditure

Parts of some items of property, plant and equipment may require replacement at regular intervals. IAS 16 gives examples of a furnace which may require relining after a specified number of hours or aircraft interiors which may require replacement several times during the life of the aircraft.

This cost is recognised in full when it is incurred and added to the carrying amount of the asset. It will be depreciated over its expected life, which may be different from the expected life of the other components of the asset. The carrying amount of the item being replaced, such as the old furnace lining, is derecognised when the replacement takes place. (IAS 16: para. 13)

Expenditure incurred in replacing or renewing a component of an item of property, plant and equipment must be **recognised in the carrying amount of the item**. The carrying amount of the replaced or renewed component must be derecognised. A similar approach is also applied when a separate component of an item of property, plant and equipment is identified in respect of a major inspection to enable the continued use of the item. (IAS 16: para. 13)

1.6.3 Exchanges of assets

IAS 16 specifies that exchange of items of property, plant and equipment, regardless of whether the assets are similar, are measured at **fair value, unless the exchange transaction lacks commercial substance** or the fair value of neither of the assets exchanged can be **measured reliably**. If the acquired item is not measured at fair value, its cost is measured at the carrying amount of the asset given up. (IAS 16: para. 24)

1.7 Measurement subsequent to initial recognition

The standard offers two possible treatments here, essentially a choice between keeping an asset recorded at **cost** or revaluing it to **fair value**.

(a)   **Cost model.** Carry the asset at its cost less depreciation and any accumulated impairment loss.

(b)   **Revaluation model.** Carry the asset at a revalued amount, being its fair value at the date of the revaluation less any subsequent accumulated depreciation and subsequent accumulated impairment losses. The revised IAS 16 makes clear that the **revaluation model is available only if the fair value of the item can be measured reliably**.

(IAS 16: paras. 29–30)

1.7.1 Revaluations

The **market value** of land and buildings usually represents fair value, assuming existing use and line of business. Such valuations are usually carried out by professionally qualified valuers.

In the case of **plant and equipment**, fair value can also be taken as **market value**. Where a market value is not available, however, depreciated replacement cost should be used. There may be no market value where types of plant and equipment are sold only rarely or because of their specialised nature (ie they would normally only be sold as part of an ongoing business).

The frequency of valuation depends on the **volatility of the fair values** of individual items of property, plant and equipment. The more volatile the fair value, the more frequently revaluations should be carried out. Where the current fair value is very different from the carrying value then a revaluation should be carried out.

Most importantly, when an item of property, plant and equipment is revalued, **the whole class of assets to which it belongs should be revalued**.

All the items within a class should be **revalued at the same time**, to prevent selective revaluation of certain assets and to avoid disclosing a mixture of costs and values from different dates in the financial statements. A rolling basis of revaluation is allowed if the revaluations are kept up to date and the revaluation of the whole class is completed in a short period of time.

How should any **increase in value** be treated when a revaluation takes place? The debit will be the increase in value in the statement of financial position, but what about the credit? IAS 16 requires the increase to be credited to a **revaluation surplus** (ie part of owners' equity), **unless** the increase is reversing a previous decrease which was recognised as an expense. To the extent that this offset is made, the increase is recognised as income; any excess is then taken to the revaluation surplus.

(IAS 16: paras. 31–36)

1.8 Example: revaluation surplus

Binkie Co has an item of land carried in its books at $13,000. Two years ago a slump in land values led the company to reduce the carrying value from $15,000. This was taken as an expense in profit or loss. There has been a surge in land prices in the current year, however, and the land is now worth $20,000.

Account for the revaluation in the current year.

Solution

The double entry is:

DEBIT	Asset value (statement of financial position)	$7,000	
CREDIT	Profit or loss		$2,000
	Other Comprehensive Income (revaluation surplus)		$5,000

The case is similar for a **decrease in value** on revaluation. Any decrease should be recognised as an expense, except where it offsets a previous increase taken as a revaluation surplus in owners' equity. Any decrease greater than the previous upwards increase in value must be taken as an expense in the profit or loss.

1.9 Example: revaluation decrease

Let us simply swap round the example given above. The original cost was $15,000, revalued upwards to $20,000 two years ago. The value has now fallen to $13,000.

Account for the decrease in value.

Solution

The double entry is:

DEBIT	Other Comprehensive Income (revaluation surplus)	$5,000	
DEBIT	Profit or loss	$2,000	
CREDIT	Asset value (statement of financial position)		$7,000

There is a further complication when a **revalued asset is being depreciated**. As we have seen, an upward revaluation means that the depreciation charge will increase. Normally, a revaluation surplus is only realised when the asset is sold, but when it is being depreciated, part of that surplus is being realised as the asset is used. The amount of the surplus realised is the difference between depreciation charged on the revalued amount and the (lower) depreciation which would have been charged on the asset's original cost. **This amount can be transferred to retained (ie realised) earnings but NOT through profit or loss.**

1.10 Example: revaluation and depreciation

Crinckle Co bought an asset for $10,000 at the beginning of 20X6. It had a useful life of five years. On 1 January 20X8 the asset was revalued to $12,000. The expected useful life has remained unchanged (ie three years remain).

Account for the revaluation and state the treatment for depreciation from 20X8 onwards.

Solution

On 1 January 20X8 the carrying value of the asset is $10,000 – (2 × $10,000 ÷ 5) = $6,000. For the revaluation:

DEBIT	Accumulated depreciation	$4,000	
DEBIT	Asset value	$2,000	
CREDIT	Other Comprehensive Income (revaluation surplus)		$6,000

The depreciation for the next three years will be $12,000 ÷ 3 = $4,000, compared to depreciation on cost of $10,000 ÷ 5 = $2,000. So each year, the extra $2,000 can be treated as part of the surplus which has become realised:

DEBIT	Other Comprehensive Income (revaluation surplus)	$2,000	
CREDIT	Retained earnings		$2,000

This is a movement on owners' equity only, not an item in profit or loss.

Exam focus point

> Note that when a revaluation takes place, the depreciation for the period up to the date of revaluation should be deducted from the carrying value **before** calculating the revaluation surplus. The examining team have drawn attention to this as an error frequently made in exams.

1.11 Depreciation

The standard states:

- The **depreciable amount** of an item of property, plant and equipment should be allocated on a systematic basis over its useful life.
- The **depreciation method** used should reflect the pattern in which the asset's economic benefits are consumed by the entity.
- The **depreciation charge** for each period should be recognised as an expense unless it is included in the carrying amount of another asset.

(IAS 16: para. 48)

Land and buildings are dealt with separately even when they are acquired together because land normally has an unlimited life and is therefore not depreciated. In contrast buildings do have a limited life and must be depreciated. Any increase in the value of land on which a building is standing will have no impact on the determination of the building's useful life. (IAS 16: para. 58)

1.11.1 Review of useful life

A review of the **useful life** of property, plant and equipment should be carried out **at least at each financial year end** and the depreciation charge for the current and future periods should be adjusted if expectations have changed significantly from previous estimates. Changes are changes in accounting estimates and are accounted for prospectively as adjustments to future depreciation. (IAS 16: para. 51)

1.11.2 Example: review of useful life

Bashful Co acquired a non-current asset on 1 January 20X2 for $80,000. It had no residual value and a useful life of ten years.

On 1 January 20X5 the remaining useful life was reviewed and revised to four years.

What will be the depreciation charge for 20X5?

Solution

	$
Original cost	80,000
Depreciation 20X2 – 20X4 (80,000 × 3/10)	(24,000)
Carrying amount at 31 December 20X4	56,000
Remaining life	4 years
Depreciation charge years 20X5 – 20X8 (56,000/4)	14,000

1.11.3 Review of depreciation method

The **depreciation method** should also be reviewed **at least at each financial year end** and, if there has been a significant change in the expected pattern of economic benefits from those assets, the method should be changed to suit this changed pattern. When such a change in depreciation method takes place the change should be accounted for as a **change in accounting estimate** and the depreciation charge for the current and future periods should be adjusted. (IAS 16: para. 61)

1.11.4 Impairment of asset values

An **impairment loss** should be treated in the same way as a **revaluation decrease** ie the decrease should be **recognised as an expense**. However, a revaluation decrease (or impairment loss) should be charged directly against any related revaluation surplus to the extent that the decrease does not exceed the amount held in the revaluation surplus in respect of that same asset.

A **reversal of an impairment** loss should be treated in the same way as a **revaluation increase**, ie a revaluation increase should be recognised as income to the extent that it reverses a revaluation decrease or an impairment loss of the same asset previously recognised as an expense. (IAS 16: para. 63)

1.12 Complex assets

These are assets which are made up of separate components. Each component is separately depreciated over their useful life (IAS 16: para. 13). An example which appeared in a recent examination was that of an aircraft. An aircraft could be considered as having the following components.

	Cost	Useful life
	$'000	
Fuselage	20,000	20 years
Undercarriage	5,000	500 landings
Engines	8,000	1,600 flying hours

Depreciation at the end of the first year, in which 150 flights totalling 400 hours were made would then be:

	$'000
Fuselage	1,000
Undercarriage (5,000 × 150/500)	1,500
Engines (8,000 × 400/1,600)	2,000
	4,500

1.13 Overhauls

Where an asset requires regular overhauls in order to continue to operate, the cost of the overhaul is treated as an additional component and depreciated over the period to the next overhaul. (IAS 16: para.14)

If, in the case of the aircraft above, an overhaul was required at the end of year 3 and every third year thereafter at a cost of $1.2m this would be capitalised as a separate component. $1.2m would be added to the cost and the depreciation (assuming 150 flights again) would therefore be:

	$'000
Total as above	4,500
Overhaul ($1,200,000/3)	400
	4,900

1.14 Retirements and disposals

When an asset is permanently **withdrawn from use, or sold or scrapped**, and no future economic benefits are expected from its disposal, it should be withdrawn from the statement of financial position.

(IAS 16: para. 67)

Gains or losses are the difference between the estimated net disposal proceeds and the carrying amount of the asset. They should be recognised as income or expense in profit or loss. (IAS 16: para. 71)

1.15 Derecognition

An entity is required to **derecognise the carrying amount** of an item of property, plant or equipment that it disposes of on the date the **criteria for the sale** in IFRS 15 *Revenue from contracts with customers* would be met. This also applies to parts of an asset. (IAS 16: para. 68)

An entity cannot classify as revenue a gain it realises on the disposal of an item of property, plant and equipment. (IAS 16: para. 68)

1.16 Disclosure

The standard has a long list of disclosure requirements, for each class of property, plant and equipment.

(a) **Measurement bases** for determining the gross carrying amount (if more than one, the gross carrying amount for that basis in each category)

(b) **Depreciation methods** used

(c) **Useful lives** or depreciation rates used

(d) **Gross carrying amount** and accumulated depreciation (aggregated with accumulated impairment losses) at the beginning and end of the period

(e) **Reconciliation** of the carrying amount at the beginning and end of the period showing:

(i) Additions
(ii) Disposals
(iii) Acquisitions through business combinations
(iv) Increases/decreases during the period from revaluations and from impairment losses
(v) Impairment losses recognised in profit or loss
(vi) Impairment losses reversed in profit or loss
(vii) Depreciation
(viii) Net exchange differences (from translation of statements of a foreign entity)
(ix) Any other movements

The financial statements should also disclose the following.

(a) Any recoverable amounts of property, plant and equipment
(b) Existence and amounts of **restrictions on title**, and items pledged as security for liabilities
(c) Accounting policy for **the estimated costs of restoring the site**
(d) Amount of expenditures on account of **items in the course of construction**
(e) Amount of commitments to **acquisitions**

Revalued assets require further disclosures.

(a) Basis used to revalue the assets
(b) Effective date of the revaluation
(c) Whether an independent valuer was involved
(d) Nature of any indices used to determine replacement cost

(e)   Carrying amount of each class of property, plant and equipment that would have been included in the financial statements had the assets been carried at cost less accumulated depreciation and accumulated impairment losses

(f)   Revaluation surplus, indicating the movement for the period and any restrictions on the distribution of the balance to shareholders

The standard also **encourages disclosure** of additional information, which the users of financial statements may find useful.

(a)   The carrying amount of temporarily idle property, plant and equipment

(b)   The gross carrying amount of any fully depreciated property, plant and equipment that is still in use

(c)   The carrying amount of property, plant and equipment retired from active use and held for disposal

(d)   The fair value of property, plant and equipment when this is materially different from the carrying amount

(IAS 16: paras. 73–77)

The following format (with notional figures) is commonly used to disclose non-current assets movements.

	Total $	Land and buildings $	Plant and equipment $
Cost or valuation			
At 1 January 20X4	50,000	40,000	10,000
Revaluation surplus	12,000	12,000	–
Additions in year	4,000	–	4,000
Disposals in year	(1,000)	–	(1,000)
At 31 December 20X4	65,000	52,000	13,000
Depreciation			
At 1 January 20X4	16,000	10,000	6,000
Charge for year	4,000	1,000	3,000
Eliminated on disposals	(500)	–	(500)
At 31 December 20X4	19,500	11,000	8,500
Carrying amount			
At 31 December 20X4	45,500	41,000	4,500
At 1 January 20X4	34,000	30,000	4,000

 Question   Non-current assets

(a)   In a statement of financial position prepared in accordance with IAS 16, what does the carrying amount represent?

(b)   In a set of financial statements prepared in accordance with IAS 16, is it correct to say that the carrying amount in a statement of financial position cannot be greater than the market (net realisable) value of the partially used asset as at the end of the reporting period? Explain your reasons for your answer.

Answer

(a)   In simple terms the carrying amount of an asset is the cost of an asset less the 'accumulated depreciation', that is, all depreciation charged so far. It should be emphasised that the main purpose of charging depreciation is to ensure that profits are fairly reported. Thus depreciation is concerned with the statement of profit or loss rather than the statement of financial position. In consequence the carrying amount in the statement of financial position can be quite arbitrary. In particular, it does not necessarily bear any relation to the market value of an asset and is of little use for planning and decision making.

An obvious example of the disparity between carrying amount and market value is found in the case of buildings, which may be worth more than ten times as much as their carrying amount.

(b)   Carrying amount can in some circumstances be higher than market value (net realisable value). IAS 16 *Property, plant and equipment* states that the value of an asset cannot be greater than its 'recoverable amount'. However 'recoverable amount' as defined in IAS 16 is the amount recoverable from further use. This may be higher than the market value.

This makes sense if you think of a specialised machine which could not fetch much on the secondhand market but which will produce goods which can be sold at a profit for many years.

Exam focus point

Property and/or other non-current assets are likely to be tested as they have come up on a number of papers.

2 IAS 16 *Property, plant and equipment* – Depreciation accounting

FAST FORWARD

Where assets held by an entity have a **limited useful life** to that entity it is necessary to apportion the value of an asset over its useful life.

2.1 Non-current assets

If an asset's life extends over more than one accounting period, it earns profits over more than one period. It is a **non-current asset**.

With the exception of land, **every non-current asset eventually wears out over time**. Machines, cars and other vehicles, fixtures and fittings, and even buildings do not last for ever. When a business acquires a non-current asset, it will have some idea about how long its useful life will be, and it might decide what to do with it.

(a)   Keep on using the non-current asset until it becomes **completely worn out**, useless, and worthless.

(b)   **Sell off** the non-current asset at the end of its useful life, either by selling it as a second-hand item or as scrap.

Since a non-current asset has a cost, and a limited useful life, and its value eventually declines, it follows that a charge should be made in profit or loss to reflect the use that is made of the asset by the business. This charge is called **depreciation**.

2.2 Scope

Depreciation accounting is governed by IAS 16 *Property, plant and equipment*. These are some of the IAS 16 definitions concerning depreciation.

Key terms

- **Depreciation** is the result of systematic allocation of the depreciable amount of an asset over its estimated useful life. Depreciation for the accounting period is charged to net profit or loss for the period either directly or indirectly.

- **Depreciable assets** are assets which:
    - Are expected to be used during more than one accounting period
    - Have a limited useful life
    - Are held by an entity for use in the production or supply of goods and services, for rental to others, or for administrative purposes

- **Useful life** is one of two things:
    - The period over which a depreciable asset is expected to be used by the entity, or
    - The number of production or similar units expected to be obtained from the asset by the entity.

> - **Depreciable amount** of a depreciable asset is the historical cost or other amount substituted for cost in the financial statements, less the estimated residual value.
>
> (IAS 16: paras. 43–62)

An 'amount substituted for cost' will normally be a **current market value** after a revaluation has taken place.

2.3 Depreciation

IAS 16 requires the depreciable amount of a depreciable asset to be allocated on a **systematic basis** to each accounting period during the useful life of the asset. **Every part of an item of property, plant and equipment with a cost that is significant in relation to the total cost of the item must be depreciated separately.**

(IAS 16: para. 44)

One way of defining depreciation is to describe it as a means of **spreading the cost** of a non-current asset over its useful life, and so matching the cost against the full period during which it earns profits for the business. Depreciation charges are an example of the application of the accrual assumption to calculate profits.

The need for depreciation of non-current assets arises from the accruals assumption. If money is expended in purchasing an asset then the amount expended must at some time be charged against profits. If the asset is one which contributes to an entity's revenue over a number of accounting periods, it would be inappropriate to charge any single period with the whole of the expenditure. Thus this is a method where the cost is spread over the useful life of the asset.

There are situations where, over a period, an asset has **increased in value**, ie its current value is greater than the carrying value in the financial statements. You might think that in such situations it would not be necessary to depreciate the asset. The standard states, however, that this is irrelevant, and that depreciation should still be charged to each accounting period, based on the depreciable amount, irrespective of a rise in value.

(IAS 16: para. 52)

An entity is required to begin depreciating an item of property, plant and equipment when it is available for use and to continue depreciating it until it is derecognised even if it is idle during the period.

(IAS 16: para. 55)

2.4 Useful life

The following factors should be considered when **estimating the useful life** of a depreciable asset.

- Expected **physical wear and tear**
- **Obsolescence**
- Legal or other **limits** on the use of the assets

Once decided, the useful life should be **reviewed at least every financial year end** and depreciation rates adjusted for the current and future periods if expectations vary significantly from the original estimates. The effect of the change should be disclosed in the accounting period in which the change takes place.

The assessment of useful life requires **judgement** based on previous experience with similar assets or classes of asset. When a completely new type of asset is acquired (ie through technological advancement or through use in producing a brand new product or service) it is still necessary to estimate useful life, even though the exercise will be much more difficult.

The standard also points out that the physical life of the asset might be longer than its useful life to the entity in question. One of the main factors to be taken into consideration is the **physical wear and tear** the asset is likely to endure. This will depend on various circumstances, including the number of shifts for which the asset will be used, the entity's repair and maintenance programme and so on. Other factors to be considered include obsolescence (due to technological advances/improvements in production/ reduction in demand for the product/service produced by the asset) and legal restrictions, eg length of a related lease.

(IAS 16: para. 57)

2.5 Residual value

In most cases the residual value of an asset is **likely to be immaterial**. If it is likely to be of any significant value, that value must be estimated at the date of purchase or any subsequent revaluation. The amount of residual value should be estimated based on the current situation with other similar assets, used in the same way, which are now at the end of their useful lives. Any expected costs of disposal should be offset against the gross residual value.

2.6 Depreciation methods

Consistency is important. The depreciation method selected should be applied consistently from period to period unless altered circumstances justify a change. When the method **is** changed, the effect should be quantified and disclosed and the reason for the change should be stated.

Various methods of allocating depreciation to accounting periods are available, but whichever is chosen must be applied **consistently** (as required by IAS 1: see Chapter 1), to ensure comparability from period to period. Change of policy is not allowed simply because of the profitability situation of the entity.

You should be familiar with the various **accepted methods of allocating depreciation** and the relevant calculations and accounting treatments, which are revised in questions at the end of this section.

2.7 Disclosure

An accounting policy note should disclose the **valuation bases** used for determining the amounts at which depreciable assets are stated, along with the other accounting policies.

IAS 16 also requires the following to be disclosed for each major class of depreciable asset.

- **Depreciation methods** used
- **Useful lives** or the depreciation rates used
- **Total depreciation** allocated for the period
- **Gross amount** of depreciable assets and the related accumulated depreciation

(IAS 16: paras. 73–78)

2.8 What is depreciation?

The need to depreciate non-current assets arises from the **accruals assumption**. If money is expended in purchasing an asset then the amount expended must at some time be charged against profits. If the asset is one which contributes to an entity's revenue over a number of accounting periods it would be inappropriate to charge any single period (eg the period in which the asset was acquired) with the whole of the expenditure. Instead, some method must be found of spreading the cost of the asset over its useful economic life.

This view of depreciation as a process of allocation of the cost of an asset over several accounting periods is the view adopted by IAS 16. It is worth mentioning here two **common misconceptions** about the purpose and effects of depreciation.

(a) It is sometimes thought that the carrying amount of an asset is equal to its net realisable value and that the object of charging depreciation is to **reflect the fall in value of an asset over its life**. This misconception is the basis of a common, but incorrect, argument which says that freehold properties (say) need not be depreciated in times when property values are rising. It is true that historical cost statements of financial position often give a misleading impression when a property's carrying amount is much below its market value, but in such a case it is open to a business to incorporate a revaluation into its books, or even to prepare its accounts based on current costs. This is a separate problem from that of allocating the property's cost over successive accounting periods.

(b) Another misconception is that depreciation is provided **so that an asset can be replaced at the end of its useful life**. This is not the case:

(i) If there is no intention of replacing the asset, it could then be argued that there is no need to provide for any depreciation at all

(ii) If prices are rising, the replacement cost of the asset will exceed the amount of depreciation provided

The following questions are for revision purposes only.

Question	Depreciation methods

A lorry bought for Titan Co cost $17,000. It is expected to last for five years and then be sold for scrap for $2,000. Usage over the five years is expected to be:

Year 1	200 days
Year 2	100 days
Year 3	100 days
Year 4	150 days
Year 5	40 days

Required

Work out the depreciation to be charged each year under:

(a) The straight line method
(b) The reducing balance method (using a rate of 35%)
(c) The machine hour method
(d) The sum-of-the digits method

Answer

(a) Under the straight line method, depreciation for each of the five years is:

$$\text{Annual depreciation} = \frac{\$(17,000 - 2,000)}{5} = \$3,000$$

(b) Under the reducing balance method, depreciation for each of the five years is:

Year	Depreciation		
1	35% × $17,000	=	$5,950
2	35% × ($17,000 – $5,950) = 35% × $11,050	=	$3,868
3	35% × ($11,050 – $3,868) = 35% × $7,182	=	$2,514
4	35% × ($7,182 – $2,514) = 35% × $4,668	=	$1,634
5	Balance to bring book value down to $2,000 = $4,668 – $1,634 – $2,000	=	$1,034

(c) Under the machine hour method, depreciation for each of the five years is calculated as follows.

Total usage (days) = 200 + 100 + 100 + 150 + 40 = 590 days

$$\text{Depreciation per day} = \frac{\$(17,000 - 2,000)}{590} = \$25.42$$

Year	Usage (days)	Depreciation ($) (days × $25.42)
1	200	5,084.00
2	100	2,542.00
3	100	2,542.00
4	150	3,813.00
5	40	1,016.80
		14,997.80

Note. The answer does not come to exactly $15,000 because of the rounding carried out at the 'depreciation per day' stage of the calculation.

(d)   The sum-of-the digits method begins by adding up the years of expected life. In this case,
        5 + 4 + 3 + 2 + 1 = 15.

        The depreciable amount of $15,000 will then be allocated as follows:

        Year   1   15,000 × 5/15 = 5,000
                2   15,000 × 4/15 = 4,000
                3   15,000 × 3/15 = 3,000
                4   15,000 × 2/15 = 2,000
                5   15,000 × 1/15 = 1,000

**Exam focus
point**

> The December 2008 exam had a question which included machine-hour depreciation. Some candidates
> failed to deduct the residual value before calculating the machine hour rate.

Question   Depreciation discussion

(a)   What are the purposes of providing for depreciation?

(b)   In what circumstances is the reducing balance method more appropriate than the straight-line
        method? Give reasons for your answer.

Answer

(a)   The accounts of a business try to recognise that the cost of a non-current asset is gradually
        consumed as the asset wears out. This is done by gradually writing off the asset's cost to profit or
        loss over several accounting periods. This process is known as depreciation, and is an example of
        the accruals assumption. IAS 16 *Property, plant and equipment* requires that depreciation should
        be allocated on a systematic basis to each accounting period during the useful life of the asset
        (para. 50).

        With regard to the accrual principle, it is fair that the profits should be reduced by the depreciation
        charge; this is not an arbitrary exercise. Depreciation is not, as is sometimes supposed, an attempt
        to set aside funds to purchase new non-current assets when required. Depreciation is not generally
        provided on freehold land because it does not 'wear out' (unless it is held for mining etc).

(b)   The reducing balance method of depreciation is used instead of the straight line method when it is
        considered fair to allocate a greater proportion of the total depreciable amount to the earlier years
        and a lower proportion to the later years on the assumption that the benefits obtained by the
        business from using the asset decline over time.

        In favour of this method it may be argued that it links the depreciation charge to the costs of
        maintaining and running the asset. In the early years these costs are low and the depreciation
        charge is high, while in later years this is reversed.

Question   Depreciation accounting

AlumCo purchased two rivet-making machines on 1 January 20X5 at a cost of $15,000 each. Each had an
estimated life of five years and a nil residual value. The straight line method of depreciation is used.

Owing to an unforeseen slump in market demand for rivets, AlumCo decided to reduce its output of rivets,
and switch to making other products instead. On 31 March 20X7, one rivet-making machine was sold (on
credit) to a buyer for $8,000.

Later in the year, however, it was decided to abandon production of rivets altogether, and the second
machine was sold on 1 December 20X7 for $2,500 cash.

Prepare the machinery account, provision for depreciation of machinery account and disposal of
machinery account for the accounting year to 31 December 20X7.

MACHINERY ACCOUNT

		$				$
20X7			20X7			
1 Jan	Balance b/f	30,000	31 Mar	Disposal of machinery account		15,000
			1 Dec	Disposal of machinery account		15,000
		30,000				30,000

ACCUMULATED DEPRECIATION OF MACHINERY

		$				$
20X7			20X7			
31 Mar	Disposal of machinery account*	6,750	1 Jan	Balance b/f		12,000
1 Dec	Disposal of machinery account**	8,750	31 Dec	Profit or loss***		3,500
		15,500				15,500

```
*     Depreciation at date of disposal = $6,000 + $750
**    Depreciation at date of disposal = $6,000 + $2,750
***   Depreciation charge for the year = $750 + $2,750
```

DISPOSAL OF MACHINERY

		$			$
20X7			20X7		
31 Mar	Machinery account	15,000	31 Mar	Account receivable (sale price)	8,000
			31 Mar	Charge for depreciation	6,750
1 Dec	Machinery	15,000	1 Dec	Cash (sale price)	2,500
			1 Dec	Charge for depreciation	8,750
			31 Dec	Profit or loss (loss on disposal)	4,000
		30,000			30,000

You should be able to calculate that there was a loss on the first disposal of $250, and on the second disposal of $3,750, giving a total loss of $4,000.

Workings

1   At 1 January 20X7, accumulated depreciation on the machines will be:

$$2 \text{ machines} \times 2 \text{ years} \times \frac{\$15,000}{5} \text{ per machine pa} = \$12,000, \text{ or } \$6,000 \text{ per machine}$$

2   Monthly depreciation is $\frac{\$3,000}{12} = \$250$ per machine per month

3   The machines are disposed of in 20X7.

   (a)   On 31 March – after three months of the year. Depreciation for the year on the machine
         = 3 months × $250 = $750

   (b)   On 1 December – after 11 months of the year. Depreciation for the year on the machine
         = 11 months × $250 = $2,750

3 IAS 40 *Investment property*

An entity may own land or a building **as an investment** rather than for use in the business. It may therefore generate cash flows largely independently of other assets which the entity holds. The treatment of investment property is covered by IAS 40.

3.1 Definitions

[handwritten: carrying amount → Balance in (S.O.F.P). = cost (or valuation) = Accumulated depreciation or impairment]

Consider the following definitions.

Key terms

> **Investment property** is property (land or a building – or part of a building – or both) held (by the owner or by the lessee as a right-of-use asset) to earn rentals or for capital appreciation or both, rather than for:
>
> (a)   Use in the production or supply of goods or services or for administrative purposes, or
> (b)   Sale in the ordinary course of business.
>
> **Owner-occupied property** is property held by the owner (or by the lessee as a right-of-use asset) for use in the production or supply of goods or services or for administrative purposes.
>
> **Fair value** is the price that would be received to sell an asset or paid to transfer a liability in an orderly transaction between market participants at the measurement date.
>
> **Cost** is the amount of cash or cash equivalents paid or the fair value of other consideration given to acquire an asset at the time of its acquisition or construction.
>
> **Carrying amount** is the amount at which an asset is recognised in the statement of financial position. *[handwritten: NBV]*
>
> (IAS 40: para. 5)

Examples of investment property include:

(a)   **Land held for long-term capital appreciation** rather than for short-term sale in the ordinary course of business

(b)   A **building** owned by the reporting entity (or held by the entity as a right-of-use asset) and **leased out under an operating lease**

(c)   A building held by a **parent** and leased to a **subsidiary**. Note, however, that while this is regarded as an investment property in the individual parent company financial statements, in the **consolidated** financial statements this property will be regarded as owner-occupied (because it is occupied by the group) and will therefore be treated in accordance with IAS 16.

(d)   Property that is being constructed or developed for future use as an investment property

(IAS 40: para. 8)

Question   Investment

Rich Co owns a piece of land. The directors have not yet decided whether to build a factory on it for use in its business or to keep it and sell it when its value has risen.

Would this be classified as an investment property under IAS 40?

Answer

Yes. If an entity has not determined that it will use the land either as an owner-occupied property or for short-term sale in the ordinary course of business, the land is considered to be held for capital appreciation.

3.2 IAS 40

IAS 40 *Investment property* prescribes the accounting treatment for investment property and related disclosure requirements. It has been amended following the issue of IFRS 16 *Leases*.

An asset held by an entity as a right-of-use asset under IFRS 16 and leased out under an operating lease is treated as investment property. (IFRS 16: para. 8)

You now know what **is** an investment property under IAS 40. Below are examples of items that are **not investment property**.

Type of non-investment property	Applicable IAS
Property intended for sale in the ordinary course of business	IAS 2 *Inventories*
Property being constructed or developed on behalf of third parties	IFRS 15 *Revenue from contracts with customers*
Owner-occupied property	IAS 16 *Property, plant and equipment*

3.3 Recognition

Investment property should be recognised as an asset when **two conditions** are met:

(a)   It is **probable** that the **future economic benefits** that are associated with the investment property will **flow to the entity**.

(b)   The **cost** of the investment property can be **measured reliably**. (IAS 40: para. 8)

3.4 Initial measurement

An investment property should be measured initially at its **cost,** including transaction costs.

A right-of-use asset classified as an investment property should be measured in accordance with IFRS 16.

3.5 Measurement subsequent to initial recognition

IAS 40 requires an entity to **choose between two models:**

- The fair value model
- The cost model (IAS 40: para. 32)

Whatever policy it chooses should be applied to **all of its investment property**.

3.5.1 Fair value model

Key terms

(a)   After initial recognition, an entity that chooses the **fair value model** should measure all of its investment property at fair value, except in the extremely rare cases where this cannot be measured reliably. In such cases it should apply the IAS 16 cost model.

(b)   A gain or loss arising from a change in the fair value of an investment property should be recognised in net profit or loss for the period in which it arises.

(c)   The fair value of investment property should reflect market conditions at the end of the reporting period. (IAS 40: para. 33)

This was the first time that the IASB has allowed a fair value model for non-financial assets. This is not the same as a revaluation, where increases in carrying amount above a cost-based measure are recognised as revaluation surplus. Under the fair-value model all changes in fair value are recognised in profit or loss.

The standard elaborates on **issues relating to fair value**.

(a)   Fair value assumes that an orderly transaction has taken place between market participants, ie both buyer and seller are reasonably informed about the nature and characteristics of the investment property.

(b)   A buyer participating in an orderly transaction is **motivated but not compelled** to buy. A seller participating in an orderly transaction is neither an over-eager nor a forced seller, nor one prepared to sell at any price or to hold out for a price not considered reasonable in the current market.

(c)   **Fair value is not the same as 'value in use'** as defined in IAS 36 *Impairment of assets*. Value in use reflects factors and knowledge specific to the entity, while fair value reflects factors and knowledge relevant to the market.

(d)   In determining fair value an entity **should not double count assets**. For example, elevators or air conditioning are often an integral part of a building and should be included in the investment property, rather than recognised separately.

(e)   When a lessee uses the fair value model to measure an investment property that is held as a right-of-use asset, it shall measure the right-of-use asset, and not the underlying property, at fair value.

(f)   In those rare cases where the **entity cannot determine the fair value of an investment property reliably**, the cost model in **IAS 16** must be applied until the investment property is disposed of. The **residual value must be assumed to be zero**.

(g)   When lease payments are at market rates, the fair value of an investment property held by a lessee as a right-of-use asset, net of all expected lease payments, should be zero.   (IAS 40: paras. 50–55)

3.5.2 Cost model

The cost model is the **cost model in IAS 16** for owned assets. Assets held by lessees as right-of-use assets are measured at cost in accordance with IFRS 16. Investment property should be measured at **depreciated cost, less any accumulated impairment losses**. An entity that chooses the cost model should **disclose the fair value of its investment property**.   (IAS 40: paras. 56,79)

3.5.3 Changing models

Once the entity has chosen the fair value or cost model, it should apply it to all its investment property. It **should not change from one model to the other unless the change will result in a more appropriate presentation**. IAS 40 states that it is highly unlikely that a change from the fair value model to the cost model will result in a more appropriate presentation.   (IAS 40: para. 31)

3.6 Transfers

Transfers to or from investment property should **only** be made **when there is a change in use**. For example, owner occupation commences so the investment property will be treated under IAS 16 as an owner-occupied property.

When there is a transfer from investment property carried at fair value to owner-occupied property or inventories, the property's cost for subsequent accounting under IAS 16 or IAS 2 should be its fair value at the date of change of use.

Conversely, an owner-occupied property may become an investment property and need to be carried at fair value. An entity should apply IAS 16 up to the date of change of use. It should treat any difference at that date between the carrying amount of the property under IAS 16 and its fair value as a revaluation under IAS 16.
                              (IAS 40: paras. 57–65)

3.7 Worked example: Transfer to investment property

Kapital Co owns a building which it has been using as a head office. In order to reduce costs, on 30 June 20X9 it moved its head office functions to one of its production centres and is now letting out its head office. Company policy is to use the fair value model for investment property.

The building had an original cost on 1 January 20X0 of $250,000 and was being depreciated over 50 years. At 31 December 20X9 its fair value was judged to be $350,000.

How will this appear in the financial statements of Kapital Co at 31 December 20X9?

Solution

The building will be depreciated up to 30 June 20X9.

	$
Original cost	250,000
Depreciation 1.1.X0 – 1.1.X9 (250/50 × 9)	(45,000)
Depreciation to 30.6.X9 (250/50 × 6/12)	(2,500)
Carrying amount at 30.6.X9	202,500
Revaluation surplus	147,500
Fair value at 30.6.X9	350,000

The difference between the carrying amount and fair value is taken to a **revaluation surplus**.

However the building will be subjected to a fair value exercise at each year end and these gains or losses will go to **profit or loss**. If at the end of the following year the fair value of the building is found to be $380,000, $30,000 will be credited to profit or loss.

3.8 Disposals

Derecognise (eliminate from the statement of financial position) an investment property on disposal or when it is permanently withdrawn from use and no future economic benefits are expected from its disposal.

Any **gain or loss** on disposal is the difference between the net disposal proceeds and the carrying amount of the asset. It should generally be **recognised as income or expense in profit or loss**.

Compensation from third parties for investment property that was impaired, lost or given up shall be recognised in profit or loss when the compensation becomes receivable.   (IAS 40: paras. 66–69)

3.9 Disclosure requirements

These relate to:

- Choice of fair value model or cost model
- Criteria for classification as investment property
- Assumptions in determining fair value
- Use of independent professional valuer (encouraged but not required)
- Rental income and expenses
- Any restrictions or obligations   (IAS 40: paras. 74–79)

3.9.1 Fair value model – additional disclosures

An entity that adopts this must also disclose a **reconciliation** of the carrying amount of the investment property at the beginning and end of the period.   (IAS 40: paras. 77–78)

3.9.2 Cost model – additional disclosures

These relate mainly to the depreciation method. In addition, an entity which adopts the cost model **must disclose the fair value** of the investment property.   (IAS 40: para. 79)

4 IAS 23 *Borrowing costs*

FAST FORWARD

> IAS 23 looks at the treatment of **borrowing costs**, particularly where the related borrowings are applied to the construction of certain assets. These are what are usually called 'self-constructed assets', where an entity builds its own inventory or non-current assets over a substantial period of time.

4.1 Definitions

IAS 23 *Borrowing costs* was revised in March 2007. Previously it gave a choice of methods in dealing with borrowing costs: capitalisation or expense. The revised standard requires capitalisation.

Only two definitions are given by the standard:

> **Borrowing costs.** Interest and other costs incurred by an entity in connection with the borrowing of funds.
>
> **Qualifying asset.** An asset that necessarily takes a substantial period of time to get ready for its intended use or sale. (IAS 23: para. 5)

The standard does not define 'substantial period of time' but an asset that normally takes more than a year to be ready for use will usually be a qualifying asset. Generally, borrowing costs will be capitalised where the impact is material.

The standard lists what may be **included in borrowing costs**.

- Interest on bank overdrafts and short-term and long-term borrowings
- Amortisation of discounts or premiums relating to borrowings
- Amortisation of ancillary costs incurred in connection with the arrangement of borrowings
- Finance charges in respect of leases recognised in accordance with IFRS 16
- Exchange differences arising from foreign currency borrowings to the extent that they are regarded as an adjustment to interest costs (IAS 23: para. 6)

Depending on the circumstances, any of the following may be qualifying assets.

- Inventories
- Manufacturing plants
- Power generation facilities
- Intangible assets
- Investment properties (IAS 23: para. 7)

Financial assets and inventories that are manufactured, or otherwise produced over a short period of time are **not qualifying assets**. Assets that are ready for their intended use or sale when purchased are not qualifying assets.

4.2 IAS 23: Capitalisation

All eligible borrowing costs must be **capitalised**.

Only borrowing costs that are **directly attributable** to the acquisition, construction or production of a qualifying asset can be capitalised as part of the cost of that asset. The standard lays out the criteria for determining which borrowing costs are eligible for capitalisation. (IAS 23: para. 8)

4.2.1 Borrowing costs eligible for capitalisation

Those borrowing costs directly attributable to the acquisition, construction or production of a qualifying asset must be identified. These are the borrowing costs that **would have been avoided** had the expenditure on the qualifying asset not been made. This is obviously straightforward where funds have been borrowed for the financing of one particular asset.

Difficulties arise, however, where the entity uses a **range of debt instruments** to finance a wide range of assets, so that there is no direct relationship between particular borrowings and a specific asset. For example, all borrowings may be made centrally and then lent to different parts of the group or entity. Judgement is therefore required, particularly where further complications can arise (eg foreign currency loans).

Once the relevant borrowings are identified, which relate to a specific asset, then the **amount of borrowing costs available for capitalisation** will be the actual borrowing costs incurred on those borrowings during the period, **less** any investment income on the temporary investment of those borrowings. It would not be unusual for some or all of the funds to be invested before they are actually used on the qualifying asset.

(IAS 23: paras.10–15)

Question

Capitalisation

On 1 January 20X6 Stremans Co borrowed $1.5m to finance the production of two assets, both of which were expected to take a year to build. Work started during 20X6. The loan facility was drawn down and incurred on 1 January 20X6, and was utilised as follows, with the remaining funds invested temporarily.

	Asset Alpha	Asset Bravo
	$'000	$'000
1 January 20X6	250	500
1 July 20X6	250	500

The loan rate was 9% and Stremans Co can invest surplus funds at 7%.

Required

Ignoring compound interest, calculate the borrowing costs which may be capitalised for each of the assets and consequently the cost of each asset as at 31 December 20X6.

Answer

		Asset Alpha	Asset Bravo
		$	$
Borrowing costs			
To 31 December 20X6	$500,000/$1,000,000 × 9%	45,000	90,000
Less investment income			
To 30 June 20X6	$250,000/$500,000 × 7% × 6/12	(8,750)	(17,500)
		36,250	72,500
Cost of assets			
Expenditure incurred		500,000	1,000,000
Borrowing costs		36,250	72,500
		536,250	1,072,500

In a situation where **borrowings are obtained generally**, but are applied in part to obtaining a qualifying asset, then the amount of borrowing costs eligible for capitalisation is found by applying the 'capitalisation rate' to the expenditure on the asset.

The **capitalisation rate** is the weighted average of the borrowing costs applicable to the entity's borrowings that are outstanding during the period, **excluding** borrowings made specifically to obtain a qualifying asset. However, there is a cap on the amount of borrowing costs calculated in this way: it must not exceed actual borrowing costs incurred.

Sometimes one overall weighted average can be calculated for a group or entity, but in some situations it may be more appropriate to use a weighted average for borrowing costs for **individual parts of the group or entity**.

(IAS 23: para. 14)

Question

Construction

Acruni Co had the following loans in place at the beginning and end of 20X6.

	1 January 20X6	31 December 20X6
	$m	$m
10% Bank loan repayable 20X8	120	120
9.5% Bank loan repayable 20X9	80	80
8.9% debenture repayable 20X7	–	150

The 8.9% debenture was issued to fund the construction of a qualifying asset (a piece of mining equipment), construction of which began on 1 July 20X6.

On 1 January 20X6, Acruni Co began construction of a qualifying asset, a piece of machinery for a hydro-electric plant, using existing borrowings. Expenditure drawn down for the construction was: $30m on 1 January 20X6, $20m on 1 October 20X6.

Required

Calculate the borrowing costs that can be capitalised for the hydro-electric plant machine.

Answer

Capitalisation rate = weighted average rate = $(10\% \times \frac{120}{120+80}) + (9.5\% \times \frac{80}{120+80}) = 9.8\%$

$$\text{Borrowing costs} = (\$30m \times 9.8\%) + (\$20m \times 9.8\% \times 3/12)$$
$$= \$3.43m$$

4.2.2 Carrying amount exceeds recoverable amount

A situation may arise whereby the carrying amount (or expected ultimate cost) of the qualifying asset exceeds its recoverable amount or net realisable value. In these cases, the carrying amount must be **written down or written off**, as required by other IASs. In certain circumstances (again as allowed by other IASs), these amounts may be written back in future periods.   (IAS 23: para. 16)

4.2.3 Commencement of capitalisation

Three events or transactions must be taking place for capitalisation of borrowing costs to be started.

(a)   Expenditure on the asset is being incurred
(b)   Borrowing costs are being incurred
(c)   Activities are in progress that are necessary to prepare the asset for its intended use or sale

Expenditure must result in the payment of cash, transfer of other assets or assumption of interest-bearing liabilities. **Deductions from expenditure** will be made for any progress payments or grants received in connection with the asset. IAS 23 allows the **average carrying amount** of the asset during a period (including borrowing costs previously capitalised) to be used as a reasonable approximation of the expenditure to which the capitalisation rate is applied in the period. Presumably more exact calculations can be used.

Activities necessary to prepare the asset for its intended sale or use extend further than physical construction work. They encompass technical and administrative work prior to construction, eg obtaining permits. They do **not** include holding an asset when no production or development that changes the asset's condition is taking place, eg where land is held without any associated development activity.
                                                                       (IAS 23: paras. 17–19)

4.2.4 Suspension of capitalisation

If active development is **interrupted for any extended periods**, capitalisation of borrowing costs should be suspended for those periods.

Suspension of capitalisation of borrowing costs is not necessary for **temporary delays** or for periods when substantial technical or administrative work is taking place.   (IAS 23: paras. 20–21)

4.2.5 Cessation of capitalisation

Once substantially all the activities necessary to prepare the qualifying asset for its intended use or sale are complete, then capitalisation of borrowing costs should cease. This will normally be when **physical construction of the asset is completed**, although minor modifications may still be outstanding.

The asset may be completed in **parts or stages**, where each part can be used while construction is still taking place on the other parts. Capitalisation of borrowing costs should cease for each part as it is completed. The example given by the standard is a business park consisting of several buildings.

(IAS 23: paras. 22–25)

4.2.6 Disclosure

The following should be disclosed in the financial statements in relation to borrowing costs.

(a) Amount of borrowing costs **capitalised during the period**
(b) **Capitalisation rate** used to determine the amount of borrowing costs eligible for capitalisation

(IAS 23: para. 26)

Chapter Roundup

- IAS 16 covers all aspects of accounting for property, plant and equipment. This represents the bulk of items which are **'tangible' non-current assets**.

- Where assets held by an entity have a **limited useful life** it is necessary to apportion the value of an asset over its useful life.

- An entity may own land or a building **as an investment** rather than for use in the business. It may therefore generate cash flows largely independently of other assets which the entity holds. The treatment of investment property is covered by IAS 40.

- IAS 23 looks at the treatment of **borrowing costs**, particularly where the related borrowings are applied to the construction of certain assets. These are what are usually called 'self-constructed assets', where an entity builds its own inventory or non-current assets over a substantial period of time.

Quick Quiz

1   Define depreciation.

2   Which of the following elements can be included in the production cost of a non-current asset?
(i)   Purchase price of raw materials
(ii)   Architect's fees
(iii)   Import duties
(iv)   Installation costs

3   Market value can usually be taken as fair value.

True ☐

False ☐

4   Investment properties must always be shown at fair value.

True ☐

False ☐

5   What is the correct treatment for property being constructed for future use as investment property?

Answers to Quick Quiz

1   See Section 2.2
2   All of them
3   True
4   False. The cost model may be used, provided it is used consistently.
5   It is treated as an investment property under IAS 40.

Now try the Section C questions below from the Practice Question Bank

Number	Level	Marks	Time
5		10	20 mins

4

Intangible assets

Topic list	Syllabus reference
1 IAS 38 *Intangible assets* – recognition and amortisation	B2
2 IAS 38 *Intangible assets* – Research and development costs	B2
3 IFRS 3 *Goodwill*	B2

Introduction

We begin our examination of intangible non-current assets with a discussion of the IAS on the subject (**IAS 38**).

Goodwill and its treatment is a controversial area, as is the accounting for items similar to goodwill, such as brands. Goodwill is very important in **group accounts** and we will look at it again in Chapter 9.

Study guide

		Intellectual level
B2	**Intangible assets**	
(a)	Discuss the nature and accounting treatment of internally generated and purchased intangibles	2
(b)	Distinguish between goodwill and other intangible assets	2
(c)	Describe the criteria for the initial recognition and measurement of intangible assets	2
(d)	Describe the subsequent accounting treatment, including the principle of impairment tests in relation to goodwill	2
(e)	Indicate why the value of purchase consideration for an investment may be less than the value of the acquired identifiable net assets and how the difference should be accounted for	2
(f)	Describe and apply the requirements of relevant accounting standards to research and development expenditure	2

1 IAS 38 *Intangible assets* – recognition and amortisation

> **FAST FORWARD**
>
> Intangible assets are defined by IAS 38 as non-monetary assets without physical substance (para. 8).

1.1 The objectives of the standard

(a) To establish the criteria for when an intangible asset may or should be **recognised**
(b) To specify how intangible assets should be **measured**
(c) To specify the **disclosure requirements** for intangible assets (IAS 38: para. 1)

1.2 Definition of an intangible asset

The definition of an intangible asset is a key aspect of the standard, because the rules for deciding whether or not an intangible asset may be **recognised** in the accounts of an entity are based on the definition of what an intangible asset is.

Key term

> An **intangible asset** is an identifiable non-monetary asset without physical substance The asset must be:
>
> (a) Controlled by the entity as a result of events in the past
> (b) Something from which the entity expects future economic benefits to flow (IAS 38: para. 8)

Examples of items that might be considered as intangible assets include computer software, patents, copyrights, motion picture films, customer lists, franchises and fishing rights. An item should not be recognised as an intangible asset, however, unless it **fully meets the definition** in the standard. The guidelines go into great detail on this matter. (IAS 38: para. 9)

1.3 Intangible asset: must be identifiable

An intangible asset must be identifiable in order to distinguish it from goodwill. With non-physical items, there may be a problem with **'identifiability'**.

(a) If an intangible asset is **acquired separately through purchase**, there may be a transfer of a legal right that would help to make an asset identifiable.
(b) An intangible asset may be identifiable if it is **separable**, ie if it could be rented or sold separately. However, 'separability' is not an essential feature of an intangible asset. (IAS 38: para. 11)

1.4 Intangible asset: control by the entity

Another element of the definition of an intangible asset is that it must be under the control of the entity as a result of a past event. The entity must therefore be able to enjoy the future economic benefits from the asset, and prevent the access of others to those benefits. A **legally enforceable right** is evidence of such control, but is not always a **necessary** condition.   *patents / copyrights.*

(a)   Control over **technical knowledge or know-how** only exists if it is protected by a **legal right**.

(b)   The skill of employees, arising out of the benefits of **training costs**, are most unlikely to be recognisable as an intangible asset, because an entity does not control the future actions of its staff.

(c)   Similarly, **market share and customer loyalty** cannot normally be intangible assets, since an entity cannot control the actions of its customers.   (IAS 38: paras. 13–16)

1.5 Intangible asset: expected future economic benefits

An item can only be recognised as an intangible asset if economic benefits are expected to flow in the future from ownership of the asset. Economic benefits may come from the **sale** of products or services, or from a **reduction in expenditures** (cost savings).   (IAS 38: para. 17)

An intangible asset, when recognised initially, must be measured at **cost**. It should be recognised if, and only if **both** the following occur.

(a)   It is probable that the **future economic benefits** that are attributable to the asset will **flow to the entity**.

(b)   The **cost can be measured reliably**.

Management has to exercise its judgement in assessing the degree of certainty attached to the flow of economic benefits to the entity. External evidence is best.

(a)   If an intangible asset is **acquired separately**, its cost can usually be measured reliably as its purchase price (including incidental costs of purchase such as legal fees, and any costs incurred in getting the asset ready for use).

(b)   When an intangible asset is acquired as **part of a business combination** (ie an acquisition or takeover), the cost of the intangible asset is its fair value at the date of the acquisition.

                                                                (IAS 38: para. 33)

IFRS 3 explains that the fair value of intangible assets acquired in business combinations can normally be measured with sufficient reliability to be **recognised separately** from goodwill.   (IFRS 3: para. B31)

In accordance with IAS 20, intangible assets acquired by way of government grant and the grant itself may be recorded initially either at cost (which may be zero) or fair value.   (IAS 38: para. 44)

1.6 Exchanges of assets

If one intangible asset is exchanged for another, the cost of the intangible asset is measured at fair value unless:

(a)   The exchange transaction lacks commercial substance, or
(b)   The fair value of neither the asset received nor the asset given up can be measured reliably.

Otherwise, its cost is measured at the carrying amount of the asset given up.   (IAS 38: para. 45)

1.7 Internally generated goodwill

Rule to learn

> Internally generated goodwill may **not** be recognised as an **asset**.

The standard deliberately precludes recognition of internally generated goodwill because it requires that, for initial recognition, the cost of the asset rather than its fair value should be capable of being measured reliably and that it should be identifiable and controlled. Thus you do not recognise an asset which is subjective and cannot be measured reliably.   (IAS 38: paras. 48–50)

2 IAS 38 *Intangible assets* – Research and development costs

Development costs can be recognised as an asset if they meet certain criteria.

2.1 Research

Research activities by definition do not meet the criteria for recognition under IAS 38. This is because, at the research stage of a project, it cannot be certain that future economic benefits will probably flow to the entity from the project. There is too much uncertainty about the likely success or otherwise of the project. **Research costs should therefore be written off as an expense as they are incurred.**

Examples of research costs

(a) Activities aimed at obtaining new knowledge

(b) The search for, evaluation and final selection of, applications of research findings or other knowledge

(c) The search for alternatives for materials, devices, products, processes, systems or services

(d) The formulation, design evaluation and final selection of possible alternatives for new or improved materials, devices, products, systems or services   (IAS 38: paras. 54–56)

2.2 Development

Development costs may qualify for recognition as intangible assets provided that the following strict criteria can be demonstrated.

(a) The technical feasibility of completing the intangible asset so that it will be available for use or sale

(b) Its intention to complete the intangible asset and use or sell it

(c) Its ability to use or sell the intangible asset

(d) How the intangible asset will generate probable future economic benefits. Among other things, the entity should demonstrate the existence of a market for the output of the intangible asset or the intangible asset itself or, if it is to be used internally, the usefulness of the intangible asset.

(e) Its ability to measure the expenditure attributable to the intangible asset during its development reliably

In contrast with research costs development costs are incurred at a later stage in a project, and the probability of success should be more apparent. Examples of development costs include:

(a) The design, construction and testing of pre-production or pre-use prototypes and models

(b) The design of tools, jigs, moulds and dies involving new technology

(c) The design, construction and operation of a pilot plant that is not of a scale economically feasible for commercial production

(d) The design, construction and testing of a chosen alternative for new or improved materials, devices, products, processes, systems or services   (IAS 38: paras. 57–62)

2.3 Other internally generated intangible assets

The standard prohibits the recognition of internally generated brands, mastheads, publishing titles and customer lists and similar items as intangible assets. These all fail to meet one or more (in some cases all) the definition and recognition criteria and in some cases are probably indistinguishable from internally generated goodwill.   (IAS 38: para. 63)

[Handwritten margin notes: "PRIOR to this P+L", "NB" (beside criteria a–e); "after you can capitalise your cost"]

2.4 Cost of an internally generated intangible asset

Intangible assets should initially be measured at cost, but subsequently they can be carried at **cost** or at a **revalued amount**.

The costs allocated to an internally generated intangible asset should be only costs that can be directly attributed or allocated on a reasonable and consistent basis to creating, producing or preparing the asset for its intended use. The principles underlying the costs which may or may not be included are similar to those for other non-current assets and inventory.

The cost of an internally generated intangible asset is the sum of the expenditure incurred from the date when the intangible asset first meets the recognition criteria. If, as often happens, considerable costs have already been recognised as expenses before management could demonstrate that the criteria have been met, this earlier expenditure should not be retrospectively recognised at a later date as part of the cost of an intangible asset. (IAS 38: paras. 65–67)

Question   Treatment

Doug Co is developing a new production process. During 20X3, expenditure incurred was $100,000, of which $90,000 was incurred before 1 December 20X3 and $10,000 between 1 December 20X3 and 31 December 20X3. Doug Co can demonstrate that, at 1 December 20X3, the production process met the criteria for recognition as an intangible asset. The recoverable amount of the know-how embodied in the process is estimated to be $50,000.

Required

How should the expenditure be treated?

Answer

At the end of 20X3, the production process is recognised as an intangible asset at a cost of $10,000. This is the expenditure incurred since the date when the recognition criteria were met, that is 1 December 20X3. The $90,000 expenditure incurred before 1 December 20X3 is expensed, because the recognition criteria were not met. It will never form part of the cost of the production process recognised in the statement of financial position.

2.5 Recognition of an expense

All expenditure related to an intangible which does not meet the criteria for recognition either as an identifiable intangible asset or as goodwill arising on an acquisition should be **expensed as incurred**. The IAS gives examples of such expenditure:

- Start up costs   *P+L as expense.*
- Training costs
- Advertising costs
- Business relocation costs

Prepaid costs for services, for example advertising or marketing costs for campaigns that have been prepared but not launched, can still be recognised as a **prepayment**. (IAS 38: paras. 68–70)

2.6 Measurement of intangible assets subsequent to initial recognition

The standard allows two methods of valuation for intangible assets after they have been first recognised.

Applying the **cost model**, an intangible asset should be **carried at its cost**, less any accumulated amortisation and less any accumulated impairment losses. (IAS 38: para. 74)

The **revaluation model** allows an intangible asset to be carried at a revalued amount, which is its **fair value** at the date of revaluation, less any subsequent accumulated amortisation and any subsequent accumulated impairment losses.

(a)   The fair value must be able to be measured reliably with reference to an **active market** in that type of asset.

(b)   The **entire class** of intangible assets of that type must be revalued at the same time (to prevent selective revaluations).

(c)   If an intangible asset in a class of revalued intangible assets cannot be revalued because there is **no active market** for this asset, the asset should be carried at its **cost less any accumulated amortisation and impairment losses**.

(d)   Revaluations should be made with such **regularity** that the carrying amount does not differ from that which would be determined using fair value at the end of the reporting period.

(IAS 38: paras. 75–77)

Point to note

> This treatment is not available for the initial recognition of intangible assets. This is because the cost of the asset must be reliably measured.

The guidelines state that there will not usually be an active market in an intangible asset; therefore the revaluation model will usually not be available. For example, although copyrights, publishing rights and film rights can be sold, each has a unique sale value. In such cases, revaluation to fair value would be inappropriate. A fair value might be obtainable however for assets such as fishing rights or quotas or taxi cab licences.

(IAS 38: para. 78)

Where an intangible asset is revalued upwards to a fair value, the amount of the revaluation should be credited directly to equity under the heading of a **revaluation surplus**.

However, if a revaluation surplus is a **reversal of a revaluation decrease** that was previously charged against income, the increase can be recognised as income.

Where the carrying amount of an intangible asset is revalued downwards, the amount of the **downward revaluation** should be charged as an expense against income, unless the asset has previously been revalued upwards. A revaluation decrease should be first charged against any previous revaluation surplus in respect of that asset.

(IAS 38: para. 80)

Question

Downward revaluation

An intangible asset is measured by Nisi Co at fair value. The asset was revalued by $400 in 20X3, and there is a revaluation surplus of $400 in the statement of financial position. At the end of 20X4, the asset is valued again, and a downward valuation of $500 is required.

Required

State the accounting treatment for the downward revaluation.

Answer

In this example, the downward valuation of $500 can first be set against the revaluation surplus of $400. The revaluation surplus will be reduced to $nil and a charge of $100 made as an expense in 20X4.

When the revaluation model is used, and an intangible asset is revalued upwards, the cumulative revaluation **surplus may be transferred to retained earnings** when the surplus is eventually realised. The surplus would be realised when the asset is disposed of. However, the surplus may also be realised over time as the **asset is used** by the entity. The amount of the surplus realised each year is the difference between the amortisation charge for the asset based on the revalued amount of the asset, and the amortisation that would be charged on the basis of the asset's historical cost. The realised surplus in such

cases should be transferred from revaluation surplus directly to retained earnings, and should not be taken through profit or loss. (IAS 38: para. 87)

2.7 Useful life

An entity should assess the useful life of an intangible asset, which may be **finite or indefinite**. An intangible asset has an indefinite useful life when there is **no foreseeable limit** to the period over which the asset is expected to generate net cash inflows for the entity.

Many factors are considered in determining the useful life of an intangible asset, including:

- Expected usage
- Typical product life cycles
- Technical, technological, commercial or other types of obsolescence
- The stability of the industry; expected actions by competitors
- The level of maintenance expenditure required
- Legal or similar limits on the use of the asset, such as the expiry dates of related leases

Computer software and many other intangible assets normally have short lives because they are susceptible to technological obsolescence. However, uncertainty does not justify choosing a life that is unrealistically short.

The useful life of an intangible asset that arises from **contractual or other legal rights** should not exceed the period of the rights, but may be shorter depending on the period over which the entity expects to use the asset. (IAS 38: paras. 88–96)

2.8 Amortisation period and amortisation method

An intangible asset with a finite useful life should be amortised over its **expected useful life**.

(a)   Amortisation should start when the asset is **available for use**.

(b)   Amortisation should cease at the earlier of the date that the asset is classified **as held for sale** in accordance with IFRS 5 *Non-current assets held for sale and discontinued operations* and the date that the asset is **derecognised**.

(c)   The amortisation method used should reflect the **pattern in which the asset's future economic benefits are consumed**. If such a pattern cannot be predicted reliably, the straight-line method should be used.

(d)   The amortisation charge for each period should normally be recognised **in profit or loss**.
(IAS 38: paras. 97–99)

The **residual value** of an intangible asset with a finite useful life is **assumed to be zero** unless a third party is committed to buying the intangible asset at the end of its useful life or unless there is an active market for that type of asset (so that its expected residual value can be measured) and it is probable that there will be a market for the asset at the end of its useful life.

The amortisation period and the amortisation method used for an intangible asset with a finite useful life should be **reviewed at each financial year end**. (IAS 38: para. 100)

2.9 Intangible assets with indefinite useful lives

An intangible asset with an indefinite useful life **should not be amortised**. (IAS 36 requires that such an asset is tested for impairment at least annually.) (IAS 38: para. 107)

The useful life of an intangible asset that is not being amortised should be **reviewed each year** to determine whether it is still appropriate to assess its useful life as indefinite. Reassessing the useful life of an intangible asset as finite rather than indefinite is an indicator that the asset may be impaired and therefore it should be tested for impairment. (IAS 38: para. 109)

**Exam focus
point**

Intangible assets could appear as part of an accounts preparation question or in an MCQ. Make sure you know the capitalisation criteria.

Question

Intangible asset

It may be difficult to establish the useful life of an intangible asset, and judgement will be needed.

Required

Consider how to determine the useful life of a **purchased** brand name.

Answer

Factors to consider would include the following.

(a) Legal protection of the brand name and the control of the entity over the (illegal) use by others of the brand name (ie control over pirating)

(b) Age of the brand name

(c) Status or position of the brand in its particular market

(d) Ability of the management of the entity to manage the brand name and to measure activities that support the brand name (eg advertising and PR activities)

(e) Stability and geographical spread of the market in which the branded products are sold

(f) Pattern of benefits that the brand name is expected to generate over time

(g) Intention of the entity to use and promote the brand name over time (as evidenced perhaps by a business plan in which there will be substantial expenditure to promote the brand name)

2.10 Disposals/retirements of intangible assets

An intangible asset should be eliminated from the statement of financial position when it is disposed of or when there is no further expected economic benefit from its future use. On disposal the gain or loss arising from the **difference between the net disposal proceeds and the carrying amount** of the asset should be taken to profit or loss as a gain or loss on disposal (ie treated as income or expense).

(IAS 38: paras. 112–117)

2.11 Section summary

- An intangible asset should be recognised if, and only if, it is probable that future economic benefits will flow to the entity and the cost of the asset can be measured reliably.
- An asset is initially recognised at cost and subsequently carried either at cost or revalued amount.
- Costs that do not meet the recognition criteria should be expensed as incurred.
- An intangible asset with a finite useful life should be amortised over its useful life. An intangible asset with an indefinite useful life should not be amortised.

Question

R&D

As an aid to your revision, list the examples given in IAS 38 of activities that might be included in either research or development.

IAS 38 gives these examples.

Research

- Activities aimed at obtaining new knowledge
- The search for, evaluation and final selection of, applications of research findings or other knowledge
- The search for alternatives for materials, devices, product, processes, systems or services
- The formulation and design, evaluation and final selection of possible alternatives for new or improved materials, devices, products, processes, systems or services

Development

- The design, construction and testing of a chosen alternative for new or improved materials, products, processes, systems or services
- The design, construction and testing of pre-production prototypes and models
- The design of tools, jigs, moulds and dies involving new technology
- The design, construction and operation of a pilot plant that is not of a scale economically feasible for commercial production (paras. 56–59)

3 IFRS 3 *Goodwill*

Purchased goodwill arising on consolidation is retained in the statement of financial position as an intangible asset under IFRS 3. It must then be reviewed annually for impairment.

3.1 What is goodwill?

Goodwill is **created by good relationships** between a business and its customers.

(a)   By building up a **reputation** (by word of mouth perhaps) for high quality products or high standards of service

(b)   By **responding promptly and helpfully** to queries and complaints from customers

(c)   Through the **personality of the staff** and their attitudes to customers

The value of goodwill to a business might be considerable. However, goodwill is not usually valued in the accounts of a business at all, and we should not normally expect to find an amount for goodwill in its statement of financial position. For example, the welcoming smile of the bar staff may contribute more to a bar's profits than the fact that a new electronic cash register has recently been acquired. Even so, whereas the cash register will be recorded in the accounts as a non-current asset, the value of staff would be ignored for accounting purposes.

On reflection, we might agree with this omission of goodwill from the accounts of a business.

(a)   The goodwill is **inherent** in the business but it has not been paid for, and it does not have an 'objective' value. We can guess at what such goodwill is worth, but such guesswork would be a matter of individual opinion, and not based on hard facts.

(b)   Goodwill **changes** from day to day. One act of bad customer relations might damage goodwill and one act of good relations might improve it. Staff with a favourable personality might retire or leave to find another job, to be replaced by staff who need time to find their feet in the job, etc. Since goodwill is continually changing in value, it cannot realistically be recorded in the accounts of the business.

3.2 Purchased goodwill

There is one exception to the general rule that goodwill has no objective valuation. This is **when a business is sold**. People wishing to set up in business have a choice of how to do it – they can either buy their own long-term assets and inventory and set up their business from scratch, or they can buy up an existing business from a proprietor willing to sell it. When a buyer purchases an existing business, he will have to purchase not only its long-term assets and inventory (and perhaps take over its accounts payable and receivable too) but also the goodwill of the business.

Purchased goodwill is shown in the statement of financial position because it has been paid for. It has no tangible substance, and so it is an **intangible non-current asset**.

3.3 How is the value of purchased goodwill decided?

When a business is sold, there is likely to be some purchased goodwill in the selling price. But **how is the amount of this purchased goodwill decided**?

This is not really a problem for accountants, who must simply record the goodwill in the accounts of the new business. The value of the goodwill is a **matter for the purchaser and seller to agree upon in fixing the purchase/sale price**. However, two methods of valuation are worth mentioning here:

(a)   The seller and buyer agree on a price for the business **without specifically quantifying the goodwill**. The purchased goodwill will then be the difference between the price agreed and the value of the identifiable net assets in the books of the new business.

(b)   However, the calculation of goodwill often precedes the fixing of the purchase price and becomes a **central element of negotiation**. There are many ways of arriving at a value for goodwill and most of them are related to the profit record of the business in question.

No matter how goodwill is calculated within the total agreed purchase price, the goodwill shown by the purchaser in his accounts will be **the difference between the purchase consideration and his own valuation of the net assets acquired**. If A values his net assets at $40,000, goodwill is agreed at $21,000 and B agrees to pay $61,000 for the business but values the net assets at only $38,000, then the goodwill in B's books will be $61,000 – $38,000 = $23,000.

3.4 IFRS 3 Business combinations

IFRS 3 covers the accounting treatment of goodwill acquired in a business combination.

Key term

> **Goodwill.** Future economic benefits arising from assets that are not capable of being individually identified and separately recognised.
>
> (IFRS 3 App A)

Goodwill acquired in a business combination is **recognised as an asset** and is initially measured at **cost**. Cost is the excess of the cost of the combination over the acquirer's interest in the net fair value of the acquiree's identifiable assets, liabilities and contingent liabilities.

After initial recognition goodwill acquired in a business combination is measured **at cost less any accumulated impairment losses**. It is **not amortised**. Instead it is tested for impairment at least annually, in accordance with IAS 36 *Impairment of assets*.

Gain on a bargain purchase (negative goodwill) arises when the acquirer's interest in the net fair value of the acquiree's identifiable assets, liabilities and contingent liabilities exceeds the cost of the business combination. IFRS 3 defines a gain on a bargain purchase as the 'excess of acquirer's interest in the net fair value of acquiree's identifiable assets, liabilities and contingent liabilities over cost'. (IFRS 3: para. 34)

Gain on a bargain purchase can arise as the result of **errors** in measuring the fair value of either the cost of the combination or the acquiree's identifiable net assets. Therefore the following action must be taken:

(a)   an entity should first **reassess** the amounts at which it has measured both the cost of the combination and the acquiree's identifiable net assets. This exercise should identify any errors.

(b)   Any **excess remaining** should be **recognised** immediately in profit or loss.

IFRS 3 requires extensive **disclosures**. These include a **reconciliation** of the carrying amount of goodwill at the beginning and end of the period, showing separately:

(a)   The gross amount and accumulated impairment losses at the beginning of the period
(b)   Additional goodwill recognised during the period
(c)   Impairment losses recognised during the period
(d)   Net exchange differences arising during the period, and
(e)   The gross amount and accumulated impairment losses at the end of the period

(IFRS 3: paras. 59–63)

Question   Characteristics of goodwill

What are the main characteristics of goodwill which distinguish it from other intangible non-current assets? To what extent do you consider that these characteristics should affect the accounting treatment of goodwill? State your reasons.

Answer

Goodwill may be distinguished from other intangible non-current assets by reference to the following characteristics.

(a)   It is incapable of realisation separately from the business as a whole.

(b)   Its value has no reliable or predictable relationship to any costs which may have been incurred.

(c)   Its value arises from various intangible factors such as skilled employees, effective advertising or a strategic location. These indirect factors cannot be valued.

(d)   The value of goodwill may fluctuate widely according to internal and external circumstances over relatively short periods of time.

(e)   The assessment of the value of goodwill is highly subjective.

It could be argued that, because goodwill is so different from other intangible non-current assets it does not make sense to account for it in the same way. Thus the capitalisation and amortisation treatment would not be acceptable. Furthermore, because goodwill is so difficult to value, any valuation may be misleading, and it is best eliminated from the statement of financial position altogether. However, there are strong arguments for treating it like any other intangible non-current asset. This issue remains controversial.

Chapter Roundup

- Intangible assets are defined by IAS 38 as non-monetary assets without physical substance.

- Development costs can be recognised as an asset if they meet certain criteria.

- Intangible assets should initially be measured at cost, but subsequently they can be carried at **cost** or at a **revalued amount**.

- Purchased goodwill arising on consolidation is retained in the statement of financial position as an intangible asset under IFRS 3. It must then be reviewed annually for impairment.

- Purchased goodwill is shown in the statement of financial position because it has been paid for. It has no tangible substance, and so it is an **intangible non-current asset**.

Quick Quiz

1   Intangible assets can only be recognised in a company's accounts if:
    - It is probable that .... will flow to the entity.
    - The cost can be ....

2   What are the criteria which must be met before development expenditure can be deferred?

3   Start up costs must be expensed.

    True ☐

    False ☐

4   Peggy buys Phil's business for $30,000. The business assets are a bar valued at $20,000, inventories at $3,000 and receivables of $3,000. How much is goodwill valued at?

5   What method of accounting for goodwill arising on consolidation is required by IFRS 3?

6   How should bargain purchase be accounted for under IFRS 3?

Answers to Quick Quiz

1   Future economic benefits; measured reliably
2   See Section 2.2
3   True
4   $30,000 – $20,000 – $3,000 – $3,000 = $4,000
5   Cost less impairment losses
6   Recognised in profit or loss immediately

Now try the Section C questions below from the Practice Question Bank

Number	Level	Marks	Time
6		10	20 mins

Impairment of assets

Topic list	Syllabus reference
1 IAS 36 *Impairment of assets*	B3
2 Cash-generating units	B3
3 Goodwill and the impairment of assets	B3
4 Accounting treatment of an impairment loss	B3

Introduction

IAS 36 is an important standard. In this standard, the impairment rules applying to both tangible and intangible assets, are covered in detail.

Study guide

B3	Impairment of assets	Intellectual level
(a)	Define, calculate and account for an impairment loss	2
(b)	Account for the reversal of an impairment loss on an individual asset	
(c)	Identify the circumstances that may indicate impairments to assets	2
(d)	Describe what is meant by a cash-generating unit	2
(e)	State the basis on which impairment losses should be allocated, and allocate an impairment loss to the assets of a cash-generating unit	2

1 IAS 36 *Impairment of assets*

FAST FORWARD

Impairment is determined by comparing the carrying amount of the asset with its recoverable amount. This is the higher of its **fair value less costs of disposal** and its **value in use**.

There is an established principle that assets should not be carried at above their recoverable amount. An entity should write down the carrying amount of an asset to its recoverable amount if the carrying amount of an asset is not recoverable in full. IAS 36 puts in place a detailed methodology for carrying out impairment reviews and related accounting treatments and disclosures.

1.1 Scope

IAS 36 applies to all tangible, intangible and financial assets except inventories, assets arising from construction contracts, deferred tax assets, assets arising under IAS 19 *Employee benefits* and financial assets within the scope of IAS 32 *Financial instruments: presentation*. This is because those IASs already have rules for recognising and measuring impairment. Note also that IAS 36 does not apply to non-current assets held for sale, which are dealt with under IFRS 5 *Non-current assets held for sale and discontinued operations*.

(IAS 36: para. 2)

Key terms

- **Impairment.** A fall in the value of an asset, so that its 'recoverable amount' is now less than its carrying amount in the statement of financial position.
- **Carrying amount.** The net value at which the asset is included in the statement of financial position (ie after deducting accumulated depreciation and any impairment losses).

(IAS 36: para. 6)

The basic principle underlying IAS 36 is relatively straightforward. If an asset's value in the accounts is higher than its realistic value, measured as its 'recoverable amount' (IAS 36: paras. 18–24), the asset is judged to have suffered an impairment loss. It should therefore be reduced in value, by the amount of the **impairment loss**. The amount of the impairment loss should be **written off against profit** immediately.

The main accounting issues to consider are therefore:

(a) How is it possible to **identify when** an impairment loss may have occurred?
(b) How should the **recoverable amount** of the asset be measured?
(c) How should an 'impairment loss' be **reported in the accounts**?

1.2 Identifying a potentially impaired asset

An entity should assess at the end of each reporting period whether there are any indications of impairment to any assets. The concept of **materiality** applies, and only material impairment needs to be identified.

(IAS 36: para. 10)

If there are indications of possible impairment, the entity is required to make a formal estimate of the **recoverable amount** of the assets concerned.

IAS 36 suggests how **indications of a possible impairment** of assets might be recognised. The suggestions are based largely on common sense.

(a) **External sources of information**

    (i) A fall in the asset's market value that is more significant than would normally be expected from passage of time over normal use

    (ii) A significant change in the technological, market, legal or economic environment of the business in which the assets are employed

    (iii) An increase in market interest rates or market rates of return on investments likely to affect the discount rate used in calculating value in use *NPV calc*

    (iv) The carrying amount of the entity's net assets being more than its market capitalisation.

(IAS 36: para. 12)

(b) **Internal sources of information**: evidence of obsolescence or physical damage, adverse changes in the use to which the asset is put, or the asset's economic performance. *(IAS 36: para. 12)*

Even if there are no indications of impairment, the following assets must **always** be tested for impairment annually.

(a) An intangible asset with an **indefinite useful life**

(b) **Goodwill** acquired in a business combination. *(IAS 36: para. 10)*

1.3 Measuring the recoverable amount of the asset

What is an asset's recoverable amount?

Key term

> The **recoverable amount of an asset** should be measured as the **higher value** of:
>
> (a) The asset's fair value less costs of disposal
> (b) Its value in use *(IAS 36: para. 18)*

An asset's fair value less costs of disposal is the price that would be received to sell the asset in an orderly transaction between market participants at the measurement date, less direct disposal costs, such as legal expenses. *(IFRS13: para. 15)*

(a) If there is an **active market** in the asset, the fair value should be based on the market price, or on the price of the recent transactions in similar assets

(b) If there is **no active market** in the asset it might be possible to **estimate** fair value using best estimates of what market participants might pay in an orderly transaction

Fair value less costs of disposal **cannot** be reduced, however, by including within costs of disposal any **restructuring or reorganisation expenses**, or any costs that have already been recognised in the accounts as liabilities.

The concept of 'value in use' is very important.

Key term

> The **value in use** of an asset is the present value of the future cash flows expected to be derived from an asset or cash-generating unit. *(IAS 36: para. 6)*

1.4 Recognition and measurement of an impairment loss

The rule for assets at historical cost is:

Rule to learn

> If the recoverable amount of an asset is lower than the carrying amount, the carrying amount should be reduced by the difference (ie the impairment loss) which should be charged as an expense in profit or loss. *(IAS 36: para. 59)*

The rule for assets held at a revalued amount (such as property revalued under IAS 16) is:

Rule to learn

> The impairment loss is to be treated as a revaluation decrease under the relevant IAS.   (IAS 36: para. 60)

In practice this means:

- To the extent that there is a revaluation surplus held in respect of the asset, the impairment loss should be charged to Other Comprehensive Income (revaluation surplus)

- Any excess should be charged to profit or loss

1.5 Reversal of an impairment loss

In some cases, the recoverable amount of an asset that has previously been impaired might turn out to be **higher** than the asset's current carrying amount. In other words, there might have been a reversal of some of the previous impairment loss.

(a) The reversal of the impairment loss should be **recognised immediately** as income in profit or loss for the year.

(b) The carrying amount of the asset should be increased to its **new recoverable amount**.

(IAS 36: para. 119)

Rule to learn

> An impairment loss recognised for an asset in prior years should be recovered if, and only if, there has been a change in the estimates used to determine the asset's recoverable amount since the last impairment loss was recognised.   (IAS 36: para. 114)

The asset cannot be revalued to a carrying amount that is higher than its value would have been if the asset had not been impaired originally, ie its **depreciated carrying amount** had the impairment not taken place. Depreciation of the asset should now be based on its new revalued amount, its estimated residual value (if any) and its estimated remaining useful life.

An exception to the rule above is for **goodwill**. An impairment loss for goodwill should not be reversed in a subsequent period.

Question
Reversal of impairment loss

A head office building with a carrying amount of $140m is estimated to have a recoverable amount of $90m due to falling property values in the area. An impairment loss of $50m is recognised.

After three years, property prices in the area have risen, and the recoverable amount of the building increases to $120m. The carrying amount of the building had the impairment not occurred would have been $110m.

Required

Calculate the reversal of the impairment loss.

Answer

The reversal of the impairment loss is recognised to the extent that it increases the carrying amount of the building to what it would have been had the impairment not taken place, ie a reversal of impairment loss of $20m is recognised and the building written back to $110m.

2 Cash-generating units

FAST FORWARD

> When it is not possible to calculate the recoverable amount of a single asset, then that of its **cash-generating unit** should be measured instead.

2.1 Use of cash-generating unit

The IAS goes into quite a large amount of detail about the important concept of cash-generating units. As a basic rule, the recoverable amount of an asset should be calculated for the **asset individually**. However, there will be occasions when it is not possible to estimate such a value for an individual asset, particularly in the calculation of value in use. This is because cash inflows and outflows cannot be attributed to the individual asset.

If it is not possible to calculate the recoverable amount for an individual asset, the recoverable amount of the asset's cash-generating unit should be measured instead. (IAS 36: paras. 66–67)

Key term

> A **cash-generating unit** is the smallest identifiable group of assets for which independent cash flows can be identified and measured. (IAS 36: para. 6)

Question — Cash-generating unit I

Can you think of some examples of how a cash-generating unit would be identified?

Answer

Here are two possibilities.

(a) A mining company owns a private railway that it uses to transport output from one of its mines. The railway now has no market value other than as scrap, and it is impossible to identify any separate cash inflows with the use of the railway itself. Consequently, if the mining company suspects an impairment in the value of the railway, it should treat the mine as a whole as a cash-generating unit, and measure the recoverable amount of the mine as a whole.

(b) A bus company has an arrangement with a town's authorities to run a bus service on four routes in the town. Separately identifiable assets are allocated to each of the bus routes, and cash inflows and outflows can be attributed to each individual route. Three routes are running at a profit and one is running at a loss. The bus company suspects that there is an impairment of assets on the loss-making route. However, the company will be unable to close the loss-making route, because it is under an obligation to operate all four routes, as part of its contract with the local authority. Consequently, the company should treat all four bus routes together as a cash-generating unit, and calculate the recoverable amount for the unit as a whole.

Question — Cash-generating unit II

Minimart Co belongs to a retail store chain MagnusCo. Minimart Co makes all its retail purchases through Magnus Co's purchasing centre. Pricing, marketing, advertising and human resources policies (except for hiring Minimart Co's cashiers and salesmen) are decided by Magnus Co. Magnus Co also owns five other stores in the same city as Minimart Co (although in different neighbourhoods) and 20 other stores in other cities. All stores are managed in the same way as Minimart Co. Minimart Co and four other stores were purchased five years ago and goodwill was recognised.

Required

What is the cash-generating unit for Minimart Co?

In identifying Minimart Co's cash-generating unit, an entity considers whether, for example:

(a)   Internal management reporting is organised to measure performance on a store-by-store basis.

(b)   The business is run on a store-by-store profit basis or on a region/city basis.

All Magnus Co's stores are in different neighbourhoods and probably have different customer bases. So, although Minimart Co is managed at a corporate level, Minimart Co generates cash inflows that are largely independent from those of Magnus Co's other stores. Therefore, it is likely that Minimart Co is a cash-generating unit.

If an active market exists for the output produced by the asset or a group of assets, this asset or group should be identified as a cash-generating unit, even if some or all of the output is used internally.

(IAS 36: para. 70)

Cash-generating units should be identified consistently from period to period for the same type of asset unless a change is justified.

(IAS 36: para. 72)

The group of net assets less liabilities that are considered for impairment should be the same as those considered in the calculation of the recoverable amount.

(IAS 36: para. 75)

(For the treatment of goodwill and corporate assets see below.)

2.2 Example: Recoverable amount and carrying amount

Fourways Co is made up of four cash-generating units. All four units are being tested for impairment. Assets and liabilities will be allocated to them as follows.

(a)   Property, plant and equipment and separate intangibles will be allocated to the cash-generating units as far as possible.

(b)   Current assets such as inventories, receivables and prepayments will be allocated to the relevant cash-generating units.

(c)   Liabilities (eg payables) will be deducted from the net assets of the relevant cash-generating units.

(d)   The net figure for each cash-generating unit resulting from this exercise will be compared to the relevant recoverable amount, computed on the same basis.

3 Goodwill and the impairment of assets

3.1 Allocating goodwill to cash-generating units

Goodwill acquired in a business combination does not generate cash flows independently of other assets. It must be **allocated** to each of the acquirer's **cash-generating units** (or groups of cash-generating units) that are expected to benefit from the synergies of the combination. Each unit to which the goodwill is so allocated should:

(a)   Represent the **lowest level** within the entity at which the goodwill is monitored for internal management purposes

(b)   Not be **larger than a reporting segment** determined in accordance with IFRS 8 *Operating segments*

It may be impracticable to complete the allocation of goodwill before the first reporting date after a business combination, particularly if the acquirer is accounting for the combination for the first time using provisional values. The initial allocation of goodwill must be completed before the end of the first reporting period after the acquisition date.

(IAS 36: paras. 80–84)

3.2 Testing cash-generating units with goodwill for impairment

A cash-generating unit to which goodwill has been allocated is tested for impairment annually. The **carrying amount** of the unit, including goodwill, is **compared with the recoverable amount**. If the carrying amount of the unit exceeds the recoverable amount, the entity must recognise an impairment loss.

The annual impairment test may be performed at any time during an accounting period, but must be performed at the **same time every year**.
(IAS 36: para. 88)

3.3 Example: allocation of impairment loss

[handwritten: Goodwill is the first thing you get Rid of. unless specifically impaired assets.]

A cash-generating unit comprises the following:

	$m
Building	30
Plant and equipment	6
Goodwill	10
Current assets	20 *[handwritten: - Distraction]*
	66

Following a recession, an impairment review has estimated the recoverable amount of the cash-generating unit to be $50m.

How do we allocate the impairment loss?

The loss will be applied first against the goodwill and then against the tangible non-current assets on a **pro-rata** basis. After writing off the goodwill, the balance to be allocated is $6m. This is pro-rated over the total of $36m for the remaining non-current assets at a rate of $1m per $6m.

	Carrying amount $m	Impairment loss $m	Carrying amount post-impairment $m
Building	30	(5)	25
Plant and equipment	6	(1)	5
Goodwill	10	(10)	–
Current assets	20	–	20
	66	(16)	50

4 Accounting treatment of an impairment loss

If, and only if, the recoverable amount of an asset is less than its carrying amount in the statement of financial position, an impairment loss has occurred. This loss should be **recognised immediately**.
(IAS 36: para. 60)

(a) The asset's **carrying amount** should be reduced to its recoverable amount in the statement of financial position.

(b) The **impairment loss** should be recognised immediately in profit or loss (unless the asset has been revalued in which case the loss is treated as a revaluation decrease). (IAS 36: para. 60)

After reducing an asset to its recoverable amount, the **depreciation charge** on the asset should then be based on its new carrying amount, its estimated residual value (if any) and its estimated remaining useful life.
(IAS 36: para. 63)

An impairment loss should be recognised for a **cash-generating unit** if (and only if) the recoverable amount for the cash-generating unit is less than the carrying amount in the statement of financial position for all the assets in the unit. When an impairment loss is recognised for a cash-generating unit, the loss should be allocated between the assets in the unit in the following order.

(a) First, to any assets that are obviously damaged or destroyed
(b) Next, to the **goodwill** allocated to the cash-generating unit
(c) Then to all other assets in the cash-generating unit, on a **pro rata basis**

[handwritten margin notes: Remaining impairment / Plant 1/6 x 6 (1) / Building 30/36 x 3/6 (5)]

In allocating an impairment loss, the carrying amount of an asset should not be reduced below the highest of:

(a)   Its fair value less costs of disposal
(b)   Its value in use (if determinable)
(c)   Zero

Any remaining amount of an impairment loss should be recognised as a liability if required by other IASs.

(IAS 36: paras. 104/105)

4.1 Example 1: impairment loss

Grohl Co that extracts natural gas and oil has a drilling platform in the Caspian Sea. It is required by legislation of the country concerned to remove and dismantle the platform at the end of its useful life. Accordingly, Grohl Co has included an amount in its accounts for removal and dismantling costs, and is depreciating this amount over the platform's expected life.

Grohl Co is carrying out an exercise to establish whether there has been an impairment of the platform.

(a)   Its carrying amount in the statement of financial position is $3m.

(b)   The company has received an offer of $2.8m for the platform from another oil company. The bidder would take over the responsibility (and costs) for dismantling and removing the platform at the end of its life. _fair value._

(c)   The present value of the estimated cash flows from the platform's continued use is $3.3m (before adjusting for dismantling costs).

value in use

(d)   The carrying amount in the statement of financial position for the provision for dismantling and removal is currently $0.6m.

What should be the value of the drilling platform in the statement of financial position, and what, if anything, is the impairment loss?

Solution

Fair value less costs of disposal	=	$2.8m
Value in use	=	PV of cash flows from use less the carrying amount of the provision/liability = $3.3m – $0.6m = $2.7m
Recoverable amount	=	Higher of these two amounts, ie $2.8m
Carrying value	=	$3m
Impairment loss	=	$0.2m

The carrying value should be reduced to $2.8m.

4.2 Example 2: impairment loss

Biscuit Co has acquired another business for $4.5m: tangible assets are valued at $4.0m and goodwill at $0.5m.

An asset with a carrying value of $1m is destroyed in a terrorist attack. The asset was not insured. The loss of the asset, without insurance, has prompted the company to assess whether there has been an impairment of assets in the acquired business and what the amount of any such loss is.

The recoverable amount of the business (a single cash-generating unit) is measured as $3.1m.

Solution

There has been an impairment loss of $1.4m ($4.5m – $3.1m).

The impairment loss will be recognised in profit or loss. The loss will be allocated between the assets in the cash-generating unit as follows.

(a)   A loss of $1m can be attributed directly to the uninsured asset that has been destroyed.

(b)   The remaining loss of $0.4m should be allocated to goodwill.

The carrying value of the assets will now be $3m for tangible assets and $0.1m for goodwill.

An exam question may ask you to calculate and allocate an impairment loss. Make sure you know the order in which to allocate the loss.

4.3 Summary

The main aspects of IAS 36 to consider are:

- **Indications** of impairment of assets
- **Measuring recoverable amount**, as fair value less costs of disposal or value in use
- **Measuring value in use**
- **Cash-generating units**
- **Accounting treatment** of an impairment loss, for individual assets and cash-generating units

Chapter Roundup

- Impairment is determined by comparing the carrying amount of the asset with its recoverable amount. This is the higher of its **fair value less costs of disposal** and its **value in use**.

- When it is not possible to calculate the recoverable amount of a single asset, then that of its **cash-generating unit** should be measured instead.

Quick Quiz

1 Define **recoverable amount** of an asset.
2 How is an impairment loss on a revalued asset treated?
3 How is an impairment loss allocated to the assets in a cash-generating unit?

Answers to Quick Quiz

1   Higher of **fair value less costs of disposal** and **value in use**

2   As a revaluation decrease

3   In the following order: (a) against any damaged or destroyed assets; then (b) against goodwill; then (c) against all other non-current assets on a *pro rata* basis.

Now try the Section C questions below from the Practice Question Bank

Number	Level	Marks	Time
7	Examination	15	29 mins

Revenue

Topic list	Syllabus reference
1 Introduction	B10
2 IFRS 15 *Revenue from contracts with customers*	B10
3 Recognition and measurement	B10
4 Common types of transaction	B10
5 Presentation and disclosure	B10
6 Performance obligations satisfied over time	B10
7 IAS 20 *Government grants and disclosure of Government Assistance*	B11

Introduction

Revenue is now the subject of a new standard: IFRS 15 *Revenue from contracts with customers*.

This replaces both IAS 18 *Revenue* and IAS 11 *Construction contracts*.

Another issue considered in this chapter is the treatment of government grants.

Study guide

		Intellectual level
B10	**Revenue**	
(a)	Explain and apply the principles of recognition of revenue:	
	(i) Identification of contracts	
	(ii) Identification of performance obligations	
	(iii) Determination of transaction price	
	(iv) Allocation of the price to performance obligations	
	(v) Recognition of revenue when/as performance obligations are satisfied	
(b)	Explain and apply the criteria for recognising revenue generated from contracts where performance obligations are satisfied over time or at a point in time.	2
(c)	Describe the acceptable methods for measuring progress towards complete satisfaction of a performance obligation.	2
(d)	Explain and apply the criteria for the recognition of contract costs.	2
(e)	Apply the principles of recognition of revenue, and specifically account for the following types of transaction:	
	(i) Principal versus agent	2
	(ii) Repurchase agreements	2
	(iii) Bill and hold arrangements	2
	(iv) Consignments	2
(f)	Prepare financial statement extracts for contracts where performance obligations are satisfied over time.	2
B11	**Government grants**	
(a)	Apply the provisions of relevant accounting standards in relation to accounting for government grants.	2

1 Introduction

Revenue recognition is straightforward in most business transactions, but it is open to manipulation.

1.1 Revenue

Income, as defined by the IASB *Conceptual Framework* includes both revenues and gains. Revenue is income arising in the ordinary course of an entity's activities and it may be called different names, such as sales, fees, interest, dividends or royalties.

Revenue is usually the largest amount in a statement of profit or loss so it is important that it is correctly stated. US studies have shown that over half of all financial statement frauds and requirements for restatements of previously published financial information involved revenue manipulation.

(fraudulent / manipulated)

The most blatant recent example was the Satyam Computer Services fraud in 2010, in which false invoices were used to record fictitious revenue amounting to $1.5bn.

Revenue recognition fraud also featured in the Enron and Worldcom cases.

The directors of Enron inflated the value of 'agency' services by reporting the entire value of each of its trades as revenue, rather than just the agency commission on the sale. Other energy companies then adopted this 'model' in a bid to keep up with Enron's results.

Worldcom was an entity in which all executive bonuses were tied to revenue targets and dubious accounting adjustments were constantly made to keep revenue 'on target'. By the time Worldcom filed for bankruptcy, revenue had been overstated by about $960m.

In the UK we have recently seen Tesco admit to profits for the half-year overstated by £250m partly due to 'accelerated' revenue recognition.

So it is not surprising that it was decided that a 'comprehensive and robust framework' for accounting for revenue was needed.

2 IFRS 15 *Revenue from contracts with customers*

FAST FORWARD

IFRS 15 sets out rules for the recognition of revenue based on transfer of **control** to the customer from the entity supplying the goods or services.

IFRS 15 *Revenue from contracts with customers* was issued in May 2014. It is the result of a joint IASB and FASB project on revenue recognition. It seeks to strike a balance between the IASB rules in IAS 18, which were felt to be too general, leading to a lot of diversity in practice, and the FASB regulations, which were too numerous.

IFRS 15 replaces both IAS 18 *Revenue* and IAS 11 *Construction contracts*. It is effective for reporting periods beginning on or after 1 January 2017. Its core principle is that revenue is recognised to depict the transfer of goods or services to a customer in an amount that reflects the consideration to which the entity expects to be entitled in exchange for those goods or services. (IFRS 15: para. IN4)

Under IFRS 15 the transfer of goods and services is based upon the transfer of **control**, rather than the transfer of risks and rewards as in IAS 18. **Control of an asset** is described in the standard as the ability to direct the use of, and obtain substantially all of the remaining benefits from, the asset.

For straightforward retail transactions IFRS 15 will have little, if any, effect on the amount and timing of revenue recognition. For contracts such as long-term service contracts and multi-element arrangements it could result in changes either to the amount or to the timing of revenue recognised.

2.1 Scope

IFRS 15 applies to all contracts with customers except:

- Leases within the scope of IFRS 16
- Insurance contracts within the scope of IFRS 4
- Financial instruments and other contractual rights and obligations within the scope of IFRS 9, IFRS 10, IFRS 11, IAS 27 or IAS 28
- Non-monetary exchanges between entities in the same line of business. (IFRS 15: para. 5)

2.2 Definitions

The following definitions are given in the standard.

Key terms

> **Income.** Increases in economic benefits during the accounting period in the form of inflows or enhancements of assets or decreases of liabilities that result in an increase in equity, other than those relating to contributions from equity participants.
>
> **Revenue.** Income arising in the course of an entity's ordinary activities.
>
> **Contract.** An agreement between two or more parties that creates enforceable rights and obligations.
>
> **Contract asset.** An entity's right to consideration in exchange for goods or services that the entity has transferred to a customer when that right is conditioned on something other than the passage of time (for example the entity's future performance).
>
> **Receivable.** An entity's right to consideration that is unconditional – ie only the passage of time is required before payment is due.

> **Contract liability.** An entity's obligation to transfer goods or services to a customer for which the entity has received consideration (or the amount is due) from the customer.
>
> **Customer.** A party that has contracted with an entity to obtain goods or services that are an output of the entity's ordinary activities in exchange for consideration.
>
> **Performance obligation.** A promise in a contract with a customer to transfer to the customer either:
>
> (a)   a good or service (or a bundle of goods or services) that is distinct; or
>
> (b)   a series of distinct goods or services that are substantially the same ad that have the same pattern of transfer to the customer.
>
> **Stand-alone selling price.** The price at which an entity would sell a promised good or service separately to a customer.
>
> **Transaction price.** The amount of consideration to which an entity expects to be entitled in exchange for transferring promised goods or services to a customer, excluding amounts collected on behalf of third parties.
>
> (IFRS 15: App A)

Revenue **does not include** sales taxes, value added taxes or goods and service taxes which are only collected for third parties, because these do not represent an economic benefit flowing to the entity.

3 Recognition and measurement

FAST FORWARD

> Generally revenue is recognised when the entity has transferred promised goods or services to the customer. IFRS 15 sets out five steps for the recognition process.

Keep phone example in mind

3.1 The five-step model

Under IFRS 15 revenue is recognised and measured using a five step model.

Step 1   Identify the contract with the customer.

A contract with a customer is within the scope of IFRS 15 only when:

(a)   The parties have approved the contract and are committed to carrying it out.

(b)   Each party's rights regarding the goods and services to be transferred can be identified.

(c)   The payment terms for the goods and services can be identified.

(d)   The contract has commercial substance.

(e)   It is probable that the entity will collect the consideration to which it will be entitled.

(f)   The contract can be written, verbal or implied.   (IFRS 15: para. 9)

Step 2   Identify the separate performance obligations.

The key point is distinct goods or services. A contract includes promises to provide goods or services to a customer. Those promises are called performance obligations. A company would account for a performance obligation separately only if the promised good or service is distinct. A good or service is distinct if it is sold separately or if it could be sold separately because it has a distinct function and a distinct profit margin.

IFRS 15 states that a good or service that is promised to a customer is distinct if both of the following criteria are met:

(a)   The customer can benefit from the good or service either on its own or together with other resources that are readily available to the customer (ie the good or service is capable of being distinct); and

(b)   The entity's promise to transfer the good or service to the customer is separately identifiable from other promises in the contract (ie the good or service is distinct with in the context of the contract)

(IFRS 15: para.27)

Factors for consideration as to whether an entity's promise to transfer the good or service to the customer is separately identifiable include, but are not limited to:

(a)   The entity does not provide a significant service of integrating the good or service with other goods or services promised in the contract.

(b)   The good or service does not significantly modify or customise another good or service promised in the contract.

(c)   The good or service is not highly dependent on or highly interrelated with other goods or services promised in the contract.   (IFRS 15: paras. 22,23)

Step 3   Determine the transaction price.

The transaction price is the amount of consideration a company expects to be entitled to from the customer in exchange for transferring goods or services. The transaction price would reflect the company's probability-weighted estimate of **variable consideration** (including reasonable estimates of contingent amounts) in addition to the effects of the customer's credit risk and the time value of money (if material).

Variable contingent amounts are only included where it is highly probable that there will not be a reversal of revenue when any uncertainty associated with the variable consideration is resolved. Examples of where a variable consideration can arise include: discounts, rebates, refunds, price concessions, credits and penalties.   (IFRS 15: para. 47)

Step 4   Allocate the transaction price to the performance obligations.

Where a contract contains more than one distinct performance obligation a company allocates the transaction price to all separate performance obligations in proportion to the stand-alone selling price of the good or service underlying each performance obligation. If the good or service is not sold separately, the company would have to estimate its stand-alone selling price.   (IFRS 15: paras. 73–75)

So, if any entity sells a bundle of goods and/or services which it also supplies unbundled, the separate performance obligations in the contract should be priced in the same proportion as the unbundled prices. This would apply to mobile phone contracts where the handset is supplied 'free'. The entity must look at the stand-alone price of such a handset and some of the consideration for the contract should be allocated to the handset.

Step 5   Recognise revenue when (or as) a performance obligation is satisfied.

The entity satisfies a performance obligation by transferring **control** of a promised good or service to the customer (IFRS 15: para. 31). A performance obligation can be satisfied **at a point in time**, such as when goods are delivered to the customer (IFRS 15: para. 38), or **over time**. An obligation satisfied **over time** will meet one of the following criteria:

- The customer simultaneously receives and consumes the benefits as the performance takes place.

- The entity's performance creates or enhances an asset that the customer controls as the asset is created or enhanced.

- The entity's performance does not create an asset with an alternative use to the entity and the entity has an enforceable right to payment for performance completed to date.   (IFRS 15: para. 35)

The amount of revenue recognised is the amount allocated to that performance obligation in Step 4.

An entity must be able to **reasonably measure** the outcome of a performance obligation before the related revenue can be recognised.

In some circumstances, such as in the early stages of a contract, it may not be possible to reasonably measure the outcome of a performance obligation, but the entity expects to recover the costs incurred. In these circumstances, revenue is recognised only to the extent of costs incurred.

(IFRS 15: para. 45)

3.2 Example: identifying the separate performance obligation

Office Solutions Co, a limited company, has developed a communications software package called CommSoft. Office Solutions Co has entered into a contract with Logisticity Co to supply the following:

(a)   Licence to use Commsoft

(b)   Installation service. This may require an upgrade to the computer operating system, but the software package does not need to be customised.

(c)   Technical support for three years

(d)   Three years of updates for Commsoft

Office Solutions Co is not the only company able to install CommSoft, and the technical support can also be provided by other companies. The software can function without the updates and technical support.

Required

Explain whether the goods or services provided to Logisticity Co are **distinct** in accordance with IFRS 15 *Revenue from contracts with customers*.

Solution

CommSoft Co was delivered before the other goods or services and remains functional without the updates and the technical support. It may be concluded that Logisticity Co can benefit from each of the goods and services either on their own or together with the other goods and services that are readily available.

The promises to transfer each good and service to the customer are separately identifiable. In particular, the installation service does not significantly modify the software itself and, as such, the software and the installation service are separate outputs promised by Office Solutions Co rather than inputs used to produce a combined output.

In conclusion, the goods and services are distinct and amount to four performance obligations in the contract under IFRS 15.

3.3 Example: determining the transaction price

Taplop Co supplies laptop computers to large businesses. On 1 July 20X5, Taplop Co entered into a contract with TrillCo, under which TrillCo was to purchase laptops at $500 per unit. The contract states that if TrillCo purchases more than 500 laptops in a year, the price per unit is reduced retrospectively to $450 per unit. Taplop's year end is 30 June.

(a)   As at 30 September 20X5, TrillCo had bought 70 laptops from Taplop. Taplop Co therefore estimated that TrillCo's purchases would not exceed 500 in the year to 30 June 20X6, and TrillCo would therefore not be entitled to the volume discount.

(b)   During the quarter ended 31 December 20X5, TrillCo expanded rapidly as a result of a substantial acquisition, and purchased an additional 250 laptops from Taplop Co. Taplop Co then estimated that TrillCo's purchases would exceed the threshold for the volume discount in the year to 30 June 20X6.

Required

Calculate the revenue Taplop Co would recognise in:

(a)   Quarter ended 30 September 20X5
(b)   Quarter ended 31 December 20X5

We need to apply the principles of IFRS 15 *Revenue from contracts with customers*.

Solution

(a)   Applying the requirements of IFRS 15 to TrillCo's purchasing pattern at 30 September 20X5, Taplop should conclude that it was highly probable that a significant reversal in the cumulative amount of revenue recognised ($500 per laptop) would not occur when the uncertainty was resolved, that is when the total amount of purchases was known.

Consequently, Taplop Co should recognise revenue of 70 × $500 = $35,000 for the first quarter ended 30 September 20X5.

(b)   In the quarter ended 31 December 20X5, TrillCo's purchasing pattern changed such that it would be legitimate for Taplop Co to conclude that TrillCo's purchases would exceed the threshold for the volume discount in the year to 30 June 20X6, and therefore that it was appropriate to reduce the price to $450 per laptop.

Taplop Co should therefore recognise revenue of $109,000 for the quarter ended 31 December 20X5. The amount is calculated as from $112,500 (250 laptops × $450) less the change in transaction price of $3,500 (70 laptops × $50 price reduction) for the reduction of the price of the laptops sold in the quarter ended 30 September 20X5.

3.4 Example: allocating the transaction price to the performance obligations

[handwritten: Previous Exam question.]

A mobile phone company, Deltawave Co, gives customers a free handset when they sign a two-year contract for provision of network services. The handset has a stand-alone price of $100 and the contract is for $20 per month.

Prior to IFRS 15, Deltawave Co would recognise no revenue in relation to the handset and a total of $240 per annum in relation to the contract.

Under IFRS 15, revenue must be allocated to the handset because delivery of the handset constitutes a performance obligation. This will be calculated as follows:

	$	%
Handset	100	17
Contract – two years	480	83
Total value	580	100

As the total receipts are $480, this is the amount which must be allocated to the separate performance obligations. Revenue will be recognised as follows (rounded to nearest $).

	$
Year 1	
Handset (480 × 17%)	82
Contract (480 – 82)/2	199
	281
Year 2	
Contract as above	199

So application of IFRS 15 has moved revenue of $41 from Year 2 to Year 1.

3.5 Contract costs

The incremental costs of **obtaining** a contract (such as sales commission) are **recognised as an asset** if the entity expects to recover those costs. (IFRS 15: para. 91)

Costs that would have been incurred regardless of whether the contract was obtained are recognised as an expense as incurred. (IFRS 15: para. 93)

Costs incurred in **fulfilling** a contract, unless within the scope of another standard (such as IAS 2 *Inventories*, IAS 16 *Property, plant and equipment* or IAS 38 *Intangible assets*) are recognised as an asset if they meet the following criteria:

(a) The costs relate directly to an identifiable contract (costs such as labour, materials, management costs)

(b) The costs generate or enhance resources of the entity that will be used in satisfying (or continuing to satisfy) performance obligations in the future; and

(c) The costs are expected to be recovered. (IFRS 15: para. 95)

Costs recognised as assets are amortised on a systematic basis consistent with the transfer to the customer of the goods or services to which the asset relates. (IFRS 15: para. 99)

3.6 Performance obligations satisfied over time

A performance obligation satisfied over time meets the criteria in Step 5 above and, if it entered into more than one accounting period, would previously have been described as a long-term contract.

In this type of contract an entity often has an enforceable right to payment for performance completed to date. The standard describes this as an amount that approximates the selling price of the goods or services transferred to date (for example recovery of the costs incurred by the entity in satisfying the performance plus a reasonable profit margin). (IFRS 15: para. B9)

Methods of measuring the amount of performance completed to date encompass **output methods** and **input methods**.

Output methods recognise revenue on the basis of the value to the **customer** of the goods or services transferred. They include surveys of performance completed, appraisal of units produced or delivered etc.

Input methods recognise revenue on the basis of the **entity's** inputs, such as labour hours, resources consumed, costs incurred. If using a cost-based method, the costs incurred must contribute to the entity's progress in satisfying the performance obligation. (IFRS 15: para. 41)

3.7 Performance obligations satisfied at a point in time

A performance obligation not satisfied over time will be satisfied at a point in time. This will be the point in time at which the customer obtains control of the promised asset and the entity satisfies a performance obligation.

Some indicators of the transfer of control are:

(a) The entity has a present right to payment for the asset.
(b) The customer has legal title to the asset.
(c) The entity has transferred physical possession of the asset.
(d) The significant risks and rewards of ownership have been transferred to the customer.

(IFRS 15: para. 38)

4 Common types of transaction

FAST FORWARD

The application notes to IFRS 15 provide guidance on how to deal with a number of different transactions.

4.1 Warranties

If a customer has the option to purchase a warranty separately from the product to which it relates, it constitutes a distinct service and is accounted for as a separate performance obligation. This would apply to a warranty which provides the customer with a service in addition to the assurance that the product complies with agreed-upon specifications.

If the customer does not have the option to purchase the warranty separately, for instance if the warranty is required by law, that does not give rise to a performance obligation and the warranty is accounted for in accordance with IAS 37. (IFRS 15: paras. B28–43)

4.2 Principal versus agent

An entity must establish in any transaction whether it is acting as principal or agent.

It is a principal if it controls the promised good or service before it is transferred to the customer. When the performance obligation is satisfied, the entity recognises revenue in the gross amount of the consideration to which it expects to be entitled for those goods or services.

It is acting as an agent if its performance obligation is to arrange for the provision of goods or services by another party. Satisfaction of this performance obligation will give rise to the recognition of revenue in the amount of any fee or commission to which it expects to be entitled in exchange for arranging for the other party to provide its goods or services.

Indicators that an entity is an agent rather than a principal include the following:

(a)   Another party is primarily responsible for fulfilling the contract.

(b)   The entity does not have inventory risk before or after the goods have been ordered by a customer, during shipping or on return.

(c)   The entity does not have discretion in establishing prices for the other party's goods or services and, therefore, the benefit that the entity can receive from those goods or services is limited.

(d)   The entity's consideration is in the form of a commission.

(e)   The entity is not exposed to credit risk for the amount receivable from a customer in exchange for the other party's goods or services. (IFRS 15: paras. B35–38)

4.3 Example: principal versus agent

This example is taken from the standard. (IFRS 15: Illustrative Examples)

An entity operates a website that enables customers to purchase goods from a range of suppliers. The suppliers deliver directly to the customers, who have paid in advance, and the entity receives a commission of 10% of the sales price.

The entity's website also processes payments from the customer to the supplier at prices set by the supplier. The entity has no further obligation to the customer after arranging for the products to be supplied.

Is the entity a principal or an agent?

The following points are relevant:

(a)   Goods are supplied directly from the supplier to the customer, so the entity does not obtain control of the goods.

(b)   The supplier is primarily responsible for fulfilling the contract.

(c)   The entity's consideration is in the form of commission.

(d)   The entity does not establish prices and bears no credit risk.

The entity would therefore conclude that it is acting as an agent and that the only revenue to be recognised is the amounts received as commission.

4.4 Repurchase agreements

Under a repurchase agreement an entity sells an asset and promises, or has the option, to repurchase it. Repurchase agreements generally come in three forms.

(a) An entity has an obligation to repurchase the asset (a forward contract).
(b) An entity has the right to repurchase the asset (a call option).
(c) An entity must repurchase the asset if requested to do so by the customer (a put option).

In the case of a forward or a call option the customer does not obtain control of the asset, even if it has physical possession. The entity will account for the contract as:

(a) A lease in accordance with IFRS 16, if the repurchase price is below the original selling price; or

(b) A financing arrangement if the repurchase price is equal to or greater than the original selling price. In this case the entity will recognise both the asset and a corresponding liability.

If the entity is obliged to repurchase at the request of the customer (a put option), it must consider whether or not the customer is likely to exercise that option.

If the repurchase price is lower than the original selling price and it is considered that the customer does not therefore have significant economic incentive to exercise the option, the contract should be accounted for as an outright sale, with a right of return. If the customer is considered to have a significant economic incentive to exercise the option, the entity should account for the agreement as a lease in accordance with IFRS 16.

If the repurchase price is greater than or equal to the original selling price and is above the expected market value of the option, the contract is treated as a financing arrangement.   (IFRS 15: paras. B64–76)

4.5 Example: contract with a call option

This example is taken from the standard.   (IFRS 15: Illustrative Examples)

An entity enters into a contract with a customer for the sale of a tangible asset on 1 January 20X7 for $1m. The contract includes a call option that gives the entity the right to repurchase the asset for $1.1m on or before 31 December 20X7.

This means that the customer does not obtain control of the asset, because the repurchase option means that it is limited in its ability to use and obtain benefit from the asset.

As control has not been transferred, the entity accounts for the transaction as a **financing arrangement**, because the exercise price is above the original selling price. The entity continues to recognise the asset and recognises the cash received as a financial liability. The difference of $0.1m is recognised as interest expense.

If on 31 December 20X7 the option lapses unexercised, the customer now obtains control of the asset. The entity will derecognise the asset and recognise revenue of $1.1m (the $1m already received plus the $0.1m charged to interest).

4.6 Example: contract with a put option

The same contract as above includes instead a put option that obliges the entity to repurchase the asset at the customer's request for $900,000 on or before 31 December 20X7, at which time the market value is expected to be $750,000.

In this case the customer has a significant economic incentive to exercise the put option because the repurchase price exceeds the market value at the repurchase date. This means that control does not pass to the customer. Since the customer will be exercising the put option, this limits its ability to use or obtain benefit from the asset.

In this situation the entity accounts for the transaction as a lease in accordance with IFRS 16. The asset has been leased to the customer for the period up to the repurchase and the difference of $100,000 will be accounted for as payments received under an operating lease.

4.7 Consignment arrangements

When a product is delivered to a customer under a consignment arrangement, the customer (dealer) does not obtain control of the product at that point in time, so no revenue is recognised upon delivery.

(IFRS 15: paras. B77–78)

Indicators of a consignment arrangement include:

(a) The product is controlled by the entity until a specified event occurs, such as the product is sold on, or a specified period expires.

(b) The entity can require the return of the product, or transfer it to another party.

(c) The customer (dealer/distributor) does not have an unconditional obligation to pay for the product.

4.7.1 Required accounting

The following apply where it is concluded that control of the inventory **has been transferred** to the dealer.

(a) The inventory should be recognised as such in the dealer's statement of financial position, together with a corresponding liability to the manufacturer.

(b) Any deposit should be deducted from the liability and the excess classified as a trade payable.

Where it is concluded that control of the inventory **has not been transferred** to the dealer, the following apply.

(a) The inventory should not be included in the dealer's statement of financial position until the transfer of control has taken place.

(b) Any deposit should be included under 'other receivables'.

4.8 Example: Consignment arrangement

WholesalerCo supplies goods to a Bob's Convenience Store Co (BCS) on a consignment basis. WholesalerCo retains title until the goods are sold by BCS. BCS does not pay WholesalerCo until the goods are sold and any unsold goods can be returned.

In this situation control of the goods is not transferred to the BSC until the goods are sold to the end-user, so it is only at that point that WholesalerCo can recognise the revenue.

Question	Recognition

Daley Motors Co owns a number of car dealerships throughout a geographical area. The terms of the arrangement between the dealerships and the manufacturer are:

(a) Legal title passes when the cars are either used by Daley Motors Co for demonstration purposes or sold to a third party.

(b) The dealer has the right to return vehicles to the manufacturer without penalty. (Daley Motors Co has rarely exercised this right in the past.)

(c) The transfer price is based on the manufacturer's list price at the date of delivery.

(d) Daley Motors Co makes a substantial interest-free deposit based on the number of cars held.

Required

Should the asset and liability be recognised by Daley Motors Co at the date of delivery?

Answer

(a) Legal form is irrelevant
(b) Yes: only because rarely exercised (otherwise 'no')
(c) Yes
(d) Yes: the dealership is effectively forgoing the interest which could be earned on the cash sum

4.9 Bill-and-hold arrangements

Under a bill-and-hold arrangement goods are sold but remain in the possession of the seller for a specified period, perhaps because the customer lacks storage facilities.   (IFRS 15: para. B79)

An entity will need to determine at what point the customer obtains control of the product. For some contracts, control will not be transferred until the goods are delivered to the customer. For others, a customer may obtain control even though the goods remain in the entity's physical possession. In this case the entity would be providing custodial services (which may constitute a separate performance obligation) to the customer over the customer's asset.

For a customer to have obtained control of a product in a bill and hold arrangement, the following criteria must all be met:

(a)   The reason for the bill-and-hold must be substantive (for example, requested by the customer).
(b)   The product must be separately identified as belonging to the customer.
(c)   The product must be ready for physical transfer to the customer.
(d)   The entity cannot have the ability to use the product or to transfer it to another customer.

                    (IFRS 15: para. B81)

4.10 Example: bill and hold arrangement

This example is taken from the standard.   (IFRS 15: Illustrative Examples)

An entity enters into a contract with a customer on 1 January 20X8 for sale of a machine and spare parts. It takes two years to manufacture these and on 31 December 20X9 the customer pays for both the machine and the spare parts but only takes physical possession of the machine. The customer inspects and accepts the spare parts but requests that they continue to be stored at the entity's warehouse.

There are now three performance obligations – transfer of the machine, transfer of the spare parts and the custodial services. The transaction price is allocated to the three performance obligations and revenue is recognised when (or as) control passes to the customer.

The machine and the spare parts are both performance obligations satisfied at a point in time, and for both of them that point in time is 31 December 20X9. In the case of the spare parts, the customer has paid for them, the customer has legal title to them and the customer has control of them as they can remove them from storage at any time.

The custodial services are a performance obligation satisfied over time, so revenue will be recognised over the period during which the spare parts are stored.

5 Presentation and disclosure

FAST FORWARD

> The presentation and disclosure requirements are important in relation to contracts where performance obligations are satisfied over time, where there are likely to be contract assets and liabilities to be accounted for at the end of the reporting period.

5.1 Presentation

Contracts with customers will be presented in an entity's statement of financial position as a contract liability, a contract asset or a receivable, depending on the relationship between the entity's performance and the customer's payment.   (IFRS 15: para. 105)

A **contract liability** is recognised and presented in the statement of financial position where a customer has paid an amount of consideration prior to the entity performing by transferring control of the related good or service to the customer.   (IFRS 15: para. 106)

When the entity has performed but the customer has not yet paid the related consideration, this will give rise to either a **contract asset** or a **receivable**. A contract asset is recognised when the entity's right to consideration is conditional on something other than the passage of time, for instance future performance. A receivable is recognised when the entity's right to consideration is unconditional except for the passage of time. (IFRS 15: para. 107)

Where revenue has been invoiced a receivable is recognised. Where revenue has been earned but not invoiced, it is recognised as a contract asset.

5.2 Disclosure

The objective is for an entity to disclose sufficient information to enable users of financial statements to understand the nature, amount, timing and uncertainty of revenue and cash flows arising from contracts with customers. The following amounts should be disclosed unless they have been presented separately in the financial statements in accordance with other standards.

(a) Revenue recognised from contracts with customers, disclosed separately from other sources of revenue. (IFRS 15: para. 113)

(b) Any impairment losses recognised (in accordance with IFRS 9) on any receivables or contract assets arising from an entity's contracts with customers, disclosed separately from other impairment losses. (IFRS 15: para. 113)

(c) The opening and closing balances of receivables, contract assets and contract liabilities from contracts with customers. (IFRS 15: para. 116)

(d) Revenue recognised in the reporting period that was included in the contract liability balance at the beginning of the period. (IFRS 15: para. 116)

(e) Revenue recognised in the reporting period from performance obligations satisfied in previous periods (such as changes in transaction price). (IFRS 15: para. 116)

Other information that should be provided:

(a) An explanation of significant changes in the contract asset and liability balances during the reporting period. (IFRS 15: para. 118)

(b) Information regarding the entity's performance obligations, including when they are typically satisfied (upon delivery, upon shipment, as services are rendered etc), significant payment terms (such as when payment is typically due) and details of any agency transactions, obligations for returns or refunds and warranties granted. (IFRS 15: para. 119)

(c) The aggregate amount of the transaction price allocated to the performance obligations that are not fully satisfied at the end of the reporting period and an explanation of when the entity expects to recognise these amounts as revenue. (IFRS 15: para. 120)

(d) Judgements, and changes in judgements, made in applying the standard that significantly affect the determination of the amount and timing of revenue from contracts with customers. (IFRS 15: para. 123)

(e) Assets recognised from the costs to obtain or fulfil a contract with a customer. This would include pre-contract costs and set-up costs. The method of amortisation should also be disclosed. (IFRS 15: para. 127)

6 Performance obligations satisfied over time

FAST FORWARD

Where performance obligations are satisfied over time, an entity must determine what amounts to include as revenue and costs in each accounting period.

6.1 Contracts where performance obligations are satisfied over time

A company is building a large tower block that will house offices, under a contract with an investment company. It will take three years to build the block and over that time it will obviously have to pay for building materials, wages of workers on the building, architects' fees and so on. It will receive periodic payments from the investment company at various predetermined stages of the construction. How does it decide, in each of the three years, **what to include as income and expenditure** for the contract in profit or loss? *Recognise loss as soon as they become known to us.*

6.2 Example: contract

Suppose that a contract is started on 1 January 20X5, with an estimated completion date of 31 December 20X6. The final contract price is $1,500,000. In the first year, to 31 December 20X5:

(a)   Costs incurred amounted to $600,000.

(b)   Half the work on the contract was completed.

(c)   Certificates of work completed have been issued, to the value of $750,000.

(d)   It is estimated with reasonable certainty that further costs to completion in 20X6 will be $600,000.

What is the contract profit in 20X5, and what entries would be made for the contract at 31 December 20X5?

Solution

This is a contract in which the performance obligation is satisfied **over time**. The entity is carrying out the work for the benefit of the customer rather than creating an asset for its own use and in this case it has an enforceable right to payment for work completed to date. We can see this from the fact that certificates of work completed have been issued.

IFRS 15 states that the amount of payment that the entity is entitled to corresponds to the amount of performance completed to date (ie goods and/or services transferred), which approximates to the costs incurred in satisfying the performance obligation plus a reasonable profit margin.

In this case the contract is certified as 50% complete, measuring progress under the output method. At 31 December 20X5 the entity will recognise revenue of $750,000 and cost of sales of $600,000, leaving profit of $150,000. The **contract asset** will be the costs to date plus the profit, that is $750,000. We are not told that any of this amount has yet been invoiced, so none of this amount is classified as receivables.

6.3 Summary of accounting treatment

Statement of profit or loss

(a)   **Revenue and costs**

    (i)   Sales revenue and associated costs should be recorded in profit or loss as the contract activity progresses.

    (ii)   Include an appropriate proportion of total contract value as sales revenue in profit or loss.

    (iii)   The costs incurred in completing that amount of the performance obligation are matched with this sales revenue, resulting in the reporting of results which can be attributed to the proportion of work completed.

    (iv)   Sales revenue is the value of work carried out to date.

(b)   **Profit recognised in the contract**

    (i)   It must reflect the proportion of work carried out, which will be equivalent to the amount of performance obligation satisfied.

    (ii)   It should take into account any known inequalities in profitability in the various stages of a contract.

Statement of financial position

(a) **Contract asset** (presented separately, under current assets)

	$
Costs to date	X
Plus recognised profits	(X)
	X
Less any recognised losses	(X)
	X
Less receivables (amounts invoiced)	(X)
Contract asset (amount due from the customer)	X

(b) **Receivables**
Unpaid invoices

(c) **Contract liability**
Where (a) gives a net amount due **to** the customer this amount should be included as a contract liability, presented separately under current liabilities. *- Big deposit upfront.*

Example: contract profits

Pappa Co has the following contract in progress:

Learn

	$m
Total contract price	750
Costs incurred to date	225
Estimated costs to completion	340
Payments invoiced and received	290

Now we will calculate the amounts to be recognised for the contract in the statement of profit or loss and statement of financial position assuming the amount of performance obligation satisfied is calculated using the proportion of costs incurred method.

1   *Estimated profit*

	$m
Total contract price	750
Less costs incurred to date	(225)
Less estimated costs to completion	(340)
Estimated profit	185

2   *Percentage complete*
Costs to date/total estimated costs: 225/(225 + 340) = 40%

3   *Statement of profit or loss*

	$m
Revenue (40% × $750)	300
Cost of sales (40% × (225 + 340))	(226)
Profit (40% × 185)	74

4   *Statement of financial position*

	$m
Costs incurred to date	225
Recognised profits	74
Less receivable	(290)
Contract asset	9

How would we account for this if it was a loss-making contract?

IFRS 15 states that an entity's right to payment for performance completed to date should approximate the selling price of the service completed to date (para. B9). Selling price would be recovery of costs incurred plus a reasonable profit margin. Where no profit can be estimated, revenue is limited to recoverable costs.

Where a loss is anticipated, this means that a proportion of the entity's costs will not be recovered, and this needs to be recognised.

We will reduce Pappa Co's contract price to $550m.

1 *Estimated loss*

	$m
Total contract price	550
Less costs incurred to date	(225)
Less estimated costs to completion	(340)
Estimated loss – costs not recoverable	(15)

2 *Percentage complete*

Costs to date/total estimated costs: 225/(225 + 340) = 40%

3 *Statement of profit or loss*

	$m
Revenue (40% × $550)	220
Cost of sales (balancing figure)	(235)*
Loss	(15)

even though the contract is 40 we must show 100% of the loss is recognised.

4 *Statement of financial position*

	$m
Costs incurred to date	225
Recognised loss	(15)
Less receivable	(290)
Contract liability	(80)

Question

Contract profits

The main business of Santolina Co is building work. At the end of September 20X3 there is an uncompleted contract on the books, details of which are as follows.

Date commenced	1.4.X1
Expected completion date	23.12.X3

	$
Total contract revenue	290,000
Costs to 30.9.X3	210,450
Value of performance obligations satisfied to 30.9.X3	230,000
Amounts invoiced for work certified to 30.9.X3	210,000
Cash received to 30.9.X3	194,000
Estimated costs to completion at 30.9.X3	20,600

Santolina Co calculates satisfaction of performance obligations based on work certified as a percentage of contract price.

Required

Prepare calculations showing the amount to be included in the statement of profit or loss and statement of financial position at 30 September 20X3 in respect of the above contract.

Answer

This is a contract where performance obligations are recognised over time. It will be included in the statement of financial position at cost plus recognised profit less amounts invoiced.

The estimated final profit is:

	$
Final contract price	290,000
Less: costs to date	(210,450)
estimated future costs	(20,600)
Estimated final profit	58,950

The recognised profit is found as follows:

$$\text{Estimated final profit} \times \frac{\text{Work certified}}{\text{Total contract price}}$$

$$\$58,950 \times \frac{230,000}{290,000} = \$58,950 \times 79.31\%$$

Profit recognised = $46,753

STATEMENT OF PROFIT OR LOSS

	$
Revenue (work certified)	230,000
Cost of sales ((210,450 + 20,600) × 79.31%)	(183,247)
Gross profit	46,753

STATEMENT OF FINANCIAL POSITION

Contract asset

	$
Costs to date	210,450
Attributable profit	46,753
	257,203
Amounts invoiced	(210,000)
Contract asset	47,203
Contract receivables (210 – 194)	16,000

Exam focus point

Contracts where performance obligations are satisfied over time are likely to appear in a single-entity financial statements preparation question, or as an MCQ.

 ## Question

IFRS 15 calculations

Haggrun Co has two contracts in progress, the details of which are as follows.

	Happy (profitable) $'000	Grumpy (loss-making) $'000
Total contract revenue	300	300
Costs incurred to date	90	150
Estimated costs to completion	135	225
Payments invoiced and received	116	116

Haggrun Co measures satisfaction of performance obligations based on percentage of work certified as complete.

Required

Show extracts from the statement of profit or loss and other comprehensive income and the statement of financial position for each contract, assuming they are both certified as:

(a)   40% complete; and

(b)   36% complete.

Answer

Happy contract

(a)   40% complete

	$'000
Statement of profit or loss	
Revenue (300 × 40%)	120
Cost of sales ((90 + 135) × 40%)	(90)
	30

Working

Profit to date

	$'000
Total contract revenue	300
Costs to date	(90)
Cost to completion	(135)
Total expected profit	75
Profit to date (75 × 40%)	30

Statement of financial position

	$'000
Costs to date	90
Profit recognised to date	30
Amounts invoiced	(116)
Contract asset	4

(b)   36% complete

	$'000
Statement of profit or loss	
Revenue (300 × 36%)	108
Cost of sales ((90 + 135) × 36%)	(81)
Profit to date (75 × 36%)	27

Statement of financial position

	$'000
Costs to date	90
Profit recognised to date	27
Amounts invoiced	(116)
Contract asset	1

Grumpy contract

(a)   40% complete

	$'000
Statement of profit or loss	
Revenue (300 × 40%)	120
Cost of sales (balancing figure*)	(195)
Foreseeable loss (W)	(75)

Working

	$'000
Total contract revenue	300
Costs to date	(150)
Costs to complete	(225)
Foreseeable loss – costs which will not be recovered	(75)

Statement of financial position

Costs to date	150
Foreseeable loss	(75)
Amounts invoiced	(116)
Contract liability	(41)
*Costs to date (150 + 225) × 40%	150
Foreseeable loss (75) × 60%**	45
	195

The other 40% is taken into account in costs to date. We make this adjustment to bring in the **whole of the foreseeable loss.

(b)　*36% complete*

	$'000

Statement of profit or loss

Revenue (300 × 36%)	108
Cost of sales*	(183)
Foreseeable loss	(75)

Statement of financial position

Costs to date	150
Foreseeable loss	(75)
Amounts invoiced	(116)
Contract liability	(41)
*Costs to date (150 + 225) × 36%	135
Foreseeable loss (75) × 64%**	48
	183

7 IAS 20 *Government grants and disclosure of Government Assistance*

FAST FORWARD

It is common for entities to receive government grants for various purposes (grants may be called subsidies, premiums, etc). They may also receive other types of assistance which may be in many forms.

7.1 Scope

The treatment of government grants is covered by IAS 20 *Accounting for government grants and disclosure of government assistance.*

IAS 20 does **not** cover the following situations.

- Accounting for government grants in financial statements reflecting the effects of **changing prices**
- Government assistance given in the form of **'tax breaks'**
- Government acting as **part-owner** of the entity
- Grants covered by IAS 41 *Agriculture*　　　　　　　　　　　(IAS 20: para. 2)

7.2 Definitions

These definitions are given by the standard.

Key terms

> - **Government.** Government, government agencies and similar bodies whether local, national or international.
>
> - **Government assistance.** Action by government designed to provide an economic benefit specific to an entity or range of entities qualifying under certain criteria.
>
> - **Government grants.** Assistance by government in the form of transfers of resources to an entity in return for past or future compliance with certain conditions relating to the operating activities of the entity. They exclude those forms of government assistance which cannot reasonably have a value placed upon them and transactions with government which cannot be distinguished from the normal trading transactions of the entity.
>
> - **Grants related to assets.** Government grants whose primary condition is that an entity qualifying for them should purchase, construct or otherwise acquire non-current assets. Subsidiary conditions may also be attached restricting the type or location of the assets or the periods during which they are to be acquired or held.
>
> - **Grants related to income.** Government grants other than those related to assets.
>
> - **Forgivable loans.** Loans for which the lender undertakes to waive repayment under certain prescribed conditions.
>
>   (IAS 20: para. 3)
>
> - **Fair value.** The price that would be received to sell an asset or paid to transfer a liability in an orderly transaction between market participants at the measurement date. (IFRS 13: para. 9)

You can see that there are many **different forms** of government assistance: both the type of assistance and the conditions attached to it will vary. Government assistance may have encouraged an entity to undertake something it otherwise would not have done.

How will the receipt of government assistance affect the financial statements?

(a) An appropriate method must be found to account for any **resources transferred**.

(b) The extent to which an entity has **benefited** from such assistance during the reporting period should be shown.

7.3 Government grants

An entity should not recognise government grants (including non-monetary grants at fair value) until it has **reasonable assurance** that:

- The entity will comply with any **conditions** attached to the grant
- The entity will **actually receive** the grant

(IAS 20: para. 7)

Even if the grant has been received, this does not prove that the conditions attached to it have been or will be fulfilled.

(IAS 20: para. 8)

It makes no difference in the treatment of the grant whether it is received in cash or given as a reduction in a liability to government, ie the **manner of receipt is irrelevant**.

(IAS 20: para. 9)

Any related **contingency** should be recognised under IAS 37 *Provisions, contingent liabilities and contingent assets*, once the grant has been recognised.

(IAS 20: para. 11)

In the case of a **forgivable loan** (as defined in key terms above) from government, it should be treated in the same way as a government grant when it is reasonably assured that the entity will meet the relevant terms for forgiveness.

(IAS 20: para. 10)

7.3.1 Accounting treatment of government grants

IAS 20 requires grants to be recognised as income over the relevant periods to match them with related costs which they have been received to compensate. This should be done on a systematic basis. **Grants should not, therefore, be credited directly to equity.** (IAS 20: para. 12)

It would be against the accruals assumption to credit grants to income on a receipts basis, so a **systematic basis of matching** must be used. A receipts basis would only be acceptable if no other basis was available.

It will usually be easy to identify the **costs related to a government grant**, and thereby the period(s) in which the grant should be recognised as income, ie when the costs are incurred. Where grants are received in relation to a depreciating asset, the grant will be recognised over the periods in which the asset is depreciated **and** in the same proportions.

Question	Recognition

Arturo Co receives a government grant representing 50% of the cost of a depreciating asset which costs $40,000. How will the grant be recognised if Arturo Co depreciates the asset:

(a) Over four years straight line; or
(b) At 40% reducing balance?

The residual value is nil. The useful life is four years.

Answer	

The grant should be recognised in the same proportion as the depreciation.

(a) Straight line

	Depreciation $	Grant income $
Year 1	10,000	5,000
2	10,000	5,000
3	10,000	5,000
4	10,000	5,000

(b) Reducing balance

	Depreciation $	Grant income $
Year 1	16,000	8,000
2	9,600	4,800
3	5,760	2,880
4 (remainder)	8,640	4,320

In the case of **grants for non-depreciable assets**, certain obligations may need to be fulfilled, in which case the grant should be recognised as income over the periods in which the cost of meeting the obligation is incurred. For example, if a piece of land is granted on condition that a building is erected on it, then the grant should be recognised as income over the building's life. (IAS 20: para. 18)

There may be a **series of conditions** attached to a grant, in the nature of a package of financial aid. An entity must take care to identify precisely those conditions which give rise to costs which in turn determine the periods over which the grant will be earned. When appropriate, the grant may be split and the parts allocated on different bases. (IAS 20: para. 15)

An entity may receive a grant as compensation for expenses or losses which it has **already incurred**. Alternatively, a grant may be given to an entity simply to provide immediate financial support where no future related costs are expected. In cases such as these, the grant received should be recognised as income of the period in which it becomes receivable. (IAS 20: para. 20)

7.3.2 Non-monetary government grants

A non-monetary asset may be transferred by government to an entity as a grant, for example a piece of land, or other resources. The **fair value** of such an asset is usually assessed and this is used to account for both the asset and the grant. Alternatively, both may be valued at a nominal amount. (IAS 20: para. 23)

7.3.3 Presentation of grants related to assets

There are two choices here for how government grants related to assets (including non-monetary grants at fair value) should be shown in the statement of financial position:

(a) Set up the grant as **deferred income**.

(b) **Deduct the grant** in arriving at the **carrying amount** of the asset.

These are considered to be acceptable alternatives and we can look at an example showing both.

(IAS 20: paras. 24–28)

Example: accounting for grants related to assets

StarStruck Co receives a 20% grant towards the cost of a new item of machinery, which cost $100,000. The machinery has an expected life of four years and a nil residual value. The expected profits of Starstruck Co, before accounting for depreciation on the new machine or the grant, amount to $50,000 per annum in each year of the machinery's life.

Solution

The results of Starstruck Co for the four years of the machine's life would be as follows.

(a) *Reducing the cost of the asset*

	Year 1 $	Year 2 $	Year 3 $	Year 4 $	Total $
Profit before depreciation	50,000	50,000	50,000	50,000	200,000
Depreciation*	20,000	20,000	20,000	20,000	80,000
Profit	30,000	30,000	30,000	30,000	120,000

*The depreciation charge on a straight line basis, for each year, is ¼ of $(100,000 − 20,000) = $20,000.

Statement of financial position at year end (extract)

	$	$	$	$
Non-current asset	80,000	80,000	80,000	80,000
Depreciation 25%	20,000	40,000	60,000	80,000
Carrying amount	60,000	40,000	20,000	–

(b) *Treating the grant as deferred income*

	Year 1 $	Year 2 $	Year 3 $	Year 4 $	Total $
Profit as above	50,000	50,000	50,000	50,000	200,000
Depreciation	(25,000)	(25,000)	(25,000)	(25,000)	(100,000)
Grant	5,000	5,000	5,000	5,000	20,000
Profit	30,000	30,000	30,000	30,000	120,000

Statement of financial position at year end (extract)

	Year 1 $	Year 2 $	Year 3 $	Year 4 $
Non-current asset at cost	100,000	100,000	100,000	100,000
Depreciation 25%	(25,000)	(50,000)	(75,000)	(100,000)
Carrying amount	75,000	50,000	25,000	–
Government grant deferred income	15,000	10,000	5,000	–

BPP
LEARNING MEDIA

Whichever of these methods is used, the **cash flows** in relation to the purchase of the asset and the receipt of the grant are often disclosed separately because of the significance of the movements in cash flow.

Deducting the grant from the cost of the asset is simpler, but the deferred income method has the advantage that the non-current asset continues to be carried at cost in the financial statements.

7.3.4 Presentation of grants related to income

These grants are a credit in profit or loss, but there is a choice in the method of disclosure:

(a) Present as a **separate credit** or under a general heading, eg 'other income'
(b) **Deduct from the related expense**

Some would argue that offsetting income and expenses in the statement of profit or loss is not good practice. Others would say that the expenses would not have been incurred had the grant not been available, so offsetting the two is acceptable. Although both methods are acceptable, disclosure of the grant may be necessary for a **proper understanding** of the financial statements, particularly the effect on any item of income or expense which is required to be separately disclosed.   (IAS 20: paras. 29–31)

7.3.5 Repayment of government grants

If a grant must be repaid it should be accounted for as a **revision of an accounting estimate** (see IAS 8).

(a) **Repayment of a grant related to income:** apply first against any unamortised deferred income set up in respect of the grant; any excess should be recognised immediately as an expense.

(b) **Repayment of a grant related to an asset**: increase the carrying amount of the asset or reduce the deferred income balance by the amount repayable. The cumulative additional depreciation that would have been recognised to date in the absence of the grant should be immediately recognised as an expense.

It is possible that the circumstances surrounding repayment may require a review of the **asset value** and an impairment of the new carrying amount of the asset.   (IAS 20: paras. 32,33)

7.4 Government assistance

Some forms of government assistance are excluded from the definition of government grants.

(a) Some forms of government assistance **cannot reasonably have a value placed on them**, eg free technical or marketing advice, provision of guarantees.

(b) There are transactions with government which **cannot be distinguished from the entity's normal trading transactions**, eg government procurement policy resulting in a portion of the entity's sales. Any segregation would be arbitrary.

Disclosure of such assistance may be necessary because of its significance; its nature, extent and duration should be disclosed. Loans at low or zero interest rates are a form of government assistance, but the imputation of interest does not fully quantify the benefit received.   (IAS 20: paras. 34–38)

7.5 Disclosure

Disclosure is required of the following.

* **Accounting policy** adopted, including method of presentation
* **Nature and extent** of government grants recognised and other forms of assistance received
* **Unfulfilled conditions and other contingencies** attached to recognised government assistance
     (IAS 20: para. 39)

7.6 SIC 10 Government assistance – no specific relation to operating activities

In some countries government assistance to entities may be aimed at encouragement or long-term support of business activities either in certain regions or industry sectors. Conditions to receive such assistance may not be specifically related to the operating activities of the entity. Examples of such assistance are transfers of resources by governments to entities which:

(a)   Operate in a particular industry
(b)   Continue operating in recently privatised industries
(c)   Start or continue to run their business in underdeveloped areas

The issue is whether such government assistance is a 'government grant' within the scope of IAS 20 and, therefore, should be accounted for in accordance with this Standard.

Government assistance to entities meets the definition of government grants in IAS 20, even if there are no conditions specifically relating to the operating activities of the entity other than the requirement to operate in certain regions or industry sectors. Such grants should therefore not be credited directly to equity.

Chapter Roundup

- Revenue recognition is straightforward in most business transactions, but it is open to manipulation.

- IFRS 15 sets out rules for the recognition of revenue based on transfer of **control** to the customer from the entity supplying the goods or services.

- Generally revenue is recognised when the entity has transferred promised goods or services to the customer. IFRS 15 sets out five steps for this recognition process.

- The application notes to IFRS 15 provide guidance on how to deal with a number of different transactions.

- The presentation and disclosure requirements are important in relation to contracts where performance obligations are satisfied over time, where there are likely to be contract assets and liabilities to be accounted for at the end of the reporting period.

- Where performance obligations are satisfied over time, an entity must determine what amounts to include as revenue and costs in each accounting period.

- It is common for entities to receive government grants for various purposes (grants may be called subsidies, premiums, etc). They may also receive other types of assistance which may be in many forms.

Quick Quiz

1   Why was a new standard on revenue needed?

2   What are **output methods** of measuring satisfaction of performance obligations?

3   What are the two types of contract dealt with in IFRS 15?

4   What is the transfer that must take place before revenue can be recognised?

5   What is a repurchase agreement?

6   List the five steps for recognising revenue under IFRS 15.

7   What are the two methods available for treatment of government grants related to assets?

Answers to Quick Quiz

1   Because the existing standards on revenue were felt to be inadequate. The IFRS standard (IAS 18) was too general and the FASB regulations were too numerous and detailed. It was considered that better regulation was needed for this area which was vulnerable to fraud and manipulation.

2   Methods of measurement based on value to the customer of goods or services transferred. Examples would be surveys of work performed.

3   Contracts where performance obligations are satisfied at a point in time

    Contracts where performance obligations are satisfied over time

4   **Control** must be transferred before revenue can be recognised.

5   A repurchase agreement is one in which an entity sells an asset and promises, or has the option, to repurchase it.

6   (i)   Identify the contract with the customer

    (ii)   Identify the separate performance obligations

    (iii)   Determine the transaction price

    (iv)   Allocate the transaction price to the performance obligations

    (v)   Recognise revenue when (or as) a performance obligation is satisfied

7   Reduce carrying amount of the asset or treat the grant as deferred income

Now try the Section C questions below from the Practice Question Bank

Number	Level	Marks	Time
20	–	18	35 mins
21	–	10	20 mins
22	Examination	10	20 mins

Introduction to groups

7

Topic list	Syllabus reference
1 Group accounts	A4
2 Consolidated financial statements	A4
3 Content of group accounts and group structure	A4

Introduction

Consolidation is an extremely important area of your Financial Reporting syllabus.

The key to consolidation questions in the examination is to adopt a logical approach and to practise as many questions as possible.

In this chapter we will look at the major definitions in consolidation. These matters are fundamental to your comprehension of group accounts, so make sure you can understand them and then **learn them**.

Study guide

		Intellectual level
A4	**The concepts and principles of groups and consolidated financial statements**	
(a)	Describe the concept of a group as a single economic unit	2
(b)	Explain and apply the definition of a subsidiary within relevant accounting standards	2
(c)	Using accounting standards and other regulation, identify and outline the circumstances in which a group is required to prepare consolidated financial statements	2
(d)	Describe the circumstances when a group may claim exemption from the preparation of consolidated financial statements	2
(e)	Explain why directors may not wish to consolidate a subsidiary and when this is permitted by accounting standards and other applicable regulation	2
(f)	Explain the need for using coterminous year ends and uniform accounting policies when preparing consolidated financial statements	2
(h)	Explain the objective of consolidated financial statements	2

Exam guide

The principles of group accounting can be tested in any of sections A, B or C. Section C questions will require the preparation of financial statements for **either** a single entity or a group.

1 Group accounts

FAST FORWARD

> Many large businesses consist of several companies controlled by one central or administrative company. Together these companies are called a **group**. The controlling company, called the parent or **holding company**, will own some or all of the shares in the other companies, called **subsidiaries**.

1.1 Introduction

There are many reasons for businesses to operate as groups; for the goodwill associated with the names of the subsidiaries, for tax or legal purposes and so forth. In many countries, company law requires that the results of a group should be presented as a whole. Unfortunately, it is not possible simply to add all the results together and this chapter and those following will teach you how to **consolidate** all the results of companies within a group.

In traditional accounting terminology, a **group of companies** consists of a **parent company** and one or more **subsidiary companies** which are controlled by the parent company.

1.2 Accounting standards

We will be looking at five accounting standards in this and the next three chapters.

- IFRS 3 *Business combinations*
- IFRS 10 *Consolidated financial statements*
- IFRS 13 *Fair value measurement*
- IAS 28 *Investments in associates and joint ventures**
- IAS 27 *Separate financial statements*

*Joint ventures are not examinable in Financial Reporting.

These standards are all concerned with different aspects of group accounts, but there is some overlap between them, particularly between IFRS 3 and IFRS 10.

In this and the next chapter we will concentrate on IAS 27 and IFRS 10, which cover the basic group definitions and consolidation procedures of a parent-subsidiary relationship. First of all, however, we will look at all the important definitions involved in group accounts, which **determine how to treat each particular type of investment** in group accounts.

1.3 Definitions

We will look at some of these definitions in more detail later, but they are useful here in that they give you an overview of all aspects of group accounts.

Exam focus point

All the definitions relating to group accounts are extremely important. You must **learn them** and **understand** their meaning and application.

Key terms

- **Control.** An investor controls an investee when the investor is exposed, or has rights, to variable returns from its involvement with the investee and has the ability to affect those returns through power over the investee. (IFRS 10: App A)

- **Power.** Existing rights that give the current ability to direct the relevant activities of the investee (IFRS 10: App A)

- **Subsidiary.** An entity that is controlled by another entity. (IFRS 10: App A)

- **Parent.** An entity that controls one or more subsidiaries. (IFRS 10: App A)

- **Group.** A parent and all its subsidiaries. (IFRS 10: App A)

- **Associate.** An entity over which an investor has significant influence and which is neither a subsidiary nor an interest in a joint venture. (IFRS 10: App A)

- **Significant influence.** The power to participate in the financial and operating policy decisions of an investee but it is not control or joint control over those policies. (IAS 28: para 3)

We can summarise the different types of investment **and** the required accounting for them as follows.

Investment	Criteria	Required treatment in group accounts
Subsidiary	Control	Full consolidation
Associate	Significant influence	Equity accounting (see Chapter 11)
Investment which is none of the above	Asset held for accretion of wealth	As for single company accounts per IFRS 9

1.4 Investments in subsidiaries

The important point here is **control**. In most cases, this will involve the holding company or parent owning a majority of the ordinary shares in the subsidiary (to which normal voting rights are attached). There are circumstances, however, when the parent may own only a minority of the voting power in the subsidiary, **but** the parent still has control.

IFRS 10 provides a definition of control and identifies three separate elements of control:

An investor controls an investee if and only if it has all of the following.

(a) **Power** over the investee
(b) Exposure to, or rights to, **variable returns** from its involvement with the investee
(c) **The ability to use its power** over the investee to affect the amount of the investor's returns

If there are changes to one or more of these three elements of control, then an investor should reassess whether it controls an investee. (IFRS 10: para. 7)

1.4.1 Accounting treatment in group accounts

IFRS 10 requires a parent to present consolidated financial statements, in which the accounts of the parent and subsidiary (or subsidiaries) are combined and presented **as a single entity**.   (IFRS 10: App A)

1.5 Investments in associates

This type of investment is something less than a subsidiary, but more than a simple investment. The key criterion here is **significant influence**. (IAS 28: para. 3) This is defined as the 'power to participate', but **not** to 'control' (which would make the investment a subsidiary).

Significant influence can be determined by the holding of voting rights (usually attached to shares) in the entity. IAS 28 states that if an investor holds **20% or more** of the voting power of the investee, it can be presumed that the investor has significant influence over the investee, **unless** it can be clearly shown that this is not the case.   (IAS 28: para. 5)

Significant influence can be presumed **not** to exist if the investor holds **less than 20%** of the voting power of the investee, unless it can be demonstrated otherwise.

The **existence of significant influence** is evidenced in one or more of the following ways.

(a)   Representation on the **board of directors** (or equivalent) of the investee
(b)   Participation in the **policy making process**
(c)   **Material transactions** between investor and investee
(d)   Interchange of management personnel
(e)   Provision of essential technical information   (IAS 28: para. 6)

IAS 28 requires the use of the **equity method** of accounting for investments in associates. This method will be explained in detail in Chapter 11.

| Question | Treatments |

The section summary after this question will give an augmented version of the table given in Section 1.3 above. Before you look at it, see if you can write out the table yourself.

1.6 Section summary

Investment	Criteria	Required treatment in group accounts
Subsidiary	Control (> 50% rule)	Full consolidation (IFRS 10)
Associate	Significant influence (20% + rule)	Equity accounting (IAS 28)
Investment which is none of the above	Asset held for accretion of wealth	As for single company accounts (IFRS 9)

2 Consolidated financial statements

FAST FORWARD

IFRS 10 requires a parent to present **consolidated** financial statements (para. 2).

2.1 Introduction

Key term

> **Consolidated financial statements.** The financial statements of a group in which the assets, liabilities, equity, income, expenses and cash flows of the parent and its subsidiaries are presented as those of a single economic entity.
> (IFRS 10: App A)

When a parent issues consolidated financial statements, it should consolidate **all subsidiaries**, both foreign and domestic.

2.2 Power

Power is defined as existing rights that give the current ability to direct the relevant activities of the investee. There is no requirement for that power to have been exercised.

Relevant activities may include:

- Selling and purchasing goods or services
- Managing financial assets
- Selecting, acquiring and disposing of assets
- Researching and developing new products and processes
- Determining a funding structure or obtaining funding

In some cases, assessing power is straightforward, such as where power is obtained directly and solely from having the majority of voting rights (or potential voting rights) and as a result the ability to direct relevant activities.

Sometimes, assessment is more complex and more than one factor must be considered. IFRS 10 gives the following examples of **rights**, other than voting rights (potential or realised) which individual, or alone, can give the investor power.

- Rights to appoint, reassign or remove key management personnel who can direct the relevant activities

- Rights to appoint or remove another entity that directs the relevant activities

- Rights to direct the investee to enter into, or veto changes to, transactions for the benefit of the investor

- Other rights, such as those specified in a management contract.

IFRS 10 suggests that the **ability rather than the contractual right** to achieve the above may also indicate that an investor has power over an investee. An investor can have power over an investee even where other entities have significant influence or other ability to participate in the direction of relevant activities.

(IFRS 10: paras. 10–14)

Exam focus point

> You should learn the contents of the above paragraph as you may be asked to apply them in the exam.

2.3 Potential voting rights

An entity may own share warrants, share call options, or other similar instruments that are **convertible into ordinary shares** in another entity. If these are exercised or converted they may give the entity voting power or reduce another party's voting power over the financial and operating policies of the other entity (potential voting rights). The **existence and effect** of potential voting rights, including potential voting rights held by another entity, should be considered when when assessing whether an entity has control over another entity (and therefore has a subsidiary). Potential voting rights are considered only if the rights are substantive (meaning that the holder must have the practical ability to exercise the right).

(IFRS 10: para. B47)

In assessing whether potential voting rights give rise to control, the investor should consider the **purpose and design of the instrument**. This includes an assessment of the various terms and conditions of the instrument as well as the investor's apparent expectations, motives and reasons for agreeing to those terms and conditions.

(IFRS 10: para. B51)

2.4 Returns

An investor must have exposure, or rights, to variable returns from its involvement with the investee in order to establish control.

This is the case where the investor's returns from its involvement have the potential to vary as a result of the investee's performance.

Returns may include:

- Dividends

- Remuneration

- Fees and exposure to loss from providing credit support

- Returns as a result of achieving synergies or economies of scale through an investor combining use of their assets with use of the investee's assets.

In order to establish control, an investor must be able to use its power to affect its returns from the investee. This is the case even where the investor delegates its decision making powers to an agent.

(IFRS 10: para.15-18)

2.5 Exemption from preparing group accounts

A parent **need not present** consolidated financial statements if and only if all of the following hold.

(a)   The parent is itself a **wholly-owned subsidiary** or it is a **partially owned subsidiary** of another entity and its other owners, including those not otherwise entitled to vote, have been informed about, and do not object to, the parent not presenting consolidated financial statements.

(b)   Its securities are **not publicly traded**.

(c)   It is **not in the process of issuing securities** in public securities markets.

(d)   The **ultimate or intermediate parent** publishes consolidated financial statements that comply with International Financial Reporting Standards.   (IFRS 10: para. 4)

A parent that does not present consolidated financial statements must comply with the IAS 27 rules on separate financial statements (discussed later in this section).

2.6 Exclusion of a subsidiary from consolidation

The rules on exclusion of subsidiaries from consolidation are necessarily strict, because this is a common method used by entities to manipulate their results. If a subsidiary which carries a large amount of debt can be excluded, then the gearing of the group as a whole will be improved. In other words, this is a way of taking debt **out of the consolidated statement of financial position**.

IAS 27 did originally allow a subsidiary to be excluded from consolidation where **control is intended to be temporary**. This exclusion was then removed by IFRS 5.

Subsidiaries held for sale are accounted for in accordance with IFRS 5 *Non-current assets held for sale and discontinued operations*.

It has been argued in the past that subsidiaries should be excluded from consolidation on the grounds of **dissimilar activities**, ie the activities of the subsidiary are so different to the activities of the other companies within the group that to include its results in the consolidation would be misleading. IFRS 10 rejects this argument: exclusion on these grounds is not justified because better (relevant) information can be provided about such subsidiaries by consolidating their results and then giving additional information about the different business activities of the subsidiary.

The previous version of IAS 27 permitted exclusion where the subsidiary operates under **severe long-term restrictions** and these significantly impair its ability to transfer funds to the parent. This exclusion has now been **removed**. Control must actually be lost for exclusion to occur.   (IFRS 10: para. 25)

2.7 Different reporting dates

In most cases, all group companies will prepare accounts to the same reporting date. One or more subsidiaries may, however, prepare accounts to a different reporting date from the parent and the bulk of other subsidiaries in the group.

In such cases the subsidiary may prepare additional statements to the reporting date of the rest of the group, for consolidation purposes. If this is not possible, the subsidiary's accounts may still be used for the consolidation, **provided that** the gap between the reporting dates is **three months or less**.

Where a subsidiary's accounts are drawn up to a different accounting date, **adjustments should be made** for the effects of significant transactions or other events that occur between that date and the parent's reporting date.   (IFRS 10: para. B92–3)

2.8 Uniform accounting policies

Consolidated financial statements should be prepared using **uniform accounting policies** for like transactions and other events in similar circumstances.

Adjustments must be made where members of a group use different accounting policies, so that their financial statements are suitable for consolidation.   (IFRS 10: para. 19)

2.9 Date of inclusion/exclusion

IFRS 10 requires the results of subsidiary undertakings to be included in the consolidated financial statements from:

(a)   The date of 'acquisition', ie the **date on which the investor obtains control of the investee**, to
(b)   The date of 'disposal', ie the **date the investor loses control of the investee**.   (IFRS 10: para. 20)

Once an investment is no longer a subsidiary, it should be treated as an associate under IAS 28 (if applicable) or as an investment under IFRS 9 (see Chapter 11).

2.10 Accounting for subsidiaries and associates in the parent's separate financial statements

A parent company will usually produce its own single company financial statements and these should be prepared in accordance with IAS 27 (revised) *Separate financial statements*. In these statements, investments in subsidiaries and associates included in the consolidated financial statements should be **either**:

(a)   Accounted for at **cost**, *or*
(b)   In accordance with **IFRS 9** (see Chapter 11); *or*
(c)   Using the **equity method** as described in **IAS 28**.

Where subsidiaries are **classified as held for sale** in accordance with IFRS 5 they should be accounted for in accordance with IFRS 5 (see Chapter 17) in the parent's separate financial statements.(IAS 27: para. 10)

2.11 Disclosure – individual financial statements

Where a parent chooses to take advantage of the exemptions from preparing consolidated financial statements (see above) under IAS 27 the **separate financial statements** must disclose:

(a)   The fact that the financial statements are separate financial statements; that the exemption from consolidation has been used; the name and country of incorporation of the entity whose consolidated financial statements that comply with IFRSs have been published; and the address where those consolidated financial statements are obtainable

(b)   A list of significant investments in subsidiaries, jointly controlled entities and associates, including the name, country of incorporation, proportion of ownership interest and, if different, proportion of voting power held

(c)   A description of the method used to account for the investments listed under (b)

When a parent prepares separate financial statements in addition to consolidated financial statements, the separate financial statements must disclose:

(a)   The fact that the statements are separate financial statements and the reasons why they have been prepared if not required by law

(b)   Information about investments and the method used to account for them, as above

(IFRS 10: paras. 15–17)

3 Content of group accounts and group structure

FAST FORWARD It is important to distinguish between the parent company **individual accounts** and the **group accounts**.

3.1 Introduction

The information contained in the individual financial statements of a parent company and each of its subsidiaries does not give a picture of the group's total activities. A **separate set of group statements** can be prepared from the individual ones. Remember that a group has no separate (legal) existence, except for accounting purposes.

Consolidated accounts are one form of group accounts which combines the information contained in the separate accounts of a holding company and its subsidiaries as if they were the accounts of a single entity. 'Group accounts' and 'consolidated accounts' are terms often used synonymously.

In simple terms a set of consolidated accounts is prepared by **adding together** the assets and liabilities of the parent company and each subsidiary. The **whole** of the assets and liabilities of each company are included, even though some subsidiaries may be only partly owned. The 'equity and liabilities' section of the statement of financial position will indicate how much of the net assets are attributable to the group and how much to outside investors in partly owned subsidiaries. These **outside investors** are known as the **non-controlling interest**.

Key term

> **Non-controlling interest.** The equity in a subsidiary not attributable, directly or indirectly, to a parent.
> (IFRS 3: App A)

Non-controlling interest should be presented in the consolidated statement of financial position **within equity, separately from the parent shareholders' equity**.

Most parent companies present their own individual accounts and their group accounts in a single **package**. The package typically comprises the following.

*   **Parent company financial statements**, which will include 'investments in subsidiary undertakings' as an asset in the statement of financial position, and income from subsidiaries (dividends) in the statement of profit or loss

*   **Consolidated statement of financial position**

*   **Consolidated statement of profit or loss and other comprehensive income**

*   **Consolidated statement of cash flows**

It may not be necessary to publish all of the parent company's financial statements, depending on local or national regulations.

3.2 Group structure

With the difficulties of definition and disclosure dealt with, let us now look at group structures. The simplest are those in which a parent company has only a **direct interest** in the shares of its subsidiary companies. For example:

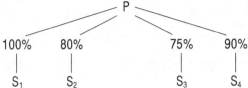

S_1 Co is a wholly owned subsidiary of P Co. S_2 Co, S_3 Co and S_4 Co are partly owned subsidiaries; a proportion of the shares in these companies is held by outside investors.

Often a parent will have **indirect holdings** in its subsidiary companies. This can lead to more complex group structures, involving sub-subsidiaries.

P Co owns 51% of the equity shares in S Co, which is therefore its subsidiary. S Co in its turn owns 51% of the equity shares in SS Co. SS Co is therefore a subsidiary of S Co and consequently a subsidiary of P Co. SS Co would describe S Co as its parent (or holding) company and P Co as its ultimate parent company.

Note that although P Co can control the assets and business of SS Co by virtue of the chain of control, its interest in the assets of SS Co is only 26%. This can be seen by considering a dividend of $100 paid by SS Co: as a 51% shareholder, S Co would receive $51; P Co would have an interest in 51% of this $51 = $26.01.

During the time until your examination you should obtain as many sets of the published accounts of large companies in your country as possible. Examine the accounting policies in relation to subsidiary and associated companies and consider how these policies are shown in the accounting and consolidation treatment. Also, look at all the disclosures made relating to fair values, goodwill etc and match them to the disclosure requirements outlined in this chapter and in subsequent chapters on IFRS 3 and IAS 28.

Alternatively (or additionally) you should attempt to obtain such information from the financial press.

Exam focus point

> You will not be tested on complex group structures at Financial Reporting. Your exam will not feature sub-subsidiaries, but you will meet this topic again at Strategic Business Reporting.

Chapter Roundup

- Many large businesses consist of several companies controlled by one central or administrative company. Together these companies are called a **group**. The controlling company, called the **parent** or **holding company**, will own some or all of the shares in the other companies, called **subsidiaries**.

- IFRS 10 requires a parent to present **consolidated** financial statements (para. 2).

- It is important to distinguish between the parent company **individual accounts** and the **group accounts**.

Quick Quiz

1   Define a 'subsidiary'.

2   When can control be assumed?

3   What accounting treatment does IFRS 10 require of a parent company?

4   When is a parent exempted from preparing consolidated financial statements?

5   Under what circumstances should subsidiary undertakings be excluded from consolidation?

6   How should an investment in a subsidiary be accounted for in the separate financial statements of the parent?

7   What is a non-controlling interest?

Answers to Quick Quiz

1   An entity that is controlled by another entity

2   When the investor has rights to variable returns from the investee and is able to affect those returns by its power over the investee.

3   The accounts of parent and subsidiary are combined and presented as a single entity.

4   When the parent is itself a wholly owned subsidiary, or a partially owned subsidiary and the non-controlling interests do not object, when its securities are not publicly traded and when its ultimate or intermediate parent publishes IFRS-compliant financial statements.

5   Very rarely, if at all. See Section 2.4.

6   (a)   At cost, or
    (b)   In accordance with IFRS 9.

7   The equity in a subsidiary not attributable, directly or indirectly, to a parent.

The consolidated statement of financial position

Topic list	Syllabus reference
1 IFRS 10: Summary of consolidation procedures	D2
2 Non-controlling interests	D2
3 Dividends paid by a subsidiary	D2
4 Goodwill arising on consolidation	D2
5 Non-controlling interest at fair value	D2
6 Intra-group trading	A4, D2
7 Intra-group sales of non-current assets	A4, D2
8 Summary: consolidated statement of financial position	D2
9 Acquisition of a subsidiary during its accounting period	D2
10 Fair values in acquisition accounting	A4, D2

Introduction

This chapter introduces the **basic procedures** required in consolidation and gives a formal step plan for carrying out a statement of financial position consolidation. This step procedure should be useful to you as a starting guide for answering any question, but remember that you cannot rely on it to answer the question for you.

Each question must be approached and **answered on its own merits**. The examination team often put small extra or different problems in because, as they are always reminding students, it is not possible to 'rote-learn' consolidation.

The **method of consolidation** shown here uses schedules for workings (retained earnings, non-controlling interest etc) rather than the ledger accounts used in some other texts. This is because we believe that ledger accounts lead students to 'learn' the consolidation journals without thinking about what they are doing – always a dangerous practice in consolidation questions.

There are plenty of questions in this chapter – work through **all** of them carefully.

Study guide

		Intellectual level
A4	**The concepts and principles of groups and consolidated financial statements**	
(g)	Explain why it is necessary to eliminate intra-group transactions	2
(i)	Explain why it is necessary to use fair values for the consideration for an investment in a subsidiary together with the fair values of a subsidiary's identifiable assets and liabilities when preparing consolidated financial statements	2
D2	**Preparation of consolidated financial statements including an associate**	
(a)	Prepare a consolidated statement of financial position for a simple group (parent and one subsidiary and associate) dealing with pre and post acquisition profits, non-controlling interests and consolidated goodwill	2
(c)	Explain and account for other reserves (eg share premium and revaluation surplus)	1
(d)	Account for the effects in the financial statements of intra-group trading	2
(e)	Account for the effects of fair value adjustments (including their effect on consolidated goodwill) to:	2
	(i) Depreciating and non-depreciating non-current assets	
	(ii) Inventory	
	(iii) Monetary liabilities	
	(iv) Assets and liabilities not included in the subsidiary's own statement of financial position, including contingent assets and liabilities	
(f)	Account for goodwill impairment	2
(g)	Describe and apply the required accounting treatment of consolidated goodwill	2

1 IFRS 10: Summary of consolidation procedures

> **FAST FORWARD**
>
> IFRS 10 lays out the basic procedures for preparing consolidated financial statements.

1.1 Basic procedure

The financial statements of a parent and its subsidiaries are **combined on a line-by-line basis** by adding together like items of assets, liabilities, equity, income and expenses.

The following steps are then taken, in order that the consolidated financial statements should **show financial information about the group as if it was a single entity**.

(a)   The carrying amount of the parent's **investment in each subsidiary** and the parent's **portion of equity** of each subsidiary are **eliminated or cancelled**.

(b)   **Non-controlling interests in the net income of consolidated subsidiaries** are adjusted against group income, to arrive at the net income attributable to the owners of the parent.

(c)   **Non-controlling interests** in the net assets of consolidated subsidiaries should be presented separately in the consolidated statement of financial position.

Other matters to be dealt with include:

(a) **Goodwill on consolidation** should be dealt with according to IFRS 3
(b) **Dividends paid** by a subsidiary must be accounted for

IFRS 10 states that all intragroup balances and transactions, and the resulting **unrealised profits**, should be **eliminated in full**. **Unrealised losses** resulting from intragroup transactions should also be eliminated **unless** cost can be recovered (IFRS 10: B86). This will be explained later in this chapter.

1.2 Cancellation and part cancellation

The preparation of a consolidated statement of financial position, in a very simple form, consists of two procedures:

(a) Take the individual accounts of the parent company and each subsidiary and **cancel out items** which appear as an asset in one company and a liability in another.

(b) Add together all the uncancelled assets and liabilities throughout the group.

Items requiring cancellation may include:

(a) The asset **'shares in subsidiary companies'** which appears in the parent company's accounts will be matched with the liability 'share capital' in the subsidiaries' accounts.

(b) There may be **intra-group trading** within the group. For example, S Co may sell goods on credit to P Co. P Co would then be a receivable in the accounts of S Co, while S Co would be a payable in the accounts of P Co.

1.3 Example: cancellation

Park Co regularly sells goods to its one subsidiary company, Suyin Co, which it has owned since Suyin Co's incorporation. The statement of financial position of the two companies on 31 December 20X6 are given below.

STATEMENT OF FINANCIAL POSITION AS AT 31 DECEMBER 20X6

	Park Co $	Suyin Co $
Assets		
Non-current assets		
Property, plant and equipment	35,000	45,000
Investment in 40,000 $1 shares in S Co at cost	40,000	
	75,000	
Current assets		
Inventories	16,000	12,000
Trade receivables: Suyin Co	2,000	–
Other	6,000	9,000
Cash and cash equivalents	1,000	
Total assets	100,000	66,000
Equity and liabilities		
Equity		
40,000 $1 ordinary shares	–	40,000
70,000 $1 ordinary shares	70,000	–
Retained earnings	16,000	19,000
	86,000	59,000
Current liabilities		
Bank overdraft		3,000
Trade and other payables: Park Co		2,000
Trade and other payables: Other	14,000	2,000
Total equity and liabilities	100,000	66,000

Required

Prepare the consolidated statement of financial position of Park Co at 31 December 20X6.

Solution

The cancelling items are:

(a) Park Co's asset 'investment in shares of Suyin Co' ($40,000) cancels with Suyin Co's liability 'share capital' ($40,000)

(b) Park Co's asset 'trade receivables: Suyin Co' ($2,000) cancels with Suyin Co's liability 'trade and other payables: Park Co' ($2,000)

The remaining assets and liabilities are added together to produce the following consolidated statement of financial position.

PARK CO
CONSOLIDATED STATEMENT OF FINANCIAL POSITION AS AT 31 DECEMBER 20X6

Assets	$	$
Non-current assets		
Property, plant and equipment		80,000
Current assets		
Inventories	28,000	
Trade receivables	15,000	
Cash and cash equivalents	1,000	
		44,000
Total assets		124,000
Equity and liabilities		
Equity		
70,000 $1 ordinary shares	70,000	
Retained earnings	35,000	
	105,000	
Current liabilities		
Bank overdraft	3,000	
Trade and other payables	16,000	
		19,000
Total equity and liabilities		124,000

Notes

1   Park Co's bank balance is **not netted off** with Suyin Co's bank overdraft. To offset one against the other would be less informative and would conflict with the principle that assets and liabilities should not be netted off.

2   The share capital in the consolidated statement of financial position is the **share capital of the parent company alone**. This must **always** be the case, no matter how complex the consolidation, because the share capital of subsidiary companies must **always** be a wholly cancelling item.

1.4 Part cancellation

An item may appear in the statements of financial position of a parent company and its subsidiary, but not at the same amounts.

(a) The parent company may have acquired **shares in the subsidiary** at a price **greater or less than their par value**. The asset will appear in the parent company's accounts at cost, while the liability will appear in the subsidiary's accounts at par value. This raises the issue of **goodwill**, which is dealt with later in this chapter.

(b) Even if the parent company acquired shares at par value, it **may not** have **acquired all the shares of the subsidiary** (so the subsidiary may be only partly owned). This raises the issue of **non-controlling interests**, which are also dealt with later in this chapter.

BPP
LEARNING MEDIA

(c) The inter-company trading balances may be out of step because of **goods or cash in transit**.

(d) One company may have **issued loan stock** of which a **proportion only** is taken up by the other company.

The following question illustrates the techniques needed to deal with items (c) and (d) above. The procedure is to **cancel as far as possible**. The remaining uncancelled amounts will appear in the consolidated statement of financial position.

(a) **Uncancelled loan stock** will appear as a **liability of the group**.

(b) **Uncancelled balances on intra-group accounts** represent **goods or cash in transit**, which will appear in the consolidated statement of financial position.

Question		Cancellation

The statements of financial position of Paula Co and of its subsidiary Shen Co have been made up to 30 June. Paula Co has owned all the ordinary shares and 40% of the loan stock of Shen Co since its incorporation.

STATEMENT OF FINANCIAL POSITION AS AT 30 JUNE

	Paula Co $	Shen Co $
Assets		
Non-current assets		
Property, plant and equipment	120,000	100,000
Investment in Shen Co, at cost		
80,000 ordinary shares of $1 each	80,000	
$20,000 of 12% loan stock in Shen Co	20,000	
	220,000	
Current assets		
Inventories	50,000	60,000
Trade receivables	40,000	30,000
Current account with Shen Co	18,000	
Cash and cash equivalents	4,000	6,000
	112,000	96,000
Total assets	332,000	196,000
Equity and liabilities		
Equity		
Ordinary shares of $1 each, fully paid	100,000	80,000
Retained earnings	95,000	28,000
	195,000	108,000
Non-current liabilities		
10% loan stock	75,000	
12% loan stock		50,000
Current liabilities		
Trade and other payables	47,000	16,000
Taxation	15,000	10,000
Current account with Paula Co		12,000
	62,000	38,000
Total equity and liabilities	332,000	196,000

The difference on current account arises because of goods in transit.

Required

Prepare the consolidated statement of financial position of Paula Co.

PAULA CO
CONSOLIDATED STATEMENT OF FINANCIAL POSITION AS AT 30 JUNE

	$	$
Assets		
Non-current assets		
Property, plant and equipment (120,000 + 100,000)		220,000
Current assets		
Inventories (50,000 + 60,000)	110,000	
Goods in transit (18,000 – 12,000)	6,000	
Trade receivables(40,000 + 30,000)	70,000	
Cash and cash equivalents (4,000 + 6,000)	10,000	
		196,000
Total assets		416,000
Equity and liabilities		
Equity		
Ordinary shares of $1 each, fully paid (parent)	100,000	
Retained earnings (95,000 + 28,000)	123,000	
		223,000
Non-current liabilities		
10% loan stock	75,000	
12% loan stock (50,000 × 60%)	30,000	
		105,000
Current liabilities		
Trade and other payables (47,000 + 16,000)	63,000	
Taxation (15,000 + 10,000)	25,000	
		88,000
Total equity and liabilities		416,000

Note especially how:

(a)   The uncancelled loan stock in Shen Co becomes a liability of the group
(b)   The goods in transit is the difference between the current accounts ($18,000 – $12,000)
(c)   The investment in Shen Co's shares is cancelled against Shen Co's share capital

2 Non-controlling interests

FAST FORWARD

In the consolidated statement of financial position it is necessary to distinguish **non-controlling interests** from those net assets attributable to the group and financed by shareholders' equity.

2.1 Introduction

It was mentioned earlier that the total assets and liabilities of subsidiary companies are included in the consolidated statement of financial position, even in the case of subsidiaries which are only partly owned. A proportion of the net assets of such subsidiaries in fact belongs to investors from outside the group (**non-controlling interests**).

IFRS 3 allows two alternative ways of calculating non-controlling interest in the group statement of financial position. Non-controlling interest can be valued at:

(a)   Its proportionate share of the fair value of the subsidiary's net assets; or

(b)   Full (or fair) value (usually based on the market value of the shares held by the non-controlling interest).

(IFRS 3: B44)

You are required to be able to apply both of these methods in Financial Reporting. The exam question will tell you which method to use. If you are required to use the 'full (or fair) value' method, then you will be given the share price or told what the fair value of the non-controlling interest is. You will normally be required to use the fair value method.

The following example shows non-controlling interest calculated at its proportionate share of the subsidiary's net assets.

2.2 Example: non-controlling interest

Perfect Co has owned 75% of the share capital of Superior Co since the date of Superior Co's incorporation. Their latest statements of financial position are given below.

	Perfect Co $	Superior Co $
Assets		
Non-current assets		
Property, plant and equipment	50,000	35,000
30,000 $1 ordinary shares in Superior Co at cost	30,000	
	80,000	
Current assets	45,000	35,000
Total assets	125,000	70,000
Equity and liabilities		
Equity		
$1 ordinary shares	80,000	40,000
Retained earnings	25,000	10,000
	105,000	50,000
Current liabilities	20,000	20,000
Total equity and liabilities	125,000	70,000

Required

Prepare the consolidated statement of financial position.

Solution

All of Superior Co's net assets are consolidated despite the fact that the company is only 75% owned. The amount of net assets attributable to non-controlling interests is calculated as follows.

	$
Non-controlling share of share capital (25% × $40,000)	10,000
Non-controlling share of retained earnings (25% × $10,000)	2,500
	12,500

Of Superior Co's share capital of $40,000, $10,000 is included in the figure for non-controlling interest, while $30,000 is cancelled with Perfect Co's asset 'investment in Superior Co'.

The consolidated statement of financial position can now be prepared.

	$	$
Assets		
Property, plant and equipment		85,000
Current assets		80,000
Total assets		165,000
Equity and liabilities		
Equity attributable to owners of the parent		
Share capital	80,000	
Retained earnings $(25,000 + (75% × $10,000))	32,500	
		112,500
Non-controlling interest		12,500
		125,000
Current liabilities		40,000
Total equity and liabilities		165,000

2.3 Procedure

(a) Aggregate the assets and liabilities in the statement of financial position ie 100% Perfect Co + 100% Superior Co irrespective of how much Perfect Co actually owns.

This shows the amount of net assets **controlled** by the group.

(b) Share capital is that of the parent only.

(c) Balance of subsidiary's reserves are consolidated (after cancelling any intra-group items).

(d) Calculate the non-controlling interest share of the subsidiary's net assets (share capital plus reserves).

3 Dividends paid by a subsidiary

When a subsidiary company pays a **dividend** during the year the accounting treatment is not difficult. Suppose Subsidiary Co, a 60% subsidiary of Parent Co, pays a dividend of $1,000 on the last day of its accounting period. Its total reserves before paying the dividend stood at $5,000.

(a) $400 of the dividend is paid to non-controlling shareholders. The cash leaves the group and will not appear anywhere in the consolidated statement of financial position.

(b) The parent company receives $600 of the dividend, debiting cash and crediting profit or loss. This will be cancelled on consolidation.

(c) The remaining balance of retained earnings in Subsidiary Co's statement of financial position ($4,000) will be consolidated in the normal way. The group's share (60% × $4,000 = $2,400) will be included in group retained earnings in the statement of financial position; the non-controlling interest share (40% × $4,000 = $1,600) is credited to the non-controlling interest account in the statement of financial position.

4 Goodwill arising on consolidation

Goodwill is the excess of the amount transferred plus the amount of non-controlling interests over the fair value of the net assets of the subsidiary.

4.1 Accounting

To begin with, **we will examine the entries made by the parent company in its own statement of financial position when it acquires shares.**

When a company Parsley Co wishes to **purchase shares** in a company Sage Co it must pay the previous owners of those shares. The most obvious form of payment would be in **cash**. Suppose Parsley Co purchases all 40,000 $1 shares in Sage Co and pays $60,000 cash to the previous shareholders in consideration. The entries in Parsley Co's books would be:

DEBIT	Investment in Sage Co at cost	$60,000	
CREDIT	Bank		$60,000

However, the previous shareholders might be prepared to accept some other form of consideration. For example, they might accept an agreed number of **shares** in Parsley Co. Parsley Co would then issue new shares in the agreed number and allot them to the former shareholders of Sage Co. This kind of deal might be attractive to Parsley Co since it avoids the need for a heavy cash outlay. The former shareholders of Sage Co would retain an indirect interest in that company's profitability via their new holding in its parent company.

Continuing the example, suppose that instead of $60,000 cash the shareholders of S Co agreed to accept one $1 ordinary share in P Co for every two $1 ordinary shares in S Co. P Co would then need to issue and allot 20,000 new $1 shares. How would this transaction be recorded in the books of P Co?

The former shareholders of Sage Co have presumably agreed to accept 20,000 shares in Parsley Co because they consider each of those shares to have a value of $3. This gives us the following method of recording the transaction in Parsley Co's books.

DEBIT	Investment in Sage Co	$60,000	
CREDIT	Share capital		$20,000
	Share premium account		$40,000

The amount which Parsley Co records in its books as the cost of its investment in Sage Co may be more or less than the carrying amount of the assets it acquires. Suppose that Sage Co in the previous example has nil reserves and nil liabilities, so that its share capital of $40,000 is balanced by tangible assets with a carrying amount of $40,000. For simplicity, assume that the carrying amount of Sage Co's assets is the same as their market or fair value.

Now when the directors of Parsley Co agree to pay $60,000 for a 100% investment in Sage Co they must believe that, in addition to its tangible assets of $40,000, Sage Co must also have intangible assets worth $20,000. This amount of $20,000 paid over and above the value of the tangible assets acquired is called **goodwill arising on consolidation** (sometimes **premium on acquisition**).

Following the normal cancellation procedure the $40,000 share capital in Sage Co's statement of financial position could be cancelled against $40,000 of the 'investment in Sage Co' in the statement of financial position of Parsley Co. This would leave a $20,000 debit uncancelled in the parent company's accounts and this $20,000 would appear in the consolidated statement of financial position under the caption 'Intangible non-current assets: goodwill arising on consolidation'.

4.2 Goodwill and pre-acquisition profits

Up to now we have assumed that Sage Co had nil retained earnings when its shares were purchased by Parsley Co. Assuming instead that Sage Co had earned profits of $8,000 in the period before acquisition, its statement of financial position just before the purchase would look as follows.

	$
Total assets	48,000
Share capital	40,000
Retained earnings	8,000
	48,000

If Parsley Co now purchases all the shares in Sage Co it will acquire total assets worth $48,000 at a cost of $60,000. Clearly in this case Sage Co's intangible assets (goodwill) are being valued at $12,000. It should be apparent that any earnings retained by the subsidiary **prior to its acquisition** by the parent company must be **incorporated in the cancellation** process so as to arrive at a figure for goodwill arising on consolidation. In other words, not only Sage Co's share capital, but also its **pre-acquisition** retained earnings, must be cancelled against the asset 'investment in Sage Co' in the accounts of the parent company. The uncancelled balance of $12,000 appears in the consolidated statement of financial position.

The consequence of this is that **any pre-acquisition retained earnings of a subsidiary company are not aggregated with the parent company's retained earnings** in the consolidated statement of financial position. The figure of consolidated retained earnings comprises the retained earnings of the parent company plus the **post-acquisition retained earnings only of subsidiary companies**. The post-acquisition retained earnings are simply retained earnings now **less** retained earnings at acquisition.

The subsidiary may also have share premium or revaluation surplus balances at the acquisition date. These will be brought into the goodwill calculation along with other pre-acquisition reserves. Any post-acquisition movement on these balances will be split between group and NCI.

4.3 Example: goodwill and pre-acquisition profits

Sing Co acquired the ordinary shares of Wing Co on 31 March when the draft statements of financial position of each company were as follows.

SING CO
STATEMENT OF FINANCIAL POSITION AS AT 31 MARCH

	$
Assets	
Non-current assets	
Investment in 50,000 shares of Wing Co at cost	80,000
Current assets	40,000
Total assets	120,000
Equity and liabilities	
Equity	
Ordinary shares	75,000
Retained earnings	45,000
Total equity and liabilities	120,000

WING CO
STATEMENT OF FINANCIAL POSITION AS AT 31 MARCH

	$
Current assets	60,000
Equity	
50,000 ordinary shares of $1 each	50,000
Retained earnings	10,000
	60,000

Required

Prepare the consolidated statement of financial position as at 31 March.

Solution

The technique to adopt here is to produce a new working: 'Goodwill'. A proforma working is set out below.

Goodwill

	$	$
Consideration transferred		X
Net assets acquired as represented by:		
Ordinary share capital	X	
Share premium	X	
Retained earnings on acquisition	X	
		(X)
Goodwill		X

Applying this to our example the working will look like this.

	$	$
Consideration transferred		80,000
Net assets acquired as represented by:		
Ordinary share capital	50,000	
Retained earnings on acquisition	10,000	
		(60,000)
Goodwill		20,000

SING CO
CONSOLIDATED STATEMENT OF FINANCIAL POSITION AS AT 31 MARCH

	$
Assets	
Non-current assets	
Goodwill arising on consolidation (W)	20,000
Current assets (40,000 + 60,000)	100,000
Total assets	120,000
Equity and liabilities	
Ordinary shares	75,000
Retained earnings	45,000
Total equity and liabilities	120,000

4.4 Goodwill and non-controlling interest

Now let us look at what would happen if Sing Co had obtained less than 100% of the shares of Wing Co.

If Sing Co had paid $70,000 for 40,000 shares in Wing Co, the goodwill working would be as follows:

	$
Consideration transferred	70,000
Non-controlling interest (60,000 × 20%)	12,000
Net assets acquired	(60,000)
Goodwill	22,000

4.5 Non-controlling interest at fair value

IFRS 3 (revised) gives entities the option of valuing non-controlling interest (NCI) at fair value (para. B44). The thinking behind this is that the NCI also owns some of the goodwill in the subsidiary, and that the traditional method of consolidation does not show this goodwill.

IFRS 3 (revised) suggests that the closest approximation to fair value will be the market price of the shares held by non-controlling shareholders just before acquisition by the parent (para. B44).

Continuing our example above, we will assume that the market price of the shares was $1.25. The goodwill calculation will then be as follows:

	$
Consideration transferred	70,000
Fair value of NCI (10,000 × $1.25)	12,500
Net assets at acquisition	(60,000)
Goodwill	22,500

Goodwill (total $22,500) is $500 higher than goodwill calculated measuring NCI at its share of the net assets of the subsidiary. This $500 represents the **goodwill attributable to the NCI**.

4.6 Non-controlling interest at year end

Where the option is used to value non-controlling interest at fair value, the goodwill attributable to the NCI will also be added to the NCI at the year end. The most straightforward way to calculate this is to start with the fair value of the NCI at acquisition and add the NCI share of post-acquisition retained earnings.

This is illustrated in the following worked example.

4.7 Worked example

Pumpkin Co acquired 75% of the shares in SesameCo on 1 January 20X7 when SesameCo had retained earnings of $15,000. The market price of SesameCo's shares just before the date of acquisition was $1.60. Pumpkin Co values NCI at fair value. Goodwill is not impaired.

The statements of financial position of Pumpkin Co and SesameCo at 31 December 20X7 were as follows:

	Pumpkin Co $	SesameCo $
Property, plant and equipment	60,000	50,000
Shares in SesameCo	68,000	–
	128,000	50,000
Current assets	52,000	35,000
	180,000	85,000
Share capital – $1 shares	100,000	50,000
Retained earnings	70,000	25,000
	170,000	75,000
Current liabilities	10,000	10,000
	180,000	85,000

Required

Prepare the consolidated statement of financial position of the Pumpkin Co Group.

4.8 Solution

CONSOLIDATED STATEMENT OF FINANCIAL POSITION

	$
Assets	
Property plant and equipment (60,000 + 50,000)	110,000
Goodwill (W1)	23,000
Current assets (52,000 + 35,000)	87,000
Total assets	220,000
Equity and liabilities	
Equity attributable to the owners of Pumpkin Co	
Share capital	100,000
Retained earnings (W2)	77,500
	177,500
NCI (W3)	22,500
Total equity	200,000
Current liabilities (10,000 + 10,000)	20,000
	220,000

Workings

1   *Goodwill*

	Group $
Consideration transferred	68,000
Fair value of NCI (12,500 × $1.60)	20,000
Net assets of SesameCo at acquisition (50,000 + 15,000)	(65,000)
Goodwill	23,000

2   *Retained earnings*

	Pumpkin Co $	SesameCo $
Per statement of financial position	70,000	25,000
Less pre-acquisition		(15,000)
		10,000
Group share of SesameCo (10,000 × 75%)	7,500	
Group retained earnings	77,500	

3	*NCI at year end*	$
	NCI at acquisition	20,000
	Share of post-acquisition retained earnings (10,000 × 25%)	2,500
		22,500

4.9 Effect of non-controlling interest at fair value

You can see from the above example that the use of the fair value option increases goodwill and non-controlling interest by the same amount. That amount represents goodwill attributable to the shares held by non-controlling shareholders. It is not necessarily proportionate to the goodwill attributed to the parent. The parent may have paid proportionately more to acquire a controlling interest. If NCI was valued at share of net assets, goodwill and NCI in the example above would be as follows:

W1 Goodwill

	$
Considered transferred	68,000
NCI ((50,000 + 15,000) × 25%)	16,250
Net assets of SesameCo at acquisition (50,000 + 15,000)	(65,000)
	19,250

W3 NCI at year end

	$
NCI at acquisition	16,250
Share of post-acquisition retained earnings	2,500
	18,750

Compare these with goodwill and NCI in the solution above and you will see that both have been reduced by $3,750 – the goodwill attributable to the NCI. So whether NCI is valued at share of net assets or at fair value, the statement of financial position will still balance.

Exam focus point

> The option to value non-controlling interest at fair value is allowed by the revised IFRS 3, but it is just an **option**. Companies can choose to adopt it or to continue to value non-controlling interest at share of net assets. In the exam you will probably be directed to apply the fair value option. If you are required to use the fair value option, the ACCA examination team has stated that there are two possible options:
>
> (1) You may be given the share price of the subsidiary just before acquisition.
> (2) You may be told that the non-controlling interest is valued at a certain amount.
>
> In the exam, the consolidation question will tell you which method to use. It will state either:
>
> • 'It is the group policy to value the non-controlling interest at full (or fair) value'; or
>
> • 'It is the group policy to value the non-controlling interest at its proportionate share of the (fair value of the) subsidiary's identifiable net assets'.
>
> You are more likely to be tested on non-controlling interest at full (fair) value.

4.10 Impairment of goodwill

Goodwill arising on consolidation is subjected to an annual impairment review and impairment may be expressed as an amount or as a percentage. The double entry to write off the impairment is:

DEBIT Group retained earnings   CREDIT Goodwill

However, when NCI is valued at **fair value** the goodwill in the statement of financial position includes goodwill attributable to the NCI. In this case the double entry will reflect the NCI proportion based on their shareholding as follows.

DEBIT Group retained earnings   CREDIT Goodwill
DEBIT Non-controlling interest

In our solution above in Section 4.8 the NCI holds 25%. If the total goodwill of $23,000 was impaired by 20% the double entry for this would be:

	$		$
DEBIT Retained earnings	3,450	CREDIT Goodwill	4,600
DEBIT Non-controlling interest	1,150		

NCI at the year-end would then be $21,350.

4.11 Gain on a bargain purchase

Goodwill arising on consolidation is one form of **purchased goodwill**. It should **be capitalised in the consolidated statement of financial position** and **reviewed for impairment every year**.

Goodwill arising on consolidation is the difference between the cost of an acquisition and the value of the subsidiary's net assets acquired. This difference can be **negative**: the aggregate of the fair values of the separable net assets acquired may **exceed** what the parent company paid for them. This is often referred to as **negative** goodwill. IFRS 3 refers to it as a **'gain on a bargain purchase'** (IFRS 10: para 34). In this situation:

(a) An entity should first **re-assess** the amounts at which it has measured both the cost of the combination and the acquiree's identifiable net assets. This exercise should **identify any errors.**

(b) Any **excess remaining** should be **recognised immediately in profit or loss.**

4.12 Forms of consideration

The consideration paid by the parent for the shares in the subsidiary can take different forms and this will affect the calculation of goodwill. Here are some examples:

4.12.1 Contingent consideration

FAST FORWARD

IFRS 3 requires recognition of all contingent consideration, measured at fair value, at the acquisition date.

Contingent consideration is 'of the acquirer to transfer additional assets or equity interests to the former owners of an acquiree as part of the exchange for control of the acquiree if specified future events occur or conditions are met. However, contingent consideration also may give the acquirer the right to the return of previously transferred consideration if specified conditions are met.' (IFRS 3: Appendix A)

IFRS 3 requires that **all contingent consideration, measured at fair value, is recognised at the acquisition date** (IFRS 3: para. 39).

The acquirer may be required to pay contingent consideration in the form of equity or of a debt instrument or cash. A debt instrument should be presented in accordance with IAS 32. Contingent consideration can also be an asset, if the consideration has already been transferred and the acquirer has the right to require the return of some of it, if certain considerations are met.

IFRS 3 sets out the treatment according to the circumstances

(a) If the change in fair value is due to **additional information** obtained that affects the position at the acquisition date, goodwill should be re-measured.

(b) If the change is due to **events** which took place after the acquisition date then:

(i) Account under IFRS 9 if the consideration is in the form of a financial instrument (such as loan notes)

(ii) Account under IAS 37 if the consideration is in the form of cash

(iii) Equity instruments are not re-measured.

4.12.2 Deferred consideration

An agreement may be made that part of the consideration for the combination will be paid at a future date. This consideration will therefore be discounted to its present value using the acquiring entity's cost of capital.

Example

The parent acquired 75% of the subsidiary's 80m $1 shares on 1 January 20X6. It paid $3.50 per share and agreed to pay a further $108m on 1 January 20X7.

The parent company's cost of capital is 8%.

In the financial statements for the year to 31 December 20X6 the cost of the combination will be:

	$m
80m shares × 75% × $3.50	210
Deferred consideration:	
$108m × 1/1.08	100
Total consideration	310

At 31 December 20X6 $8m will be charged to finance costs, being the **unwinding of the discount** on the deferred consideration. The deferred consideration was discounted by $8m to allow for the time value of money. At 1 January 20X7 the full amount becomes payable.

4.12.3 Share exchange

The parent has acquired 12,000 $1 shares in the subsidiary by issuing 5 of its own $1 shares for every 4 shares in the subsidiary. The market value of the parent company's shares is $6.

Cost of the combination:

	$
12,000 × 5/4 × $6	90,000

Note that this is credited to the share capital and share premium of the parent company as follows.

	Debit	Credit
Investment in subsidiary	90,000	
Share capital ($12,000 × 5/4)		15,000
Share premium ($12,000 × 5/4 × 5)		75,000

4.12.4 Expenses and issue costs

Expenses of the combination, such as lawyers and accountants fees are written off as incurred. However, IFRS 3 requires that the costs of issuing equity are treated as a deduction from the proceeds of the equity issue (IFRS 3: para. 53). Share issue costs will therefore be debited to the share premium account. Issue costs of financial instruments are deducted from the proceeds of the financial instrument.

4.13 Consolidation adjustments

At the date of acquisition the parent recognises the assets, liabilities and contingent liabilities of the subsidiary at their fair value at the date when control is acquired. It may be that some of these assets or liabilities had not previously been recognised by the acquiree.

For instance, the subsidiary may have tax losses brought forward, but had not recognised these as an asset because it could not foresee future profits against which they could be offset. If the tax losses can now be utilised by the acquirer they will be recognised as an identifiable asset and included in the goodwill calculation.

5 Non-controlling interest at fair value

Now we will look at a full consolidation question including non-controlling interest at fair value.

Question   Consolidated statement of financial position

The draft statements of financial position of Ping Co and Pong Co on 30 June 20X8 were as follows.

STATEMENT OF FINANCIAL POSITION AS AT 30 JUNE 20X8

	Ping Co $	Pong Co $
Assets		
Non-current assets		
Property, plant and equipment	50,000	40,000
20,000 ordinary shares in Pong Co at cost	30,000	
	80,000	
Current assets		
Inventories	3,000	8,000
Owed by Ping Co		10,000
Trade receivables	16,000	7,000
Cash and cash equivalents	2,000	–
	21,000	25,000
Total assets	101,000	65,000
Equity and liabilities		
Equity		
Ordinary shares of $1 each	45,000	25,000
Revaluation surplus	12,000	5,000
Retained earnings	26,000	28,000
	83,000	58,000
Current liabilities		
Owed to Pong Co	8,000	–
Trade and other payables	10,000	7,000
	18,000	7,000
Total equity and liabilities	101,000	65,000

Ping Co acquired its investment in Pong Co on 1 July 20X7 when the retained earnings of Pong Co stood at $6,000. The agreed consideration was $30,000 cash and a further $10,000 on 1 July 20X9. Ping Co's cost of capital is 7%. Pong Co has an internally-developed brand name – 'Pongo' – which was valued at $5,000 at the date of acquisition. There have been no changes in the share capital or revaluation surplus of Pong Co since that date. At 30 June 20X8 Pong Co had invoiced Ping Co for goods to the value of $2,000 and Ping Co had sent payment in full but this had not been received by Pong Co.

There is no impairment of goodwill. It is group policy to value NCI at full fair value. At the acquisition date the NCI was valued at $9,000.

Required

Prepare the consolidated statement of financial position of Ping Co as at 30 June 20X8.

1 Calculate goodwill

Goodwill

		Group $
Consideration transferred (W2)		38,734
Fair value of NCI		9,000
Net assets acquired as represented by:		
Ordinary share capital	25,000	
Revaluation surplus on acquisition	5,000	
Retained earnings on acquisition	6,000	
Intangible asset – brand name	5,000	
		(41,000)
Goodwill		6,734

This goodwill must be capitalised in the consolidated statement of financial position.

2 Consideration transferred

	$
Cash paid	30,000
Fair value of deferred consideration ($10,000 \times 1/(1.07^{2}*)$)	8,734
	38,734

*Note that the deferred consideration has been discounted at 7% for two years (1 July 20X7 to 1 July 20X9).

However, at the date of the current financial statements, 30 June 20X8, the discount for one year has unwound. The amount of the discount unwound is:

	$
($10,000 \times 1/1.07$) − 8,734	612

So this amount will be charged to finance costs in the consolidated financial statements and the deferred consideration under liabilities will be shown as $9,346 (8,734 + 612).

3 Calculate consolidated reserves

Consolidated revaluation surplus

	$
Ping Co	12,000
Share of Pong Co's post acquisition revaluation surplus	–
	12,000

Consolidated retained earnings

	Ping $	Pong $
Retained earnings per question	26,000	28,000
Less pre-acquisition		(6,000)
Discount unwound – finance costs	(612)	22,000
Share of Pong: 80% × $22,000	17,600	
	42,988	

4 Calculate non-controlling interest at year end

	$
Fair value of NCI	9,000
Share of post-acquisition retained earnings (22,000 × 20%)	4,400
	13,400

5   **Agree current accounts**

Pong Co has cash in transit of $2,000 which should be added to cash and deducted from the amount owed by Ping Co.

Cancel common items: these are the current accounts between the two companies of $8,000 each.

6   **Prepare the consolidated statement of financial position.**

PING CO
CONSOLIDATED STATEMENT OF FINANCIAL POSITION AS AT 30 JUNE 20X8

	$	$
Assets		
Non-current assets		
Property, plant and equipment (50,000 + 40,000)		90,000
Intangible assets: Goodwill (W1)		6,734
Brand name (W1)		5,000
Current assets		
Inventories (3,000 + 8,000)	11,000	
Trade receivables (16,000 + 7,000)	23,000	
Cash and cash equivalents (2,000 + 2,000)	4,000	
		38,000
Total assets		139,734
Equity and liabilities		
Equity		
Ordinary shares of $1 each	45,000	
Revaluation surplus (W3)	12,000	
Retained earnings (W3)	42,988	
		99,988
NCI (W4)		13,400
		113,388
Current liabilities		
Trade and other payables (10,000 + 7,000)		17,000
Deferred consideration (W2)		9,346
Total equity and liabilities		139,734

6 Intra-group trading

FAST FORWARD

Intra-group trading can give rise to **unrealised profit** which is eliminated on consolidation.

6.1 Unrealised profit

Any receivable/payable balances outstanding between the companies are cancelled on consolidation. No further problem arises if all such intra-group transactions are **undertaken at cost**, without any mark-up for profit.

However, each company in a group is a separate trading entity and may wish to treat other group companies in the same way as any other customer. In this case, a company (say Apple Co) may buy goods at one price and sell them at a higher price to another group company (Banana Co). The accounts of Apple Co will quite properly include the profit earned on sales to Banana Co; and similarly Banana Co's statement of financial position will include inventories at their cost to Banana Co, ie at the amount at which they were purchased from Apple Co.

This gives rise to two problems:

(a) Although Apple Co makes a profit as soon as it sells goods to Banana Co, the group does not make a sale or achieve a profit until an outside customer buys the goods from Banana Co.

(b) Any purchases from Apple Co which remain unsold by Banana Co at the year end will be included in Banana Co's inventory. Their value in the statement of financial position will be their cost to Banana Co, which is not the same as their cost to the group.

The objective of consolidated accounts is to present the financial position of several connected companies as that of a single entity, the group. This means that **in a consolidated statement of financial position the only profits recognised should be those earned by the group** in providing goods or services to outsiders; and similarly, inventory in the consolidated statement of financial position should be valued at cost to the group.

Suppose that a parent company Snow Co buys goods for $1,600 and sells them to a wholly owned subsidiary Stark Co for $2,000. The goods are in Stark Co's inventory at the year end and appear in Stark Co's statement of financial position at $2,000. In this case, Snow Co will record a profit of $400 in its individual accounts, but from the group's point of view the figures are:

Cost	$1,600
External sales	nil
Closing inventory at cost	$1,600
Profit/loss	nil

If we add together the figures for retained earnings and inventory in the individual statements of financial position of Snow Co and Stark Co the resulting figures for consolidated retained earnings and consolidated inventory will each be overstated by $400. A **consolidation adjustment** is therefore necessary as follows:

DEBIT   Group retained earnings,
CREDIT   Group inventory (statement of financial position),

with the amount of **profit unrealised** by the group.

6.2 Non-controlling interests in unrealised intra-group profits

A further problem occurs where a subsidiary company which is **not wholly owned is involved in intra-group trading** within the group. If a subsidiary Keith Co is 75% owned and sells goods to the parent company for $16,000 cost plus $4,000 profit, ie for $20,000 and if these items are unsold by Mick Co at the end of the reporting period, the 'unrealised' profit of $4,000 earned by Keith Co and charged to Mick Co will be partly owned by the NCI of Keith Co.

The correct treatment of these intragroup profits is to remove the whole profit, charging the NCI with their proportion.

Note that where the sale has been made **by the parent** none of the unrealised profit will be charged to the NCI.

Entries to learn

DEBIT	Group retained earnings
DEBIT	Non-controlling interest
CREDIT	Group inventory (statement of financial position)

6.3 Example: non-controlling interests and intra-group profits

Powell Co has owned 75% of the shares of Sinclair Co since the incorporation of that company. During the year to 31 December 20X2, Sinclair Co sold goods costing $16,000 to Powell Co at a price of $20,000 and these goods were still unsold by Powell Co at the end of the year. Draft statements of financial position of each company at 31 December 20X2 were:

	Powell Co		Sinclair Co	
	$	$	$	$
Assets				
Non-current assets				
Property, plant and equipment	125,000		120,000	
Investment: 75,000 shares in Sinclair Co at cost	75,000		–	
		200,000		120,000
Current assets				
Inventories	50,000		48,000	
Trade receivables	20,000		16,000	
		70,000		64,000
Total assets		270,000		184,000
Equity and liabilities				
Equity				
Ordinary shares of $1 each fully paid	80,000		100,000	
Retained earnings	150,000		60,000	
		230,000		160,000
Current liabilities		40,000		24,000
Total equity and liabilities		270,000		184,000

Required

Prepare the consolidated statement of financial position of Powell Co at 31 December 20X2. The fair value of the non-controlling interest at acquisition was $25,000.

Solution

The profit earned by Sinclair Co but unrealised by the group is $4,000 of which $3,000 (75%) is attributable to the group and $1,000 (25%) to the NCI.

	Powell Co	Sinclair Co
	$	$
Retained earnings		
Per question	150,000	60,000
Less unrealised profit		(4,000)
		56,000
Share of Sinclair Co: $56,000 × 75%	42,000	
	192,000	
Non-controlling interest		
Fair value at acquisition		25,000
Share of post-acquisition retained earnings (56,000 × 25%)		14,000
		39,000

CONSOLIDATED STATEMENT OF FINANCIAL POSITION AS AT 31 DECEMBER 20X2

	$	$
Assets		
Property, plant and equipment		245,000
Current assets		
Inventories $(50,000 + 48,000 – 4,000)$	94,000	
Trade receivables	36,000	
		130,000
Total assets		375,000
Equity and liabilities		
Ordinary shares of $1 each	80,000	
Retained earnings	192,000	
		272,000
NCI		39,000
		311,000
Current liabilities		64,000
Total equity and liabilities		375,000

Question	Unrealised profit

Patsy Co acquired 80% of the shares in Saffy Co one year ago when the reserves of Saffy Co stood at $10,000. Draft statements of financial position for each company are:

	Patsy Co		Saffy Co	
	$	$	$	$
Assets				
Non-current assets				
Property, plant and equipment	80,000			40,000
Investment in Saffy Co at cost	46,000			
		126,000		
Current assets		40,000		30,000
Total assets		166,000		70,000
Equity and liabilities				
Equity				
Ordinary shares of $1 each	100,000		30,000	
Retained earnings	45,000		22,000	
		145,000		52,000
Current liabilities		21,000		18,000
Total equity and liabilities		166,000		70,000

During the year Saffy Co sold goods to Patsy Co for $50,000, the profit to Saffy Co being 20% of selling price. At the end of the reporting period, $15,000 of these goods remained unsold in the inventories of Patsy Co. At the same date, Patsy Co owed Saffy Co $12,000 for goods bought and this debt is included in the trade payables of Patsy Co and the receivables of Saffy Co. NCI is valued at full fair value. It was valued at $9,000 at the date of acquisition.

Required

Prepare a draft consolidated statement of financial position for Patsy Co.

PATSY CO
CONSOLIDATED STATEMENT OF FINANCIAL POSITION

	$	$
Assets		
Non-current assets		
Property, plant and equipment (80,000 + 40,000)	120,000	
Goodwill (W1)	15,000	
		135,000
Current assets (W3)		55,000
Total assets		190,000
Equity and liabilities		
Equity		
Ordinary shares of $1 each	100,000	
Retained earnings (W2)	52,200	
		152,200
NCI (W5)		10,800
Current liabilities (W4)		27,000
Total equity and liabilities		190,000

Workings

1   *Goodwill*

	$	$
Consideration transferred		46,000
Fair value of NCI		9,000
Net assets acquired as represented by		
Share capital	30,000	
Retained earnings	10,000	
		(40,000)
Goodwill		15,000

2   *Retained earnings*

	Patsy Co $	Saffy Co $
Retained earnings per question	45,000	22,000
Unrealised profit: 20% × $15,000		(3,000)
Pre-acquisition		(10,000)
		9,000
Share of Saffy Co 80%	7,200	
	52,200	

3   *Current assets*

	$	$
In Patsy Co's statement of financial position		40,000
In Saffy Co's statement of financial position	30,000	
Less Saffy Co's current account with Patsy Co cancelled	(12,000)	
		18,000
		58,000
Less unrealised profit excluded from inventory valuation		(3,000)
		55,000

4   *Current liabilities*

	$
In Patsy Co's statement of financial position	21,000
Less Patsy Co's current account with Saffy Co cancelled	(12,000)
	9,000
In Saffy Co's statement of financial position	18,000
	27,000

5   *NCI*

	$
Fair value at date of acquisition	9,000
Share of post-acquisition retained earnings (9,000 × 20%)	1,800
	10,800

7 Intra-group sales of non-current assets

> As well as engaging in trading activities with each other, group companies may on occasion wish to **transfer non-current assets**.

7.1 Accounting treatment

In their individual accounts the companies concerned will treat the transfer just like a sale between unconnected parties: the selling company will record a profit or loss on sale, while the purchasing company will record the asset at the amount paid to acquire it, and will use that amount as the basis for calculating depreciation.

On consolidation, the usual **'group entity' principle applies**. The consolidated statement of financial position must show assets at their cost to the group, and any depreciation charged must be based on that cost. Two consolidation adjustments will usually be needed to achieve this.

(a)   An adjustment to alter retained earnings and non-current assets cost so as to remove any element of unrealised profit or loss. This is similar to the adjustment required in respect of unrealised profit in inventory.

(b)   An adjustment to alter retained earnings and accumulated depreciation is made so that consolidated depreciation is based on the asset's cost to the group.

The retained earnings of the entity making the sale are debited with the unrealised profit and the additional depreciation is credited back to the entity holding the asset.

The double entry is as follows.

(a)   Sale by parent

DEBIT   Group retained earnings
CREDIT   Non-current assets

with the profit on disposal

DEBIT   Non current assets
CREDIT   Subsidiary's retained earnings

with the excess depreciation.

(b)   Sale by subsidiary

DEBIT   Subsidiary's retained earnings
CREDIT   Non-current assets

with the profit on disposal

DEBIT   Non-current assets
CREDIT   Group retained earnings

with the additional depreciation

7.2 Example: intra-group sale of non-current assets

Percy Co owns 60% of Edmund Co and on 1 January 20X1 S Co sells plant costing $10,000 to Percy Co for $12,500. The companies make up accounts to 31 December 20X1 and the balances on their retained earnings at that date are:

Percy Co after charging depreciation of 10% on plant	$27,000
Edmund Co including profit on sale of plant	$18,000

Required

Show the working for consolidated retained earnings.

Solution

Retained earnings

	Percy Co	Edmund Co
	$	$
Per question	27,000	18,000
Disposal of plant		
Profit		(2,500)
Depreciation: 10% × $2,500	250	
		15,500
Share of Edmund Co: $15,500 × 60%	9,300	
	36,550	

Notes

1   The NCI in the retained earnings of Edmund Co is 40% × $15,500 = $6,200.

2   The profit on the transfer less related depreciation of $2,250 (2,500 – 250) will be deducted from the carrying amount of the plant to write it down to cost to the group.

8 Summary: consolidated statement of financial position

Purpose	To show the net assets which P controls and the ownership of those assets
Net assets	Always 100% P plus 100% S providing P holds a majority of voting rights
Share capital	P only
Reason	Simply reporting to the parent company's shareholders in another form
Retained earnings	100% P plus group share of post-acquisition retained earnings of S less consolidation adjustments
Reason	To show the extent to which the group actually owns total assets less liabilities
Non-controlling interest	Fair value at acquisition plus share of post-acquisition retained profit (loss)
Reason	To show the equity in a subsidiary not attributable to the parent

9 Acquisition of a subsidiary during its accounting period

When a parent company acquires a subsidiary during its accounting period the only accounting entries made at the time will be those recording the **cost of acquisition in the parent company's books**. At the end of the accounting period the consolidation adjustments will be made.

9.1 Pre-acquisition profits

As we have already seen, at the end of the accounting year it will be necessary to prepare consolidated accounts.

The subsidiary company's accounts to be consolidated will show the subsidiary's profit or loss for the whole year. For consolidation purposes, however, it will be necessary to distinguish between:

(a) Profits earned before acquisition
(b) Profits earned after acquisition

In practice, a subsidiary company's profit may not accrue evenly over the year; for example, the subsidiary might be engaged in a trade, such as toy sales, with marked seasonal fluctuations. Nevertheless, the assumption can be made that **profits accrue evenly** whenever it is impracticable to arrive at an accurate split of pre- and post-acquisition profits.

Once the amount of pre-acquisition profit has been established the appropriate consolidation workings (goodwill, retained earnings) can be produced.

It is worthwhile to summarise what happens on consolidation to the retained earnings figures extracted from a subsidiary's statement of financial position. Suppose the accounts of Subject Co, a 60% subsidiary of Prince Co, show retained earnings of $20,000 at the end of the reporting period, of which $14,000 were earned prior to acquisition. The figure of $20,000 will appear in the consolidated statement of financial position as follows.

	$
Non-controlling interests working: their share of post-acquisition retained earnings (40% × 6,000)	2,400
Goodwill working: pre-acquisition retained earnings	14,000
Consolidated retained earnings working: group share of post-acquisition retained earnings (60% × $6,000)	3,600
	20,000

Exam focus point

The ACCA examination team has reported that many candidates fail to apportion the results of the subsidiary to include only its post-acquisition results.

Question

Acquisition

Hinge Co acquired 80% of the ordinary shares of Singe Co on 1 April 20X5. On 31 December 20X4 Singe Co's accounts showed a share premium account of $4,000 and retained earnings of $15,000. The statements of financial position of the two companies at 31 December 20X5 are set out below. Neither company has paid any dividends during the year. NCI should be valued at full fair value. The market price of the subsidiary's shares was $2.50 prior to acquisition by the parent.

Required

You are required to prepare the consolidated statement of financial position of Hinge Co at 31 December 20X5. There has been no impairment of goodwill.

STATEMENT OF FINANCIAL POSITION AS AT 31 DECEMBER 20X5

	Hinge Co $	Singe Co $
Assets		
Non-current assets		
Property, plant and equipment	32,000	30,000
16,000 ordinary shares of 50c each in Singe Co	50,000	
	82,000	
Current assets	85,000	43,000
Total assets	167,000	73,000
Equity and liabilities		
Equity		
Ordinary shares of $1 each	100,000	
Ordinary shares of 50c each		10,000
Share premium account	7,000	4,000
Retained earnings	40,000	39,000
	147,000	53,000
Current liabilities	20,000	20,000
Total equity and liabilities	167,000	73,000

Answer

Singe Co has made a profit of $24,000 ($39,000 – $15,000) for the year. In the absence of any direction to the contrary, this should be assumed to have arisen evenly over the year; $6,000 in the three months to 31 March and $18,000 in the nine months after acquisition. The company's pre-acquisition retained earnings are therefore as follows.

	$
Balance at 31 December 20X4	15,000
Profit for three months to 31 March 20X5	6,000
Pre-acquisition retained earnings	21,000

The balance of $4,000 on share premium account is all pre-acquisition.

The consolidation workings can now be drawn up.

1   *Goodwill*

	$	$
Consideration transferred		50,000
NCI ($2.50 × 4,000)		10,000
Net assets acquired		
represented by		
Ordinary share capital	10,000	
Retained earnings (pre-acquisition)	21,000	
Share premium	4,000	
		(35,000)
Goodwill at acquisition		25,000

2   *Retained earnings*

	Hinge Co $	Singe Co $
Per question	40,000	39,000
Pre-acquisition (see above)		(21,000)
		18,000
Share of Singe Co: $18,000 × 80%	14,400	
	54,400	

3   NCI at reporting date

	$
NCI at acquisition	10,000
Share of post-acquisition retained earnings (18,000 x 20%)	3,600
	13,600

HINGE CO
CONSOLIDATED STATEMENT OF FINANCIAL POSITION AS AT 31 DECEMBER 20X5

	$	$
Assets		
Property, plant and equipment		62,000
Goodwill (W1)		25,000
Current assets		128,000
Total assets		215,000
Equity and liabilities		
Equity		
Ordinary shares of $1 each	100,000	
Share premium account	7,000	
Retained earnings (W2)	54,400	
		161,400
NCI (W3)		13,600
		175,000
Current liabilities		40,000
Total equity and liabilities		215,000

9.2 Example: pre-acquisition losses of a subsidiary

As an illustration of the entries arising when a subsidiary has pre-acquisition **losses**, suppose Push Co acquired all 50,000 $1 ordinary shares in Scramble Co for $20,000 on 1 January 20X1 when there was a debit balance of $35,000 on Scramble Co's retained earnings. In the years 20X1 to 20X4 Scramble Co makes profits of $40,000 in total, leaving a credit balance of $5,000 on retained earnings at 31 December 20X4. Push Co's retained earnings at the same date are $70,000.

Solution

The consolidation workings would appear as follows.

1   Goodwill

	$	$
Consideration transferred		20,000
Net assets acquired		
as represented by		
Ordinary share capital	50,000	
Retained earnings	(35,000)	
		(15,000)
Goodwill		5,000

2   Retained earnings

	P Co	S Co
	$	$
At the end of the reporting period	70,000	5,000
Pre-acquisition loss	–	35,000
		40,000
Scramble Co – share of post-acquisition retained earnings		
(40,000 × 100%)	40,000	
	110,000	

10 Disposals of subsidiaries

Only 'full disposals' where the entire shareholding is sold are examinable under Financial Reporting.

The subsidiary will be removed from the consolidated statement of financial positions and a profit or loss on disposal will need to be calculated and accounted for.

Disposals are considered in Chapter 9 where we look at the preparation of the consolidated statement of profit or loss and other comprehensive income.

11 Fair values in acquisition accounting

Fair values are very important in calculating goodwill.

11.1 Goodwill

Key term

> **Goodwill.** An asset representing the future economic benefits arising from other assets acquired in a business combination that are not individually identified and separately recognised.   (IFRS 3: App A)

The **statement of financial position of a subsidiary company** at the date it is acquired may not be a guide to the fair value of its net assets. For example, the market value of a freehold building may have risen greatly since it was acquired, but it may appear in the statement of financial position at historical cost less accumulated depreciation.

11.2 What is fair value?

Fair value is defined as follows by IFRS 13 *Fair value measurement*. It is an important definition.

Key term

> **Fair value.** The price that would be received to sell an asset or paid to transfer a liability in an orderly transaction between market participants at the measurement date.   (IFRS 13: para. 9)

11.3 Fair value adjustment calculations

Until now we have calculated goodwill as the difference between the consideration transferred and the **book value** of net assets acquired by the group. If this calculation is to comply with the definition above we must ensure that the book value of the subsidiary's net assets is the same as their **fair value**. There are two possible ways of achieving this:

(a)   The **subsidiary company** might **incorporate any necessary revaluations** in its own books of account. In this case, we can proceed directly to the consolidation, taking asset values and reserves figures straight from the subsidiary company's statement of financial position.

(b)   The **revaluations** may be made as a **consolidation adjustment without being incorporated** in the subsidiary company's books. In this case, we must make the necessary adjustments to the subsidiary's statement of financial position as a working. Only then can we proceed to the consolidation.

Remember that when depreciating assets are revalued there may be a corresponding alteration in the amount of depreciation charged and accumulated.

11.4 Example: fair value adjustments

Pine Co acquired 75% of the ordinary shares of Sequoia Co on 1 September 20X5. At that date the fair value of Sequoia Co's non-current assets was $23,000 greater than their carrying amount, and the balance of retained earnings was $21,000. The statements of financial position of both companies at 31 August 20X6 are given below. Sequoia Co has not incorporated any revaluation in its books of account. NCI is valued at full fair value which was deemed to be $18,000 at the acquisition date.

PINE CO
STATEMENT OF FINANCIAL POSITION AS AT 31 AUGUST 20X6

	$	$
Assets		
Non-current assets		
Property, plant and equipment	63,000	
Investment in Sequoia Co at cost	51,000	
		114,000
Current assets		82,000
Total assets		196,000
Equity and liabilities		
Equity		
Ordinary shares of $1 each	80,000	
Retained earnings	96,000	
		176,000
Current liabilities		20,000
Total equity and liabilities		196,000

SEQUOIA CO
STATEMENT OF FINANCIAL POSITION AS AT 31 AUGUST 20X6

	$	$
Assets		
Property, plant and equipment		28,000
Current assets		43,000
Total assets		71,000
Equity and liabilities		
Equity		
Ordinary shares of $1 each	20,000	
Retained earnings	41,000	
		61,000
Current liabilities		10,000
Total equity and liabilities		71,000

If Sequoia Co had revalued its non-current assets at 1 September 20X5, an addition of $3,000 would have been made to the depreciation charged for 20X5/X6.

Required

Prepare Pine Co's consolidated statement of financial position as at 31 August 20X6.

Solution

PINE CO CONSOLIDATED STATEMENT OF FINANCIAL POSITION AS AT 31 AUGUST 20X6

	$	$
Non-current assets		
Property, plant and equipment (63,000 + 28,000 + 23,000 – 3,000)	111,000	
Goodwill (W1)	5,000	
		116,000
Current assets		125,000
		241,000
Equity and liabilities		
Equity		
Ordinary shares of $1 each	80,000	
Retained earnings (W2)	108,750	
		188,750
NCI (W3)		22,250
		211,000
Current liabilities		30,000
		241,000

Workings

1   *Goodwill*

		Group
		$
Consideration transferred		51,000
Fair value of NCI		18,000
Net assets acquired as represented by		
Ordinary share capital	20,000	
Retained earnings	21,000	
Fair value adjustment	23,000	
		(64,000)
Goodwill		5,000

2   *Retained earnings*

	Pine Co	Sequoia Co
	$	$
Per question	96,000	41,000
Pre acquisition profits		(21,000)
Depreciation adjustment		(3,000)
Post acquisition Sequoia Co		17,000
Group share in Sequoia Co		
($17,000 × 75%)	12,750	
Group retained earnings	108,750	

3   *NCI at reporting date*

	$
Fair value at acquisition	18,000
Share of post-acquisition retained earnings (17,000 × 25%)	4,250
	22,250

Question

Fair value

An asset is recorded in Spice Co's books at its historical cost of $4,000. On 1 January 20X5 Paprika Co bought 80% of Spice Co's equity. Its directors attributed a fair value of $3,000 to the asset as at that date. It had been depreciated for two years out of an expected life of four years on the straight line basis. There was no expected residual value. On 30 June 20X5 the asset was sold for $2,600. What is the profit or loss on disposal of this asset to be recorded in Spice Co's accounts and in Paprika Co's consolidated accounts for the year ended 31 December 20X5?

Answer

Spice Co: Carrying amount at disposal (at historical cost) = $4,000 × 1½/4 = $1,500
∴ Profit on disposal = $1,100 (depreciation charge for the year = $500)

Paprika Co: Carrying amount at disposal (at fair value) = $3,000 × 1½/2 = $2,250
∴ Profit on disposal for consolidation = $350 (depreciation for the year = $750).

The NCI would be credited with 20% of both the profit on disposal and the depreciation charge as part of the one line entry in the consolidated statement of profit or loss.

11.5 IFRS 3 and IFRS 13: Fair values

FAST FORWARD

IFRS 3 sets out the accounting requirements and disclosures of the fair value exercise

IFRS 13 *Fair value measurement* gives guidance on how the fair value of assets and liabilities should be established.

The general rule under **IFRS 3** is that the subsidiary's assets and liabilities must be measured at fair value except in limited, stated cases. The assets and liabilities must:

(a) Meet the definitions of assets and liabilities in the Conceptual Framework

(b) Be part of what the acquiree (or its former owners) exchanged in the business combination rather than the result of separate transactions

IFRS 13 provides extensive guidance on **how the fair value of assets and liabilities should be established**.

This standard requires that the following are considered in determining fair value.

(a) The asset or liability being measured (IFRS 13: para. 11)

(b) The principal market (ie that where the most activity takes place) or where there is no principal market, the most advantageous market (ie that in which the best price could be achieved) in which an orderly transaction would take place for the asset or liability (IFRS 13: para. 16)

(c) The highest and best use of the asset or liability and whether it is used on a standalone basis or in conjunction with other assets or liabilities (IFRS 13: para. 27)

(d) Assumptions that market participants would use when pricing the asset or liability

Having considered these factors, IFRS 13 provides a **hierarchy of inputs** for arriving at fair value. It requires that level 1 inputs are used where possible:

Level 1 Quoted prices in active markets for identical assets that the entity can access at the measurement date (IFRS 13: para. 76)

Level 2 Inputs other than quoted prices that are directly or indirectly observable for the asset (IFRS 13: para. 81)

Level 3 Unobservable inputs for the asset (IFRS 13: para. 86)

We will look at the requirements of IFRS 3 regarding fair value in more detail below. First let us look at a practical example.

Example: Land

Anscome Co has acquired land in a business combination. The land is currently developed for industrial use as a site for a factory. The current use of land is presumed to be its highest and best use unless market or other factors suggest a different use. Nearby sites have recently been developed for residential use as sites for high-rise apartment buildings. On the basis of that development and recent zoning and other changes to facilitate that development, Anscome determines that the land currently used as a site for a factory could be developed as a site for residential use (ie for high-rise apartment buildings) because market participants would take into account the potential to develop the site for residential use when pricing the land.

How would the highest and best use of the land be determined?

Solution

The highest and best use of the land would be determined by comparing both of the following:

(a) The value of the land as currently developed for industrial use (ie the land would be used in combination with other assets, such as the factory, or with other assets and liabilities).

(b)   The value of the land as a vacant site for residential use, taking into account the costs of demolishing the factory and other costs (including the uncertainty about whether the entity would be able to convert the asset to the alternative use) necessary to convert the land to a vacant site (ie the land is to be used by market participants on a stand-alone basis).

The highest and best use of the land would be determined on the basis of the higher of those values.

11.5.1 IFRS 3 Fair values

IFRS 3 sets out **general principles** for arriving at the fair values of a subsidiary's assets and liabilities. (IFRS 3: para. 18) The acquirer should recognise the acquiree's identifiable assets, liabilities and contingent liabilities at the acquisition date **only** if they satisfy the following criteria.

(a)   In the case of an **asset** other than an intangible asset, it is **probable** that any associated **future economic benefits** will flow to the acquirer, and its fair value can be **measured reliably**.

(b)   In the case of a **liability** other than a contingent liability, it is probable that an **outflow** of resources embodying economic benefits will be required to settle the obligation, and its fair value can be **measured reliably**.

(c)   In the case of an **intangible asset** or a **contingent liability**, its fair value can be **measured reliably**.

(IFRS 3: para. 11)

The acquiree's identifiable assets and liabilities might include assets and liabilities **not previously recognised** in the acquiree's financial statements. For example, a tax benefit arising from the acquiree's tax losses that was not recognised by the acquiree may be recognised by the group if the acquirer has future taxable profits against which the unrecognised tax benefit can be applied.

11.5.2 Restructuring and future losses

An acquirer **should not recognise liabilities for future losses** or other costs expected to be incurred as a result of the business combination.   (IFRS 3: para. 11)

IFRS 3 explains that a plan to restructure a subsidiary following an acquisition is not a present obligation of the acquiree at the acquisition date. Neither does it meet the definition of a contingent liability. Therefore an acquirer **should not recognise a liability for** such **a restructuring plan** as part of allocating the cost of the combination unless the subsidiary was already committed to the plan before the acquisition.

(IFRS 3: para. 11)

This **prevents creative accounting**. An acquirer cannot set up a provision for restructuring or future losses of a subsidiary and then release this to the profit or loss in subsequent periods in order to reduce losses or smooth profits.

11.5.3 Intangible assets

The acquiree may have **intangible assets**, such as development expenditure. These can be recognised separately from goodwill only if they are **identifiable**. An intangible asset is identifiable only if it:

(a)   Is **separable**, ie capable of being separated or divided from the entity and sold, transferred, or exchanged, either individually or together with a related contract, asset or liability, or

(b)   Arises from contractual or other legal rights.   (IAS 38: IN6)

The acquiree may also have internally-generated assets such as brand names which have not been recognised as intangible assets. As the acquiring company is giving valuable consideration for these assets, they are now recognised as assets in the consolidated financial statements.

11.5.4 Contingent liabilities

Contingent liabilities of the acquiree are **recognised** if their **fair value can be measured reliably**. This is a departure from the normal rules in IAS 37; contingent liabilities are not normally recognised, but only disclosed.

After their initial recognition, the acquirer should measure contingent liabilities that are recognised separately at the higher of:

(a)   The amount that would be recognised in accordance with IAS 37
(b)   The amount initially recognised   (IFRS 3: para. 56)

11.5.5 Cost of a business combination

The general principle is that the acquirer should measure the cost of a business combination as the total of the **fair values**, at the date of exchange, **of assets given**, liabilities incurred or assumed, and equity instruments issued by the acquirer, in exchange for control of the acquiree.

Sometimes all or part of the cost of an acquisition is deferred (ie does not become payable immediately). The fair value of any deferred consideration is determined by **discounting** the amounts payable to their **present value** at the date of exchange.

Where equity instruments (eg ordinary shares) of a quoted entity form part of the cost of a combination, the **published price** at the date of exchange normally provides the best evidence of the instrument's fair value and except in rare circumstances this should be used.

Future losses or other costs expected to be incurred as a result of a combination should not be included in the cost of the combination.

Costs **attributable** to the combination, for example professional fees and administrative costs, should not be included: they are recognised as an expense when incurred. **Costs of issuing debt instruments and equity shares** should **reduce the proceeds from the debt issue or the equity issue**.   (IFRS 3: para. 53)

11.5.6 Other exceptions to the recognition or measurement principles

(a)   **Deferred tax:** use IAS 12 values.
(b)   **Assets held for sale**: use IFRS 5 values.

Question	Goodwill on consolidation

On 1 September 20X7 Tyzo Co acquired 6 million $1 shares in Kono Co at $2.00 per share. At that date Kono Co produced the following interim financial statements.

	$m		$m
Property, plant and equipment		Trade payables	3.2
(note (i))	16.0	Taxation	0.6
Inventories (note (ii))	4.0	Bank overdraft	3.9
Receivables	2.9	Long-term loans	4.0
Cash in hand	1.2	Share capital ($1 shares)	8.0
		Retained earnings	4.4
	24.1		24.1

Notes

1   The following information relates to the property, plant and equipment of Kono Co at 1 September 20X7.

	$m
Gross replacement cost	28.4
Net replacement cost (gross replacement cost less depreciation)	16.6
Economic value	18.0
Net realisable value	8.0

2   The inventories of Kono Co which were shown in the interim financial statements are raw materials at cost to Kono Co of $4m. They would have cost $4.2m to replace at 1 September 20X7.

3   On 1 September 20X7 Tyzo Co took a decision to rationalise the group so as to integrate Kono Co. The costs of the rationalisation were estimated to total $3.0m and the process was due to start on 1 March 20X8. No provision for these costs has been made in the financial statements given above.

4   It is group policy to recognise NCI at full (fair) value.

Required

Compute the goodwill on consolidation of Kono Co that will be included in the consolidated financial statements of the Tyzo Co group for the year ended 31 December 20X7, explaining your treatment of the items mentioned above. You should refer to the provisions of relevant accounting standards.

Answer

Goodwill on consolidation of Kono Co

	$m	$m
Consideration transferred ($2.00 × 6m)		12.0
NCI ($2.00 × 2m)		4.0
Fair value of net assets acquired		
Share capital	8.0	
Pre-acquisition reserves	4.4	
Fair value adjustments		
Property, plant and equipment (16.6 – 16.0)	0.6	
Inventories (4.2 – 4.0)	0.2	
		(13.2)
Goodwill		2.8

Notes on treatment

1   Share capital and pre-acquisition profits represent the book value of the net assets of Kono Co at the date of acquisition. Adjustments are then required to this book value in order to give the fair value of the net assets at the date of acquisition. For short-term monetary items, fair value is their carrying value on acquisition.

2   IFRS 3 states that the fair value of property, plant and equipment should be determined by market value or, if information on a market price is not available (as is the case here), then by reference to depreciated replacement cost, reflecting normal business practice. The net replacement cost (ie $16.6m) represents the gross replacement cost less depreciation based on that amount, and so further adjustment for extra depreciation is unnecessary.

3   IFRS 3 also states that raw materials should be valued at replacement cost. In this case that amount is $4.2m.

4   The rationalisation costs cannot be reported in pre-acquisition results under IFRS 3 as they are not a liability of Kono Co at the acquisition date.

One of the competences you require to fulfil Performance Objective 7 of the PER is the ability to classify information in accordance with the requirements for external financial statements or for inclusion in disclosure notes in the statements. You can apply the knowledge you obtain from this chapter to help to demonstrate this competence.

Chapter Roundup

- IFRS 10 lays out the basic procedures for preparing consolidated financial statements.
- In the consolidated statement of financial position it is necessary to distinguish **non-controlling interests** from those net assets attributable to the group and financed by shareholders' equity.
- **Goodwill** is the excess of the amount transferred plus the amount of non-controlling interests over the fair value of the net assets of the subsidiary.
- IFRS 3 requires recognition of all contingent consideration, measured at fair value, at the acquisition date.
- Intra-group trading can give rise to **unrealised profit** which is eliminated on consolidation.
- As well as engaging in trading activities with each other, group companies may on occasion wish to **transfer non-current assets**.
- When a parent company acquires a subsidiary during its accounting period the only accounting entries made at the time will be those recording the **cost of the acquisition in the parent company's books**. At the end of the accounting period the consolidation adjustments will be made.
- Only 'full disposals' where the entire shareholding is sold are examinable under Financial Reporting.
- **Fair values** are very important in calculating goodwill.
- **IFRS 3** sets out the accounting requirements and disclosures of the fair value exercise
- **IFRS 13** Fair value measurement gives guidance on how the fair value of assets and liabilities should be established.

Quick Quiz

1   Chicken Co owns 80% of Egg Co. Egg Co sells goods to Chicken Co at cost plus 50%. The total invoiced sales to Chicken Co by Egg Co in the year ended 31 December 20X9 were $900,000 and, of these sales, goods which had been invoiced at $60,000 were held in inventory by Chicken Co at 31 December 20X9. What is the reduction in aggregate group gross profit?

2   Major Co, which makes up its accounts to 31 December, has an 80% owned subsidiary Minor Co. Minor Co sells goods to Major Co at a mark-up on cost of 33.33%. At 31 December 20X8, Major had $12,000 of such goods in its inventory and at 31 December 20X9 had $15,000 of such goods in its inventory.

    What is the amount by which the consolidated profit attributable to Major Co's shareholders should be adjusted in respect of the above?

    Ignore taxation.

    A $1,000 Debit
    B $800 Credit
    C $750 Credit
    D $600 Debit

3   Goodwill is always positive.

    True ☐
    False ☐

4   A parent company can assume that, for a subsidiary acquired during its accounting period, profits accrue evenly during the year.

    True ☐
    False ☐

5   What entries are made in the workings to record the pre-acquisition profits of a subsidiary?

6   Describe the requirement of IFRS 3 in relation to the revaluation of a subsidiary company's assets to fair value at the acquisition date.

7   What guidelines are given by IFRS 3 in relation to valuing land and buildings fairly?

1   $\$60,000 \times \dfrac{50}{150} = \$20,000$

2   D $(15,000 - 12,000) \times \dfrac{33.3}{133.3} \times 80\%$

3   False. Goodwill can be negative if the purchaser has 'got a bargain'.

4   Not necessarily – the ACCA examination team will advise you on this.

5   See Section 4.2.

6   See Section 10.5.

7   Land and buildings should be valued in accordance with IFRS 13 (generally market value).

Now try the questions below from the Practice Question Bank

Number	Level	Marks	Time
9	–	12	23 mins
10	–	14	27 mins
14	–	25	49 mins

The consolidated statement of profit or loss and other comprehensive income

Introduction

This chapter deals with the consolidated statement of profit or loss and the consolidated statement of profit or loss and other comprehensive income.

Most of the consolidation adjustments will involve the **statement of profit or loss**, so that is the focus of this chapter.

A subsidiary that has been disposed of will no longer be included in the consolidated statement of financial position, but its results up to the date of disposal will form part of consolidated profit or loss.

Study guide

		Intellectual level
D2	Preparation of consolidated financial statements including an associate	
(b)	Prepare a consolidated statement of profit or loss and consolidated statement of profit or loss and other comprehensive income for a simple group dealing with an acquisition in the period and non-controlling interest	2

1 The consolidated statement of profit or loss

The source of the consolidated statement of profit or loss is the individual statements of profit or loss of the separate companies in the group.

1.1 Consolidation procedure

The consolidated statement of profit or loss combines the financial statements of parent and subsidiary (subsidiaries) to present the results for the accounting period as the results of a **single economic unit**.

It is customary in practice to prepare a working paper (known as a **consolidation schedule**) on which the individual statements of profit or loss are set out side by side and totalled to form the basis of the consolidated statement of profit or loss.

Exam focus point

In an examination it is very much quicker not to do this. Use workings to show the calculation of complex figures such as the non-controlling interest and show the derivation of others on the face of the statement of profit or loss, as shown in our examples.

In the consolidated statement of profit or loss, non-controlling interest is brought in as a one-line adjustment at the end of the statement.

1.2 Simple example: consolidated statement of profit or loss

Tom Co acquired 75% of the ordinary shares of Jerry Co on that company's incorporation in 20X3. The summarised statements of profit or loss and movement on retained earnings of the two companies for the year ending 31 December 20X6 are set out below.

	Tom Co $	Jerry Co $
Revenue	75,000	38,000
Cost of sales	(30,000)	(20,000)
Gross profit	45,000	18,000
Administrative expenses	(14,000)	(8,000)
Profit before tax	31,000	10,000
Income tax expense	(10,000)	(2,000)
Profit for the year	21,000	8,000

Note: *Movement on retained earnings*

Retained earnings brought forward	87,000	17,000
Profit for the year	21,000	8,000
Retained earnings carried forward	108,000	25,000

Required

Prepare the consolidated statement of profit or loss and extract from the statement of changes in equity showing retained earnings and non-controlling interest.

Solution

TOM CO
CONSOLIDATED STATEMENT OF PROFIT OR LOSS
FOR THE YEAR ENDED 31 DECEMBER 20X6

	$
Revenue (75 + 38)	113,000
Cost of sales (30 + 20)	(50,000)
Gross profit	63,000
Administrative expenses (14 + 8)	(22,000)
Profit before tax	41,000
Income tax expense	(12,000)
Profit for the year	29,000
Profit attributable to:	
Owners of the parent	27,000
Non-controlling interest ($8,000 × 25%)	2,000
	29,000

STATEMENT OF CHANGES IN EQUITY (EXTRACT)

	Retained earnings $	Non-controlling interest $	Total equity $
Balance at 1 January 20X6	99,750	4,250	104,000
Total comprehensive income for the year	27,000	2,000	29,000
Balance at 31 December 20X6	126,750	6,250	133,000

Notice how the non-controlling interest is dealt with.

(a) Down to the line **'profit for the year'** the **whole** of Jerry Co's results is included without reference to group share or non-controlling share. A **one-line adjustment** is then inserted to deduct the non-controlling share of Jerry Co's profit.

(b) The non-controlling share ($4,250) of Jerry Co's retained earnings brought forward (17,000 × 25%) is **excluded** from group retained earnings. This means that the carried forward figure of $126,750 is the figure which would appear in the statement of financial position for group retained earnings.

This last point may be clearer if we construct the working for group retained earnings.

Group retained earnings

	Tom Co $	Jerry Co $
At year end	108,000	25,000
Less pre-acquisition retained earnings		–
		25,000
Tom Co – share of post acquisition retained earnings (25,000 × 75%)	18,750	
	126,750	

The non-controlling share of Jerry Co's retained earnings comprises the non-controlling interest in the $17,000 profits brought forward plus the non-controlling interest ($2,000) in $8,000 retained profits for the year.

We will now look at the complications introduced by **intra-group trading**, **intra-group dividends** and **pre-acquisition profits** in the subsidiary.

1.3 Intra-group trading

Intra-group sales and purchases are eliminated from the consolidated statement of profit or loss.

Like the consolidated statement of financial position, the consolidated statement of profit or loss should deal with the results of the group as those of a single entity. When one company in a group sells goods to another the relevant amount is added to the revenue of the first company and to the cost of sales of the second. Yet as far as the entity's dealings with outsiders are concerned no sale has taken place.

The consolidated figures for revenue and cost of sales should represent **sales to**, and **purchases from, outsiders**. An adjustment is therefore necessary to reduce the revenue and cost of sales figures by the value of intra-group sales during the year.

We have also seen in an earlier chapter that any unrealised profits on intra-group trading should be excluded from the figure for group profits. This will occur whenever goods sold at a profit within the group remain in the inventory of the purchasing company at the year end. The best way to deal with this is to **calculate the unrealised profit on unsold inventories at the year end and reduce consolidated gross profit by this amount**. Cost of sales will be the balancing figure.

1.4 Example: intra-group trading

Suppose in our earlier example that Jerry Co had recorded sales of $5,000 to Tom Co during 20X6. Jerry Co had purchased these goods from outside suppliers at a cost of $3,000. One half of the goods remained in Tom Co's inventory at 31 December 20X6.

Prepare the revised consolidated statement of profit or loss.

Solution

The consolidated statement of profit or loss for the year ended 31 December 20X6 would now be as follows.

	$
Revenue (75 + 38 – 5)	108,000
Cost of sales (30 + 20 – 5 + 1*)	(46,000)
Gross profit (45 + 18 – 1*)	62,000
Administrative expenses	(22,000)
Profit before taxation	40,000
Income tax expense	(12,000)
Profit for the year	28,000
Profit attributable to :	
Owners of the parent	26,250
Non-controlling interest (8,000 – 1,000) × 25%	1,750
	28,000

Note

Retained earnings brought forward	99,750
Profit for the year	26,250
Retained earnings carried forward	126,000

*Unrealised profit: ½ × ($5,000 – $3,000)

An adjustment will be made for the unrealised profit against the inventory figure in the consolidated statement of financial position.

1.5 Intra-group dividends

In our example so far we have assumed that Jerry Co retains all of its after-tax profit. It may be, however, that Jerry Co distributes some of its profits as dividends. As before, the **non-controlling interest** in the subsidiary's profit should be calculated immediately after the figure of after-tax profit. For this purpose, no account need be taken of how much of the non-controlling interest is to be distributed by Jerry Co as dividend.

Note that group retained earnings are only adjusted for dividends paid to the parent company shareholders. Dividends paid by the subsidiary to the parent are cancelled on consolidation and dividends paid to the non-controlling interest are replaced by the allocation to the non-controlling interest of their share of the profit for the year of the subsidiary.

1.6 Pre-acquisition profits

FAST FORWARD ▶ Only the **post-acquisition** profits of the subsidiary are brought into the consolidated profit or loss.

As explained above, the figure for retained earnings carried forward must be the same as the figure for retained earnings in the consolidated statement of financial position. We have seen in previous chapters that retained earnings in the consolidated statement of financial position comprise:

(a) The **whole of the parent company's** retained earnings

(b) A **proportion of the subsidiary company's** retained earnings. The proportion is the **group's share of post-acquisition retained earnings** in the subsidiary. From the total retained earnings of the subsidiary we must therefore **exclude** both the **non-controlling share** of total retained earnings and the **group's share of pre-acquisition** retained earnings.

A **similar procedure is necessary in the consolidated statement of profit or loss** if it is to link up with the consolidated statement of financial position. Previous examples have shown how the non-controlling share of profits is treated in the statement of profit or loss. Their share of profits for the year is deducted from profit after tax, while the figure for profits brought forward in the consolidation schedule includes only the group share of the subsidiary's profits.

In the same way, when considering examples which include pre-acquisition profits in a subsidiary, the figure for profits brought forward should include only the group share of the post-acquisition retained profits. If the subsidiary is **acquired during the accounting year**, it is therefore necessary to apportion its profit for the year between pre-acquisition and post-acquisition elements. This can be done by simple time apportionment (ie assuming that profits arose evenly throughout the year) but there may be seasonal trading or other effects which imply a different split than by time apportionment.

With a mid-year acquisition, the entire statement of profit or loss of the subsidiary is split between pre-acquisition and post-acquisition amounts. Only the post-acquisition figures are included in the consolidated statement of profit or loss.

Question			Acquisition

Dougal Co acquired 60% of the $100,000 equity of Ted Co on 1 April 20X5. The statements of profit or loss of the two companies for the year ended 31 December 20X5 are set out below.

	Dougal Co	Ted Co	Ted Co ($^9/_{12}$)
	$	$	$
Revenue	170,000	80,000	60,000
Cost of sales	(65,000)	(36,000)	(27,000)
Gross profit	105,000	44,000	33,000
Other income – dividend received Ted Co	3,600		
Administrative expenses	(43,000)	(12,000)	(9,000)
Profit before tax	65,600	32,000	24,000
Income tax expense	(23,000)	(8,000)	(6,000)
Profit for the year	42,600	24,000	18,000
Note			
Dividends (paid 31 December)	12,000	6,000	
Profit retained	30,600	18,000	
Retained earnings brought forward	81,000	40,000	
Retained earnings carried forward	111,600	58,000	

Required

Prepare the consolidated statement of profit or loss and the retained earnings and non-controlling interest extracts from the statement of changes in equity.

Answer

The shares in Ted Co were acquired three months into the year. Only the post-acquisition proportion (9/12ths) of Ted Co's statement of profit or loss is included in the consolidated statement of profit or loss. This is shown above for convenience.

DOUGAL CO CONSOLIDATED STATEMENT OF PROFIT OR LOSS
FOR THE YEAR ENDED 31 DECEMBER 20X5

	$
Revenue (170 + 60)	230,000
Cost of sales (65 + 27)	(92,000)
Gross profit	138,000
Administrative expenses (43 + 9)	(52,000)
Profit before tax	86,000
Income tax expense (23 + 6)	(29,000)
Profit for the year	57,000
Profit attributable to:	
Owners of the parent	49,800
Non-controlling interest (18 × 40%)	7,200
	57,000

STATEMENT OF CHANGES IN EQUITY

	Retained earnings	Non-controlling interest
	$	$
Balance at 1 January 20X5	81,000	–
Dividends paid (6,000 – 3,600)	(12,000)	(2,400)
Total comprehensive income for the year	49,800	7,200
Added on acquisition of subsidiary (W)	–	58,400
Balance at 31 December 20X5	118,800	63,200

Note that all of Ted Co's profits brought forward are pre-acquisition.

Working

	$
Added on acquisition of subsidiary:	
Share capital	100,000
Retained earnings brought forward	40,000
Profits Jan-March 20X5 (24,000 – 18,000)	6,000
	146,000
Non-controlling share 40%	58,400

The following information relates to Brodick Co and its subsidiary Lamlash Co for the year to 30 April 20X7.

	Brodick Co $'000	Lamlash Co $'000
Revenue	1,100	500
Cost of sales	(630)	(300)
Gross profit	470	200
Administrative expenses	(105)	(150)
Dividend from Lamlash Co	24	–
Profit before tax	389	50
Income tax expense	(65)	(10)
Profit for the year	324	40

	Brodick Co $'000	Lamlash Co $'000
Note		
Dividends paid	200	30
Profit retained	124	10
Retained earnings brought forward	460	48
Retained earnings carried forward	584	58

Additional information

(a) The issued share capital of the group was as follows.

Brodick Co: 5,000,000 ordinary shares of $1 each
Lamlash Co: 1,000,000 ordinary shares of $1 each

(b) Brodick Co purchased 80% of the issued share capital of Lamlash Co on 1 November 20X6. At that time, the retained earnings of Lamlash stood at $52,000.

Required

Insofar as the information permits, prepare the Brodick group consolidated statement of profit or loss for the year to 30 April 20X7, and extracts from the statement of changes in equity showing group retained earnings and the non-controlling interest.

Answer

BRODICK GROUP
CONSOLIDATED STATEMENT OF PROFIT OR LOSS
FOR THE YEAR TO 30 APRIL 20X7

	$'000
Revenue (1,100 + (500 × 6/12))	1,350
Cost of sales (630 + (300 × 6/12))	(780)
Gross profit	570
Administrative expenses (105 + (150 × 6/12))	(180)
Profit before tax	390
Income tax expense (65 + (10 × 6/12))	(70)
Profit for the year	320
Profit attributable to:	
Owners of the parent	316
Non-controlling interest (W1)	4
	320

STATEMENT OF CHANGES IN EQUITY

	Retained earnings $'000	Non-controlling interest $'000
Balance brought forward 1 May 20X6	460	–
Added on acquisition of subsidiary (W2)	–	210
Dividends paid – per Qn/(30,000 – 24,000)	(200)	(6)
Total comprehensive income for the year (W1)	316	4
Balance carried forward 30 April 20X7	576	208

Workings

1   *Non-controlling interests*

	$'000
In Lamlash (20% × 40) × 6/12	4

2   *Added on acquisition of subsidiary*

	$'000
Share capital	1,000
Retained earnings	52
	1,052
Non-controlling share 20%	210

1.7 Section summary

The table below summarises the main points about the consolidated statement of profit or loss.

Purpose	To show the results of the group for an accounting period as if it were a single entity
Revenue to profit for year	100% P Co + 100% S Co (excluding adjustments for intra-group transactions)
Reason	To show the results of the group which were controlled by the parent company
Intra-group sales	Strip out intra-group activity from both sales revenue and cost of sales
Unrealised profit on intra-group sales	(a) Goods sold by P Co Increase cost of sales by unrealised profit (b) Goods sold by S Co Increase cost of sales by full amount of unrealised profit and decrease non-controlling interest by their share of unrealised profit
Depreciation	If the value of S Co's non-current assets have been subjected to a fair value uplift then any additional depreciation must be charged to profit or loss. The non-controlling interest will need to be adjusted for their share.
Transfer of non-current assets	Expenses must be increased by any profit on the transfer and reduced by any additional depreciation arising from the increased carrying value of the asset.

Non-controlling interests	S Co's profit after tax (PAT) X
	Less: *unrealised profit (X)
	          *profit on disposal of non-current assets (X)
	          additional depreciation following FV uplift (X)
	Add: **additional depreciation following disposal of
	          non-current assets X
	                                                                                                        X
	
	NCI% X
	
	*Only applicable if sales of goods and non-current assets made by subsidiary.
	
	**Only applicable if sale of non-current assets made by subsidiary.

Reason	To show the extent to which profits generated through P Co's control are in fact owned by other parties

2 The consolidated statement of profit or loss and other comprehensive income

FAST FORWARD

The consolidated statement of profit or loss and other comprehensive income is produced using the consolidated statement of profit or loss as a basis.

The only items of other comprehensive income that are included in your syllabus are revaluation gains and losses, so a consolidated statement of profit or loss and other comprehensive income will be easy to produce once you have done the consolidated statement of profit or loss.

We will take the last question and add an item of comprehensive income to illustrate this.

2.1 Example: Comprehensive income

The consolidated statement of profit or loss of the Brodrick Group is as in the answer to the last question. In addition, Lamlash made a $200,000 revaluation gain on one of its properties during the year following acquisition.

2.2 Solution

BRODRICK GROUP
CONSOLIDATED STATEMENT OF PROFIT OR LOSS AND OTHER COMPREHENSIVE INCOME
FOR THE YEAR TO 30 APRIL 20X7

	$'000
Revenue	1,350
Cost of sales	(780)
Gross profit	570
Administrative expenses	(180)
Profit before tax	390
Income tax expense	(70)
Profit for the year	320
Other comprehensive income:	
Gain on property revaluation	200
Total comprehensive income for the year	520
Profit attributable to:	
Owners of the parent	316
Non-controlling interest	4
	320
Total comprehensive income attributable to:	
Owners of the parent (316 + (200 × 80%))	476
Non-controlling interest (4 + (200 × 20%))	44
	520

2.3 Consolidated statement of profit or loss and other comprehensive income (separate statement)

If we were using the two-statement format (as explained in Chapter 3) we would produce a separate statement of profit or loss and statement of other comprehensive income.

2.4 Example: Other comprehensive income

BRODRICK GROUP
CONSOLIDATED STATEMENT OF PROFIT OR LOSS AND OTHER COMPREHENSIVE INCOME

Profit for the year	320
Other comprehensive income:	
Gain on property revaluation	200
Total comprehensive income for the year	520
Total comprehensive income attributable to:	
Owners of the parent (316 + (200 × 80%))	476
Non-controlling interest (4 + (200 × 20%)	44
	520

2.5 Full worked example

On 1 July 20X8 Crystal Co acquired 60,000 of the 100,000 shares in Pebble Co, its only subsidiary. The draft statements of profit or loss and other comprehensive income of both companies at 31 December 20X8 are shown below:

	Crystal Co	Pebble Co
	$'000	$'000
Revenue	43,000	26,000
Cost of sales	(28,000)	(18,000)
Gross profit	15,000	8,000
Other income – dividend received from Pebble Co	2,000	–
Distribution costs	(2,000)	(800)
Administrative expenses	(4,000)	(2,200)
Finance costs	(500)	(300)
Profit before tax	10,500	4,700
Income tax expense	(1,400)	(900)
Profit for the year	9,100	3,800
Other comprehensive income:		
Gain on property revaluation (Note (i))	–	2,000
Investment in equity instrument	200	–
Total comprehensive income for the year	9,300	5,800

Additional information:

(i)   At the date of acquisition the fair values of Pebble Co's assets were equal to their carrying amounts with the exception of a building which had a fair value $1m in excess of its carrying amount. At the date of acquisition the building had a remaining useful life of 20 years. Building depreciation is charged to administrative expenses. The building was revalued again at 31 December 20X8 and its fair value had increased by an additional $1m.

(ii) Sales from Crystal Co to Pebble Co were $6m during the post-acquisition period. All of these goods are still held in inventory by Pebble Co. Crystal Co marks up all sales by 20%.

(iii) Despite the property revaluation, Crystal Co has concluded that goodwill in Pebble Co has been impaired by $500,000.

(iv) It is Crystal Co's policy to value the non-controlling interest at full (fair) value.

(v)   Income and expenses can be assumed to have arisen evenly throughout the year.

Prepare the consolidated statement of profit or loss and other comprehensive income for the year ended 31 December 20X8.

Solution

CONSOLIDATED STATEMENT OF PROFIT OR LOSS AND OTHER COMPREHENSIVE INCOME

	$'000
Revenue (43,000 + (26,000 × 6/12) – 6,000 (W1))	50,000
Cost of sales (28,000 + (18,000 × 6/12) – 6,000 + 1,000 (W1))	(32,000)
Gross profit	18,000
Distribution costs (2,000 + (800 × 6/12))	(2,400)
Administrative expenses (4,000 + (2,200 × 6/12) + 25 (W2) + 500 impairment)	(5,625)
Finance costs (500 + (300 × 6/12))	(650)
Profit before tax	9,325
Income tax expense (1,400 + (900 × 6/12))	(1,850)
Profit for the year	7,475
Other comprehensive income:	
Gain on property revaluation (post-acquisition)	1,000
Investment in equity instrument	200
Total comprehensive income for the year	8,675
Profit attributable to:	
Owners of the parent	6,925
Non-controlling interest (W3)	550
	7,475
Total comprehensive income attributable to:	
Owners of the parent	7,725
Non-controlling interest (550 + (1,000 × 40%)	950
	8,675

Workings

1 *Unrealised profit*

Remove intercompany trading:

DR Revenue $6m/CR Cost of sales $6m

Unrealised profit = 6,000 × 20/120 = 1,000 – add to cost of sales

2 *Movement on fair value adjustment*

The fair value adjustment of $1m will be depreciated over the remaining life of the building. The amount to be charged at 31 December is:

1,000,000 / 20 × 6/12 = 25,000

40% of this (10,000) will be charged to the NCI.

3 *Non-controlling interest – share of profit for the year*

	$'000
Share of post-acquisition profit (3,800 × 6/12 × 40%)	760
Movement on fair value adjustment (25 × 40%)	(10)
Share of goodwill impairment (500 × 40%)	(200)
	550

3 Disposals

> The consolidated statement of profit or loss will include the results of subsidiaries disposed of up to the date of disposal.

When a subsidiary is disposed of, this must be accounted for in both the parent's separate financial statements and the consolidated financial statements.

3.1 Parent's separate financial statements

This calculation is straightforward: the proceeds are compared with the carrying amount of the investment sold. The investment will be held at cost or at fair value if held as an investment in equity instruments:

	$
Fair value of consideration received	X
Less carrying amount of investment disposed of	(X)
Profit/(loss) on disposal	X/(X)

3.2 Group financial statements

(a) **Statement of profit or loss and other comprehensive income**

    (i)   Consolidate results and non-controlling interest to the date of disposal.

    (ii)   Show the group profit or loss on disposal.

(b) **Statement of financial position**

    There will be no non-controlling interest and no consolidation as there is no subsidiary at the date the statement of financial position is being prepared.

3.3 Group profit/loss on disposal

The group profit or loss on disposal is the difference between the sales proceeds and the group's investment in the subsidiary. This investment consists of the group's share of the subsidiary's net assets up to the date of disposal, plus any remaining goodwill in the subsidiary.

The basic proforma is as follows:

	$	$
Consideration transferred		X
Less: share of consolidated carrying amount at date of disposal		
Net assets at date of disposal	X	
Goodwill at date of sale	X	
less non-controlling interests	(X)	
		(X)
Group profit/(loss) on disposal		X/(X)

Horse Co bought 80% of the share capital of Hoof Co for $648,000 on 1 October 20X5. At that date Hoof Co's retained earnings balance stood at $360,000. The statements of financial position at 30 September 20X8 and the summarised statements of profit or loss to that date are given below. (There is no other comprehensive income.

The fair value of the non-controlling interest is determined to be $160,000 at acquisition.

	Horse Co $'000	Hoof Co $'000
Non-current assets	704	540
Investment in Hoof Co	648	–
Current assets	740	740
	2,092	1,280
Equity		
$1 ordinary shares	1,080	360
Retained earnings	812	720
Current liabilities	200	200
	2,092	1,280
Profit before tax	306	252
Tax	(90)	(72)
Profit for the year	216	180

Assume that profits accrue evenly throughout the year and no dividends have been paid.

It is the group's policy to value the non-controlling interest at its fair value.

Ignore taxation.

Required

Prepare the consolidated statement of financial position and statement of profit or loss at 30 September 20X8 assuming that Horse Co sells its entire holding in Hoof Co for $1,300,000 on 30 September 20X8. (Assume no impairment of goodwill.)

Answer

CONSOLIDATED STATEMENT OF FINANCIAL POSITION AS AT 30 SEPTEMBER 20X8

	$'000
Non-current assets	704
Current assets (740 + 1,300)	2,040
	2,744
Equity	
$1 ordinary shares	1,080
Retained earnings (W3)	1,464
Current liabilities	200
	2,744

CONSOLIDATED STATEMENT OF PROFIT OR LOSS FOR THE YEAR ENDED 30 SEPTEMBER 20X8

	$'000
Profit before tax (306 + 252)	558
Profit on disposal (W1)	364
Tax (90 + 72)	(162)
	760
Profit attributable to:	
Owners of the parent	724
Non-controlling interest (20% × 180)	36
	760

Workings

1   *Profit on disposal of Hoof Co*

	$'000	$'000
Fair value of consideration received		1,300
Less: fair value of net assets of subsidiary at date of disposal		
Net assets (360 + 720)	1,080	
Goodwill (W3)	88	
Less; non-controlling interests (1,080 × 20%)	(232)	
		(936)
		364

2   *Goodwill*

	$'000
Fair value of the consideration transferred	648
Fair value of the NCI at acquisition	160
Less: fair value of Hoof net assets at acquisition (100%) = R/E $360k + SC $360k	(720)
	88

3   *Retained earnings carried forward*

	Horse $'000	Hoof $'000
Per question/date of disposal	812	720
Add group gain on disposal (W1)	364	–
Reserves at acquisition	–	(360)
		360
Share of post-acq'n reserves up to the disposal (80% × 360)	288	
	1,464	

3.4 Mid-year disposal

If Horse Co had disposed of its holding in Hoof Co on 31 March 20X8 for the same amount, at a point when Hoof Co's post-tax profits were $90,000 (180,000 × 6/12), the results would be as follows:

CONSOLIDATED STATEMENT OF FINANCIAL POSITION AS AT 30 SEPTEMBER 20X8

	$'000
Non-current assets	720
Current assets (740 + 1,300)	2,040
	2,760
Equity	
$1 ordinary shares	1,080
Retained earnings (W4)	1,480
Current liabilities	200
	2,760

CONSOLIDATED STATEMENT OF PROFIT OR LOSS FOR THE YEAR ENDED 30 SEPTEMBER 20X8

	$'000
Profit before tax (306 + (252 × 6/12))	432
Profit on disposal (W2)	436
Tax (90 + (72 × 6/12))	(126)
	742
Profit attributable to:	
Owners of the parent	724
Non-controlling interest (20% × 90)	18
	742

Workings

1   *Timeline*

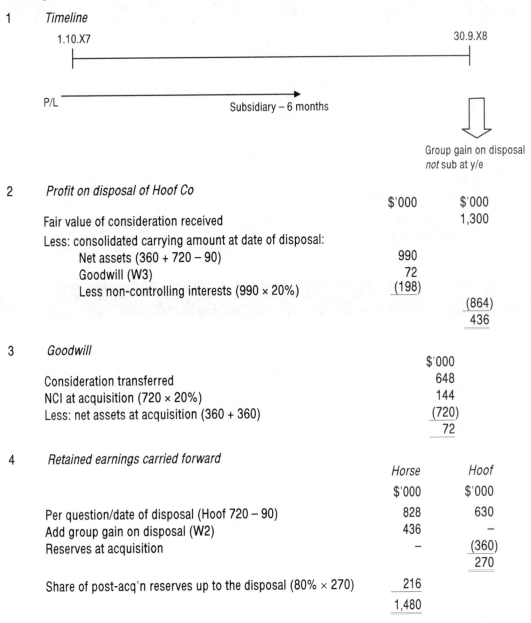

2   *Profit on disposal of Hoof Co*

	$'000	$'000
Fair value of consideration received		1,300
Less: consolidated carrying amount at date of disposal:		
Net assets (360 + 720 – 90)	990	
Goodwill (W3)	72	
Less non-controlling interests (990 × 20%)	(198)	
		(864)
		436

3   *Goodwill*

	$'000
Consideration transferred	648
NCI at acquisition (720 × 20%)	144
Less: net assets at acquisition (360 + 360)	(720)
	72

4   *Retained earnings carried forward*

	Horse	*Hoof*
	$'000	$'000
Per question/date of disposal (Hoof 720 – 90)	828	630
Add group gain on disposal (W2)	436	–
Reserves at acquisition	–	(360)
		270
Share of post-acq'n reserves up to the disposal (80% × 270)	216	
	1,480	

Exam focus point

The 20-mark group accounts preparation questions will **not** include disposals of subsidiaries, but aspects of this can be tested elsewhere in the exam, including in the interpretation questions.

Chapter Roundup

- The source of the consolidated statement of profit or loss is the individual statements of profit or loss of the separate companies in the group.

- In the consolidated statement of profit or loss, non-controlling interest is brought in as a one-line adjustment at the end of the statement.

- Intra-group sales and purchases are eliminated from the consolidated statement of profit or loss.

- Only the **post-acquisition** profits of the subsidiary are brought into the consolidated profit or loss.

- The consolidated statement of profit or loss and other comprehensive income is produced using the consolidated statement of profit or loss as a basis.

- The consolidated statement of profit or loss will include the results of the subsidiaries disposed of up to the date of disposal.

Quick Quiz

1   Where does unrealised profit on intra-group trading appear in the statement of profit or loss?

2   At the beginning of the year a 75% subsidiary transfers a non-current asset to the parent for $500,000. Its carrying value was $400,000 and it has four years of useful life left. How is this accounted for at the end of the year in the consolidated statement of profit or loss?

3   What amount should be presented in the consolidated statement of financial position in respect of a subsidiary which has been sold?

Answers to Quick Quiz

1   As a deduction from consolidated gross profit.

2
		$
Unrealised profit		100,000
Additional depreciation (100 ÷ 4)		(25,000)
Net charge to profit or loss		75,000

	Debit	Credit
	$	$
Non-current asset		100,000
Additional depreciation	25,000	
Group profit (75%)	56,250	
Non-controlling interest (25%)	18,750	
	100,000	100,000

3   A subsidiary which has been sold is not owned at the end of the year, so no amount will be shown in the statement of financial position.

Now try the questions below from the Practice Question Bank

Number	Level	Marks	Time
11		15	29 mins
12		15	29 mins

Financial Reporting | **9: The consolidated statement of profit or loss and other comprehensive income**   173

10

Accounting for associates

Topic list	Syllabus reference
1 Accounting for associates	A4, D2
2 The equity method	A4, D2
3 Statement of profit or loss and statement of financial position	D2

Introduction

In this chapter we deal with the treatment of associates in the consolidated financial statements. As the group's share of profit in the associate appears under profit or loss rather than other comprehensive income, we have concentrated on the separate statement of profit or loss.

Study guide

		Intellectual level
A4	**The concepts and principles of groups and consolidated financial statements**	
(j)	Define an associate and explain the principles and reasoning for the use of equity accounting	2
D2	**Preparation of consolidated financial statements including an associate**	
(a)	Prepare a consolidated statement of profit or loss and consolidated statement of profit or loss and other comprehensive income for a simple group dealing with an acquisition in the period and non-controlling interest	2

1 Accounting for associates

FAST FORWARD

This is covered by IAS 28 *Investments in associates and joint ventures*. The investing company does not have control, as it does with a subsidiary, but it does have **significant influence**.

1.1 Definitions

We looked at some of the important definitions in Chapter 8; these are repeated here with some additional important terms.

Key terms

- **Associate.** An entity, including an unincorporated entity such as a partnership, over which an investor has significant influence and which is neither a subsidiary nor an interest in a joint venture.
- **Significant influence.** The power to participate in the financial and operating policy decisions of the investee but it is not control or joint control over those policies.
- **Equity method.** A method of accounting whereby the investment is initially recorded at cost and adjusted thereafter for the post-acquisition change in the investor's share of net assets of the investee. The profit or loss of the investor includes the investor's share of the profit or loss of the investee.

(IAS 28: para. 3)

We have already looked at how the **status** of an investment in an associate should be determined. Go back to Section 1 of Chapter 8 to revise it. (Note that as for an investment in a subsidiary, any **potential voting rights** should be taken into account in assessing whether the investor has **significant influence** over the investee.)

IAS 28 requires all investments in associates to be accounted for in the consolidated accounts using the equity method, **unless** the investment is classified as 'held for sale' in accordance with IFRS 5 in which case it should be accounted for under IFRS 5 (IAS 28: para. 20) (see Chapter 17), or the exemption in the paragraph below applies.

An investor is exempt from applying the equity method if:

(a) It is a parent exempt from preparing consolidated financial statements under IFRS 10, or

(b) All of the following apply:

- (i) The investor is a **wholly-owned subsidiary** or it is a **partially owned subsidiary** of another entity and its other owners, including those not otherwise entitled to vote, have been informed about, and do not object to, the investor not applying the equity method
- (ii) The investor's securities are **not publicly traded**
- (iii) It is **not in the process of issuing securities** in public securities markets
- (iv) The **ultimate or intermediate parent** publishes consolidated financial statements that comply with International Financial Reporting Standards

(IAS 28: para. 17)

IAS 28 **does not allow** an investment in an associate to be excluded from equity accounting when an investee operates under severe long-term restrictions that significantly impair its ability to transfer funds to the investor. Significant influence must be lost before the equity method ceases to be applicable.

The use of the equity method should be **discontinued** from the date that the investor **ceases to have significant influence**.

From that date, the investor shall account for the investment in accordance with IFRS 9 *Financial instruments*. The carrying amount of the investment at the date that it ceases to be an associate shall be regarded as its cost on initial measurement as a financial asset under IFRS 9. (IAS 28: para. 22)

1.2 Separate financial statements of the investor

If an investor **issues consolidated financial statements** (because it has subsidiaries), an investment in an associate should be **either**:

(a) Accounted for at **cost**, or
(b) In accordance with **IFRS 9** (at fair value); or
(c) Using the equity method as described in IAS 28

in its separate financial statements. (IAS 27: para. 10)

If an investor that does *not* **issue consolidated financial statements** (ie it has no subsidiaries) but has an investment in an associate this should similarly be included in the financial statements of the investor either at cost, or in accordance with IFRS 9 (see Chapter 11) or using the equity method as described in IAS 28.

2 The equity method

2.1 Application of the equity method: consolidated accounts

Many of the procedures required to apply the equity method are the same as are required for full consolidation. In particular, **intra-group unrealised profits** must be excluded.

2.1.1 Consolidated statement of profit or loss

The basic principle is that the investing company (Xray Co) should take account of its **share of the earnings** of the associate, Yankee Co, whether or not Yankee Co distributes the earnings as dividends. Xray Co achieves this by adding to consolidated profit the group's share of Y Co's profit after tax.

Notice the difference between this treatment and the **consolidation** of a subsidiary company's results. If Yankee Co were a subsidiary Xray Co would take credit for the whole of its sales revenue, cost of sales etc and would then make a one-line adjustment to remove any non-controlling share.

Under equity accounting, the associate's sales revenue, cost of sales and so on are *not* **amalgamated** with those of the group. Instead the group share only of the associate's profit after tax for the year is added to the group profit.

2.1.2 Consolidated statement of financial position

A figure for **investment in associates** is shown which at the time of the acquisition must be stated at cost. At the end of each accounting period the group share of the retained reserves of the associate is added to the original cost to get the total investment to be shown in the consolidated statement of financial position.

2.2 Example: associate

Peanut Co, a company with subsidiaries, acquires 25,000 of the 100,000 $1 ordinary shares in Almond Co for $60,000 on 1 January 20X8. In the year to 31 December 20X8, Almond Co earns profits after tax of $24,000, from which it pays a dividend of $6,000.

How will Almond Co's results be accounted for in the individual and consolidated accounts of Peanut Co for the year ended 31 December 20X8?

Solution

In the **individual accounts** of Peanut Co, the investment will be recorded on 1 January 20X8 at cost. Unless there is an impairment in the value of the investment (see below), this amount will remain in the individual statement of financial position of Peanut Co permanently. The only entry in Peanut Co's individual statement of profit or loss will be to record dividends received. For the year ended 31 December 20X8, Peanut Co will:

DEBIT	Cash	$1,500	
CREDIT	Income from shares in associates		$1,500

In the **consolidated financial statements** of Peanut Co equity accounting principles will be used to account for the investment in Almond Co. Consolidated profit after tax will include the group's share of Almond Co's profit after tax (25% × $24,000 = $6,000). To the extent that this has been distributed as dividend, it is already included in Peanut Co's individual accounts and will automatically be brought into the consolidated results. That part of the group's share of profit in the associate which has not been distributed as dividend ($4,500) will be brought into consolidation by the following adjustment.

DEBIT	Investment in associates	$4,500	
CREDIT	Share of profit of associates		$4,500

The asset 'Investment in associates' is then stated at $64,500, being cost plus the group share of post-acquisition retained profits.

> **Exam focus point**
>
> A common mistake made by students is to add the associate's accounts line by line into the rest of the group (as it were for a subsidiary). Make sure that you apply the equity accounting rule to associates.

3 Statement of profit or loss and statement of financial position

3.1 Consolidated statement of profit or loss

> **FAST FORWARD**
>
> In the **consolidated statement of profit or loss** the investing group takes credit for its **share of the after-tax profits** of associates, whether or not they are distributed as dividends.

A **consolidation schedule** may be used to prepare the consolidated statement of profit or loss of a group with associates. Note the treatment of the associate's profits in the following example.

3.2 Illustration

The following **consolidation schedule** relates to the Gru Co group, consisting of the parent company, Kevin Co, an 80% owned subsidiary (Stuart Co) and an associate (Bob Co) in which the group has a 30% interest.

CONSOLIDATION SCHEDULE

	Group $'000	Kevin Co $'000	Stuart Co $'000	Bob Co $'000
Revenue	1,400	600	800	300
Cost of sales	(770)	(370)	(400)	(120)
Gross profit	630	230	400	180
Administrative expenses	(290)	(110)	(180)	(80)
	340	120	220	100
Interest receivable	30	30	–	–
	370	150	220	100
Interest payable	(20)	–	(20)	–
Share of profit of associate Bob Co (57 × 30%)	17	–	–	
	367	150	200	100

Income tax expense				
Group	(145)	(55)	(90)	
Associate		–	–	(43)
Profit for the year	222	95	110	57
Non-controlling interest (110 × 20%)	(22)			
	200			

Notes

1 Group sales revenue, group gross profit and costs such as depreciation etc exclude the sales revenue, gross profit and costs etc of associated companies.

2 The group share of the associated company profits is credited to group profit or loss. If the associated company has been acquired during the year, it would be necessary to deduct the pre-acquisition profits (remembering to allow for tax on current year profits).

3 The non-controlling interest will only ever apply to subsidiary companies.

3.3 Pro-forma consolidated statement of profit or loss

The following is a **suggested layout** (using the figures given in the illustration above) for the consolidated statement of profit or loss of a company having subsidiaries as well as associated companies.

	$'000
Revenue	1,400
Cost of sales	(770)
Gross profit	630
Other income: interest receivable	30
Administrative expenses	(290)
Finance costs	(20)
Share of profit of associate	17
Profit before tax	367
Income tax expense	(145)
Profit for the year	222
Profit attributable to:	
Owners of the parent	200
Non-controlling interest	22
	222

3.4 Consolidated statement of financial position

FAST FORWARD

In the **consolidated statement of financial position** the investment in associates should be shown as:

- **Cost of the investment in the associate**; plus
- Group share of post-acquisition profits; less
- Any amounts paid out as dividends; less
- Any amount written off the investment

As explained earlier, the consolidated statement of financial position will contain an **asset 'Investment in associates'**. The amount at which this asset is stated will be its original cost plus the group's share of any **post-acquisition profits** which have not been distributed as dividends.

3.5 Example: consolidated statement of financial position

On 1 January 20X6 the net tangible assets of Alaska Co amount to $220,000, financed by 100,000 $1 ordinary shares and revenue reserves of $120,000. Penn Co, a company with subsidiaries, acquires 30,000 of the shares in Alaska Co for $75,000. During the year ended 31 December 20X6 Alaska Co's profit after tax is $30,000, from which dividends of $12,000 are paid.

Show how Penn Co's investment in Alaska Co would appear in the consolidated statement of financial position at 31 December 20X6.

Solution

CONSOLIDATED STATEMENT OF FINANCIAL POSITION AS AT 31 DECEMBER 20X6 (extract)

	$
Non-current assets	
Investment in associated company	
Cost	75,000
Group share of post-acquisition retained profits	
(30% × $18,000)	5,400
	80,400

Question	Associate I

Set out below are the draft accounts of Pishpash Co and its subsidiaries and of AbbiCo. Pishpash Co acquired 40% of the equity capital of AbbiCo three years ago when the latter's reserves stood at $40,000.

SUMMARISED STATEMENTS OF FINANCIAL POSITION

	Pishpash Co & subsidiaries $'000	AbbiCo $'000
Tangible non-current assets	220	170
Investment in Associate at cost	60	–
Loan to AbbiCo	20	–
Current assets	100	50
Loan from Pishpash Co	–	(20)
	400	200
Share capital ($1 shares)	250	100
Retained earnings	150	100
	400	200

SUMMARISED STATEMENTS OF PROFIT OR LOSS

	Pishpash Co & subsidiaries $'000	AbbiCo $'000
Profit before tax	95	80
Income tax expense	35	30
Net profit for the year	60	50

Required

You are required to prepare the summarised consolidated accounts of Pishpash Co.

Notes

1   Assume that the associate's assets/liabilities are stated at fair value.
2   Assume that there are no non-controlling interests in the subsidiary companies.

PISHPASH CO
CONSOLIDATED STATEMENT OF PROFIT OR LOSS

	$'000
Net profit	95
Share of profits of associated company (50 × 40%)	20
Profit before tax	115
Income tax expense	(35)
Profit attributable to the members of Pishpash Co	80

PISHPASH CO
CONSOLIDATED STATEMENT OF FINANCIAL POSITION

	$'000
Assets	
Tangible non-current assets	220
Investment in associate (see note)	84
Loan to associate	20
Current assets	100
Total assets	424
Equity and liabilities	
Share capital	250
Retained earnings (W)	174
Total equity and liabilities	424

Note

	$'000
Investment in associate	
Cost of investment	60
Share of post-acquisition retained earnings (W)	24
	84

Working

Retained earnings	Pishpash Co& Subsidiaries $'000	AbbiCo $'000
Per question	150	100
Pre-acquisition		40
Post-acquisition		60
Group share in associate		
($60 × 40%)	24	
Group retained earnings	174	

Alfred Co bought a 25% shareholding on 31 December 20X8 in Grimbald Co at a cost of $38,000.

During the year to 31 December 20X9 Grimbald Co made a profit before tax of $82,000 and the taxation charge on the year's profits was $32,000. A dividend of $20,000 was paid on 31 December out of these profits.

Required

Calculate the entries for the associate which would appear in the consolidated accounts of the Alfred group, in accordance with the requirements of IAS 28.

CONSOLIDATED STATEMENT OF PROFIT OR LOSS

	$
Group share of profit of associate (82,000 × 25%)	20,500
Less taxation (32,000 × 25%)	(8,000)
Share of profit of associate	12,500

CONSOLIDATED STATEMENT OF FINANCIAL POSITION

	$
Investment in associate (W)	45,500

Working

	$
Cost of investment	38,000
Share of post-acquisition retained earnings ((82,000 – 32,000 – 20,000) × 25%)	7,500
	45,500

The following points are also relevant and are similar to a parent-subsidiary consolidation situation.

(a)   Use financial statements drawn up to the **same reporting date**

(b)   If this is impracticable, adjust the financial statements for **significant transactions/events** in the intervening period. The difference between the reporting date of the associate and that of the investor must be no more than three months.

(c)   Use **uniform accounting policies** for like transactions and events in similar circumstances, adjusting the associate's statements to reflect group policies if necessary

3.6 'Upstream' and 'downstream' transactions

'Upstream' transactions are, for example, sales of assets from an associate to the investor. 'Downstream' transactions are, for example, sales of assets from the investor to an associate.

Profits and losses resulting from 'upstream' and 'downstream' transactions between an investor (including its consolidated subsidiaries) and an associate are eliminated to the extent of the investor's interest in the associate. This is very similar to the procedure for eliminating intra-group transactions between a parent and a subsidiary. The important thing to remember is that **only the group's share is eliminated**.

3.7 Example: downstream transaction

Astral Co, a parent with subsidiaries, holds 25% of the equity shares in Belt Co. During the year, Astral Co makes sales of $1,000,000 to Belt Co at cost plus a 25% mark-up. At the year end, Belt Co has all these goods still in inventories.

Solution

Astral Co has made an unrealised profit of $200,000 (1,000,000 × 25/125) on its sales to the associate. The group's share (25%) of this must be eliminated:

DEBIT   Share of profit of associate (consolidated profit or loss) $50,000
CREDIT   Investment in associate (consolidated statement of financial position) $50,000

Note that if the sale had been made by the associate to the group (an upstream transaction) the posting would have been **exactly the same**.

3.8 Associate's losses

When the equity method is being used and the investor's share of losses of the associate equals or exceeds its interest in the associate, the investor should **discontinue** including its share of further losses. The investment is reported at nil value. After the investor's interest is reduced to nil, **additional losses** should only be recognised where the investor has incurred obligations or made payments on behalf of the associate (for example, if it has guaranteed amounts owed to third parties by the associate).

(IAS 28: para. 39)

3.9 Impairment losses

Any impairment loss is recognised in accordance with IAS 36 *Impairment of assets* for each associate individually.

(IAS 28: para. 42)

In the case of an associate, any impairment loss will be deducted from the carrying value in the statement of financial position.

The working would be:

	$
Cost of investment	X
Share of post-acquisition retained earnings	X
	X
Impairment loss	(X)

Exam focus point

> It is not unusual in the exam to have both an associate and a subsidiary to account for in a consolidation.

Question	Consolidated statement of financial position

The statements of financial position of John Co and its investee companies, Paul Co and S Co, at 31 December 20X5 are shown below.

STATEMENTS OF FINANCIAL POSITION AS AT 31 DECEMBER 20X5

	John Co $'000	*Paul Co* $'000	*George Co* $'000
Non-current assets			
Freehold property	1,950	1,250	500
Plant and machinery	795	375	285
Investments	1,500	–	–
	4,245	1,625	785
Current assets			
Inventories	575	300	265
Trade receivables	330	290	370
Cash and cash equivalents	50	120	20
	955	710	655
Total assets	5,200	2,335	1,440
Equity and liabilities			
Equity			
Share capital – $1 shares	2,000	1,000	750
Retained earnings	1,460	885	390
	3,460	1,885	1,140

	John Co $'000	Paul Co $'000	George Co $'000
Non-current liabilities			
12% loan stock	500	100	
Current liabilities			
Trade and other payables	680	350	300
Bank overdraft	560	–	–
	1,240	350	300
Total equity and liabilities	5,200	2,335	1,440

Additional information

1   John Co acquired 600,000 ordinary shares in Paul Co on 1 January 20X0 for $1,000,000 when the retained earnings of Paul Co were $200,000.

2   At the date of acquisition of Paul Co, the fair value of its freehold property was considered to be $400,000 greater than its value in Paul Co's statement of financial position. Paul Co had acquired the property in January 20W0 and the buildings element (comprising 50% of the total value) is depreciated on cost over 50 years.

3   John Co acquired 225,000 ordinary shares in George Co on 1 January 20X4 for $500,000 when the retained earnings of George Co were $150,000.

4   Paul Co manufactures a component, the Ringo, used by both John Co and George Co. Transfers are made by Paul Co at cost plus 25%. John Co held $100,000 inventory of the Ringo at 31 December 20X5. In the same period John Co sold goods to George Co of which George Co had $80,000 in inventory at 31 December 20X5. John Co had marked these goods up by 25%.

5   The goodwill in Paul Co is impaired and should be fully written off. An impairment loss of $92,000 is to be recognised on the investment in George Co.

6   Non-controlling interest is valued at full fair value. Paul Co shares were trading at $1.60 just prior to the acquisition by John Co.

Required

Prepare, in a format suitable for inclusion in the annual report of the John Group, the consolidated statement of financial position at 31 December 20X5.

Answer

JOHN GROUP CONSOLIDATED STATEMENT OF FINANCIAL POSITION AS AT 31 DECEMBER 20X5

	$'000
Non-current assets	
Freehold property (W2)	3,570.00
Plant and machinery (795 + 375)	1,170.00
Investment in associate (W7)	475.20
	5,215.20
Current assets	
Inventories (W3)	855.00
Receivables (330 + 290)	620.00
Cash and cash equivalents (50 + 120)	170.00
	1,645.00
Total assets	6,860.20
Equity and liabilities	
Equity	
Share capital	2,000.00
Retained earnings (W8)	1,792.20
	3,792.20
Non-controlling interest (W9)	878.00
	4,670.20

	$'000
Non-current liabilities	
12% loan stock (500 + 100)	600.00
Current liabilities (680 + 560 + 350)	1,590.00
Total equity and liabilities	6,860.20

Workings

1   Group structure

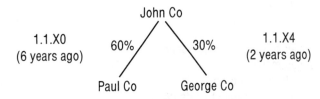

2   *Freehold property*

	$'000
John Co	1,950
Paul Co	1,250
Fair value adjustment	400
Additional depreciation (400 × 50% ÷ 40) × 6 years (20X0–20X5)	(30)
	3,570

3   *Inventory*

	$'000
John Co	575
Paul Co	300
PUP (100 × $^{25}/_{125}$) (W4)	(20)
	855

4   *Unrealised profit (PUP)*

	$'000
On sales by Paul Co to John Co (parent co) 100 × 25/125	20.0
On sales by John Co to George Co (associate) 80 × 25/125 × 30%	4.8

5   *Fair value adjustments*

	Difference at acquisition $'000	Difference now $'000
Property	400	400
Additional depreciation: 200 × 6/40	–	(30)
	400	370

∴ Charge $30,000 to retained earnings

6   *Goodwill*

	$'000	$'000
Paul Co		
Consideration transferred		1,000
Non-controlling interest (400 × $1.60)		640
Net assets acquired:		
Share capital	1,000	
Retained earnings	200	
Fair value adjustment	400	
		(1,600)
Goodwill at acquisition		40
Impairment loss		(40)
		0

7   *Investment in associate*

	$'000
Cost of investment	500.00
Share of post-acquisition profit (390 – 150) × 30%	72.00
Less PUP	(4.80)
Less impairment loss	(92.00)
	475.20

8   *Retained earnings*

	John Co $'000	Paul Co $'000	George Co $'000
Retained earnings per question	1,460.0	885.0	390.0
Adjustments			
Unrealised profit (W4)	(4.8)	(20.0)	
Fair value adjustments (W5)		(30.0)	
Impairment loss (Paul Co)		(40.0)	
		795.0	390.0
Less pre-acquisition reserves		(200.0)	(150.0)
	1,455.20	595.0	240.0
Paul Co: 60% × 595	357.00		
George Co: 30% × 240	72.00		
Impairment loss George Co	(92.00)		
	1,792.20		

9   *Non-controlling interest at reporting date*

	$'000
NCI at acquisition (W6)	640.00
Share of post-acquisition retained earnings (595 × 40%)	238.00
	878.00

Chapter Roundup

- This is covered by IAS 28 *Investments in associates and joint ventures*. The investing company does not have control, as it does with a subsidiary, but it does have **significant influence**.

- In the **consolidated statement of profit or loss** the investing group takes credit for its **share of the after-tax profits** of associates, whether or not they are distributed as dividends.

- In the **consolidated statement of financial position** the investment in associates should be shown as:

  - **Cost of the investment in the associate**; plus
  - Group share of post-acquisition profits; less
  - Any amounts paid out as dividends; less
  - Any amount written off the investment

Quick Quiz

1 Define an associate.
2 How should associates be accounted for in the separate financial statements of the investor?
3 What is the effect of the equity method on the consolidated statement of profit or loss and statement of financial position?

Answers to Quick Quiz

1. An entity in which an investor has a significant influence, but which is not a subsidiary or a joint venture of the investor.

2. Either at cost or in accordance with IFRS 9

3. (a) *Consolidated statement of profit or loss.* Investing company includes its share of the earnings of the associate, by adding its share of profit after tax.

   (b) *Consolidated statement of financial position.* Investment in associates is initially included in assets at cost. This will increase or decrease each year according to whether the associated company makes a profit or loss.

Now try the question below from the Practice Question Bank

Number	Level	Marks	Time
13	–	20	39 mins

Financial instruments

Introduction

IAS 32: *Financial instruments: presentation*
IFRS 7: *Financial instruments: disclosure*

IFRS 9: *Financial instruments*

The introduction of IFRS 9 was to simplify much of this complex and controversial area of accounting.

This chapter aims to break this daunting subject into manageable pieces.

Study guide

		Intellectual level
B5	**Financial instruments**	
(a)	Explain the need for an accounting standard on financial instruments	1
(b)	Define financial instruments in terms of financial assets and financial liabilities	1
(c)	Explain and account for the factoring of receivables	2
(d)	Indicate for the following categories of financial instruments how they should be measured and how any gains and losses from subsequent measurement should be treated in the financial statements:	1
	(i) Amortised cost	2
	(ii) Fair value through other comprehensive income (including where an irrevocable election has been made for equity instruments that are not held for trading)	2
	(iii) Fair value through profit or loss	
(e)	Distinguish between debt and equity capital	2
(f)	Apply the requirements of relevant accounting standards to the issue and finance costs of:	2
	(i) Equity	
	(ii) Redeemable preference shares and debt instruments with no conversion rights (principle of amortised cost)	
	(iii) Convertible debt	

Exam guide

Financial instruments are generally tested as part of a question rather than as a full question.

1 Financial instruments

FAST FORWARD

A financial instrument gives rise to a financial asset of one entity and a financial liability or equity instrument of another.

(IAS 32: para. 11)

1.1 Introduction

If you read the financial press you will probably be aware of **rapid international expansion** in the use of financial instruments. These vary from straightforward, traditional instruments, eg bonds, through to various forms of so-called 'derivative instruments'.

We can perhaps summarise the reasons why a project on accounting for financial instruments was considered necessary as follows.

(a)   The **significant growth of financial instruments** over recent years has outstripped the development of guidance for their accounting.

(b)   The topic is of **international concern**, other national standard-setters are involved as well as the IASB.

(c)   There have been recent **high-profile disasters** involving derivatives which, while not caused by accounting failures, have raised questions about accounting and disclosure practices.

Three accounting standards deal with financial instruments:

(a)   IAS 32 *Financial instruments: presentation*, which deals with:

(i)   The classification of financial instruments between liabilities and equity

(ii)   Presentation of certain compound instruments (instruments combining debt and equity)

(b)   IFRS 7 *Financial instruments: disclosure*

(c)   IFRS 9 *Financial instruments.* IFRS 9 deals with:

(i)   Recognition and derecognition

(ii)   Measurement of financial instruments

(iii)   Impairment

(iv)   General hedging accounting

1.2 Definitions

The most important definitions are common to all three standards.

The important definitions to learn are:

- Financial asset
- Financial liability
- Equity instrument

Key terms

- **Financial instrument.** Any contract that gives rise to both a financial asset of one entity and a financial liability or equity instrument of another entity.

- **Financial asset.** Any asset that is:

(a)   Cash

(b)   An equity instrument of another entity

(c)   A contractual right to receive cash or another financial asset from another entity; or to exchange financial instruments with another entity under conditions that are potentially favourable to the entity

- **Financial liability.** Any liability that is:

(a)   A contractual obligation:

(i)   To deliver cash or another financial asset to another entity, or

(ii)   To exchange financial instruments with another entity under conditions that are potentially unfavourable.

- **Equity instrument.** Any contract that evidences a residual interest in the assets of an entity after deducting all of its liabilities.

- **Fair value.** Price that would be received to sell an asset or paid to transfer a liability in an orderly transaction between market participants at the measurement date.   (IAS 32: para. 11)

Exam focus point

These definitions are very important – so learn them.

We should clarify some points arising from these definitions. Firstly, one or two terms above should be themselves defined:

(a) A 'contract' need not be in writing, but it must comprise an agreement that has 'clear economic consequences' and which the parties to it cannot avoid, usually because the agreement is enforceable in law.

(b) An 'entity' here could be an individual, partnership, incorporated body or government agency.

The definitions of **financial assets** and **financial liabilities** may seem rather circular, referring as they do to the terms financial asset and financial instrument. The point is that there may be a chain of contractual rights and obligations, but it will lead ultimately to the receipt or payment of cash *or* the acquisition or issue of an equity instrument.

Examples of **financial assets** include:

(a) Trade receivables
(b) Options
(c) Shares (when held as an investment)

Examples of **financial liabilities** include:

(a) Trade payables
(b) Debenture loans payable
(c) Redeemable preference (non-equity) shares

IAS 32 makes it clear that the following items are **not** financial instruments.

(a) **Physical assets**, eg inventories, property, plant and equipment, leased assets and **intangible assets** (patents, trademarks etc)

(b) **Prepaid expenses**, deferred revenue and most warranty obligations

(c) Liabilities or assets that are **not contractual** in nature

(IAS 32: AG10)

Question

Definitions

Can you give the reasons why physical assets and prepaid expenses do not qualify as financial instruments?

Answer

Refer to the definitions of financial assets and liabilities given above.

(a) **Physical assets**: control of these creates an opportunity to generate an inflow of cash or other assets, but it does not give rise to a present right to receive cash or other financial assets.

(b) **Prepaid expenses, etc**: the future economic benefit is the receipt of goods/services rather than the right to receive cash or other financial assets.

Contingent rights and obligations meet the definition of financial assets and financial liabilities respectively, even though many do not qualify for recognition in financial statements. This is because the contractual rights or obligations exist because of a past transaction or event (eg assumption of a guarantee).

(IAS 32: para. 25)

2 Presentation of financial instruments

FAST FORWARD

The objective of IAS 32 is to establish principles for presenting financial instruments or equity.

(IAS 32: para. 2)

2.1 Scope

IAS 32 should be applied in the presentation and disclosure of **all types of financial instruments**.

Certain items are **excluded** for example interests in subsidiaries (IAS 27), associates (IAS 28) and joint ventures (out of scope for this syllabus but covered in IFRS 11), pensions and insurance contracts (both out of scope for this syllabus). Also, contracts for contingent consideration in a business combination and financial instruments, contracts and obligations under share based payment transactions (IFRS 2)

(IAS 32: para. 4)

2.2 Liabilities and equity

The main principle of IAS 32 is that financial instruments should be presented according to their **substance, not merely their legal form**. In particular, entities which issue financial instruments should classify them (or their component parts) as **either financial liabilities, or equity**.   (IAS 32: para. 15)

The classification of a financial instrument as a liability or as equity depends on the following.

- The **substance of the contractual arrangement** on initial recognition
- The definitions of a **financial liability** and an **equity instrument**   (IAS 32: para. 15)

How should a **financial liability be distinguished from an equity instrument**? The critical feature of a **liability** is an **obligation** to transfer economic benefit. Therefore a financial instrument is a financial liability if there is a **contractual obligation** on the issuer either to deliver cash or another financial asset to the holder or to exchange another financial instrument with the holder under potentially unfavourable conditions to the issuer.   (IAS 32: para. 16)

The financial liability exists regardless of the way in which the contractual obligation will be settled.

The issuer's ability to satisfy an obligation may be restricted, eg by lack of access to foreign currency, but this is irrelevant as it does not remove the issuer's obligation or the holder's right under the instrument.

Where the above critical feature is **not** met, then the financial instrument is an **equity instrument**. IAS 32 explains that although the holder of an equity instrument may be entitled to a *pro rata* share of any distributions out of equity, the issuer does **not** have a contractual obligation to make such a distribution.

Although substance and legal form are often **consistent with each other**, this is not always the case. In particular, a financial instrument may have the legal form of equity, but in substance it is in fact a liability. Other instruments may combine features of both equity instruments and financial liabilities. (IAS 32: para. 16)

For example, many entities issue **preference shares** which must be **redeemed** by the issuer for a fixed (or determinable) amount at a fixed (or determinable) future date. Alternatively, the holder may have the right to require the issuer to redeem the shares at or after a certain date for a fixed amount. In such cases, the issuer has an **obligation**. Therefore the instrument is a **financial liability** and should be classified as such.

(IAS 32: para. 16)

The distinction between redeemable and non-redeemable preference shares is important. Most preference shares are redeemable and are therefore classified as a **financial liability**. Expect to see this in your exam.

2.3 Compound financial instruments

Some financial instruments contain both a liability and an equity element. In such cases, IAS 32 requires the component parts of the instrument to be **classified separately**, according to the substance of the contractual arrangement and the definitions of a financial liability and an equity instrument.

(IAS 32: para. 28)

One of the most common types of compound instrument is **convertible debt**. This creates a primary financial liability of the issuer and grants an option to the holder of the instrument to convert it into an equity instrument (usually ordinary shares) of the issuer. This is the economic equivalent of the issue of conventional debt plus a warrant to acquire shares in the future.

Although in theory there are several possible ways of calculating the split, IAS 32 requires the following method.

(a) Calculate the value for the liability component.
(b) Deduct this from the instrument as a whole to leave a residual value for the equity component.

(IAS 32: para. 32)

The reasoning behind this approach is that an entity's equity is its residual interest in its assets amount after deducting all its liabilities.

The **sum of the carrying amounts** assigned to liability and equity will always be equal to the carrying amount that would be ascribed to the instrument **as a whole**.

2.4 Example: valuation of compound instruments

Rathbone Co issues 2,000 convertible bonds at the start of 20X2. The bonds have a three year term, and are issued at par with a face value of $1,000 per bond, giving total proceeds of $2,000,000. Interest is payable annually in arrears at a nominal annual interest rate of 6%. Each bond is convertible at any time up to maturity into 250 ordinary shares.

When the bonds are issued, the prevailing market interest rate for similar debt without conversion options is 9%.

Required

What is the value of the equity component in the bond?

Solution

The liability component is valued first, and the **difference** between the proceeds of the bond issue and the fair value of the liability is assigned to the **equity component**. The present value of the liability component is calculated using a discount rate of 9%, the market interest rate for similar bonds having no conversion rights, as shown.

	$
Present value of the principal: $2,000,000 payable at the end of three years ($2m × 0.772183)*	1,544,367
Present value of the interest: $120,000 payable annually in arrears for three years ($120,000 × 2.5313)*	303,755
Total liability component	1,848,122
Equity component (balancing figure)	151,878
Proceeds of the bond issue	2,000,000

* These figures can be obtained from discount and annuity tables or simply calculated arithmetically as follows.

		$
Principal		
$2,000,000 discounted at 9% over 3 years: 2,000,000 ÷ 1.09 ÷ 1.09 ÷ 1.09 (or 2,000,000 × $1/1.09^3$)		1,544,367
Interest		
Year 1 120,000 ÷ 1.09	110,091	
Year 2 110,091 ÷ 1.09	101,002	
Year 3 101,002 ÷ 1.09	92,662	
		303,755
Value of liability component		1,848,122
Equity component (balancing figure)		151,878
Proceeds of bond issue		2,000,000

The split between the liability and equity components remains the same throughout the term of the instrument, even if there are changes in the **likelihood of the option being exercised**. This is because it is not always possible to predict how a holder will behave. The issuer continues to have an obligation to make future payments until conversion, maturity of the instrument or some other relevant transaction takes place.

Question

Ishmail Co issues $20m of 4% convertible loan notes at par on 1 January 20X7. The loan notes are redeemable for cash or convertible into equity shares on the basis of 20 shares per $100 of debt at the option of the loan note holder on 31 December 20X9. Similar but non-convertible loan notes carry an interest rate of 9%.

The present value of $1 receivable at the end of the year based on discount rates of 4% and 9% can be taken as:

		4%	9%
		$	$
End of year	1	0.96	0.92
	2	0.93	0.84
	3	0.89	0.77
Cumulative		2.78	2.53

Required

Show how these loan notes should be accounted for in the financial statements at 31 December 20X7.

Answer

	$
Statement of profit or loss	
Finance costs (W2)	1,568
Statement of financial position	
Equity – option to convert (W1)	2,576
Non-current liabilities	
4% convertible loan notes (W2)	18,192

Workings

1	Equity and liability elements	
		$'000
	3 years interest (20,000 × 4% × 2.53)	2,024
	Redemption (20,000 × 0.77)	15,400
	Liability element	17,424
	Equity element (β)	2,576
	Proceeds of loan notes	20,000

2	Loan note balance	
		$'000
	Liability element (W1)	17,424
	Interest for the year at 9%	1,568
	Less interest paid (20,000 × 4%)	(800)
	Carrying value at 31 December 20X7	18,192

2.5 Interest, dividends, losses and gains

As well as looking at presentation in the statement of financial position, IAS 32 considers how financial instruments affect the statement of profit or loss and other comprehensive income (and changes in equity). The treatment varies according to whether interest, dividends, losses or gains relate to a **financial liability** or an **equity instrument**. (IAS 32: para. 35)

(a) Interest, dividends, losses and gains relating to a financial instrument (or component part) classified as a **financial liability** should be recognised as **income or expense** in profit or loss.
(IAS 32: para. 35)

(b)   Distributions to holders of a financial instrument classified as an **equity instrument** (dividends to ordinary shareholders) should be **debited directly to equity** by the issuer. These will appear in the statement of changes in equity.

(IAS 32: para. 35)

(c)   **Transaction costs** of an equity transaction should be accounted for as a **deduction from equity**, usually debited to the share premium account.

(IAS 32: para. 39)

2.6 Section summary

- Issuers of financial instruments must classify them as **liabilities** or **equity**.

- The **substance** of the financial instrument is more important than its **legal form**.

- The **critical feature of a financial liability** is the contractual obligation to deliver cash or another financial asset.

- **Compound instruments** are split into equity and liability parts and presented accordingly.

- **Interest, dividends, losses and gains** are treated according to whether they relate to a financial liability or an equity instrument.

3 Disclosure of financial instruments

FAST FORWARD

IFRS 7 replaces the disclosure requirements which were previously in IAS 32.

3.1 IFRS 7

As well as specific monetary disclosures, **narrative commentary** by issuers is encouraged by the Standard (IFRS 7: para. 33). This will enable users to understand management's attitude to risk, whatever the current transactions involving financial instruments are at the period end.

The standard does not prescribe the **format or location** for disclosure of information. A combination of narrative descriptions and specific quantified data should be given, as appropriate.

The **level of detail** required is a matter of judgement. Where a large number of very similar financial instrument transactions are undertaken, these may be grouped together. Conversely, a single significant transaction may require full disclosure.

Classes of instruments will be grouped together by management in a manner appropriate to the information to be disclosed.

(IAS 32: para. 6)

Exam focus point

The examining team have indicated that they will not set questions on the **risks** of financial instruments.

4 Recognition of financial instruments

FAST FORWARD

IFRS 9 *Financial instruments* establishes principles for recognising and measuring financial assets and liabilities.

(IFRS 9: IN1)

4.1 Scope

IFRS 9 applies to **all entities** and to **all types of financial instruments except** those specifically excluded, for example investments in subsidiaries, associates, joint ventures and other joint arrangements.

(IFRS 9: para. 2.1)

4.2 Initial recognition

A financial asset or financial liability should be recognised in the statement of financial position when the reporting entity becomes a party to the contractual provisions of the instrument.   (IFRS 9: para 3. 1.1)

Notice that this is **different** from the recognition criteria in the *Conceptual Framework* and in most other standards. Items are normally recognised when there is a probable inflow or outflow of resources and the item has a cost or value that can be measured reliably.

4.3 Derecognition

Derecognition is the removal of a previously recognised financial instrument from an entity's statement of financial position.

An entity should derecognise a **financial asset** when:

(a)   The **contractual rights** to the cash flows from the financial asset **expire**; or

(b)   It transfers substantially all the risks and rewards of ownership of the financial asset to another party.

An entity should derecognise a **financial liability** when it is **extinguished** – ie when the obligation specified in the contract is discharged or cancelled or expires.

It is possible for only **part** of a financial asset or liability to be derecognised. This is allowed if the part comprises:

(a)   Only specifically identified cash flows; or
(b)   Only a fully proportionate (pro rata) share of the total cash flows.

For example, if an entity holds a bond it has the right to two separate sets of cash inflows: those relating to the principal and those relating to the interest. It could sell the right to receive the interest to another party while retaining the right to receive the principal.

On derecognition, the amount to be included in net profit or loss for the period is calculated as follows:

	$	$
Carrying amount of asset/liability (or the portion of asset/liability) transferred		X
Less proceeds received/paid		(X)
Difference to profit or loss		X

Where only part of a financial asset is derecognised, the carrying amount of the asset should be allocated between the part retained and the part transferred based on their relative fair values on the date of transfer. A gain or loss should be recognised based on the proceeds for the portion transferred. (IFRS 9: para. 3.2)

4.4 Classification of financial assets

On **recognition**, IFRS 9 requires that financial assets are **classified as measured** at either:

- **Amortised cost**
- **Fair value through other comprehensive income; or**
- **Fair value through profit or loss**   (IFRS 9: para. 4.1)

4.4.1 Classification basis

The IFRS 9 classification is made on the basis of both:

(a)   The **entity's business model** for managing the financial assets, and
(b)   The **contractual cash flow** characteristics of the financial asset.   (IFRS 9: para. 4.1)

A financial asset is classified as measured at **amortised cost** where:

(a)   The objective of the business model within which the asset is held is to hold assets in order to collect contractual cash flows

(b)   The contractual terms of the financial asset give rise on specified dates to cash flows that are solely payments of principal and interest on the principal outstanding.   (IFRS 9: para. 4.1.2)

An application of these rules means that **equity investments may not be classified as measured at amortised cost** and must be measured at fair value. This is because contractual cash flows on specified dates are not a characteristic of equity instruments. They are held at fair value with changes going through profit or loss unless the investment is **not held for trading** and the entity makes an **irrevocable election at initial recognition to recognise it at fair value through other comprehensive income**, with only dividend income recognised in profit or loss.

A financial asset must be classified as measured at **fair value through other comprehensive income** (unless designated at inception as measured at fair value through profit or loss) where:

(a)   The objective of the business model within which the asset is held is achieved by **both** collecting contractual cash flows and selling financial assets; and

(b)   The contractual terms of the financial asset give rise on specified dates to cash flows that are solely payments of principal and interest.

(IFRS 9: para. 4.1.2)

A **debt instrument** may be classified as measured at either amortised cost or fair value **depending on whether it meets the criteria above**. Even where the criteria are met at initial recognition, a debt instrument may in certain circumstances be classified as measured at fair value through profit or loss.

As noted above, IFRS 9 allows debt instruments that pass the cash flow test for measurement at amortised cost but are also held for trading to be carried at **fair value through other comprehensive income**. For these instruments, fair value changes will go through other comprehensive income; interest charges will be measured at amortised cost and go through **profit or loss**.

(IFRS 9: para. 4.1.2)

4.4.2 Business model test in more detail

IFRS 9 introduces a business model test that requires an entity to assess whether its **business objective for a debt instrument is to collect the contractual cash flows of the instrument as opposed to realising any change in its fair value by selling it prior to its contractual maturity**. Note the following key points:

(a)   The assessment of a 'business model' is not made at an individual financial instrument level.

(b)   The assessment is based on how key management personnel actually manage the business, rather than management's intentions for specific financial assets.

(c)   An entity may have more than one business model for managing its financial assets and the classification need not be determined at the reporting entity level. For example, it may have one portfolio of investments that it manages with the objective of collecting contractual cash flows and another portfolio of investments held with the objective of trading to realise changes in fair value. It would be appropriate for entities like these to carry out the assessment for classification purposes at portfolio level, rather than at entity level.

(d)   Although the objective of an entity's business model may be to hold financial assets in order to collect contractual cash flows, the entity need not hold all of those assets until maturity. Thus an entity's business model can be to hold financial assets to collect contractual cash flows even when sales of financial assets occur.

(IFRS 9: para. B4.1)

4.4.3 Contractual cash flow test in more detail

The requirement in IFRS 9 to assess the contractual cash flow characteristics of a financial asset is based on the concept that **only instruments with contractual cash flows of principal and interest on principal may qualify for amortised cost measurement**. By interest, IFRS 9 means consideration for the time value of money and the credit risk associated with the principal outstanding during a particular period of time.

(IFRS 9: para. B4.1)

Question   Contractual cash flows

Would an investment in a convertible loan qualify to be measured at amortised cost under IFRS 9?

No because of the inclusion of the conversion option which is not deemed to represent payments of principal and interest.

4.5 Factoring of receivables

The business model test must be considered in the case of factoring.

Where debts or receivables are factored, the original creditor **sells the debts to the factor**. The sales price may be fixed at the outset or may be adjusted later. It is also common for the factor to offer a credit facility that allows the seller to draw upon a proportion of the amounts owed.

An entity may have a past practice of factoring its receivables. If the significant risks and rewards are transferred from the entity, resulting in the original receivable being derecognised, the entity is not holding these receivables to collect the contractual cash flows but to sell them.

However, if the significant risks and rewards of these receivables are not transferred from the entity, and the receivables do not therefore qualify for derecognition, the entity's business objective is to hold the assets to collect contractual cash flows. (IFRS 9: para. 3.2.15/16)

In order to determine the correct accounting treatment it is necessary to consider whether the control of the debts has been passed on to the factor, or whether the factor is, in effect, providing a loan on the security of the receivable balances. If the seller has to **pay interest** on the difference between the amounts advanced to him and the amounts that the factor has received, and if the seller bears the **risks of non-payment** by the debtor, then the indications would be that the transaction is, in effect, a loan.

4.5.1 Summary of indications of appropriate treatment

The following is a summary of indicators of the appropriate treatment.

Indications that the debts are *not* an asset of the seller	Indications that the debts *are* an asset of the seller
Transfer is for a single non-returnable fixed sum.	Finance cost varies with speed of collection of debts, eg: • By adjustment to consideration for original transfer, or • Subsequent transfers priced to recover costs of earlier transfers.
There is no recourse to the seller for losses.	There is full recourse to the seller for losses.
Factor is paid all amounts received from the factored debts (and no more). Seller has no rights to further sums from the factor.	Seller is required to repay amounts received from the factor on or before a set date, regardless of timing or amounts of collections from debtors.

4.5.2 Required accounting

Where the seller has retained no significant risks and rewards relating to the debts and has no obligation to repay amounts received from the factor, the receivables should be removed from its statement of financial position and no liability shown in respect of the proceeds received from the factor. A profit or loss should be recognised, calculated as the difference between the carrying amount of the debts and the proceeds received. (IFRS 9: para. 3.2)

Where the seller does retain significant benefits and risks, a gross asset (equivalent in amount to the gross amount of the receivables) should be shown in the statement of financial position of the seller within assets, and a corresponding liability in respect of the proceeds received from the factor should be shown within liabilities. The interest element of the factor's charges should be recognised as it accrues and included in profit or loss with other interest charges. Other factoring costs should be similarly accrued. (IFRS 9: para. 3.2)

4.6 Example: factoring

Receivables can be factored **with recourse** (significant benefits and risks retained) or **without recourse** (benefits and risks not retained).

A company has a cash shortage and $50,000 of receivables collectible within the next three months. It sells the receivables to a factoring company for $40,000. The factoring company will collect and retain the full $50,000 as it falls due. The factoring company bears the liability for any bad debts. This is factoring **without recourse**.

A company has a cash shortage and $50,000 of receivables collectible within the next three months. It assigns the receivables to a factoring company in exchange for an advance totalling $42,000. If any of the debts are not paid within the three months, the advance paid for those debts must be repaid to the factor. The company therefore bears the liability for bad debts. This is factoring **with recourse**.

4.7 Re-classification of financial assets

Although on initial recognition financial instruments must be classified in accordance with the requirements of IFRS 9, in some cases they may be subsequently reclassified. IFRS 9 requires that **when an entity changes its business model for managing financial assets, it should reclassify all affected financial assets**. This reclassification applies only to **debt instruments**, as equity instruments must be classified as measured at fair value.

(IFRS 9: para. 4.4)

4.8 Classification of financial liabilities

On **recognition**, IFRS 9 requires that financial liabilities are **classified as measured** either:

(a)   **At fair value through profit or loss**, or
(b)   **At amortised cost**.

A financial liability is classified at fair value through profit or loss if:

(a)   It is **held for trading**, or
(b)   Upon initial recognition it is **designated at fair value through profit or loss**.   (IFRS 9: para. 4.2)

Derivatives are always measured at fair value through profit or loss.

Exam focus point

> A financial instrument can appear as an MCQ or as part of an accounts preparation question.

5 Measurement of financial instruments

FAST FORWARD

> Under IFRS 9 all financial assets should be initially measured at cost = fair value plus transaction costs. Financial liabilities should be measured at transaction price ie fair value of the consideration received.

5.1 Initial measurement

Financial instruments are initially measured at the **fair value** of the consideration given or received (ie, **cost**) **plus** (or minus in the case of financial liabilities) **transaction costs** that are **directly attributable** to the acquisition or issue of the financial instrument.

The **exception** to this rule is where a financial instrument is designated as **at fair value through profit or loss** (this term is explained below). In this case, **transaction costs** are **not** added to fair value at initial recognition.

(IFRS 9: para. 5.1)

The fair value of the consideration is normally the transaction price or market prices. If market prices are not reliable, the fair value may be **estimated** using a valuation technique (for example, by discounting cash flows).

5.2 Subsequent measurement of financial assets – debt instruments

After initial recognition, IFRS 9 requires an entity to measure financial assets at either **amortised cost**, **fair value through other comprehensive income** or **fair value through profit or loss** based on:

(a)   The entity's business model for managing the financial assets

(b)   The contractual cash flow characteristics of the financial asset

A financial asset is measured at **amortised cost** if both of the following conditions are met:

(a)   The asset is held within a business model whose objective is to hold assets in order to collect contractual cash flows.

(b)   The contractual terms of the financial asset give rise on specified dates to cash flows that are solely payments of principal and interest on the principal amount outstanding.

After initial recognition, all financial assets other than those held at fair value through profit or loss should be re-measured to either **fair value** or **amortised cost**.   (IFRS 9: para. 5.2)

IFRS 9 allows the option to **initially** measure a financial asset at **fair value through profit or loss** where a mismatch would otherwise arise between the asset and a related liability. In this case, the asset will also be **subsequently** measured at fair value through profit or loss.   (IFRS 9: para. 4.2)

Key terms

> A **financial asset or liability at fair value through profit or loss** meets either of the following conditions.
>
> (a)   It is classified as held for trading. A financial instrument is classified as held for trading if it is:
>
>   (i)   Acquired or incurred principally for the purpose of selling or repurchasing it in the near term
>
>   (ii)   Part of a portfolio of identified financial instruments that are managed together and for which there is evidence of a recent actual pattern of short-term profit-taking
>
> (b)   Upon initial recognition it is **designated** by the entity as at fair value through profit or loss.
>
> (IFRS 9: para. B4.1)

5.3 Financial assets at amortised cost

Assets held at **amortised cost** are measured using the **effective interest method**.

Key terms

> **Amortised cost of a financial asset or financial liability** is the amount at which the financial asset or liability is measured at initial recognition minus principal repayments, plus or minus the cumulative amortisation of any difference between that initial amount and the maturity amount, and minus any write-down for impairment or uncollectability.
>
> The **effective interest method** is a method of calculating the amortised cost of a financial instrument and of allocating the interest income or interest expense over the relevant period.
>
> The **effective interest rate** is the rate that exactly discounts estimated future cash payments or receipts through the expected life of the financial instrument to the net carrying amount.   (IFRS 9: App A)

5.4 Example: amortised cost

On 1 January 20X1 Abacus Co purchases a debt instrument for its fair value of $1,000. The debt instrument is due to mature on 31 December 20X5. The instrument has a principal amount of $1,250 and the instrument carries fixed interest at 4.72% that is paid annually. The effective rate of interest is 10%.

How should Abacus Co account for the debt instrument over its five year term?

Solution

Abacus Co will receive interest of $59 (1,250 × 4.72%) each year and $1,250 when the instrument matures.

Abacus Co must allocate the discount of $250 and the interest receivable over the five year term at a constant rate on the carrying amount of the debt. To do this, it must apply the effective interest rate of 10%.

The following table shows the allocation over the years.

Year	Amortised cost at beginning of year $	Profit or loss: Interest income for year (@10%) $	Interest received during year (cash inflow) $	Amortised cost at end of year $
20X1	1,000	100	(59)	1,041
20X2	1,041	104	(59)	1,086
20X3	1,086	109	(59)	1,136
20X4	1,136	113	(59)	1,190
20X5	1,190	119	(1,250 + 59)	–

Each year the carrying amount of the financial asset is increased by the interest income for the year and reduced by the interest actually received during the year.

This is a financial asset that has passed the cash flow test for measurement at amortised cost. If Abacus Co was **also** holding this instrument for trading, the IFRS 9 business model would allow it to be carried at fair value through other comprehensive income.

In this case, fair value changes will go through other comprehensive income; interest charges will be measured at amortised cost and go through **profit or loss**.

For instance, if at 1 January 20X2 the fair value of the debt instrument was $1,080, the difference of $39 (1,080 – 1,041) would go to OCI and the asset would be shown in the statement of financial position at $1,080.

5.5 Equity instruments

After initial recognition equity instruments are measured at either **fair value through profit or loss** (FVTPL) or **fair value through other comprehensive income** (FVTOCI).

If equity instruments are held at FVTPL no transaction costs are included in the carrying amount.

Equity instruments can be held at FVTOCI if:

(a)   They are not held for trading (ie the intention is to hold them for the long term to collect dividend income)

(b)   An irrevocable election is made at initial recognition to measure the investment at FVTOCI

If the investment is held at FVTOCI, all changes in fair value go through other comprehensive income. Only dividend income will appear in profit or loss.   (IFRS 9: para. 4.1.4)

| Question | Equity instrument |

In February 20X8 Bonce Co purchased 20,000 $1 listed equity shares at a price of $4 per share. Transaction costs were $2,000. At the year end of 31 December 20X8, these shares were trading at $5.50. A dividend of 20c per share was received on 30 September 20X8.

Show the financial statement extracts of Bonce Co at 31 December 20X8 relating to this investment on the basis that:

(a)   The shares were bought for trading (conditions for FVTOCI have not been met)
(b)   Conditions for FVTOCI have been met

Answer

(a)

	$
Statement of profit or loss	
Investment income (20,000 × (5.5 − 4.0))	30,000
Dividend income (20,000 × 20c)	4,000
Transaction costs	(2,000)
Statement of financial position	
Investments in equity instruments (20,000 × 5.5)	110,000

(b)

	$
Statement of profit or loss	
Dividend income	4,000
Other comprehensive income	
Gain on investment in equity instruments (20,000 × 5.5) − ((20,000 × 4) + 2,000)	28,000
Statement of financial position	
Investments in equity instruments (20,000 × 5.5)	110,000

Note that the solution would be the same (b) if an irrevocable election for FVTOCI had been made.

5.6 Subsequent measurement of financial liabilities

After initial recognition all financial liabilities should be measured at **amortised cost**, with the exception of financial liabilities at fair value through profit or loss. These should be measured at **fair value**, but where the fair value **is not capable of reliable measurement**, they should be measured at **cost**.

(IFRS 9: para. 4.2.1)

Question

Bond

Galaxy Co issues a bond for $503,778 on 1 January 20X2. No interest is payable on the bond, but it will be held to maturity and redeemed on 31 December 20X4 for $600,000. The bond has **not** been designated as at fair value through profit or loss. The effective interest rate is 6%.

Required

Calculate the charge to profit or loss in the financial statements of Galaxy Co for the year ended 31 December 20X2 and the balance outstanding at 31 December 20X2.

Answer

The bond is a 'deep discount' bond and is a financial liability of Galaxy Co. It is measured at amortised cost. Although there is no interest as such, the difference between the initial cost of the bond and the price at which it will be redeemed is a finance cost. This must be allocated over the term of the bond at a constant rate on the carrying amount. This is done by applying the effective interest rate.

The charge to profit or loss is $30,226 (503,778 × 6%).

The balance outstanding at 31 December 20X2 is $534,004 (503,778 + 30,226).

Stargazer Co issues 6% loan notes with a nominal value of $200,000. They are issued at a 5% discount and $1,700 of issue costs are incurred. The loan notes will be repayable at a premium of 10% after four years. The effective interest rate is 10%.

What amounts will be shown in the statement of profit or loss and statement of financial position at the end of years 1–4?

Answer

Year	Statement of profit or loss – Finance costs	Statement of financial position – 6% loan notes
	$	$
1	18,830	195,130
2	19,513	202,643
3	20,264	210,907
4	21,093	–

Working

		$
Year 1	Capital balance *	188,300
	Interest 10%	18,830
	Interest paid (200,000 × 6%)	(12,000)
Year 2 b/f		195,130
	Interest 10%	19,513
	Interest paid	(12,000)
Year 3 b/f		202,643
	Interest 10%	20264
	Interest paid	(12,000)
Year 4 b/f		210,907
	Interest (ß)**	21,093
	Interest paid	(12,000)
		220,000
	Capital repaid	(220,000)
		–

*((200,000 × 95%) − 1,700)

** Final interest amount is a balancing figure incorporating a $2 rounding.

In the exam you will **not** be expected to produce a full table like this, you will only need to produce relevant amounts for one or two years, but this is a useful layout to remember.

5.7 Own credit

IFRS 9 requires that financial liabilities which are **designated as measured at fair value through profit or loss are treated differently**. In this case the gain or loss in a period must be classified into:

- Gain or loss **resulting from credit risk**, and
- **Other** gain or loss.

This change to IFRS 9 was made in response to an anomaly regarding changes in the credit risk of a financial liability.
(IFRS 9: para. 5.5)

Changes in a financial liability's credit risk affect the fair value of that financial liability. This means that when an entity's creditworthiness deteriorates, the fair value of its issued debt will decrease (and *vice versa*). For financial liabilities measured using the fair value option, this causes **a gain (or loss) to be recognised in profit or loss for the year**. For example:

STATEMENT OF PROFIT OR LOSS AND OTHER COMPREHENSIVE INCOME (EXTRACT)
PROFIT OR LOSS FOR THE YEAR

	$'000
Liabilities at fair value (except derivatives and liabilities held for trading)	
Change in fair value	100

Many users of financial statements found this result to be **counter-intuitive** and confusing. Accordingly, IFRS 9 requires the gain or loss as a result of credit risk to be recognised in other comprehensive income (unless it creates or enlarges an **accounting mismatch**, in which case it is recognised in profit or loss). The other gain or loss (not the result of credit risk) is recognised in profit or loss.   (IFRS 9: para. 5.5.2)

IFRS 9 presentation

STATEMENT OF PROFIT OR LOSS AND OTHER COMPREHENSIVE INCOME (EXTRACT)

Profit or loss for the year

	$'000
Liabilities at fair value (except derivatives and liabilities held for trading)	
Change in fair value from own credit	90
Profit (loss) for the year	90

Other comprehensive income (not reclassified to profit or loss)

Fair value gain on financial liability attributable to change in credit risk	10
Total comprehensive income	100

5.8 Gains and losses

Instruments at **fair value through profit or loss**: gains and losses are recognised **in profit or loss**.

Financial instruments held at fair value: gains and losses are recognised in **profit or loss** unless the financial asset is an **equity instrument** and the entity made an election upon initial recognition to present gains and losses **directly in equity** through other comprehensive income. Dividends from the investment will be recognised in profit or loss.

Note that when an investment held at FVTOCI is sold, any gain or loss on disposal will also go through OCI and be held in reserves. At disposal entities are permitted to transfer the total gains and/or losses on the investment to retained earnings, but these amounts will not appear in any statement of profit or loss.

Financial instruments carried at **amortised cost**: gains and losses are recognised **in profit or loss** as a result of the amortisation process **and** when the asset is derecognised.

Financial assets held within a business model whose objective is achieved by **both collecting contractual cash flows** and selling financial assets **must** be measured at **fair value** with gains and losses recognised in **other comprehensive income**.   (IFRS 9: para. 5.7)

5.9 Impairment and uncollectability of financial assets

The new impairment model in IFRS 9 is based on providing for **expected** losses (rather than dealing with losses after they have arisen) and applies to financial assets held at **amortised cost and FVTOCI**. The financial statements should reflect the general pattern of deterioration or improvement in the credit quality of financial instruments.

On **initial recognition** of the asset the entity creates a credit loss allowance equal to **12 months' expected credit losses**. This is calculated by multiplying the probability of a default occurring in the next 12 months by the expected credit losses that would result from that default.

If credit risk increases significantly **subsequent to** initial recognition, the allowance recorded to represent 12 months' expected credit losses is replaced by an allowance for **lifetime expected credit losses**. If credit quality then improves, the 12 month loss basis is reinstated.

The movement in the allowance is recognised as an impairment gain or loss in profit or loss.

(IFRS 9: para. 5.5)

5.9.1 Financial assets carried at fair value through profit or loss

On financial assets carried at fair value gains and losses are recognised in **profit or loss**. Any impairment loss should be **recognised in net profit or loss for the year** even though the financial asset has not been derecognised.

The impairment loss is the difference between its **acquisition cost** (net of any principal repayment and amortisation) and **current fair value** (for equity instruments) or recoverable amount (for debt instruments), less any impairment loss on that asset previously recognised in profit or loss.

(IFRS 9: para. 5.7)

Chapter Roundup

- A financial instrument gives rise to a financial asset of one entity and a financial liability or equity instrument of another. (IAS 32: para. 11)

- The important definitions to learn are:
  - Financial asset
  - Financial liability
  - Equity instrument

- The objective of IAS 32 is to establish principles for presenting financial instruments or equity. (IAS 32: para. 2)

- IFRS 7 replaces the disclosure requirements which were previously in IAS 32.

- IFRS 9 *Financial instruments* establishes principles for recognising and measuring financial assets and liabilities. (IFRS 9: IN1)

- Under IFRS 9 all financial assets should be initially measured at cost = fair value plus transaction costs. Financial liabilities should be measured at transaction price ie fair value of the consideration received.

Quick Quiz

1. Which issues are dealt with by IAS 32?

2. Define the following.

   (a) Financial asset
   (b) Financial liability
   (c) Equity instrument

3. What is the critical feature used to identify a financial liability?

4. How should compound instruments be classified by the issuer?

5. When should a financial asset be de-recognised?

6. How are financial instruments initially measured?

7. Where should redeemable preference shares appear in the statement of financial position?

Answers to Quick Quiz

1   Classification between liabilities and equity; presentation

2   See Key Terms, Section 1.2.

3   The contractual obligation to deliver cash or another financial asset to the holder

4   By calculating the present value of the liability component and then deducting this from the instrument as a whole to leave a residual value for the equity component

5   Financial assets should be derecognised when the rights to the cash flows from the asset expire or where substantially all the risks and rewards of ownership are transferred to another party.

6   At fair value plus transaction costs

7   Under non-current liabilities (not equity)

Now try the question below from the Practice Question Bank

Number	Level	Marks	Time
18	–	10	20 mins

Leasing

12

Topic list	Syllabus reference
1 IFRS 16	B6
2 Lessee accounting	B6
3 Sale and leaseback	B6

Introduction

Leasing transactions are extremely common so this is an important practical subject. Lease accounting is regulated by IFRS 16, which replaces IAS 17.

IFRS 16 represents the completion of the IASB's project to end off balance sheet accounting for leases.

Lessor – owns the Asset
Lessee – leases the Asset

Study guide

		Intellectual level
B6	**Leasing**	
(a)	Account for right-of-use assets and lease liabilities in the records of the lessee.	2
(b)	Explain the exemption from the recognition criteria for leases in the records of the lessee.	2
(c)	Account for sale and leaseback agreements	2

Exam guide

You are quite likely to meet a lease in an accounts preparation question.

1 IFRS 16

FAST FORWARD IFRS 16 was brought in to remedy the non-recognition of liabilities for assets held under operating leases.

1.1 Objective

IFRS 16 sets out the principles for the recognition, measurement, presentation and disclosure of leases. The objective is to ensure that lessees and lessors provide relevant information in a manner that faithfully represents those transactions (IFRS 16: para. IN1).

It replaces IAS 17, which required lessees and lessors to classify their leases as either finance leases or operating leases and account for these two types of lease differently. IAS 17 did not require lessees to recognise assets and liabilities arising from operating leases (IFRS 16: para. IN5). IFRS 16 was brought in to remedy this.

1.2 Main features

MateRiaLity

IFRS 16 introduces a single lessee accounting model and requires a lessee to recognise assets and liabilities for all leases with a term of more than twelve months, unless the underlying asset is of low value. For short-term leases or low value assets, the lease payments are simply charged to profit or loss as an expense (see below).

For all other leases, the lessee recognises a right-of-use asset, representing its right to use the underlying asset and a lease liability representing its obligation to make lease payments (IFRS 16: para. IN10). For lessors, there is little change from the IAS 17 requirements. Lessors will continue to recognise the distinction between finance and operating leases.

1.3 Recognition exemptions

IFRS 16 provides an optional exemption from the full requirements of the standard for:

(a) **Short-term leases.** These are leases with a lease term of twelve months or less. This election is made by class of underlying asset. A lease that contains a purchase option cannot be a short-term lease.

9'''' pg3i short term lease less than 12month being rentals to ptc

(b) **Low value leases.** These are leases where the underlying asset has a low value when new (such as tablet and personal computers or small items of office furniture and telephones). This election can be made on a lease-by-lease basis. An underlying asset qualifies as low value only if two conditions apply:

(i) The lessee can benefit from using the underlying asset.

(ii) The underlying asset is not highly dependent on, or highly interrelated with, other assets. (IFRS 16: para. B5)

There is not a specific amount stated under IFRS 16 defining 'low value', but examples given include personal computers and telephones (IFRS 16: para.B8)

If the entity elects to take the exemption, **lease payments are recignised as an expense** on a straight-line basis over the lease term (or other systematic basis) (IFRS 16: para.6)

1.4 Identifying a lease

A contract is, or contains, a lease if the contract conveys the **right to control** the use of an identified asset for a period of time in exchange for consideration (IFRS 16: para. 9). The contract may contain other elements which are not leases, such as a service contract. These other components must be separated out from the lease and separately accounted for, allocating the consideration on the basis of the stand-alone prices of the lease and non-lease components (IFRS 16: para. 13).

Leasing a car over 5 years

The right to control the use of an identified asset depends on the lessee having:

(a) The right to obtain substantially all of the economic benefits from use of the identified asset; and

(b) The right to direct the use of the identified asset (IFRS 16: para. B9). This arises if either:

(i) The customer has the right to direct how and for what purpose the asset is used during the whole of its period of use, or

(ii) The relevant decisions about use are pre-determined and the customer can operate the asset without the supplier having the right to change those operating instructions.

A lessee does not control the use of an identified asset if the lessor can substitute the underlying asset for another asset during the lease term and would benefit economically from doing so. (IFRS 16: para. B14)

Key terms

> **Lease.** A contract, or part of a contract, that conveys the right to use an asset, **the underlying asset**, for a period of time in exchange for consideration.
>
> **Underlying asset.** An asset that is the subject of a lease, for which the right to use that asset has been provided by a **lessor** to a **lessee**.
>
> **Right-of-use asset.** An asset that represents a lessee's right to use an **underlying asset** for the **lease term**.
>
> - **Lease payments.** Payments made by a **lessee** to a **lessor** relating to the right to use an **underlying asset** during the **lease term**, comprising:
>   (a) fixed payments, less any **lease incentives**
>   (b) **variable lease payments** that depend on an index or rate
>   (c) the exercise price of a purchase option if the lessee is reasonably certain to exercise that option
>   (d) payment of lease termination penalties if applicable
>
> - **Interest rate implicit in the lease.**
>   The discount rate that, at the inception of the lease, causes the aggregate present value of:
>   (a) The lease payments, and
>   (b) The **unguaranteed residual value**

to be equal to the sum of:

(a)   The fair value of the **underlying asset**, and

(b)   Any initial direct costs.

- **Lessee's incremental borrowing rate**. The rate of interest that a **lessee** would have to pay to borrow over a similar term, and with a similar security, the funds necessary to obtain an asset of similar value to the **right of use asset** in a similar economic environment.

- **Unguaranteed residual value**. That portion of the residual value of the underlying asset, the realisation of which by the lessor is not assured.

- **Variable lease payments**. The portion of payments made by a **lessee** to a **lessor** for the right to use an **underlying asset** during the **lease term** that varies because of changes in facts or circumstances occurring after the commencement date, other than the passage of time.

- **Lease term.** The non-cancellable period for which the lessee has contracted to lease the asset together with any further terms for which the lessee has the option to continue to lease the asset, with or without further payment, when at the inception of the lease it is reasonably certain that the lessee will exercise the option and any periods covered by an option to terminate the lease if the lessee is reasonably certain not to exercise that option   (IFRS 16: para. 18)

- **Short-term lease**. A lease that at the commencement date has a term of 12 months or less and does not contain a purchase option.

- **Lease incentives**. Payments made by the **lessor** to the **lessee**, or the reimbursement or assumption by the lessor of costs of the lessee.   (IFRS 16: Appendix A)

Note. In an exam question you will be given the interest rate implicit in the lease.

1.5 Identifying a lease: examples

[Handwritten note: Previous exam question. Who's controlling the asset? Who gets all the economic benefit of the asset?]

The following flowchart, taken from IFRS 16 Appendix B (para. B31)

```
┌─────────────────────────────────────┐
│  Is there an identified asset?       │──── No ────┐
│  Consider paragraphs B13–B20.        │            │
└─────────────────────────────────────┘            │
                │ Yes                               │
                ▼                                    │
┌─────────────────────────────────────┐            │
│  Does the customer have the right to │            │
│  obtain substantially all of the     │            │
│  economic benefits from use of the   │──── No ────┤
│  asset throughout the period of use? │            │
│  Consider paragraphs B21–B23.        │            │
└─────────────────────────────────────┘            │
                │ Yes                               │
                ▼                                    │
┌─────────────────────────────────────┐            │
│  Does the customer, the supplier or  │            │
│  neither party have the right to     │            │
Customer│  direct how and for what purpose │ Supplier│
│  the asset is used throughout the    │            │
│  period of use?                      │            │
│  Consider paragraphs B25–B30.        │            │
└─────────────────────────────────────┘            │
                │                                    │
        Neither; how and for what                   │
        purpose the asset will be                   │
        used is predetermined                       │
                ▼                                    │
┌─────────────────────────────────────┐            │
│  Does the customer have the right to │            │
│  operate the asset throughout the    │            │
Yes│  period of use, without the supplier │         │
│  having the right to change those    │            │
│  operating instructions?             │            │
│  Consider paragraph B24(b)(i).       │            │
└─────────────────────────────────────┘            │
                │ No                                 │
                ▼                                    │
┌─────────────────────────────────────┐            │
│  Did the customer design the asset   │            │
│  in a way that predetermines how and │──── No ────┤
│  for what purpose the asset will be  │            │
│  used throughout the period of use?  │            │
│  Consider paragraph B24(b)(ii).      │            │
└─────────────────────────────────────┘            │
                │                                    │
                ▼                                    ▼
    ( The contract contains a lease )   ( The contract does not
                                          contain a lease )
```

1.5.1 Example 1: Is it a lease?

Coketown Council has entered into a five-year contract with Carefleet Co, under which Carefleet Co supplies the council with ten vehicles for the purposes of community transport. Carefleet Co owns the relevant vehicle, all ten of which are specified in the contract. Coketown Council determines the routes taken for community transport and the charges and eligibility for discounts. The council can choose to use the vehicles for purposes other than community transport. When the vehicles are not being used, they are kept at the council's offices and cannot be retrieved by Carefleet Co unless Coketown Council defaults on payment. If a vehicle needs to be serviced or repaired, Carefleet Co is obliged to provide a temporary replacement vehicle of the same type.

Conclusion: this is a lease. There is an identifiable asset, the ten vehicles specified in the contract. The council has a right to use the vehicles for the period of the contract. Carefleet Co does not have the right to substitute any of the vehicles unless they are being serviced or repaired. Therefore Coketown Council would need to recognise a right-of-use asset and a lease liability in its statement of financial position.

1.5.2 Example 2: Is it a lease?

Broketown Council has recently made substantial cuts to its community transport service. It will now provide such services only in cases of great need, assessed on a case by case basis. It has entered into a two-year contract with Fleetcar Co for the use of one of its minibuses for this purpose. The minibus must seat ten people, but Fleetcar Co can use any of its ten-seater minibuses when required. The minibuses are held on Fleetcar Co's premises and are only made available to Broketown Council on request.

Conclusion: this is not a lease. There is no identifiable asset. Fleetcar Co can exchange one minibus for another. Therefore, Broketown Council should account for the rental payments as an expense in profit or loss.

1.5.3 Example 3: Is it a lease?

This example is based on illustrative example 3 from IFRS 16 illustrative examples.

Kabal Co enters into a ten-year contract with a utilities company (TelenewCo) for the right to use three specified, physically distinct dark fibres within a larger fibre-optic cable connecting North Town to South Town. Kabal Co makes the decisions about the use of the fibres by connecting each end of the fibres to its electronic equipment (ie Kabal Co 'lights' the fibres and decides what data, and how much data, those fibres will transport). If the fibres are damaged, TelenewCo is responsible for the repairs and maintenance. TelenewCo owns extra fibres, but can substitute those for Kabal Co's fibres only for reasons of repairs, maintenance or malfunction (and is obliged to substitute the fibres in these cases).

Conclusion: this is a lease. The contract contains a lease of dark fibres. Kabal Co has the right to use the three dark fibres for ten years.

There are three identified fibres. The fibres are explicitly specified in the contract and are physically distinct from other fibres within the cable. TelenewCo cannot substitute the fibres other than for reasons of repairs, maintenance or malfunction (IFRS 16: para. B18).

Kabal Co has the right to control the use of the fibres throughout the ten-year period of use because:

(a)   Kabal Co has the right to obtain substantially all of the economic benefits from use of the fibres over the ten-year period of use and Kabal Co has exclusive use of the fibres throughout the period of use.

(b)   Kabal Co has the right to direct the use of the fibres because IFRS 16: Para B24 applies:

   (i)   The customer has the right to direct how and for what purpose the asset is used during the whole of its period of use, or

   (ii)   The relevant decisions about use are pre-determined and the customer can operate the asset without the supplier having the right to change those operating instructions.

Kabal Co makes the relevant decisions about how and for what purpose the fibres are used by deciding (i) when and whether to light the fibres and (ii) when and how much output the fibres will produce (ie what data, and how much data, those fibres will transport). Kabal Co has the right to change these decisions during the ten-year period of use.

Although TelenewCo's decisions about repairing and maintaining the fibres are essential to their efficient use, those decisions do not give TelenewCo the right to direct how and for what purpose the fibres are used. Consequently, TelenewCo does not control the use of the fibres during the period of use.

1.6 Initial measurement of the right-of-use asset

The right-of-use asset is initially measured at cost. This comprises:

(a)   The amount of the initial measurement of the lease liability

(b)   Any lease payments made before the commencement date, less any lease incentives received

(c)   Any initial direct costs incurred by the lessee

(d)   Any costs which the lessee will incur for dismantling and removing the underlying asset or restoring the site at the end of the lease term

[Handwritten margin notes: Lease term 4 years. Intended to use the asset in production 3 years.]

Subsequently, the right-of-use asset is **normally measured** at **cost less accumulated depreciation and impairment losses** in accordance with the cost model of IAS 16 *Property, plant and equipment* (IFRS 16: para. 29).

Under this model, the right-of-use asset is **depreciated** from the commencement date to the **earlier of** the **end of its useful life** or the **end of the lease term.** However, if ownership of the underlying asset is expected to be transferred to the lessee at the end of the lease, the right-of-use asset should be depreciated over the **useful life** of the underlying asset (IFRS 16: paras. 31 and 32).

Alternatively, the right-of-use asset is accounted for in accordance with:

(a)   The **revaluation model of IAS 16.** This is **optional** where the right-of-use asset relates to a class of property, plant and equipment which is measured under the revaluation model, and where elected, must apply to all right-of-use assets relating to that class; or

(b)   The **fair value model of IAS 40** *Investment property.* This is **compulsory** if the right-of-use asset meets the definition of investment property and the lessee uses the fair value model for its investment property.

1.7 Initial measurement of the lease liability

At the commencement date the lease liability is measured at the present value of future lease payments, including any expected payments at the end of the lease, discounted at the interest rate implicit in the lease (IFRS 16: para. 24). If that rate cannot be readily determined, the lessee's incremental borrowing rate should be used (IFRS 16: para. 26).

1.8 Subsequent measurement of the right-of-use asset

After the commencement date the right-of-use asset should be measured using the cost model in IAS 16, unless it is an investment property or belongs to a class of assets to which the revaluation model applies (IFRS 16: para. 29).

If the lease transfers ownership of the underlying asset at the end of the lease term or if the cost reflects a purchase option which the lessee is expected to exercise, the right-of-use asset should be depreciated over the useful life of the underlying asset. *[Handwritten: if there is a purchase option you depreciate]*

If there is no transfer of ownership and no purchase option, the right-of-use asset should be depreciated from the commencement date to the earlier of the end of the useful life and the end of the lease term (IFRS 16: paras. 31, 32).

1.9 Subsequent measurement of lease liability
[Handwritten: Bank loan increased by interest decreased by repayments]

After the commencement date the carrying amount of the lease liability is increased by interest charges on the outstanding liability and reduced by lease payments made (IFRS 16: para. 36).

2 Lessee accounting

FAST FORWARD

For lessees, IFRS 16 removes the distinction between finance leases and operating leases which was a feature of IAS 17.

2.1 Presentation
[Handwritten: you have to disclose value of leased asset]

In the statement of financial position right-of use assets can be presented on a separate line under non-current assets or they can be included in the total of corresponding underlying assets and disclosed in the notes.

Lease liabilities should be either presented separately from other liabilities or disclosed in the notes (IFRS 16: para. 47).

IFRS 16 does not specify that lease liabilities should be split between non-current and current liabilities, but this should be done as best practice.

2.2 Allocating the finance charge

As the company benefits from paying the lease over a period of time, when the lessee makes a rental payment, it will comprise two elements:

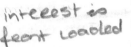 *interest is front loaded*

(a) **Interest portion of the payment**. The interest is referred to as an interest charge or finance charge and it appears in the statement of profit or loss of the lessee.

(b) A repayment of part of the **capital cost** of the asset. In the lessee's books this proportion of each rental payment must be debited to the lessor's account to reduce the outstanding liability.

The accounting problem is to decide what proportion of each instalment paid by the lessee represents interest, and what proportion represents a repayment of the capital advanced by the lessor. This is done using the actuarial method, where the interest rate implicit in the lease is used to determine the finance charge and the balance of the payment is the repayment of capital.

The **actuarial method**, used by IFRS 16, requires the finance charge to be **allocated** to periods during the lease term so as to produce a constant periodic rate of interest on the remaining balance of the liability for each period, ie applying the interest rate implicit in the lease (the lease's internal rate of return) to the amount of capital outstanding to calculate the finance charge for the period. (The lessee's incremental borrowing rate may be used if the interest rate implicit in the lease cannot be determined.)

Consequently, at the **start** of the lease the **finance charges will be large** as the outstanding lease liability is large. Towards **the end** of the lease's life, the **finance charge will be smaller** as the outstanding lease liability is smaller.

2.3 Example: allocating the finance charge

[This example is based on IFRS 16 Illustrative example 13]

Lion Co enters into a five-year lease of a building which has a remaining useful life of ten years. Lease payments are $50,000 per annum, payable at the beginning of each year.

Lion Co incurs initial direct costs of $20,000 and receives lease incentives of $5,000. There is no transfer of the asset at the end of the lease and no purchase option.

The interest rate implicit in the lease is not immediately determinable but the lessee's incremental borrowing rate is 5%.

At the commencement date Lion Co pays the initial $50,000, incurs the direct costs and receives the lease incentives. *– gives you money back lessee.*

Step 1: Calculate the lease liability

The lease liability is measured at the present value of the remaining four payments:

	$
$50,000/1.05 *year 2*	47,619
$50,000/1.05² *year 3*	45,351
$50,000/1.05³ *year 4*	43,192
$50,000/1.05⁴ *year 5*	41,135
	177,297

Step 2: Calculate the value of the Right-of-use asset

	$
Initial payment	50,000
Discounted liability	177,297
Initial direct costs	20,000
Incentives received	(5,000)
	242,297

Record the transaction in the financial statements

Assets and liabilities would initially be recognised as follows:

		Debit $	Credit $
Right-to-use asset		242,297	
Lease liability			177,297
Cash	(50,000 + 20,000 – 5,000)		65,000
		242,297	242,297

At the end of year 1, the liability will be measured as:

	$
Opening balance	177,297
Interest 5%	8,865 ✳
	186,162
Current liability	50,000
Non-current liability	136,162
	186,162

The right of use asset will be depreciated over five years, being the shorter of the lease term and the useful life of the underlying asset.

Now we will see how this would work out if the lease payments were made **in arrears**.

At the commencement date the lessee would incur the direct costs and receive the lease incentives.

Step 1: Calculate the lease liability

The lease would be measured at the present value of **five** payments:

	$
$50,000/1.05	47,619
$50,000/1.05^2	45,351
$50,000/1.05^3	43,192
$50,000/1.05^4	41,135
$50,000/1.05^5	39,176
	216,473

Step 2: Calculate the value of the Right-of-use asset

Discounted liability	216,473
Direct costs	20,000
Lease incentives	(5,000)
	231,473

Record the transaction in the financial statements

Assets and liabilities would initially be recognised as follows:

	Debit $	Credit $
Right-of-use asset	231,473	
Lease liability		216,473
Cash (20,000 – 5,000)		15,000
	231,473	231,473

At the end of year 1, the liability will be measured as:

	$
Opening balance	216,473
Interest 5%	10,824
Lease payment year 1	(50,000)
Year-end balance	177,297

In order to ascertain the split between non-current and current liabilities, we work out the balance at the end of year 2:

	$
Opening balance	177,297
Interest 5%	8,865
Lease payment year 2	(50,000)
Year-end balance	136,162

The statement of financial position will show:

	$
Non-current liability	136,162
Current liability (177,297 – 136,162)	41,135
	177,297

Note that when payments are made in arrears the next instalment due will contain interest, so this is effectively deducted to arrive at the capital repayment.

2.4 Calculation of the lease liability

The calculation of the lease liability to be included in the financial statements can be summarised as follows. Here the lease commencement date is 1.1.X1 and the interest rate implicit in the lease is x%.

If lease payments are made in arrears:

		$
1.1.X1	Lease liability (present value of future lease payments)	X
1.1.X1 – 31.12.X1	Interest at x%	X
31.12.X1	Instalment in arrears	(X)
31.12.X1	**Liability carried down**	**X**
1.1.X2 – 31.12.X2	Interest at x%	X
31.12.X2	Instalment in arrears	(X)
31.12.X2	**Liability due in more than 1 year**	**X**

If lease payments are made in advance:

		$
1.1.X1	Lease liability (present value of future lease payments)	X
1.1.X1 – 31.12.X1	Interest at x%	X $\longrightarrow$
31.12.X1	**Liability carried down**	**X**
1.1.X2	Instalment in advance	(X)
	Liability due in more than 1 year	**X**

Aqua Co makes up its accounts to 31 December each year. It enters into a lease (as a lessee) to lease an item of equipment with the following terms:

Inception of lease:	1 January 20X1
Term:	Five years: $2,000 paid at commencement of lease, followed by four payments of $2,000 payable at the start of each subsequent year
Fair value:	$8,000
Present value of future lease payments:	$6,075
Useful life:	Eight years
Interest rate implicit in the lease:	12%

Required

Show how should this lease should be accounted for in Aqua Co's statement of financial position as at 31 December 20X1.

Answer

STATEMENT OF FINANCIAL POSITION AS AT 31 DECEMBER 20X1 (EXTRACT)

	$
Non-current assets	
Right-of-use asset (W1)	6,460
Non-current liabilities	
Lease liability (W2)	4,804
Current liabilities	
Lease liability ((6,804 – 4,804) W2)	2,000

Workings

1   Right-of-use asset

	$
Initial measurement of lease liability	6,075
Payments made before or at commencement of lease	2,000
Right-of-use asset	8,075

Depreciate over the shorter of the useful life or the lease term:

Depreciation charge = $8,075/5 = $1,615

Carrying amount at 31.12.X1 = $8,075 – $1,615 = $6,460

2   Lease liability

		$
1.1.X1	Liability b/d	6,075
1.1.X1 – 31.12.X1	Interest at 12%	729
31.12.X1	**Liability c/d**	**6,804**
1.1.X2	Instalment 2 (in advance)	(2,000)
1.1.X2	**Liability due in more than one year**	**4,804**

2.5 Disclosure requirements for lessees

The objective of the disclosure requirements is to allow users to assess the effect that leases have on the financial position, financial performance and cash flows of the lessee (IFRS 16: para. 51).
Amounts to be disclosed include:

- Depreciation charge for right-of-use assets

- Interest expense on lease liabilities

- Expenses relating to short-term and low-value leases

- Details of sale and leaseback transactions

- The carrying amount of right-of-use assets at the end of the reporting period, by class of underlying asset

- Additions to right-of-use assets

3 Sale and leaseback

FAST FORWARD

A sale and leaseback transaction involves the sale of an asset and the leasing back of the same asset.

IFRS 16 requires an initial assessment to be made regarding whether or not the transfer constitutes a sale. This is done by determining when the performance obligation is satisfied in accordance with IFRS 15 *Revenue from Contracts with Customers* (IFRS 16: para. 98).

3.1 Transfer is a sale

If the transfer satisfies the IFRS 15 requirement to be accounted for as a sale:

- The seller/lessee measures the right-of-use asset arising from the leaseback at the proportion of the previous carrying amount of the asset that relates to the **right-of use retained** by the seller/lessee. This is calculated as:

$$\text{Carrying amount} \times \frac{\text{discounted lease payments}}{\text{fair value}}$$

- The seller/lessee **only recognises the amount of any gain or loss** on the sale that relates to the **rights transferred** to the buyer (IFRS 16: para. 100). This can be calculated in three stages:

Stage 1: Calculate the total gain   Total gain = fair value – carrying amount

Stage 2: Calculate the gain that relates to the **rights retained**:

$$\text{Gain} \times \frac{\text{discounted lease payments}}{\text{fair value}} = \text{Gain relating to rights retained}$$

Stage 3: The gain relating to **rights transferred** is the balancing figure:

Gain on rights transferred = total gain (Stage 1) – gain on rights retained (Stage 2)

The right-of-use asset continues to be **depreciated as normal**, although a revision of its remaining useful life may be necessary to restrict it to the lease term.

3.1.1 Example: sale and leaseback where the transfer is a sale

On 1 April 20X2, Wigton Co bought an injection moulding machine for $600,000. The carrying amount of the machine as at 31 March 20X3 was $500,000. On 1 April 20X3, Wigton Co sold it to Whitehaven Co for $740,000, its fair value. Wigton Co immediately leased the machine back for five years, the remainder of its useful life, at $160,000 per annum payable in arrears. The present value of the annual lease payments is $700,000 and the transaction satisfies the IFRS 15 criteria to be recognised as a sale.

Required

What gain should Wigton Co recognise for the year ended 31 March 20X4 as a result of the sale and leaseback?

Solution

Stage 1: Total gain on the sale

= fair value − carrying amount

= $740,000 − $500,000 = $240,000

Stage 2: Gain relating to the rights retained

$= \text{Gain} \times \dfrac{\text{discounted lease payments}}{\text{fair value}}$

= $(240,000 × 700,000/740,000)

= $227,027

Stage 3: Gain relating to the rights transferred = total gain (Stage 1) − gain on rights retained (Stage 2)

= $240,000 − $227,027

= $12,973

Wigton Co should recognise a gain of $12,973 for the year ended 31 March 20X4 as a result of the sale and leaseback.

If the fair value of the consideration for the sale does not equal the fair value of the asset, or if the lease payments are not at market rates, the following adjustments should be made:

- Any below-market terms should be accounted for as a prepayment of lease payments (the shortfall in consideration received from the lessor is treated as a lease payment made by the lessee)

- Any above-market terms are accounted for as additional financing provided by the buyer/lessor (the additional amount paid by the lessor is treated as additional liability, **not** as gain on the sale) (IFRS 16: para. 101)

3.2 Transfer is not a sale

If the transfer does not satisfy the IFRS 15 requirements to be accounted for as a sale, the seller continues to recognise the transferred asset and the transfer proceeds are treated as a financial liability, accounted for in accordance with IFRS 9. The transaction is more in the nature of a secured loan.

3.3 Example: sale and leaseback not on market terms

[Adapted from IFRS 16 Illustrated example 24]

Bungle Co sells a building to the Zippy Co for $800,000 cash. The carrying amount of the building prior to the sale was $600,000. Bungle Co arranges to lease the building back for five years at $120,000 per annum, payable in arrears. The remaining useful life is 15 years. At the date of sale the fair value of the building was $750,000 and the interest rate implicit in the lease is 4.5%.

The transaction **satisfies the performance obligations in IFRS 15**, so will be accounted for as a sale and leaseback.

At the date of sale the fair value of the building was $750,000, so the **excess** $50,000 paid by Zippy Co is **recognised as additional financing** provided by Bungle Co

Step 1. The lease liability must be calculated.

The interest rate implicit in the lease is 4.5% therefore the present value of the annual payments is calculate as follows:

	$
120,000/1.045	114,833
120,000/1.045^2	109,888
120,000/1.045^3	105,155
120,000/1.045^4	100,627
120,000/1.045^5	96,294
	526,797

Of this, **$476,797 ($526,797 – $50,000) relates to the lease** and **$50,000 relates to the additional financing**.

Step 2. The right-of-use assets must be measured

At the commencement date, Bungle Co measures the right-of-use asset arising from the leaseback of the building at the proportion of the previous carrying amount of the building that relates to the right-of-use retained.

This is calculated as

Right-of-use asset (arising from leaseback) = carrying amount × discounted lease payments/fair value.

Therefore: $600,000 × 476,797/750,000 = $381,437

The right-of-use asset will be **depreciated** over five years, being the shorter of the lease term and the useful life of the asset.

Step 3. The gain on the sale and leaseback must be calculated.

Bungle Co only recognises the amount of gain that relates to the rights transferred:

Stage 1: Total gain on the sale	= fair value – carrying amount
	= $750,000 – $600,000
	= $150,000
Stage 2: Gain relating to the rights retained	= Gain × $\dfrac{\text{discounted lease payments}}{\text{fair value}}$
	= $(150,000 × 476,797/750,000)
	= $95,360
Stage 3: Gain relating to the rights transferred	= total gain (Stage 1) – gain on rights retained (Stage 2)
	= $150,000 – $95,360
	= $54,640

Step 4. The transaction must be recorded in Bungle Co's accounts

At the commencement date the transaction is recorded as follows:

	Debit $	Credit $
Cash	800,000	
Right-of-use asset	381,437	
Building		600,000
Financial liability		526,797
Gain on rights transferred		54,640
	1,181,437	1,181,437

The right-of-use asset will be depreciated over five years, the gain will be recognised in profit or loss and the financial liability will be increased each year by the interest charge and reduced by the lease payments.

Capital Co entered into a sale and leaseback on 1 April 20X7. It sold a lathe with a carrying amount of $300,00 for $400,000 (equivalent to fair value) and leased it back over a five-year period, equivalent to its remaining useful life. The transaction constitutes a sale in accordance with IFRS 15.

The lease provided for five annual payments in arrears of $90,000. The rate of interest implicit in the lease is 5%.

Required

What are the amounts to be recognised in the financial statements at 31 March 20X8 in respect of this transaction?

Answer

(1)   Calculate the lease liability at the commencement date

	$
90,000/1.05	85,714
90,000/1.05^2	81,633
90,000/1.05^3	77,745
90,000/1.05^4	74,043
90,000/1.05^5	70,517
	389,652

(2)   Measure the right-of-use asset = carrying amount × discounted lease payments/fair value

= 300,000 × 389,652/400,000

= $292,239

(3)   Calculate the gain on the sale and leaseback

Stage 1: Total gain on the sale	= fair value − carrying amount
	= $400,000 − $300,000
	= $100,000

Stage 2: Gain relating to the rights retained $= \text{Gain} \times \dfrac{\text{discounted lease payments}}{\text{fair value}}$

= $(100,000 × 389,652/400,000)

= $97,413

Stage 3: Gain relating to the rights transferred = total gain (Stage 1) − gain on rights retained (Stage 2)

= $100,000 − $97,413

= $2,587

(4)   Record the transaction in the accounts

	Debit $	Credit $
Cash	400,000	
Right of use asset	292,239	
Underlying asset		300,000
Liability		389,652
Gain on transfer		2,587
	692,239	692,239

The transaction will be shown in the financial statements as follows:

$

Statement of profit or loss

	$
Gain on transfer	2,587
Depreciation (292,239/5)	(38,448)
Interest (W)	(19,483)

Statement of financial position

Non-current asset

	$
Right-of-use asset	292,239

Non-current liabilities

	$
Lease liability (W)	245,092

Current liabilities

	$
Lease liability (319,135 – 245,092) (W)	74,043

Working – lease liability

		$
1.4.X7	Lease liability (present value of future lease payments)	389,652
1.4.X7 – 31.3.X8	Interest at 5%	19,483
31.3.X8	Instalment paid in arrears	(90,000)
31.3.X8	**Liability carried down**	319,135
1.4.X8 – 31.3.X9	Interest at 5%	15,957
31.3.X9	Instalment paid in arrears	(90,000)
31.3.X9	**Liability due in more than 1 year**	245,092

Current liabilities reflect the amount of the finance lease liability that will become due within 12 months.

Chapter Roundup

- IFRS 16 was brought in to remedy the non-recognition of liabilities for assets held under operating leases.

- For lessees, IFRS 16 removes the distinction between finance and operating leases which was a feature of IAS 17.

- A sale and leaseback transaction involves the sale of an asset and the leasing back of the same asset.

Quick Quiz

1   A contract is, or contains, a lease if the contract conveys the right to …. an identified asset for a period of time in exchange for …. (IFRS 16: para. 9).

2   Business Co acquires an asset under a high-value, five-year lease. What is the double entry?

3   List the disclosures required under IFRS 16 for lessees.

4   A lorry has an expected useful life of six years. It is acquired under a four year finance lease. Over which period should it be depreciated?

5   Space Co leases a tablet computer. How should this lease be treated in its financial statements?

Answers to Quick Quiz

1   A contract is, or contains, a lease if the contract conveys the right to **control the use of** an identified asset for a period of time in exchange for **consideration** (IFRS 16: para. 9).

2   DEBIT   Right-of-use asset account
             CREDIT   Lease liability

3   See Section 2.4.

4   The four year term, being the shorter of the lease term and the useful life

5   This is a low-value lease, so Space Co should recognise the lease rentals as an expense over the lease term.

Now try the questions below from the Practice Question Bank

Number	Level	Marks	Time
24	–	10	20 mins
25	–	10	20 mins

13

Provisions and events after the reporting period

Topic list	Syllabus reference
1 Provisions	B7
2 Provisions for restructuring	B7
3 Contingent liabilities and contingent assets	B7
4 IAS 10: *Events after the reporting period*	B7

Introduction

You will have met IAS 37 and IAS 10 in your earlier studies. However, you will be asked in more detail about them for Financial Reporting

Study guide

		Intellectual level
B7	**Provisions and events after the reporting period**	
(a)	Explain why an accounting standard on provisions is necessary	2
(b)	Distinguish between legal and constructive obligations	2
(c)	State when provisions may and may not be made and demonstrate how they should be accounted for	2
(d)	Explain how provisions should be measured	1
(e)	Define contingent assets and liabilities and describe their accounting treatment and required disclosures	2
(f)	Identify and account for:	2
	(i) Warranties/guarantees	
	(ii) Onerous contracts	
	(iii) Environmental and similar provisions	
	(iv) Provisions for future repairs or refurbishments	
(g)	Events after the reporting period	
	(i) Distinguish between and account for adjusting and non-adjusting events after the reporting period	2
	(ii) Identify items requiring separate disclosure, including their accounting treatment and required disclosures	2

1 Provisions

FAST FORWARD

Under **IAS 37** a provision should be recognised when:

- An entity has a **present obligation**, legal or constructive

- It is probable that a **transfer of resources embodying economic benefits** will be required to settle it

- A **reliable estimate** can be made of its amount

(IAS 37: para. 14)

1.1 Objective

IAS 37 *Provisions, contingent liabilities and contingent assets* aims to ensure that appropriate **recognition criteria** and **measurement bases** are applied to provisions, contingent liabilities and contingent assets and that **sufficient information** is disclosed in the **notes** to the financial statements to enable users to understand their nature, timing and amount.

1.2 Provisions

Before IAS 37, there was no accounting standard dealing with provisions. Companies wanting to show their results in the most favourable light used to make large 'one off' provisions in years where a high level of underlying profits was generated. These provisions, often known as 'big bath' provisions, were then available to shield expenditure in future years when perhaps the underlying profits were not as good.

In other words, provisions were used for profit smoothing. Profit smoothing is misleading.

Important

The key aim of IAS 37 is to ensure that **provisions are made only** where there are valid grounds for them.

IAS 37 views a provision as a liability.

A **provision** is a **liability** of uncertain timing or amount.

Reduces the scope for profit smoothing (handwritten)

A **liability** is a present obligation of the entity arising from past events, the settlement of which is expected to result in an outflow from the entity of resources embodying economic benefits. (IAS 37 para. 10)

The IAS distinguishes provisions from other liabilities such as trade creditors and accruals. This is on the basis that for a provision there is **uncertainty** about the timing or amount of the future expenditure. Whilst uncertainty is clearly present in the case of certain accruals the uncertainty is generally much less than for provisions.

*DR Expense
CR Provision
(Liability)* (handwritten)

1.3 Recognition

IAS 37 states that a provision should be **recognised** as a liability in the financial statements when:

- An entity has a **present obligation** (legal or constructive) as a result of a past event

- It is probable that an **outflow of resources embodying economic benefits** will be required to settle the obligation

- A **reliable estimate** can be made of the amount of the obligation (IAS 37: para. 14)

1.4 Meaning of obligation

It is fairly clear what a legal obligation is. However, you may not know what a **constructive obligation** is.

IAS 37 defines a **constructive obligation** as

'An obligation that derives from an entity's actions where:

- by an established pattern of past practice, published policies or a sufficiently specific current statement the entity has indicated to other parties that it will accept certain responsibilities; and

- as a result, the entity has created a valid expectation on the part of those other parties that it will discharge those responsibilities.' (IAS 37: para. 10)

For instance, an oil company may have an established practice of always making good any environmental damage caused by drilling, even though it is not legally obliged to do so. In this way, it has created a valid expectation that it will do this and it will have to recognise the constructive obligation and make a corresponding provision each time it drills a new well.

1.4.1 Probable transfer of resources

For the purpose of the IAS, a transfer of resources embodying economic benefits is regarded as **'probable'** if the event is **more likely than not** to occur (IAS 37: para. 15). This appears to indicate a probability of more than 50%. However, the standard makes it clear that where there is a number of similar obligations the probability should be based on considering the population as a whole, rather than one single item. (IAS 37: para. 24)

1.4.2 Example: transfer of resources

If a company has entered into a warranty obligation then the probability of transfer of resources embodying economic benefits may well be extremely small in respect of one specific item. However, when considering the population as a whole the probability of some transfer of resources is quite likely to be much higher. If there is a **greater than 50% probability** of some transfer of economic benefits then a **provision** should be made for the **expected amount**.

1.4.3 Measurement of provisions

Important

> The amount recognised as a provision should be the best estimate of the expenditure required to settle the present obligation at the end of the reporting period.
> (IAS 37: para. 36)

The estimates will be determined by the **judgement** of the entity's management supplemented by the experience of similar transactions.
(IAS 37: para. 38)

Allowance is made for **uncertainty**. Where the provision being measured involves a large population of items, the obligation is estimated by weighting all possible outcomes by their associated probabilities, ie **expected value**.
(IAS 37: para. 39)

Where the provision involves a single item, such as the outcome of a legal case, provision is made **in full** for the most likely outcome.
(IAS 37: para. 40)

Question

Warranty

Parker Co sells goods with a warranty under which customers are covered for the cost of repairs of any manufacturing defect that becomes apparent within the first six months of purchase. The company's past experience and future expectations indicate the following pattern of likely repairs.

Expected value

Statistical expected value

% of goods sold	Defects	Cost of repairs if all items suffered from these defects $m
75	None	–
20	Minor	1.0
5	Major	4.0

Required

What is the provision required?

Answer

The cost is found using 'expected values' (75% × $nil) + (20% × $1.0m) + (5% × $4.0m) = $400,000.

Time value of money

Present value = discount to year 0 if an amount is expected in year 5

Where the effect of the **time value of money** is material, the amount of a provision should be the **present value** of the expenditure required to settle the obligation. An appropriate **discount** rate should be used.
(IAS 37: para. 45)

$\frac{1}{(1+R)^N}$

The discount rate should be a pre-tax rate that reflects current market assessments of the time value of money. The discount rate(s) should not reflect risks for which future cash flow estimates have been adjusted.
(IAS 37: para. 47)

Note. You will be given any relevant discount rates in the exam.

Theoretical explanation on 232 Ex 1.5 E Decommissioning or abandonment costs

Example

Cambridge Co knows that when it ceases a certain operation in five years' time it will have to pay environmental cleanup costs of $5m.

The provision to be made now will be the present value of $5m in five years' time.

The relevant discount rate in this case is 10%.

Therefore a provision will be made for:

	$
$5m × 0.62092*	3,104,600

*The discount rate for five years at 10%.

The following year the provision will be:

$5m × 0.68301**   3,415,050
                                                                                310,540

**The discount rate for four years at 10%

The increase in the second year of $310,450 will be charged to profit or loss. It is referred to as the **unwinding** of the discount. This is accounted for as a finance cost. The original provision of $3,104,600 will be added to the cost of the assets involved in the operation and depreciated over five years.

1.4.4 Future events

Future events which are reasonably expected to occur (eg new legislation, changes in technology) may affect the amount required to settle the entity's obligation and should be taken into account.

(IAS 37: para. 48)

1.4.5 Expected disposal of assets

Gains from the expected disposal of assets should not be taken into account in measuring a provision.

(IAS 37: para. 51)

1.4.6 Reimbursements

Some or all of the expenditure needed to settle a provision may be expected to be recovered from a third party. If so, the reimbursement should be recognised only when it is virtually certain that reimbursement will be received if the entity settles the obligation.

- The reimbursement should be treated as a separate asset, and the amount recognised should not be greater than the provision itself.

- The provision and the amount recognised for reimbursement may be netted off in profit or loss.

(IAS 37: para. 53)

1.4.7 Changes in provisions No need to carry provision just get rid of it

Provisions should be reviewed at the end of each reporting period and adjusted to reflect the current best estimate. If it is no longer probable that a transfer of resources will be required to settle the obligation, the provision should be reversed.

(IAS 37: para. 59)

1.4.8 Use of provisions

A provision should be used only for expenditures for which the provision was originally recognised. Setting expenditures against a provision that was originally recognised for another purpose would conceal the impact of two different events.

(IAS 37: para. 61)

1.4.9 Future operating losses

Provisions should not be recognised for future operating losses. They do not meet the definition of a liability and the general recognition criteria set out in the standard.

(IAS 37: para. 63)

1.4.10 Onerous contracts where you have a lot of deliverables to deliver on

If an entity has a contract that is onerous, the present obligation under the contract **should be recognised and measured** as a provision. (IAS 37: para. 66) An example might be vacant leasehold property. The entity holding the lease is under an obligation to maintain the property but is receiving no income or benefit from it.

Key term

> An **onerous contract** is a contract entered into with another party under which the unavoidable costs of fulfilling the terms of the contract exceed any revenues expected to be received from the goods or services supplied or purchased directly or indirectly under the contract and where the entity would have to compensate the other party if it did not fulfil the terms of the contract.
>
> (IAS 37: para. 68)

1.5 Examples of possible provisions

It is easier to see what IAS 37 is driving at if you look at examples of those items which are possible provisions under this standard. Some of these we have already touched on.

(a) **Warranties**. These are argued to be genuine provisions as on past experience it is probable, ie more likely than not, that some claims will emerge. The provision must be estimated, however, on the basis of the class as a whole and not on individual claims. There is a clear legal obligation in this case. Warranties are also covered by IFRS 15 *Revenue from contracts with customers* (see Chapter 6). The nature of the warranty granted will determine whether the warranty should be accounted for under IAS 37 or IFRS 15.

(b) **Major repairs**. In the past it has been quite popular for companies to provide for expenditure on a major overhaul to be accrued gradually over the intervening years between overhauls. Under IAS 37 this is no longer possible as IAS 37 would argue that this is a mere intention to carry out repairs, not an obligation. The entity can always sell the asset in the meantime. The only solution is to treat major assets such as aircraft, ships, furnaces etc as a series of smaller assets where each part is depreciated over shorter lives. Thus any major overhaul may be argued to be replacement and therefore capital rather than revenue expenditure.

(c) **Self insurance**. A number of companies have created a provision for self insurance based on the expected cost of making good fire damage etc instead of paying premiums to an insurance company. Under IAS 37 this provision is no longer justifiable as the entity has no obligation until a fire or accident occurs. No obligation exists until that time.

(d) **Environmental contamination**. If the company has an environmental policy such that other parties would expect the company to clean up any contamination or if the company has broken current environmental legislation then a provision for environmental damage must be made.

(e) **Decommissioning or abandonment costs**. When an oil company initially purchases an oilfield it is put under a legal obligation to decommission the site at the end of its life. Prior to IAS 37 most oil companies set up the provision gradually over the life of the field so that no one year would be unduly burdened with the cost.

IAS 37, however, insists that a legal obligation exists on the initial expenditure on the field and therefore a liability exists immediately. This would appear to result in a large charge to profit and loss in the first year of operation of the field. However, the IAS takes the view that the cost of purchasing the field in the first place is not only the cost of the field itself but also the costs of putting it right again. Thus all the costs of decommissioning may be capitalised.

(f) **Restructuring**. This is considered in detail below.

<table>
<tr><td>**Exam focus point**</td><td>These examples are the sort of situation you may get in the exam. The December 2008 exam had a question dealing with an oilfield and related clean-up costs, which had to be discounted.</td></tr>
</table>

2 Provisions for restructuring Possible exam question

<table>
<tr><td>**FAST FORWARD**</td><td>One of the main purposes of IAS 37 was to target abuses of provisions for restructuring. Accordingly, IAS 37 lays down **strict criteria** to determine when such a provision can be made.</td></tr>
</table>

<table>
<tr><td>**Key term**</td><td>IAS 37 defines a **restructuring** as:

A programme that is planned and is controlled by management and materially changes one of two things.

• The scope of a business undertaken by an entity
• The manner in which that business is conducted

(IAS 37: para. 10)</td></tr>
</table>

The IAS gives the following **examples** of events that may fall under the definition of restructuring.

- The **sale or termination** of a line of business
- The **closure of business locations** in a country or region or the **relocation** of business activities from one country region to another *Banks left ireland during the Recession.*
- **Changes in management structure**, for example, the elimination of a layer of management
- **Fundamental reorganisations** that have a material effect on the **nature and focus** of the entity's operations

(IAS 37: para. 70)

The question is whether or not an entity has an obligation – legal or constructive – at the end of the reporting period. For this to be the case:

- An entity must have a **detailed formal plan** for the restructuring.
- It must have **raised a valid expectation** in those affected that it will carry out the restructuring by starting to implement that plan or announcing its main features to those affected by it.

(IAS 37: para. 72)

Important

> **A mere management decision is not normally sufficient.** Management decisions may sometimes trigger recognition, but only if earlier events such as negotiations with employee representatives and other interested parties have been concluded subject only to management approval. (IAS 37: para. 72)

Where the restructuring involves the **sale of an operation** then IAS 37 states that no obligation arises until the entity has entered into a **binding sale agreement**. This is because until this has occurred the entity will be able to change its mind and withdraw from the sale even if its intentions have been announced publicly.

(IAS 37: para. 78)

2.1 Costs to be included within a restructuring provision

The IAS states that a restructuring provision should include only the **direct expenditures** arising from the restructuring, which are those that are both:

- **Necessarily entailed** by the restructuring; and
- Not associated with the **ongoing activities** of the entity.

(IAS 37: para. 80)

The following costs should specifically **not** be included within a restructuring provision.

- **Retraining** or relocating continuing staff
- **Marketing**
- **Investment in new systems** and distribution networks

(IAS 37: para. 81)

2.2 Disclosure

Disclosures for provisions fall into two parts.

- Disclosure of details of the **change in carrying value** of a provision from the beginning to the end of the year
- Disclosure of the **background** to the making of the provision and the uncertainties affecting its outcome

(IAS 37: paras. 84–5)

Question

Provision

In which of the following circumstances might a provision be recognised?

(a) On 13 December 20X9 the board of an entity decided to close down a division. The accounting date of the company is 31 December. Before 31 December 20X9 the decision was not communicated to any of those affected and no other steps were taken to implement the decision.

(b) The board agreed a detailed closure plan on 20 December 20X9 and details were given to customers and employees.

(c)   A company is obliged to incur clean up costs for environmental damage (that has already been caused).

(d)   A company intends to carry out future expenditure to operate in a particular way in the future.

Answer

(a)   No provision would be recognised as the decision has not been communicated.

(b)   A provision would be made in the 20X9 financial statements.

(c)   A provision for such costs is appropriate.

(d)   No present obligation exists and under IAS 37 no provision would be appropriate. This is because the entity could avoid the future expenditure by its future actions, maybe by changing its method of operation.

3 Contingent liabilities and contingent assets

FAST FORWARD

> An entity should not **recognise** a **contingent asset or liability**, but they should be **disclosed**.
> (IAS 37: para. 27)

Now you understand provisions it will be easier to understand contingent assets and liabilities.

Key term

[handwritten: Something that may arise in the future]

IAS 37 defines a **contingent liability** as:

- A possible obligation that arises from past events and whose existence will be confirmed only by the occurrence or non-occurrence of one or more uncertain future events not wholly within the control of the entity; or

- A present obligation that arises from past events but is not recognised because:

    - It is not probable that an outflow of resources embodying economic benefits will be required to settle the obligation; or

    - The amount of the obligation cannot be measured with sufficient reliability. (IAS 37: para. 10)

As a rule of thumb, probable means more than 50% likely. If an obligation is probable, it is not a contingent liability – instead, a provision is needed.

3.1 Treatment of contingent liabilities

Contingent liabilities **should not be recognised in financial statements** but they **should be disclosed**. The required disclosures are:

[handwritten: Don't anticipate gains until your certain then they're then contingent]

- A brief description of the nature of the contingent liability
- An estimate of its financial effect
- An indication of the uncertainties that exist
- The possibility of any reimbursement   *[handwritten: if comp A sues comp B (supplier) for product defect, comp B sues comp C]*
(IAS 37: para. 86)

3.2 Contingent assets   *[handwritten: There are no contingent assets (really)]*

Key term

IAS 37 defines a **contingent asset** as:

A possible asset that arises from past events and whose existence will be confirmed by the occurrence or non-occurrence of one or more uncertain future events not wholly within control of the entity.

(IAS 37: para. 10)

A contingent asset must not be recognised. (IAS 37: para. 31) Only when the realisation of the related economic benefits is **virtually certain** should recognition take place. At that point, **the asset is no longer a contingent asset!**

3.3 Example

A company is engaged in a legal dispute. The outcome is not yet known. A number of possibilities arise:

- It expects to have to pay about $100,000. **A provision is recognised.**

- Possible damages are $100,000 but it is not expected to have to pay them. **A contingent liability is disclosed.**

- The company expects to have to pay damages but is unable to estimate the amount. **A contingent liability is disclosed.**

- The company expects to receive damages of $100,000 and this is virtually certain. **An asset is recognised.**

- The company expects to probably receive damages of $100,000. **A contingent asset is disclosed.**

- The company thinks it may receive damages, but it is not probable. **No disclosure.**

3.4 Disclosure

3.4.1 Disclosure: contingent liabilities

A **brief description** must be provided of all material contingent liabilities unless they are likely to be remote. In addition, provide:

- An estimate of their **financial effect**
- Details of **any uncertainties**
- The possibility of any reimbursement

(IAS 37: para. 86)

3.4.2 Disclosure: contingent assets

Contingent assets must only be disclosed in the notes if they are **probable**. In that case a brief description of the contingent asset should be provided along with an estimate of its likely financial effect.

(IAS 37: para. 89)

3.5 'Let out'

IAS 37 permits reporting entities to avoid disclosure requirements relating to provisions, contingent liabilities and contingent assets if they would be expected to **seriously prejudice** the position of the entity in dispute with other parties. However, this should only be employed in **extremely rare** cases. Details of the general nature of the provision/contingencies must still be provided, together with an explanation of why it has not been disclosed.

(IAS 37: para. 92)

3.6 Flow chart

You must practise the questions below to get the hang of IAS 37. But first, study the flow chart, taken from IAS 37, which is a good summary of its requirements concerning provisions and contingent liabilities.

(IAS 37: IGB)

Exam focus point

> If you learn this flow chart you should be able to deal with most questions you are likely to meet in an exam.

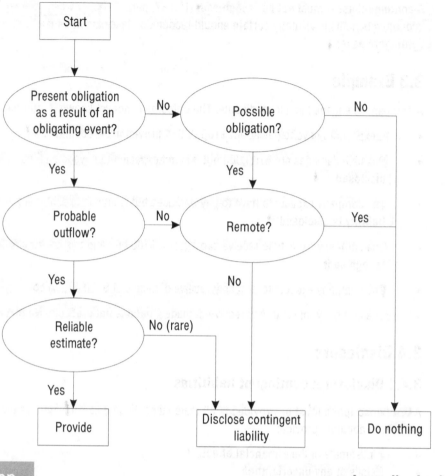

Question

During 20X0 Smack Co gives a guarantee of certain borrowings of Pony Co, whose financial condition at that time is sound. During 20X1, the financial condition of Pony Co deteriorates and at 30 June 20X1 Pony Co files for protection from its creditors.

Required

What accounting treatment is required:

(a)   At 31 December 20X0?
(b)   At 31 December 20X1?

Answer

(a)   *At 31 December 20X0*

There is a present obligation as a result of a past obligating event. The obligating event is the giving of the guarantee, which gives rise to a legal obligation. However, at 31 December 20X0 no transfer of resources is probable in settlement of the obligation.

No provision is recognised. The guarantee is disclosed as a contingent liability unless the probability of any transfer is regarded as remote.

(b)   *At 31 December 20X1*

As above, there is a present obligation as a result of a past obligating event, namely the giving of the guarantee.

At 31 December 20X1 it is probable that a transfer of resources will be required to settle the obligation. A provision is therefore recognised for the best estimate of the obligation.

Question

Warren Co gives warranties at the time of sale to purchasers of its products. Under the terms of the warranty the manufacturer undertakes to make good, by repair or replacement, manufacturing defects that become apparent within a period of three years from the date of the sale. Should a provision be recognised?

Answer

Warren Co **cannot avoid** the cost of repairing or replacing all items of product that manifest manufacturing defects in respect of which warranties are given before the end of the reporting period, and a provision for the cost of this should therefore be made.

Warren Co is obliged to repair or replace items that fail within the entire warranty period. Therefore, in respect of **this year's sales**, the obligation provided for at the end of the reporting period should be the cost of making good items for which defects have been notified but not yet processed, **plus** an estimate of costs in respect of the other items sold for which there is sufficient evidence that manufacturing defects **will** manifest themselves during their remaining periods of warranty cover.

Question

After a wedding in 20X0 ten people became very ill, possibly as a result of food poisoning from products sold by Callow Co. Legal proceedings are started seeking damages from Callow Co but it disputes liability. Up to the date of approval of the financial statements for the year to 31 December 20X0, Callow Co's lawyers advise that it is probable that it will not be found liable. However, when Callow Co prepares the financial statements for the year to 31 December 20X1 its lawyers advise that, owing to developments in the case, it is probable that it will be found liable.

Required

What is the required accounting treatment:

(a)   At 31 December 20X0?
(b)   At 31 December 20X1?

Answer

(a)   *At 31 December 20X0*

On the basis of the evidence available when the financial statements were approved, there is no obligation as a result of past events. No provision is recognised. The matter is disclosed as a contingent liability unless the probability of any transfer is regarded as remote.

(b)   *At 31 December 20X1*

On the basis of the evidence available, there is a present obligation. A transfer of resources in settlement is probable.

A provision is recognised for the best estimate of the amount needed to settle the present obligation.

3.7 Summary

- The objective of IAS 37 is to ensure that appropriate recognition criteria and measurement bases are applied to provisions and contingencies and that sufficient information is disclosed.
- The IAS seeks to ensure that provisions are **only recognised** when a **measurable obligation** exists. It includes detailed rules that can be used to ascertain when an obligation exists and how to measure the obligation.
- The standard attempts to **eliminate** the **'profit smoothing'** which has gone on before it was issued.

4 IAS 10: *Events after the reporting period*

FAST FORWARD

IAS 10 sets out the criteria for recognising **events occurring after the reporting date**.

The standard gives the following definition.

Key terms

> **Events occurring after the reporting period** are those events, both favourable and unfavourable, that occur between the end of the reporting period and the date on which the financial statements are authorised for issue. Two types of events can be identified:
>
> - Those that provide evidence of conditions that existed at the end of the reporting period – **adjusting**
> - Those that are indicative of conditions that arose after the reporting period – **non-adjusting**
>
> (IAS 10: para. 3)

The financial statements are significant indicators of a company's success or failure. It is important, therefore, that they include all the information necessary for an understanding of the company's position.

Between the end of the reporting period and the date the financial statements are authorised (ie for issue outside the organisation), **events may occur** which show that assets and liabilities at the end of the reporting period should be adjusted, or that disclosure of such events should be given.

4.1 Events requiring adjustment

The standard requires adjustment of assets and liabilities in certain circumstances.

An entity shall adjust the amounts recognised in its financial statements to reflect **adjusting events** after the reporting period. An entity shall not adjust the amounts recognised in its financial statements to reflect non-adjusting events after the reporting period. (IAS 10: paras. 8,10)

An **example** of additional evidence which becomes available after the reporting period is where a **customer goes into liquidation, thus confirming that the trade account receivable balance at the year end is uncollectable**. (IAS 10: para. 9)

In relation to **going concern**, the standard states that, where operating results and the financial position have deteriorated after the reporting period, it may be necessary to reconsider whether the going concern assumption is appropriate in the preparation of the financial statements. (IAS 10: para. 14)

Examples of **adjusting events** would be:

- Evidence of a permanent diminution in property value prior to the year end
- Sale of inventory after the reporting period for less than its carrying value at the year end
- Insolvency of a customer with a balance owing at the year end
- Amounts received or paid in respect of legal or insurance claims which were in negotiation at the year end
- Determination after the year end of the sale or purchase price of assets sold or purchased before the year end

- Evidence of a permanent diminution in the value of a long-term investment prior to the year end

- Discovery of error or fraud which shows that the financial statements were incorrect

(IAS 10: para. 9)

4.2 Events not requiring adjustment

The standard then looks at events which do **not** require adjustment.

The standard gives the following examples of events which do **not** require adjustments:

- Acquisition of, or disposal of, a subsidiary after the year end
- Announcement of a plan to discontinue an operation
- Major purchases and disposals of assets
- Destruction of a production plant by fire after the reporting period
- Announcement or commencing implementation of a major restructuring
- Share transactions after the reporting period
- Litigation commenced after the reporting period

(IAS 10: para. 22)

But note that, while they may be non-adjusting, some events after the reporting period will require **disclosure**.

(IAS 10: para. 22)

If non-adjusting events after the reporting period are material, non-disclosure could influence the economic decisions of users taken on the basis of the financial statements. Accordingly, an entity shall disclose the following for each material category of non-adjusting event after the reporting period:

(a) The nature of the event
(b) An estimate of its financial effect, or a statement that such an estimate cannot be made

(IAS 10: para. 21)

The **example** given by the standard of such an event is where the **value of an investment falls between the end of the reporting period and the date the financial statements are authorised** for issue. The fall in value represents circumstances during the current period, not conditions existing at the end of the previous reporting period, so it is not appropriate to adjust the value of the investment in the financial statements. Disclosure is an aid to users, however, indicating 'unusual changes' in the state of assets and liabilities after the reporting period.

(IAS 10: para. 11)

The rule for **disclosure** of events occurring after the reporting period which relate to conditions that arose after that date, is that disclosure should be made if non-disclosure would hinder the user's ability to make **proper evaluations** and decisions based on the financial statements. An example might be the acquisition of another business.

(IAS 10: para. 21)

Chapter Roundup

- Under **IAS 37** a **provision** should be recognised when:

  - When an entity has a **present obligation**, legal or constructive

  - It is probable that a **transfer of resources embodying economic benefits** will be required to settle it

  - A reliable estimate can be made of its amount

- One the main purposes of IAS 37 was to target abuses of provisions for restructuring. Accordingly, IAS 37 lays down **strict criteria** to determine when such a provision can be made.

- An entity should not **recognise** a **contingent asset or liability**, but they should be **disclosed**. (IAS 37: para.27)

- IAS 10 sets out the criteria for recognising **events occurring after the reporting date**.

Quick Quiz

1   A provision is a .... of .... timing or amount.

2   A programme is undertaken by management which converts the previously wholly owned chain of restaurants they ran into franchises. Is this restructuring?

3   Define contingent asset and contingent liability.

4   How should decommissioning costs on an oilfield be accounted for under IAS 37?

5   'Provisions for major overhauls should be accrued for over the period between overhauls'. Is this correct?

Answers to Quick Quiz

1   A provision is a **liability** of **uncertain** timing or amount.

2   Yes. The manner in which the business is conducted has changed.

3   Refer to Sections 3.1 and 3.2.

4   They should be capitalised as part of the initial expenditure on the oilfield.

5   No. It is not correct. See Section 1.5.

Now try the question below from the Practice Question Bank

Number	Level	Marks	Time
17	–	25	49 mins

14

Inventories and biological assets

Topic list	Syllabus reference
1 Inventories and short-term WIP (IAS 2)	B4
2 IAS 41 *Agriculture*	B4

Introduction

You have encountered inventory and its valuation in your earlier studies.
Inventory and short-term work-in-progress valuation has a direct impact on a
company's gross profit and it is usually a material item in any company's
accounts. This is therefore an important subject area. If you have any doubts
about accounting for inventories and methods of inventory valuation you would
be advised to go back to your earlier study material and revise this topic.

Section 1 of this chapter goes over some of this ground again, concentrating
on the effect of IAS 2. Section 2 goes on to discuss a new area, agriculture.
You should find this topic fairly logical as long as you work through the
material carefully.

Study guide

		Intellectual level
B4	**Inventory and biological assets**	
(a)	Describe and apply the principles of inventory valuation	2
(b)	Apply the requirements of relevant accounting standards for biological assets	2

Exam guide

Questions on inventory or biological assets could appear as OTQs and may also feature in longer questions.

1 Inventories and short-term WIP (IAS 2)

FAST FORWARD

The use of **LIFO** is **prohibited** under IAS 2. (IAS 2: IN13)

1.1 Introduction

In most businesses the value put on inventory is an important factor in the determination of profit. Inventory valuation is, however, a highly subjective exercise and consequently there is a wide variety of different methods used in practice.

1.2 IAS 2 Inventories

IAS 2 lays out the required accounting treatment for inventories. The major area of contention is the cost **value of inventory** to be recorded. This is recognised as an asset of the entity until the related revenues are recognised (ie the item is sold) at which point the inventory is recognised as an expense (ie cost of sales). Part or all of the cost of inventories may also be expensed if a write-down to **net realisable value** is necessary. The IAS also provides guidance on the cost formulas that are used to assign costs to inventories.

In other words, the fundamental accounting assumption of **accruals** requires costs to be matched with associated revenues. In order to achieve this, costs incurred for goods which remain unsold at the year end must be carried forward in the statement of financial position and matched against future revenues.

1.3 Scope

The following items are **excluded** from the scope of the standard.

- Work in progress under **long-term contracts** (covered by IFRS 15 *Revenue from contracts with customers,* see Chapter 6)

- **Financial instruments** (ie shares, bonds)

- **Biological assets**

(IAS 2: para. 2)

Accruals concept (matching) – match expenditure with income in the period the income is earned

1.4 Definitions

The following definitions are important.

- **Inventories** are assets:
  - Held for sale in the ordinary course of business;
  - In the process of production for such sale; or
  - In the form of materials or supplies to be consumed in the production process or in the rendering of services.
- **Net realisable value** is the estimated selling price in the ordinary course of business less the estimated costs of completion and the estimated costs necessary to make the sale. (IAS 2: para. 6)
- **Fair value** is the price that would be received to sell an asset or paid to transfer a liability in an orderly transaction between market participants at the measurement date. (IFRS 13: App A)

Inventories can **include** any of the following.

- **Goods purchased and held for resale**, eg goods held for sale by a retailer, or land and buildings held for resale
- **Finished goods** produced
- **Work in progress** being produced
- Materials and supplies awaiting use in the production process (**raw materials**)

1.5 Measurement of inventories

The standard states that '**Inventories should be measured at the lower of cost and net realisable value.**'
(IAS 2: para. 6)

This is a very important rule and you will be expected to apply it in the exam.

1.6 Cost of inventories

The cost of inventories will consist of all costs of:

- **Purchase**
- **Costs of conversion**
- **Other costs** incurred in bringing the inventories to their **present location and condition**
(IAS 2: para. 10)

1.6.1 Costs of purchase

The standard lists the following as comprising the costs of purchase of inventories.

- **Purchase price** PLUS
- **Import duties** and other taxes PLUS
- Transport, handling and any other cost **directly attributable** to the acquisition of finished goods, services and materials LESS
- **Trade discounts**, rebates and other similar amounts (IAS 2: para. 119)

1.6.2 Costs of conversion

Costs of conversion of inventories consist of two main parts.

(a) Costs **directly related** to the units of production, eg direct materials, direct labour

(b)   Fixed and variable **production overheads** that are incurred in converting materials into finished goods, allocated on a systematic basis.   (IAS 2: para. 12)

You may have come across the terms 'fixed production overheads' or 'variable production overheads' elsewhere in your studies. The standard defines them as follows.

Key terms

> - **Fixed production overheads** are those indirect costs of production that remain relatively constant regardless of the volume of production, eg the cost of factory management and administration.
>
> - **Variable production overheads** are those indirect costs of production that vary directly, or nearly directly, with the volume of production, eg indirect materials and labour.   (IAS 2: para. 12)

The standard emphasises that fixed production overheads must be allocated to items of inventory on the basis of the **normal capacity of the production facilities**. This is an important point.

(a)   **Normal capacity** is the expected achievable production based on the average over several periods/seasons, under normal circumstances.

(b)   The above figure should take account of the capacity lost through **planned maintenance**.

(c)   If it approximates to the normal level of activity then the **actual level of production** can be used.

(d)   **Low production** or **idle plant** will **not** result in a higher fixed overhead allocation to each unit.

(e)   **Unallocated overheads** must be recognised as an expense in the period in which they were incurred.

(f)   When production is **abnormally high**, the fixed production overhead allocated to each unit will be reduced, so avoiding inventories being stated at more than cost.

(g)   The allocation of variable production overheads to each unit is based on the **actual use** of production facilities.   (IAS 2: para. 13)

1.6.3 Other costs

Any other costs should only be recognised if they are incurred in bringing the inventories to their **present location and condition**.   (IAS 2: para. 15)

The standard lists types of cost which **would not be included** in cost of inventories. Instead, they should be recognised as an **expense** in the period they are incurred.

(a)   **Abnormal amounts** of wasted materials, labour or other production costs

(b)   **Storage costs** (except costs which are necessary in the production process before a further production stage)

(c)   **Administrative overheads** not incurred to bring inventories to their present location and conditions

(d)   **Selling costs**   (IAS 2: para. 16)

1.6.4 Techniques for the measurement of cost

Two techniques are mentioned by the standard, both of which produce results which **approximate to cost**, and so both of which may be used for convenience.   (IAS 2: para. 21)

(a)   **Standard costs** are set up to take account of normal production values: amount of raw materials used, labour time etc. They are reviewed and revised on a regular basis.

(b)   **Retail method**: this is often used in the retail industry where there is a large turnover of inventory items, which nevertheless have similar profit margins. The only practical method of inventory valuation may be to take the total selling price of inventories and deduct an overall average profit margin, thus reducing the value to an approximation of cost. The percentage will take account of reduced price lines. Sometimes different percentages are applied on a department basis.

1.7 Cost formulae

Cost of inventories should be assigned by **specific identification** of their individual costs for:

(a) Items that are **not ordinarily interchangeable**
(b) Goods or services produced and segregated for **specific projects** (IAS 2: para. 23)

Specific costs should be attributed to individual items of inventory when they are segregated for a specific project, but not where inventories consist of a large number of interchangeable (ie identical or very similar) items. In the latter case the rule is as specified below. (IAS 2: para. 24)

1.7.1 Interchangeable items

Rule to learn

> The cost of inventories should be assigned by using the **first-in, first-out (FIFO)** or **weighted average** cost formulas. The LIFO formula (last in, first out) is **not permitted** by IAS 2. (IAS 2: para. 25)

You should be familiar with these methods from your earlier studies. Under the weighted average cost method, a recalculation can be made after each purchase, **or alternatively only at the period end**.

1.8 Net realisable value (NRV)

As a general rule assets should not be carried at amounts greater than those expected to be realised from their sale or use. In the case of inventories this amount could fall below cost when items are **damaged or become obsolete**, or where the **costs to completion have increased** in order to make the sale. (IAS 2: para. 28)

In fact we can identify the principal situations in which **NRV is likely to be less than cost**, ie where there has been:

(a) An **increase in costs** or a **fall in selling price**
(b) A **physical deterioration** in the condition of inventory
(c) **Obsolescence** of products
(d) A decision as part of the company's marketing strategy to manufacture and sell products at a **loss**
(e) **Errors in production or purchasing**

A write down of inventories would normally take place on an item by item basis, but similar or related items may be **grouped together**. This grouping together is acceptable for, say, items in the same product line, but it is not acceptable to write down inventories based on a whole classification (eg finished goods) or a whole business. (IAS 2: para. 29)

The assessment of NRV should take place **at the same time** as estimates are made of selling price, using the most reliable information available. Fluctuations of price or cost should be taken into account if they relate directly to **events after the reporting period,** which confirm conditions existing at the end of the period. (IAS 2: para. 30)

The reasons why inventory is held must also be taken into account. Some inventory, for example, may be held to satisfy a firm contract and its NRV will therefore be the **contract price**. Any additional inventory of the same type held at the period end will, in contrast, be assessed according to general sales prices when NRV is estimated. (IAS 2: para. 31)

Net realisable value must be reassessed at the end of each period and compared again with cost. If the NRV has risen for inventories held over the end of more than one period, then the previous write down must be **reversed** to the extent that the inventory is then valued at the lower of cost and the new NRV. This may be possible when selling prices have fallen in the past and then risen again. (IAS 2: para. 33)

1.9 Recognition as an expense

The following treatment is required **when inventories are sold**.

(a) The **carrying amount** is recognised as an expense in the period in which the related revenue is recognised.

(b) The amount of any **write-down of inventories** to NRV and all losses of inventories are recognised as an expense in the period the write-down or loss occurs.

(c) The amount of any **reversal of any write-down of inventories**, arising from an increase in NRV, is recognised as a reduction in the amount of inventories recognised as an expense in the period in which the reversal occurs. (IAS 2: para. 34)

Question	Inventory valuation

A company has inventory on hand at the end of the reporting period as follows.

	Units	Raw material cost $	Attributable production overheads $	Attributable selling costs $	Expected selling $
Item A	300	160	15	12	185
Item B	250	50	10	10	75

Required

At what amount will inventories be stated in the statement of financial position in accordance with IAS 2?

Answer					
	Units	Cost $	NRV $	Lower $	Total $
Item A	300	175	173	173	51,900
Item B	250	60	65	60	15,000
					66,900

1.10 Consistency – different cost formulas for inventories

IAS 2 allows two cost formulas (FIFO or weighted average cost) for inventories that are ordinarily interchangeable or are not produced and segregated for specific projects. The issue is whether an entity may use different cost formulas for different types of inventories.

IAS 2 provides that an entity should use **the same cost formula for all inventories having similar nature and use to the entity.** For inventories with different nature or use (for example, certain commodities used in one business segment and the same type of commodities used in another business segment), different cost formulas may be justified. A difference in geographical location of inventories (and in the respective tax rules), by itself, is not sufficient to justify the use of different cost formulas. (IAS 2: para. 25)

2 IAS 41 *Agriculture*

> **FAST FORWARD**
>
> IAS 41 applies the requirements of IFRS to the treatment of biological assets.

2.1 Overview

The importance of the agricultural sector in a country's economy will vary. It is reasonable to assume, however, that although agriculture is important in first world countries, it is likely to be of greater significance to developing countries.

IAS 41 *Agriculture* was issued in February 2001.

The main reason for developing a standard on agriculture was because there was great diversity in practice in accounting for agriculture at both a transnational and national level. It is quite difficult to apply **traditional accounting methods** to agricultural activities, which explains why agriculture is excluded from many IFRSs.

(a) When and how do you account for the **critical events** associated with biological transformation (growth, procreation, production and degeneration), which alter the substance of biological assets?

(b) **Statement of financial position classification** is made difficult by the variety and characteristics of the living assets of agriculture.

(c) The nature of the management of agricultural activities also causes problems, particularly determination of the **unit of measurement**, ie whether biological assets are a perpetual group of assets or a number of limited life assets.

IAS 41 seeks to improve and harmonise practice in accounting for agriculture, which demonstrates fundamental **differences in its nature and characteristics** to other business activities.

2.2 Definitions

The following definitions are used in IAS 41.

Key terms

> • **Agricultural activity** is the management by an entity of the biological transformation of biological assets for sale, into agricultural produce or into additional biological assets.
>
> • **Agricultural produce** is the harvested product of an entity's biological assets.
>
> • **Biological assets** are living animals or plants.
>
> • **Biological transformation** compromises the processes of growth, degeneration, production and procreation that cause qualitative and quantitative changes in a biological asset.
>
> • A **group of biological assets** is an aggregation of similar living animals or plants.
>
> • **Harvest** is the detachment of produce from a biological asset or the cessation of a biological asset's life processes.
>
> • **Fair value** is the price that would be received to sell an asset or paid to transfer a liability in an orderly transaction between market participants at the measurement date. (IFRS 13)
>
> • **Carrying amount** is the amount at which an asset is recognised in the statement of financial position. (IAS 41: para. 5)

Note the key parts of the definition of **agriculture**:

(a) **Biological**: agriculture relates to 'life phenomena', living animals and plants with an innate capacity of biological transformation which are dependent upon a combination of natural resources (sunlight, water, etc). (IAS 41: para. 6)

(b) **Transformation**: agriculture involves physical transformation, whereby animals and plants undergo a change in biological quantity (fat cover, density, etc) and/or quantity (progeny, live weight etc) over time, which is measured and monitored (increasingly objectively) as part of management control. (IAS 41: para. 6)

(c) **Management**: biological transformation is managed.

(i) Conditions are stabilised or enhanced.

(ii) The transparency of the relationship between inputs and outputs is determined by the degree of control (intensive versus extensive).

(iii) It is different from exploitation through extraction, where no attempt is made to facilitate the transformation.

(iv)   Biological assets are managed in groups of plant or animal classes, using individual assets to ensure the sustainability of the group.

(v)   Sustainability of an agricultural activity is a function of quality and quantity.

(IAS 41: para. 6)

(d)   **Produce**: agricultural produce is diverse and may require further processing before ultimate consumption.

(IAS 41: para. 6)

2.3 Scope

The standard applies to the three elements that form part of, or result from, agricultural activity.

* Biological assets
* Agricultural produce at the point of harvest
* Government grants

(IAS 41: para. 1)

The standard does not apply to agricultural land or intangible assets related to agricultural activity (IAS 38). After harvest, IAS 2 is applied (IAS 41: para. 2).

2.4 Biological assets

We have seen the definition given above. Biological assets are the core income-producing assets of agricultural activities, held for their transformative capabilities. Biological transformation leads to various different outcomes:

* **Asset changes:**

    – Growth: increase in quantity and or quality
    – Degeneration: decrease in quantity and/or quality

* **Creation of new assets:**

    – Production: producing separable non-living products
    – Procreation: producing separable living animals

(IAS 41: para. 7)

We can distinguish between the importance of these by saying that asset changes are **critical to the flow of future economic benefits** both in and beyond the current period, but the relative importance of new asset creation will depend on the purpose of the agricultural activity.

The IAS distinguishes therefore between two broad categories of agricultural production system.

(a)   **Consumable**: animals/plants themselves are harvested.
(b)   **Bearer**: animals/plants bear produce for harvest.

(IAS 41: para. 44)

A few further points are made:

(a)   Biological assets are usually managed in groups of animal or plant classes, with characteristics (eg male/female ratio) which allow **sustainability in perpetuity**.

(b)   **Land often forms an integral part** of the activity itself in pastoral and other land-based agricultural activities.

(IAS 41: para. 25)

2.4.1 Bearer biological assets

An amendment has been issued to IAS 41 regarding **plant-based bearer biological assets**, which would include trees grown in plantations, such as grape vines, rubber trees and oil palms (IASB, *Agriculture: Bearer Plants (Amendments to IAS 16 and IAS 41)*).

These plants are used solely to grow produce crops over several periods and are not in themselves consumed. When no longer productive they are usually scrapped.

It was decided that fair value was not an appropriate measurement for these assets as, once they reach maturity, the only economic benefit they produce comes from the agricultural produce they create. In this respect, they are similar to assets in a manufacturing activity.

Consequently, these assets have been removed from the scope of IAS 41 and should be accounted for under IAS 16 *Property, plant and equipment.* They are measured at accumulated costs until maturity and are then subject to depreciation and impairment charges. The IAS 16 revaluation model could also be applied. Agricultural produce from these plants continues to be recognised under IAS 41/IAS 2.

2.4.2 Recognition of biological assets

The recognition criteria are very **similar to those for other assets**, in that animals or plants should be recognised as assets in the following circumstances.

(a) The entity **controls** the asset as a result of past events.
(b) It is probable that the **future economic benefits** associated with the asset will flow to the entity.
(c) The fair value or cost of the asset to the entity can be **measured reliably**.   (IAS 41: para. 10)

The significant physical attributes of biological assets can be measured using various methods (which are used by markets to measure value) and generally indicate the source of future economic benefits. The **certainty** of the flow of rewards can be determined by formal ownership records, eg land title, branding. The availability of both cost and value for biological assets indicates the reliability aspect of the measurement criteria is fulfilled.   (IAS 41: para. 11)

2.4.3 Measurement of biological assets

The IAS requires that at each year end all biological assets within the scope should be **measured at fair value** less estimated point-of-sale costs.   (IAS 41: para. 12)

The IAS allows an alternative method of valuation, if a fair value cannot be determined because market-determined prices or values are not available. Then the biological asset can be measured at cost less accumulated depreciation and impairment losses.   (IAS 41: para. 30)

This alternative basis is only allowed on **initial recognition** (IAS 41: para. 31).

The **measurement basis** used to depict the fair value of a biological asset will differ depending on the existence of an active market, market efficiency and the use made of the asset. In summary, it is felt that **fair value**, when compared to historical cost, has greater relevance, reliability, comparability and understandability as a measure of future economic benefits.   (IAS 41: B16)

2.4.4 Measuring fair value

The standard states that the primary indicator of fair value should be **net market value**. This is reasonable as efficient markets exist for most biological assets in most locations and net market value is usually considered as providing the best evidence of fair value where an active market exists. Markets will generally differentiate between differing **qualities and quantities**. Market value is not generally predicated on management's intended use, however, but recognises alternative uses.   (IAS 41: B16)

IFRS 13 requires the fair value of a biological asset to be determined by reference to the **principal market** for the asset. This may or may not be the most favourable market.   (IFRS 13: para. 16)

An active and efficient market may not be available for a class of biological assets in a specific location, or there may be imperfections in the market. The standard goes into some detail about **how fair value should be measured** in such circumstances, but in summary the valuation techniques should be consistent with the objectives of measuring fair value and should attain an appropriate balance between relevance and reliability.   (IFRS 13: paras. 17–19)

2.4.5 Recognition

In the **statement of financial position** the biological assets must be shown at fair value less estimated point of sale costs, incorporating the consequences of all biological transformations.

A gain or loss arising on initial recognition of a biological asset at fair value less estimated point of sale costs and from a change in fair value less estimated point of sale costs is included in profit or loss in the period in which it arises.   (IAS 41: para. 26)

Changes to fair value can arise due to both physical changes in the asset and price changes in the market. Entities are encouraged to make separate disclosure of these two elements in order to facilitate performance appraisal.   (IAS 41: para. B74)

There are **exceptions to this approach** in certain situations. For example, in some agricultural systems the predominant activity has a production cycle of less than a year (eg broiler chickens, mushroom growing, cereal crops). In such cases the total change in carrying amount is reported in profit or loss as a single item of income or expense.   (IAS 41: para. B76)

2.4.6 Presentation and disclosure

In the statement of financial position biological assets should be classified as a separate class of assets falling under neither current nor non-current classifications. This reflects the view of such assets as having an unlimited life on a collective basis; it is the total exposure of the entity to this type of asset that is important.

Biological assets should also be **sub-classified** (either in the statement of financial position or as a note to the accounts):

(a)   Class of animal or plant
(b)   Nature of activities (consumable or bearer)
(c)   Maturity or immaturity for intended purpose   (IAS 41: para. 41)

Where activities are **consumable**, the maturity criterion will be attainment of harvestable specifications, whereas in **bearer** activities, it will be attainment of sufficient maturity to sustain economic harvests.

2.5 Agricultural produce

This was defined in the key terms above. It is **recognised at the point of harvest** (eg detachment from the biological asset). Agricultural produce is either incapable of biological process or such processes remain dormant (eg stored grain). **Recognition ends** once the produce enters trading activities or production processes within integrated agribusinesses, although processing activities that are incidental to agricultural activities and that do not materially alter the form of the produce (eg drying or cleaning) are not counted as processing. Following harvest, the provisions of IAS 2 apply.

2.5.1 Measurement and presentation

Following the treatment of biological assets above, the IAS states that agricultural produce should be **measured at each year end at fair value** less estimated point-of-sale costs, to the extent that it is sourced from an entity's biological assets, which are also valued at fair value. This is logical when you consider that, until harvest, the agricultural produce was valued at fair value anyway as part of the biological asset.

The **change in the carrying amount** of the agricultural produce held at year end should be recognised as **income or expense** in profit or loss. This will be rare as such produce is usually sold or processed within a short time, so that produce held over two reporting dates is being held for a specific management purpose and the consequences of that should be reflected in the current period.

Agricultural produce that is harvested for **trading or processing activities** within integrated agricultural/agribusiness operations should be measured at **fair value** at the date of harvest and this amount is deemed cost for application of IAS 2 to consequential inventories.   (IAS 41: para. 13)

2.5.2 Presentation in the statement of financial position

Agricultural produce should be classified as inventory in the statement of financial position and disclosed separately either in the statement of financial position or in the notes.   (IAS 41: para. 13)

2.6 Government grants

An unconditional government grant related to a biological asset measured at its fair value less estimated point-of-sale costs should be recognised as income when, and only when, the grant becomes receivable.
(IAS 41: para. 34)

If a government grant requires an entity not to engage in specified agricultural activity (eg the EU's set aside grant), an entity should only recognise the grant as income when, and only when, the conditions are met.   (IAS 41: para. 35)

IAS 20 does not apply to a government grant on biological assets measured at fair value less estimated point-of-sale costs. However if a biological asset is measured at cost less accumulated depreciation and accumulated impairment losses then IAS 20 does apply.   (IAS 41: para. 37)

2.7 Section summary

In relation to agriculture you should be able to discuss:

- Accounting for **biological assets**
- **Transformation** and changes in substance
- **Unit of measurement** and changes in the carrying amount

Chapter Roundup

- The use of **LIFO** is **prohibited** under IAS 2 (IAS 2: IN13).
- IAS 41 applies the requirements of IFRS to the treatment of biological assets.

Quick Quiz

1   Net realisable value = Selling price **less** .... **less** ....

2   Which inventory costing method is allowed under IAS 2?

   (a)   FIFO

   (b)   LIFO

3   IAS 41 has abolished the concept of cost for measurement purposes.

   True   ☐

   False   ☐

4   What are the two categories in the agricultural production system?

Answers to Quick Quiz

1   Net realisable value = selling price **less** *costs to completion* **less** *costs necessary to make the sale.*
2   (a) FIFO. LIFO is not allowed.
3   False. Cost is allowed if fair value is not available at initial recognition.
4   Consumable and bearer. See Section 2.4.

Now try the questions below from the Practice Question Bank

Number	Level	Marks	Time
15	–	10	20 mins
16	–	10	20 mins

15

Taxation

Introduction

In almost all countries entities are taxed on the basis of their trading income. In some countries this may be called corporation or corporate tax, but we will follow the terminology of IAS 12 *Income taxes* and call it income tax.

There are two aspects of income tax which must be accounted for: **current tax** and **deferred tax**. These will be discussed in Sections 1 and 2 respectively.

Study guide

		Intellectual level
B8	**Taxation**	
(a)	Account for current taxation in accordance with relevant accounting standards	2
(b)	Explain the effect of taxable temporary differences on accounting and taxable profits	2
(c)	Compute and record deferred tax amounts in the financial statements	2

1 Current tax

FAST FORWARD

Current tax is the amount payable to the tax authorities in relation to the trading activities of the period. It is generally straightforward.

1.1 Introduction

You may have assumed until now that accounting for income tax was a very simple matter for companies. You would calculate the amount of tax due to be paid on the company's taxable profits and with this amount you would:

DEBIT   Tax charge (statement of profit or loss)
CREDIT   Tax liability (statement of financial position)

Indeed, this aspect of corporate taxation – **current tax** – **is** ordinarily straightforward. Complexities arise, however, when we consider the future tax consequences of what is going on in the accounts now. This is an aspect of tax called **deferred tax**, which we will look at in the next section.

1.2 IAS 12 Income taxes

IAS 12 covers both current and deferred tax. The parts relating to current tax are fairly brief, because this is the simple and uncontroversial area of tax.

1.3 Definitions

These are some of the definitions given in IAS 12. We will look at the rest later.

Key terms

> - **Accounting profit.** Net profit or loss for a period before deducting tax expense.
>
> - **Taxable profit (tax loss).** The profit (loss) for a period, determined in accordance with the rules established by the taxation authorities, upon which income taxes are payable (recoverable).
>
> - **Tax expense (tax income).** The aggregate amount included in the determination of net profit or loss for the period in respect of current tax and deferred tax.
>
> - **Current tax.** The amount of income taxes payable (recoverable) in respect of the taxable profit (tax loss) for a period.
>
> (IAS 12: para. 5)

Before we go any further, let us be clear about the difference between current and deferred tax.

(a) **Current tax** is the amount **actually payable** to the tax authorities in relation to the trading activities of the entity during the period.

(b) **Deferred tax** is an **accounting measure**, used to match the tax effects of transactions with their accounting impact and thereby produce less distorted results.

You should understand this a little better after working through Section 2.

1.4 Recognition of current tax liabilities and assets

IAS 12 requires any **unpaid tax** in respect of the current or prior periods to be recognised as a **liability**.
Conversely, any **excess tax** paid in respect of current or prior periods over what is due should be
recognised as an **asset**.   (IAS 12: para. 12)

Question	Current tax

In 20X8 Darton Co had taxable profits of $120,000. In the previous year (20X7) income tax on 20X7
profits had been estimated as $30,000. The corporate income tax rate is 30%.

Required

Calculate tax payable and the charge for 20X8 if the tax due on 20X7 profits was subsequently agreed with
the tax authorities as:

(a) $35,000; or
(b) $25,000.

Any under or over payments are not settled until the following year's tax payment is due.

Answer

(a)

	$
Tax due on 20X8 profits ($120,000 × 30%)	36,000
Underpayment for 20X7	5,000
Tax charge and liability	41,000

(b)

	$
Tax due on 20X8 profits (as above)	36,000
Overpayment for 20X7	(5,000)
Tax charge and liability	31,000

Alternatively, the rebate due could be shown separately as income in the statement of comprehensive
income and as an asset in the statement of financial position. An offset approach like this is, however,
most likely.

Taking this a stage further, IAS 12 also requires recognition as an asset of the benefit relating to any tax
loss that can be **carried back** to recover current tax of a previous period. This is acceptable because it is
probable that the benefit will flow to the entity **and** it can be reliably measured.   (IAS 12: para. 13)

1.5 Example: tax losses carried back

In 20X7 Eramu Co paid $50,000 in tax on its profits. In 20X8 the company made tax losses of $24,000.
The local tax authority rules allow losses to be carried back to offset against current tax of prior years.
The tax rate is 30%.

Required

Show the tax charge and tax liability for 20X8.

Solution

Tax repayment due on tax losses = 30% × $24,000 = $7,200.

The double entry will be:

DEBIT	Tax receivable (statement of financial position)	$7,200	
CREDIT	Tax repayment (statement of profit or loss)		$7,200

The tax receivable will be shown as an asset until the repayment is received from the tax authorities.

1.6 Measurement

Measurement of current tax liabilities (assets) for the current and prior periods is very simple. They are measured at the **amount expected to be paid to (recovered from) the tax authorities** (IAS 12: para. 46).

1.7 Recognition of current tax

Normally, current tax is recognised as income or expense and included in the net profit or loss for the period, (IAS 12: para. 77) except in two cases:

(a) Tax arising from a **business combination** is treated differently (tax assets or liabilities of the acquired subsidiary will form part of the goodwill calculation). (IAS 12: para. 19)

(b) Tax arising from a transaction or event which is recognised **directly in equity** (in the same or a different period). (IAS 12: Obj)

The rule in (b) is logical. If a transaction or event is charged or credited directly to equity, rather than to profit or loss, then the related tax should be also. An example of such a situation is where, under IAS 8, an adjustment is made to the **opening balance of retained earnings** due to either a change in accounting policy that is applied retrospectively, or to the correction of a material prior period error (see Chapter 7).

1.8 Presentation

In the statement of financial position, **tax assets and liabilities** should be shown separately from other assets and liabilities.

Current tax assets and liabilities can be **offset**, but this should happen only when certain conditions apply.

(a) The entity has a **legally enforceable right** to set off the recognised amounts.

(b) The entity intends to settle the amounts on a **net basis**, or to realise the asset and settle the liability at the same time. (IAS 12: para. 71)

The **tax expense (income)** related to the profit or loss from ordinary activities should be shown in the statement of profit or loss. (IAS 12: para. 77)

The **disclosure requirements** of IAS 12 are extensive and we will look at these later in the chapter.

2 Deferred tax

FAST FORWARD

Deferred tax is an accounting measure used to match the tax effects of transactions with their accounting impact. It is quite complex.

Exam focus point

Students invariably find deferred tax very confusing. You are unlikely to be asked any very complicated questions on deferred tax in Financial Reporting, so concentrate on understanding and being able to explain the purpose of deferred tax and to carry out basic calculations.

2.1 What is deferred tax?

Deferred tax is an accounting adjustment. It is not a tax which is payable to the tax authorities.

When a company recognises an asset or liability, it expects to **recover or settle the carrying amount** of that asset or liability. In other words, it expects to sell or use up assets, and to pay off liabilities. What happens if that recovery or settlement is likely to make future tax payments larger (or smaller) than they would otherwise have been if the recovery or settlement had no tax consequences? In these circumstances, IAS 12 requires companies to recognise a **deferred tax liability** (or **deferred tax asset**).

2.2 Definitions

Don't worry too much if you don't understand the concept of deferred tax yet; things should become clearer as you work through this section. First of all, here are the definitions relating to deferred tax given in IAS 12.

Key terms

Deferred tax liabilities are the amounts of income taxes payable in future periods in respect of taxable temporary differences.

Deferred tax assets are the amounts of income taxes recoverable in future periods in respect of:

- Deductible temporary differences
- The carry forward of unused tax losses
- The carry forward of unused tax credits

Temporary differences are differences between the carrying amount of an asset or liability in the statement of financial position and its tax base. Temporary differences may be either:

- **Taxable temporary differences**, which are temporary differences that will result in taxable amounts in determining taxable profit (tax loss) of future periods when the carrying amount of the asset or liability is recovered or settled

- **Deductible temporary differences**, which are temporary differences that will result in amounts that are deductible in determining taxable profit (tax loss) of future periods when the carrying amount of the asset or liability is recovered or settled

The **tax base** of an asset or liability is the amount attributed to that asset or liability for tax purposes.

(IAS 12: para. 5)

We need to look at some of these definitions in more detail.

2.3 Tax base

We can expand on the definition given above by stating that the **tax base of an asset** is the amount that will be deductible for tax purposes against any taxable economic benefits that will flow to the entity when it recovers the carrying amount of the asset. Where those economic benefits are not taxable, the tax base of the asset is the same as its carrying amount. So where the carrying amount and the tax base of the asset are **different**, a temporary difference exists.

(IAS 12: para. 7)

Question   Tax base (1)

State the tax base of each of the following assets and any temporary difference arising.

(a) A machine cost $10,000 and has a carrying amount of $8,000. For tax purposes, depreciation of $3,000 has already been deducted in the current and prior periods and the remaining cost will be deductible in future periods, either as depreciation or through a deduction on disposal. Revenue generated by using the machine is taxable, any gain on disposal of the machine will be taxable and any loss on disposal will be deductible for tax purposes.

(b) Interest receivable has a carrying amount of $1,000. The related interest revenue will be taxed on a cash basis.

(c) Trade receivables have a carrying amount of $10,000. The related revenue has already been included in taxable profit (tax loss).

(d) A loan receivable has a carrying amount of $1m. The repayment of the loan will have no tax consequences.

(a)   The tax base of the machine is $7,000. The temporary difference is $1,000.
(b)   The tax base of the interest receivable is nil. The temporary difference is $1,000.
(c)   The tax base of the trade receivables is $10,000. No temporary difference.
(d)   The tax base of the loan is $1m. No temporary difference.

In the case of a **liability**, the tax base will be its carrying amount, less any amount that will be deducted for tax purposes in relation to the liability in future periods. For revenue received in advance, the tax base of the resulting liability is its carrying amount, less any amount of the revenue that will **not** be taxable in future periods.

Question

Tax base (2)

State the tax base of each of the following liabilities and any resulting temporary difference.

(a)   Current liabilities include accrued expenses with a carrying amount of $1,000. The related expense will be deducted for tax purposes on a cash basis.

(b)   Current liabilities include interest revenue received in advance, with a carrying amount of $10,000. The related interest revenue was taxed on a cash basis.

(c)   Current liabilities include accrued expenses with a carrying amount of $2,000. The related expense has already been deducted for tax purposes.

(d)   Current liabilities include accrued fines and penalties with a carrying amount of $100. Fines and penalties are not deductible for tax purposes.

(e)   A loan payable has a carrying amount of $1m. The repayment of the loan will have no tax consequences.

Answer

(a)   The tax base of the accrued expenses is nil. The temporary difference is $1,000.
(b)   The tax base of the interest received in advance is nil. The temporary difference is $10,000.
(c)   The tax base of the accrued expenses is $2,000. No temporary difference.
(d)   The tax base of the accrued fines and penalties is $100. No temporary difference.
(e)   The tax base of the loan is $1m. No temporary difference.

IAS 12 gives the following examples of circumstances in which the carrying amount of an asset or liability will be **equal to its tax base** and **no temporary difference will arise**.

•   **Accrued expenses** which have already been deducted in determining an entity's current tax liability for the current or earlier periods

•   A **loan payable** which is measured at the amount originally received and this amount is the same as the amount repayable on final maturity of the loan

•   **Accrued expenses** which will never be deductible for tax purposes

•   **Accrued income** which will never be taxable   (IAS 12: para. 8)

2.4 Temporary differences

You may have found the definition of temporary differences somewhat confusing. Remember that accounting profits form the basis for computing **taxable profits**, on which the tax liability for the year is calculated; however, accounting profits and taxable profits are different. There are two reasons for the differences.

(a) **Permanent differences**. These occur when certain items of revenue or expense are excluded from the computation of taxable profits (for example, entertainment expenses may not be allowable for tax purposes).

(b) **Temporary differences**. These occur when items of revenue or expense are included in both accounting profits and taxable profits, but not for the same accounting period. For example, an expense which is allowable as a deduction in arriving at taxable profits for 20X7 might not be included in the financial accounts until 20X8 or later. In the long run, the total taxable profits and total accounting profits will be the same (except for permanent differences) so that timing differences originate in one period and are capable of reversal in one or more subsequent periods. Deferred tax is the tax attributable to **temporary differences.**

(IAS 12: para. 9)

The distinction made in the definition between **taxable temporary differences** and **deductible temporary differences** can be made clearer by looking at whether the difference will cause **more** or **less** tax to be paid in future periods.

2.5 Section summary

- Deferred tax is an **accounting device**. It does **not** represent tax payable to the tax authorities.
- The **tax base** of an asset or liability is the value of that asset or liability for tax purposes.
- You should understand the difference between **permanent and temporary differences**.
- Deferred tax is the tax attributable to **temporary differences**.

3 Taxable temporary differences

FAST FORWARD

Deferred tax assets and liabilities arise from taxable and deductible temporary differences.

Exam focus point

The rule to remember here is that:

'All taxable temporary differences give rise to a deferred tax liability.'   (IAS 12: para. 5)

3.1 Examples

The following are examples of circumstances that give rise to taxable temporary differences. They will all result in a higher tax charge in one or more future periods.

3.1.1 Transactions that affect the statement of profit or loss

(a) **Interest revenue** received in arrears and included in accounting profit on the basis of time apportionment. It is included in taxable profit, however, on a cash basis.

(b) **Sale of goods revenue** is included in accounting profit when the goods are delivered, but only included in taxable profit when cash is received.

(c) **Depreciation** of an asset is accelerated for tax purposes. When new assets are purchased, allowances may be available against taxable profits which exceed the amount of depreciation chargeable on the assets in the financial accounts for the year of purchase.

(d) **Development costs** which have been capitalised will be amortised in the statement of profit or loss, but they were deducted in full from taxable profit in the period in which they were incurred.

(e) **Prepaid expenses** have already been deducted on a cash basis in determining the taxable profit of the current or previous periods.   (IAS 12: IEA1–5)

3.1.2 Transactions that affect the statement of financial position

(a) **Accounting depreciation of an asset** is not deductible for tax purposes. Deduction for tax purposes will be allowed through tax depreciation.

(b) A borrower records a **loan** at proceeds received (amount due at maturity) less transaction costs. The carrying amount of the loan is subsequently increased by amortisation of the transaction costs against accounting profit. The transaction costs were, however, deducted for tax purposes in the period when the loan was first recognised.

(IAS 12: IEA6–9)

3.1.3 Fair value adjustments and revaluations

(a) **Current investments** or financial instruments are carried at fair value. This exceeds cost, but no equivalent adjustment is made for tax purposes.

(b) Property, plant and equipment can be **revalued** by an entity (under IAS 16), but no equivalent adjustment is made for tax purposes. This also applies to long-term investments. As the tax base remains at the original value, there will be a difference between the carrying amount and the tax base, leading to an increase in the deferred tax provision.

In these cases, the deferred tax provision recognises that additional profit will be realised on the use or eventual disposal of these assets, leading to a higher tax charge.

(IAS 12: IEA10/11)

3.2 Taxable temporary differences

Try to **understand the reasoning** behind the recognition of deferred tax liabilities on taxable temporary differences.

(a) When an **asset is recognised**, it is expected that its carrying amount will be recovered in the form of economic benefits that flow to the entity in future periods.

(b) If the carrying amount of the asset is **greater than** its tax base, then taxable economic benefits will also be greater than the amount that will be allowed as a deduction for tax purposes.

(c) The difference is therefore a **taxable temporary difference** and the obligation to pay the resulting income taxes in future periods is a **deferred tax liability**.

(d) As the entity recovers the carrying amount of the asset, the taxable temporary difference will **reverse** and the entity will have taxable profit.

(e) It is then probable that economic benefits will flow from the entity in the form of **tax payments**, and so the recognition of deferred tax liabilities is required by IAS 12.

3.3 Example: taxable temporary differences

Custard Co purchased an asset costing $1,500. At the end of 20X8 the carrying amount is $1,000. The cumulative depreciation for tax purposes is $900 and the current tax rate is 25%.

Required
Calculate the deferred tax liability for the asset.

Solution

Firstly, what is the tax base of the asset? It is $1,500 – $900 = $600.

In order to recover the carrying amount of $1,000, Custard Co must earn taxable income of $1,000, but it will only be able to deduct $600 as a taxable expense. Custard Co must therefore pay income tax of $400 × 25% = $100 when the carrying amount of the asset is recovered.

Custard Co must therefore recognise a deferred tax liability of $400 × 25% = $100, recognising the difference between the carrying amount of $1,000 and the tax base of $600 as a taxable temporary difference.

3.4 Timing differences

Some temporary differences are often called **timing differences**, when income or expense is included in accounting profit in one period, but is included in taxable profit in a different period. The main types of taxable temporary differences which are timing differences and which result in deferred tax liabilities are:

- **Interest received** which is accounted for on an accruals basis, but which for tax purposes is included on a cash basis

- **Accelerated depreciation** for tax purposes

- Capitalised and amortised **development costs**

3.5 Revalued assets

Under IAS 16 assets may be revalued. This changes the carrying amount of the asset but the tax base of the asset is not adjusted. Consequently, the taxable flow of economic benefits to the entity as the carrying value of the asset is recovered will differ from the amount that will be deductible for tax purposes.

The difference between the carrying amount of a revalued asset and its tax base is a temporary difference and gives rise to a **deferred tax liability or asset**. (IAS 12: IEA10/11)

The following question on accelerated depreciation should clarify some of the issues and introduce you to the calculations which may be necessary in the exam.

Question   Current and deferred tax

Jonquil Co buys equipment for $50,000 on 1 January 20X1 and depreciates it on a straight-line basis over its expected useful life of five years. It has no other non-current assets.

For tax purposes, the equipment is depreciated at 25% per annum on a straight-line basis.

Accounting profit before tax for the years 20X1 to 20X5 is $20,000 per annum.

The tax rate is 40%.

Required:

Show the calculations of current and deferred tax for the years 20X1 to 20X5.

Answer

The differences between accounting and tax depreciation on the equipment will be:

	20X1	20X2	20X3	20X4	20X5
	$	$	$	$	$
Accounting depreciation	10,000	10,000	10,000	10,000	10,000
Tax depreciation	12,500	12,500	12,500	12,500	–
Taxable difference	2,500	2,500	2,500	2,500	(10,000)
Cumulative difference	2,500	5,000	7,500	10,000	–

Note that the taxable difference reverses in 20X5, when the equipment is fully depreciated for tax purposes.

This will give the following differences between the carrying amount and the tax base of the asset at the end of each year.

	20X1	20X2	20X3	20X4	20X5
	$	$	$	$	$
Carrying amount at Y/E	40,000	30,000	20,000	10,000	–
Tax base at Y/E	37,500	25,000	12,500	–	–
Cumulative difference	2,500	5,000	7,500	10,000	
Deferred tax 40%	1,000	2,000	3,000	4,000	–

The tax charge to profit or loss will be as follows:

	20X1 $	20X2 $	20X3 $	20X4 $	20X5 $
Profit for the year	20,000	20,000	20,000	20,000	20,000
Add back depreciation	10,000	10,000	10,000	10,000	10,000
Deduct tax depreciation	(12,500)	(12,500)	(12,500)	(12,500)	–
Taxable amount	17,500	17,500	17,500	17,500	30,000
Tax charge 40%	7,000	7,000	7,000	7,000	12,000
Deferred tax adjustment*	1,000	1,000	1,000	1,000	(4,000)
Tax charge in profit or loss	8,000	8,000	8,000	8,000	8,000

*2,500 × 40%

The effect of the deferred tax adjustment is to recognise the additional tax which will be due in 20X5 evenly over years 20X1 to 20X5.

At the end of 20X5 there will be no remaining temporary difference and the balance on the deferred tax account in the statement of financial position will be credited back to profit or loss.
The statements of financial position will show:

	20X1 $	20X2 $	20X3 $	20X4 $	20X5 $
Non current liabilities					
Deferred tax	1,000	2,000	3,000	4,000	–
Current liabilities					
Income tax payable	7,000	7,000	7,000	7,000	12,000

3.6 Section summary

- Taxable temporary differences give rise to a **deferred tax liability**.
- Many taxable temporary differences are **timing differences**.
- Timing differences arise when income or an expense is included in accounting profit in one period, but in taxable profit in a **different period**.

4 Deductible temporary differences

4.1 Definition

Refer again to the definition given in Section 2 above.

There is a proviso, however. The deferred tax asset must also satisfy the **recognition criteria** given in IAS 12. This is that a deferred tax asset should be recognised for all deductible temporary differences to the extent that it is **probable that taxable profit will be available** against which it can be utilised (IAS 12: para. 24). Before we look at this issue in more detail, let us consider the examples of deductible temporary differences given in the standard.

4.2 Transactions that affect the statement of profit or loss

(a) **Retirement benefit costs** (pension costs) are deducted from accounting profit as service is provided by the employee. They are not deducted in determining taxable profit until the entity pays either retirement benefits or contributions to a fund. (This may also apply to similar expenses.)

(b) **Accumulated depreciation** of an asset in the financial statements is greater than the accumulated depreciation allowed for tax purposes up to the end of the reporting period.

(c) The **cost of inventories** sold before the end of the reporting period is deducted from accounting profit when goods/services are delivered, but is deducted from taxable profit when the cash is received.

(d) The **NRV** of inventory, or the **recoverable amount** of an item of property, plant and equipment falls and the carrying value is therefore **reduced**, but that reduction is ignored for tax purposes until the asset is sold.

(e) **Research costs** (or organisation/other start-up costs) are recognised as an expense for accounting purposes but are not deductible against taxable profits until a later period.

(f) Income is **deferred** in the statement of financial position, but has already been included in taxable profit in current/prior periods. (IAS 12: IEB1–7)

4.3 Fair value adjustments and revaluations

Current investments or **financial instruments** may be carried at fair value which is less than cost, but no equivalent adjustment is made for tax purposes. (IAS 12: IEB8)

4.4 Recognition of deductible temporary differences

Let us lay out the reasoning behind the recognition of deferred tax assets arising from deductible temporary differences.

(a) When a **liability is recognised**, it is assumed that its carrying amount will be settled in the form of outflows of economic benefits from the entity in future periods.

(b) When these resources flow from the entity, part or all may be deductible in determining taxable profits of a **period later** than that in which the liability is recognised.

(c) A **temporary tax difference** then exists between the carrying amount of the liability and its tax base.

(d) A **deferred tax asset** therefore arises, representing the income taxes that will be recoverable in future periods when that part of the liability is allowed as a deduction from taxable profit.

(e) Similarly, when the carrying amount of an asset is **less than its tax base**, the difference gives rise to a deferred tax asset in respect of the income taxes that will be recoverable in future periods.

4.5 Example: deductible temporary differences

Pargatha Co recognises a liability of $10,000 for accrued product warranty costs on 31 December 20X7. These product warranty costs will not be deductible for tax purposes until the entity pays claims. The tax rate is 25%.

Required

State the deferred tax implications of this situation.

Solution

What is the tax base of the liability? It is nil (carrying amount of $10,000 less the amount that will be deductible for tax purposes in respect of the liability in future periods).

When the liability is settled for its carrying amount, the entity's future taxable profit will be reduced by $10,000 and so its future tax payments by $10,000 × 25% = $2,500.

The difference of $10,000 between the carrying amount ($10,000) and the tax base (nil) is a deductible temporary difference. Pargatha Co should therefore recognise a deferred tax asset of $10,000 × 25% = $2,500 **provided that** it is probable that the entity will earn sufficient taxable profits in future periods to benefit from a reduction in tax payments.

4.6 Taxable profits in future periods

For a deferred tax asset to be recognised, sufficient future taxable profits must be available against which the deductible difference can be utilised.

(IAS 12: para. 24)

4.7 Unused tax losses and unused tax credits

An entity may have unused tax losses or credits (ie which it can offset against taxable profits) at the end of a period. Should a deferred tax asset be recognised in relation to such amounts? IAS 12 states that a deferred tax asset may be recognised in such circumstances **to the extent that it is probable future taxable profit will be available against which the unused tax losses/credits can be utilised**.

(IAS 12: para. 24)

4.8 Section summary

- Deductible temporary differences give rise to a **deferred tax asset**.
- Deferred tax assets can only be recognised when **sufficient future taxable profits** exist against which they can be utilised.

5 Measurement and recognition of deferred tax

5.1 Basis of provision of deferred tax

The entity recognises that each timing difference at the end of the reporting period has an effect on future tax payments. If a company claims an accelerated tax allowance on an item of plant, future tax assessments will be bigger than they would have been otherwise. Future transactions may well affect those assessments still further, but that is not relevant in assessing the position at the end of the reporting period.

5.2 Example

Suppose that Girdo Co begins trading on 1 January 20X7. In its first year it makes profits of $5m, the depreciation charge is $1m and the tax allowances on those assets amount to $1.5m. The rate of income tax is 30%.

Solution

The tax liability is $1.35m (30% × $m(5.0 + 1.0 − 1.5)), but the debit to profit or loss is increased by the deferred tax liability of 30% × $0.5m = $150,000. The total charge to profit or loss is therefore $1.5m which is an effective tax rate of 30% on accounting profits (ie 30% × $5.0m).

5.3 Changes in tax rates

Where the corporate rate of income tax **fluctuates from one year to another**, a problem arises in respect of the amount of deferred tax to be credited (debited) to the statement of profit or loss in later years.

IAS 12 requires deferred tax assets and liabilities to be measured at the tax rates expected to apply in the period **when the asset is realised or liability settled**, based on tax rates and laws enacted (or substantively enacted) at the end of the reporting period.

(IAS 12: para. 47)

5.4 Example

Ginger Co has an asset with a carrying amount of $80,000 and a tax base of $50,000. The current tax rate is 30% and the rate is being reduced to 25% in the next tax year. Ginger Co plans to dispose of the asset for its carrying amount and will do so after the tax rate falls.

The deferred tax on the temporary difference is therefore $30,000 × 25% = $7,500.

5.5 Discounting

Discounting is used to allow for the effect of the time value of money.

IAS 12 states that deferred tax assets and liabilities **should not be discounted** because of the complexities and difficulties involved. Discounting is applied to other non-current liabilities such as provisions and deferred payments. (IAS 12: paras. 53–4)

5.6 Carrying amount of deferred tax assets

The carrying amount of deferred tax assets should be **reviewed at the end of each reporting period** and reduced where appropriate (insufficient future taxable profits). Such a reduction may be reversed in future years. (IAS 12: para. 56)

5.7 Recognition

As with current tax, deferred tax should normally be recognised as income or an expense and included in the net profit or loss for the year in the **statement of profit or loss**. Current and deferred tax will together make up the tax charge. The exception is where the tax arises from a transaction or event which is recognised (in the same or a different period) **directly in equity** such as a revaluation where the surplus is credited to the revaluation surplus. (IAS 12: para. 58)

The figures shown for deferred tax in the statement of profit or loss will consist of **two components**:

(a) Deferred tax relating to **timing differences**

(b) Adjustments relating to **changes in the carrying amount of deferred tax assets/liabilities** (where there is no change in timing differences), eg changes in tax rates/laws, reassessment of the recoverability of deferred tax assets, or a change in the expected recovery of an asset

Items in (b) will be recognised in profit or loss, **unless** they relate to items previously charged/credited to equity. (IAS 12: para. 60)

Deferred tax (and current tax) should be **charged/credited directly to equity** if the tax relates to items also charged/credited directly to equity (in the same or a different period).

Examples of IASs which allow certain items to be credited/charged directly to equity include:

(a) **Revaluations** of property, plant and equipment (IAS 16)

(b) The effect of a **change in accounting policy** (applied retrospectively) or correction of a **material error** (IAS 8)

Revaluations will appear under 'other comprehensive income' in the statement of profit or loss and other comprehensive income and the tax element will be shown separately as 'Income tax relating to components of other comprehensive income'. (IAS 12: para. 61)

5.7.1 Example

Zebra Co owns a property which has a carrying amount at the beginning of 20X9 of $1,500,000. At the year end it has entered into a contract to sell the property for $1,800,000. The tax rate is 30%. How will this be shown in the financial statements?

Solution

STATEMENT OF PROFIT OR LOSS AND OTHER COMPREHENSIVE INCOME (EXTRACT)

	$'000
Profit for the year	X
Other comprehensive income:	
Gains on property revaluation	300
Income tax relating to components of other comprehensive income (300 × 30%)	(90)
Other comprehensive income for the year net of tax	210

The amounts will be posted as follows:

	Debit $'000	Credit $'000
Property, plant and equipment	300	
Deferred tax		90
Revaluation surplus		210

In this case the deferred tax has been deducted from the revaluation surplus rather than being charged to profit or loss.

5.8 Why do we recognise deferred tax?

(a) Adjustments for deferred tax are made in accordance with the **accruals concept** and in accordance with the definition of a **liability** in the Conceptual Framework, ie a past event has given rise to an obligation in the form of increased taxation which will be payable in the future. (IASB Conceptual Framework: paras 4.15–4.19)

The amount can be reliably estimated. A deferred tax asset similarly meets the definition of an **asset**.

(b) If the future tax consequences of transactions are not recognised, profit can be overstated, leading to overpayment of dividends and distortion of share price and EPS.

6 Taxation in company accounts

FAST FORWARD

> In the statement of financial position the liability for tax payable is the tax on the current year profits. In the statement of profit or loss the tax on the current year profits is adjusted for transfers to or from the deferred tax balance and for prior year under- or overprovisions.

We have now looked at the 'ingredients' of taxation in company accounts. There are two aspects to consider:

(a) Taxation on profits in the statement of profit or loss
(b) Taxation payments due, shown as a liability in the statement of financial position

6.1 Taxation in the statement of profit or loss

The tax on profit on ordinary activities is calculated by **aggregating**:

(a) **Income tax** on taxable profits
(b) **Transfers to or from deferred taxation**
(c) Any **under provision or overprovision** of income tax on profits of previous years

When income tax on profits is calculated, **the calculation is only an estimate of what the company thinks its tax liability will be. In subsequent dealings with the tax authorities, a different income tax charge might eventually be agreed.**

The difference between the estimated tax on profits for one year and the actual tax charge finally agreed for the year is made as an adjustment to taxation on profits in the following year, **resulting in the disclosure of either an underprovision or an overprovision of tax.**

Question

In the accounting year to 31 December 20X3, Neil Down Co made an operating profit before taxation of $110,000.

Income tax on the operating profit has been estimated as $45,000. In the previous year (20X2) income tax on 20X2 profits had been estimated as $38,000 but it was subsequently agreed at $40,500.

A transfer to the credit of the deferred taxation account of $16,000 will be made in 20X3.

Required

(a) Calculate the tax on profits for 20X3 for disclosure in the accounts.
(b) Calculate the amount of tax payable.

Answer

		$
(a)	Income tax on profits (liability in the statement of FP)	45,000
	Deferred taxation	16,000
	Underprovision of tax in previous year $(40,500 – 38,000)	2,500
	Tax on profits for 20X3 (profit or loss charge)	63,500
		$
(b)	Tax payable on 20X3 profits (liability)	45,000

6.2 Taxation in the statement of financial position

It should already be apparent from the previous examples that the income tax charge in the statement of profit or loss will not be the same as income tax liabilities in the statement of financial position.

In the statement of financial position, there are several items which we might expect to find.

(a) **Amounts underprovided/overprovided in the prior year**. These will appear as debits/credits to the tax payable account.

(b) If no tax is payable (or very little), then there might be an **income tax recoverable asset** disclosed in current assets (income tax is normally recovered by offset against the tax liability for the year).

(c) There will usually be a **liability for tax** assessed as due for the current year.

(d) We may also find a **liability on the deferred taxation account**. Deferred taxation is shown under 'non-current liabilities' in the statement of financial position.

Question

For the year ended 31 July 20X4 Norman Kronkest Co made taxable trading profits of $1,200,000 on which income tax is payable at 30%.

(a) A transfer of $20,000 will be made to the deferred taxation account. The balance on this account was $100,000 before making any adjustments for items listed in this paragraph.

(b) The estimated tax on profits for the year ended 31 July 20X3 was $80,000, but tax has now been agreed at $84,000 and fully paid.

(c) Tax on profits for the year to 31 July 20X4 is payable on 1 May 20X5.

(d) In the year to 31 July 20X4 the company made a capital gain of $60,000 on the sale of some property. This gain is taxable at a rate of 30%.

Required

(a) Calculate the tax charge for the year to 31 July 20X4.

(b) Calculate the tax liabilities in the statement of financial position of Norman Kronkest as at 31 July 20X4.

(a) *Tax charge for the year*

			$
(i)	Tax on trading profits (30% of 1,200,000)		360,000
	Tax on capital gain (30% of 60,000)		18,000
	Deferred taxation		20,000
			398,000
	Underprovision of taxation in previous years $(84,000 – 80,000)		4,000
	Tax charge on profit for the period		402,000

(ii) The statement of profit or loss will show the following:

	$
Profit before tax (1,200,000 + 60,000)	1,260,000
Income tax expense	(402,000)
Profit for the year	858,000

(b)

	$
Deferred taxation	
Balance brought forward	100,000
Transferred from profit or loss	20,000
Deferred taxation in the statement of financial position	120,000

The tax liability is as follows.

	$
Payable on 1 May 20X5	
Tax on profits (30% of $1,200,000)	360,000
Tax on capital gain (30% of $60,000)	18,000
Due on 1 May 20X5	378,000

	$
Summary	
Current liabilities	
Tax, payable on 1 May 20X5	378,000
Non-current liabilities	
Deferred taxation	120,000

It may be helpful to show the journal entries for these items.

		$	$
DEBIT	Tax charge (statement of profit or loss)	402,000	
CREDIT	Tax payable		*382,000
	Deferred tax		20,000

*This account will show a debit balance of $4,000 until the underprovision is recorded, since payment has already been made: (360,000 + 18,000 + 4,000). The closing balance will therefore be $378.000.

6.3 Presentation of tax assets and liabilities

These should be **presented separately** from other assets and liabilities in the statement of financial position. Deferred tax assets and liabilities should be distinguished from current tax assets and liabilities.

In addition, deferred tax assets/liabilities should **not** be classified as current assets/liabilities, where an entity makes such a distinction.

There are only limited circumstances where **current tax** assets and liabilities may be **offset**. This should only occur if two things apply:

(a)   The entity has a legally enforceable right to set off the recognised amounts.

(b)   The entity intends either to settle on a net basis, or to realise the asset and settle the liability simultaneously.

Similar criteria apply to the **offset of deferred tax assets and liabilities**. (IAS 12: paras. 71–4)

6.4 Presentation of tax expense

The tax expense or income related to the profit or loss for the year should be presented in the statement of profit or loss. (IAS 12: para. 77)

Chapter Roundup

- **Current tax** is the amount payable to the tax authorities in relation to the trading activities during the period. It is generally straightforward.

- **Deferred tax** is an accounting measure, used to match the tax effects of transactions with their accounting impact. It is quite complex.

- **Deferred tax assets and liabilities** arise from deductible and taxable temporary differences.

- In the statement of financial position the liability for tax payable is the tax on the current year profits. In the statement of profit or loss the tax on current year profits is adjusted for transfers to or from the deferred tax balance and for prior year under- and overprovisions.

Quick Quiz

1   The tax expense related to the profit for the year should be shown in the statement of profit or loss.

   True ☐

   False ☐

2   Deferred tax liabilities are the amounts of income taxes payable in future periods in respect of ....

3   Give three examples of temporary differences.

4   Harry Co has a tax overprovision relating to the prior year of $3,000. Taxable temporary differences have increased by $6,000 and profit for the year is $150,000. Tax is at 30%.
    What is the charge to profit or loss?

Answers to quick quiz

1 True

2 Taxable temporary differences

3 Any three of:

- Interest revenue received in arrears
- Depreciation accelerated for tax purposes
- Development costs capitalised in the statement of financial position
- Prepayments
- Sale of goods revenue recognised before the cash is received

4 $43,800

	$
Tax on profit (150,000 × 30%)	45,000
Overprovision	(3,000)
Deferred tax increase (6,000 × 30%)	1,800
	43,800

Now try the question below from the Practice Question Bank

Number	Level	Marks	Time
26	–	6	12 mins

Presentation of published financial statements

Topic list	Syllabus reference
1 IAS 1 *Presentation of financial statements*	D1
2 Statement of financial position	D1
3 The current/non-current distinction	D1
4 Statement of profit or loss and other comprehensive income	D1
5 Statement of profit or loss	D1
6 Revision of basic accounts	D1
7 Changes in equity	D1
8 Notes to the financial statements	D1

Introduction

The bulk of this Study Text looks at the accounts of limited liability companies, either single companies or groups of companies.

We begin in this chapter by looking at the overall **content and format** of company financial statements. These are governed by IAS 1 (revised) *Presentation of financial statements*.

Study guide

		Intellectual level
D1	**Preparation of single entity financial statements**	
(a)	Prepare an entity's statement of financial position and statement of profit or loss and other comprehensive income in accordance with the structure and content prescribed within IFRS and with accounting treatments as identified within syllabus sections A, B and C	2
(b)	Prepare and explain the contents and purpose of the statement of changes in equity	2

1 IAS 1 *Presentation of financial statements*

FAST FORWARD

IAS 1 covers the form and content of financial statements. The main components are:

- Statement of financial position
- Statement of profit or loss and other comprehensive income
- Statement of changes in equity
- Statement of cash flows
- Notes to the financial statements

1.1 Profit or loss for the year

The statement of profit or loss and other comprehensive income is the most significant indicator of a company's financial performance. So it is important to ensure that it is not misleading.

IAS 1 stipulates that all items of income and expense recognised in a period shall be included in profit or loss unless a **Standard** requires otherwise. (IAS 1: para. 88)

Circumstances where items may be excluded from profit or loss for the current year include the correction of errors and the effect of changes in accounting policies. These are covered in IAS 8. (IAS 1: para. 89)

1.2 How items are disclosed

IAS 1 specifies disclosures of certain items in certain ways:

- Some items must appear on the face of the statement of financial position or statement of profit or loss and other comprehensive income.

- Other items can appear in a **note to the financial statements** instead.

- **Recommended formats** are given which entities may or may not follow, depending on their circumstances. (IAS 1: paras. 79, 97)

Obviously, disclosures specified by **other standards** must also be made, and we will mention the necessary disclosures when we cover each statement in turn. Disclosures in both IAS 1 and other standards must be made either on the face of the statement or in the notes unless otherwise stated, ie disclosures cannot be made in an accompanying commentary or report.

1.3 Identification of financial statements

As a result of the above point, it is most important that entities **distinguish the financial statements** very clearly from any other information published with them. This is because all IASs/IFRSs apply **only** to the financial statements (ie the main statements and related notes), so readers of the annual report must be able to differentiate between the parts of the report which are prepared under IFRSs, and other parts which are not. (IAS 1: para. 50)

The entity should **identify each** financial statement and the notes very clearly. IAS 1 also requires disclosure of the following information in a prominent position. If necessary it should be repeated wherever it is felt to be of use to the reader in his understanding of the information presented.

- **Name** of the reporting entity (or other means of identification)
- Whether the accounts cover the **single entity** only or a group of entities
- The **date of the end of the reporting period** or the period covered by the financial statements (as appropriate)
- The **presentation currency**
- The **level of rounding** used in presenting amounts in the financial statements   (IAS 1: para. 51)

Judgement must be used to determine the best method of presenting this information. In particular, the standard suggests that the approach to this will be very different when the financial statements are communicated electronically.   (IAS 1: para. 52)

The **level of rounding** is important, as presenting figures in thousands or millions of units makes the figures more understandable. The level of rounding must be disclosed, however, and it should not obscure necessary details or make the information less relevant.   (IAS 1: para. 53)

1.4 Reporting period

It is normal for entities to present financial statements **annually** and IAS 1 states that they should be prepared at least as often as this. If (unusually) the end of an entity's reporting period is changed, for whatever reason, the period for which the statements are presented will be less or more than one year. In such cases the entity should also disclose:

(a)   The **reason(s) why** a period other than one year is used
(b)   The fact that the comparative figures given **are not in fact comparable**   (IAS 1: para. 36)

For practical purposes, some entities prefer to use a period which **approximates to a year**, eg 52 weeks, and the IAS allows this approach as it will produce statements not materially different from those produced on an annual basis.   (IAS 1: para. 37)

1.5 Timeliness

If the publication of financial statements is delayed too long after the reporting period, their usefulness will be severely diminished. An entity with consistently complex operations cannot use this as a reason for its failure to report on a timely basis. Local legislation and market regulation imposes specific deadlines on certain entities.

IAS 1 looks at the statement of financial position and statement of profit or loss and other comprehensive income. We will not give all the detailed disclosures as some are outside the scope of your syllabus. Instead we will look at a **'proforma' set of accounts** based on the Standard.

2 Statement of financial position

FAST FORWARD

IAS 1 suggests a format for the statement of financial position. Certain items are specified for **disclosure on the face of the financial statements**.

IAS 1 discusses the distinction between current and non-current items in some detail, as we shall see in the next section. First of all we can look at the **suggested format** of the statement of financial position (given in an appendix to the Standard) and then look at further disclosures required.

2.1 Statement of financial position example

The example given by IAS 1 is as follows.   (IAS 1: IG)

GENERIC GROUP – STATEMENT OF FINANCIAL POSITION AT 31 DECEMBER

	20X7 $'000	20X6 $'000
Assets		
Non-current assets		
Property, plant and equipment	350,700	360,020
Goodwill	80,800	91,200
Other intangible assets	227,470	227,470
Investments in associates	100,150	110,770
Investments in equity instruments	142,500	156,000
	901,620	945,460
Current assets		
Inventories	135,230	132,500
Trade receivables	91,600	110,800
Other current assets	25,650	12,540
Cash and cash equivalents	312,400	322,900
	564,880	578,740
Total assets	1,466,500	1,524,200
Equity and liabilities		
Equity attributable to owners of the parent		
Share capital	650,000	600,000
Retained earnings	243,500	161,700
Other components of equity	10,200	21,200
	903,700	782,900
Non-controlling interest	70,050	48,600
Total equity	973,750	831,500
Non-current liabilities		
Long-term borrowings	120,000	160,000
Deferred tax	28,800	26,040
Long-term provisions	28,850	52,240
Total non-current liabilities	177,650	238,280
Current liabilities		
Trade and other payables	115,100	187,620
Short-term borrowings	150,000	200,000
Current portion of long-term borrowings	10,000	20,000
Current tax payable	35,000	42,000
Short-term provisions	5,000	4,800
Total current liabilities	315,100	454,420
Total liabilities	492,750	692,700
Total equity and liabilities	1,466,500	1,524,200

IAS 1 (revised) specifies various items which must appear on the **face of the statement of financial position** as a minimum disclosure.

(a)   Property, plant and equipment (Chapter 4)
(b)   Investment property (Chapter 4)
(c)   Intangible assets (Chapter 5)
(d)   Financial assets (excluding amounts shown under (e), (h) and (i)) (Chapter 14)
(e)   Investments accounted for using the equity method (Chapter 11)
(f)   Biological assets (Chapter 12)
(g)   Inventories (Chapter 12)
(h)   Trade and other receivables
(i)   Cash and cash equivalents (Chapter 21)
(j)   Assets classified as held for sale under IFRS 5 (Chapter 7)

(k)   Trade and other payables
(l)   Provisions (Chapter 13)
(m) Financial liabilities (other than (j) and (k))
(n)   Current tax liabilities and assets as in IAS 12 (Chapter 17)
(o)   Deferred tax liabilities and assets (Chapter 17)
(p)   Liabilities included in disposal groups under IFRS 5 (Chapter 7)
(q)   Non-controlling interests (Chapter 9)
(r)   Issued capital and reserves   (IAS 1: para. 54)

We will look at these items in the chapters marked.

Any **other line items**, headings or sub-totals should be shown on the face of the statement of financial position when it is necessary for an understanding of the entity's financial position.   (IAS 1: para. 55)

The example shown above is for illustration only (although we will follow the format in this Study Text). The IAS, however, does not prescribe the order or format in which the items listed should be presented. It simply states that they **must be presented separately** because they are so different in nature or function from each other.

Whether additional items are presented separately depends on judgements based on the assessment of the following factors.

(a)   **Nature and liquidity of assets and their materiality.** Thus goodwill and assets arising from development expenditure will be presented separately, as will monetary/non-monetary assets and current/non-current assets.

(b)   **Function within the entity.** Operating and financial assets, inventories, receivables and cash and cash equivalents are therefore shown separately.

(c)   **Amounts, nature and timing of liabilities.** Interest-bearing and non-interest-bearing liabilities and provisions will be shown separately, classified as current or non-current as appropriate.
                                                                                   (IAS 1: para. 58)

The standard also requires separate presentation where **different measurement bases** are used for assets and liabilities which differ in nature or function. According to IAS 16, for example, it is permitted to carry certain items of property, plant and equipment at cost or at a revalued amount.   (IAS 1: para. 59)

2.2 Information presented either on the face of the statement of financial position or by note

Further **sub-classification** of the line items listed above should be disclosed either on the face of the statement of financial position or in the notes. The classification will depend upon the nature of the entity's operations. As well as each item being sub-classified by its nature, any amounts payable to or receivable from any **group company or other related party** should also be disclosed separately.

The sub-classification details will in part depend on the requirements of IFRSs. The size, nature and function of the amounts involved will also be important and the factors listed above should be considered. **Disclosures** will vary from item to item and IAS 1 gives the following examples.

(a)   **Property, plant and equipment** are classified by class as described in IAS 16, *Property, plant and equipment.*

(b)   **Receivables** are analysed between amounts receivable from trade customers, other members of the group, receivables from related parties, prepayments and other amounts.

(c)   **Inventories** are sub-classified, in accordance with IAS 2 *Inventories,* into classifications such as merchandise, production supplies, materials, work in progress and finished goods.

(d)   **Provisions** are analysed showing separately provisions for employee benefit costs and any other items classified in a manner appropriate to the entity's operations.

(e)   **Equity capital and reserves** are analysed showing separately the various classes of paid in capital, share premium and reserves.   (IAS 1: para. 78)

The standard then lists some **specific disclosures** which must be made, either on the face of the statement of financial position or in the related notes.

(a)   **Share capital disclosures** (for each class of share capital)

    (i)   Number of shares authorised

    (ii)   Number of shares issued and fully paid, and issued but not fully paid

    (iii)   Par value per share, or that the shares have no par value

    (iv)   Reconciliation of the number of shares outstanding at the beginning and at the end of the year

    (v)   Rights, preferences and restrictions attaching to that class including restrictions on the distribution of dividends and the repayment of capital

    (vi)   Shares in the entity held by the entity itself or by related group companies

    (vii)   Shares reserved for issuance under options and sales contracts, including the terms and amounts
(IAS 1: para. 79)

(b)   Description of the nature and purpose of **each reserve** within owners' equity   (IAS 1: para. 79)

Some types of entity have no share capital, eg partnerships. Such entities should disclose information which is **equivalent** to that listed above. This means disclosing the movement during the period in each category of equity interest and any rights, preferences or restrictions attached to each category of equity interest.
(IAS 1: para. 80)

3 The current/non-current distinction

FAST FORWARD ▶▶

You should appreciate the distinction between current and non-current assets and liabilities and their different treatments.

3.1 The current/non-current distinction

An entity must present **current** and **non-current** assets as separate classifications on the face of the statement of financial position. A presentation based on liquidity should only be used where it provides more relevant and reliable information, in which case all assets and liabilities must be presented broadly **in order of liquidity**.
(IAS 1: para. 60)

In either case, the entity should disclose any portion of an asset or liability which is expected to be recovered or settled **after more than 12 months**. For example, for an amount receivable which is due in instalments over 18 months, the portion due after more than 12 months must be disclosed.
(IAS 1: para. 61)

The IAS emphasises how helpful information on the **operating cycle** is to users of financial statements. Where there is a clearly defined operating cycle within which the entity supplies goods or services, then information disclosing those net assets that are continuously circulating as **working capital** is useful.
(IAS 1: para. 62)

This distinguishes them from those net assets used in the long-term operations of the entity. Assets that are expected to be realised and liabilities that are due for settlement within the operating cycle are therefore highlighted.
(IAS 1: para. 62)

The liquidity and solvency of an entity is also indicated by information about the **maturity dates** of assets and liabilities. As we will see later, IFRS 7 *Financial instruments: disclosures* requires disclosure of maturity dates of both financial assets and financial liabilities. (Financial assets include trade and other receivables; financial liabilities include trade and other payables.)
(IAS 1: para. 63)

3.2 Current assets

An asset should be classified as a **current asset** when it:

- Is expected to be realised in, or is held for sale or consumption in, the normal course of the entity's operating cycle; or

- Is held primarily for trading purposes or for the short-term and expected to be realised within 12 months of the end of the reporting period; or

- Is cash or a cash equivalent asset which is not restricted in its use.

All other assets should be classified as non-current assets. (IAS 1: para. 66)

Non-current assets includes tangible, intangible, operating and financial assets of a long-term nature. Other terms with the same meaning can be used (eg 'fixed', 'long-term'). (IAS 1: para. 67)

The term 'operating cycle' has been used several times above and the standard defines it as follows.

The **operating cycle** of an entity is the time between the acquisition of assets for processing and their realisation in cash or cash equivalents. (IAS 1: para. 68)

Current assets therefore include inventories and trade receivables that are sold, consumed and realised as part of the normal operating cycle. **This is the case even where they are not expected to be realised within 12 months**. (IAS 1: para. 68)

Current assets will also include **marketable securities** if they are expected to be realised within 12 months after the reporting period. If expected to be realised later, they should be included in non-current assets. (IAS 1: para. 68)

3.3 Current liabilities

A liability should be classified as a **current liability** when it:

- Is expected to be settled in the normal course of the entity's operating cycle; or

- Is held primarily for the purpose of trading; or

- Is due to be settled within 12 months after the end of the reporting period; or when

- The entity does not have an unconditional right to defer settlement of the liability for at least 12 months after the end of the reporting period.

All other liabilities should be classified as non-current liabilities. (IAS 1: para. 69)

The categorisation of current liabilities is very similar to that of current assets. Thus, some current liabilities are part of the **working capital** used in the normal operating cycle of the business (ie trade payables and accruals for employee and other operating costs). Such items will be classed as current liabilities **even where they are due to be settled more than 12 months after the end of the reporting period**. (IAS 1: para. 70)

There are also current liabilities which are not settled as part of the normal operating cycle, but which are due to be settled within 12 months of the end of the reporting period. These include bank overdrafts, income taxes, other non-trade payables and the current portion of interest-bearing liabilities. Any interest-bearing liabilities that are used to finance working capital on a long-term basis, and that are not due for settlement within 12 months, should be classed as **non-current liabilities**. (IAS 1: para. 71)

A **non-current financial liability** due to be **settled within 12 months** of the end of the reporting period should be classified as a **current liability**, even if an agreement to refinance, or to reschedule payments, on a long-term basis is completed after the end of the reporting period and before the financial statements are authorised for issue. (IAS 1: para. 72)

End of the reporting period	Agreement to refinance on long-term basis	Date financial statements authorised for issue	Settlement date <12 months after end of the reporting period therefore current liability

A **non-current financial liability** that is payable on **demand** because the entity **breached** a **condition** of its loan agreement should be classified as **current** at the end of the reporting period even if the **lender** has agreed **after the end of the reporting period**, and **before** the financial statements are **authorised for issue**, **not** to **demand payment** as a consequence of the breach.

Condition of loan agreement breached. Non-current liability becomes payable on demand	End of the reporting period	Lender agrees not to enforce payment resulting from breach	Date financial statements are authorised for issue. Loan shown as **current** liability

However, if the **lender** has **agreed** by the **end of the reporting period** to provide a **period of grace** ending **at least 12 months after the end of the reporting period** within which the entity can rectify the breach and during that time the lender cannot demand immediate repayment, the liability is classified as **non-current**.

4 Statement of profit or loss and other comprehensive income

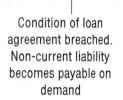

In June 2011 the IASB published an amendment to IAS 1 called 'Presentation of items of other comprehensive income' (IASB, 2011). This changed the name of the 'statement of comprehensive income' to the 'statement of profit or loss and other comprehensive income'.

4.1 Format

IAS 1 (revised) allows income and expense items to be presented either:

(a)   In a single statement of profit or loss and other comprehensive income; or

(b)   In two statements: a separate statement of profit or loss and statement of other comprehensive income.

                                                                                        (IAS 1: para. 81)

The format for a single statement of profit or loss and other comprehensive income is shown as follows in the standard. The section down to 'profit for the year' can be shown as a separate 'statement of profit or loss' with an additional 'statement of other comprehensive income'. Note that not all of the items which would appear under 'other comprehensive income' are included in your syllabus.

Exam focus point

In the examinations, if a 'statement of profit or loss and other comprehensive income' is referred to, this will always relate to the single statement format. If 'statements of profit or loss' are referred to, this relates to the statement from 'revenue' to 'profit for the year'. Exams may refer to 'other comprehensive income' which relates to the 'other comprehensive income' section of the statement. In practice, the item of 'other comprehensive income' you are most likely to meet is a revaluation gain. Where we have used 'statement of profit or loss' in this Text, this can be taken to refer to the profit or loss section of the full statement or separate statement of profit or loss.

GENERIC GROUP – STATEMENT OF PROFIT OR LOSS AND OTHER COMPREHENSIVE INCOME
FOR THE YEAR ENDED 31 DECEMBER 20X7

	20X7 $'000	20X6 $'000
Revenue	390,000	355,000
Cost of sales	(245,000)	(230,000)
Gross profit	145,000	125,000
Other income	20,667	11,300
Distribution costs	(9,000)	(8,700)
Administrative expenses	(20,000)	(21,000)
Other expenses	(2,100)	(1,200)
Finance costs	(8,000)	(7,500)
Share of profit of associates	35,100	30,100
Profit before tax	161,667	128,000
Income tax expense	(40,417)	(32,000)
Profit for the year from continuing operations	121,250	96,000
Loss for the year from discontinued operations	–	(30,500)
Profit for the year	121,250	65,500

	20X7	20X6
Other comprehensive income:		
Items that will not be reclassified to profit or loss:		
Gains on property revaluation	933	3,367
Investments in equity instruments	(24,000)	26,667
Remeasurement gains (losses) on defined benefit pension plans	(667)	1,333
Share of gain(loss) on property revaluation of associates	400	(700)
Income tax relating to items that will not be reclassified	5,834	(7,667)
	(17,500)	23,000
Items that may be reclassified subsequently to profit or loss		
*Exchange differences on translating foreign operations	5,334	10,667
*Cash flow hedges	(667)	(4,000)
Income tax relating to items that may be reclassified	(1,167)	(1,667)
	3,500	5,000
Other comprehensive income for the year, net of tax	(14,000)	28,000
Total comprehensive income for the year	107,250	93,500
Profit attributable to:		
Owners of the parent	97,000	52,400
Non-controlling interest	24,250	13,100
	121,250	65,500
Total comprehensive income attributable to		
Owners of the parent	85,800	74,800
Non-controlling interest	21,450	18,700
	107,250	93,500
Earnings per share (in currency units)	0.46	0.30

*Not in the Financial Reporting syllabus

This is the full statement as issued by the IASB.   (IAS 1: IG)

Note that the amendment to IAS 1 now splits items of other comprehensive income into those which can be reclassified to profit or loss and those which can not be reclassified. In practice, none of the items which can be reclassified are examinable at Financial Reporting, so this is not an issue that you will encounter in your exam.

Companies are given the option of presenting this information in two statements:

GENERIC GROUP – STATEMENT OF PROFIT OR LOSS FOR THE YEAR ENDED 31 DECEMBER 20X7

	20X7 $'000	20X6 $'000
Revenue	390,000	355,000
Cost of sales	(245,000)	(230,000)
Gross profit	145,000	125,000
Other income	20,667	11,300
Distribution costs	(9,000)	(8,700)
Administrative expenses	(20,000)	(21,000)
Other expenses	(2,100)	(1,200)
Finance costs	(8,000)	(7,500)
Share of profit of associates	35,100	30,100
Profit before tax	161,667	128,000
Income tax expense	(40,417)	(32,000)
Profit for the year from continuing operations	121,250	96,000
Loss for the year from discontinued operations	–	(30,500)
Profit for the year	121,250	65,500
Profit attributable to:		
Owners of the parent	97,000	52,400
Non-controlling interest	24,250	13,100
	121,250	65,500

GENERIC GROUP STATEMENT OF PROFIT OR LOSS AND OTHER COMPREHENSIVE INCOME FOR THE YEAR ENDED 31 DECEMBER 20X7 (TWO STATEMENT FORMAT)

	20X7 $'000	20X6 $'000
Profit for the year	121,250	65,500
Other comprehensive income:		
Items that will not be reclassified to profit or loss:		
Gains on property revaluation	933	3,367
Investments in equity instruments	(24,000)	26,667
*Actuarial gains (losses) on defined benefit pension plans	(667)	1,333
Share of gain(loss) on property revaluation of associates	400	(700)
Income tax relating to items that will not be reclassified	5,834	(7,667)
	(17,500)	23,000
Items that may be reclassified to profit or loss:		
*Exchange differences on translating foreign operations	5,334	10,667
*Cash flow hedges	(667)	(4,000)
Income tax relating to items that may be reclassified	(1,167)	(1,667)
	3,500	5,000
Other comprehensive income for the year, net of tax	(14,000)	28,000
Total comprehensive income for the year	107,250	93,500
Total comprehensive income attributable to		
Owners of the parent	85,800	74,800
Non-controlling interest	21,450	18,700
	107,250	93,500

*Not in the Financial Reporting syllabus

5 Statement of profit or loss

IAS 1 offers two possible formats for the statement of profit or loss or separate profit or loss section – by function or by nature. Classification by function is more common.

5.1 Examples of separate statements of profit or loss

GENERIC GROUP
STATEMENT OF PROFIT OR LOSS FOR THE YEAR ENDED 31 DECEMBER 20X8

Illustrating the classification of expenses by function

	20X8 $'000	20X7 $'000
Revenue	X	X
Cost of sales	(X)	(X)
Gross profit	X	X
Other income	X	X
Distribution costs	(X)	(X)
Administrative expenses	(X)	(X)
Other expenses	(X)	(X)
Finance costs	(X)	(X)
Share of profit of associates	X	X
Profit before tax	X	X
Income tax expense	(X)	(X)
Profit for the year	X	X
Profit attributable to:		
Owners of the parent	X	X
Non-controlling interest	X	X
	X	X

Illustrating the classification of expenses by nature

	20X8 $'000	20X7 $'000
Revenue	X	X
Other operating income	X	X
Changes in inventories of finished goods and work in progress	(X)	X
Work performed by the entity and capitalised	X	X
Raw material and consumables used	(X)	(X)
Employee benefits expense	(X)	(X)
Depreciation and amortisation expense	(X)	(X)
Impairment of property, plant and equipment	(X)	(X)
Other expenses	(X)	(X)
Finance costs	(X)	(X)
Share of profit of associates	X	X
Profit before tax	X	X
Income tax expense	(X)	(X)
Profit for the year	X	X
Profit attributable to:		
Owners of the parent	X	X
Non-controlling interest	X	X
	X	X

Note. The usual method of presentation is expenses by function and this is the format likely to appear in your exam.

5.2 Information presented in the statement of profit or loss

The standard lists the following as the **minimum** to be disclosed on the face of the statement of profit or loss.

(a) Revenue
(b) Finance costs
(c) Share of profits and losses of associates and joint ventures accounted for using the equity method
(d) A single amount for the total of discontinued operations
(e) Tax expense

(IAS 1: para. 82)

The following items must be disclosed as allocations of profit or loss for the period.

(a) Profit or loss attributable to non-controlling interest
(b) Profit or loss attributable to owners of the parent   (IAS 1: para. 81)

The allocated amounts must not be presented as items of income or expense. (These relate to group accounts, covered later in this Text.)

5.3 Information presented either in the statement or in the notes

An analysis of expenses must be shown either in the profit or loss section (as above, which is encouraged by the standard) or by note, using a classification based on **either** the nature of the expenses or their function. This **sub-classification of expenses** indicates a range of components of financial performance; these may differ in terms of stability, potential for gain or loss and predictability.   (IAS 1: paras. 99–106)

5.3.1 Nature of expense method

Expenses are not reallocated amongst various functions within the entity, but are aggregated in the statement of profit or loss **according to their nature** (eg purchase of materials, depreciation, wages and salaries, transport costs). This is by far the easiest method, especially for smaller entities.

(IAS 1: para. 102)

5.3.2 Function of expense/cost of sales method

You are likely to be more familiar with this method. Expenses are classified according to their function as part of cost of sales, distribution or administrative activities. This method often gives **more relevant information** for users, but the allocation of expenses by function requires the use of judgement and can be arbitrary. Consequently, perhaps, when this method is used, entities should disclose **additional information** on the nature of expenses, including staff costs, and depreciation and amortisation expense.

(IAS 1: para. 103)

Which of the above methods is chosen by an entity will depend on **historical and industry factors**, and also the **nature of the organisation**. Under each method, there should be given an indication of costs which are likely to vary (directly or indirectly) with the level of sales or production. The choice of method should fairly reflect the main elements of the entity's performance (IAS 1: para.105). **This is the method you should expect to see in your exam.**

Exam focus point

Note that you get **no** marks for writing out the format for a financial statement. However, you must write out the format so that you can then fill in the numbers and earn the marks.

5.4 Dividends

IAS 1 also requires disclosure of the amount of **dividends paid** during the period covered by the financial statements. This is shown either in the statement of changes in equity or in the notes.   (IAS 1: para. 107)

Further points

(a) All requirements previously set out in other Standards for the presentation of particular line items in the statement of financial position and statement of profit or loss and other comprehensive income are now dealt with in IAS 1. These line items are: biological assets; liabilities and assets for current tax and deferred tax; and pre-tax gain or loss recognised on the disposal of assets or settlement of liabilities attributable to discontinued operations.

(b) An entity must disclose, in the summary of significant accounting policies and/or other notes, the **judgements** made by management in **applying** the **accounting policies** that have the **most significant effect** on the amounts of items recognised in the financial statements.

(IAS 1: para. 122)

(c) An entity must disclose in the notes information regarding **key assumptions** about the **future**, and other sources of **measurement uncertainty**, that have a significant **risk of** causing a **material adjustment** to the carrying amounts of assets and liabilities within the **next financial year**.

(IAS 1: para. 125)

 One of the competences you require to fulfil performance objective 10 of the PER is the ability to compile financial statements and accounts in line with appropriate standards and guidelines. You can apply the knowledge you obtain from this section of the text to help you demonstrate this competence.

6 Revision of basic accounts

FAST FORWARD

The Study Guide requires you to be able to prepare a basic set of company accounts from a trial balance.

In the next part of this text we move on to the mechanics of preparing financial statements. It would be useful at this point to refresh your memory of the basic accounting you have already studied and these questions will help you. Make sure that you understand everything before you go on.

 Question

Basics

A friend has bought some shares in a company quoted on a local stock exchange and has received the latest accounts. There is one page he is having difficulty in understanding.

Required

Briefly, but clearly, answer his questions.

(a) What is a statement of financial position?
(b) What is an asset?
(c) What is a liability?
(d) What is share capital?
(e) What are reserves?
(f) Why does the statement of financial position balance?
(g) To what extent does the statement of financial position value my investment?

Answer

(a) A **statement of financial position** is a statement of the assets, liabilities and capital of a business as at a stated date. It is laid out to show either total assets as equivalent to total liabilities and capital or net assets as equivalent to capital. Other formats are also possible but the top half (or left hand) total will always equal the bottom half (or right hand) total.

(b)   An **asset** is a resource controlled by a business and is expected to be of some future benefit. Its value is determined as the historical cost of producing or obtaining it (unless an attempt is being made to reflect rising prices in the accounts, in which case a replacement cost might be used). Examples of assets are:

(i)   Plant, machinery, land and other **non-current assets**

(ii)   **Current** assets such as inventories, cash and debts owed to the business with reasonable assurance of recovery: these are assets which are not intended to be held on a continuing basis in the business

(c)   A **liability** is an amount owed by a business, other than the amount owed to its proprietors (capital). Examples of liabilities are:

(i)   Amounts owed to the government (sales or other taxes)

(ii)   Amounts owed to suppliers

(iii) Bank overdraft

(iv)   Long-term loans from banks or investors

It is usual to differentiate between 'current' and 'long-term' liabilities. The former fall due within a year of the end of the reporting period.

(d)   **Share capital** is the permanent investment in a business by its owners. In the case of a limited company, this takes the form of **shares** for which investors subscribe on formation of the company. Each share has a **nominal** or **par** (ie face) **value** (say $1). In the statement of financial position, total issued share capital is shown at its par value.

(e)   If a company issues shares for more than their par value (at a **premium**) then (usually) by law this premium must be recorded separately from the par value in a 'share premium account'. This is an example of a reserve. It belongs to the shareholders but cannot be distributed to them, because it is a **capital reserve**. Other capital reserves include the revaluation surplus, which shows the surpluses arising on revaluation of assets which are still owned by the company.

Share capital and capital reserves are not distributable except on the winding up of the company, as a guarantee to the company's creditors that the company has enough assets to meet its debts. This is necessary because shareholders in limited liability companies have 'limited liability'; once they have paid the company for their shares they have no further liability to it if it becomes insolvent. The proprietors of other businesses are, by contrast, personally liable for business debts.

Retained earnings constitute accumulated profits (less losses) made by the company and can be distributed to shareholders as **dividends**. They too belong to the shareholders, and so are a claim on the resources of the company.

(f)   Statements of financial position do not always balance on the first attempt, as all accountants know! However, once errors are corrected, all statements of financial position balance. This is because in **double entry bookkeeping** every transaction recorded has a dual effect. Assets are always equal to liabilities plus capital and so capital is always equal to assets less liabilities. This makes sense as the owners of the business are entitled to the net assets of the business as representing their capital plus accumulated surpluses (or less accumulated deficit).

(g)   The statement of financial position is not intended as a statement of a business's worth at a given point in time. This is because, except where some attempt is made to adjust for the effects of rising prices, assets and liabilities are recorded at **historical cost** and on a prudent basis. For example, if there is any doubt about the recoverability of a debt, then the value in the accounts must be reduced to the likely recoverable amount. In addition, where non-current assets have a finite useful life, their cost is gradually written off to reflect the use being made of them.

Sometimes non-current assets are **revalued** to their market value but this revaluation then goes out of date as few assets are revalued every year.

The figure in the statement of financial position for capital and reserves therefore bears **no relationship** to the market value of shares. Market values are the product of a large number of factors, including general economic conditions, alternative investment returns (eg interest rates), likely future profits and dividends and, not least, market sentiment.

The accountant of Fiddles Co, a limited liability company, has begun preparing final accounts but the work is not yet complete. At this stage the items included in the list of account balances are as follows.

	$'000
Land	100
Buildings	120
Plant and machinery	170
Depreciation provision	120
Ordinary shares of $1	100
Retained earnings brought forward	380
Trade accounts receivable	200
Trade accounts payable	110
Inventory	190
Profit before tax	80
Allowance for receivables	3
Bank balance (asset)	12
Suspense	1

Notes (i) to (v) below are to be taken into account.

(i)   The accounts receivable control account figure, which is used in the list of account balances, does not agree with the total of the sales ledger. A contra of $5,000 has been entered correctly in the individual ledger accounts but has been entered on the wrong side of both control accounts.

A batch total of sales of $12,345 had been entered in the double entry system as $13,345, although the individual ledger accounts entries for these sales were correct. The balance of $4,000 on the sales returns account has inadvertently been omitted from the trial balance though correctly entered in the ledger records.

(ii)   A standing order of receipt from a regular customer for $2,000, and bank charges of $1,000, have been completely omitted from the records.

(iii)   A receivable for $1,000 is to be written off. The allowance for receivables balance is to be adjusted to 1% of receivables.

(iv)   The opening inventory figure had been overstated by $1,000 and the closing inventory figure had been understated by $2,000.

(v)   Any remaining balance on the suspense account should be treated as purchases if a debit balance and as sales if a credit balance.

Required

(a)   Prepare journal entries to cover items in notes (i) to (v) above. You are not to open any new accounts and may use only those accounts included in the list of account balances as given.

(b)   Prepare final accounts for internal use within the limits of the available information. For presentation purposes all the items arising from notes (i) to (v) above should be regarded as material.

Answer

(a) JOURNAL ENTRIES FOR ADJUSTMENTS

		Debit $	Credit $
(i)	Trade accounts payable	10,000	
	Trade accounts receivable		10,000
	Profit before tax	1,000	
	Trade accounts receivable		1,000
	Profit before tax	4,000	
	Suspense		4,000
(ii)	Bank	2,000	
	Trade accounts receivable		2,000
	Profit before tax	1,000	
	Bank		1,000
(iii)	Profit before tax	1,000	
	Trade accounts receivable		1,000
	Allowance for receivables (W1)	1,140	
	Profit before tax		1,140
(iv)	Inventories	2,000	
	Profit before tax		2,000
	Retained earnings brought forward	1,000	
	Profit before tax		1,000
(v)	Suspense	3,000	
	Profit before tax		3,000

(b) STATEMENT OF FINANCIAL POSITION

	$	$	$
Assets			
Non-current assets			
Land and buildings		220,000	
Plant and machinery		170,000	
Depreciation		(120,000)	
			270,000
Current assets			
Inventories (190 + 2)		192,000	
Accounts receivable (W1)	186,000		
Less allowance	(1,860)		
		184,140	
Bank (12 + 2 – 1)		13,000	
			389,140
Total assets			659,140
Equity and liabilities			
Equity			
Share capital		100,000	
Retained earnings (see profit or loss)		459,140	
			559,140
Current liabilities			
Accounts payable (110 – 10)			100,000
Total equity and liabilities			659,140

FIDDLES CO

STATEMENT OF PROFIT OR LOSS (This is not as per IAS 1, it is purely for internal purposes)

	$
Profit before tax (W2)	80,140
Retained earnings brought forward ($380,000 – 1,000)	379,000
Retained earnings carried forward	459,140

Workings

		$
1	**Accounts receivable**	
	Per opening trial balance	200,000
	Contra	(10,000)
	Miscasting	(1,000)
	Standing order	(2,000)
	Written off	(1,000)
		186,000
	Allowance b/f	3,000
	Allowance required	1,860
	Journal	1,140

		$
2	**Profit before tax**	
	Per question	80,000
	Wrong batch total	(1,000)
	Returns	(4,000)
	Bank charges	(1,000)
	Irrecoverable debt	(1,000)
	Allowance for receivables	1,140
	Inventory (2,000 + 1,000)	3,000
	Suspense (sales)	3,000
		80,140

This question dealt with accounts for **internal** purposes. In accounts produced for publication the statement of profit or loss would comply with the IAS 1 format. In the following chapter we will be dealing with all the issues involved in producing financial statements for publication.

7 Changes in equity

IAS 1 requires a statement of changes in equity. This shows the movement in the equity section of the statement of financial position. A full set of financial statements includes a statement of changes in equity.

7.1 Format

This is the format of the statement of changes in equity as per IAS 1. For clarity, we have left out those columns relating to items not in the Financial Reporting syllabus as highlighted in Section 4, and amended totals accordingly.

(IAS 1: IG)

GENERIC GROUP – STATEMENT OF CHANGES IN EQUITY FOR THE YEAR ENDED 31 DECEMBER 20X7

	Share capital	Retained earnings	Investments in equity instruments	Revaluation surplus	Total	Non-controlling interest	Total equity
	$'000	$'000	$'000	$'000	$'000	$'000	$'000
Balance at 1 January 20X6	600,000	118,100	1,600	–	719,700	29,800	749,500
Changes in accounting policy	–	400	–	–	400	100	500
Restated balance	600,000	118,500	1,600	–	720,100	29,900	750,000
Changes in equity							
Dividends	–	(10,000)	–	–	(10,000)	–	(10,000)
Total comprehensive income for the year	–	53,200	16,000	1,600	70,800	18,700	89,500
Balance at 31 December 20X6	600,000	161,700	17,600	1,600	780,900	48,600	829,500

	Share capital	Retained earnings	Investments in equity instruments	Revaluation surplus	Total	Non-controlling interest	Total equity
Changes in equity for 20X7							
Issue of share capital	50,000	–	–	–	50,000	–	50,000
Dividends	–	(15,000)	–	–	(15,000)	–	(15,000)
Total comprehensive income for the year	–	96,600	(14,400)	800	83,000	21,450	104,450
Transfer to retained earnings	–	200	–	(200)	–	–	–
Balance at 31 December 20X7	650,000	243,500	3,200	2,200	898,900	70,050	968,950

Note that where there has been a change of accounting policy necessitating a retrospective restatement, the adjustment is disclosed for each period. So, rather than just showing an adjustment to the balance b/f on 1.1.X7, the balances for 20X6 are restated.

8 Notes to the financial statements

FAST FORWARD

Some items need to be disclosed by way of note.

8.1 Contents of notes

The notes to the financial statements will **amplify** the information given in the statement of financial position, statement of profit or loss and other comprehensive income and statement of changes in equity. We have already noted above the information which the IAS allows to be shown by note rather than in the statements. To some extent, then, the contents of the notes will be determined by the level of detail shown on the **face of the statements**.

8.2 Structure

The notes to the financial statements should perform the following functions.

(a) Present information about the **basis on which the financial statements were prepared** and which **specific accounting policies** were chosen and applied to significant transactions/events

(b) Disclose any information, not shown elsewhere in the financial statements, which is **required by IFRSs**

(c) Show any additional information that is relevant to understanding which is not shown elsewhere in the financial statements
(IAS 1: para. 112)

The way the notes are presented is important. They should be given in a **systematic manner** and **cross referenced** back to the related figure(s) in the statement of financial position, statement of comprehensive income or statement of cash flows.
(IAS 1: para. 113)

Notes to the financial statements will amplify the information shown therein by giving the following.

(a) More **detailed analysis** or breakdowns of figures in the statements
(b) **Narrative information** explaining figures in the statements
(c) **Additional information**, eg contingent liabilities and commitments

IAS 1 suggests a **certain order** for notes to the financial statements. This will assist users when comparing the statements of different entities.

(a) Statement of **compliance** with IFRSs

(b) Statement of the **measurement basis** (bases) and accounting policies applied

(c) **Supporting information** for items presented in each financial statement in the same order as each line item and each financial statement is presented

(d) Other disclosures, eg:

    (i) Contingent liabilities, commitments and other financial disclosures

    (ii) Non-financial disclosures

The order of specific items may have to be varied occasionally, but a systematic structure is still required.

(IAS 1: para. 114)

8.3 Disclosure of accounting policies

The accounting policies section should describe the following.

(a) The **measurement basis** (or bases) used in preparing the financial statements

(b) The **other accounting policies** used, as required for a proper understanding of the financial statements *(IAS 1: para. 117)*

This information may be shown in the notes or sometimes as a **separate component** of the financial statements.

The information on measurement bases used is obviously fundamental to an understanding of the financial statements. Where **more than one basis is used**, it should be stated to which assets or liabilities each basis has been applied. *(IAS 1: para. 118)*

Note. Accounting policies are covered in Chapter 7.

8.4 Other disclosures

An entity must disclose in the notes:

(a) The amount of dividends proposed or declared before the financial statements were authorised for issue but not recognised as a distribution to owners during the period, and the amount per share

(b) The amount of any cumulative preference dividends not recognised *(IAS 1: para. 137)*

IAS 1 ends by listing some **specific disclosures** which will always be required if they are not shown elsewhere in the financial statements.

(a) The domicile and legal form of the entity, its country of incorporation and the address of the registered office (or, if different, principal place of business)

(b) A description of the nature of the entity's operations and its principal activities

(c) The name of the parent entity and the ultimate parent entity of the group *(IAS 1: para. 138)*

Exam focus point

> You will have to produce financial statements suitable for publication in your exam, so this chapter is important and you should refer back to it.

Question   **Financial statements**

The accountant of Wislon Co has prepared the following list of account balances as at 31 December 20X7.

	$'000
50c ordinary shares (fully paid)	450
10% loan notes (secured)	200
Retained earnings 1.1.X7	242
General reserve 1.1.X7	171
Land and buildings 1.1.X7 (cost)	430
Plant and machinery 1.1.X7 (cost)	830

	$'000
Accumulated depreciation	
Buildings 1.1.X7	20
Plant and machinery 1.1.X7	222
Inventory 1.1.X7	190
Sales	2,695
Purchases	2,152
Ordinary dividend	15
Loan note interest	10
Wages and salaries	254
Light and heat	31
Sundry expenses	113
Suspense account	135
Trade accounts receivable	179
Trade accounts payable	195
Cash	126

Additional information

(i) Sundry expenses include $9,000 paid in respect of insurance for the year ending 1 September 20X8. Light and heat does not include an invoice of $3,000 for electricity for the three months ending 2 January 20X8, which was paid in February 20X8. Light and heat also includes $20,000 relating to salesmen's commission.

(ii) The suspense account is in respect of the following items.

	$'000
Proceeds from the issue of 100,000 ordinary shares	120
Proceeds from the sale of plant	300
	420
Less consideration for the acquisition of Mary & Co	285
	135

(iii) The net assets of Mary & Co were purchased on 3 March 20X7. Assets were valued as follows.

	$'000
Equity investments	231
Inventory	34
	265

All the inventory acquired was sold during 20X7. The equity investments were still held by Wislon at 31.12.X7. Goodwill has not been impaired in value.

(iv) The property was acquired some years ago. The buildings element of the cost was estimated at $100,000 and the estimated useful life of the assets was 50 years at the time of purchase. As at 31 December 20X7 the property is to be revalued at $800,000.

(v) The plant which was sold had cost $350,000 and had a carrying amount of $274,000 as on 1.1.X7. $36,000 depreciation is to be charged on plant and machinery for 20X7.

(vi) The management wish to provide for:

    (1) Loan note interest due
    (2) A transfer to general reserve of $16,000
    (3) Audit fees of $4,000

(vii) Inventory as at 31 December 20X7 was valued at $220,000 (cost).

(viii) Taxation is to be ignored.

Required

Prepare the financial statements of Wislon Co as at 31 December 20X7. You do not need to produce notes to the statements.

(a) Normal adjustments are needed for accruals and prepayments (insurance, light and heat, loan note interest and audit fees). The loan note interest accrued is calculated as follows.

	$'000
Charge needed in profit or loss (10% × $200,000)	20
Amount paid so far, as shown in list of account balances	10
Accrual: presumably six months' interest now payable	10

The accrued expenses shown in the statement of financial position comprise:

	$'000
Loan note interest	10
Light and heat	3
Audit fee	4
	17

(b) The misposting of $20,000 to light and heat is also adjusted, by reducing the light and heat expense, but charging $20,000 to salesmen's commission.

(c) Depreciation on the building is calculated as $\dfrac{\$100,000}{50} = \$2,000$.

The carrying amount of the building is then $430,000 – $20,000 – $2,000 = $408,000 at the end of the year. When the property is revalued a reserve of $800,000 – $408,000 = $392,000 is then created.

(d) The profit on disposal of plant is calculated as proceeds $300,000 (per suspense account) less carrying amount $274,000, ie $26,000. The cost of the remaining plant is calculated at $830,000 – $350,000 = $480,000. The depreciation provision at the year end is:

	$'000
Balance 1.1.X7	222
Charge for 20X7	36
Less depreciation on disposals (350 – 274)	(76)
	182

(e) Goodwill arising on the purchase of Mary & Co is:

	$'000
Consideration (per suspense account)	285
Assets at valuation	265
Goodwill	20

This is shown as an asset in the statement of financial position. The equity investments, being owned by Wislon Co at the year end, are also shown on the statement of financial position, whereas Mary & Co's inventory, acquired and then sold, is added to the purchases figure for the year.

(f) The other item in the suspense account is dealt with as follows.

	$'000
Proceeds of issue of 100,000 ordinary shares	120
Less nominal value 100,000 × 50c	50
Excess of consideration over par value (= share premium)	70

(g) The transfer to general reserve increases it to $171,000 + $16,000 = $187,000.

We can now prepare the financial statements.

WISLON CO
STATEMENT OF PROFIT OR LOSS AND OTHER COMPREHENSIVE INCOME FOR THE YEAR ENDED
31 DECEMBER 20X7

	$'000
Revenue	2,695
Cost of sales (W1)	(2,156)
Gross profit	539
Other income (profit on disposal of plant)	26
Administrative expenses (W2)	(437)
Finance costs	(20)
Profit for the year	108
Other comprehensive income:	
Gain on property revaluation	392
Total comprehensive income for the year	500

Note

The only item of 'other comprehensive income' for the year was the revaluation gain. If there had been no revaluation gain, only a statement of profit or loss would have been required.

Workings

1 *Cost of sales*

	$'000
Opening inventory	190
Purchases (2,152 + 34)	2,186
Closing inventory	(220)
	2,156

2 *Administrative expenses*

	$'000
Wages, salaries and commission (254 + 20)	274
Sundry expenses (113 – 6)	107
Light and heat (31 – 20 + 3)	14
Depreciation: buildings	2
plant	36
Audit fees	4
	437

WISLON CO
STATEMENT OF FINANCIAL POSITION AS AT 31 DECEMBER 20X7

	$'000	$'000
Assets		
Non-current assets		
Property, plant and equipment		
Property at valuation		800
Plant: cost	480	
accumulated depreciation	(182)	
		298
Goodwill		20
Equity investments		231
Current assets		
Inventories	220	
Trade accounts receivable	179	
Prepayments	6	
Cash and cash equivalents	126	
		531
Total assets		1,880

	$'000	$'000
Equity and liabilities		
Equity		
50c ordinary shares	500	
Share premium	70	
Revaluation surplus	392	
General reserve	187	
Retained earnings	319	
		1,468
Non-current liabilities		
10% loan stock (secured)		200
Current liabilities		
Trade and other payables	195	
Accrued expenses	17	
		212
Total equity and liabilities		1,880

WISLON CO
STATEMENT OF CHANGES IN EQUITY
FOR THE YEAR ENDED 31 DECEMBER 20X7

	Share capital $'000	Share premium $'000	Retained earnings $'000	General reserve $'000	Revaluation Surplus $'000	Total $'000
Balance at 1.1.X7	450	–	242	171	–	863
Issue of share capital	50	70				120
Dividends			(15)			(15)
Total comprehensive income for the year			108		392	500
Transfer to reserve			(16)	16		
Balance at 31.12.X7	500	70	319	187	392	1,468

Note that the total comprehensive income is analysed into its components.

Chapter Roundup

- IAS 1 covers the form and content of financial statements. The main components are:
  - Statement of financial position
  - Statement of profit or loss and other comprehensive income
  - Statement of changes in equity
  - Statement of cash flows
  - Notes to the financial statements

- IAS 1 suggests a **format** for the statement of financial position. Certain items are specified for **disclosure on the face of the financial statements**.

- You should appreciate the distinction between current and non-current assets and liabilities and their different treatments.

- In June 2011 the IASB published an amendment to IAS 1 called 'Presentation of items of other comprehensive income'. This changed the name of the 'statement of comprehensive income' to 'statement of profit or loss and other comprehensive income'.

- IAS 1 offers two possible formats for the statement of profit or loss or separate profit or loss section – by function or by nature. Classification by function is more common.

- The Study Guide requires you to be able to prepare a basic set of company accounts from a trial balance.

- IAS 1 requires a statement of changes in equity. This shows the movement in the equity section of the statement of financial position. A full set of financial statements includes a statement of changes in equity.

- Some items need to be disclosed by way of note.

Quick Quiz

1   Which of the following are examples of current assets?
   (a)   Property, plant and equipment
   (b)   Prepayments
   (c)   Cash equivalents
   (d)   Manufacturing licences
   (e)   Retained earnings

2   Provisions must be disclosed in the statement of financial position.

   True   ☐

   False ☐

3   Which of the following must be disclosed on the face of the statement of profit or loss?
   (a)   Tax expense
   (b)   Analysis of expenses
   (c)   Net profit or loss for the year

4   Where are revaluation gains shown in the financial statements?

Answers to Quick Quiz

1   (b) and (c) only
2   True
3   (a) and (c) only. (b) may be shown in the notes.
4   In other comprehensive income and in the statement of changes in equity.

Now try the question below from the Practice Question Bank

Number	Level	Marks	Time
4	–	25	49 mins

Reporting financial performance

Topic list	Syllabus reference
1 IAS 8 *Accounting policies, changes in accounting estimates and errors*	B9
2 Changes in accounting polices	A1/B9
3 Errors	B9
4 IFRS 5 *Non-current assets held for sale and discontinued operations*	B9
5 IAS 21 Foreign currency transactions	B12

Introduction

IAS 8 deals with accounting policies. It also looks at certain circumstances and transactions which require different treatment to normal profit or loss items.

IFRS 5 on assets held for sale and discontinued operations is an important standard which gives users additional information regarding the sources of the entity's profit and losses.

IAS 21 on foreign currency is a new addition to the Financial Reporting syllabus but will only be tested at a basic level.

Study guide

		Intellectual level
A1	**The need for a conceptual framework and the characteristics of useful information**	
(g)	Discuss the principle of comparability in accounting for changes in accounting policies	2
B9	**Reporting financial performance**	
(a)	Discuss the importance of identifying and reporting the results of discontinued operations	2
(b)	Define and account for non-current assets held for sale and discontinued operations	2
(c)	Indicate the circumstances where separate disclosure of material items of income and expense is required	2
(d)	Account for changes in accounting estimates, changes in accounting policy and correction of prior period errors	2
B12	**Foreign currency transactions**	
(a)	Explain the difference between functional and presentation currency and explain why adjustments for foreign currency transactions are necessary.	2
(b)	Account for the translation of foreign currency transactions and monetary/non-monetary foreign currency items at the reporting date.	2

1 IAS 8 *Accounting policies, changes in accounting estimates and errors*

FAST FORWARD

> IAS 8 deals with changes in accounting estimates, changes in accounting policies and errors.

1.1 Definitions

The following definitions are given in the standard.

Key terms

- **Accounting policies** are the specific principles, bases, conventions, rules and practices adopted by an entity in preparing and presenting financial statements.

- A **change in accounting estimate** is an adjustment of the carrying amount of an asset or a liability or the amount of the periodic consumption of an asset, that results from the assessment of the present status of, and expected future benefits and obligations associated with, assets and liabilities. Changes in accounting estimates result from new information or new developments and, accordingly, are not corrections of errors.

- **Material.** Omissions or misstatements of items are material if they could, individually or collectively, influence the economic decisions that users make on the basis of the financial statements.

- **Prior period errors** are omissions from, and misstatements in, the entity's financial statements for one or more prior periods arising from a failure to use, or misuse of, reliable information that:

    - Was available when financial statements for those periods were authorised for issue
    - Could reasonably be expected to have been obtained and taken into account in the preparation and presentation of those financial statements

Such errors include the effects of mathematical mistakes, mistakes in applying accounting policies, oversights or misinterpretations of facts, and fraud.

- **Retrospective application** is applying a new accounting policy to transactions, other events and conditions as if that policy had always been applied.

- **Retrospective restatement** is correcting the recognition, measurement and disclosure of amounts of elements of financial statements as if a prior period error had never occurred.

- **Prospective application** of a change in accounting policy and of recognising the effect of a change in an accounting estimate, respectively, are:

  - Applying the new accounting policy to transactions, other events and conditions occurring after the date as at which the policy is changed

  - Recognising the effect of the change in the accounting estimate in the current and future periods affected by the change

- **Impracticable.** Applying a requirement is impracticable when the entity cannot apply it after making every reasonable effort to do so. It is impracticable to apply a change in an accounting policy retrospectively or to make a retrospective restatement to correct an error if one of the following apply.

  - The effects of the retrospective application or retrospective restatement are not determinable.

  - The retrospective application or retrospective restatement requires assumptions about what management's intent would have been in that period.

  - The retrospective application or retrospective restatement requires significant estimates of amounts and it is impossible to distinguish objectively information about those estimates that:

    (i) Provides evidence of circumstances that existed on the date(s) at which those amounts are to be recognised, measured or disclosed

    (ii) Would have been available when the financial statements for that prior period were authorised for issue, from other information

(IAS 8: para. 5)

1.2 Accounting policies

Accounting policies are determined by **applying the relevant IFRS** and considering any relevant Implementation Guidance issued by the IASB for that IFRS. (IAS 8: paras. 7–9)

Where there is no applicable IFRS or Interpretation management should use its **judgement** in developing and applying an accounting policy that results in information that is **relevant** and **reliable**. Management should refer to:

(a) The requirements and guidance in IFRSs dealing with **similar** and **related issues**

(b) The definitions, recognition criteria and measurement concepts for assets, liabilities and expenses in the *Conceptual Framework* (IAS 8: paras. 10–11)

Management may also consider the most recent pronouncements of **other standard setting bodies** that use a similar conceptual framework to develop standards, other accounting literature and accepted industry practices if these do not conflict with the sources above. (IAS 8: para. 12)

An entity must select and apply its accounting policies for a period **consistently** for similar transactions, other events and conditions, unless an IFRS specifically requires or permits categorisation of items for which different policies may be appropriate. If an IFRS requires or permits categorisation of items, an appropriate accounting policy must be selected and applied consistently to each category.

(IAS 8: para. 13)

BPP
LEARNING MEDIA

2 Changes in accounting policies

Changes in accounting policy are applied **retrospectively**.

2.1 Accounting for changes of policy

The same accounting policies are usually adopted from period to period, to allow users to analyse trends over time in profit, cash flows and financial position. **Changes in accounting policy will therefore be rare** and should be made only if:

(a) The change is required by an IFRS; or

(b) The change will result in a **more appropriate presentation** of events or transactions in the financial statements of the entity, providing more reliable and relevant information.   (IAS 8: para. 14)

The standard highlights two types of event which do not constitute changes in accounting policy:

(a) Adopting an accounting policy for a **new type of transaction** or event not dealt with previously by the entity

(b) Adopting a **new accounting policy** for a transaction or event which has not occurred in the past or which was not material   (IAS 8: para. 16)

In the case of tangible non-current assets, if a policy of revaluation is adopted for the first time then this is treated, not as a change of accounting policy under IAS 8, but as a revaluation under IAS 16 Property, plant and equipment (see Chapter 3). The following paragraphs do not therefore apply to a change in policy to adopt revaluations.   (IAS 8: para. 17)

A change in accounting policy **must be applied retrospectively**. **Retrospective application** means that the new accounting policy is applied to transactions and events as if it had always been in use. In other words, at the earliest date such transactions or events occurred, the policy is applied from that date.
(IAS 8: para. 19)

Prospective application is **no longer allowed** under IAS 8 unless it is **impracticable** (see Key Terms) to determine the cumulative effect of the change.   (IAS 8: para. 27)

2.2 Worked example: change of accounting policy

Tabby Co has always valued inventory on a FIFO (first in, first out) basis. In 20X9 it decides to switch to the weighted average method of valuation. Gross profit in the 20X8 financial statements was calculated as follows.

		$'000
Revenue		869
Cost of sales:		
Opening inventory	135	
Purchases	246	
Closing inventory	(174)	(207)
Gross profit		662

In order to prepare comparative figures for 20X8 showing the change of accounting policy, it is necessary to recalculate the amounts for 20X7, so that the opening inventory for 20X8 is valued on a weighted average basis.

It is established that opening inventory for 20X8 based on the weighted average method would be $122,000 and closing inventory would be $143,000. So the 20X8 gross profit now becomes:

		$'000
Revenue		869
Cost of sales:		
Opening inventory	122	
Purchases	246	
Closing inventory	(143)	(225)
		644

This shows $18,000 lower gross profit for 20X8 which will reduce net profit and retained earnings by the same amount. The opening inventory for 20X9 will be $143,000 rather than $174,000 and the statement of changes in equity for 20X9 will show an $18,000 adjustment to opening retained earnings.

2.3 Adoption of an IFRS

Where a new IFRS is adopted, resulting in a change of accounting policy, IAS 8 requires any transitional provisions in the new IFRS itself to be followed. If none are given in the IFRS which is being adopted, then you should follow the general principles of IAS 8.   (IAS 8: para. 19)

2.4 Disclosure

Certain **disclosures** are required when a change in accounting policy has a material effect on the current period or any prior period presented, or when it may have a material effect in subsequent periods.

(a)   Reasons for the change/nature of change
(b)   Reasons why new policy provides more relevant/reliable information
(c)   Amount of the adjustment for the current period and for each period presented
(d)   Amount of the adjustment relating to periods prior to those included in the comparative information
(e)   The fact that comparative information has been restated or that it is impracticable to do so
                                                                        (IAS 8: para. 29)

An entity should also disclose information relevant to assessing the **impact of new IFRS** on the financial statements where these have **not yet come into force**.   (IAS 8: para. 28)

Disclosure is important to maintain the principle of **comparability**. Users should be able to compare the financial statements of an entity over time and to compare the financial statements of entities in the same line of business. Changes of accounting policy affect comparability, so it is important that they are disclosed.

2.5 Changes in accounting estimates

Changes in accounting estimate are **not** applied retrospectively.

Estimates arise in relation to business activities because of the **uncertainties inherent within them**. Judgements are made based on the most up to date information and the use of such estimates is a necessary part of the preparation of financial statements. It does not undermine their reliability. Here are some examples of accounting estimates:

(a)   A necessary **irrecoverable debt allowance**
(b)   **Useful lives** of depreciable assets
(c)   Provision for **obsolescence of inventory**   (IAS 8: para. 32)

The rule here is that the **effect of a change in an accounting estimate** should be included in the determination of net profit or loss in one of:

(a)   The period of the change, if the change affects that period only
(b)   The period of the change and future periods, if the change affects both   (IAS 8: para. 36)

Changes may occur in the circumstances which were in force at the time the estimate was calculated, or perhaps additional information or subsequent developments have come to light.

An example of a change in accounting estimate which affects only the **current period** is the bad debt estimate. However, a revision in the life over which an asset is depreciated would affect both the **current and future periods**, in the amount of the depreciation expense.

Reasonably enough, the effect of a change in an accounting estimate should be included in the **same expense classification** as was used previously for the estimate. This rule helps to ensure **consistency** between the financial statements of different periods.

The **materiality** of the change is also relevant. The nature and amount of a change in an accounting estimate that has a material effect in the current period (or which is expected to have a material effect in subsequent periods) should be disclosed. If it is not possible to quantify the amount, this impracticability should be disclosed.
(IAS 8: para. 40)

3 Errors

FAST FORWARD

Prior period errors must be corrected **retrospectively** (IAS 8: para. 42).

3.1 Introduction

Errors discovered during a current period which **relate to a prior period** may arise through:

(a) Mathematical mistakes
(b) Mistakes in the application of accounting policies
(c) Misinterpretation of facts
(d) Oversights
(e) Fraud

A more formal definition is given in the Key Terms in Section 1.1.

Most of the time these errors can be **corrected through net profit or loss for the current period**. Where they are material prior period errors, however, this is not appropriate. The standard considers two possible treatments.

3.2 Accounting treatment

Prior period errors: correct retrospectively. There is no longer any allowed alternative treatment. This involves:

(a) Either restating the comparative amounts for the prior period(s) in which the error occurred, or
(b) When the error occurred before the earliest prior period presented, restating the opening balances of assets, liabilities and equity for that period,
(IAS 8: para. 42)

so that the financial statements are presented **as if the error had never occurred**.

Only where it is **impracticable** to determine the cumulative effect of an error on prior periods can an entity correct an error **prospectively**.
(IAS 8: para. 43)

Various **disclosures** are required:

(a) **Nature** of the prior period error

(b) For each prior period, to the extent practicable, the **amount** of the correction:

(i) For each financial statement line item affected
(ii) If IAS 33 applies, for basic and diluted earnings per share

(c) The amount of the correction at the **beginning of the earliest prior period** presented

(d) If **retrospective restatement is impracticable** for a particular prior period, the **circumstances** that led to the existence of that condition and a description of how and from when the error has been corrected. Subsequent periods need not repeat these disclosures.
(IAS 8: para. 49)

Exam focus point

If you have to deal with a change of accounting policy or an error in an accounts preparation question, remember to adjust the balance of retained earnings brought forward.

During 20X7 Global Co discovered that certain items had been included in inventory at 31 December 20X6, valued at $4.2m, which had in fact been sold before the year end. The following figures for 20X6 (as reported) and 20X7 (draft) are available.

	20X6	20X7 (draft)
	$'000	$'000
Revenue	47,400	67,200
Cost of goods sold	(34,570)	(55,800)
Profit before taxation	12,830	11,400
Income taxes	(3,880)	(3,400)
Profit for the period	8,950	8,000

Retained earnings at 1 January 20X6 were $13m. The cost of goods sold for 20X7 includes the $4.2m error in opening inventory. The income tax rate was 30% for 20X6 and 20X7. No dividends have been declared or paid.

Required

Show the statement of profit or loss for 20X7, with the 20X6 comparative, and retained earnings.

Answer

STATEMENT OF PROFIT OR LOSS

	20X6	20X7
	$'000	$'000
Revenue	47,400	67,200
Cost of goods sold (W1)	(38,770)	(51,600)
Profit before tax	8,630	15,600
Income tax (W2)	(2,620)	(4,660)
Profit for the year	6,010	10,940

RETAINED EARNINGS

	20X6	20X7
Opening retained earnings	$'000	$'000
As previously reported (13,000 + 8,950)	13,000	21,950
Correction of prior period		
error (4,200 – 1,260)	–	(2,940)
As restated	13,000	19,010
Profit for the year	6,010	10,940
Closing retained earnings	19,010	29,950

Workings

1	Cost of goods sold	20X6	20X7
		$'000	$'000
	As stated in question	34,570	55,800
	Inventory adjustment	4,200	(4,200)
		38,770	51,600

2	Income tax	20X6	20X7
		$'000	$'000
	As stated in question	3,880	3,400
	Inventory adjustment (4,200 × 30%)	(1,260)	1,260
		2,620	4,660

4 IFRS 5 *Non-current assets held for sale and discontinued operations*

FAST FORWARD IFRS 5 requires assets 'held for sale' to be presented separately in the statement of financial position. It sets out the criteria for recognising a **discontinued operation**.

4.1 Background

IFRS 5 is the result of a short-term convergence project with the US Financial Accounting Standards Board (FASB). It replaced IAS 35 *Discontinuing operations*.

IFRS 5 requires assets and groups of assets that are 'held for sale' to be **presented separately** in the statement of financial position and the results of discontinued operations to be presented separately in the statement of profit or loss and other comprehensive income. This is required so that users of financial statements will be better able to make **projections** about the financial position, profits and cash flows of the entity.

Key terms

> **Disposal group.** A group of assets to be disposed of, by sale or otherwise, together as a group in a single transaction, and liabilities directly associated with those assets that will be transferred in the transaction. (In practice a disposal group could be a subsidiary, a cash-generating unit or a single operation within an entity.)
>
> **Cash-generating unit.** The smallest identifiable group of assets for which independent cash flows can be identified and measured
> (IFRS 5: App A)

IFRS 5 does not apply to certain assets covered by other accounting standards:

(a) Deferred tax assets (IAS 12)
(b) Assets arising from employee benefits (IAS 19)
(c) Financial assets (IFRS 9)
(d) Investment properties accounted for in accordance with the fair value model (IAS 40)
(e) Agricultural and biological assets (IAS 41)
(f) Insurance contracts (IFRS 4)
                                                                                        (IFRS 5: para. 5)

4.2 Classification of assets held for sale

A non-current asset (or disposal group) should be classified as **held for sale** if its carrying amount will be recovered **principally through a sale transaction** rather than **through continuing use** (IFRS 5: para. 6). A number of detailed criteria must be met:

(a) The asset must be **available for immediate sale** in its present condition.
(b) Its sale must be **highly probable** (ie significantly more likely than not).   (IFRS 5: para. 7)

For the sale to be highly probable, the following must apply:

(a) Management must be **committed** to a plan to sell the asset.
(b) There must be an active programme to **locate a buyer**.
(c) The asset must be marketed for sale at a **price that is reasonable** in relation to its current fair value.
(d) The sale should be expected to take place **within one year** from the date of classification.
(e) It is unlikely that significant changes to the plan will be made or that the plan will be withdrawn.
                                                                                        (IFRS 5: para. 8)

An asset (or disposal group) can still be classified as held for sale, even if the sale has not actually taken place within one year. However, the delay must have been **caused by events or circumstances beyond the entity's control** and there must be sufficient evidence that the entity is still committed to sell the asset or disposal group. Otherwise the entity must cease to classify the asset as held for sale. (IFRS 5: para. 9)

If an entity acquires a disposal group (eg, a subsidiary) exclusively with a view to its subsequent disposal it can classify the asset as held for sale only if the sale is expected to take place within one year and it is highly probable that all the other criteria will be met within a short time (normally three months).

(IFRS 5: para. 11)

An asset that is to be **abandoned** should not be classified as held for sale. This is because its carrying amount will be recovered principally through continuing use. However, a disposal group to be abandoned may meet the definition of a discontinued operation and therefore separate disclosure may be required (see below).

(IFRS 5: para. 13)

Question	Held for sale

On 1 December 20X3, ManiCo became committed to a plan to sell a manufacturing facility and has already found a potential buyer. ManiCo does not intend to discontinue the operations currently carried out in the facility. At 31 December 20X3 there is a backlog of uncompleted customer orders. The company will not be able to transfer the facility to the buyer until after it ceases to operate the facility and has eliminated the backlog of uncompleted customer orders. This is not expected to occur until spring 20X4.

Required

Can the manufacturing facility be classified as 'held for sale' at 31 December 20X3?

Answer

The facility will not be transferred until the backlog of orders is completed; this demonstrates that the facility is not available for immediate sale in its present condition. The facility cannot be classified as 'held for sale' at 31 December 20X3. It must be treated in the same way as other items of property, plant and equipment: it should continue to be depreciated and should not be separately disclosed.

4.3 Measurement of assets held for sale

Key terms

> **Fair value.** The price that would be received to sell an asset or paid to transfer a liability in an orderly transaction between market participants at the measurement date.
>
> **Costs of disposal.** The incremental costs directly attributable to the disposal of an asset (or disposal group), excluding finance costs and income tax expense.
>
> **Recoverable amount.** The higher of an asset's fair value less costs of disposal and its value in use.
>
> **Value in use.** The present value of estimated future cash flows expected to arise from the continuing use of an asset and from its disposal at the end of its useful life.   (IFRS 5: App A)

A non-current asset (or disposal group) that is held for sale should be measured at the **lower of** its **carrying amount** and **fair value less costs of disposal**. Fair value less costs of disposal is equivalent to net realisable value.

(IFRS 5: para. 15)

An impairment loss should be recognised where fair value less costs of disposal is lower than carrying amount. Note that this is an exception to the normal rule. IAS 36 *Impairment of assets* requires an entity to recognise an impairment loss only where an asset's recoverable amount is lower than its carrying value. Recoverable amount is defined as the higher of fair value less costs of disposal and value in use. IAS 36 does not apply to assets held for sale. An impairment loss on an asset held under IFRS 5 is charged to **profit or loss**.

(IFRS 5: paras. 20/21)

Non-current assets held for sale **should not be depreciated**, even if they are still being used by the entity.

A non-current asset held for sale should be **remeasured** at the lower of its carrying amount and fair value less costs of disposal at each reporting date at which it is still classified as held for sale. Any impairment (arising for instance from an increase in costs of disposal) is recognised and charged to profit or loss. If

the fair value less costs of disposal of the asset increases, then the carrying amount of the asset can be increased and the resulting gain should be recognised in profit or loss, effectively reversing the impairment loss. However, this gain should not be in excess of impairment losses previously recognised under IFRS 5 or under IAS 36 (before the asset was classified as held for sale) (IFRS 5: para. 21).

(IFRS 5: para. 25)

A non-current asset (or disposal group) that is **no longer classified as held for sale** (for example, because the sale has not taken place within one year) is measured at the **lower of**:

(a)   Its **carrying amount** before it was classified as held for sale, adjusted for any depreciation that would have been charged had the asset not been held for sale

(b)   Its **recoverable amount** at the date of the decision not to sell   (IFRS 5: para. 27)

4.4 Presentation of a non-current asset or disposal group classified as held for sale

Non-current assets and disposal groups classified as held for sale should be **presented separately** from other assets in the statement of financial position. The liabilities of a disposal group should be presented separately from other liabilities in the statement of financial position.

(a)   Assets and liabilities held for sale **should not be offset**.

(b)   The **major classes** of assets and liabilities held for sale should be **separately disclosed** either on the face of the statement of financial position or in the notes.

(c)   IFRS 5 requires non-current assets or disposal groups held for sale to be shown as a separate component of **current assets/current liabilities**.   (IFRS 5: para. 38)

For example (taken from standard):   (IFRS 5: IG Example 12)

ASSETS

Non-current assets
AAA   X

Current assets
BBB   X
CCC   X
            X

Non-current assets classified as held for sale   X
            X

Total assets   X

EQUITY AND LIABILITIES
Equity
DDD   X

Non-current liabilities
EEE   X

Current liabilities
FFF   X
GGG   X
            X
Liabilities directly associated with non-current assets classified
as held for sale

            X
Total equity and liabilities   X

4.5 Additional disclosures

In the period in which a non-current asset (or disposal group) has been either classified as held for sale or sold the following should be disclosed.

(a)   A **description** of the non-current asset (or disposal group)

(b)   A description of the **facts and circumstances** of the disposal

(c)   Any **gain or loss** recognised when the item was classified as held for sale

Where an asset previously classified as held for sale is **no longer held for sale**, the entity should disclose a description of the facts and circumstances leading to the decision and its effect on results.

(IFRS 5: para. 41)

4.6 Presenting discontinued operations

Key terms

> **Discontinued operation.** A component of an entity that has either been disposed of, or is classified as held for sale, and:
>
> (a)   Represents a separate major line of business or geographical area of operations
>
> (b)   Is part of a single co-ordinated plan to dispose of a separate major line of business or geographical area of operations, or
>
> (c)   Is a subsidiary acquired exclusively with a view to resale.
>
> **Component of an entity.** Operations and cash flows that can be clearly distinguished, operationally and for financial reporting purposes, from the rest of the entity.   (IFRS 5: App A)

An entity should **present and disclose information** that enables users of the financial statements to evaluate the financial effects of **discontinued operations** and disposals of non-current assets or disposal groups.   (IFRS 5: para. 30)

This allows users to distinguish between operations which will continue in the future and those which will not, and makes it more possible to predict future results.

An entity should disclose a **single amount** in the statement of profit or loss comprising the total of:

(a)   The **post-tax profit or loss** of discontinued operations

(b)   The post-tax gain or loss recognised on the **measurement to fair value less costs of disposal** or on the disposal of the assets or disposal group(s) constituting the discontinued operation

An entity should also disclose an **analysis** of this single amount into:

(a)   The revenue, expenses and pre-tax profit or loss of discontinued operations

(b)   The related income tax expense

(c)   The gain or loss recognised on the measurement to fair value less costs of disposal or on the disposal of the assets of the discontinued operation

(d)   The related income tax expense   (IFRS 5: para. 33)

This may be presented either in the statement of profit or loss or in the notes. If it is presented in the statement of profit or loss it should be presented in a section identified as relating to discontinued operations, ie separately from continuing operations. This analysis is not required where the discontinued operation is a newly acquired subsidiary that has been classified as held for sale.

An entity should disclose the **net cash flows** attributable to the operating, investing and financing activities of discontinued operations. These disclosures may be presented either on the face of the statement of cash flows or in the notes.   (IFRS 5: para. 33)

Gains and losses on the remeasurement of a disposal group that is not a discontinued operation but is held for sale should be included in profit or loss from continuing operations.   (IFRS 5: para. 37)

4.7 Illustration

The following illustration is taken from the implementation guidance to IFRS 5. Profit for the period from discontinued operations would be analysed in the notes. (IFRS 5: IG)

LARGE GROUP
STATEMENT OF PROFIT OR LOSS FOR THE YEAR ENDED 31 DECEMBER 20X2

	20X2 $'000	20X1 $'000
Continuing operations		
Revenue	X	X
Cost of sales	(X)	(X)
Gross profit	X	X
Other income	X	X
Distribution costs	(X)	(X)
Administrative expenses	(X)	(X)
Other expenses	(X)	(X)
Finance costs	(X)	(X)
Share of profit of associates	X	X
Profit before tax	X	X
Income tax expense	(X)	(X)
Profit for the year from continuing operations	X	X
Discontinued operations		
Profit for the year from discontinued operations	X	X
Profit for the year	X	X
Profit attributable to:		
Owners of the parent	X	X
Non-controlling interest	X	X
	X	X

Note that if there were items of 'other comprehensive income' this would be shown as a full 'statement of profit or loss and other comprehensive income' as per the format in IAS 1.

Question

Closure

On 20 October 20X3 the directors of Largo Co made a public announcement of plans to close a steel works. The closure means that the group will no longer carry out this type of operation, which until recently has represented about 10% of its total revenue. The works will be gradually shut down over a period of several months, with complete closure expected in July 20X4. At 31 December output had been significantly reduced and some redundancies had already taken place. The cash flows, revenues and expenses relating to the steel works can be clearly distinguished from those of the subsidiary's other operations.

Required

How should the closure be treated in the financial statements for the year ended 31 December 20X3?

Answer

Because the steel works is being closed, rather than sold, it cannot be classified as 'held for sale'. In addition, the steel works is not a discontinued operation. Although at 31 December 20X3 Largo Co was firmly committed to the closure, this has not yet taken place nor can its assets be classified as held for sale, therefore the steel works must be included in continuing operations. Information about the planned closure could be disclosed in the notes to the financial statements.

5 Foreign currency transactions

> Transactions involving foreign currency are very common in practice. IAS 21 sets out the accounting treatment for foreign currency transactions.

If a company trades overseas, it will buy or sell assets in foreign currencies. For example, an American company might buy materials from Canada, and pay for them in US dollars, and then sell its finished goods in Germany, receiving payment in Euros, or perhaps in some other currency. If the company owes money in a foreign currency at the end of the accounting year, or holds assets which were bought in a foreign currency, those liabilities or assets must be translated into the local currency, in order to be included in the financial statements.

A company might have a subsidiary abroad (ie a foreign entity that it owns), and the subsidiary will trade in its own local currency. The subsidiary will keep books of account and prepare its annual accounts in its own currency. However, at the year end, the holding company must 'consolidate' the results of the overseas subsidiary into its group accounts, so that somehow, the assets and liabilities and the annual profits of the subsidiary must be translated from the foreign currency into $.

Note. The Financial Reporting exam will only be testing foreign currency in the context of single entities, so we will not be covering group aspects.

If foreign currency exchange rates remained constant, there would be no accounting problem. However, foreign exchange rates are continually changing, for instance the rate of exchange between the Japanese yen and sterling might be Y183 to £1 at the start of the accounting year, and Y174 to £1 at the end of the year.

5.1 Definitions

These are some of the definitions given by IAS 21.

Key terms

> **Foreign currency.** A currency other than the functional currency of the entity.
>
> **Functional currency.** The currency of the primary economic environment in which the entity operates.
>
> **Presentation currency.** The currency in which the financial statements are presented.
>
> **Exchange rate.** The ratio of exchange for two currencies.
>
> **Exchange difference.** The difference resulting from translating a given number of units of one currency into another currency at different exchange rates.
>
> **Closing rate.** The spot exchange rate at the year-end date.
>
> **Spot exchange rate.** The exchange rate for immediate delivery.
>
> **Monetary items.** Units of currency held and assets and liabilities to be received or paid in a fixed or determinable number of units of currency. (IAS 21: para. 8)

5.2 Functional currency

Each entity – whether an individual company, a parent of a group, or an operation within a group (such as a subsidiary, associate or branch) – should determine its **functional currency** and **measure its results and financial position in that currency**.

For most individual companies the functional currency will be the currency of the country in which they are located and in which they carry out most of their transactions. Determining the functional currency is much more likely to be an issue where an entity operates as part of a group. IAS 21 contains detailed guidance on how to determine an entity's functional currency. (IAS 21: paras. 9–13)

IAS 21 states that an entity should consider the following factors in determining its functional currency:

(a) The currency that mainly **influences sales prices** for goods and services (often the currency in which prices are denominated and settled)

(b) The currency of the **country whose competitive forces and regulations** mainly determine the sales prices of its goods and services

(c) The currency that mainly **influences labour, material and other costs** of providing goods or services (often the currency in which prices are denominated and settled)   (IFRS 21: para. 9)

Sometimes the functional currency of an entity is not immediately obvious. Management must then exercise judgement and may also need to consider:

(a) The currency in which **funds from financing activities** (raising loans and issuing equity) are generated

(b) The currency in which **receipts from operating activities** are usually retained   (IFRS 21: para. 10)

An entity can present its financial statements in any currency (or currencies) it chooses. IAS 21 deals with the situation in which financial statements are presented in a currency other than the functional currency.

(IFRS 21: para. 17)

Again, this is unlikely to be an issue for most individual companies. Their presentation currency will normally be the same as their functional currency (the currency of the country in which they operate).

5.3 Foreign currency transactions

There are two distinct types of foreign currency transaction, **conversion and translation**.

5.3.1 Conversion gains and losses

Conversion is the process of exchanging amounts of one foreign currency for another. For example, suppose MerryCan Co, a US company, buys a consignment of goods from a supplier in Germany. The order is placed on 1 May and the agreed price is €124,250. At the time of delivery the rate of foreign exchange was €2 to $1. MerryCan Co would record the amount owed in its books as follows.

DEBIT	Purchases (124,250 ÷ 2)	$62,125	
CREDIT	Trade Payables		$62,125

When MerryCan Cocomes to pay the supplier, it needs to obtain some foreign currency. By this time, however, if the rate of exchange has altered to €2.05 to $1, the cost of raising €124,250 would be (÷ 2.05) $60,610. MerryCan Co would need to spend only $60,610 to settle a debt for inventories 'costing' $62,125. MerryCan Co will record a profit on conversion (or exchange gain) of $1,515.

DEBIT	Trade Payables	$62,125	
CREDIT	Cash		$60,610
CREDIT	Profit on conversion		$1,515

Profits (or losses) on conversion would be included in profit or loss for the year in which conversion (whether payment or receipt) takes place.

Suppose that another YankiFed Co sells goods to a Mexican company and it is agreed that payment should be made in Mexican pesos at a price of MXN116,000. We will further assume that the exchange rate at the time of sale is MXN17.2 to $1, but when the debt is eventually paid, the rate has altered to MXN 18.1 to $1. YankiFed Co would record the sale as follows.

DEBIT	Trade Receivables (116,000 ÷ 17.2)	$6,744	
CREDIT	Revenue		$6,744

When the MXN116,000 are paid, YankiFed Co will convert them into $, to obtain (÷ 18.1) $6,409. In this example, there has been a loss on conversion of $335 which will be written off to profit of loss for the year:

DEBIT	Cash	$6,409	
DEBIT	Loss on conversion	$335	
CREDIT	Trade Receivables		$6,744

BPP
LEARNING MEDIA

5.3.2 Translation

Foreign currency translation, as distinct from conversion, does not involve the act of exchanging one currency for another. **Translation is required at the end of an accounting period when a company still holds assets or liabilities in its statement of financial position which were obtained or incurred in a foreign currency.**

These assets or liabilities might consist of:

(a) An individual home company holding individual **assets** or **liabilities** originating in a foreign currency 'deal'.

(b) An individual home company with a separate **branch** of the business operating abroad which keeps its own books of account in the local currency.

There has been great **uncertainty** about the method which should be used to translate the value of assets and liabilities from a foreign currency into $ for the year end statement of financial position.

Suppose, for example, that a Belgian subsidiary purchases a piece of property for €2,100,000 on 31 December 20X7. The rate of exchange at this time was €70 to $1. During 20X8, the subsidiary charged depreciation on the building of €16,800, so that at 31 December 20X8, the subsidiary recorded the asset as follows.

	€
Property at cost	2,100,000
Less accumulated depreciation	16,800
Carrying amount	2,083,200

At this date, the rate of exchange has changed to €60 to $1.

The local holding company must translate the asset's value into $, but there is a **choice of exchange rates**.

(a) Should the rate of exchange for translation be the rate which existed at the date of purchase, which would give a carrying amount of 2,083,200 ÷ 70 = $29,760?

(b) Should the rate of exchange for translation be the rate existing at the end of 20X8 (the closing rate of €60 to $1)? This would give a carrying amount of $34,720.

Similarly, should depreciation be charged to group profit or loss at the rate of €70 to $1 (the historical rate), €60 to $1 (the closing rate), or at an average rate for the year (say, €64 to $1)?

5.4 Foreign currency transactions: initial recognition

IAS 21 states that a foreign currency transaction should be recorded, on initial recognition in the functional currency, by applying the exchange rate between the reporting currency and the foreign currency **at the date of the transaction** to the foreign currency amount. (IFRS 21: para. 21)

An **average rate** for a period may be used if exchange rates do not fluctuate significantly. (IFRS 21: para. 22)

5.5 Reporting at subsequent year ends

It is important to distinguish between monetary and non-monetary items. **Monetary items** involve the right to receive or the obligation to deliver a fixed or determinable amount of currency. This would include receivables, payables, loans etc. **Non-monetary items** would be items such as non-current assets and inventories.

The following rules apply at each subsequent year end.

(a) Report foreign currency **monetary items** using the **closing rate**

(b) Report **non-monetary items** (eg non-current assets, inventories) which are carried at **historical cost** in a foreign currency using the **exchange rate at the date of the transaction** (historical rate)

(c) Report **non-monetary items** which are carried at **fair value** in a foreign currency using the exchange rates that existed **when the values were measured**. (IFRS 21: para. 23)

5.6 Recognition of exchange differences

Exchange differences occur when there is a **change in the exchange rate** between the transaction date and the date of settlement of monetary items arising from a foreign currency transaction.

Exchange differences arising on the settlement of monetary items (receivables, payables, loans, cash in a foreign currency) or on translating an entity's monetary items at rates different from those at which they were translated initially, or reported in previous financial statements, should be **recognised in profit or loss** in the period in which they arise. (IFRS 21: para. 28)

There are two situations to consider:

(a) The transaction is **settled in the same period** as that in which it occurred: all the exchange difference is recognised in that period.

(b) The transaction is **settled in a subsequent accounting period**: the exchange difference recognised in each intervening period up to the period of settlement is determined by the change in exchange rates during that period.

In other words, where a monetary item has not been settled at the end of a period, it should be **restated using the closing exchange rate** and any gain or loss taken to profit or loss. (IFRS 21: para. 29)

Question

Entries

Seattle Co, whose year-end is 31 December, buys some goods from Telomere SA of France on 30 September. The invoice value is €60,000 and is due for settlement in equal instalments on 30 November and 31 January. The exchange rate moved as follows.

	€ = $1
30 September	1.60
30 November	1.80
31 December	1.90
31 January	1.85

Required

State the accounting entries in the books of Seattle Co.

Answer

The purchase will be recorded in the books of Seattle Co using the rate of exchange ruling on 30 September.

DEBIT	Purchases	$37,500	
CREDIT	Trade payables		$37,500

Being the $ cost of goods purchased for €60,000 (€60,000 ÷ €1.60/$1)

On 30 November, Seattle Co must pay €30,000. This will cost €30,000 ÷ €1.80/$1 = $16,667 and the company has therefore made an exchange gain of $18,750 – $16,667 = $2,083.

DEBIT	Trade payables	$18,750	
CREDIT	Exchange gains: profit or loss		$2,083
CREDIT	Cash		$16,667

On 31 December, the year end, the outstanding liability will be recalculated using the rate applicable to that date: €30,000 ÷ €1.90/$1 = $15,789. A further exchange gain of $2,961 has been made and will be recorded as follows.

DEBIT	Trade payables	$2,961	
CREDIT	Exchange gains: profit or loss		$2,961

The total exchange gain of $5,044 will be included in the operating profit for the year ending 31 December.

On 31 January, Seattle Co must pay the second instalment of €30,000. This will cost them $16,216 (€30,000 ÷ €1.85/$1).

DEBIT	Trade payables	$15,789	
	Exchange losses: profit or loss	$427	
CREDIT	Cash		$16,216

When a gain or loss on a non-monetary item is recognised **in other comprehensive income** (for example, where property is revalued), any **related exchange differences** should also be **recognised in other comprehensive income**.

One of the competences you require to fulfil Performance Objective 7 of the PER is the ability to select and disclose accounting policies to be applied in the preparation of external financial statements. This chapter deals with important disclosures and you can apply the knowledge you obtain from this chapter to help to demonstrate this competence.

Chapter Roundup

- IAS 8 deals with changes in accounting estimates, changes in accounting policies and errors.
- Changes in accounting policy are applied **retrospectively**.
- Changes in accounting estimate are **not** applied retrospectively.
- Prior period errors must be corrected **retrospectively** (IAS 8: para. 42).
- IFRS 5 requires assets 'held for sale' to be presented separately in the statement of financial position. It sets out the criteria for recognising a **discontinued operation**.
- Transactions involving foreign currency are very common in practice. IAS 21 sets out the accounting treatment for foreign currency transactions.

Quick Quiz

1   How should a prior period error be corrected under IAS 8?
2   Give the circumstances when a change in accounting policy might be required.
3   When can a non-current asset be classified as held for sale?
4   How should an asset held for sale be measured?
5   How does IFRS 5 define a discontinued operation?
6   What is meant by functional currency?

Answers to Quick Quiz

1. By adjusting the opening balance of retained earnings (Section 3.2)

2. (a) The change is required by an IFRS; or

   (b) The change will result in a **more appropriate presentation** of events or transactions in the financial statements of the entity, providing more reliable and relevant information.

3. (a) The asset must be **available for immediate sale** in its present condition.

   (b) Its sale must be **highly probable** (ie significantly more likely than not).

4. At the lower of carrying amount and fair value less costs of disposal

5. See Key Term Section 4.6

6. The currency of the primary economic environment in which the entity operates

Now try the question below from the Practice Question Bank

Number	Level	Marks	Time
8	–	25	49 mins

18

Earnings per share

Topic list	Syllabus reference
1 IAS 33 *Earnings per share*	B9
2 Basic EPS	B9
3 Effect on EPS of changes in capital structure	B9
4 Diluted EPS	B9
5 Presentation, disclosure and other matters	B9, C3

Introduction

Earnings per share (EPS) is widely used by investors as a measure of a company's performance and is of particular importance in:

(a) **Comparing the results** of a company over a **period of time**

(b) **Comparing the performance** of one company's equity against the performance of **another company's equity**, and also against the returns obtainable from loan stock and other forms of investment

The purpose of any earnings yardstick is to achieve as far as possible clarity of meaning, comparability between one company and another, one year and another, and attributability of profits to the equity shares. IAS 33 *Earnings per share* goes some way to ensuring that all these aims are achieved.

Study guide

			Intellectual level
B9	**Reporting financial performance**		
(e)	Earnings per share (eps)		
	(i)	Calculate the eps in accordance with relevant accounting standards (dealing with bonus issues, full market value issues and rights issues)	2
	(ii)	Explain the relevance of the diluted eps and calculate the diluted eps involving convertible debt and share options (warrants)	2
C3	**Limitations of interpretation techniques**		
(f)	(i)	Explain why the trend of eps may be a more accurate indicator of performance than a company's profit trend and the importance of eps as a stock market indicator	2
	(ii)	Discuss the limitations of using eps as a performance measure	2

1 IAS 33 *Earnings per share*

Earnings per share is a measure of the amount of profits earned by a company for each ordinary share. Earnings are profits after tax and preference dividends.

1.1 Objective

The objective of IAS 33 is to improve the **comparison** of the performance of different entities in the same period and of the same entity in different accounting periods by prescribing methods for determining the number of shares to be included in the calculation of earnings per share and other amounts per share and by specifying their presentation.

1.2 Definitions

The following definitions are given in IAS 33 and IAS 32.

Key terms

- **Ordinary shares.** An equity instrument that is subordinate to all other classes of equity instruments.

- **Potential ordinary share.** A financial instrument or other contract that may entitle its holder to ordinary shares.

- **Options, warrants and their equivalents.** Financial instruments that give the holder the right to purchase ordinary shares.
  (IAS 33: para. 5)

- **Financial instrument.** Any contract that gives rise to both a financial asset of one entity and a financial liability or equity instrument of another entity.

- **Equity instrument.** Any contract that evidences a residual interest in the assets of an entity after deducting all of its liabilities.
  (IAS 32: para. 11)

1.2.1 Ordinary shares

There may be more than one class of ordinary shares, but ordinary shares of the same class will have the same rights to receive dividends. Ordinary shares participate in the net profit for the period **only after other types of shares**, eg preference shares.
(IAS 33: para. 5)

1.2.2 Potential ordinary shares

IAS 33 identifies the following examples of financial instruments and other contracts generating potential ordinary shares.

(a) **Debt or equity instruments**, including preference shares, that are convertible into ordinary shares

(b) **Share warrants and options**

(c) **Employee plans** that allow employees to receive ordinary shares as part of their remuneration and other share purchase plans

(d) Shares that would be issued upon the satisfaction of **certain conditions** resulting from contractual arrangements, such as the purchase of a business or other assets (IAS 33: para. 7)

1.3 Scope

IAS 33 has the following scope restrictions:

(a) Only companies with (potential) ordinary shares which are **publicly traded** need to present EPS (including companies in the process of being listed).

(b) EPS need only be presented on the basis of **consolidated results** where the parent's results are shown as well.

(c) Where companies **choose** to present EPS, even when they have no (potential) ordinary shares which are traded, they must do so in accordance with IAS 33. (IAS 33: paras. 2–4)

2 Basic EPS

FAST FORWARD

> **Basic EPS** is calculated by dividing the net profit or loss for the period attributable to ordinary shareholders by the weighted average number of ordinary shares outstanding during the period.

2.1 Measurement

Basic EPS should be calculated by dividing the **net profit** or loss for the period attributable to ordinary shareholders by the **weighted average number of ordinary shares** outstanding during the period.
(IAS 33: para. 10)

$$\text{Basic EPS} = \frac{\text{Net profit /(loss) attributable to ordinary shareholders}}{\text{Weighted average number of ordinary shares outstanding during the period}}$$

2.2 Earnings

Earnings includes **all items of income and expense** (including tax and non-controlling interests) **less** net profit attributable to **preference shareholders**, including preference dividends. (IAS 33: para. 12)

Preference dividends deducted from net profit consist of:

(a) Preference dividends on non-cumulative preference shares declared in respect of the period

(b) The full amount of the required preference dividends for cumulative preference shares for the period, **whether or not** they have been declared (**excluding** those paid/declared during the period in respect of previous periods) (IAS 33: para. 14)

Note. In an exam question any preference shares will be redeemable and the dividend will already have been accounted for under finance costs.

2.3 Per share

The number of ordinary shares used should be the weighted average number of ordinary shares during the period. This figure (for all periods presented) should be **adjusted for events**, other than the conversion of potential ordinary shares, that have changed the number of shares outstanding without a corresponding change in resources. (IAS 33: para. 19)

The **time-weighting factor** is the number of days the shares were outstanding compared with the total number of days in the period; a reasonable approximation is usually adequate. (IAS 33: para. 20)

2.4 Example: weighted average number of shares

Justina Co, a listed company, has the following share transactions during 20X7.

Date	Details	Shares issued
1 January 20X7	Balance at beginning of year	170,000
31 May 20X7	Issue of new shares for cash	80,000
31 December 20X7	Balance at year end	250,000

Required

Calculate the weighted average number of shares outstanding for 20X7.

Solution

The weighted average number of shares can be calculated in two ways.

(a) $(170,000 \times 5/12) + (250,000 \times 7/12) = 216,666$ shares
(b) $(170,000 \times 12/12) + (80,000 \times 7/12) = 216,666$ shares

2.5 Consideration

Shares are usually included in the weighted average number of shares from the **date consideration is receivable** which is usually the date of issue. The treatment for the issue of ordinary shares in different circumstances is as follows. (IAS 33: para. 21)

Ordinary shares issued as **purchase consideration** in an acquisition should be included as of the date of acquisition because the acquired entity's results will also be included from that date. (IAS 33: para. 22)

If ordinary shares are **partly paid**, they are treated as a fraction of an ordinary share to the extent they are entitled to dividends relative to fully paid ordinary shares.

Contingently issuable shares (including those subject to recall) are included in the computation when all necessary conditions for issue have been satisfied. (IAS 33: para. 24)

Question | Basic EPS

Flame Co is a company with a called up and paid up capital of 100,000 ordinary shares of $1 each and 20,000 10% redeemable preference shares of $1 each.

The gross profit was $200,000 and trading expenses were $50,000. Flame Co paid the required preference share dividend and an ordinary dividend of 42c per share. The tax charge for the year was estimated at $40,000.

Calculate basic EPS for the year.

FLAME CO
TRADING RESULTS FOR YEAR TO 31 DECEMBER

	$
Gross profit	200,000
Expense (50,000 + 2,000 preference dividend)	(52,000)
Profit before tax	148,000
Income tax expense	(40,000)
Profit for the year	108,000

EARNINGS PER SHARE

$$\frac{108,000}{100,000} = \$1.08$$

3 Effect on EPS of changes in capital structure

FAST FORWARD

You should know how to calculate **basic EPS** and how to deal with related complications (issue of shares for cash, bonus issues, rights issues).

3.1 Introduction

We looked at the effect of issues of new shares on basic EPS above. In these situations, the corresponding figures for EPS for the previous year will be comparable with the current year because, as the weighted average number of shares has risen, there has been a **corresponding increase in resources**. Money has been received when shares were issued. It is assumed that shares are issued at full market price.

3.2 Example: earnings per share with a new issue

On 30 September 20X2, Boffin Co made an issue at full market price of 1,000,000 ordinary shares. The company's accounting year runs from 1 January to 31 December. Relevant information for 20X1 and 20X2 is as follows.

	20X2	20X1
Shares in issue as at 31 December	9,000,000	8,000,000
Profits after tax and preference dividend	$3,300,000	$3,280,000

Required

Calculate the EPS for 20X2 and the corresponding figure for 20X1.

Solution

	20X2	20X1
Weighted average number of shares		
8 million × 9/12	6,000,000	
9 million × 3/12	2,250,000	
	8,250,000	8,000,000
Earnings	$3,300,000	$3,280,000
EPS	$0.40	$0.41

In spite of the increase in total earnings by $20,000 in 20X2, the EPS is not as good as in 20X1, because there was extra capital employed for the final three months of 20X2.

There are other events, however, which change the number of shares outstanding, **without a corresponding change in resources**. In these circumstances it is necessary to make adjustments so that the current and prior period EPS figures are comparable.

Four such events are considered by IAS 33.

(a) **Capitalisation or bonus issue** (sometimes called a stock dividend)
(b) Bonus element in any other issue, eg a **rights issue** to existing shareholders
(c) **Share split**
(d) **Reverse share split** (consolidation of shares)   (IAS 33: para. 27)

3.3 Capitalisation/bonus issue and share split/reverse share split

These two types of event can be considered together as they have a similar effect. In both cases, ordinary shares are issued to existing shareholders for **no additional consideration**. The number of ordinary shares has increased without an increase in resources.   (IAS 33: para. 27)

This problem is solved by **adjusting the number of ordinary shares outstanding before the event** for the proportionate change in the number of shares outstanding as if the event had occurred at the beginning of the earliest period reported.   (IAS 33: para. 28)

3.4 Example: earnings per share with a bonus issue

Greymatter Co had 400,000 shares in issue, until on 30 September 20X2 it made a bonus issue of 100,000 shares. Calculate the EPS for 20X2 and the corresponding figure for 20X1 if total earnings were $80,000 in 20X2 and EPS for 20X1 was $0.1875. The company's accounting year runs from 1 January to 31 December.

Solution

	20X2
Earnings	$80,000
Shares at 1 January	400,000
Bonus issue	100,000
	500,000 shares
EPS	$0.16

The number of shares for 20X1 must also be adjusted if the figures for EPS are to remain comparable.

The EPS for 20X1 is therefore restated as:

$$\$0.1875 \times \frac{400}{500} = \$0.15$$

3.5 Rights issue

A rights issue of shares is an issue of new shares to existing shareholders **at a price below the current market value**. The offer of new shares is made on the basis of x new shares for every y shares currently held; eg a 1 for 3 rights issue is an offer of one new share at the offer price for every three shares currently held. This means that there is a bonus element included.   (IAS 33: App A2)

To arrive at figures for EPS when a rights issue is made, we need to calculate first of all the **theoretical ex-rights value**. This is a weighted average value per share, and is perhaps explained most easily with a numerical example.

3.6 Example: theoretical ex-rights value

Suppose that Egghead Co has 10,000,000 shares in issue. It now proposes to make a 1 for 4 rights issue at a price of $3 per share. The market value of existing shares on the final day before the issue is made is $3.50 (this is the 'with rights' value). What is the theoretical ex-rights value per share?

Solution

	$
Before issue 4 shares, value $3.50 each	14.00
Rights issue 1 share, value $3	3.00
Theoretical value of 5 shares	17.00

Theoretical ex-rights value = $\dfrac{\$17.00}{5}$ = $3.40 per share

Note that this calculation can alternatively be performed using the total value and number of outstanding shares.

3.7 Procedures

The procedures for calculating the EPS for the current year and a corresponding figure for the previous year are:

(a) The **EPS for the corresponding previous period** should be multiplied by the following fraction. (**Note**. The market price on the last day of quotation is taken as the fair value immediately prior to exercise of the rights, as required by the standard.)

Formula to learn

$$\frac{\text{Theoretical ex} - \text{rights fair value per share}}{\text{Fair value per share immediately before the exercise of rights (cum rights price)}}$$

(b) To obtain the **EPS for the current year** you should:

(i) Multiply the number of shares before the rights issue by the fraction of the year before the date of issue and by the following fraction

Formula to learn

$$\frac{\text{Fair value per share immediately before the exercise of rights (cum rights price)}}{\text{Theoretical ex} - \text{rights fair value per share}}$$

(ii) Multiply the number of shares after the rights issue by the fraction of the year after the date of issue and add to the figure arrived at in (i)

The total earnings should then be divided by the total number of shares so calculated.

3.8 Example: earnings per share with a rights issue

Brains Co had 100,000 shares in issue, but then makes a 1 for 5 rights issue on 1 October 20X2 at a price of $1. The market value on the last day of quotation with rights was $1.60.

Calculate the EPS for the year ended 31 December 20X2 and the corresponding figure for 20X1 given total earnings of $50,000 in 20X2 and $40,000 in 20X1.

Solution

Calculation of theoretical ex-rights value:

	$
Before issue 5 shares, value × $1.60	8.00
Rights issue 1 share, value × $1.00	1.00
Theoretical value of 6 shares	9.00

Theoretical ex-rights value = $\dfrac{\$9}{6}$ = $1.50

EPS for 20X1

EPS as calculated before taking into account the rights issue = 40c ($40,000 divided by 100,000 shares).

$$\text{EPS} = \frac{1.50}{1.60} \times \$0.4 = \$0.375$$

(Remember: This is the corresponding value for 20X1 which will be shown in the financial statements for Brains Co at the end of 20X2.)

EPS for 20X2

Number of shares before the rights issue was 100,000. 20,000 shares were issued.

Stage 1:	$100,000 \times \frac{9}{12} \times \frac{1.60}{1.50}$	80,000
Stage 2:	$120,000 \times \frac{3}{12}$	30,000
		110,000

$$\text{EPS} = \frac{\$50,000}{110,000} = \$0.45$$

The figure for total earnings is the actual earnings for the year.

Question — Rights issue

Marcoli Co has produced the following net profit figures for the years ending 31 December.

	$m
20X6	1.1
20X7	1.5
20X8	1.8

On 1 January 20X7 the number of shares outstanding was 500,000. During 20X7 the company announced a rights issue with the following details.

Rights:	1 new share for each 5 outstanding (100,000 new shares in total)
Exercise price:	$5.00
Last date to exercise rights:	1 March 20X7

The market (fair) value of one share in Marcoli immediately prior to exercise on 1 March 20X7 = $11.00.

Required

Calculate the EPS for 20X6, 20X7 and 20X8.

Answer

Computation of theoretical ex-rights value

This computation uses the total fair value and number of shares.

$$\frac{\text{Fair value of all outstanding shares} + \text{total received from exercise of rights}}{\text{No shares outstanding prior to exercise} + \text{no shares issued in exercise}}$$

$$= \frac{(\$11.00 \times 500,000) + (\$5.00 \times 100,000)}{500,000 + 100,000} = \$10.00$$

Computation of EPS

		20X6 $	20X7 $	20X8 $
20X6	EPS as originally reported $\dfrac{\$1,100,000}{500,000}$	2.20		
20X6	EPS restated for rights issue $\dfrac{\$1,100,000}{500,000} \times \dfrac{10}{11}$ (or $2.20 \times \dfrac{10}{11}$)	2.00		
20X7	EPS including effects of rights issue $\dfrac{\$1,500,000}{(500,000 \times 2/12 \times 11/10) + (600,000 \times 10/12)}$		2.54	
20X8	EPS $= \dfrac{\$1,800,000}{600,000}$			3.00

Exam focus point

> You should know how to deal with the effect on EPS of bonus and rights issues and be able to calculate diluted EPS. Diluted EPS calculation and EPS calculations are often included as part of a larger question or as a MCQ. In September 2016, EPS was a part of two of the longer written questions. Ensure you can calculate it correctly and understand what it means.

4 Diluted EPS

FAST FORWARD

> **Diluted EPS** is calculated by adjusting the net profit due to continuing operations attributable to ordinary shareholders and the weighted average number of shares outstanding for the effects of all dilutive potential ordinary shares.
>
> (IAS 33: para. 31)

4.1 Introduction

At the end of an accounting period, a company may have in issue some **securities** which do not (at present) have any 'claim' to a share of equity earnings, but **may give rise to such a claim in the future**. These securities include:

(a)   A **separate class of equity shares** which at present is not entitled to any dividend, but will be entitled after some future date

(b)   **Convertible loan stock** or **convertible preferred shares** which give their holders the right at some future date to exchange their securities for ordinary shares of the company, at a pre-determined conversion rate

(c)   **Options** or **warrants**

In such circumstances, the future number of ordinary shares in issue might increase, which in turn results in a fall in the EPS. In other words, a **future increase** in the **number of ordinary shares will cause a dilution or 'watering down' of equity**, and it is possible to calculate a **diluted earnings per share** (ie the EPS that would have been obtained during the financial period if the dilution had already taken place). This will indicate to investors the possible effects of a future dilution.

4.2 Earnings

The earnings calculated for basic EPS should be based on **continuing operations** and adjusted by the **post-tax** (including deferred tax) effect of:

(a)   Any **dividends** on dilutive potential ordinary shares that were deducted to arrive at earnings for basic EPS

(b)   **Interest recognised** in the period for the dilutive potential ordinary shares (convertible debt)

(c) Any **other changes in income or expenses** (fees or discount) that would result from the conversion of the dilutive potential ordinary shares

The conversion of some potential ordinary shares may lead to changes in **other income or expenses**. For example, the reduction of interest expense related to potential ordinary shares and the resulting increase in net profit for the period may lead to an increase in the expense relating to a non-discretionary employee profit-sharing plan. When calculating diluted EPS, the net profit or loss for the period is adjusted for any such consequential changes in income or expense.   (IAS 33: para. 33)

4.3 Per share

The number of ordinary shares is the weighted average number of ordinary shares calculated for basic EPS plus the weighted average number of ordinary shares that would be issued on the conversion of all the **dilutive potential ordinary shares** into ordinary shares.   (IAS 33: para. 36)

It should be assumed that dilutive ordinary shares were converted into ordinary shares at the **beginning of the period** or, if later, at the actual date of issue. (IAS 33: para.36) There are two other points:

(a) The computation assumes the most **advantageous conversion rate** or exercise rate from the standpoint of the holder of the potential ordinary shares.   (IAS 33: para. 39)

(b) **Contingently issuable** (potential) ordinary shares are treated as for basic EPS; if the conditions have not been met, the number of contingently issuable shares included in the computation is based on the number of shares that would be issuable if the end of the reporting period was the end of the contingency period. Restatement is not allowed if the conditions are not met when the contingency period expires.   (IAS 33: para. 52)

4.4 Example: diluted EPS

In 20X7 Farrah Co had a basic EPS of $1.05 based on earnings of $105,000 and 100,000 ordinary $1 shares. It also had in issue $40,000 15% convertible loan stock which is convertible in two years' time at the rate of 4 ordinary shares for every $5 of stock. The rate of tax is 30%.

Required

Calculate the diluted EPS.

Solution

Diluted EPS is calculated as follows.

Step 1 **Number of shares**: the additional equity on conversion of the loan stock will be 40,000 × 4/5 = 32,000 shares.

Step 2 **Earnings**: Farrah Co will save interest payments of $6,000 (40,000 × 15%) but this increase in profits will be taxed. Hence the earnings figure may be recalculated:

$(105,000 + (6,000 \times 70\%)) = \$109,200$

Step 3 **Calculation**: Diluted EPS = $\dfrac{\$109,200}{132,000}$ = $0.83

Step 4 **Dilution**: the dilution in earnings would be $1.05 − $0.83 = $0.22 per share.

Question   Diluted EPS

Ardent Co has 5,000,000 ordinary shares of 25 cents each in issue, and also had in issue in 20X4:

(a) $1,000,000 of 14% convertible loan stock, convertible in three years' time at the rate of two shares per $10 of stock

(b) $2,000,000 of 10% convertible loan stock, convertible in one year's time at the rate of three shares per $5 of stock

The total earnings in 20X4 were $1,750,000.

The rate of income tax is 35%.

Required

Calculate the basic EPS and diluted EPS.

Answer

(a)   Basic EPS = $\dfrac{\$1,750,000}{5 \text{ million}}$ = $0.35

(b)   We must decide which of the potential ordinary shares (ie the loan stocks) are dilutive (ie would decrease the EPS if converted).

For the 14% loan stock, incremental EPS = $\dfrac{0.65 \times \$140,000}{200,000 \text{ shares}}$ = $0.46

For the 10% loan stock, incremental EPS = $\dfrac{0.65 \times \$200,000}{1.2\text{m shares}}$ = $0.11

The effect of converting the 14% loan stock is therefore to **increase** the EPS figure, since the incremental EPS of $0.46 is greater than the basic EPS of $0.35. The 14% loan stock is not dilutive and is therefore excluded from the diluted EPS calculation.

The 10% loan stock is dilutive.

Diluted EPS = $\dfrac{\$1.75\text{m} + \$0.13\text{m}}{5\text{m} + 1.2\text{m}}$ = $0.3

Note. The calculation of DEPS should always be based on the **maximum** number of shares that can be issued. For instance, if the 14% loan stock above had the following conversion rights.

- 20X5: 4 shares per $10
- 20X6: 3 shares per $10
- 20X7: 2 shares per $10

DEPS would be calculated at 4 shares per $10.

4.5 Treatment of options

It should be assumed that options are exercised and that the assumed proceeds would have been received from the issue of shares at **fair value**. Fair value for this purpose is calculated on the basis of the average price of the ordinary shares during the period. Options are brought into the dilution calculation in the year in which they are issued, **weighted as appropriate**. For instance, if the year end is 31 December 20X6 and options had been granted on 1 July 20X6, the number of dilutive shares under the options will be × 6/12.

(IAS 33: para. 63)

Options and other share purchase arrangements are dilutive when they would result in the issue of ordinary shares for **less than fair value**. The amount of the dilution is fair value less the issue price. In order to calculate diluted EPS, each transaction of this type is treated as consisting of two parts:

(a)   A contract to issue a certain number of ordinary shares at their **average market price** during the period. These shares are fairly priced and are assumed to be neither dilutive nor antidilutive. They are **ignored** in the computation of diluted earnings per share.

(b)   A contract to issue the remaining ordinary shares for **no consideration**. Such ordinary shares generate no proceeds and have no effect on the net profit attributable to ordinary shares outstanding. Therefore such shares are **dilutive** and they are added to the number of ordinary shares outstanding in the computation of diluted EPS.

To the extent that **partly paid shares** are not entitled to participate in dividends during the period, they are considered the equivalent of **warrants** or **options**. (IAS 33: App A15)

Brand Co has the following results for the year ended 31 December 20X7.

Net profit for year	$1,200,000
Weighted average number of ordinary shares outstanding during year	500,000 shares
Average fair value of one ordinary share during year	$20.00
Weighted average number of shares under option during year	100,000 shares
Exercise price for shares under option during year	$15.00

Required

Calculate both basic and diluted earnings per share.

Answer

	Per share $	Earnings $	Shares
Net profit for year		1,200,000	
Weighted average shares outstanding during 20X7			500,000
Basic earnings per share	2.40		
Number of shares under option			100,000
Number of shares that would have been issued At fair value: (100,000 × $15.00 / $20.00)			(75,000)*
Diluted earnings per share	2.29	1,200,000	525,000

*The earnings have not been increased as the total number of shares has been increased only by the number of shares (25,000) deemed for the purpose of the computation to have been issued for no consideration.

4.6 Dilutive potential ordinary shares

According to IAS 33, potential ordinary shares should be treated as dilutive when, and only when, their conversion to ordinary shares would **decrease net profit per share** from continuing operations. This point was illustrated in the question above. (IAS 33: para. 41)

5 Presentation, disclosure and other matters

> **FAST FORWARD**
>
> IAS 33 contains a number of requirements on presentation and disclosure.

5.1 Presentation

Basic and diluted EPS should be presented by an entity in the statement of profit or loss and other comprehensive income for each class of ordinary share that has a different right to share in the net profit for the period. The basic and diluted EPS should be presented with **equal prominence** for all periods presented. (IAS 33: para. 66)

Disclosure must still be made where the EPS figures (basic and/or diluted) are **negative** (ie a loss per share).

5.2 Disclosure

An entity should disclose the following.

(a)   The amounts used as the **numerators** in calculating basic and diluted EPS, and a **reconciliation** of those amounts to the net profit or loss for the period

(b)   The weighted average number of ordinary shares used as the **denominator** in calculating basic and diluted EPS, and a **reconciliation** of these denominators to each other   (IAS 33: para. 70)

5.3 Alternative EPS figures

An entity may present **alternative EPS figures if it wishes**. However, IAS 33 lays out certain rules where this takes place.

(a)   The weighted average number of shares as calculated under IAS 33 **must** be used.

(b)   A **reconciliation** must be given if necessary between the component of profit used in the alternative EPS and the line item for profit reported in the statement of profit or loss and other comprehensive income.

(c)   Basic and diluted EPS must be shown with **equal prominence**.   (IAS 33: para. 73)

5.4 Significance of earnings per share

Earnings per share (EPS) is one of the most frequently quoted statistics in financial analysis. Because of the widespread use of the price earnings **(P/E) ratio** as a yardstick for investment decisions, it became increasingly important. It is certainly true that EPS gives a more accurate picture of the actual return to investors than reported profits, which do not show the dilutive effect of share issues.

Reported and forecast EPS can, through the P/E ratio, have a **significant effect on a company's share price**. Thus, a share price might fall if it looks as if EPS is going to be low.

There are a number of reasons why EPS should not be used to determine the value of a company's shares. IAS 33 concentrates on the **denominator** of EPS – ie the number of shares. However, it is more difficult to regulate the **numerator** – earnings. Reported earnings can be affected by a number or factors – choice of accounting policy, asset valuation, taxation issues. Directors who want to present favourable EPS can find ways to boost reported earnings, as happened with Enron.

EPS has also served as a means of assessing the **stewardship and management** role performed by company directors and managers. Remuneration packages might be linked to EPS growth, thereby increasing the pressure on management to improve EPS. The danger of this, however, is that management effort may go into distorting results to produce a favourable EPS.

It should also be noted that EPS takes no account of other issues that affect whether a company is worth investing in, such as its risk profile and its investment requirements. Nevertheless, the market is sensitive to EPS.

Chapter Roundup

- **Earnings per share** is a measure of the amount of profits earned by a company for each ordinary share. Earnings are profits after tax and preference dividends.

- **Basic EPS** is calculated by dividing the net profit or loss for the period attributable to ordinary shareholders by the weighted average number of ordinary shares outstanding during the period.

- You should know how to calculate **basic EPS** and how to deal with related complications (issue of shares for cash, bonus issues, rights issues).

- **Diluted EPS** is calculated by adjusting the net profit due to continuing operations attributable to ordinary shareholders and the weighted average number of shares outstanding for the effects of all dilutive potential ordinary shares (IAS 33: para. 31).

- **IAS 33** contains a number of requirements on presentation and disclosure.

Quick Quiz

1   How is basic EPS calculated?

2   Give the formula for the 'bonus element' of a rights issue.

3   Define 'dilutive potential ordinary share'.

4   Which numerator is used to decide whether potential ordinary shares are dilutive?

5   Why is the numerator adjusted for convertible bonds when calculating diluted EPS?

1   $$\frac{\text{Net profit /(loss) attributable to ordinary shareholders}}{\text{Weighted average number of ordinary shares outstanding during the period}}$$

2   $$\frac{\text{Actual cum} - \text{rights price}}{\text{Theoretical ex} - \text{rights price}}$$

3   See Section 4.1.

4   Net profit attributable to ordinary shareholders

5   Because the issue of shares will affect earnings (the interest will no longer have to be paid)

Now try the questions below from the Practice Question Bank

Number	Level	Marks	Time
23 (b)	–	5	10 mins
27	–	10	20 mins

19

Calculation and interpretation of accounting ratios and trends

Introduction

This chapter looks at **interpretation of accounts**. We deal here with the calculation of ratios, how they can be analysed and interpreted, and how the results should be presented to management.

Study guide

		Intellectual level
C2	**Calculation and interpretation of accounting ratios and trends to address users' and stakeholders' needs**	
(a)	Define and compute relevant financial ratios	2
(b)	Explain what aspects of performance specific ratios are intended to assess	2
(c)	Analyse and interpret ratios to give an assessment of an entity's/group's performance and financial position in comparison with:	2
	(i) An entity's previous periods' financial statements	
	(ii) Another similar entity/group for the same reporting period	
	(iii) Industry average ratios	
(d)	Interpret an entity's financial statements to give advice from the perspectives of different stakeholders	2
(e)	Discuss how the interpretation of current value based financial statements would differ from those using historical cost based accounts	1

1 The broad categories of ratio

FAST FORWARD

> You must be able to **appraise and communicate** the position and prospects of a business based on given and prepared statements and ratios.

If you were to look at a statement of financial position or statement of profit or loss and other comprehensive income, how would you decide whether the company was doing well or badly? Or whether it was financially strong or financially vulnerable? And what would you be looking at in the figures to help you to make your judgement?

Ratio analysis involves **comparing one figure against another** to produce a ratio, and assessing whether the ratio indicates a weakness or strength in the company's affairs.

1.1 The broad categories of ratios

Broadly speaking, basic ratios can be grouped into five categories:

- Profitability and return
- Long-term solvency and stability
- Short-term solvency and liquidity
- Efficiency (turnover ratios)
- Shareholders' investment ratios

Within each heading we will identify a number of standard measures or ratios that are normally calculated and generally accepted as meaningful indicators. One must stress however that each individual business must be considered separately, and a ratio that is meaningful for a manufacturing company may be completely meaningless for a financial institution. **Try not to be too mechanical** when working out ratios and constantly think about what you are trying to achieve.

The key to obtaining meaningful information from ratio analysis is **comparison**. This may involve comparing ratios over time within the same business to establish whether things are improving or declining, and comparing ratios between similar businesses to see whether the company you are analysing is better or worse than average within its specific business sector.

It must be stressed that ratio analysis on its own is not sufficient for interpreting company accounts, and that there are **other items of information** which should be looked at, for example:

(a) The content of any **accompanying commentary** on the accounts and other statements

(b) The age and nature of the **company's assets**

(c) **Current and future developments** in the company's markets, at home and overseas, recent acquisitions or disposals of a subsidiary by the company

(d) **Unusual** items separately disclosed in the financial statements

(e) Any other **noticeable features** of the report and accounts, such as events after the end of the reporting period, contingent liabilities, a qualified auditors' report, the company's taxation position, and so on

1.2 Example: calculating ratios

To illustrate the calculation of ratios, the following **draft** statement of financial position and statement of profit or loss figures will be used. We are using a separate statement of profit or loss for this example as no items of other comprehensive income are involved.

FURLONG CO STATEMENT OF PROFIT OR LOSS
FOR THE YEAR ENDED 31 DECEMBER 20X8

	Notes	20X8 $	20X7 $
Revenue	1	3,095,576	1,909,051
Operating profit	1	359,501	244,229
Interest	2	17,371	19,127
Profit before taxation		342,130	225,102
Income tax expense		74,200	31,272
Profit for the year		267,930	193,830
Earnings per share		12.8c	9.3c

FURLONG CO STATEMENT OF FINANCIAL POSITION
AS AT 31 DECEMBER 20X8

	Notes	20X8 $	20X7 $
Assets			
Non-current assets			
Property, plant and equipment		802,180	656,071
Current assets			
Inventories		64,422	86,550
Trade receivables	3	1,002,701	853,441
Cash at bank and in hand		1,327	68,363
		1,068,450	1,008,354
Total assets		1,870,630	1,664,425
Equity and liabilities			
Equity			
Ordinary shares 10c each	5	210,000	210,000
Share premium account		48,178	48,178
Retained earnings		651,721	410,591
		909,899	668,769
Non-current liabilities			
10% loan stock 20X4/20Y0		100,000	100,000
Current liabilities	4	860,731	895,656
Total equity and liabilities		1,870,630	1,664,425

Notes to the financial statements

		20X8	20X7
1	*Sales revenue and profit*	$	$
	Sales revenue	3,095,576	1,909,051
	Cost of sales	2,402,609	1,441,950
	Gross profit	692,967	467,101
	Administration expenses	333,466	222,872
	Operating profit	359,501	244,229
	Depreciation charged	151,107	120,147
2	*Interest*		
	Payable on bank overdrafts and other loans	8,115	11,909
	Payable on loan stock	10,000	10,000
		18,115	21,909
	Receivable on short-term deposits	744	2,782
	Net payable	17,371	19,127
3	*Trade Receivables*		
	Amounts falling due within one year		
	Trade receivables	905,679	807,712
	Prepayments and accrued income	97,022	45,729
		1,002,701	853,441
4	*Current liabilities*		
	Trade payables	627,018	545,340
	Accruals and deferred income	81,279	280,464
	Corporate taxes	108,000	37,200
	Other taxes	44,434	32,652
		860,731	895,656
5	*Called-up share capital*		
	Authorised ordinary shares of 10c each	1,000,000	1,000,000
	Issued and fully paid ordinary shares of 10c each	210,000	210,000
6	Dividends paid	20,000	–

2 Profitability and return on capital

Return on capital employed (ROCE) may be used by the shareholders or the Board to assess the performance of management.

In our example, the company made a profit in both 20X8 and 20X7, and there was an increase in profit between one year and the next:

(a)   Of 52% before taxation
(b)   Of 39% after taxation

Profit before taxation is generally thought to be a better figure to use than profit after taxation, because there might be unusual variations in the tax charge from year to year which would not affect the underlying profitability of the company's operations.

Another profit figure that should be calculated is PBIT, **profit before interest and tax**. This is the amount of profit which the company earned before having to pay interest to the providers of loan capital, such as loan notes and medium-term bank loans, which will be shown in the statement of financial position as non-current liabilities.

Formula to learn

Profit before interest and tax is therefore:

(a)   The profit on ordinary activities before taxation; **plus**
(b)   Interest charges on loan capital.

Published accounts do not always give sufficient detail on interest payable to determine how much is interest on long-term finance. We will assume in our example that the whole of the interest payable ($18,115, Note 2) relates to long-term finance.

PBIT in our example is therefore:

	20X8	20X7
	$	$
Profit on ordinary activities before tax	342,130	225,102
Interest payable	18,115	21,909
PBIT	360,245	247,011

This shows a 46% growth between 20X7 and 20X8.

2.1 Return on capital employed (ROCE)

It is impossible to assess profits or profit growth properly without relating them to the **amount of funds (capital) that were employed in making the profits**. The most important profitability ratio is therefore return on capital employed (ROCE), which states the profit as a percentage of the amount of capital employed.

Formula to learn

> $$\text{ROCE} = \frac{\text{Profit before interest and taxation}}{\text{Total assets less current liabilities}} \times 100\%$$
>
> **Capital employed** = Shareholders' equity plus non-current liabilities
> (**or** total assets less current liabilities)

The underlying principle is that we must **compare like with like**, and so if capital means share capital and reserves plus non-current liabilities and debt capital, profit must mean the profit earned by all this capital together. This is PBIT, since interest is the return for loan capital.

In our example, capital employed = 20X8 $1,870,630 – $860,731 = $1,009,899
20X7 $1,664,425 – $895,656 = $768,769

These total figures are the total assets less current liabilities figures for 20X8 and 20X7 in the statement of financial position.

	20X8	20X7
ROCE	$\dfrac{\$360,245}{\$1,009,899} = 35.7\%$	$\dfrac{\$247,011}{\$768,769} = 32.1\%$

What does a company's ROCE tell us? What should we be looking for? There are three comparisons that can be made.

(a) The **change in ROCE from one year to the next** can be examined. In this example, there has been an increase in ROCE by about 4 percentage points from its 20X7 level.

(b) The **ROCE being earned by other companies**, if this information is available, can be compared with the ROCE of this company. Here the information is not available.

(c) A comparison of the ROCE with **current market borrowing rates** may be made.

(i) What would be the cost of extra borrowing to the company if it needed more loans, and is it earning a ROCE that suggests it could make profits to make such borrowing worthwhile?

(ii) Is the company making a ROCE which suggests that it is getting value for money from its current borrowing?

(iii) Companies are in a risk business and commercial borrowing rates are a good independent yardstick against which company performance can be judged.

In this example, if we suppose that current market interest rates, say, for medium-term borrowing from banks, are around 10%, then the company's actual ROCE of 36% in 20X8 would not seem low. On the contrary, it might seem high.

However, it is easier to spot a low ROCE than a high one, because there is always a chance that the company's non-current assets, especially property, are **undervalued** in its statement of financial position, and so the capital employed figure might be unrealistically low. If the company had earned a ROCE, not of 36%, but of, say only 6%, then its return would have been below current borrowing rates and so disappointingly low.

2.2 Return on equity (ROE)

Return on equity gives a more restricted view of capital than ROCE, but it is based on the same principles.

Formula to learn

$$ROE = \frac{\text{Profit after tax and preference dividend}}{\text{Equity shareholders funds}} \times 100\%$$

In our example, ROE is calculated as follows.

	20X8	20X7
ROE	$\frac{\$267,930}{\$909,899} = 29.4\%$	$\frac{\$193,830}{\$668,769} = 29\%$

ROE is **not a widely used ratio**, however, because there are more useful ratios that give an indication of the return to shareholders, such as earnings per share, dividend per share, dividend yield and earnings yield, which are described later.

2.3 Analysing profitability and return in more detail: the secondary ratios

We often sub-analyse ROCE, to find out more about why the ROCE is high or low, or better or worse than last year. There are two factors that contribute towards a return on capital employed, both related to sales revenue.

(a) **Profit margin**. A company might make a high or low profit margin on its sales. For example, a company that makes a profit of 25c per $1 of sales is making a bigger return on its revenue than another company making a profit of only 10c per $1 of sales.

(b) **Asset turnover**. Asset turnover is a measure of how well the assets of a business are being used to generate sales. For example, if two companies each have capital employed of $100,000 and Company A makes sales of $400,000 per annum whereas Company B makes sales of only $200,000 per annum, Company A is making a higher revenue from the same amount of assets (twice as much asset turnover as Company B) and this will help A to make a higher return on capital employed than B. Asset turnover is expressed as 'x times' so that assets generate x times their value in annual sales. Here, Company A's asset turnover is four times and B's is two times.

Profit margin and asset turnover together explain the ROCE and if the ROCE is the primary profitability ratio, these other two are the secondary ratios. The relationship between the three ratios can be shown mathematically.

Formula to learn

Profit margin × Asset turnover = ROCE

$$\therefore \quad \frac{\text{PBIT}}{\text{Sales}} \times \frac{\text{Sales}}{\text{Capital employed}} = \frac{\text{PBIT}}{\text{Capital employed}}$$

In our example:

		Profit margin		Asset turnover		ROCE
(a)	20X8	$\frac{\$360,245}{\$3,095,576}$	×	$\frac{\$3,095,576}{\$1,009,899}$	=	$\frac{\$360,245}{\$1,009,899}$
		11.64%	×	3.07 times	=	35.7%

		Profit margin		Asset turnover		ROCE
(b)	20X7	$\dfrac{\$247{,}011}{\$1{,}909{,}051}$	×	$\dfrac{\$1{,}909{,}051}{\$768{,}769}$	=	$\dfrac{\$247{,}011}{\$768{,}769}$
		12.94%	×	2.48 times	=	32.1%

In this example, the company's improvement in ROCE between 20X7 and 20X8 is attributable to a higher asset turnover. Indeed the profit margin has fallen a little, but the higher asset turnover has more than compensated for this.

It is also worth commenting on the change in sales revenue from one year to the next. You may already have noticed that Furlong achieved sales growth of over 60% from $1.9m to $3.1m between 20X7 and 20X8. This is very strong growth, and this is certainly one of the most significant items in the statement of profit or loss and statement of financial position.

2.3.1 A warning about comments on profit margin and asset turnover

It might be tempting to think that a high profit margin is good, and a low asset turnover means sluggish trading. In broad terms, this is so. But there is a trade-off between profit margin and asset turnover, and you cannot look at one without allowing for the other.

(a)   A **high profit margin** means a high profit per $1 of sales, but if this also means that sales prices are high, there is a strong possibility that sales revenue will be depressed, and so asset turnover lower.

(b)   A **high asset turnover** means that the company is generating a lot of sales, but to do this it might have to keep its prices down and so accept a low profit margin per $1 of sales.

Consider the following.

Alpha Co		Brava Co	
Sales revenue	$1,000,000	Sales revenue	$4,000,000
Capital employed	$1,000,000	Capital employed	$1,000,000
PBIT	$200,000	PBIT	$200,000

These figures would give the following ratios.

ROCE	=	$\dfrac{\$200{,}000}{\$1{,}000{,}000}$	= 20%	ROCE	=	$\dfrac{\$200{,}000}{\$1{,}000{,}000}$	= 20%
Profit margin	=	$\dfrac{\$200{,}000}{\$1{,}000{,}000}$	= 20%	Profit margin	=	$\dfrac{\$200{,}000}{\$4{,}000{,}000}$	= 5%
Asset turnover	=	$\dfrac{\$1{,}000{,}000}{\$1{,}000{,}000}$	= 1	Asset turnover	=	$\dfrac{\$4{,}000{,}000}{\$1{,}000{,}000}$	= 4

The companies have the same ROCE, but it is arrived at in a very different fashion. Alpha Co operates with a low asset turnover and a comparatively high profit margin whereas Brava Co carries out much more business, but on a lower profit margin. Alpha Co could be operating at the luxury end of the market, whilst Brava Co is operating at the popular end of the market.

2.4 Gross profit margin, net profit margin and profit analysis

Depending on the format of the statement of profit or loss, you may be able to calculate the gross profit margin as well as the net profit margin. **Looking at the two together** can be quite informative.

For example, suppose that Fashion Co has the following summarised statement of profit or loss for two consecutive years.

	Year 1	Year 2
	$	$
Revenue	70,000	100,000
Cost of sales	42,000	55,000
Gross profit	28,000	45,000
Expenses	21,000	35,000
Profit for the year	7,000	10,000

BPP LEARNING MEDIA

Financial Reporting | **19: Calculation and interpretation of accounting ratios and trends**   345

Although the net profit margin is the same for both years at 10%, the gross profit margin is not.

In year 1 it is: $\dfrac{\$28,000}{\$70,000}$ = 40%

and in year 2 it is: $\dfrac{\$45,000}{\$100,000}$ = 45%

The improved gross profit margin has not led to an improvement in the net profit margin. This is because expenses as a percentage of sales have risen from 30% in year 1 to 35% in year 2.

2.5 Historical vs current cost

In this chapter we are dealing with interpretation of financial statements based on historical cost accounts.

It is worth considering how the analysis would change if we were dealing with financial statements based on some form of current value accounting (which we will go on to look at in Chapter 22).

These are some of the issues that would arise:

- Non-current asset values would probably be stated at fair value. This may be higher than depreciated historical cost. Therefore capital employed would be higher. This would lead to a reduction in ROCE.

- Higher asset values would lead to a higher depreciation charge, which would reduce net profit.

- If opening inventory were shown at current value, this would increase cost of sales and reduce net profit.

So you can see that ROCE based on historical cost accounts is probably overstated in real terms.

3 Liquidity, gearing/leverage and working capital

FAST FORWARD

Banks and other lenders will be interested in a company's gearing level.

3.1 Long-term solvency: debt and gearing ratios

Debt ratios are concerned with **how much the company owes in relation to its size**, whether it is getting into heavier debt or improving its situation, and whether its debt burden seems heavy or light.

(a) When a company is heavily in debt banks and other potential lenders may be unwilling to advance further funds.

(b) When a company is earning only a modest profit before interest and tax, and has a heavy debt burden, there will be very little profit left over for shareholders after the interest charges have been paid. And so if interest rates were to go up (on bank overdrafts and so on) or the company were to borrow even more, it might soon be incurring interest charges in excess of PBIT. This might eventually lead to the liquidation of the company.

These are two big reasons why companies should keep their debt burden under control. There are four ratios that are particularly worth looking at, the debt ratio, gearing ratio, interest cover and cash flow ratio.

3.2 Debt ratio

Formula to learn

The **debt ratio** is the ratio of a company's total debts to its total assets.

(a) Assets consist of non-current assets at their carrying amount, plus current assets
(b) Debts consist of all payables, whether they are due within one year or after more than one year

You can ignore other non-current liabilities, such as deferred taxation.

There is no absolute guide to the maximum safe debt ratio, but as a very general guide, you might regard 50% as a safe limit to debt. In practice, many companies operate successfully with a higher debt ratio than this, but 50% is nonetheless a helpful benchmark. In addition, if the debt ratio is over 50% and getting worse, the company's debt position will be worth looking at more carefully.

In the case of Furlong the debt ratio is:

	20X8	20X7
Total debts	$ (860,731 + 100,000)	$ (895,656 + 100,000)
Total assets	$1,870,630	$1,664,425
	= 51%	= 60%

In this case, the debt ratio is quite high, mainly because of the large amount of current liabilities. However, the debt ratio has fallen from 60% to 51% between 20X7 and 20X8, and so the company appears to be improving its debt position.

3.3 Gearing/leverage

Gearing or leverage is concerned with a company's **long-term capital structure**. We can think of a company as consisting of non-current assets and net current assets (ie working capital, which is current assets minus current liabilities). These assets must be financed by long-term capital of the company, which is one of two things:

(a) Issued share capital which can be divided into:

    (i) Ordinary shares plus other equity (eg reserves)
    (ii) Non-redeemable preference shares (unusual)

(b) Long-term debt including redeemable preference shares

Preference share capital is normally classified as a non-current liability in accordance with IAS 32 (IAS 32: AG35), and preference dividends (paid or accrued) are included in finance costs in profit or loss.

The **capital gearing ratio** is a measure of the proportion of a company's capital that is debt. It is measured as follows.

Formula to learn

$$\text{Gearing} = \frac{\text{Interest bearing debt}}{\text{Shareholders' equity} + \text{interest bearing debt}} \times 100\%$$

As with the debt ratio, there is **no absolute limit** to what a gearing ratio ought to be. A company with a gearing ratio of more than 50% is said to be high-geared (whereas low gearing means a gearing ratio of less than 50%). Many companies are high geared, but if a high geared company is becoming increasingly high geared, it is likely to have difficulty in the future when it wants to borrow even more, unless it can also boost its shareholders' capital, either with retained profits or by a new share issue.

Leverage is an alternative term for gearing; the words have the same meaning. Note that leverage (or gearing) can be looked at conversely, by calculating the proportion of total assets financed by equity, and which may be called the equity to assets ratio. It is calculated as follows.

Formula to learn

$$\text{Equity to assets ratio} = \frac{\text{Shareholders' equity}}{\text{Shareholders' equity} + \text{interest bearing debt}} \times 100\%$$

$$\text{or} \quad \frac{\text{Shareholders' equity}}{\text{Total assets less current liabilities}} \times 100\%$$

In the example of Furlong Co, we find that the company, although having a high debt ratio because of its current liabilities, has a low gearing ratio. It has no preference share capital and its only long-term debt is the 10% loan stock. The equity to assets ratio is therefore high.

		20X8	20X7
Gearing ratio	=	$\dfrac{\$100,000}{\$1,009,899}$	$\dfrac{\$100,000}{\$768,769}$
		= 10%	= 13%
Equity to assets ratio	=	$\dfrac{\$909,899}{\$1,009,899}$	$\dfrac{\$668,769}{\$768,769}$
		= 90%	= 87%

As you can see, the equity to assets ratio is the mirror image of gearing.

3.4 The implications of high or low gearing/leverage

We mentioned earlier that **gearing or leverage** is, amongst other things, an attempt to **quantify the degree of risk involved in holding equity shares in a company**, risk both in terms of the company's ability to remain in business and in terms of expected ordinary dividends from the company. The problem with a highly geared company is that by definition there is a lot of debt. Debt generally carries a fixed rate of interest (or fixed rate of dividend if in the form of preference shares), hence there is a given (and large) amount to be paid out from profits to holders of debt before arriving at a residue available for distribution to the holders of equity. The riskiness will perhaps become clearer with the aid of an example.

	Alpha Co	Brava Co	Charlie Co
	$'000	$'000	$'000
Ordinary shares	600	400	300
Retained earnings	200	200	200
Revaluation surplus	100	100	100
	900	700	600
6% preference shares (redeemable)	–	–	100
10% loan stock	100	300	300
Capital employed	1,000	1,000	1,000
Gearing ratio	10%	30%	40%
Equity to assets ratio	90%	70%	60%

Now suppose that each company makes a profit before interest and tax of $50,000, and the rate of tax on company profits is 30%. Amounts available for distribution to equity shareholders will be as follows.

	Alpha Co	Brava Co	Charlie Co
	$'000	$'000	$'000
Profit before interest and tax	50	50	50
Interest/preference dividend	10	30	36
Taxable profit	40	20	14
Taxation at 30%	12	6	4
Profit for the year	28	14	10

If in the subsequent year profit before interest and tax falls to $40,000, the amounts available to ordinary shareholders will become as follows.

	Alpha Co	Brava Co	Charlie Co
	$'000	$'000	$'000
Profit before interest and tax	40	40	40
Interest/preference dividend	10	30	36
Taxable profit	30	10	4
Taxation at 30%	9	3	1
Profit for the year	21	7	3

Note the following:

Gearing ratio	10%	30%	40%
Equity to assets ratio	90%	70%	60%
Change in PBIT	–20%	–20%	–20%
Change in profit available for ordinary shareholders	–25%	–50%	–70%

The more highly geared the company, the greater the risk that little (if anything) will be available to distribute by way of dividend to the ordinary shareholders. The example clearly displays this fact in so far as the more highly geared the company, the greater the percentage change in profit available for ordinary shareholders for any given percentage change in profit before interest and tax. The relationship similarly holds when profits increase, and if PBIT had risen by 20% rather than fallen, you would find that once again the largest percentage change in profit available for ordinary shareholders (this means an increase) will be for the highly geared company. This means that there will be greater **volatility** of amounts available for ordinary shareholders, and presumably therefore greater volatility in dividends paid to those shareholders, where a company is highly geared. That is the risk: you may do extremely well or extremely badly without a particularly large movement in the PBIT of the company.

The risk of a company's ability to remain in business was referred to earlier. Gearing or leverage is relevant to this. A highly geared company has a large amount of interest to pay annually (assuming that the debt is external borrowing rather than preference shares). If those borrowings are **'secured'** in any way (and loan notes in particular are secured), then the **holders of the debt are perfectly entitled to force the company** to **realise assets to pay their interest** if funds are not available from other sources. Clearly the more highly geared a company the more likely this is to occur when and if profits fall.

3.5 Interest cover

The interest cover ratio shows whether a company is earning enough profits before interest and tax to pay its interest costs comfortably, or whether its interest costs are high in relation to the size of its profits, so that a fall in PBIT would then have a significant effect on profits available for ordinary shareholders.

Formula to learn

$$\text{Interest cover} = \frac{\text{Profit before interest and tax}}{\text{Interest charges}}$$

An interest cover of two times or less would be low, and should really exceed three times before the company's interest costs are to be considered within acceptable limits.

Returning first to the example of Alpha Co, Brava Co and Charlie Co, the interest cover was:

		Alpha Co	*Brava Co*	*Charlie Co*
(a)	When PBIT was $50,000 =	$\dfrac{\$50,000}{\$10,000}$	$\dfrac{\$50,000}{\$30,000}$	$\dfrac{\$50,000}{\$36,000}$
		5 times	1.67 times	1.39 times
(b)	When PBIT was $40,000 =	$\dfrac{\$40,000}{\$10,000}$	$\dfrac{\$40,000}{\$30,000}$	$\dfrac{\$40,000}{\$36,000}$
		4 times	1.33 times	1.11 times

Both Brava Co and Charlie Co have a low interest cover, which is a warning to ordinary shareholders that their profits are highly vulnerable, in percentage terms, to even small changes in PBIT.

Question

Returning to the example of Furlong Co in Paragraph 1.2, what is the company's interest cover?

Answer

Interest payments should be taken gross, from the note to the accounts, and not net of interest receipts as shown in the statement of profit or loss.

	20X8	20X7
PBIT	360,245	247,011
Interest payable	18,115	21,909
	= 20 times	= 11 times

Furlong Co has more than sufficient interest cover. In view of the company's low gearing, this is not too surprising and so we finally obtain a picture of Furlong Co as a company that does not seem to have a debt problem, in spite of its high (although declining) debt ratio.

3.6 Cash flow ratio

The cash flow ratio is the ratio of a company's **net cash inflow to its total debts**.

(a) **Net cash inflow** is the amount of cash which the company has coming into the business from its operations. A suitable figure for net cash inflow can be obtained from the statement of cash flows.

(b) **Total debts** are short-term and long-term payables, including provisions. A distinction can be made between debts payable within one year and other debts and provisions.

Obviously, a company needs to be earning enough cash from operations to be able to meet its foreseeable debts and future commitments, and the cash flow ratio, and changes in the cash flow ratio from one year to the next, provide a **useful indicator of a company's cash position**.

3.7 Short-term solvency and liquidity

Profitability is of course an important aspect of a company's performance and gearing or leverage is another. Neither, however, addresses directly the key issue of *liquidity*.

Key term

> **Liquidity** is the amount of cash a company can put its hands on quickly to settle its debts (and possibly to meet other unforeseen demands for cash payments too).

Liquid funds consist of:

(a) Cash

(b) Short-term investments for which there is a ready market

(c) Fixed-term deposits with a bank or other financial institution, for example, a six month high-interest deposit with a bank

(d) Trade receivables (because they will pay what they owe within a reasonably short period of time)

(e) Bills of exchange receivable (because like ordinary trade receivables, these represent amounts of cash due to be received within a relatively short period of time)

In summary, **liquid assets are current asset items that will or could soon be converted into cash, and cash itself.** Two common definitions of liquid assets are:

- All current assets without exception
- All current assets with the exception of inventories

A company can obtain liquid assets from sources other than sales of goods and services, such as the issue of shares for cash, a new loan or the sale of non-current assets. But a company cannot rely on these at all times, and in general, obtaining liquid funds depends on making sales revenue and profits. Even so, profits do not always lead to increases in liquidity. This is mainly because funds generated from trading may be immediately invested in non-current assets or paid out as dividends.

The reason why a company needs liquid assets is so that it can meet its debts when they fall due. Payments are continually made for operating expenses and other costs, and so there is a **cash cycle** from trading activities of cash coming in from sales and cash going out for expenses.

3.8 The cash cycle

To help you to understand liquidity ratios, it is useful to begin with a brief explanation of the cash cycle. The cash cycle describes **the flow of cash out of a business and back into it again as a result of normal trading operations.**

Cash goes out to pay for supplies, wages and salaries and other expenses, although payments can be delayed by taking some credit. A business might hold inventory for a while and then sell it. Cash will come back into the business from the sales, although customers might delay payment by themselves taking some credit.

The main points about the cash cycle are:

(a)   The timing of cash flows in and out of a business does not coincide with the time when sales and costs of sales occur. **Cash flows out can be postponed by taking credit. Cash flows in can be delayed by having receivables.**

(b)   **The time between making a purchase and making a sale also affects cash flows**. If inventories are held for a long time, the delay between the cash payment for inventory and cash receipts from selling it will also be a long one.

(c)   **Holding inventories and having receivables can therefore be seen as two reasons why cash receipts are delayed.** Another way of saying this is that if a company invests in working capital, its cash position will show a corresponding decrease.

(d)   Similarly, **taking credit from creditors can be seen as a reason why cash payments are delayed**. The company's liquidity position will worsen when it has to pay the suppliers, unless it can get more cash in from sales and receivables in the meantime.

The liquidity ratios and working capital turnover ratios are used to test a company's liquidity, length of cash cycle, and investment in working capital. The cash cycle is also referred to as the operating cycle. There is a question on this following Section 3.14.

3.9 Liquidity ratios: current ratio and quick ratio

The 'standard' test of liquidity is the **current ratio**. It can be obtained from the statement of financial position.

Formula to learn

Current ratio = $\dfrac{\text{Current assets}}{\text{Current liabilities}}$

The idea behind this is that a company should have enough current assets that give a promise of 'cash to come' to meet its future commitments to pay off its current liabilities. Obviously, a **ratio in excess of 1 should be expected**. Otherwise, there would be the prospect that the company might be unable to pay its debts on time. In practice, a ratio comfortably in excess of 1 should be expected, but what is 'comfortable' varies between different types of businesses.

Companies are not able to convert all their current assets into cash very quickly. In particular, some manufacturing companies might hold large quantities of raw material inventories, which must be used in production to create finished goods inventory. These might be warehoused for a long time, or sold on lengthy credit. In such businesses, where inventory turnover is slow, most inventories are not very 'liquid' assets, because the cash cycle is so long. For these reasons, we calculate an additional liquidity ratio, known as the quick ratio or acid test ratio.

The **quick ratio**, or **acid test ratio**, is calculated as follows.

$$\text{Quick ratio} = \frac{\text{Current assets less inventory}}{\text{Current liabilities}}$$

This ratio should ideally be **at least 1** for companies with a slow inventory turnover. For companies with a fast inventory turnover, a quick ratio can be comfortably less than 1 without suggesting that the company could be in cash flow trouble.

Both the current ratio and the quick ratio offer an indication of the company's liquidity position, but the absolute figures **should not be interpreted too literally**. It is often theorised that an acceptable current ratio is 1.5 and an acceptable quick ratio is 0.8, but these should only be used as a guide. Different businesses operate in very different ways. A supermarket group for example might have a current ratio of 0.52 and a quick ratio of 0.17. Supermarkets have low receivables (people do not buy groceries on credit), low cash (good cash management), medium inventories (high inventories but quick turnover, particularly in view of perishability) and very high payables.

Compare this with a manufacturing and retail organisation, with a current ratio of 1.44 and a quick ratio of 1.03. Such businesses operate with liquidity ratios closer to the standard.

What is important is the **trend** of these ratios. From this, one can easily ascertain whether liquidity is improving or deteriorating. If a supermarket has traded for the last ten years (very successfully) with current ratios of 0.52 and quick ratios of 0.17 then it should be supposed that the company can continue in business with those levels of liquidity. If in the following year the current ratio were to fall to 0.38 and the quick ratio to 0.09, then further investigation into the liquidity situation would be appropriate. It is the relative position that is far more important than the absolute figures.

Don't forget the other side of the coin either. A current ratio and a quick ratio can get **bigger than they need to be**. A company that has large volumes of inventories and receivables might be over-investing in working capital, and so tying up more funds in the business than it needs to. This would suggest poor management of receivables (credit) or inventories by the company.

3.10 Efficiency ratios: control of receivables and inventories

A rough measure of the average length of time it takes for a company's customers to pay what they owe is the **accounts receivable collection period**.

The estimated average accounts receivable collection period is calculated as:

$$\frac{\text{Trade receivables}}{\text{Sales}} \times 365 \text{ days}$$

The figure for sales should be taken as the sales revenue figure in the statement of profit or loss. Note that any **cash sales should be excluded** – this ratio only uses credit sales. The trade receivables are not the total figure for receivables in the statement of financial position, which includes prepayments and non-trade receivables. The trade receivables figure will be itemised in an analysis of the receivable total, in a note to the accounts.

The estimate of the accounts receivable collection period is **only approximate**.

(a) The value of receivables in the statement of financial position might be abnormally high or low compared with the 'normal' level the company usually has.

(b) Sales revenue in the statement of profit or loss is exclusive of sales taxes, but receivables in the statement of financial position are inclusive of sales tax. We are not strictly comparing like with like.

Sales are usually made on 'normal credit terms' of payment within 30 days. A collection period significantly in excess of this might be representative of poor management of funds of a business. However, some companies must allow generous credit terms to win customers. Exporting companies in particular may have to carry large amounts of receivables, and so their average collection period might be well in excess of 30 days.

The **trend of the collection period over time** is probably the best guide. If the collection period is increasing year on year, this is indicative of a poorly managed credit control function (and potentially therefore a poorly managed company).

3.11 Accounts receivable collection period: examples

Using the same types of company as examples, the collection period for each of the companies was as follows.

Company	Trade receivables / Sales	Collection period (× 365)	Previous year	Collection period (× 365)
Supermarket	$\dfrac{\$5,016K}{\$284,986K}=$	6.4 days	$\dfrac{\$3,977K}{\$290,668K}=$	5.0 days
Manufacturer	$\dfrac{\$458.3m}{\$2,059.5m}=$	81.2 days	$\dfrac{\$272.4m}{\$1,274.2m}=$	78.0 days
Sugar refiner and seller	$\dfrac{\$304.4m}{\$3,817.3m}=$	29.1 days	$\dfrac{\$287.0m}{\$3,366.3m}=$	31.1 days

The differences in collection period reflect the differences between the types of business. Supermarkets have hardly any trade receivables at all, whereas the manufacturing companies have far more. The collection periods are fairly constant from the previous year for all three companies.

3.12 Inventory turnover period

Another ratio worth calculating is the inventory turnover period. This is another estimated figure, obtainable from published accounts, which indicates the average number of days that items of inventory are held for. As with the average receivable collection period, however, it is only an approximate estimated figure, but one which should be reliable enough for comparing changes year on year.

Formula to learn

The inventory turnover period is calculated as:

$$\frac{\text{Inventory}}{\text{Cost of sales}} \times 365 \text{ days}$$

This is another measure of how vigorously a business is trading. A lengthening inventory turnover period from one year to the next indicates:

(a) A slowdown in trading; or

(b) A build-up in inventory levels, perhaps suggesting that the investment in inventories is becoming excessive.

Generally the **higher the inventory turnover the better**, ie the lower the turnover period the better, but several aspects of inventory holding policy have to be balanced.

(a) Lead times
(b) Seasonal fluctuations in orders
(c) Alternative uses of warehouse space
(d) Bulk buying discounts
(e) Likelihood of inventory perishing or becoming obsolete

Presumably if we add together the inventory turnover period and receivables collection period, this should give us an indication of how soon inventory is converted into cash. Both receivables collection period and inventory turnover period therefore give us a further indication of the company's liquidity.

3.13 Inventory turnover period: example

The estimated inventory turnover periods for a supermarket are as follows.

Company	$\dfrac{\text{Inventory}}{\text{Cost of sales}}$	Iventory turnover period (days × 365)		Previous year		
Supermarket	$\dfrac{\$15,554K}{\$254,571K}$	22.3 days		$\dfrac{\$14,094K}{\$261,368K}$	×	365 = 19.7 days

3.14 Accounts payable payment period

Formula to learn

Accounts payable payment period is ideally calculated by the formula:

$$\frac{\text{Trade accounts payable}}{\text{Purchases}} \times 365 \text{ days}$$

It is rare to find purchases disclosed in published accounts and so **cost of sales serves as an approximation**. The payment period often helps to assess a company's liquidity; an increase is often a sign of lack of long-term finance or poor management of current assets, resulting in the use of extended credit from suppliers, increased bank overdraft and so on.

Question	Liquidity and working capital

Calculate liquidity and working capital ratios from the accounts of TEB Co, a business which provides service support (cleaning etc) to customers worldwide. Comment on the results of your calculations.

	20X7 $m	20X6 $m
Sales revenue	2,176.2	2,344.8
Cost of sales	1,659.0	1,731.5
Gross profit	517.2	613.3
Current assets		
Inventories	42.7	78.0
Receivables (Note 1)	378.9	431.4
Short-term deposits and cash	205.2	145.0
	626.8	654.4
Current liabilities		
Loans and overdrafts	32.4	81.1
Tax on profits	67.8	76.7
Accruals	11.7	17.2
Payables (Note 2)	487.2	467.2
	599.1	642.2
Net current assets	27.7	12.2

Notes

1	Trade receivables	295.2	335.5
2	Trade payables	190.8	188.1

Answer

	20X7	20X6
Current ratio	$\dfrac{626.8}{599.1} = 1.05$	$\dfrac{654.4}{642.2} = 1.02$
Quick ratio	$\dfrac{584.1}{599.1} = 0.97$	$\dfrac{576.4}{642.2} = 0.90$
Accounts receivable collection period	$\dfrac{295.2}{2,176.2} \times 365 = 49.5$ days	$\dfrac{335.5}{2,344.8} \times 365 = 52.2$ days
Inventory turnover period	$\dfrac{42.7}{1,659.0} \times 365 = 9.4$ days	$\dfrac{78.0}{1,731.5} \times 365 = 16.4$ days
Accounts payable payment period	$\dfrac{190.8}{1,659.0} \times 365 = 42.0$ days	$\dfrac{188.1}{1,731.5} \times 365 = 39.7$ days

TEB Co's current ratio is a little lower than average but its quick ratio is better than average and very little less than the current ratio. This suggests that inventory levels are strictly controlled, which is reinforced by the low inventory turnover period. It would seem that working capital is tightly managed, to avoid the poor liquidity which could be caused by a long receivables collection period and comparatively high payables.

The company in the exercise is a service company and hence it would be expected to have very low inventory and a very short inventory turnover period. The similarity of receivables collection period and payables payment period means that the company is passing on most of the delay in receiving payment to its suppliers.

Question

Operating cycle

(a) Calculate the operating cycle for Moribund plc for 20X2 on the basis of the following information.

		$
Inventory:	raw materials	150,000
	work in progress	60,000
	finished goods	200,000
Purchases		500,000
Trade accounts receivable		230,000
Trade accounts payable		120,000
Sales		900,000
Cost of goods sold		750,000

Tutorial note. You will need to calculate inventory turnover periods (total year end inventory over cost of goods sold), receivables as daily sales, and payables in relation to purchases, all converted into 'days'.

(b) List the steps which might be taken in order to improve the operating cycle.

Answer

(a) The operating cycle can be found as follows.

Inventory turnover period:
$$\frac{\text{Total closing inventory} \times 365}{\text{Cost of goods sold}}$$

plus

Accounts receivable collection period:
$$\frac{\text{Closing trade receivables} \times 365}{\text{Sales}}$$

less

Accounts payable payment period:

$$\frac{Closing\ trade\ payables \times 365}{Purchases}$$

	20X2
Total closing inventory ($)	410,000
Cost of goods sold ($)	750,000
Inventory turnover period	199.5 days
Closing receivables ($)	230,000
Sales ($)	900,000
Receivables collection period	93.3 days
Closing payables ($)	120,000
Purchases ($)	500,000
Payables payment period	(87.6 days)
Length of operating cycle (199.5 + 93.3 – 87.6)	205.2 days

(b)   The steps that could be taken to reduce the operating cycle include:

    (i)   Reducing the raw material inventory turnover period.

    (ii)   Reducing the time taken to produce goods. However, the company must ensure that quality is not sacrificed as a result of speeding up the production process.

    (iii)   Increasing the period of credit taken from suppliers. The credit period already seems very long – the company is allowed three months credit by its suppliers, and probably could not be increased. If the credit period is extended then the company may lose discounts for prompt payment.

    (iv)   Reducing the finished goods inventory turnover period.

    (v)   Reducing the receivables collection period. The administrative costs of speeding up debt collection and the effect on sales of reducing the credit period allowed must be evaluated. However, the credit period does already seem very long by the standards of most industries. It may be that generous terms have been allowed to secure large contracts and little will be able to be done about this in the short term.

4 Shareholders' investment ratios

FAST FORWARD

Ratios such as EPS and dividend per share help equity shareholders and other investors to **assess the value and quality of an investment in the ordinary shares of a company.**

They are:

(a)   Earnings per share
(b)   Dividend per share
(c)   Dividend cover
(d)   P/E ratio
(e)   Dividend yield

The value of an investment in ordinary shares in a company **listed on a stock exchange** is its market value, and so investment ratios must have regard not only to information in the company's published accounts, but also to the current price, and the fourth and fifth ratios involve using the share price.

4.1 Earnings per share

It is possible to calculate the return on each ordinary share in the year. This is the earnings per share (EPS). Earnings per share is the amount of net profit for the period that is attributable to each ordinary share which is outstanding during all or part of the period (see Chapter 18).

4.2 Dividend per share and dividend cover

The **dividend per share** in cents is self-explanatory, and clearly an item of some interest to shareholders.

Formula to learn

> **Dividend cover** is a ratio of: $\dfrac{\text{Earnings per share}}{\text{Dividend per (ordinary) share}}$

It shows the **proportion of profit for the year that is available for distribution to shareholders that has been paid (or proposed) and what proportion will be retained in the business to finance future growth.** A dividend cover of two times would indicate that the company had paid 50% of its distributable profits as dividends, and retained 50% in the business to help to finance future operations. Retained profits are an important source of funds for most companies, and so the dividend cover can in some cases be quite high.

A **significant change** in the dividend cover from one year to the next would be worth looking at closely. For example, if a company's dividend cover were to fall sharply between one year and the next, it could be that its profits had fallen, but the directors wished to pay at least the same amount of dividends as in the previous year, so as to keep shareholder expectations satisfied.

4.3 Price/earnings ratio

Key term

> The **Price/Earnings (P/E) ratio** is the ratio of a company's current share price to the earnings per share.

A high P/E ratio indicates strong shareholder **confidence** in the company and its future, eg in profit growth, and a lower P/E ratio indicates lower confidence.

The P/E ratio of one company can be compared with the P/E ratios of:

- Other companies in the same business sector
- Other companies generally

It is often used in **stock exchange reporting** where prices are readily available.

4.4 Dividend yield

Dividend yield is the return a shareholder is currently expecting on the shares of a company.

Formula to learn

> Dividend yield = $\dfrac{\text{Dividend on the share for the year}}{\text{Current market value of the share (ex div)}} \times 100\%$

(a) The dividend per share is taken as the dividend for the previous year.
(b) Ex-div means that the share price does **not** include the right to the most recent dividend.

Shareholders look for **both dividend yield and capital growth**. Obviously, dividend yield is therefore an important aspect of a share's performance.

Question
Dividend yield

In the year to 30 September 20X8, an advertising agency declares an interim ordinary dividend of 7.4c per share and a final ordinary dividend of 8.6c per share. Assuming an ex div share price of 315 cents, what is the dividend yield?

Answer

The total dividend per share is (7.4 + 8.6) = 16 cents

$\dfrac{16}{315} \times 100 = 5.1\%$

5 Group aspects

> The Financial Reporting syllabus now explicitly includes the interpretation of financial statements of *groups*, as well as single entities.

When analysing financial performance it is important to consider the effect of parent/subsidiary relationships. Ratios based on consolidated financial statements can obscure the performance of the parent or the subsidiary. It is particularly important to be able to isolate the effects of **acquisitions** or **disposals** of subsidiaries on the financial statements and on the ratios.

5.1 Acquisitions

Ratio analysis is particularly relevant when a company is considering an acquisition. In reviewing the financial statements of the acquiree, the acquirer needs to be alert to any evidence of window dressing. Have transactions been undertaken to boost the results of the acquiree prior to the sale? And are there favourable business relationships or supply chains that will no longer apply post-acquisition?

It will also be important to review the effect of the acquisition on the group financial statements. This will require calculating underlying ratios, to see what results would have looked like if the acquisition had not taken place.

5.2 Disposals

When a disposal takes place, IFRS 5 requires the results of the discontinued operation to be separately presented (IFRS 5: para. 33), so that users can assess properly the performance of the continuing operations. In carrying out ratio analysis it is also necessary to eliminate the effects of group companies or trading operations that have been disposed of.

This means removing the results of the disposal from profit or loss (including any profit or loss on disposal, which is a one-off item) and removing the net assets of the operation disposed of from capital employed. Then important ratios such as gross profit %, operating profit % and ROCE can be calculated for the remaining business.

In this way it will be possible to judge whether the disposal had a favourable result – it may even turn out that the operation disposed of was the most profitable part of the business! It may also be possible to judge whether the sale was correctly priced – perhaps that profitable subsidiary or division should have been priced a bit higher.

5.3 Example

This is a question from the June 2015 paper.

Yogi Co is a public company and extracts from its most recent financial statements are provided below:

STATEMENTS OF PROFIT OR LOSS FOR THE YEAR ENDED 31 MARCH

	20X5	20X4
	$'000	$'000
Revenue	36,000	50,000
Cost of sales	(24,000)	(30,000)
Gross profit	12,000	20,000
Profit from sale of division (note (i))	1,000	nil
Distribution costs	(3,500)	(5,300)
Administrative expenses	(4,800)	(2,900)
Finance costs	(400)	(800)
Profit before tax	4,300	11,000
Income tax expense	(1,300)	(3,300)
Profit for the year	3,000	7,700

STATEMENTS OF FINANCIAL POSITION AS AT 31 MARCH

	20X5		20X4	
	$'000	$'000	$'000	$'000
ASSETS				
Non-current assets				
Property, plant and equipment		16,300		19,000
Intangible – goodwill		nil		2,000
		16,300		21,000
Current assets				
Inventories	3,400		5,800	
Trade receivables	1,300		2,400	
Cash and cash equivalents	1,500		nil	
		6,200		8,200
Total assets		22,500		29,200
EQUITY AND LIABILITIES				
Equity				
Equity shares of $1 each		10,000		10,000
Retained earnings		3,000		4,000
		13,000		14,000
Non-current liabilities				
10% loan notes		4,000		8,000
Current liabilities				
Bank overdraft	nil		1,400	
Trade and other payables	4,300		3,100	
Current tax payable	1,200		2,700	
		5,500		7,200
Total equity and liabilities		22,500		29,200

Notes

1. On 1 April 20X4, Yogi Co sold the net assets (including goodwill) of a separately operated division of its business for $8m cash on which it made a profit of $1m. This transaction required shareholder approval and, in order to secure this, the management of Yogi Co offered shareholders a dividend of 40 cents for each share in issue out of the proceeds of the sale. The trading results of the division which are included in the statement of profit or loss for the year ended 31 March 20X4 above are:

	$'000
Revenue	18,000
Cost of sales	(10,000)
Gross profit	8,000
Distribution costs	(1,000)
Administrative expenses	(1,200)
Profit before interest and tax	5,800

2. The following selected ratios for Yogi Co have been calculated for the year ended 31 March 20X4 (as reported above):

Gross profit margin	40.0%
Operating profit margin	23.6%
Return on capital employed	
(profit before interest and tax / (total assets – current liabilities)	53.6%
Net asset turnover	2.27 times

Required

(a) Calculate the equivalent ratios for Yogi Co:

    (i) For the year ended 31 March 20X4, after excluding the contribution made by the division that has been sold; and

    (ii) For the year ended 31 March 20X5, excluding the profit on the sale of the division.

(b) Comment on the comparative financial performance and position of Yogi Co for the year ended 31 March 20X5.

5.4 Solution

(a) Calculation of equivalent ratios (figures in $'000):

	20X4 excl. division	20X5 as reported	20X4 per question
Gross profit margin			
((20,000 – 8,000)/(50,000 – 18,000) × 100)	37.5%	33.3%	40.0%
Operating profit margin			
((11,800 – 5,800)/32,000) × 100)	18.8%	10.3%	23.6%
Return on capital employed (ROCE)			
((11,800 – 5,800)/(29,200 – 7,200 – 7,000) × 100	40.0%	21.8%	53.6%
Net asset turnover (32,000/15,000)	2.13 times	2.12 times	2.27 times

Note: The capital employed in the division sold at 31 March 20X4 was $7m ($8m sale proceeds less $1m profit on sale).

The figures for the calculations of 20X4's adjusted ratios (ie excluding the effects of the sale of the division) are given in brackets; the figures for 20X5 are derived from the equivalent figures in the question, however, the operating profit margin and ROCE calculations exclude the profit from the sale of the division (as stated in the requirement) as it is a 'one off' item.

(b) The most relevant comparison is the 20X5 results (excluding the profit on disposal of the division) with the results of 20X4 (excluding the results of the division), otherwise like is not being compared with like.

Profitability

Although comparative sales have increased (excluding the effect of the sale of the division) by $4m (36,000 – 32,000), equivalent to 12.5%, the gross profit margin has fallen considerably (from 37.5% in 20X4 down to 33.3% in 20X5) and this deterioration has been compounded by the sale of the division, which was the most profitable part of the business (which earned a gross profit margin of 44.4% (8/18)). The deterioration of the operating profit margin (from 18.8% in 20X4 down to 10.3% in 20X5) is largely due to poor gross profit margins, but operating expenses are proportionately higher (as a percentage of sales) in 20X5 (23.0% compared to 18.8%) which has further reduced profitability. This is due to higher administrative expenses (as distribution costs have fallen), perhaps relating to the sale of the division.

Yogi Co's performance as measured by ROCE has deteriorated dramatically from 40.0% in 20X4 (as adjusted) to only 218% in 20X5. As the net asset turnover has remained broadly the same at 2.1 times (rounded), it is the fall in the operating profit which is responsible for the overall deterioration in performance. Whilst it is true that Yogi Co has sold the most profitable part of its business, this does not explain why the 20X5 results have deteriorated so much (by definition the adjusted 20X4 figures exclude the favourable results of the division). Consequently, Yogi Co's management need to investigate why profit margins have fallen in 20X5; it may be that customers of the sold division also bought (more profitable) goods from Yogi Co's remaining business and they have taken their custom to the new owners of the division; or it may be related to external issues which are also being experienced by other companies such as an economic recession. A study of industry sector average ratios could reveal this.

Other issues

It is very questionable to have offered shareholders such a high dividend (half of the disposal proceeds) to persuade them to vote for the disposal. At $4m (4,000 + 3,000 – 3,000, ie the movement on retained earnings or 10m shares at 40 cents) the dividend represents double the profit for the year of $2m (3,000 – 1,000) if the gain on the disposal is excluded. Another effect of the disposal is that Yogi Co appears to have used the other $4m (after paying the dividend) from the disposal proceeds to pay down half of the 10% loan notes. This has reduced finance costs and interest cover; interestingly, however, as the finance cost at 10% is much lower than the 20X5 ROCE of 21.8%, it will have had a detrimental effect on overall profit available to shareholders.

Summary

In retrospect, it may have been unwise for Yogi Co to sell the most profitable part of its business at what appears to be a very low price. It has coincided with a remarkable deterioration in profitability (not solely due to the sale) and the proceeds of the disposal have not been used to replace capacity or improve long-term prospects. By returning a substantial proportion of the sale proceeds to shareholders, it represents a downsizing of the business.

Exam focus point

The 20-mark group accounts preparation questions will **not** include disposals of subsidiaries, but aspects of this can be tested elsewhere in the exam, including, as here, in the interpretation questions.

There are additional issues to be considered when calculating and analysing ratios based on consolidated financial statements. These are non-controlling interest, goodwill and the investment in associate. It is also necessary to consider the effects of consolidation adjustments. These matter because they may distort a ratio, and it may be necessary to strip out such adjustments in order to see the picture more clearly.

For illustration purposes we will use the amended consolidated financial statements of a company called Hydan Co which has one subsidiary, Systan Co, and for our purposes, one associate.

CONSOLIDATED STATEMENT OF PROFIT OR LOSS FOR THE YEAR ENDED 30 JUNE 20X5

	$'000
Revenue	103,200
Cost of sales	(77,500)
Gross profit	25,700
Operating expenses	(20,175)
Interest receivable	150
Finance costs	(420)
Share of profit of associates	250
Profit before tax	5,505
Income tax expense	(3,200)
Profit for the year	2,305

Profit attributable to:	
Owners of the parent	1,755
Non-controlling interest	550
	2,305

CONSOLIDATED STATEMENT OF FINANCIAL POSITION AS AT 30 JUNE 20X5

	$'000
Non-current assets	
Property, plant and equipment	28,800
Goodwill	3,025
Investment in associate	1,200
Current assets	24,000
Total assets	57,025

	$'000
Equity and liabilities	
Equity attributable to owners of the parent	
Ordinary shares of $1 each	10,000
Share premium	5,000
Retained earnings	17,675
	32,675
Non-controlling interest	4,050
	36,725
Non-current liabilities	
7% bank loan	6,000
Current liabilities	14,300
Total equity and liabilities	57,025

Profitability ratios

Return on capital employed and return on equity could be calculated either including or excluding non-controlling interest. Non-controlling interest is **normally included**. The key point is that both parts of the ratio should be consistent.

Hydan Co's ROE will be calculated as:

$$\frac{\text{Profit (including attributable to NCI)}}{\text{Shareholders' equity}} = \frac{2,305}{36,725} = 6.28\%$$

If we wanted to isolate the return generated by the parent company shareholders the ratio would be:

$$\frac{\text{Profit attributable to the owners of the parent}}{\text{Shareholders' equity excluding NCI}} = \frac{1,755}{32,675} = 5.37\%$$

We can see from this that the NCI, and therefore the subsidiary, has a higher rate of return than the parent company.

Profit attributable to the owners of the parent includes the group share of the **associate's profit**. In calculating ROE the intention is to measure the return generated by the group and its shares in its associates.

In the case of **ROCE**, the ratio based on the consolidated financial statements will be:

$$\frac{\text{Profit before interest, tax, investment income and share of profit of associate}}{\text{Equity + long-term debt minus investment in associate}} = \frac{5,525^*}{41,525^{**}} = 13.3\%$$

*5,505 – 150 + 420 – 250
**36,725 + 6,000 – 1,200

Note that for ROCE we **exclude** the share of associate's profit from the numerator so we must exclude the investment in associate from the denominator.

In order to arrive at an ROCE that reflects the return on capital contributed solely by the parent company shareholders, we would need to see the subsidiary financial statements so that we could attribute interest charges and tax to the NCI. In this case we do not have those available.

The ROCE based on the consolidated financial statements can be sub-analysed into net profit % and asset turnover.

If we had calculated ROCE based solely on the return attributable to owners of the parent, we would not be able to perform this sub-analysis. This is because we are not able from the consolidated financial statements to apportion sales revenue between the group and the non-controlling interest.

When calculating group net profit %, 'share of profit of associates' should be excluded. This is because sales revenue will not include any revenue contributed by associates. Otherwise, the ratio would be distorted by the results of a company that is not part of the group.

Gearing

Hydan Co's gearing (debt/equity) is (6,000/36,725) = 16%. In calculating gearing we include NCI as part of equity. This is because the debt shown in a consolidated statement of financial position includes 100% of the debt of the subsidiary.

The inclusion of NCI increases equity and so reduces the ratio, but the inclusion of any subsidiary debt will have increased the ratio so, depending on the level of subsidiary debt, the consolidation process can have either a positive or a negative effect on gearing.

If the acquisition has been funded by a share exchange, this will have increased share capital and premium, so increasing equity and reducing gearing.

One issue that must be considered in relation to gearing is the degree to which consolidated financial statements mask the results of individual companies. A company such as Hydan Co could itself have a high gearing ratio, but the inclusion of a couple of subsidiaries with low gearing and healthy earnings, plus the addition of NCI, could bring the consolidated gearing right down. In practice, lenders will be aware of this, so any institution lending to Hydan Co will want sight of its individual financial statements.

Solvency

The current ratio based on Hydan Co's consolidated financial statements is (24,000/14,300) = 1.68:1

We don't have the information needed to produce the quick ratio.

Group current assets and current liabilities are shown after the elimination of any intragroup balances. Exclusion of intragroup transactions and balances can lead to the removal of large amounts. Large organisations have considerable amounts owed to and from group companies. We can't see any of this from the consolidated ratio.

The consolidated current ratio is also not that meaningful to creditors, who are interested in the ability of the individual company which owes them money to pay its debts. One of the group companies could be insolvent – we can't see that from the consolidated ratio.

The degree to which the consolidated current ratio gives a faithful representation of the solvency of the group companies depends on the degree of deviation of the individual ratios from the group ratio.

Hydan Co has one subsidiary, Systan Co. If we knew that Hydan Co itself had a current ratio of 1.58:1 and Systan Co had a current ratio of 1.79:1, we could assume that a group ratio of 1.68:1 gave a fair representation.

The deviation from 1.68 would be as follows:

$$\frac{(1.58-1.68)+(1.79-1.68)/2}{1.68} = \frac{(0.1+0.11)/2}{1.68} = \frac{0.11}{1.68} = 0.07$$

0.07 is closer to 0 than 1, making the group ratio of 1.68 reliable.

If, however, Hydan Co had a current ratio of 0.58 and Systan Co had a current ratio of 2.79, still giving a group ratio of 1.68, the deviation would be as follows:

$$\frac{(0.58-1.68)+(2.79-1.68)/2}{1.68} = \frac{(1.1+1.11)/2}{1.68} = \frac{1.11}{1.68} = 0.66$$

0.66 is closer to one than zero making the group ratio in this case unreliable. Simply put, the difference between 0.58 and 2.79 is so great that the average of 1.68 is not sufficiently meaningful.

Where there is no access to the individual company financial statements, the consolidated current ratio should be treated with caution.

Other issues:

Goodwill

Goodwill often appears in the consolidated statement of financial position. The existence of goodwill increases assets arfd shareholders' equity and so affects a number of ratios.

The increase in shareholders' equity will act to reduce both ROCE and ROE. Impairment losses on goodwill will reduce profits, also negatively impacting ROCE and ROE.

EPS

Earnings per share is regarded as an important measure of profitability, and is a component of the P/E ratio. For measurement against other companies, EPS is only useful if measured against other companies with the same number of shares. Where there are differing numbers of shares, the P/E ratio is a more useful means of comparison.

The trend of EPS measured over time is a useful indicator but can be distorted in the case of consolidated financial statements where an acquisition has taken place funded by a share exchange.

Other investor ratios

Other investor ratios such as dividends per share are less meaningful when applied to consolidated financial statements. Investors own shares in individual companies and receive dividends on the basis of the results of the individual company, not the group.

Dividend cover is also inapplicable, as the dividend has to be covered from the earnings of the individual company, not the group.

Consolidated vs individual financial statements

Some consolidation adjustments will lead to the recognition of additional assets. For instance, a subsidiary may have an internally-generated customer list which it does not recognise in its own financial statements. A value may be placed upon this at acquisition and it will then be recognised in the consolidated financial statements as an intangible asset. This increases assets and shareholder's equity, depressing consolidated ROCE and ROE. As the intangible asset is amortised, this will negatively impact earnings.

It is worth noting that the individual financial statements of companies in a group can also be misleading, as they are subject to intercompany transactions which may be undertaken for a variety of reasons.

Transfer pricing is one issue. Goods may have been supplied on favourable terms to another group company – or they can be supplied at inflated prices. The purpose can be simply to transfer funds from one company to another.

A subsidiary may obtain head office services free of charge – or at an inflated charge.

Loans may be advanced at non-commercial rates.

All of these issues are **resolved upon consolidation** as the entries will be eliminated, along with any resulting unrealised profit. So in some cases, the consolidated financial statements and ratios based on the consolidated financial statements, may give a more faithful representation of the financial situation of the companies in the group.

Change in group structure

When comparing financial statements year-on-year, the effect of any change in group structure must be considered. In particular, if a group has disposed of a subsidiary in the previous year, the results of the subsidiary disposed of need to be separated out in order to make any comparison meaningful. The application of IFRS 5 *Non-current assets held for sale and discontinued operations* makes it possible to separate out the results of continuing and discontinued operations (IFRS 5: para. 33). This is important for analysts as discontinued operations will not be contributing to future performance and non-current assets held for sale will be disposed of in the near future.

6 Presentation of financial performance

FAST FORWARD

However many ratios you can find to calculate **numbers alone will not answer a question**. You **must** interpret all the information available to you and support your interpretation with ratio calculations.

Exam focus point

> Examination questions on financial performance may try to simulate a real life situation. A set of accounts could be presented and you may be asked to prepare a report on them, addressed to a specific interested party, such as a bank.

You should begin your report with a heading showing who it is from, the name of the addressee, the subject of the report and a suitable date.

A good approach is often to head up a **'schedule of ratios and statistics'** which will form an appendix to the main report. Calculate the ratios in a logical sequence, dealing in turn with operating and profitability ratios, use of assets (eg turnover period for inventories, collection period for receivables), liquidity and gearing/leverage.

As you calculate the ratios you are likely to be struck by **significant fluctuations and trends**. These will form the basis of your comments in the body of the report. The report should begin with some introductory comments, setting out the scope of your analysis and mentioning that detailed figures have been included in an appendix. You should then go on to present your analysis under any categories called for by the question (eg separate sections for management, shareholders and creditors, or separate sections for profitability and liquidity).

Finally, look out for opportunities to **suggest remedial action** where trends appear to be unfavourable. Questions sometimes require you specifically to set out your advice and recommendations.

6.1 Planning your answers

This is as good a place as any to stress the importance of planning your answers. This is particularly important for 'wordy' questions. While you may feel like breathing a sigh of relief after all that number crunching, you should not be tempted to 'waffle'. The best way to avoid going off the point is to **prepare an answer plan**. This has the advantage of making you think before you write and structure your answer logically.

The following approach may be adopted when preparing an answer plan.

(a) Read the question **requirements**.

(b) **Skim through the question** to see roughly what it is about.

(c) Read through the question carefully, **underlining any key words**.

(d) Set out the **headings** for the main parts of your answer. Leave space to insert points within the headings.

(e) **Jot down points** to make within the main sections, underlining points on which you wish to expand.

(f) Write your **full answer**.

If you run out of time, a clear answer plan with points in note form will earn you more marks than an introductory paragraph written out in full.

The following information has been extracted from the recently published accounts of Doolittle Co

EXTRACTS FROM THE STATEMENTS OF PROFIT OR LOSS TO 30 APRIL

	20X9	20X8
	$'000	$'000
Revenue	11,200	9,750
Cost of sales	8,460	6,825
Net profit before tax	465	320
This is after charging:		
Depreciation	360	280
Loan note interest	80	60
Interest on bank overdraft	15	9
Audit fees	12	10

STATEMENTS OF FINANCIAL POSITION AS AT 30 APRIL

	20X9		20X8	
	$'000	$'000	$'000	$'000
Assets				
Non-current assets		1,850		1,430
Current assets				
Inventories	640		490	
Trade receivables	1,230		1,080	
Cash and cash equivalents	80		120	
		1,950		1,690
Total assets		3,800		3,120
Equity and liabilities				
Equity				
Ordinary share capital	800		800	
Retained earnings	1,310		930	
		2,110		1,730
Non-current liabilities				
10% loan stock		800		600
Current liabilities				
Bank overdraft	110		80	
Trade and other payables	750		690	
Taxation	30		20	
		890		790
Total equity and liabilities		3,800		3,120

The following ratios are those calculated for Doolittle Co, based on its published accounts for the previous year, and also the latest industry average ratios:

	Doolittle Co 30 April 20X8	Industry average
ROCE (capital employed = equity and debentures)	16.30%	18.50%
Profit/sales	3.90%	4.73%
Asset turnover	4.19	3.91
Current ratio	2.14	1.90
Quick ratio	1.52	1.27
Gross profit margin	30.00%	35.23%
Accounts receivable collection period	40 days	52 days
Accounts payable payment period	37 days	49 days
Inventory turnover (times)	13.90	18.30
Gearing	26.75%	32.71%

Required

(a)   Calculate comparable ratios (to two decimal places where appropriate) for Doolittle Co for the year ended 30 April 20X9. All calculations must be clearly shown.

(b)   Write a report to your board of directors analysing the performance of Doolittle Co, comparing the results against the previous year and against the industry average.

Answer

(a)

	20X8	20X9	Industry average
ROCE	$\dfrac{320+60}{2,330}=16.30\%$	$\dfrac{465+80}{2,910}=18.72\%$	18.50%
Profit/sales	$\dfrac{320+60}{9,750}=3.90\%$	$\dfrac{465+80}{11,200}=4.87\%$	4.73%
Asset turnover	$\dfrac{9,750}{2,330}=4.18x$	$\dfrac{11,200}{2,910}=3.85x$	3.91x
Current ratio	$\dfrac{1,690}{790}=2.10$	$\dfrac{1,950}{890}=2.20$	1.90
Quick ratio	$\dfrac{1,080+120}{790}=1.52$	$\dfrac{1,230+80}{890}=1.47$	1.27
Gross profit margin	$\dfrac{9,750-6,825}{9,750}=30.00\%$	$\dfrac{11,200-8,460}{11,200}=24.46\%$	35.23%
Accounts receivable collection period	$\dfrac{1,080}{9,750}\times365=40\text{days}$	$\dfrac{1,230}{11,200}\times365=40\text{days}$	52 days
Accounts payable payment period	$\dfrac{690}{6,825}\times365=37\text{days}$	$\dfrac{750}{8,460}\times365=32\text{days}$	49 days
Inventory turnover (times)	$\dfrac{6,825}{490}=13.9x$	$\dfrac{8,460}{640}=13.2x$	18.30x
Gearing	$\dfrac{600}{2,330}=25.75\%$	$\dfrac{800}{2,910}=27.5\%$	32.71%

(b)   (i)   REPORT

To: Board of Directors
From: Accountant   Date: xx/xx/xx
Subject: Analysis of performance of Doolittle Co

This report should be read in conjunction with the appendix attached which shows the relevant ratios (from part (a)).

Trading and profitability

Return on capital employed has improved considerably between 20X8 and 20X9 and is now higher than the industry average.

Net income as a proportion of sales has also improved noticeably between the years and is also now marginally ahead of the industry average. Gross margin, however, is considerably lower than in the previous year and is only some 70% of the industry average. This suggests either that there has been a change in the cost structure of Doolittle Co or that there has been a change in the method of cost allocation between the periods. Either way, this is a marked change that requires investigation. The company may be in a period of transition as sales have increased by nearly 15% over the year and it would appear that new non-current assets have been purchased.

Asset turnover has declined between the periods although the 20X9 figure is in line with the industry average. This reduction might indicate that the efficiency with which assets are used has deteriorated or it might indicate that the assets acquired in 20X9 have not yet fully contributed to the business. A longer term trend would clarify the picture.

(ii)   Liquidity and working capital management

The current ratio has improved slightly over the year and is marginally higher than the industry average. It is also in line with what is generally regarded as satisfactory (2:1).

The quick ratio has declined marginally but is still better than the industry average. This suggests that Doolittle Co has no short term liquidity problems and should have no difficulty in paying its debts as they become due.

Trade receivables as a proportion of revenue is unchanged from 20X8 and are considerably lower than the industry average. Consequently, there is probably little opportunity to reduce this further and there may be pressure in the future from customers to increase the period of credit given. The period of credit taken from suppliers has fallen from 37 days' purchases to 32 days' and is much lower than the industry average; thus, it may be possible to finance any additional receivables by negotiating better credit terms from suppliers.

Inventory turnover has fallen slightly and is much slower than the industry average and this may partly reflect stocking up ahead of a significant increase in sales. Alternatively, there is some danger that the inventory could contain certain obsolete items that may require writing off. The relative increase in the level of inventory has been financed by an increased overdraft which may reduce if the inventory levels can be brought down.

The high levels of inventory, overdraft and receivables compared to that of payables suggests a labour intensive company or one where considerable value is added to bought-in products.

(iii)   Gearing

The level of gearing has increased only slightly over the year and is below the industry average. Since the return on capital employed is nearly twice the rate of interest on the loan stock, profitability is likely to be increased by a modest increase in the level of gearing.

Signed: Accountant

One of the competences you require to fulfil Performance Objective 8 of the PER is the ability to assess the financial performance and position of an entity based on financial statements and disclosure notes. You can apply the knowledge you obtain from this chapter to help to demonstrate this competence.

Exam focus point

Analysis questions require the exercise of a certain amount of critical judgement. Questions are often set in which the directors propose a course of action and the ACCA examination team reports that candidates often agree with the directors' proposals. In which case, why was the question set? Critical appraisal of the proposal is required by the students, supported by calculations where appropriate.

Chapter Roundup

- You must be able to **appraise and communicate** the position and prospects of a business based on given and prepared statements and ratios.

- Return on capital employed (ROCE) may be used by shareholders or the Board to assess the performance of management.

- Banks and other lenders will be interested in a company's gearing level.

- Ratios such as EPS and dividend per share help equity shareholders and other investors to **assess the value and quality of an investment in the ordinary shares of a company**.

- However many ratios you can find to calculate **numbers alone will not answer a question**. You **must** interpret all the information available to you and support your interpretation with ratio calculations.

Quick Quiz

1   List the main categories of ratio.

2   ROCE is $\dfrac{\text{Profit before interest and tax}}{\text{Capital employed}} \times 100\%$

   True ☐

   False ☐

3   Company Q has a profit margin of 7%. Briefly comment on this.

4   The debt ratio is a company's long-term debt divided by its net assets.

   True ☐

   False ☐

5   The cash flow ratio is the ratio of:

   A   Gross cash inflow to total debt
   B   Gross cash inflow to net debt
   C   Net cash inflow to total debt
   D   Net cash inflow to net debt

6   List the formulae for:

   (a)   Current ratio
   (b)   Quick ratio
   (c)   Accounts receivable collection period
   (d)   Inventory turnover period

Answers to Quick Quiz

1   See Section 1.1.

2   True

3   You should be careful here. You have very little information. This is a low margin but you need to know what industry the company operates in. 7% may be good for a major retailer.

4   False (see Section 3.2)

5   C (see Section 3.6)

6   See Sections 3.9, 3.10 and 3.12.

Now try the question below from the Practice Question Bank

Number	Level	Marks	Time
28	–	25	49 mins

Limitations of financial statements and interpretation techniques

20

Topic list	Syllabus reference
1 Limitations of financial statements	C1
2 Accounting polices and the limitations of ratio analysis	C3

Introduction

In the last chapter we looked at how we interpret financial statements. In this chapter we take a look at how far we can rely on such interpretation.

Study guide

		Intellectual level
C	**ANALYSING AND INTERPRETING THE FINANCIAL STATEMENTS OF SINGLE ENTITIES AND GROUPS**	
C1	**Limitations of financial statements**	
(a)	Indicate the problems of using historical information to predict future performance and trends	2
(b)	Discuss how financial statements may be manipulated to produce a desired effect (creative accounting, window dressing)	2
(c)	Explain why figures in the statement of financial position may not be representative of average values throughout the period, for example, due to:	2
	(i) Seasonal trading	
	(ii) Major asset acquisitions near the end of the accounting period	
(d)	Explain how the use of consolidated financial statements might limit interpretation techniques.	
C3	**Limitations of interpretation techniques**	
(a)	Discuss the limitations in the use of ratio analysis for assessing corporate performance	2
(b)	Discuss the effect that changes in accounting policies or the use of different accounting policies between entities can have on the ability to interpret performance	2
(c)	Indicate other information, including non-financial information, that may be of relevance to the assessment of an entity's performance	1

Exam guide

These issues are unlikely to form a whole question but could well appear in a question on interpretation of accounts.

1 Limitations of financial statements

> Financial statements are affected by the obvious shortcomings of historical cost information and are also subject to manipulation.

Financial statements are intended to give a fair presentation of the financial performance of an entity over a period and its financial position at the end of that period. The IASB *Conceptual Framework* and the IFRSs are there to ensure as far as possible that they do. However, there are a number of reasons why the information in financial statements should not just be taken at its face value.

1.1 Problems of historical cost information

Historical cost information is reliable and can be verified, but it becomes less relevant as time goes by. The value shown for assets carried in the statement of financial position at historical cost may bear no relation whatever to what their current value is and what it may cost to replace them. The corresponding depreciation charge will also be low, leading to the overstatement of profits in real terms. The financial statements do not show the real cost of using such assets.

This is particularly misleading when attempting to predict future performance. It could be that a major asset will need to be replaced in two years time, at vastly more than the original cost of the asset currently shown in the statement of financial position. This will then entail much higher depreciation and interest payments (if a loan or lease is used). In addition, overstatement of profit due to the low depreciation charge could have led to too much profit having been distributed, increasing the likelihood of new asset purchases having to be financed by loans. This information could not have been obtained just from looking at the financial statements.

In a period of inflation, financial statements based on historical cost are subject to an additional distortion. Sales revenue will be keeping pace with inflation and so will the cost of purchases. However, using FIFO (and to some degree the weighted average method) inventory being used will be valued as the earliest (and therefore cheapest) purchases. This leads to understatement of cost of sales and overstatement of profits. This is the result of inventory carried at historical cost.

1.2 Creative accounting

Listed companies produce their financial statements with one eye on the stock market and, where possible, they like to produce financial statements which show analysts what they are expecting to see. For instance, a steady rise in profits, with no peaks or troughs, is reassuring to potential investors. Companies could sometimes achieve this by using provisions to smooth out the peaks and troughs. This has been largely outlawed by IAS 37 (see Chapter 13), but companies can still achieve similar effects by delaying or advancing invoicing or manipulating cut-offs or accruals. Directors who are paid performance bonuses will favour the steady rise (enough to secure the bonus each year, rather than up one year, down the next) while those who hold share options may be aiming for one spectacular set of results just before they sell.

An important aspect of improving the appearance of the statement of financial position is keeping gearing as low as possible. Investors know that interest payments reduce the amount available for distribution and potential lenders will be less willing to lend to a company which is already highly geared.

A number of creative accounting measures are aimed at reducing gearing, but regulation is increasingly catching up with these measures. In the past parent companies could find reasons to exclude highly-geared subsidiaries from the consolidation and could obtain loans in the first place via such 'quasi subsidiaries', so that the loan never appeared in the consolidated statement of financial position. This loophole was effectively closed by IAS 27. Assets could be 'sold' under a sale and leaseback agreement, which is in effect a disguised loan, or leased under an operating lease rather than a finance lease, in order to keep the liability off the balance sheet. IFRS 16, the new leasing standard, now makes it very difficult to keep liabilities off the balance sheet. If all else fails, a last minute piece of 'window dressing' can be undertaken. For instance, a loan can be repaid just before the year end and taken out again at the beginning of the next year.

1.3 Intragroup transactions

It is common for entities to carry on activities with or through subsidiaries and associates, or occasionally to engage in transactions with directors or their families. The point is that such transactions cannot be assumed to have been engaged in 'at arm's length' or in the best interests of the entity itself, which is why investors and potential investors need to be made aware of them. Transfer pricing can be used to transfer profit from one company to another and inter-company loans and transfers of non-current assets can also be used in the same way.

1.4 Seasonal trading

This is another issue that can distort reported results. Many companies whose trade is seasonal position their year end after their busy period, to minimise time spent on the inventory count. At this point in time, the statement of financial position will show a healthy level of cash and/or receivables and a low level of trade payables, assuming most of them have been paid. Thus the position is reported at the moment when the company is at its most solvent. A statement of financial position drawn up a few months earlier, or even perhaps a few months later, when trade is still slack but fixed costs still have to be paid, may give a very different picture.

1.5 Asset acquisitions

Major asset acquisitions just before the end of an accounting period can also distort results. The statement of financial position will show an increased level of assets and corresponding liabilities (probably a loan or lease payable), but the income which will be earned from utilisation of the asset will not yet have materialised. This will adversely affect the company's return on capital employed.

1.6 Acquisitions and disposals

A company may have acquired or disposed of a subsidiary or division during the year and the effect of this will need to be isolated in order to assess the underlying performance. See Chapter 19 for more details on this.

2 Accounting policies and the limitations of ratio analysis

We discussed the disclosure of accounting policies in our examination of IAS 1. The choice of accounting policy and the effect of its implementation are almost as important as its disclosure in that the results of a company can be altered significantly by the choice of accounting policy.

2.1 The effect of choice of accounting policies

Where accounting standards allow alternative treatment of items in the accounts, then the accounting policy note should declare which policy has been chosen. It should then be applied consistently.

You should be able to think of examples of how the choice of accounting policy can affect the financial statements eg whether to revalue property in IAS 16, or how to account for government grants in IAS 20.

2.2 Changes in accounting policy

The effect of a change of accounting policy is treated as a prior year adjustment according to IAS 8 para. 19) (see Chapter 17). This just means that the comparative figures are adjusted for the change in accounting policy for comparative purposes and an adjustment is put through retained earnings.

Any change in policy may only be made if it can be justified on the grounds that the new policy is preferable to the one it replaces because it will give a fairer presentation of the result and of the financial position of a reporting entity (IAS 8: para. 14).

The problem with this situation is that the directors may be able to **manipulate the results** through change(s) of accounting policies. This would be done to avoid the effect of an old accounting policy or gain the effect of a new one. It is likely to be done in a sensitive period, perhaps when the company's profits are low or the company is about to announce a rights issue. The management would have to convince the auditors that the new policy was much better, but it is not difficult to produce reasons in such cases.

The effect of such a change is very **short-term**. Most analysts and sophisticated users will discount its effect immediately, except to the extent that it will affect any dividend (because of the effect on distributable profits). It may help to avoid breaches of banking covenants because of the effect on certain ratios.

Obviously, the accounting policy for any item in the accounts could only be changed once in quite a long period of time. Auditors would not allow another change, even back to the old policy, unless there was a wholly exceptional reason.

The managers of a company can choose accounting policies **initially** to suit the company or the type of results they want to get. Any changes in accounting policy must be justified, but some managers might try to change accounting policies just to manipulate the results.

2.3 Limitations of ratio analysis

The consideration of how accounting policies may be used to manipulate company results leads us to some of the other limitations of ratio analysis.

The most important ones are:

- In a company's first year of trading there will be no comparative figures. So there will be no indication of whether or not a ratio is improving.

- Comparison against industry averages may not be that revealing. A business may be subject to factors which are not common in the industry.

- Ratios based on historic cost accounts are subject to the distortions described in 1.1 above. In particular, undervalued assets will distort ROCE and exaggerate gearing.

- Ratios are influenced by the choice of accounting policy. For instance, a company seeking to maintain or increase its ROCE may choose not to revalue its assets.

- Financial statements are subject to manipulation and so are the ratios based on them. Creative accounting is undertaken with key ratios in mind.

- Inflation over a period will distort results and ratios. Net profit, and therefore ROCE, can be inflated where FIFO is applied during an inflationary period.

- No two companies, even operating in the same industry, will have the same financial and business risk profile. For instance, one may have better access to cheap borrowing than the other and so may be able to sustain a higher level of gearing.

2.4 Other issues

Are there other issues which should be looked at when assessing an entity's performance? Factors to consider are:

- How technologically advanced is it? If it is not using the latest equipment and processes it risks being pushed out of the market at some point or having to undertake a high level of capital expenditure.

- What are its environmental policies? Is it in danger of having to pay for cleanup if the law is tightened? Does it appeal to those seeking 'ethical investment'?

- What is the reputation of its management? If it has attracted good people and kept them, that is a positive indicator.

- What is its mission statement? To what degree does it appear to be fulfilling it?

- What is its reputation as an employer? Do people want to work for this company? What are its labour relations like?

- What is the size of its market? Does it trade in just one or two countries or worldwide?

- How strong is its competition? Is it in danger of takeover?

You can probably think of other factors that you would consider important. In some cases you can also look at the quality of the product that a company produces.

Question	Company analysis

Analyse a company that you know something about against these criteria.

Exam focus point

In any interpretation of accounts question, bear the issues in this chapter in mind. In this exam you are expected to be able to look critically at financial information.

One of the competences you require to fulfil Performance Objective 8 of the PER is the ability to identify inconsistencies between information in the financial statements of an entity and accompanying narrative reports. You can apply the knowledge you obtain from this chapter to help to demonstrate this competence.

Chapter Roundup

- Financial statements are affected by the obvious shortcomings of historical cost information and are also subject to manipulation.

- We discussed the disclosure of accounting policies in our examination of IAS 1. The choice of accounting policy and the effect of its implementation are almost as important as its disclosure in that the results of a company can be altered significantly by the choice of accounting policy.

Quick Quiz

1   What is the effect of inventory carried at historical cost in a period of inflation?
2   What is 'window dressing'?
3   How can companies attempt to transfer profits from one group company to another?
4   Will two companies in the same industry have the same ROCE?

Answers to Quick Quiz

1   Overstatement of profits (see Section 1.1)

2   An accounting adjustment made just before the year end to improve the appearance of the financial statements (see Section 1.2).

3   Transfer pricing, intercompany loans, transfers of fixed assets (see Section 1.3)

4   Probably not, there may be many other differences between them.

Now try the question below from the Practice Question Bank

Number	Level	Marks	Time
29	–	20	39 mins

Statement of
cash flows

Topic list	Syllabus reference
1 IAS 7 *Statement of cash flows*	D1
2 Preparing a statement of cash flows	D1
3 Interpretation of statement of cash flows	C3

Introduction

You have already covered much of the material on statements of cash flows in your earlier studies. Much of this is repeated here for revision.

The importance of the distinction between cash and profit and the scant attention paid to this by the statement of profit or loss has resulted in the development of statements of cash flows.

This chapter adopts a systematic approach to the preparation of statements of cash flows in examinations; you should learn this method and you will then be equipped for any problems in the exam.

The third section of the chapter looks at the information which is provided by statements of cash flows and how it should be analysed.

Study guide

		Intellectual level
D1	**Preparation of single entity financial statements**	
(c)	Prepare a statement of cash flows for a single entity (not a group) in accordance with relevant accounting standards using the indirect method	2
C3	**Limitations of interpretation techniques**	
(d)	Compare the usefulness of cash flow information with that of a statement of profit or loss or a statement of profit or loss and other comprehensive income	2
(e)	Interpret a statement of cash flows (together with other financial information) to assess the performance and financial position of an entity	2

Exam guide

A statement of cash flows appear regularly in Financial Reporting, sometimes combined with interpretation of the financial statements. OTQs could also require calculation of figures for cash flows.

1 IAS 7 *Statement of cash flows*

FAST FORWARD

> **A statement of cash flows** is a useful addition to the financial statements because it is recognised that accounting profit is not the only indicator of a company's performance.

1.1 Introduction

It has been argued that 'profit' does not always give a useful or meaningful picture of a company's operations. Readers of a company's financial statements might even be **misled by a reported profit figure**.

(a) Shareholders might believe that if a company makes a profit after tax, of say, $100,000 then this is the amount which it could afford to **pay as a dividend**. Unless the company has **sufficient cash** available to stay in business and also to pay a dividend, the shareholders' expectations would be wrong.

(b) Employees might believe that if a company makes profits, it can afford to **pay higher wages** next year. This opinion may not be correct: the ability to pay wages depends on the **availability of cash**.

(c) Survival of a business entity depends not so much on profits as on its **ability to pay its debts when they fall due**. Such payments might include 'revenue' items such as material purchases, wages, interest and taxation etc, but also capital payments for new non-current assets and the repayment of loan capital when this falls due (for example on the redemption of debentures).

From these examples, it may be apparent that a company's performance and prospects depend not so much on the 'profits' earned in a period, but more realistically on liquidity or **cash flows**.

1.2 Funds flow and cash flow

Some countries, either currently or in the past, have required the disclosure of additional statements based on **funds flow** rather than cash flow. However, the definition of 'funds' can be very vague and such statements often simply require a rearrangement of figures already provided in the statement of financial position and statement of profit or loss. By contrast, a statement of cash flows is unambiguous and provides information which is additional to that provided in the rest of the accounts. It also lends itself to organisation by activity and not by classification in the statement of financial position.

A statement of cash flows is frequently given as an **additional statement**, supplementing the statement of financial position, statement of profit or loss and other comprehensive income and related notes. The group aspects of statement of cash flows (and certain complex matters) have been excluded as they are beyond the scope of your syllabus.

1.3 Objective of IAS 7

The aim of IAS 7 is to provide information to users of financial statements about the entity's **ability to generate cash and cash equivalents**, as well as indicating the cash needs of the entity. The statement of cash flows provides **historical** information about cash and cash equivalents, classifying cash flows between operating, investing and financing activities.

1.4 Scope

A statement of cash flows should be presented as an **integral part** of an entity's financial statements. All types of entity can provide useful information about cash flows as the need for cash is universal, whatever the nature of their revenue-producing activities. Therefore **all entities are required by the standard to produce a statement of cash flows**.

1.5 Benefits of cash flow information

The use of statements of cash flows is very much **in conjunction** with the rest of the financial statements. Users can gain further appreciation of the change in net assets, of the entity's financial position (liquidity and solvency) and the entity's ability to adapt to changing circumstances by affecting the amount and timing of cash flows. A statement of cash flows **enhance comparability** as they are not affected by differing accounting policies used for the same type of transactions or events.

Cash flow information of a historical nature can be used as an indicator of the amount, timing and certainty of future cash flows. Past forecast cash flow information can be **checked for accuracy** as actual figures emerge. The relationship between profit and cash flows can be analysed as can changes in prices over time.

1.6 Definitions

The standard gives the following definitions, the most important of which are **cash** and **cash equivalents**.

Key terms

- **Cash** comprises cash on hand and demand deposits.

- **Cash equivalents** are short-term, highly liquid investments that are readily convertible to known amounts of cash and which are subject to an insignificant risk of changes in value.

- **Cash flows** are inflows and outflows of cash and cash equivalents.

- **Operating activities** are the principal revenue-producing activities of the entity and other activities that are not investing or financing activities.

- **Investing activities** are the acquisition and disposal of non-current assets and other investments not included in cash equivalents.

- **Financing activities** are activities that result in changes in the size and composition of the equity capital and borrowings of the entity.

  (IAS 7: para. 6)

1.7 Cash and cash equivalents

The standard expands on the definition of cash equivalents (IAS 7: para. 7): they are not held for investment or other long-term purposes, but rather to meet short-term cash commitments. To fulfil the above definition, an investment's **maturity date should normally be within three months from its acquisition date**. It would usually be the case then that equity investments (ie shares in other companies) are **not** cash equivalents. An exception would be where preferred shares were acquired with a very close maturity date.

Loans and other borrowings from banks are classified as financing activities. (IAS 7: para. 8) In some countries, however, **bank overdrafts** are repayable on demand and are treated as part of an entity's total cash management system. In these circumstances an overdrawn balance will be included in cash and cash equivalents. Such banking arrangements are characterised by a balance which fluctuates between overdrawn and credit.

Movements between different types of cash and cash equivalent are not included in cash flows. The investment of surplus cash in cash equivalents is part of cash management, not part of operating, investing or financing activities.

(IAS 7: para. 9)

1.8 Presentation of a statement of cash flows

IAS 7 requires statements of cash flows to report cash flows during the period classified by **operating, investing and financing activities**.

(IAS 7: para. 10)

The manner of presentation of cash flows between operating, investing and financing activities **depends on the nature of the entity**. (IAS 7: para. 11) By classifying cash flows between different activities in this way users can see the impact on cash and cash equivalents of each one, and their relationships with each other. We can look at each in more detail.

1.8.1 Operating activities

This is perhaps the key part of the statement of cash flows because it shows whether, and to what extent, companies can **generate cash from their operations**. (IAS 7: para. 13) It is these operating cash flows which must, in the end pay for all cash outflows relating to other activities, ie paying loan interest, dividends and so on.

Most of the components of cash flows from operating activities will be those items which **determine the net profit or loss of the entity**, ie they relate to the main revenue-producing activities of the entity. The standard gives the following as examples of cash flows from operating activities. (IAS 7: para. 14)

(a)   Cash receipts from the sale of goods and the rendering of services
(b)   Cash receipts from royalties, fees, commissions and other revenue
(c)   Cash payments to suppliers for goods and services
(d)   Cash payments to and on behalf of employees

Certain items may be included in the net profit or loss for the period which do *not* relate to operational cash flows, for example the profit or loss on the sale of a piece of plant will be included in net profit or loss, but the cash flows will be classed as **investing**.

(IAS 7: para. 14)

1.8.2 Investing activities

The cash flows classified under this heading show the extent of new investment in **assets which will generate future profit and cash flows**. The standard gives the following examples of cash flows arising from investing activities. (IAS 7: para. 16)

(a)   Cash payments to acquire property, plant and equipment, intangibles and other non-current assets, including those relating to capitalised development costs and self-constructed property, plant and equipment

(b)   Cash receipts from sales of property, plant and equipment, intangibles and other non-current assets

(c)   Cash payments to acquire shares or debentures of other entities

(d)   Cash receipts from sales of shares or debentures of other entities

(e)   Cash advances and loans made to other parties

(f)   Cash receipts from the repayment of advances and loans made to other parties   (IAS 7: para. 16)

1.8.3 Financing activities

This section of the statement of cash flows shows the share of cash which the entity's capital providers have claimed during the period. This is an indicator of **likely future interest and dividend payments**. The standard gives the following examples of cash flows which might arise under this heading.

(a)   Cash proceeds from issuing shares

(b)   Cash payments to owners to acquire or redeem the entity's shares

(c)   Cash proceeds from issuing debentures, loans, notes, bonds, mortgages and other short or long-term borrowings

(d)   Principal repayments of amounts borrowed under leases   (IAS 7: para. 17)

Item (d) needs more explanation. Where the reporting entity uses an asset held under a lease, the amounts to go in the statement of cash flows as **financing activities** are repayments of the **principal (capital)** rather than the **interest**. The interest paid will be shown under **operating activities**.

1.9 Reporting cash flows from operating activities

The standard offers a choice of method for this part of the statement of cash flows:

(a)   **Direct method:** disclose major classes of gross cash receipts and gross cash payments

(b)   **Indirect method**: net profit or loss is adjusted for the effects of transactions of a non-cash nature, any deferrals or accruals of past or future operating cash receipts or payments, and items of income or expense associated with investing or financing cash flows   (IAS 7: para. 18)

The **direct method is the preferred method by the standard** because it discloses information, not available elsewhere in the financial statements, which could be of use in estimating future cash flows. The example below shows both methods.   (IAS 7: para. 19)

1.9.1 Using the direct method

There are different ways in which the **information about gross cash receipts and payments** can be obtained. The most obvious way is simply to extract the information from the accounting records. This may be a laborious task, however, and the indirect method below may be easier.

Exam focus point

However, you will be familiar with the direct method from your studies at Financial Accounting (FA) level. Therefore, the FR syllabus will be focusing on using the **indirect method** for preparation of a statement of cash flow.

1.9.2 Using the indirect method

This method is undoubtedly **easier** from the point of view of the preparer of the statement of cash flows. The net profit or loss for the period is adjusted for:

(a)   Changes during the period in inventories, operating receivables and payables
(b)   Non-cash items, eg depreciation, provisions, profits/losses on the sales of assets
(c)   Other items, the cash flows from which should be classified under investing or financing activities.

A **proforma** of such a calculation, taken from the IAS, is as follows and this method is more common in the exam (IAS 7 IE: para. 18(b)). (The proforma has been amended to reflect changes to IFRS.)

	$
Cash flows from operating activities	
Profit before taxation	X
Adjustments for:	
Depreciation	X
Foreign exchange loss	X
Investment income	(X)
Interest expense	X
	X
Increase in trade and other receivables	(X)
Decrease in inventories	X
Decrease in trade payables	(X)
Cash generated from operations	X
Interest paid	(X)
Income taxes paid	(X)
Net cash from operating activities	X

It is important to understand why **certain items are added and others subtracted**. Note the following.

(a) Depreciation is not a cash expense, but is deducted in arriving at profit. It makes sense, therefore, to eliminate it by adding it back.

(b) By the same logic, a loss on a disposal of a non-current asset (arising through underprovision of depreciation) needs to be added back and a profit deducted.

(c) An increase in inventories means less cash – you have spent cash on buying inventory.

(d) An increase in receivables means the company's debtors have not paid as much, and therefore there is less cash.

(e) If we pay off payables, causing the figure to decrease, again we have less cash.

1.9.3 Indirect versus direct

The direct method is encouraged where the necessary information is not too costly to obtain, but IAS 7 does not require it (IAS 7: para. 19). In practice the indirect method is more commonly used, since it is quicker and easier.

1.10 Interest and dividends

Cash flows from interest and dividends received and paid should each be **disclosed separately**. Each should be classified in a consistent manner from period to period as either operating, investing or financing activities. (IAS 7: para. 31)

Dividends paid by the entity can be classified in **one of two ways**:

(a) As a **financing cash flow**, showing the cost of obtaining financial resources

(b) As a component of **cash flows from operating activities** so that users can assess the entity's ability to pay dividends out of operating cash flows (IAS 7: para. 34)

1.11 Taxes on income

Cash flows arising from taxes on income should be **separately disclosed** and should be classified as cash flows from operating activities **unless** they can be specifically identified with financing and investing activities. (IAS 7: para. 35)

Taxation cash flows are often **difficult to match** to the originating underlying transaction, so most of the time all tax cash flows are classified as arising from operating activities. (IAS 7: para. 36)

1.12 Components of cash and cash equivalents

The components of cash and cash equivalents should be disclosed and a **reconciliation** should be presented, showing the amounts in the statement of cash flows reconciled with the equivalent items reported in the statement of financial position. (IAS 7: para. 45)

It is also necessary to disclose the **accounting policy** used in deciding the items included in cash and cash equivalents, in accordance with IAS 1 *Presentation of financial statements*, but also because of the wide range of cash management practices worldwide. (IAS 7: para. 47)

1.13 Other disclosures

All entities should disclose, together with a **commentary by management**, any other information likely to be of importance, for example:

(a) Restrictions on the use of or access to any part of cash equivalents

(b) The amount of undrawn borrowing facilities which are available

(c) Cash flows which increased operating capacity compared to cash flows which merely maintained operating capacity (IAS 7: para. 50)

1.14 Example of a statement of cash flows

In the next section we will look at the procedures for preparing a statement of cash flows. Let's look at this **example**, adapted from the example given in the standard.

Indirect method

STATEMENT OF CASH FLOWS (INDIRECT METHOD) – YEAR ENDED 31 DECEMBER 20X7

	$m	$m
Cash flows from operating activities		
Profit before taxation	3,570	
Adjustments for:		
Depreciation	450	
Investment income	(500)	
Interest expense	400	
	3,920	
Increase in trade and other receivables	(500)	
Decrease in inventories	1,050	
Decrease in trade payables	(1,740)	
Cash generated from operations	2,730	
Interest paid	(270)	
Income taxes paid	(900)	
Net cash from operating activities		1,560
Cash flows from investing activities		
Purchase of property, plant and equipment	(900)	
Proceeds from sale of equipment	20	
Interest received	200	
Dividends received	200	
Net cash used in investing activities		(480)
Cash flows from financing activities		
Proceeds from issue of share capital	250	
Proceeds from long-term borrowings	250	
Dividends paid*	(1,290)	
Net cash used in financing activities		(790)
Net increase in cash and cash equivalents		290
Cash and cash equivalents at beginning of period		120
Cash and cash equivalents at end of period		410

*This could also be shown as an operating cash flow

2 Preparing a statement of cash flows

FAST FORWARD

You need to be aware of the **format** of the statement as laid out in **IAS 7**; setting out the format is an essential first stage in preparing the statement, so this format must be learnt.

2.1 Introduction

In essence, preparing a statement of cash flows is very straightforward. You should therefore simply learn the format and apply the steps noted in the example below. Note that the following items are treated in a way that might seem confusing, but the treatment is logical if you **think in terms of cash**.

(a) **Increase in inventory** is treated as **negative** (in brackets). This is because it represents a cash **outflow**; cash is being spent on inventory.

(b) An **increase in receivables** would be treated as **negative** for the same reasons; more receivables means less cash.

(c) By contrast an **increase in payables is positive** because cash is being retained and not used to settle accounts payable. There is therefore more of it.

2.2 Example: preparation of a statement of cash flows

Kane Co's statement of profit or loss for the year ended 31 December 20X2 and statements of financial position at 31 December 20X1 and 31 December 20X2 were:

KANE CO
STATEMENT OF PROFIT OR LOSS FOR THE YEAR ENDED 31 DECEMBER 20X2

	$'000	$'000
Revenue		720
Raw materials consumed	70	
Staff costs	94	
Depreciation	118	
Loss on disposal of non-current asset	18	
		300
Operating profit		420
Interest payable		28
Profit before tax		392
Taxation		124
Profit for the year		268

KANE CO
STATEMENTS OF FINANCIAL POSITION AS AT 31 DECEMBER

	20X2	20X1
	$'000	$'000
Non-current assets		
Cost	1,596	1,560
Depreciation	(318)	(224)
	1,278	1,336
Current assets		
Inventories	24	20
Trade receivables	76	58
Cash and cash equivalents	48	56
	148	134
Total assets	1,426	1,470

	20X2 $'000	20X1 $'000
Equity and liabilities		
Equity		
Share capital	360	340
Share premium	36	24
Retained earnings	716	514
	1,112	878
Non-current liabilities		
Long-term loans	200	500
Current liabilities		
Trade and other payables	12	6
Taxation	102	86
	114	92
Total equity and liabilities	1,426	1,470

Additional information

Dividends paid were $66,000

During the year, the company paid $90,000 for a new piece of machinery.

Required

Prepare a statement of cash flows for Kane Co for the year ended 31 December 20X2 in accordance with the requirements of IAS 7, using the indirect method.

Solution

Step 1   **Set out the proforma statement of cash flows** with the headings required by IAS 7. You should leave plenty of space. Ideally, use three or more sheets of paper, one for the main statement, one for the notes and one for your workings. It is obviously essential to know the formats very well.

Step 2   Begin with the **cash flows from operating activities** as far as possible. When preparing the statement from statements of financial position, you will usually have to calculate such items as depreciation, loss on sale of non-current assets, profit for the year and tax paid (see Step 4). Note that you may not be given the tax charge in the statement of profit or loss. You will then have to assume that the tax paid in the year is last year's year-end provision and calculate the charge as the balancing figure.

Step 3   Calculate the cash flow figures for **purchase or sale of non-current assets, issue of shares and repayment of loans** if these are not already given to you (as they may be).

Step 4   Start with profit before tax. You will often be given this. If not it can be calculated by working back from the movement in retained earnings.

Step 5   You will now be able to **complete the statement** by slotting in the figures given or calculated.

KANE CO
STATEMENT OF CASH FLOWS FOR THE YEAR ENDED 31 DECEMBER 20X2

	$'000	$'000
Cash flows from operating activities		
Profit before tax	392	
Depreciation charges	118	
Loss on sale of tangible non-current assets	18	
Interest expense	28	
Increase in inventories (W4)	(4)	
Increase in trade receivables (W4)	(18)	
Increase in trade and other payables (W4)	6	

	$'000	$'000
Cash generated from operations	540	
Interest paid	(28)	
Dividends paid	(66)	
Tax paid (W3)	(108)	
Net cash from operating activities		338
Cash flows from investing activities		
Payments to acquire tangible non-current assets	(90)	
Receipts from sales of tangible non-current assets (W1)	12	
Net cash used in investing activities		(78)
Cash flows from financing activities		
Issues of share capital	32	
Long-term loans repaid (W3)	(300)	
Net cash used in financing activities		(268)
Decrease in cash and cash equivalents		(8)
Cash and cash equivalents at 1.1.X2		56
Cash and cash equivalents at 31.12.X2		48

Workings

1 Assets

	Non-current assets $'000
B/d	1,336
Addition	90
Depreciation charge	(118)
Disposals carrying amount (54 – 24)	(30)
C/d	1,278

Disposal proceeds = (30 –18) = 12

2 Equity

	Share capital $'000	Share premium $'000	Retained earnings $'000
B/d	340	24	514
Share issue	20	12	
SPL			268
Dividends paid (per Q)	–	–	(66)
	360	36	716

3 Liabilities

	Long-term loans $'000	Taxation $'000
B/d	500	86
SPL		124
Cash paid (β)	(300)	(108)
C/d	200	102

4 Working capital changes

	Inventories $'000	Trade receivables $'000	Trade payables $'000
B/d	20	58	6
Increase (decrease) (β)	4	18	6
C/d	24	76	12

Set out below are the financial statements of Emma Co.

STATEMENT OF PROFIT OR LOSS FOR THE YEAR ENDED 31 DECEMBER 20X2

	$'000
Revenue	2,553
Cost of sales	(1,814)
Gross profit	739
Other income: interest received	25
Distribution costs	(125)
Administrative expenses	(264)
Finance costs	(75)
Profit before tax	300
Income tax expense	(140)
Profit for the year	160

STATEMENTS OF FINANCIAL POSITION AS AT 31 DECEMBER

	20X2	20X1
Assets	$'000	$'000
Non-current assets		
Property, plant and equipment	380	305
Intangible assets	250	200
Investments	–	25
Current assets		
Inventories	150	102
Trade receivables	390	315
Short-term investments	50	–
Cash and cash equivalents	2	1
Total assets	1,222	948

	20X2	20X1
Equity and liabilities	$'000	$'000
Equity		
Share capital ($1 ordinary shares)	200	150
Share premium account	160	150
Revaluation surplus	100	91
Retained earnings	260	180
Non-current liabilities		
Long-term loan	130	50
Environmental provision	40	
Current liabilities		
Trade and other payables	127	119
Bank overdraft	85	98
Taxation	120	110
Total equity and liabilities	1,222	948

The following information is available.

(i)   The proceeds of the sale of non-current asset investments amounted to $30,000.

(ii)   Fixtures and fittings, with an original cost of $85,000 and a carrying amount of $45,000, were sold for $32,000 during the year.

(iii)   The following information relates to property, plant and equipment.

	31.12.20X2 $'000	31.12.20X1 $'000
Cost	720	595
Accumulated depreciation	340	290
Carrying amount	380	305

(iv)   On 31 December 20X2 Emma Co purchased a chalk quarry from which extraction will take place for five years. At the end of that time Emma Co will be obliged to close off the quarry and make the area safe. The cost of this has been estimated and discounted to a present value of $40,000, which is included in the carrying amount of the quarry and shown as a provision.

(v)   50,000 $1 ordinary shares were issued during the year at a premium of 20c per share.

(vi)   The short-term investments are highly liquid and are close to maturity.

(vii)   Dividends of $80,000 were paid during the year.

Required

Prepare a statement of cash flows for the year to 31 December 20X2 using the format laid out in IAS 7.

Answer

EMMA CO
STATEMENT OF CASH FLOWS FOR THE YEAR ENDED 31 DECEMBER 20X2

	$'000	$'000
Cash flows from operating activities		
Profit before tax	300	
Depreciation charge (W1)	90	
Loss on sale of property, plant and equipment (45 – 32)	13	
Profit on sale of non-current asset investments	(5)	
Interest expense (net)	50	
(Increase)/decrease in inventories	(48)	
(Increase)/decrease in trade receivables	(75)	
Increase/(decrease) in trade payables	8	
	333	
Interest paid	(75)	
Dividends paid	(80)	
Tax paid (110 + 140 – 120)	(130)	
Net cash from operating activities		48
Cash flows from investing activities		
Payments to acquire property, plant and equipment (W2)	(161)	
Payments to acquire intangible non-current assets	(50)	
Receipts from sales of property, plant and equipment	32	
Receipts from sale of non-current asset investments	30	
Interest received	25	
Net cash flows from investing activities		(124)
Cash flows from financing activities		
Issue of share capital	60	
Long-term loan	80	
Net cash flows from financing		140
Increase in cash and cash equivalents		64
Cash and cash equivalents at 1.1.X2		(97)
Cash and cash equivalents at 31.12.X2		(33)

Workings

1   *Depreciation charge*

	$'000	$'000
Depreciation at 31 December 20X2		340
Depreciation 31 December 20X1	290	
Depreciation on assets sold (85 – 45)	(40)	
		(250)
Charge for the year		90

2   *Assets*

	Property, plant and equipment $'000	Intangible assets $'000	Investments $'000
B/d	305	200	25
Disposals (85 – 40)*	(45)*		(25)
Depreciation (W1)	(90)		
Environmental provision	40		
Revaluation (100 – 91)	9		
Purchases for cash (β)	**161**	**50**	–
Carrying amount 31.12.X2	380	250	–

*Loss on disposal = (45 – 32) = 13

3   *Equity*

	Share capital $'000	Share premium $'000	Revaluation surplus $'000	Retained earnings $'000
B/d	150	150	91	180
Revaluation (W2)			9	
SPL				160
Dividends paid				(80)
Cash received (β)	50	10	–	–
	200	160	100	260

4   *Liabilities*

	Long-term loan $'000	Environmental provision $'000	Taxation $'000
B/d	50	-	110
Provision		40	
SPL			140
Cash received /(paid) β	80	–	(130)
C/d	130	40	120

5   *Working capital movement*

	Inventory $'000	Receivables $'000	Payables $'000
B/d	102	315	119
Increase (decrease)	48	75	8
C/d	150	390	127

In the exam you may have a number of issues to deal with in the statement of cash flows. Examples are:

- Share capital issues. The proceeds will be split between share capital and share premium.
- Bonus issues. These do **not** involve cash.

- Revaluation of non-current assets. This must be taken into account in calculating acquisitions and disposals.
- Movement on deferred tax. This must be taken into account in calculating tax paid.
- Leases. Right-of-use assets acquired under leases must be adjusted for in non-current asset calculations and the amount paid under the lease must appear as a cash flow.
- Non-current assets can include amounts for restoration/clean up costs which are not cash flows.

Make sure you attempt Question 31 in the question bank which includes a lease.

3 Interpretation of statements of cash flows

FAST FORWARD

IAS 7 was introduced to provide users with an evaluation of the ability of an entity to generate cash and cash equivalents and of its needs to utilise those cash flows.

3.1 Introduction

So what kind of information does the statement of cash flows, along with its notes, provide?

Some of the main areas where statements of cash flows should provide information not found elsewhere in the financial statements are:

(a) The **relationships between profit and cash** can be seen clearly and analysed accordingly.
(b) **Cash equivalents** are highlighted, giving a better picture of the liquidity of the company.
(c) **Financing inflows and outflows must be shown, rather than simply passed through reserves**.

One of the most important things to realise at this point is that it is wrong to try to assess the health or predict the death of a reporting entity solely on the basis of a single indicator. When analysing cash flow data, the **comparison should not just be between cash flows and profit, but also between cash flows over a period of time** (say three to five years).

Cash is not synonymous with profit on an annual basis, but you should also remember that the 'behaviour' of profit and cash flows will be very different. **Profit is smoothed out** through accruals, prepayments, provisions and other accounting conventions. This does not apply to cash, so the **cash flow figures** are likely to be **'lumpy'** in comparison. You must distinguish between this 'lumpiness' and the trends which will appear over time.

The **relationship between profit and cash flows will vary constantly**. Note that healthy companies do not always have reported profits exceeding operating cash flows. Similarly, unhealthy companies can have operating cash flows well in excess of reported profit. The value of comparing them is in determining the extent to which earned profits are being converted into the necessary cash flows.

Profit is not as important as the extent to which a company can **convert its profits into cash on a continuing basis.** This process should be judged over a period longer than one year. The cash flows should be compared with profits over the same periods to decide how successfully the reporting entity has converted earnings into cash.

Cash flow figures should also be considered in terms of their specific relationships with each other over time. A form of **'cash flow gearing'** can be determined by comparing operating cash flows and financing flows, particularly borrowing, to establish the extent of dependence of the reporting entity on external funding.

Other relationships can be examined:

(a) Operating cash flows and investment flows can be related to match cash recovery from investment to investment.
(b) Investment can be compared to distribution to indicate the proportion of total cash outflow designated specifically to investor return and reinvestment.
(c) A comparison of tax outflow to operating cash flow minus investment flow will establish a 'cash basis tax rate'.

The 'ratios' mentioned above can be monitored **inter- and intra-firm** and the analyses can be undertaken in monetary, general price-level adjusted, or percentage terms.

3.2 Worked example

Here is a full example of how the position and performance of a company can be analysed using the statement of financial position, profit or loss extracts and the statement of cash flows.

The following draft financial statements relate to Tabba Co, a private company.

Statements of financial position as at:	30 September 20X5		30 September 20X4	
	$'000	$'000	$'000	$'000
Non-current assets				
Property, plant and equipment (Note (ii))		10,600		15,800
Current assets				
Inventories	2,550		1,850	
Trade receivables	3,100		2,600	
Insurance claim (Note (iii))	1,500		1,200	
Cash and cash equivalents	850		nil	
		8,000		5,650
Total assets		18,600		21,450
Equity				
Share capital ($1 each)		6,000		6,000
Reserves:				
Revaluation (Note (ii))	nil		1,600	
Retained earnings	2,550		850	
		2,550		2,450
		8,550		8,450
Non–current liabilities				
Lease obligations (Note (ii))	2,000		1,700	
6% loan notes	800		nil	
10% loan notes	nil		4,000	
Deferred tax	200		500	
Government grants (Note (ii))	1,400		900	
		4,400		7,100
Current liabilities				
Bank overdraft	nil		550	
Trade and other payables	4,050		2,950	
Government grants (Note (ii))	600		400	
Lease obligations (Note (ii))	900		800	
Current tax payable	100		1,200	
		5,650		5,900
Total equity and liabilities		18,600		21,450

The following additional information is relevant:

(i)   Profit or loss extract for the year ended 30 September 20X5:

	$'000
Operating profit before interest and tax	270
Interest expense	(260)
Interest receivable	40
Profit before tax	50
Net income tax credit	50
Profit for the year	100

Note. The interest expense includes lease interest.

(ii) The details of the property, plant and equipment are:

	Cost $'000	Accumulated depreciation $'000	Carrying amount $'000
At 30 September 20X4	20,200	4,400	15,800
At 30 September 20X5	16,000	5,400	10,600

During the year Tabba Co sold its factory for its fair value $12m. At the date of sale it had a carrying value of $7.4m based on a previous revaluation to $8.6m less depreciation of $1.2m since the revaluation. The profit on the sale of the factory has been included in operating profit. The revaluation surplus related entirely to the factory. No other disposals of non-current assets were made during the year.

Plant acquired under leases during the year gave rise to right-of-use assets of $1.5m. Other purchases of plant during the year qualified for government grants of $950,000.

Amortisation of government grants has been credited to cost of sales.

(iii) The insurance claim related to flood damage to the company's inventories which occurred in September 20X4. The original estimate has been revised during the year after negotiations with the insurance company. The claim is expected to be settled in the near future.

Required

(a) Prepare a statement of cash flows using the indirect method for Tabba Co in accordance with IAS 7 Statement of Cash Flows for the year ended 30 September 20X5.

(b) Using the information in the question and your statement of cash flows, comment on the change in the financial position of Tabba during the year ended 30 September 20X5.

Note that you are not required to calculate any ratios.

Solution

(a) TABBA CO: STATEMENT OF CASH FLOWS FOR THE YEAR ENDED 30 SEPTEMBER 20X5

	$'000	$'000
Cash flows from operating activities		
Profit before taxation		50
Adjustments for:		
Depreciation (W1)		2,200
Profit on disposal of PPE (W1)		(4,600)
Release of grant (W3)		(250)
Increase in insurance claim receivable (1,500 – 1,200)		(300)
Interest expense		260
Investment income		(40)
		(2,680)
(Increase) decrease in inventories (W4)		(700)
(Increase) decrease in trade & other receivables (W4)		(500)
Increase (decrease) in trade payables (W4)		1,100
Cash used in operations		(2,780)
Interest paid		(260)
Income taxes paid (W3)		(1,350)
Net cash outflow from operating activities		(4,390)
Cash flows from investing activities		
Interest received	40	
Proceeds of grants (From question)	950	
Proceeds of disposal of property (From question)	12,000	
Purchase of property, plant and equipment (W1)	(2,900)	
Net cash from investing activities		10,090

	$'000	$'000
Cash flows from financing activities		
Proceeds of loan (6% loan received)	800	
Repayment of loan (10% loan repaid)	(4,000)	
Payments under leases (W3)	(1,100)	
Net cash used in financing activities		(4,300)
Net increase in cash and cash equivalents		1,400
Opening cash and cash equivalents		(550)
Closing cash and cash equivalents		850

Workings

1 Property, plant and equipment and right-of-use assets

	$'000
Carrying amount 30 September 20X4	15,800
Disposal (8,600 – 1,200)	(7,400)*
Acquisitions under leases	1,500
Depreciation (5,400 – 4,400 + 1,200)	(2,200)
Other additions (β)	2,900
Carrying amount 30 September 20X5	10,600

*Profit on disposal = (12,000 – 7,400) = 4,600

2 Equity

	Share capital	Revaluation surplus	Retained earnings
B/d	6,000		850
Factory sale, surplus realised		(1,600)	1,600
SPL	–	–	100
C/d	6,000	–	2,550

3 Liabilities

	Leases $'000	Government grant $'000	Taxation $'000
B/f – non-current	1,700	900	500
– current	800	400	1,200
New leases	1,500		
Grant received		950	
Profit or loss credit			(50)
Cash paid/movement (β)	**(1,100)**	**(250)**	**(1,350)**
C/f (non-current + current)	2,900	2,000	300

In the case of the leases and tax the movement represents cash paid, in the case of the government grant it represents grant amount released.

4 Working capital changes

	Inventories $'000	Trade receivables $'000	Trade payables $'000
b/d	1,850	2,600	2,950
Increase / (decrease)	**700**	**500**	**1,100**
c/d	2,550	3,100	4,050

(b)   **Changes in Tabba Co's financial position**

The last section of the statement of cash flows reveals a healthy increase in cash of $1.4m. However, Tabba Co is losing cash on its operating activities and its going concern status must be in doubt.

To survive and thrive businesses must generate cash from their operations; but Tabba Co has absorbed $2.68m. Whereas most companies report higher operating cash inflows than profits, Tabba Co has reported the reverse. The only reason Tabba Co was able to report a profit was because of the one-off $4.6m surplus on disposal. There were two other items that inflated profits without generating cash; a $300,000 increase in the insurance claim receivable and a $250,000 release of a government grant. Without these three items Tabba Co would have reported a $5.1m loss before tax.

Were it not for the disposal proceeds Tabba Co would be reporting a $10.6m net decrease in cash. Tabba Co has no other major assets to sell and so the coming year will see a large outflow of cash unless Tabba Co's trading position improves.

The high tax bill for the previous year suggests that Tabba Co's fall from profitability has been swift and steep. Despite this downturn in trade Tabba Co's inventories and receivables have increased, suggesting poor financial management. This in turn damages cash flow, which is indicated by the increase in the level of payables.

There are some good signs though. Investment in non-current assets has continued, although $1.5m of this was on leases which are often a sign of cash shortages. Some of the disposal proceeds have been used to redeem the expensive $4m 10% loan and replace it with a smaller and cheaper $800,000 6% loan. This will save $352,000 per annum.

Tabba Co's recovery may depend on whether the circumstances causing the slump in profits and cash flow will either disappear of their own accord or whether Tabba Co can learn to live with them. The statement of cash flows has however highlighted some serious issues for the shareholders to discuss with the directors at the annual general meeting.

Question

Intepretation of a cash flow

Refer to the financial statements and additional information relating to Emma Co provided on pages 392-393 and Emma Co's statement of cash flows on page 393-395.

Using the information referenced above, comment on the change in the financial position of Emma Co during the year ended 30 September 20X5.

Answer

Overall, the cash position has improved during the year as Emma Co has seen a cash inflow. However, the company is still in a cumulative overall negative cash position.

The company is making a positive cash flow from operations however the working capital cycle (cash from receivables, cash paid to payables and cash held in inventory) has decreased the cash inflow by $115,000. Management should investigate why so much cash is being held in the working capital of the company. It may be that sales have increased proportionately to the increase in receivables, however, if this is not the case, there may be an issue with credit control procedures. Equally, if too much cash is held in inventories, this could highlight slow moving or obsolete inventory, so there may need to be a review of the inventory level being held by the company.

Clearly management have invested in the future prospects of Emma Co as there were significant cash outflows to purchase new property, plant and equipment. This appears to have been partly financed by the long term loan that has been taken out ($80,000) and an issue of share capital (raising $60,000). Interestingly, dividends equal to the long term loan were paid during the year. It could be questioned why the directors decided to announce this dividend when the funds would have been better utilised within the business. This would have the additional bonus of saving Emma Co interest payments.

3.3 The advantages of cash flow accounting

The advantages of cash flow accounting are:

(a) Survival in business depends on the **ability to generate** cash. Cash flow accounting directs attention towards this critical issue.

(b) Cash flow is **more comprehensive** than 'profit' which is dependent on accounting conventions and concepts.

(c) **Creditors** (long and short-term) are more interested in an entity's ability to repay them than in its profitability. Whereas 'profits' might indicate that cash is likely to be available, cash flow accounting is more direct with its message.

(d) Cash flow reporting provides a better means of **comparing the results** of different companies than traditional profit reporting.

(e) Cash flow reporting **satisfies the needs of all users** better:

   (i) For **management**, it provides the sort of information on which decisions should be taken (in management accounting, 'relevant costs' to a decision are future cash flows); traditional profit accounting does not help with decision-making.

   (ii) For **shareholders and auditors**, cash flow accounting can provide a satisfactory basis for stewardship accounting.

   (iii) As described previously, the information needs of **creditors and employees** will be better served by cash flow accounting.

(f) Cash flow forecasts are **easier to prepare**, as well as more useful, than profit forecasts.

(g) They can in some respects be **audited more easily** than accounts based on the accruals concept.

(h) The accruals concept is confusing, and cash flows are **more easily understood**.

(i) Cash flow accounting should be both retrospective, and also include a forecast for the future. This is of **great information value** to all users of accounting information.

(j) **Forecasts** can subsequently be **monitored** by the publication of variance statements which compare actual cash flows against the forecast.

Question	Disadvantages

Can you think of some possible disadvantages of cash flow accounting?

Answer

The main disadvantages of cash accounting are essentially the advantages of accruals accounting (proper matching of related items). There is also the practical problem that few businesses keep historical cash flow information in the form needed to prepare a historical statement of cash flows and so extra record keeping is likely to be necessary.

Exam focus point

A statement of cash flows is very likely to come up in your exam, in one of the long questions, or at least in a couple of MCQs. In this chapter we give you the basics, but you should also do as many as possible of the statement of cash flows questions in the Practice and Revision Kit. These will give you practice at the various items that you may have to deal with in a cash flow question.

Chapter Roundup

- **Statements of cash flows** are a useful addition to the financial statements because it is recognised that accounting profit is not the only indicator of a company's performance.

- You need to be aware of the **format** of the statement as laid out in **IAS 7**; setting out the format is an essential first stage in preparing the statement, so this format must be learnt.

- IAS 7 was introduced to provide users with an evaluation of the ability of an entity to generate cash and cash equivalents and of its needs to utilise those cash flows.

Quick Quiz

1   What is the aim of a statement of cash flows?

2   The standard headings in IAS 7 *Statement of cash flows* are:

   - O.................. a................
   - I.................. a...................
   - F.................. a.....................
   - Net.................. in C..................... and ....

3   Cash equivalents are current asset investments which will mature or can be redeemed within three months of the year end.

   True   ☐

   False   ☐

4   Why are you more likely to encounter the indirect method as opposed to the direct method?

5   List five advantages of cash flow accounting.

Answers to Quick Quiz

1 To indicate an entity's ability to generate cash and cash equivalents

2 • Operating activities
   • Investing activities
   • Financing activities
   • Net increase (decrease) in cash and cash equivalents

3 False. See the definition in Section 1.6 if you are not sure about this.

4 The indirect method utilises figures which appear in the financial statements. The figures required for the direct method may not be readily available.

5 See Section 3.3.

Now try the questions below from the Practice Question Bank

Number	Level	Marks	Time
30	–	15	29 mins
31	–	14	27 mins

Accounting for inflation

Introduction

In this chapter we look at the alternatives to historical cost accounting.

Study guide

		Intellectual level
A2	**Recognition and measurement**	
(d)	Discuss the advantages and disadvantages of the use of historical cost accounting	2
(e)	Discuss whether the use of current value accounting overcomes the problems of historical cost accounting	2
(f)	Describe the concept of financial and physical capital maintenance and how this affects the determination of profits	1

Exam guide

This is a topical issue which could come up as part of a discussion question or as an OTQ.

1 Historical cost versus current value

FAST FORWARD

A number of alternatives to historical cost accounting have come under discussion in the past, mainly during periods of high inflation.

1.1 Advantages of historical cost accounting

As we are still using historical cost accounting, it may be supposed to have a number of advantages. The most important ones are:

- Amounts used are objective and free from bias.

- Amounts are reliable, they can always be verified, they exist on invoices and documents.

- Amounts in the statement of financial position can be matched perfectly with amounts in the statement of cash flows.

- Opportunities for creative accounting are less than under systems which allow management to apply their judgement to the valuation of assets.

- It has been used for centuries and is easily understood.

1.2 Disadvantages of historical cost accounting

Historical cost accounting has a number of disadvantages. They arise as particular problems in periods of inflation. The main ones are:

- It can lead to understatement of assets in the statement of financial position. A building purchased 50 years ago will appear at the price that was paid for it 50 years ago.

- Because assets are understated, depreciation will also be understated. While the purpose of depreciation is not to set aside funds for replacement of assets, if an asset has to be replaced at twice the price that was paid for its predecessor, the company may decide that it may have been prudent to make some provision for this in earlier years.

- When inventory prices are rising, and when the company is operating a FIFO system, the cheapest inventories are being charged to cost of sales and the most expensive are being designated as closing inventory in the statement of financial position. This leads to understatement of cost of sales.

- An organisation selling in an inflationary market will see its revenue and profits rise, but this is 'paper profit', distorted by the understated depreciation and cost of sales.

From these disadvantages various issues arise:

- Understatement of assets will depress a company's share price and make it vulnerable to takeover. In practice, listed companies avoid this by revaluing land and buildings in line with market values.

- Understated depreciation and understated cost of sales lead to overstatement of profits, compounded by price inflation.

- Overstated profits can lead to too much being distributed to shareholders, leaving insufficient amounts for investment.

- Overstated profits will lead shareholders to expect higher dividends and employees to demand higher wages.

- Overstated profits lead to overstated tax bills.

During periods where price inflation is low, profit overstatement will be marginal. The disadvantages of historical cost accounting become most apparent in periods of inflation. It was during the inflationary period of the 70s that alternatives were sought and that an attempt was made to introduce Current Cost Accounting (CCA). As inflation came back under control, the debate died down, but it is becoming increasingly recognised that historical cost accounting has shortcomings which need to be addressed.

1.3 Current value accounting

The move towards current value accounting has already taken a number of steps. Entities are now permitted to revalue non-current assets such as land and buildings in line with market value and financial assets and liabilities such as securities and investments can be carried at **fair value**, defined in IFRS 13 as: 'the price that would be received to sell an asset or paid to transfer a liability in an orderly transaction between market participants at the measurement date' (para. 9).

These developments, and the use of fair values in acquisition accounting (to measure the assets of the subsidiary and thus arrive at a realistic goodwill valuation) are relatively uncontroversial. However, there are those who would like fair value to be used more widely as a system of current value. The European Central Bank recently produced a paper on the possible use of Full Fair Value Accounting (FFVA) in the banking industry.

In the US a similar move is being advocated towards Current Value Accounting (CVA). Under CVA the original cost of an asset would be replaced with its discounted present value ie. the present value of its future cash flows. This is obviously suitable for monetary items such as receivables and payables. The expected inflows and outflows would be discounted to present value using an interest rate which reflects the current time value of money. For assets such as vehicles, which do not yield a pre-determined future cash flow, current cost would be a more applicable measure – based either on the current cost of the original asset or on its replacement by a more up-to-date version. For inventories, current replacement cost or NRV would be indicated. Under this measurement basis, the LIFO/FIFO distinction would no longer apply.

1.4 Historical cost accounting; does it have a future?

Investment analysts have argued that historical cost information is out of date and not relevant and that fair value information, where based on active market prices, is the best available measure of future cash flows which an asset can be expected to generate.

This is heard increasingly in the US, where investors are the most highly-regarded user group for financial information, and the issue is likely to arise in the context of the IASB/FASB convergence discussions.

We will now go on to look at two alternative systems which have sought in the past to address the shortcomings of historical cost accounting – **current purchasing power (CPP)** and **current cost accounting (CCA)**. We begin by looking at the fundamental difference between these two systems – a different concept of capital maintenance and therefore of profit.

2 Concepts of capital and capital maintenance

FAST FORWARD

Measurement of profit depends on the methods used to value capital and on the method, if any, of accounting for price level changes.

Most entities use a **financial concept of capital** when preparing their financial statements.

2.1 Concepts of capital maintenance and the determination of profit

First of all, we need to define the different concepts of capital.

Key terms

> **Capital.** Under a **financial concept of capital**, such as invested money or invested purchasing power, capital is the net assets or equity of the entity. The financial concept of capital is adopted by most entities.
>
> Under a **physical concept of capital**, such as operating capability, capital is the productive capacity of the entity based on, for example, units of output per day. (IASB, *Conceptual Framework*: para. 4.59)

The definition of profit is also important.

Key term

> **Profit.** The residual amount that remains after expenses (including capital maintenance adjustments, where appropriate) have been deducted from income. Any amount over and above that required to maintain the capital at the beginning of the period is profit. (IASB, *Conceptual Framework*: para. 4.63)

The main difference between the two concepts of capital maintenance is the treatment of the **effects of changes in the prices of assets and liabilities** of the entity (IASB, *Conceptual Framework*: para. 4.62). In general terms, an entity has maintained its capital if it has as much capital at the end of the period as it had at the beginning of the period. Any amount over and above that required to maintain the capital at the beginning of the period is profit.

(a) **Financial capital maintenance**: profit is the increase in nominal money capital over the period. This is the concept used in CPP, and used under historical cost accounting.

(b) **Physical capital maintenance**: profit is the increase in the physical productive capacity over the period. This is the concept used in CCA. (IASB, *Conceptual Framework*: para. 4.62)

2.2 Capital maintenance in times of inflation

Profit can be measured as the **difference between how wealthy a company is at the beginning and at the end of an accounting period.**

(a) This wealth can be expressed in terms of the capital of a company as shown in its opening and closing statements of financial position.

(b) A business which maintains its capital unchanged during an accounting period can be said to have broken even.

(c) Once **capital has been maintained**, **anything** achieved **in excess represents profit.**

For this analysis to be of any use, we must be able to draw up a company's statement of financial position at the beginning and at the end of a period, so as to place a value on the opening and closing capital. There are particular difficulties in doing this during a **period of rising prices**.

In conventional historical cost accounts, assets are stated in the statement of financial position at the amount it cost to acquire them (less any amounts written off in respect of depreciation or impairment in value). Capital is simply the **difference between assets and liabilities**.

Exam focus point

> If prices are rising, it is possible for a company to show a profit in its historical cost accounts despite having identical physical assets and owing identical liabilities at the beginning and end of its accounting period. Look out for this.

For example, consider the following opening and closing statements of financial position of a company.

	Opening $	Closing $
Inventory (100 items at cost)	500	600
Other net assets	1,000	1,000
Capital	1,500	1,600

Assuming that no new capital has been introduced during the year, and no capital has been distributed as dividends, the profit shown in historical cost accounts would be $100, being the excess of closing capital over opening capital. And yet in physical terms the company is no better off: it still has 100 units of inventory (which cost $5 each at the beginning of the period, but $6 each at the end) and its other net assets are identical. The 'profit' earned has merely enabled the company to keep pace with inflation.

An alternative to the concept of capital maintenance based on historical costs is to express capital in **physical** terms. On this basis, no profit would be recognised in the example above because the physical substance of the company is unchanged over the accounting period. Capital is maintained if at the end of the period the company is in a position to achieve the same physical output as it was at the beginning of the period. You should bear in mind that financial definitions of capital maintenance are not the only ones possible; in theory at least, there is no reason why profit should not be measured as the increase in a company's **physical** capital over an accounting period.

3 Current purchasing power (CPP)

FAST FORWARD

CPP accounting is a method of accounting for general (not specific) inflation. It does so by expressing asset values in a stable monetary unit, the $ of current purchasing power.

3.1 The unit of measurement

Another way to tackle the problems of capital maintenance in times of rising prices is to look at the **unit of measurement** in which accounting values are expressed.

It is an axiom of conventional accounting, as it has developed over the years, that value should be measured in terms of money. It is also **implicitly assumed** that **money values are stable**, so that $1 at the start of the financial year has the same value as $1 at the end of that year. But when **prices are rising**, this assumption is invalid: **$1 at the end of the year has less value (less purchasing power) than it had one year previously**.

This leads to problems when aggregating amounts which have arisen at different times. For example, a company's non-current assets may include items bought at different times over a period of many years. They will each have been recorded in $s, but the value of $1 will have varied over the period. In effect the **non-current asset figure in a historical cost statement of financial position is an aggregate of a number of items expressed in different units**. It could be argued that such a figure is **meaningless**.

Faced with this argument, one possibility would be to re-state all accounts items in terms of a stable monetary unit. There would be difficulties in practice, but in theory there is no reason why a stable unit ($ CPP = $s of current purchasing power) should not be devised. In this section we will look at a system of accounting (current purchasing power accounting, or CPP) based on precisely this idea.

3.2 Specific and general price changes

We can identify two different types of price inflation.

When prices are rising, it is likely that the **current value of assets will also rise**, but not necessarily by the general rate of inflation. For example, if the replacement cost of a machine on 1 January 20X2 was $5,000, and the general rate of inflation in 20X2 was 8%, we would not necessarily expect the replacement cost of the machine at 31 December 20X2 to be $5,000 plus 8% = $5,400. The rate of price increase on the machinery might have been less than 8% or more than 8%. (Conceivably, in spite of general inflation, the replacement cost of the machinery might have gone down.)

(a)   There is **specific price inflation**, which measures price changes over time for a specific asset or group of assets.

(b)   There is **general price inflation**, which is the average rate of inflation, which reduces the general purchasing power of money.

To counter the problems of specific price inflation some system of current value accounting may be used (such as current cost accounting). The capital maintenance concepts underlying current value systems do not attempt to allow for the maintenance of real value in money terms.

Current purchasing power (CPP) accounting is based on a different concept of capital maintenance.

Key term

> **CPP** measures profits as the increase in the current purchasing power of equity. Profits are therefore stated after allowing for the declining purchasing power of money due to price inflation.

When applied to historical cost accounting, CPP is a system of accounting which makes adjustments to income and capital values to allow for the general rate of price inflation.

3.3 Monetary and non-monetary items

It is obvious that during a period of inflation borrowers benefit at the expense of lenders. A sum borrowed at the beginning of the year will cost less to repay at the end of the year (although lenders will seek to allow for this in higher interest charges). Similarly, customers with balances owing benefit at the expense of suppliers. CPP accounting seeks to remove this element of 'holding gain'.

Monetary items (cash, receivables, payables) cannot be restated as their amount is fixed. Non-monetary items (not-current assets and inventories) are restated in line with the general price index (at $c) and the balancing figure is equity.

Question   CPP profits

Rice Co and Price Co set up in business on 1 January 20X5 with no non-current assets, and cash of $5,000. On 1 January they acquired inventories for the full $5,000, which they sold on 30 June 20X5 for $6,000. On 30 November they obtained a further $2,100 of inventory on credit. The index of the general price level gives the following index figures.

Date	Index
1 January 20X5	300
30 June 20X5	330
30 November 20X5	350
31 December 20X5	360

Required

Calculate the CPP profits (or losses) of Rice Co and Price Co for the year to 31 December 20X5.

Answer

The approach is to prepare a CPP statement of profit or loss.

	$c	$c
Revenue (6,000 × 360 / 330)		6,545
Less cost of goods sold (5,000 × 360 / 300)		6,000
		545
Loss on holding cash for 6 months*	(545)	
Gain by owing payables for 1 month**	60	
		(485)
CPP profit		60

*($6,000 × 360 / 330) − $6,000 = $c 545
**($2,100 × 360 / 350) − $2,100 = $c 60

Note that under historical cost accounting the gross profit would be $1,000 ($6,000 − $5,000).

3.4 The advantages and disadvantages of CPP accounting

3.4.1 Advantages

(a) The restatement of asset values in terms of a **stable money value** provides **a more meaningful basis of comparison** with other companies. Similarly, provided that previous years' profits are re-valued into CPP terms, it is also possible to compare the current year's results with past performance.

(b) **Profit** is measured in **'real' terms** and excludes 'inflationary value increments'. This enables better forecasts of future prospects to be made.

(c) CPP **avoids the subjective valuations** of current value accounting, because a single price index is applied to all non-monetary assets.

(d) CPP **provides a stable monetary** unit with which to value profit and capital; ie $c.

(e) Since it is based on historical cost accounting, **raw data is easily verified**, and measurements of value can be readily audited.

3.4.2 Disadvantages

(a) It is not **clear what $c means**. 'Generalised purchasing power' as measured by a retail price index, or indeed any other general price index, has no obvious practical significance.

(b) The use of indices inevitably involves **approximations** in the measurements of value.

(c) The value **of assets in a CPP statement of financial position has less meaning than a current value statement of financial position**. It cannot be supposed that the CPP value of net assets reflects:

    (i) The general goods and services that could be bought if the assets were released

    (ii) The consumption of general goods and services that would have to be forgone to replace those assets

In this respect, a CPP statement of financial position has similar drawbacks to an historical cost statement of financial position.

4 Current cost accounting (CCA)

FAST FORWARD CCA is based on a **physical concept of capital maintenance**. Profit is recognised after the operating capability of the business has been maintained.

4.1 Value to the business (deprival value)

Current cost accounting (CCA) reflects an approach to capital maintenance based on maintaining the **operating capability** of a business. The conceptual basis of CCA is that the value of assets consumed or sold, and the value of assets in the statement of financial position, should be stated at their **value to the business** (also known as 'deprival value').

Key term

> The **deprival value** of an asset is the loss which a business entity would suffer if it were deprived of the use of the asset.

(a) A basic assumption in CCA is that 'capital maintenance' should mean maintenance of the 'business substance' or 'operating capability' of the business entity. As we have seen already, it is generally accepted that profit is earned only after a sufficient amount has been charged against sales to ensure that the capital of the business is maintained. In CCA, a **physical** rather than financial definition of capital is used: capital maintenance is measured by the ability of the business entity to keep up the same level of operating capability.

(b) 'Value to the business' is the required method of valuation in current cost accounting, because it reflects the extra funds which would be required to maintain the operating capability of the business entity if it suddenly lost the use of an asset.

Value to the business, or deprival value, can be any of the following values.

(a) **Replacement cost**: in the case of non-current assets, it is assumed that the replacement cost of an asset would be its net replacement cost (NRC), its gross replacement cost minus an appropriate provision for depreciation to reflect the amount of its life already 'used up'.

(b) **Net realisable value** (NRV): what the asset could be sold for, net of any disposal costs.

(c) **Economic value** (EV), or value in use: what the existing asset will be worth to the company over the rest of its useful life.

The choice of deprival value from one of the three values listed will depend on circumstances. In simple terms you should remember that in **CCA deprival value is nearly always replacement cost.**

If the asset is worth replacing, its deprival value will always be net replacement cost. If the asset is not worth replacing, it might have been disposed of straight away, or else it might have been kept in operation until the end of its useful life.

You may therefore come across a statement that deprival value is the **lower of**:

- **Net replacement cost (NRC)**
- The **higher of net realisable value and economic value**

We have already seen that if an asset is not worth replacing, the deprival value will be NRV or EV. However, there are many assets which will not be replaced either:

(a) Because the asset is **technologically obsolete**, and has been (or will be) superseded by more modern equipment; or

(b) Because the business is **changing the nature of its operations** and will not want to continue in the same line of business once the asset has been used up.

Such assets, even though there are reasons not to replace them, would still be valued (usually) at net replacement cost, because this 'deprival value' still provides an estimate of the **operating capability** of the company.

4.2 CCA profits and deprival value

The deprival value of assets is reflected in the CCA statement of profit or loss by the following means.

(a) **Depreciation** is charged on non-current assets on the basis of **gross replacement cost** of the asset (where NRC is the deprival value).

(b) Where **NRV or EV** is the deprival value, the charge against CCA profits will be the **loss in value of the asset** during the accounting period; ie from its previous carrying value to its current NRV or EV.

(c) **Goods sold** are charged at their **replacement cost**. Thus if an item of inventory cost $15 to produce, and sells for $20, by which time its replacement cost has risen to $17, the CCA profit would be $3.

	$
Sales	20
Less replacement cost of goods sold	17
Current cost profit	3

4.3 Example: CCA vs accounting for inflation

Suppose that Arthur Smith Co buys an asset on 1 January for $10,000. The estimated life of the asset is five years, and straight line depreciation is charged. At 31 December the gross replacement cost of the asset is $10,500 (5% higher than on 1 January) but general inflation during the year, as measured by the retail price index, has risen 20%.

(a) To maintain the value of the business against inflation, the asset should be revalued as follows.

	$
Gross ($10,000 × 120%)	12,000
Depreciation charge for the year (@ 20%)	2,400
Net value in the statement of financial position	9,600

(b) In CCA, the business maintains its operating capability if we revalue the asset as follows.

	$
Gross replacement cost	10,500
Depreciation charge for the year (note)	2,100
NRC; value in the statement of financial position	8,400

Note	$
Historical cost depreciation	2,000
CCA depreciation adjustment (5%)	100
Total CCA depreciation cost	2,100

CCA preserves the operating capability of the company but does not necessarily preserve it against the declining value in the purchasing power of money (against inflation). As mentioned previously, CCA is a system which takes account of specific price inflation (changes in the prices of specific assets or groups of assets) but **not of general price inflation.**

A strict view of current cost accounting might suggest that a set of CCA accounts should be prepared from the outset on the basis of deprival values. In practice, current cost accounts are usually prepared by **starting from historical cost accounts and making appropriate adjustments.**

4.4 CCA accounts

CCA accounts will include the following adjustments:

(1) Depreciation adjustment – to amend depreciation in line with the gross replacement cost of the asset.

(2) Cost of sales adjustment – to take account of increases in inventory prices and remove any element of profit based on this.

(3) Working capital adjustment – to remove any element of profit or loss based on holding payables or receivables in a period of inflation.

You do not need to know how to do these adjustment, but you can see that they attempt to deal with the areas where inflation can lead to 'holding gains'.

4.5 The advantages and disadvantages of current cost accounting

4.5.1 Advantages

(a) By excluding holding gains from profit, CCA can be used to indicate whether the dividends paid to shareholders will **reduce the operating capability** of the business.

(b) Assets are valued after management has considered the **opportunity cost** of holding them, and the expected benefits from their future use. CCA is therefore a useful guide for management in deciding whether to hold or sell assets.

(c) It is **relevant** to the needs of information users in:

   (i) Assessing the stability of the business entity

   (ii) Assessing the vulnerability of the business (eg to a takeover), or the liquidity of the business

   (iii) Evaluating the performance of management in maintaining and increasing the business substance

   (iv) Judging future prospects

(d)   It can be **implemented fairly easily** in practice, by making simple adjustments to the historical cost accounting profits. A current cost statement of financial position can also be prepared with reasonable simplicity.

4.5.2 Disadvantages

(a)   It is impossible to make valuations of EV or NRV without **subjective judgements**. The measurements used are therefore not objective.

(b)   There are several problems to be overcome in deciding how to provide an **estimate of replacement** costs for non-current assets.

(c)   The mixed value approach to valuation means that some assets will be valued at replacement cost, but others will be valued at net realisable value or economic value. It is arguable that the **total assets** will, therefore, have an **aggregate value** which is **not particularly meaningful** because of this mixture of different concepts.

(d)   It can be argued that **'deprival value'** is an **unrealistic concept**, because the business entity has not been deprived of the use of the asset. This argument is one which would seem to reject the fundamental approach to 'capital maintenance' on which CCA is based.

- A number of alternatives to historical cost accounting have come under discussion in the past, mainly during periods of high inflation.

- **Measurement of profit** depends on the methods used to value capital and on the method, if any, of accounting for price level changes.

- **CPP accounting** is a method of accounting for general (not specific) inflation. It does so by expressing asset values in a stable monetary unit, the $ of current purchasing power.

- CCA is based on a **physical concept of capital maintenance**. Profit is recognised after the operating capability of the business has been maintained.

Quick Quiz

1   Can methods of current value accounting be described as systems for accounting for inflation?

2   Distinguish between specific price inflation and general price inflation.

3   What is an asset's deprival value if it is not worth replacing?

Answers to Quick Quiz

1   No

2   •   Specific price inflation measures price changes over time for a specific asset or group of assets
    •   General price inflation measures the continual reduction in the general purchasing power of money

3   The higher of net realisable value and economic value

Now try the question below from the Practice Question Bank

Number	Level	Marks	Time
32	–	25	49 mins

Specialised, not-for-profit and public sector entities

Topic list	Syllabus reference
1 Primary aims	C4
2 Regulatory framework	C4
3 Performance measurement	C4

Introduction

In this chapter we look at the application of financial reporting requirements to not-for-profit and public sector entities.

Study guide

		Intellectual level
C4	**Specialised, not-for-profit and public sector entities**	
(a)	Explain how the interpretation of the financial statement of a specialised, not-for-profit or public sector organisation might differ from that of a profit-making entity by reference to the different aims, objectives and reporting requirements.	1

Exam guide

This topic is likely to turn up as an OTQ, but could also feature in a written question.

1 Primary aims

FAST FORWARD

The accounting requirements for not-for-profit and public sector entities are moving closer to those required for profit-making entities. However, they do have different goals and purposes.

What organisations do we have in mind when we refer to **Not-for-profit and public sector entities**? These are the most obvious examples:

- (a) Central government departments and agencies
- (b) Local or federal government departments
- (c) Publicly funded bodies providing healthcare (in the UK this would be the NHS) and social housing
- (d) Further and higher education institutions
- (e) Charitable bodies

The first four are **public sector entities**. Charities are **private** not-for-profit entities.

Not-for-profit entities have different goals and purposes to profit-making entities and are responsible to different stakeholders. However, they are dealing in very large sums of money and it is important that they are properly managed and that their accounts present fairly the results of their operations.

Until recently, **public sector** accounts were prepared on a **cash basis**. A transition is still in progress which will get them operating on an **accruals basis**, in line with normal practice in the private sector.

1.1 Conceptual framework for not-for profit entities

The International Federation of Accountants (IFAC) published Phase 1 of a *Public Sector Conceptual Framework* in January 2013 (IFAC: 2013). It has four chapters as follows:

- (1) Role and authority of the Conceptual Framework
- (2) Objectives and users of general purpose financial reporting
- (3) Qualitative characteristics
- (4) Reporting entity

In preparing the conceptual framework IFAC had to bear in mind that not-for profit entities have different objectives, different operating environments and other different characteristics to private sector businesses.

Some of the issues that arise in considering financial reporting by not-for-profit entities are:

- Insufficient emphasis on accountability/stewardship
- A need to broaden the definition of users and user groups
- The emphasis on future cash flows is inappropriate to not-for-profit entities
- Insufficient emphasis on budgeting

1.2 Accountability/stewardship

Not-for-profit entities are not reporting to shareholders, but it is very important that they can account for funds received and show how they have been spent. In some cases, resources may be contributed for specific purposes and management is required to show that they have been utilised for that purpose. Perhaps most importantly, taxpayers are entitled to see how the government is spending their money.

1.3 Users and user groups

The primary user group for not-for-profit entities is providers of funds. In the case of public bodies, such as government departments, this primary group will consist of taxpayers. In the case of private bodies such as charities it will be financial supporters, and also potential future financial supporters. There is also a case for saying that a second primary user group should be recognised, being the recipients of the goods and services provided by the not-for-profit entity.

1.4 Cash flow focus

The financial statements of not-for-profit entities need to provide information which will enable users to assess an entity's ability to generate net cash inflows. Not-for-profit entities need to generate cash flows, but other aspects are generally more significant – for instance, the resources the entity has available to deliver future goods and services, the cost and effectiveness of those it has delivered in the past and the degree to which it is meeting its objectives.

1.5 Budgeting

Another issue is whether financial reporting should include forecast information. For not-for-profit entities, budgets and variance analyses are more important. In some cases, funding is supplied on the basis of a formal, published budget.

2 Regulatory framework

FAST FORWARD

There is a general move to get public bodies reporting under the accruals system. Many private not-for-profit organisations still use cash accounting.

Regulation of public not-for-profit entities, principally local and national governments and governmental agencies, is by the International Public Sector Accounting Standards Board (IPSAB), which comes under IFAC.

2.1 International public sector accounting standards

The IPSASB is developing a set of International Public Sector Accounting Standards (IPSASs), based on IFRSs. To date the following IPSASs have been issued:

(1) Presentation of Financial Statements
(2) Cash Flow Statements
(3) Net Surplus or Deficit for the Period, Fundamental Errors and Changes in Accounting Policies
(4) The Effect of Changes in Foreign Exchange Rates
(5) Borrowing Costs
(6) Consolidated Financial Statements and Accounting for Controlled Entities

(7)   Accounting for investments in Associates
(8)   Financial Reporting of Interests in Joint Ventures
(9)   Revenue from Exchange Transactions
(10)   Financial Reporting in Hyperinflationary Economies
(11)   Construction Contracts
(12)   Inventories
(13)   Leases
(14)   Events After the Reporting Date
(15)   Financial Instruments: Disclosure and Presentation
(16)   Investment Property
(17)   Property, Plant and Equipment
(18)   Segment Reporting
(19)   Provisions, Contingent Liabilities and Contingent Assets
(20)   Related Party Disclosures
(21)   Impairment of Non-Cash-Generating Assets
(22)   Disclosure of financial information about the central government
(23)   Revenue from non-exchange transactions
(24)   Presentation of budget information in the financial statements
(25)   Employee benefits
(26)   Impairment of cash-generating assets
(27)   Agriculture
(28)   Financial instruments (presentation)
(29)   Financial instruments (recognition and measurement)
(30)   Financial instruments (disclosure)
(31)   Intangible assets
(32)   Service concession arrangements
(33)   First time adoption of accrual basis IPSASs

You are not required to remember this list of IPSAs, or know any of their detailed provisions, but you can see that they closely mirror the IAS/IFRSes and each one is based on the relevant Standard.

The IPSAs are all based on the **accrual method** of accounting and one of the aims of the IPSAB is to move public sector organisations from the cash to the accruals basis of accounting.

2.2 Characteristics of Not-for-profit Entities

2.2.1 Private sector

Not-for-profit entities in the private sector have the following characteristics:

*   Their objective is to provide goods and services to various recipients and not to make a profit

*   They are generally characterised by the absence of defined ownership interests (shares) that can be sold, transferred or redeemed

*   They may have a wide group of stakeholders to consider (including the public at large in some cases)

*   Their revenues generally arise from contributions (donations or membership dues) rather than sales

*   Their capital assets are typically acquired and held to deliver services without the intention of earning a return on them

2.2.2 Public sector

Nor-for-profit entities in the public sector have similar key characteristics to those in the private sector. They are typically established by legislation and:

*   Their objective is to provide goods and services to various recipients or to develop or implement policy on behalf of governments and not to make a profit

- They are characterised by the absence of defined ownership interests that can be sold, transferred or redeemed

- They typically have a wide group of stakeholders to consider (including the public at large)

- Their revenues are generally derived from taxes or other similar contributions obtained through the exercise of coercive powers

- Their capital assets are typically acquired and held to deliver services without the intention of earning a return on them

2.3 Not-for-profit entities – specific issues

While the general trend is to get not-for-profit entities producing accounts which are based as far as possible on the provisions of IFRS and which are generally comparable to those produced for profit-making entities, there are two issues which have yet to be resolved.

2.3.1 Cost of transition

While there has been a general assumption that for public sector entities the move to the accruals basis will result in more relevant and better quality financial reporting, no actual cost-benefit analysis has been undertaken on this.

One of the arguments in favour of the adoption of the accruals basis is that it will be possible to compare the cost of providing a service against the same cost in the private sector. It will then be possible to see how goods and services can be most cheaply sourced.

2.3.2 Definition of a liability

The *Conceptual Framework* defines a liability as 'a present obligation of the entity arising from past events, the settlement of which is expected to result in an outflow from the entity of resources embodying economic benefits' (*Conceptual Framework*: para. 4.15). A liability is recognised when the amount of the outflow can be reliably measured.

Public benefit entities are subject to a commitment to provide public benefits, but there is an issue to be resolved over whether this commitment meets the definition of a liability. In this situation there has been no 'exchange'. The entity has not received any goods or services for which it is required to make 'settlement'. A distinction can be drawn between 'general commitments to provide public benefits' and 'specific commitments to provide public benefits'. The specific commitment can be regarded as a 'present obligation', but it can be argued that the obligation only arises when the entity formally undertakes to provide something such as a non-performance-related grant. (If the grant were performance-related, the entity would be able to withdraw from the agreement if the performance targets were not reached.)

There is also the issue of 'reliable measurement'. Governments in particular often find themselves funding projects which go a long way over budget, suggesting that reliable measurement was not obtained at the outset.

This issue is still being debated by the IPSAB. It is of major importance in the financial reporting of the social policies of governments.

3 Performance measurement

FAST FORWARD

Not-for-profit and public sector entities are required to manage their funds efficiently but are not expected to show a profit. Their performance is measured in terms of achievement of their stated purpose.

Not-for-profit and public sector entities produce financial statements in the same way as profit-making entities do but, while they are expected to remain solvent, their performance cannot be measured simply by the bottom line.

A public sector entity is not expected to show a profit or to underspend its budget. In practice, central government and local government departments know that if they underspend the budget, next year's allocation will be correspondingly reduced. This leads to a rash of digging up the roads and other expenditure just before the end of the financial year as councils strive to spend any remaining funds.

Private and public sector entities are judged principally on the basis of what they have achieved, not how much or how little they have spent in achieving it. So how is performance measured?

3.1 Public sector entities

These will have performance measures laid down by government. The emphasis is on economy, efficiency and effectiveness. Departments and local councils have to show how they have spent public money and what level of service they have achieved. Performance measurement will be based on Key Performance Indicators (KPIs). Examples of these for a local council could be:

- Number of homeless people rehoused
- % of rubbish collections made on time
- Number of children in care adopted

Public sector entities use the services of outside contractors for a variety of functions. They then have to be able to show that they have obtained the best possible value for what they have spent on outside services. This principle is usually referred to as Value For Money (VFM). In the UK, local authorities are required to report under a system known as Best Value. They have to show that they applied 'fair competition' in awarding contracts.

Best Value is based on the principle of the 'four Cs':

(1) **Challenging** why, how and by whom a service is provided
(2) **Comparing** performance against other local authorities
(3) **Consulting** service users, the local community etc
(4) Using fair **Competition** to secure efficient and effective services

Exam focus point

> You will not be asked anything detailed or specific on this topic. It is most likely to be examined as an MCQ.

Chapter Roundup

- The accounting requirements for not-for-profit and public sector entities are moving closer to those required for profit-making entities. However, they do have different goals and purposes.

- There is a general move to get public bodies reporting under the accruals system. Many private not-for-profit organisations still use cash accounting.

- Not-for-profit and public sector entities are required to manage their funds efficiently but are not expected to show a profit. Their performance is measured in terms of achievement of their stated purpose.

Quick Quiz

1   Give some examples of not-for-profit and public sector entities.

2   What are some of the characteristics of **private sector** not-for-profit entities?

3   What are the 'four Cs'?

Answers to Quick Quiz

1　Central and local government departments, schools, hospitals, charities.

2　See Section 2.2.1.

3　See Section 3.1.

Now try the questions below from the Practice Question Bank

Number	Level	Marks	Time
3(b)	–	5	10 mins
33	–	15	29 mins

Section A questions

1 Which one of the following is an enhancing qualitative characteristic of financial information according to the *Conceptual Framework*?

    A   Timeliness
    B   Materiality
    C   Relevance
    D   Accruals

                                                                                  (2 marks)

2 Which one of the following is **not** an item which is required to be shown on the face of the statement of financial position according to IAS 1 *Presentation of Financial Statements*?

    A   Inventories
    B   Biological assets
    C   Irrecoverable debt allowance
    D   Investment property

                                                                                       (2 marks)

3 What is the correct treatment of equity dividends paid under IAS 1?

    A   Dividends paid are shown on the face of the statement of profit or loss
    B   Dividends paid are deducted from retained earnings
    C   Dividends paid are included in administrative expenses
    D   Dividends paid are deducted from 'other comprehensive income'

                                                                                        (2 marks)

4 Watson Co acquired a property on 1 January 20X1 for $250,000, being $200,000 for the building and $50,000 for the land. The building was judged to have a useful life of 50 years. On 1 January 20X6 the property was independently valued which resulted in an increase of $100,000 to the carrying amount of the building and $50,000 to the carrying amount of the land. The useful life is unchanged.

What is the depreciation charge for the year ended 31 December 20X6?

    A $5,520
    B $6,222
    C $6,273
    D $6,818

                                                                                        (2 marks)

5 Demetrios Co disposed of Venus Co, an 80%-owned subsidiary, on 31 December 20X8. Sale proceeds were $1.5m. At the date of disposal Venus Co had 1 million $1 shares in issue and retained earnings of $460,000. Unimpaired goodwill relating to the acquisition of Venus Co was $76,000. Demetrios values non-controlling interest at share of net assets.

What amount should be recognised as profit/(loss) on disposal in the consolidated financial statements of Demetrios Co?

    A $256,000 profit
    B $36,000 loss
    C $40,000 profit
    D $332,000 profit

                                                                                        (2 marks)

6   An asset has a carrying amount of $1.2m. Its replacement cost is $1m, its fair value is $800,000 and its value in use is $950,000. The legal expenses involved in selling the asset are estimated at $20,000.

What is the amount of the impairment loss suffered by the asset?

A $250,000
B $420,000
C $200,000
D $270,000

(2 marks)

---

7   A discontinued operation was disposed of in the current year. How should this be presented in the statement of profit or loss?

A   A one-line entry showing post-tax profit or loss of the operation and the post-tax gain or loss on disposal

B   A separate column showing the results of the discontinued operation, with the gain or loss on disposal included under 'other income'

C   A one-line entry showing the pre-tax profit or loss of the operation and the pre-tax gain or loss on disposal included under 'other income'. Tax effects included in 'income tax expense'

D   A one-line entry showing pre-tax profit or loss of the operation and pre-tax gain or loss on disposal, with tax effects included under 'income tax expense'

(2 marks)

---

8   Mammoth Co acquired 80% of the 100,000 $1 equity shares of Minor Co on 1 January 20X7. The consideration consisted of one Mammoth Co share for each two shares in Minor Co and $300,000 cash. The market price of a Mammoth Co share at 1 January 20X7 was $2.50 and the market price of a Minor Co share on the same date was $1.75. Mammoth Co measure non-controlling interest at fair value based on share price. At the acquisition date Minor Co had retained earnings of $85,000 and $100,000 in revaluation surplus. Its head office building had a fair value $60,000 in excess of its carrying amount.

What was the goodwill on acquisition?

A $190,000
B $55,000
C $90,000
D $75,000

(2 marks)

---

9   Catfish Co has owned 75% of Shark Co for a number of years. During the year to 31 December 20X8 Shark Co sold goods to Catfish Co for $75,000. Catfish Co had resold 40% of these goods by the year end. Shark Co applies a 25% mark-up on all sales.

By what amount should the consolidated retained earnings of Catfish Co at 31 December 20X8 be reduced in respect of these intragroup sales?

A $33,750
B $6,750
C $8,438
D $9,000

(2 marks)

10 Frog Co acquired 80% of Tadpole Co on 1 April 20X7. The individual financial statements of Frog Co and Tadpole Co for the year ended 31 December 20X7 showed revenue of $280,000 and $190,000 respectively. In the post-acquisition period Tadpole Co sold goods priced at $40,000 to Frog. 50% of these goods were still held in inventory by Frog Co at the end of the year.

What was group revenue in the consolidated statement of profit or loss for the year ended 31 December 20X7?

A $392,500
B $402,500
C $450,000
D $382,500

(2 marks)

---

11 Python Co obtained 30% of the equity shares of Cobra Co on 1 June 20X8 for $700,000. It is able to exercise significant influence over Cobra Co. During the year to 31 May 20X9 Cobra Co made sales of $200,000 to Python Co, priced at cost plus 25% mark-up. Python Co still had 50% of these goods in inventory at the year end. Cobra Co's statement of profit or loss for the year ended 31 May 20X9 shows profit for the year of $650,000.

What amount should be shown as 'investment in associate' in the consolidated statement of financial position of Python Co as at 31 May 20X9?

A $895,000
B $875,000
C $835,000
D $870,000

(2 marks)

---

12 Which of the following will be treated as part of the cost of inventories?

(i)   Import duties on raw materials
(ii)   Labour involved in production
(iii)   Distribution costs
(iv)   Fixed production overheads
(v)   Storage costs of finished goods
(vi)   Cost of wasted materials

A   (i), (ii), (vi)
B   (ii), (iv), (v)
C   (iii), (iv), (vi)
D   (i), (ii), (iv)

(2 marks)

---

13 A contract where performance obligations are satisfied over time was commenced on 1 April 20X7 for a price of $2.5m. At 31 December 20X7 the contract was judged to be 40% complete, costs incurred to date amounted to $1.4m and further costs to complete were expected to be $1.3m.

Invoices amounting to $300,000 have been issued but no payment has yet been received.

What amount should be shown in the statement of financial position as at 31 December 20X7 in respect of 'contract asset/liability'?

A $900,000 contract liability
B $900,000 contract asset
C $1,020,000 contract liability
D $1,020,000 contract asset

(2 marks)

14 Cracker Co set up a gas exploration site on 1 January 20X1 which will operate for five years. At the end of five years the site will need to be dismantled and the landscape restored. The amount required for dismantling and restoration, discounted at the company's cost of capital of 8%, is $1.2m and a provision is set up for this amount.

What is the total amount charged to profit or loss for the year ended 31 December 20X2 in respect of these dismantling and restoration costs?

A $343,680
B $336,000
C $103,680
D $96,000

(2 marks)

15 How are financial assets **initially** measured under IFRS 9 (excluding assets held for trading or subject to a specific designation)?

A   Fair value
B   Fair value plus transaction costs
C   Fair value minus transaction costs
D   Amortised cost

(2 marks)

16 Twinkle Co sells an asset and has an obligation to repurchase it within a specified period of time at a price which is above the original sale price.

How should it account for the original sale?

A   As a consignment arrangement
B   As an outright sale
C   As a financing arrangement
D   As a lease agreement

(2 marks)

17 On 1 April 20X7 Lastgo Co rents a warehouse under a ten-month lease for $24,000 per month. As an incentive to sign the contract it is given the first month rent-free.

What amount in respect of lease rental should be charged to profit or loss for the quarter ended 30 June 20X7?

A $64,800
B $48,000
C $72,000
D $43,200

(2 marks)

18 Tangier Co had 200,000 shares in issue at 1 January 20X4. On 1 April 20X4 it made a 1 for 4 rights issue at a price of $1.20. The market value immediately prior to the issue was $1.80. Profit for the year ended 31 December 20X4 was $560,000.

What is EPS for the year?

A $2.32
B $2.24
C $2.61
D $2.80

(2 marks)

19   Which one of the following is **not** an advantage of cash flow accounting?

    A   It directs attention towards an entity's ability to generate cash, which is needed for survival

    B   It provides valuable information for creditors and lenders

    C   It matches related items in accordance with the accruals concept

    D   It provides a better means of comparing the results of different entities than the other financial statements

(2 marks)

---

20   On 1 April 20X5 Thames Co acquired 80% of Avon Co's 100,000 $1 ordinary shares. Goodwill acquired in the business combination was $50,000, of which 40% had been written off by 31 March 20X7. NCI was measured at full fair value. At the disposal date, NCI was measured at $58,000.

On 1 April 20X7 Thames Co sold all of its shares in Avon Co for $200,000, when Avon Co's retained earnings amounted to $140,000.

What is the loss on disposal that should be recognised in the consolidated statement of profit or loss of Thames Co for the year ended 31 March 20X7?

    A $16,000
    B $12,000
    C $22,000
    D $70,000

(2 marks)

(Total = 40 marks)

Section B questions

The following scenario relates to questions 21–25.

Figaro Co is preparing its financial statements for the year ended 31 December 20X6. A number of issues must be accounted for before they can be finalised.

The following circumstances have arisen during the year

(i)   Figaro Co has entered into a contract to supply a company in China with specialised vehicle components. Unfortunately the raw material that it needs to manufacture these components has risen substantially in price and Figaro Co now expects to produce and sell the components at a loss.

(ii)   Figaro Co has a machine that needs regular overhauls every year in order to be allowed to operate. Each overhaul costs $5,000.

(iii)   Figaro Co has set up a new division to produce a product for which the market is still small. It expects this division to run at a loss for two years.

(iv)   Figaro Co sells goods with a one-year warranty. Goods may require minor or major repairs during the warranty period. If all of the goods sold during the year to 30 December 20X6 were to require minor repairs, the total cost would be $50,000. If all of the goods sold required major repairs the cost would be $120,000. In any year Figaro Co expects 5% of goods sold to be returned for major repairs and 16% to be returned for minor repairs.

(v)   Figaro Co has acquired 100% of a new subsidiary. At the date of acquisition the acquiree had a contingent liability which was reliably valued at $150,000.

21   Which of circumstances (i) to (iii) above will give rise to a provision?

    A   (i) only
    B   (ii) only
    C   (i) and (ii)
    D   (ii) and (iii)

22   How do provisions differ from other liabilities?

    A   They do not arise as a result of past events.
    B   They involve uncertain timing or amount.
    C   An outflow of resources is not probable.
    D   They are not charged to profit for the year.

23   What amount should be shown as a warranty provision in the statement of financial position of Figaro Co at 31 December 20X6?

    A $2,500
    B $8,000
    C $14,000
    D $19,200

24   A provision arises from a legal or constructive obligation. In the case of Figaro Co which of the following would be an obligation giving rise to a provision?

    A   A new law will be enacted on 1 August 20X6 to combat air pollution. Figaro Co must fit new air filters to be in compliance with this law.

    B   The Board of Figaro Co in a meeting on 27 June 20X6 decided to restructure and close one of its divisions on 1 September 20X6. This will involve redundancies, but the decision has not yet been communicated outside the Board.

    C   Figaro Co carries out certain work that entails environmental damage. It is not a legal requirement to clean up this damage but most firms in the industry do so. Figaro Co does not.

    D   Figaro Co is being sued by an ex-employee on health and safety grounds. Lawyers have advised that the employee has a 55% chance of success.

25   How should the contingent liability in (v) above be accounted for by Figaro Co?

    A   It should be disclosed, but not recognised

    B   It should be recognised

    C   It should be recognised if an outflow of resources is probable, otherwise just disclosed

    D   It should not be recognised or disclosed

The following scenario relates to questions 26–30.

Fenice Co is preparing its financial statements for the year ended 30 June 20X6. It leases the following non-current assets:

- A company car held under an agreement that was taken out on 1 July 20X5. The interest rate implicit in the lease is 6%. The initial measurement of the liability is $25,000. It has a five-year useful life. Fenice Co will repay $6,000 pa in arrears for five years. The first payment was made on 30 June 20X6.

- A warehouse which has a remaining useful life of ten years. Fenice Co took out a three-year lease on 1 January 20X6. Under the lease agreement it pays $20,000 per annum in advance. The first instalment was paid on 1 January 20X6 and Fenice received an incentive of $5,000. The interest rate implicit in the lease is 8%.

- A machine which Fenice Co sold to a finance house on 1 July 20X5 and then leased back.

    –   The carrying amount of the machine at the date of sale was $140,000.

    –   The sale proceeds were $200,000, the estimated fair value.

    –   The remaining useful life of the machine was five years.

    –   The lease liability at commencement was $175,234.

26   Which one of the following circumstances would indicate that an agreement should not be classified as a lease?

    A   It is unlikely that the lessee will exercise any option to purchase the asset.

    B   The lessor can direct how the asset is used during the lease term.

    C   The asset is not so specialised in nature that it can only be used by the lessee.

    D   The lease term is for less than 50% of the useful life of the asset.

27   What amount should be shown under non-current liabilities at 30 June 20X6 in respect of the company car?

    A $25,000

    B $20,500

    C $21,730

    D $15,730

28   What amount would be shown under non-current liabilities at 30 June 20X6 in respect of the company car if payments were being made in advance, commencing on 1 July 20X5?

    A $14,140

    B $20,140

    C $19,000

    D $14,988

29   What is the initial measurement of the right-of-use asset in respect of the warehouse?

    A $46,543

    B $55,666

    C $50,666

    D $51,543

30   What is the gain that will be recognised in profit or loss on sale of the machine?

      A $60,000
      B $52,570
      C $42,000
      D $7,430

The following scenario relates to questions 31–35.

The accountant of Orfeo Co is preparing financial statements for the year ended 31 December 20X7. Before these can be completed a number of issues need to be resolved.

(i)   Orfeo Co's head office building was revalued on 1 July 20X7, giving rise to a surplus of $100,000. The building had an original cost of $1m on 1 January 20X0 and a 50-year life at that date. The useful life of the building remains unchanged.

(ii)   During the year one of Orfeo Co's machines broke down and could not be fixed. The carrying amount of the machine at that date was $30,000. The accountant must now consider the issue of impairment.

(iii) On 10 November 20X7 Orfeo Co bought a consignment of goods from an Italian company, priced at €150,000. Payment was due in two equal instalments – on 10 December 20X7 and 10 January 20X8. The first instalment was paid on time.

       Euro to dollar rates for the last two months of 20X7 were;

       10.11.20X7   €1.13 : $
       10.12.20X7   €1.18 : $
       31.12.20X7   €1.12 : $

31   What amount should be charged as depreciation on the building in (i) for the year ended 31 December 20X7?

      A $22,300
      B $22,128
      C $22,000
      D $21,176

32   What are the deferred tax implications of this revaluation?

      A   Deferred tax on the surplus of $100,000 should be charged to profit or loss for the year.
      B   Deferred tax on the surplus of $100,000 should be charged to the revaluation surplus.
      C   Deferred tax on the surplus will not arise until the building is sold.
      D   There are no deferred tax implications.

33   When carrying out an impairment review, assets are measured at their **recoverable amount**. Which of these options describes recoverable amount?

      A   Higher of fair value less costs of disposal and value in use
      B   Higher of carrying amount and fair value less costs of disposal
      C   Lower of fair value less costs of disposal and value in use
      D   Lower of carrying amount and fair value less costs of disposal

34   Because of the loss of production caused by the damaged machine, Orfeo Co lost customers and it was decided that the whole factory unit was impaired by $120,000. Orfeo Co's accountant has to decide how to allocate this impairment loss.

      The carrying amounts of the assets of the factory unit at the date of the impairment review, including the damaged machine, were:

	$
Goodwill	20,000
Factory building	440,000
Plant and machinery	160,000
Net current assets	100,000
	720,000

What will be the carrying amount of plant and machinery when the impairment loss has been allocated?

A $129,000
B $130,000
C $144,000
D $114,000

35   What should be the total amount of exchange gain or loss recognised during the year to 31 December 20X7 in respect of the transaction in (iii) above?

A $592 loss
B $2,813 gain
C $2,221 gain
D $1,186 gain

(Total = 30 marks)

Practice questions

(It should be noted that some of these questions are not in the current exam format (20 marks for Section C) but are intended as useful practice for the material in the chapters. The Practice & Revision Kit has a large number of exam format questions.)

1 Conceptual framework
20 mins

(a) Explain and give an example of the effect on a set of published financial statements if the going concern convention is held not to apply.

(b) Explain in general terms what the IASB *Conceptual Framework* is trying to achieve. **(10 marks)**

2 Regulators
20 mins

State three different regulatory influences on the preparation of the published accounts of quoted companies and briefly explain the role of each one. Comment briefly on the effectiveness of this regulatory system.
(10 marks)

3 Standard setters
20 mins

There are those who suggest that any standard setting body is redundant because accounting standards are unnecessary. Other people feel that such standards should be produced, but by the government, so that they are a legal requirement.

Required

(a) Discuss the statement that accounting standards are unnecessary for the purpose of regulating financial statements.

(b) Discuss whether or not the financial statements of not-for-profit entities should be subject to regulation.
(10 marks)

4 Polymer Co

49 mins

The following list of account balances has been prepared by Polymer, plastics manufacturers, on 31 May 20X8, which is the end of the company's accounting period.

	$	$
Authorised and issued 300,000 ordinary shares of $1 each, fully paid		300,000
100,000 8.4% cumulative redeemable preference shares of $1 each, fully paid		100,000
Revaluation surplus		50,000
Share premium reserve		100,000
General reserve		50,000
Retained earnings – 31 May 20X7		283,500
Patents and trademarks	215,500	
Freehold land at cost	250,000	
Leasehold property at cost	75,000	
Amortisation of leasehold property – 31 May 20X7		15,000
Factory plant and equipment at cost	150,000	
Accumulated depreciation – plant and equipment – 31 May 20X7		68,500
Furniture and fixtures at cost	50,000	
Accumulated depreciation – furniture and fixtures – 31 May 20X7		15,750
Motor vehicles at cost	75,000	
Accumulated depreciation – motor vehicles – 31 May 20X7		25,000
10% loan notes (20Y0 – 20Y5)		100,000
Trade receivables/ trade payables	177,630	97,500
Bank overdraft		51,250
Inventories – raw materials at cost – 31 May 20X7	108,400	
Purchases – raw materials	750,600	
Carriage inwards – raw materials	10,500	
Manufacturing wages	250,000	
Manufacturing overheads	125,000	
Cash	5,120	
Work in progress – 31 May 20X7	32,750	
Sales		1,526,750
Administrative expenses	158,100	
Selling and distribution expenses	116,800	
Legal and professional expenses	54,100	
Allowance for receivables – 31 May 20X8		5,750
Inventories – finished goods – 31 May 20X7	184,500	
	2,789,000	2,789,000

Additional information:

(i) Inventories at 31 May 20X8 were:

	$
Raw materials	112,600
Finished goods	275,350
Work in progress	37,800

(ii) Depreciation for the year is to be charged as follows:

Plant and equipment	8% on cost – charged to production
Furniture and fixtures	10% on cost – charged to admin
Motor vehicles	20% on reducing value – 25% admin
	– 75% selling and distribution

(iii) Financial, legal and professional expenses include:

	$
Solicitors' fees for purchase of freehold land during year	5,000

(iv) Provision is to be made for a full year's interest on the loan notes.

(v) Income tax on the profits for the year is estimated at $40,000 and is due for payment on 28 February 20X9.

(vi) The directors recommended on 30 June that a dividend of 3.5c per share be paid on the ordinary share capital. No ordinary dividend was paid during the year ended 31 May 20X7.

(vii) The leasehold land and buildings are held on a 50 year lease, acquired 10 years ago.

Required

From the information given above, prepare the statement of profit or loss and other comprehensive income of Polymer for the year to 31 May 20X8 and a statement of financial position at that date for publication in accordance with International Financial Reporting Standards.

Notes to the financial statements are not required. **(25 marks)**

5 Gains Co

20 mins

Required

Using the information below prepare the Statement of changes in equity for Gains Co for the year ended 31 December 20X9. **(10 marks)**

(a) *Gains Co*

STATEMENT OF PROFIT OR LOSS AND OTHER COMPREHENSIVE INCOME (EXTRACT)

	$'000
Profit before interest and tax	792
Finance income	24
Finance cost	(10)
Profit before tax	806
Income tax expense	(240)
PROFIT FOR THE YEAR	566
Other comprehensive income:	
Gain on property revaluation	120
TOTAL COMPREHENSIVE INCOME FOR THE YEAR	686

(b) *Non-current assets*

(i) Assets held at cost were impaired by $25,000.
(ii) Freehold land and buildings were revalued to $500,000 (carrying amount $380,000).
(iii) A previously revalued asset was sold for $60,000.

Details of the revaluation are:

	$
Carrying amount at revaluation	30,000
Revaluation	50,000
	80,000
Depreciation (80,000 / 10) × 3	24,000
	56,000

Gains Co has been following paragraph 41 of IAS 16 which allows a reserve transfer of the realised revaluation surplus (the difference between depreciation based on revalued amount and depreciation based on cost) as the asset is used to retained earnings.

Revaluations during the year related to land.

(iv)   Details of investment properties are as follows:

	$
Original cost	120,000
Revaluation surplus	40,000
Value at 1.1.20X9	160,000

The properties had a valuation on 31 December 20X9 of $110,000. Gains Co previously accounted for its investment properties by crediting gains to a revaluation surplus as allowed by local GAAP. Gains Co now wishes to apply the fair value model of IAS 40 which states that gains and losses should be accounted for in profit or loss. The elimination of the previous revaluation surplus is to be treated as a change in accounting policy in accordance with IAS 8. No adjustment has yet been made for the change in accounting policy or subsequent fall in value.

(c)   *Share capital*

During the year the company had the following changes to its capital structure:

(i)   An issue of 200,000 $1 ordinary bonus shares capitalising its share premium reserve
(ii)   An issue of 400,000 $1 ordinary shares (issue price $1.40 per share).

(d)   *Equity*

The carrying amount of equity at the start of the year was as follows:

	$
Share capital	2,800,000
Share premium	1,150,000
Retained earnings	2,120,000
Revaluation surplus	750,000
	6,820,000

(e)   *Dividends*

Dividends paid during the year amounted to $200,000.

6 Biogenics Co   20 mins

(a)   Over the last 20 years many companies have spent a great deal of money internally developing new intangible assets such as software. The treatment for these assets is prescribed by IAS 38 *Intangible assets*.

Required

In accordance with IAS 38, discuss whether internally-developed intangible assets should be recognised, and if so how they should be initially recorded and subsequently accounted for.

(3 marks)

(b)   Biogenics Co is a publicly listed pharmaceutical company. During the year to 31 December 20X9 the following transactions took place:

(i) $6m was spent on developing a new obesity drug which received clinical approval on 1 July 20X9 and is proving commercially successful. The directors expect the project to be in profit within 12 months of the approval date. The patent was registered on 1 July 20X9. It cost $1.5m and remains in force for three years.

(ii)   A research project was set up on 1 October 20X9 which is expected to result in a new cancer drug. $200,000 was spent on computer equipment and $400,000 on staff salaries. The equipment has an expected life of four years.

(iii)   On 1 September 20X9 Biogenics Co acquired an up-to-date list of GPs at a cost of $500,000 and has been visiting them to explain the new obesity drug. The list is expected to generate sales throughout the life-cycle of the drug.

Required

Prepare extracts from the statement of financial position of Biogenics Co at 31 December 20X9 relating to the above items and summarise the costs to be included in the statement of profit or loss for that year.

(7 marks)

(Total = 10 marks)

7 Multiplex Co   *Impairment*

29 mins

NB

On 1 January 20X0 Multiplex Co acquired Steamdays Co, a company that operates a scenic railway along the coast of a popular tourist area. The summarised statement of financial position at fair values of Steamdays Co on 1 January 20X0, reflecting the terms of the acquisition was:

	$'000
Goodwill	200
Operating licence	1,200
Property – train stations and land	300
Rail track and coaches	300
Two steam engines	1,000
Purchase consideration	3,000

The operating licence is for ten years. It was renewed on 1 January 20X0 by the transport authority and is stated at the cost of its renewal. The carrying values of the property and rail track and coaches are based on their value in use. The engines are valued at their net selling prices.

On 1 February 20X0 the boiler of one of the steam engines exploded, completely destroying the whole engine. Fortunately no one was injured, but the engine was beyond repair. Due to its age a replacement could not be obtained. Because of the reduced passenger capacity the estimated value in use of the whole of the business after the accident was assessed at $2m. *1M impairment*

Passenger numbers after the accident were below expectations even allowing for the reduced capacity. A market research report concluded that tourists were not using the railway because of their fear of a similar accident occurring to the remaining engine. In the light of this the value in use of the business was re-assessed on 31 March 20X0 at $1.8m. On this date Multiplex Co received an offer of $900,000 in respect of the operating licence (it is transferable). The realisable value of the other net assets has not changed significantly.

Required

Calculate the carrying value of the assets of Steamdays Co (in Multiplex Co's consolidated statement of financial position) at 1 February 20X0 and 31 March 20X0 after recognising the impairment losses.

(15 marks)

8 Hewlett Co

49 mins

Hewlett Co is a quoted company reporting under IFRSs. During the year end 31 December 20X2, the company changed its accounting policy with respect to property valuation. There are also a number of other issues that need to be finalised before the financial statements can be published.

Hewlett Co's trial balance from the general ledger at 31 December 20X2 showed the following balances:

	$m	$m
Revenue		2,648
Purchases	1,669	
Inventories at 1 January 20X2	444	
Distribution costs	514	
Administrative expenses	345	
Loan note interest paid	3	
Rental income		48
Land and buildings: cost (including $90m land)	840	
accumulated depreciation at 1 January 20X2		120
Plant and equipment: cost	258	
accumulated depreciation at 1 January 20X2		126
Investment property at 1 January 20X2	548	
Trade receivables	541	
Cash and cash equivalents	32	
50c ordinary shares		100
Share premium		244
Retained earnings at 1 January 20X2		753
Interim dividend paid	6	
General reserve		570
4% loan note repayable 20X8 (issued 20X0)		150
Trade and other payables		434
Proceeds from sale of equipment		7
	5,200	5,200

Further information to be taken into account:

(i) Closing inventories were counted and amounted to $388m at cost. However, shortly after the year end out-of-date inventories with a cost of $21m were sold for $14m.

(ii) At the beginning of the year, Hewlett Co disposed of some malfunctioning equipment for $7m. The equipment had cost $15m and had accumulated depreciation brought forward at 1 January 20X2 of $3m.

There were no other additions or disposal to property, plant and equipment in the year.

(iii) The company treats depreciation on plant and equipment as a cost of sale and on land and buildings as an administrative cost. Depreciation rates as per the company's accounting policy note are as follows:

Buildings   Straight line over 50 years
Plant and equipment   20% reducing balance

Hewlett Co's accounting policy is to charge a full year's depreciation in the year of an asset's purchase and none in the year of disposal. Hewlett Co's buildings were eight years old on 1 January 20X2.

(iv) On 31 December 20X2 the company revalued its land and buildings to $760m (including $100m for the land). The company follows the revaluation model of IAS 16 for its land and buildings, but no revaluations had previously been necessary. The company wishes to treat the revaluation surplus as being realised on disposal of the assets.

BPP
LEARNING MEDIA

Practice question bank   435

(v)   Due to a change in Hewlett Co's product portfolio plans, an item of plant with a carrying amount $22m at 31 December 20X2 (after adjusting for depreciation for the year) may be impaired due to a change in use. An impairment test conducted at 31 December, revealed its fair value less costs of disposal to be $16m. The asset is now expected to generate an annual net income stream of $3.8m for the next five years at which point the asset would be disposed of for $4.2m. An appropriate discount rate is 8%. Five-year discount factors at 8% are:

Simple	Cumulative
0.677	3.993

(vi)   The income tax charge (current and deferred tax) for the year is estimated at $45m (of which $17m relates to future payable tax on the revaluation, to be charged to other comprehensive income (and the revaluation surplus)).

(vii)   An interim dividend of 3c per share was paid on 30 June 20X2. A final dividend of 1.5c per share was declared by the directors on 28 January 20X3. No dividends were paid or declared in 20X1.

(viii) During the year on 1 July 20X2, Hewlett Co made a 1 for 4 bonus issue, capitalising its general reserve. This transaction had not yet been accounted for. The fair value of the company's shares on the date of the bonus issue was $7.50 each.

(ix)   Hewlett uses the fair value model of IAS 40. The fair value of the investment property at 31 December 20X2 was $588m.

Required

Prepare the statement of profit or loss and other comprehensive income and statement of changes in equity for Hewlett Co for the year to 31 December 20X2 and a statement of financial position at that date in accordance with IFRSs insofar as the information permits.

Notes to the financial statements are not required, but all workings should be clearly shown.

Work to the nearest $1m. Comparative information is not required.   **(25 marks)**

9 Barcelona Co and Madrid Co   23 mins

Barcelona Co acquired 60% of Madrid Co's ordinary share capital on 1 October 20X2 at a price of $1.06 per share. The balance on Madrid Co's retained earnings at that date was $104m and the general reserve stood at $11m.

Their respective statements of financial position as at 30 September 20X6 are:

	Barcelona Co $m	Madrid Co $m
Non-current assets		
Property, plant & equipment	2,848	354
Patents	45	–
Investment in Madrid	159	–
	3,052	354
Current assets		
Inventories	895	225
Trade and other receivables	1,348	251
Cash and cash equivalents	212	34
	2,455	510
	5,507	864

	Barcelona Co $m	Madrid Co $m
Equity		
Share capital (20c ordinary shares)	920	50
Retained earnings	2,086	394
General reserve	775	46
	3,781	490
Non-current liabilities		
Long-term borrowings	558	168
Current liabilities		
Trade and other payables	1,168	183
Current portion of long-term borrowings	–	23
	1,168	206
	5,507	864

At the date of acquisition the fair values of some of Madrid Co's assets were greater than their carrying amounts. One line of Madrid Co's inventory had a fair value of $8m above its carrying amount. This inventory had all been sold by 30 September 20X6. Madrid Co's land and buildings had a fair value $26m above their carrying amount. $20 of this is attributable to the buildings, which had a remaining useful life of ten years at the date of acquisition.

It is group policy to value non-controlling interests at full (or fair) value. The fair value of the non-controlling interests at acquisition was $86m.

Annual impairment tests have revealed cumulative impairment losses relating to recognised goodwill of $20m to date.

Required

Produce the consolidated statement of financial position for the Barcelona Group as at 30 September 20X6.

(12 marks)

10 Reprise Group   27 mins

Reprise Co purchased 75% of Encore Co for $2,000,000 ten years ago when the balance on its retained earnings was $1,044,000. The statements of financial position of the two companies as at 31 March 20X4 are:

	Reprise Co $'000	Encore Co $'000
Non-current assets		
Investment in Encore	2,000	–
Land and buildings	3,350	–
Plant and equipment	1,010	2,210
Motor vehicles	510	345
	6,870	2,555
Current assets		
Inventories	890	352
Trade receivables	1,372	514
Cash and cash equivalents	89	51
	2,351	917
	9,221	3,472

	Reprise Co $'000	Encore Co $'000
Equity		
Share capital – $1 ordinary shares	1,000	500
Retained earnings	4,225	2,610
Revaluation surplus	2,500	–
	7,725	3,110
Non-current liabilities		
10% debentures	500	–
Current liabilities		
Trade and other payables	996	362
	9,221	3,472

The following additional information is available:

(i) Included in trade receivables of Reprise Co are amounts owed by Encore Co of $75,000. The current accounts do not at present balance due to a payment for $39,000 being in transit at the year end from Encore Co.

(ii) Included in the inventories of Encore Co are items purchased from Reprise Co during the year for $31,200. Reprise Co marks up its goods by 30% to achieve its selling price.

(iii) $180,000 of the recognised goodwill arising is to be written off due to impairment losses.

(iv) Encore Co shares were trading at $4.40 just prior to acquisition by Reprise Co and this price is used to value non-controlling interests.

Required

Prepare the consolidated statement of financial position for the Reprise group of companies as at 31 March 20X4. It is the group policy to value the non-controlling interests at full (or fair) value.

(14 marks)

11 Fallowfield Co and Rusholme Co   29 mins

Fallowfield Co acquired a 60% holding in Rusholme Co three years ago when Rusholme Co's retained earnings balance stood at $16,000. Both businesses have been very successful since the acquisition and their respective statements of profit or loss for the year ended 30 June 20X8 are:

	Fallowfield Co $	Rusholme Co $
Revenue	403,400	193,000
Cost of sales	(201,400)	(92,600)
Gross profit	202,000	100,400
Distribution costs	(16,000)	(14,600)
Administrative expenses	(24,250)	(17,800)
Dividends from Rusholme	15,000	
Profit before tax	176,750	68,000
Income tax expense	(61,750)	(22,000)
PROFIT FOR THE YEAR	115,000	46,000

STATEMENT OF CHANGES IN EQUITY (EXTRACT)

	Fallowfield Co Retained earnings $	Rusholme Co Retained earnings $
Balance at 1 July 20X7	163,000	61,000
Dividends	(40,000)	(25,000)
Profit for the year	115,000	46,000
Balance at 30 June 20X8	238,000	82,000

Additional information:

During the year Rusholme Co sold some goods to Fallowfield Co for $40,000, including 25% mark-up. Half of these items were still in inventories at the year end.

Required

Produce the consolidated statement of profit or loss of Fallowfield Co and its subsidiary for the year ended 30 June 20X8, and an extract from the statement of changes in equity, showing retained earnings. Goodwill is to be ignored. **(15 marks)**

12 Panther Group   29 mins

Panther Co operated as a single company, but in 20X4 decided to expand its operations. Panther Co acquired a 60% interest in Sabre Co on 1 July 20X4 for $2,000,000.

The statements of profit or loss and other comprehensive income of Panther Co and Sabre Co for the year ended 31 December 20X4 are:

	Panther Co $'000	Sabre Co $'000
Revenue	22,800	4,300
Cost of sales	(13,600)	(2,600)
Gross profit	9,200	1,700
Distribution costs	(2,900)	(500)
Administrative expenses	(1,800)	(300)
Finance costs	(200)	(70)
Finance income	50	–
Profit before tax	4,350	830
Income tax expense	(1,300)	(220)
PROFIT FOR THE YEAR	3,050	610
Other comprehensive income for the year, net of tax	1,600	180
TOTAL COMPREHENSIVE INCOME FOR THE YEAR	4,650	790

Historically, Sabre Co had been a significant trading partner of Panther Co. During 20X4, Panther Co purchased $640,000 of goods from Sabre Co. Of these, $60,000 remained in inventories at the year end. Sabre Co makes a mark-up on cost of 20% under the transfer pricing agreement between the two companies. The fair value of the identifiable net assets of Sabre Co on purchase were $200,000 greater than their book value. The difference relates to properties with a remaining useful life of 20 years.

On 1 January 20X4 (to protect its supply lines), Panther Co had advanced a loan to Sabre Co amounting to $800,000 at a market interest rate of 5%. The loan is due for repayment in 20X9.

Statement of changes in equity (extracts) for the two companies:

	Panther Co Reserves $'000	Sabre Co Reserves $'000
Balance at 1 January 20X4	12,750	2,480
Dividend paid	(900)	–
Total comprehensive income for the year	4,650	790
Balance at 31 December 20X4	16,500	3,270

Panther Co and Sabre Cohad $400,000 and $150,000 of share capital in issue throughout the period respectively.

Required

Prepare the consolidated statement of profit or loss and other comprehensive income and statement of changes in equity (extract for reserves) for the Panther Group for the year ended 31 December 20X4.

No adjustments for impairment losses were necessary in the group financial statements.

Assume income and expenses (other than intragroup items) accrue evenly. **(15 marks)**

13 Hever Co

39 mins

Hever Co has held shares in two companies, Spiro Co and Aldridge Co, for a number of years. As at 31 December 20X4 they have the following statements of financial position:

	Hever Co $'000	Spiro Co $'000	Aldridge Co $'000
Non-current assets			
Property, plant & equipment	370	190	260
Investments	218	–	–
	588	190	260
Current assets			
Inventories	160	100	180
Trade receivables	170	90	100
Cash and cash equivalents	50	40	10
	380	230	290
	968	420	550
Equity			
Share capital ($1 ords)	200	80	50
Share premium	100	80	30
Retained earnings	568	200	400
	868	360	480
Current liabilities			
Trade and other payables	100	60	70
	968	420	550

You ascertain the following additional information:

(i)   The 'investments' in the statement of financial position comprise solely Hever's investment in Spiro Co($128,000) and in Aldridge Co($90,000).

(ii)   The 48,000 shares in SpiroCo were acquired when Spiro Co's retained earnings stood at $20,000.

The 15,000 shares in Aldridge Co were acquired when that company had a retained earnings balance of $150,000.

(iii)   When Hever Co acquired its shares in Spiro Co the fair value of Spiro Co's net assets equalled their book values with the following exceptions:

	$'000
Property, plant and equipment	50 higher
Inventories	20 lower (sold during 20X4)

Depreciation arising on the fair value adjustment to non-current assets since this date is $5,000.

(iv)   During the year, Hever Co sold inventories to Spiro Co for $16,000, which originally cost Hever Co $10,000. Three-quarters of these inventories have subsequently been sold by Spiro Co.

(v)   No impairment losses on goodwill had been necessary by 31 December 20X4.

(vi)   It is group policy to value non-controlling interests at full (or fair) value. The fair value of the non-controlling interests at acquisition was $90,000.

Required

Produce the consolidated statement of financial position for the Hever group (incorporating the associate).

(20 marks)

14 Highveldt Co

49 mins

Highveldt Co, a public listed company, acquired 75% of Samson Co's ordinary shares on 1 April 20X4. Highveldt Co paid an immediate $3.50 per share in cash and agreed to pay a further amount on 1 April 20X5 contingent upon the post-acquisition performance of Samson Co. At the date of acquisition the fair value of this contingent consideration was assessed at $108m, but by 31 March 20X5 it had become clear that the amount due would be $116m (ignore discounting). Highveldt Co has recorded the cash consideration of $3.50 per share and provided for the initial estimate of contingent consideration of $108m.

The summarised statements of financial position of the two companies at 31 March 20X5 are shown below:

	Highveldt Co		Samson Co	
	$m	$m	$m	$m
Tangible non-current assets (note(i))		420		320
Development costs (note (iv))		nil		40
Investments (note (ii))		300		20
		720		380
Current assets		133		91
Total assets		853		471
Equity and liabilities				
Ordinary shares of $1 each		270		80
Reserves:				
Share premium		80		40
Revaluation surplus		45		nil
Retained earnings – 1 April 20X4	160		134	
– year to 31 March 20X5	190		76	
		350		210
		745		330
Non-current liabilities				
10% intercompany loan (note (ii))		nil		60
Current liabilities		108		81
Total equity and liabilities		853		471

The following information is relevant:

(i)   Highveldt Co has a policy of revaluing land and buildings to fair value. At the date of acquisition Samson Co's land and buildings had a fair value $20m higher than their carrying amount and at 31 March 20X5 this had increased by a further $4m (ignore any additional depreciation).

(ii)   Included in Highveldt Co's investments is a loan of $60m made to Samson Co at the date of acquisition. Interest is payable annually in arrears. Samson Co paid the interest due for the year on 31 March 20X5, but Highveldt Co did not receive this until after the year end. Highveldt Co has not accounted for the accrued interest from Samson Co.

(iii)   Samson Co had established a line of products under the brand name of Titanware. Acting on behalf of Highveldt Co, a firm of specialists, had valued the brand name at a value of $40m with an estimated life of ten years as at 1 April 20X4. The brand is not included in Samson Co's statement of financial position.

(iv)   Samson Co's development project was completed on 30 September 20X4 at a cost of $50m. $10m of this had been amortised by 31 March 20X5. Development costs capitalised by Samson Co at the date of acquisition were $18m. Highveldt Co's directors are of the opinion that Samson Co's development costs do not meet the criteria in IAS 38 *Intangible Assets* for recognition as an asset.

(v)   Samson Co sold goods to Highveldt Co during the year at a profit of $6m. One-third of these goods were still in the inventory of Highveldt Co at 31 March 20X5.

(vi)   An impairment test at 31 March 20X5 on the consolidated goodwill concluded that it should be written down by $22m. No other assets were impaired.

(vii)   It is the group policy to value the non-controlling interest at full fair value. At the date of acquisition the directors estimated the fair value of the non-controlling interest to be $74m.

Required

(a)   Calculate the following figures as they would appear in the consolidated statement of financial position of Highveldt Co at 31 March 20X5:

  (i)   Goodwill   **(8 marks)**

  (ii)   Non-controlling interest   **(4 marks)**

  (iii)   The following consolidated reserves: **(8 marks)**

  • Share premium
  • Revaluation surplus
  • Retained earnings

  Note. Show your workings.

(b)   Explain why consolidated financial statements are useful to the users of financial statements (as opposed to just the parent company's separate (entity) financial statements).   **(5 marks)**

(Total = 25 marks)

15 Villandry Co   20 mins

(a)   Villandry Co's inventory includes three items for which the following details are available.

	Supplier's list price	Net realisable value
	$	$
Product Arctic	3,600	5,100
Product Brassy	2,900	2,800
Product Chilly	4,200	4,100

The company receives a 2.5% trade discount from its suppliers and it also takes advantage of a 2% discount for prompt payment.

Required

Calculate the total value of products Arctic, Brassy and Chilly which should be shown in inventory in the statement of financial position.

(b)   Explain the difference that changing from a weighted average to FIFO method of inventory valuation is likely to have on an entity's profit or loss.

(10 marks)

16 Biological assets   20 mins

IAS 41 *Agriculture* prescribes the accounting treatment and disclosures related to agricultural activities. An entity is encouraged, but not required, to provide a quantified description of each group of biological assets, distinguishing between consumables and bearer biological assets, or between mature and immature biological assets, as appropriate.

Required

(a)   Distinguish between a biological asset and an item of agricultural produce.
(b)   Explain how agricultural produce is measured in the financial statements of an entity.
(c)   Give five examples of biological assets and their relative agricultural produce.
(d)   Explain what is meant by consumable and bearer biological assets, giving one example for each.

(10 marks)

 **Provisions** 49 mins

IAS 37 *Provisions, contingent liabilities and contingent assets* was issued in 1998. Prior to its publication, there was no International Accounting Standard that dealt with the general subject of accounting for provisions.

Extraction Co prepares its financial statements to 31 December each year. During the years ended 31 December 20X0 and 31 December 20X1, the following event occurred.

Extraction Co is involved in extracting minerals in a number of different countries. The process typically involves some contamination of the site from which the minerals are extracted. Extraction Co makes good this contamination only where legally required to do so by legislation passed in the relevant country.

The company has been extracting minerals in Copperland since January 20W8 and expects its site to produce output until 31 December 20X5. On 23 December 20X0, it came to the attention of the directors of Extraction Co that the government of Copperland was virtually certain to pass legislation requiring the making good of mineral extraction sites. The legislation was duly passed on 15 March 20X1. The directors of Extraction Co estimate that the cost of making good the site in Copperland will be $2m. This estimate is of the actual cash expenditure that will be incurred on 31 December 20X5.

Required

(a) Explain why there was a need for an accounting standard dealing with provisions, and summarise the criteria that need to be satisfied before a provision is recognised.

(b) Compute the effect of the estimated cost of making good the site on the financial statements of Extraction Co for BOTH of the years ended 31 December 20X0 and 20X1. Give full explanations of the figures you compute.

The annual discount rate to be used in any relevant calculations is 10%.

The relevant discount factors at 10% are:

Year 4 at 10%   0.683
Year 5 at 10%   0.621   **(25 marks)**

18 Financial assets and liabilities   20 mins

(a) On 1 January 20X2, an entity issued a debt instrument with a coupon rate of 3.5% at a par value of $6,000,000. The directly attributable costs of issue were $120,000. The debt instrument is repayable on 31 December 20X7 at a premium of $1,100,000.

Required

What is the total amount of the finance cost associated with the debt instrument?   **(3 marks)**

(b) On 1 January 20X3 Dashing Co issued $600,000 loan notes. Issue costs were $200. The loan notes do not carry interest, but are redeemable at a premium of $152,389 on 31 December 20X4. The effective finance cost of the loan notes is 12%.

Required

What is the finance cost in respect of the loan notes for the year ended 31 December 20X4?   **(3 marks)**

(c) On 1 January 20X1, Flustered Co issued 10,000 5% convertible bonds at their par value of $50 each. The bonds will be redeemed on 1 January 20X6. Each bond is convertible to equity shares at the option of the holder at any time during the five year period. Interest on the bond will be paid annually in arrears.

The prevailing market interest rate for similar debt without conversion options at the date of issue was 6%.

The discount factor for 6% at year 5 is 0.747.
The cumulative discount factor for years 1–5 at 6% is 4.212.

Required

At what value should the equity element of the hybrid financial instrument be recognised in the financial statements in Flustered Co at the date of issue? **(4 marks)**

(Total = 10 marks)

19 Alpha

49 mins

In producing the *Conceptual Framework for Financial Reporting* and some of the current IFRSs, the IASB has had to address the potential problem that the management of some companies may choose to adopt inappropriate accounting policies. These could have the effect of portraying an entity's financial position in a favourable manner. In some countries this is referred to as 'creative accounting'

Required

(a) Describe in broad terms common ways in which management can manipulate financial statements to indulge in 'creative accounting' and why they would wish to do so. **(7 marks)**

(b) Explain with examples how IFRS seeks to limit creative accounting in each of the following areas of accounting.

    (i)   Group accounting

    (ii)   Financing non-current assets

    (iii) Measurement and disclosure of current assets **(8 marks)**

(c) Alpha Co, a public listed corporation, is considering how it should raise $10m of finance which is required for a major and vital non-current asset renewal scheme that will be undertaken during the current year to 31 December 20X6. Alpha Co is particularly concerned about how analysts are likely to react to its financial statements for the year to 31 December 20X6. Present forecasts suggest that Alpha Co's earnings per share and its financial gearing ratios may be worse than market expectations. Mr Wong, Alpha Co's Finance Director, is in favour of raising the finance by issuing a convertible loan. He has suggested that the coupon (interest) rate on the loan should be 5%; this is below the current market rate of 9% for this type of loan. In order to make the stock attractive to investors the terms of conversion into equity would be very favourable to compensate for the low interest rate.

Required

    (i)   Explain why the Finance Director believes the above scheme may favourably improve Alpha Co's earnings per share and gearing.

    (ii)   Describe how the requirements of IAS 33 *Earnings per share* and IAS 32 *Financial instruments: presentation* are intended to prevent the above effects. **(10 marks)**

(Total = 25 marks)

20 Jenson Co

35 mins

The timing of revenue (income) recognition has long been an area of debate and inconsistency in accounting. It has now become the subject of a new standard, IFRS 15 *Revenue from contracts with customers*.

The IASB in the *Conceptual Framework* has defined the 'elements' of financial statements, and it uses these to determine when a gain or loss occurs.

Required

(a) Explain what is meant by a performance obligation in relation to revenue recognition and discuss the criteria used in the *Conceptual Framework* for determining when a gain or loss arises.

(5 marks)

(b) Jenson Co has entered into the following transactions/agreements in the year to 31 March 20X5.

    (i)   Goods, which had a cost of $20,000, were sold to Lauda Co for $35,000 on 1 July 20X4. Jenson Co has an option to repurchase the goods from Lauda Co at any time within the next two years. The repurchase price will be $35,000 plus interest charged at 12% per annum

from the date of sale to the date of repurchase. It is expected that Jenson Co will repurchase the goods.

(ii) Jenson Co owns the rights to a fast food franchise. On 1 April 20X4 it sold the right to open a new outlet to Mr Verstappen. The franchise is for five years. Jenson Co received an initial fee of $50,000 for the first year and will receive $5,000 per annum thereafter. Jenson Co has continuing service obligations on its franchise for advertising and product development that amount to approximately $8,000 per annum for each franchised outlet. A reasonable profit margin on the provision of the continuing services is deemed to be 20% of revenues received.

(iii) On 1 September 20X4 Jenson Co received subscriptions in advance of $240,000. The subscriptions are for 24 monthly publications of a magazine produced by Jenson Co. At the year end Jenson Co had produced and despatched 6 of the 24 publications.

Required

Describe how Jenson Co should treat each of the above examples in its financial statements in the year to 31 March 20X5. **(13 marks)**

(Total = 18 marks)

21 Trontacc Co   20 mins

Trontacc Co is a company whose activities are in the field of major construction projects. During the year ended 30 September 20X7, it enters into three separate contracts, each with a fixed contract price of $1,000,000. These are contracts where performance obligations are satisfied over time and Trontacc Co has an enforceable right to payment for performance completed to date. The following information relates to these contracts at 30 September 20X7.

		Contract	
	Aspire	*Bigga*	*Construct*
	$'000	$'000	$'000
Amounts invoiced and paid up to 30.9.X7	540	475	400
Costs incurred to date	500	550	320
Estimate costs to complete the contract	300	550	580
Estimated percentage of obligations satisfied	60%	50%	35%

Required

(a) Show how each contract would be reflected in the statement of financial position of Trontacc Co at 30 September 20X7 under IFRS 15 *Revenue from contracts with customers*.

(b) Show how each contract would be reflected in the statement of profit or loss of Trontacc Co for the year ended 30 September 20X7 under IFRS 15. **(10 marks)**

22 Crayzee Co   20 mins

Crayzee Co is a civil engineering company. It started work on two construction projects during the year ended 31 December 20X0. The nature of both contracts is that the customer controls the asset as the project goes forward. Work is certified by a surveyor as performance obligations are completed. The following figures relate to those projects at the end of the reporting period.

	Maryhill bypass	*Rottenrow Centre*
	$'000	$'000
Contract price	9,000	8,000
Costs incurred to date	1,400	2,900
Estimated costs to completion	5,600	5,200
Value of work certified to date	2,800	3,000
Progress billings	2,600	3,400

An old mineshaft has been discovered under the site for the Rottenrow Centre and the costs of dealing with this have been taken into account in the calculation of estimated costs to completion. Crayzee Co's lawyers are reasonably confident that the customer will have to bear the additional costs which will be incurred in stabilising the land. If negotiations are successful then the contract price will increase to $10m.

Crayzee Co recognises revenues and profits on construction contracts on the basis of work certified to date.

Required

Calculate the figures which would appear in Crayzee Co's financial statements in respect of these two projects.

(10 marks)

23 Telenorth Co

49 mins

The following trial balance relates to Telenorth Co at 30 September 20X1.

	$'000	$'000
Revenue		283,460
Inventory 1 October 20X0	12,400	
Purchases	147,200	
Distribution expenses	22,300	
Administration expenses	34,440	
Loan note interest paid	300	
Interim dividends: ordinary	2,000	
preference	480	
Investment income		1,500
25 year leasehold building – cost	56,250	
Plant and equipment – cost	55,000	
Computer system – cost	35,000	
Investments at valuation	34,500	
Depreciation 1 October 20X0 (note (ii))		
Leasehold building		18,000
Plant and equipment		12,800
Computer system		9,600
Trade accounts receivable	35,700	
Bank overdraft		1,680
Trade accounts payable		17,770
Deferred tax (note (iii))		5,200
Ordinary shares of $1 each		20,000
Suspense account (note (iv))		26,000
6% loan notes (issued 1 October 20X0)		10,000
8% preference shares (redeemable)		12,000
Revaluation surplus (note (iii))		3,400
Retained earnings 1 October 20X0		14,160
	435,570	435,570

The following notes are relevant.

(i) An inventory count was not conducted by Telenorth Co until 4 October 20X1 due to operational reasons. The value of the inventory on the premises at this date was $16m at cost. Between the year end and the inventory count the following transactions have been identified.

	$
Normal sales at a mark up on cost of 40%	1,400,000
Sales on a sale or return basis at a mark up on cost of 30%	650,000
Goods received at cost	820,000

All sales and purchases had been correctly recorded in the period in which they occurred.

(ii) Telenorth Co has the following depreciation policy.

Leasehold building – straight-line

Plant and equipment – five years straight line with residual values estimated at $5,000,000

Computer system – 40% per annum reducing balance

Depreciation of the leasehold building and plant is treated as cost of sales; depreciation of the computer system is an administration cost.

(iii) A provision for income tax of $23.4m for the year to 30 September 20X1 is required. The deferred tax liability is to be increased by $2.2m, of which $1m is to be charged direct to the revaluation surplus.

(iv) The suspense account contains the proceeds of two share issues.

    (a) The exercise of all the outstanding directors' share options of four million shares on 1 October 20X0 at $2 each

    (b) A fully subscribed rights issue on 1 July 20X1 of 1 for 4 held at a price of $3 each. The stock market price of Telenorth's shares immediately before the rights issue was $4.

(v) The finance charge relating to the preference shares is equal to the dividend payable.

Required

(a)   (i) The statement of profit or loss of Telenorth Co for the year to 30 September 20X1 **(8 marks)**

    (ii) A statement of financial position as at 30 September 20X1 in accordance with International Financial Reporting Standards as far as the information permits. **(12 marks)**

    Notes to the financial statements are not required.

(b) Calculate the earnings per share in accordance with IAS 33 for the year to 30 September 20X1 (ignore comparatives). **(5 marks)**

(Total = 25 marks)

24 Bulwell Aggregates Co   20 mins

Bulwell Aggregates Co entered into a three-year contract to obtain three lorries on 1 January 20X1. The contract met the IFRS 16 criteria to be classified as a lease and the initial measurement of the right-of-use asset was $54,000. The agreement states that Bulwell Aggregates Co will pay a deposit of $9,000 on 1 January 20X1, and two annual instalments of $24,000 on 31 December 20X1, 20X2 and a final instalment of $20,391 on 31 December 20X3. Ownership will pass to Bulwell Aggregates Co at the end of the lease term.

Interest is to be calculated at 25% on the balance outstanding on 1 January each year and paid on 31 December each year.

The depreciation policy of Bulwell Aggregates Co is to depreciate the right-of-use asset arising from the lease of the vehicles over a four year period using the straight line method.

Required

Show the entries in the statement of profit or loss and statement of financial position for the years 20X1, 20X2, 20X3. This is the only lease transaction undertaken by this company.

Calculations to the nearest $. **(10 marks)**

25 Lis Co   20 mins

On 1 January 20X3 Lis entered into a lease agreement to rent an asset for a six-year period, at which point it will be returned to the lessor and scrapped, with annual payments of $18,420 made in advance. The initial measurement of the lease liability amounts to $84,000, discounted at the implicit interest rate shown in the lease agreement of 12.5%.

Lis Co expects to sell goods produced by the asset during the first five years of the lease term, but has leased the asset for six years as this is the requirement of the lessor, and in case this expectation changes. Lis Co has the right to determine the use of the asset during the lease term and will obtain substantially all the economic benefit from its use.

Required

Explain how the above lease would be accounted for the year ending 31 December 20X3 including producing relevant extracts from the statement of profit or loss and statement of financial position.

You are not required to prepare the notes to the financial statements.

(10 marks)

26 Carpati Co

12 mins

The following information relates to Carpati Co:

(1) The carrying amount of plant and equipment at 30 September 20X6 is $1,185,000.

(2) The tax written down value of plant and equipment at 1 October 20X5 was $405,000.

(3) During the year ended 30 September 20X6, the company bought plant and equipment of $290,000, which is eligible for tax depreciation.

(4) Carpati Co bought its freehold property in 20W5 for $600,000. It was revalued in the 20X6 accounts to $1,500,000. Ignore depreciation on buildings. No tax allowances were available to Carpati Co on the buildings.

Required

Draft the note to the statement of financial position at 30 September 20X6 omitting comparatives, in respect of deferred tax. Work to the nearest $'000. Assume a current income tax rate of 30%. Tax depreciation is at 25% on a reducing balance basis. The income tax rate enacted for 20X7 is 28%. **(6 marks)**

27 Pilum Co

20 mins

A statement showing the retained profit of Pilum Co for the year ended 31 December 20X4 is set out below.

	$	$
Profit before tax		2,530,000
Less income tax expense		(1,127,000)
		1,403,000
Transfer to reserves		(230,000)
Dividends:		
Paid preference interim dividend	138,000	
Paid ordinary interim divided	414,000	
Declared preference final dividend	138,000	
		(690,000)
Retained		483,000

On 1 January 20X4 the issued share capital of Pilum Co was 4,600,000 6% preference shares of $1 each and 4,120,000 ordinary shares of $1 each.

Required

Calculate the earnings per share (on basic and diluted basis) in respect of the year ended 31 December 20X4 for each of the following circumstances (Each of the three circumstances (a) to (c) is to be dealt with separately.).

(a) On the basis that there was no change in the issued share capital of the company during the year ended 31 December 20X4.

(b) On the basis that the company made a rights issue of $1 ordinary shares on 1 October 20X4 in the proportion of 1 for every 5 shares held, at a price of $1.20. The market price for the shares at close of trade on the last day of quotation cum rights was $1.78 per share.

(c) On the basis that Pilum Co made no new issue of shares during the year ended 31 December 20X4 but on that date it had in issue $1,500,000 10% convertible loan stock 20X8 – 20Y1. This loan stock will be convertible into ordinary $1 shares as follows.

> 20X8 90 $1 shares for $100 nominal value loan stock
> 20X9 85 $1 shares for $100 nominal value loan stock
> 20Y0 80 $1 shares for $100 nominal value loan stock
> 20Y1 75 $1 shares for $100 nominal value loan stock

Assume where appropriate that the income tax rate is 30%.   **(10 marks)**

28 Biggerbuys Co   **49 mins**

Biggerbuys Co has carried on business for a number of years as a retailer of a wide variety of consumer products. The entity operates from a number of stores around the country. In recent years the entity has found it necessary to provide credit facilities to its customers in order to maintain growth in revenue. As a result of this decision the liability to its bankers has increased substantially. The statutory financial statements for the year ended 30 June 20X9 have recently been published and extracts are provided below, together with comparative figures for the previous two years.

STATEMENTS OF PROFIT OR LOSS FOR THE YEARS ENDED 30 JUNE

	20X7	*20X8*	*20X9*
	$m	*$m*	*$m*
Revenue	1,850	2,200	2,500
Cost of sales	(1,250)	(1,500)	(1,750)
Gross profit	600	700	750
Other operating costs	(550)	(640)	(700)
Operating profit	50	60	50
Interest from credit sales	45	60	90
Interest payable	(25)	(60)	(110)
Profit before taxation	70	60	30
Tax payable	(23)	(20)	(10)
Profit for the year	47	40	20

STATEMENTS OF FINANCIAL POSITION AT 30 JUNE

	20X7	*20X8*	*20X9*
	$m	*$m*	*$m*
Property, plant and equipment	278	290	322
Inventories	400	540	620
Trade receivables	492	550	633
Cash and cash equivalents	12	12	15
	1,182	1,392	1,590
Share capital	90	90	90
Reserves	282	292	282
	372	382	372
Bank loans	320	520	610
Other interest bearing borrowings	200	200	320
Trade and other payables	270	270	280
Tax payable	20	20	8
	1,182	1,392	1,590

Other information

(i) Depreciation charged for the three years in question was:

Year ended 30 June	*20X7*	*20X8*	*20X9*
	$m	*$m*	*$m*
	55	60	70

(ii) The other interest bearing borrowings are secured by a floating charge over the assets of Biggerbuys Co. Their repayment is due on 30 June 20Y9.

(iii) Dividends of $30m were paid in 20X7 and 20X8. A dividend of $20m has been proposed.

(iv) The bank loans are unsecured. The maximum lending facility the bank will provide is $630m.

(v) Over the past three years the level of credit sales has been:

Year ended 30 June	20X7	20X8	20X9
	$m	$m	$m
	300	400	600

The entity offers extended credit terms for certain products to maintain market share in a highly competitive environment.

Given the steady increase in the level of bank loans which has taken place in recent years, the entity has recently written to its bankers to request an increase in the lending facility. The request was received by the bank on 15 October 20X9, two weeks after the financial statements were published. The bank is concerned at the steep escalation in the level of the loans and has asked for a report on the financial performance of Biggerbuys Co for the last three years.

Required

As a consultant management accountant employed by the bankers of Biggerbuys Co, prepare a report to the bank which analyses the financial performance of the company for the period covered by the financial statements. Your report may take any form you wish, but you are aware of the particular concern of the bank regarding the rapidly increasing level of lending. Therefore it may be appropriate to include aspects of prior performance that could have contributed to the increase in the level of bank lending. **(25 marks)**

29 Webster Co   39 mins

Webster Co is a publicly listed diversified holding company that is looking to acquire a suitable engineering company. Two private limited engineering companies, Cole Co and Darwin Co, are available to purchase. The summarised financial statements for the year to 31 March 20X9 of both companies are:

STATEMENT OF PROFIT OR LOSS

	Cole Co		Darwin Co	
	$'000	$'000	$'000	$'000
Sales revenue (note (i))		3,000		4,400
Opening inventory	450		720	
Purchases (note (ii))	2,030		3,080	
	2,480		3,800	
Closing inventory	(540)		(850)	
		(1,940)		(2,950)
Gross profit		1,060		1,450
Operating expenses		(480)		(964)
Profit from operations		580		486
Loan note interest		(80)		–
Overdraft interest		–		(10)
Net profit for year		500		476

STATEMENT OF FINANCIAL POSITION

	Cole Co		Darwin Co	
	$'000	$'000	$'000	$'000
Non-current assets				
Property, plant and equipment (notes (iii) and (iv))		2,340		3,100
Current assets				
Inventories	540		850	
Trade receivables	522		750	
Cash and cash equivalent	20		–	
		1,082		1,600
Total assets		3,422		4,700
Equity and liabilities				
Equity				
Equity shares of $1 each		1,000		500
Reserves				
Revaluation surplus		–		700
Retained earnings – 1 April 20X8		684		1,912
Profit – year to 31 March 20X9		500		476
		2,184		3,588
Non-current liabilities				
10% Loan note		800		–
Current liabilities				
Trade and other payables	438		562	
Overdraft	–		550	
		438		1,112
Total equity and liabilities		3,422		4,700

Webster bases its preliminary assessment of target companies on certain key ratios. These are listed below together with the relevant figures for Cole Co and Darwin Co calculated from the above financial statements:

		Cole Co		Darwin Co
Return on capital employed	(500 + 80)/(2,184 + 800)		(476/3,588)	
	× 100	19.4 %	× 100	13.3 %
Asset turnover	(3,000/2,984)	1.01 times	(4,400/3,588)	1.23 times
Gross profit margin		35.3 %		33.0 %
Net profit margin		16.7 %		10.8 %
Accounts receivable collection period		64 days		62 days
Accounts payable payment period		79 days		67 days

Capital employed is defined as shareholders' funds plus non-current debt at the year end; asset turnover is sales revenues divided by gross assets less current liabilities.

The following additional information has been obtained.

(i) Cole Co is part of the Velox Group. On 1 March 20X9 it was permitted by its holding company to sell goods at a price of $500,000 to Brander Co, a fellow subsidiary. The sale gave Cole Co a gross profit margin of 40% instead of its normal gross margin of only 20% on these types of goods. In addition Brander Co was instructed to pay for the goods immediately. Cole Co normally allows three months credit.

(ii) On 1 January 20X9 Cole Co purchased $275,000 (cost price to Cole Co) of its materials from Advent Co, another member of the Velox Group. Advent Co was also instructed by the Velox Group to depart from its normal trading terms, which would have resulted in a charge of $300,000 to Cole Co for these goods. The Group's finance director also authorised a four-month credit period on this sale. Cole Co normally receives two months credit from its suppliers. Cole Co had sold all of these goods at the year end.

(iii) Non-current assets:

Details relating to the two companies' non-current assets are:

	Cost/revaluation	Depreciation	Carrying amount
	$'000	$'000	$'000
Cole Co:property	3,000	1,860	1,140
plant	6,000	4,800	1,200
			2,340
Darwin Co: property	2,000	100	1,900
plant	3,000	1,800	1,200
			3,100

The two companies own very similar properties. Darwin Co's property was revalued to $2,000,000 at the beginning of the current year (ie 1 April 20X8). On this date Cole Co's property, which is carried at cost less depreciation, had a carrying amount of $1,200,000. Its current value (on the same basis as Darwin Co's property) was also $2,000,000. On this date (1 April 20X8) both properties had the same remaining life of 20 years.

(iv) Darwin Co purchased new plant costing $600,000 in February 20X9. In line with company policy a full year's depreciation at 20% per annum has been charged on all plant owned at year end. The equipment is still being tested and will not come on-stream until next year. The purchase of the plant was largely financed by an overdraft facility, which resulted in the interest cost shown in the statement of profit or loss. Both companies depreciate plant over a five-year life and treat all depreciation as an operating expense.

(v) The bank overdraft that would have been required but for the favourable treatment towards Cole Co in respect of items in 1 and 2 above, would have attracted interest of $15,000 in the year to 31 March 20X9.

Required

(a) Restate the financial statements of Cole Co and Darwin Co in order that they may be considered comparable for decision making purposes. State any assumptions you make. **(10 marks)**

(b) Recalculate the key ratios used by Webster Co and, referring to any other relevant points, comment on how the revised ratios may affect the assessment of the two companies. **(10 marks)**

(Total = 20 marks)

30 Xpand Co

29 mins

Xpand Co is a publicly listed company which has experienced rapid growth in recent years through the acquisition and integration of other companies. Xpand Co is interested in acquiring Hydan Co, a retailing company, which is one of several companies owned and managed by the same family.

The summarised financial statements of Hydan Co for the year ended 30 September 20X4 are:

STATEMENT OF PROFIT OR LOSS

	$'000
Revenue	70,000
Cost of sales	(45,000)
Gross profit	25,000
Operating costs	(7,000)
Directors' salaries	(1,000)
Profit before taxation	17,000
Income tax expense	(3,000)
Profit for the year	14,000

STATEMENT OF FINANCIAL POSITION

	$'000	$'000
ASSETS		
Non-current assets		
Property, plant and equipment		32,400
Current assets		
Inventories	7,500	
Cash and cash equivalents	100	
		7,600
Total assets		40,000
EQUITY AND LIABILITIES		
Equity		
Equity shares of $1 each		1,000
Retained earnings		18,700
		19,700
Non-current liabilities		
Directors' loan accounts (interest free)		10,000
Current liabilities		
Trade payables	7,500	
Current tax payable	2,800	
		10,300
Total equity and liabilities		40,000

From the above financial statements Xpand Co has calculated for Hydan Co the ratios below for the year ended 30 September 20X4. It has also obtained the equivalent ratios for the retail sector average which can be taken to represent Hydan Co's sector.

	Hydan Co	Sector average
Return on equity (ROE) (including directors' loan accounts)	47.1%	22.0%
Net asset turnover	2.36 times	1.67 times
Gross profit margin	35.7%	30.0%
Net profit margin	20.0%	12.0%

From enquiries made, Xpand Co has learned the following information:

(i) Hydan Co buys all of its trading inventory from another of the family companies at a price which is 10% less than the market price for such goods.

(ii) After the acquisition, Xpand Co would replace the existing board of directors and need to pay remuneration of $2.5m per annum.

(iii) The directors' loan accounts would be repaid by obtaining a loan of the same amount with interest at 10% per annum.

(iv) Xpand Co expects the purchase price of Hydan Co to be $30m.

Required

(a) Recalculate the ratios for Hydan Co after making appropriate adjustments to the financial statements for notes (i) to (iv) above. For this purpose, the expected purchase price of $30m should be taken as Hydan Co's equity and net assets are equal to this equity plus the loan.

(b) In relation to the ratios calculated in (a) above, and the ratios for Hydan Co given in the question, comment on the performance of Hydan Co compared to its retail sector average. **(15 marks)**

31 Dundee Co

27 mins

The summarised accounts of Dundee Co for the year ended 31 March 20X7 are:

STATEMENTS OF FINANCIAL POSITION AT 31 MARCH

	20X7 $m	20X6 $m
Non-current assets		
Property, plant and equipment	4,200	3,700
Current assets		
Inventories	1,500	1,600
Trade receivables	2,200	1,800
	3,700	3,400
	7,900	7,100
Equity		
Share capital	1,200	1,200
Retained earnings	2,200	1,900
	3,400	3,100
Non-current liabilities		
Deferred tax	1,070	850
Lease liabilities	1,300	1,200
	2,370	2,050
Current liabilities		
Trade payables	1,250	1,090
Current tax	225	205
Lease liabilities	500	450
Bank overdraft	155	205
	2,130	1,950
	7,900	7,100

STATEMENT OF PROFIT OR LOSS FOR THE YEAR ENDED 31 MARCH 20X7

	$m
Revenue	4,300
Cost of sales	(2,000)
Gross profit	2,300
Operating expenses	(1,000)
Finance costs	(250)
Profit before tax	1,050
Income tax expense	(450)
PROFIT FOR THE YEAR	600
Dividends paid in the year	300

Further information:

(i) Depreciation charged for the year totalled $970m. There were no disposals of property, plant and equipment in the period.

(ii) There was no accrual of interest at the beginning or at the end of the year.

(iii) Dundee Co finances a number (but not all) of its property, plant and equipment purchases using leases. In the period, property, plant and equipment which would have cost $600m to purchase outright was acquired under leases.

Required

Prepare the statement of cash flows for Dundee Co for the year ended 31 March 20X7 as per IAS 7 using the indirect method.

(14 marks)

32 Elmgrove Co

49 mins

As financial accountant for Elmgrove Co, you are responsible for the preparation of a statement of cash flows for the year ended 31 March 20X9.

The following information is available.

STATEMENT OF FINANCIAL POSITION AS AT 31 MARCH 20X9

	20X9 $m	20X8 $m
Non-current assets		
Property, plant and equipment	327	264
Current assets		
Inventories	123	176
Trade receivables	95	87
Short term investments	65	30
Cash at bank and in hand	29	–
	312	293
	639	557
Equity		
Share capital – $1 shares	200	120
Share premium	30	–
Revaluation surplus	66	97
Retained earnings	71	41
	367	258
Non-current liabilities		
10% Debentures	100	150
Current liabilities	172	149
	639	557

STATEMENT OF PROFIT OR LOSS FOR THE YEAR ENDED 31 MARCH 20X9

	$m
Revenue	473
Cost of sales	(229)
Gross profit	244
Distribution costs	(76)
Administrative expenses	(48)
Finance income	6
Finance costs	(17)
Profit before tax	109
Income tax expense	(47)
Profit for the year	62
Dividends paid in the period	32

The following notes are also relevant.

(i) *Property, plant and equipment*

Property, plant and equipment held by Elmgrove Co are items of plant and equipment and freehold premises. During 20X9 items of plant and equipment which originally cost $40m were disposed of, resulting in a loss of $6m. These items have a carrying amount of $28m at the date of disposal.

(ii) *Short term investments*

The short-term investments meet the definition of cash equivalents per IAS 7 *Statement of cash flows.*

(iii) *Current liabilities*

Current liabilities consist of the following.

	20X9 $m	20X8 $m
Bank overdraft	–	22
Trade payables	126	70
Interest payable	7	3
Income tax payable	39	54
	172	149

(iv) *10% debentures*

On 1 August 20X8 $50m of 10% debentures was converted into $50m of $1 ordinary shares.

(v) *Depreciation*

The depreciation charge for the year included in the statement of profit or loss was $43m.

Required

(a) Using the information provided, prepare a statement of cash flows for Elmgrove Co for the year ended 31 March 20X9 using the indirect method. **(20 marks)**

(b) Write a memorandum to a director of Elmgrove Co summarising the major benefits a user receives from a published statement of cash flows. **(5 marks)**

(Total = 25 marks)

33 CPP and CCA   29 mins

(a) 'It is important that management and other users of financial accounts should be in a position to appreciate the effects of inflation on the business with which they are concerned.'

Required

Consider the above statement and explain how inflation obscures the meaning of accounts prepared by the traditional historical cost convention, and discuss the contribution which CPP accounting could make to providing a more satisfactory system of accounting for inflation.

(b) Compare the general principles underlying CPP and CCA accounting.

(c) Define the term 'realised holding gain'. **(15 marks)**

34 Not-for-profit   10 mins

A new Academy school, Aspiration High School, has been opened in an area of high social deprivation, replacing a school which was closed as a result of poor academic performance.

Aspiration High School is funded directly by central government and some critics claim that too much money has been spent on it.

In what ways would you expect the Department of Education to monitor the performance of this school? **(5 marks)**

Multiple choice answers

1   A   Timeliness

2   C   Irrecoverable debt allowance. Inventories, biological assets and investment property should be separately presented.

3   B   Dividends paid are deducted from retained earnings. They are a distribution, not an expense. They are not shown on the face of the statement of profit or loss or deducted from other comprehensive income.

4   B

	$
Original cost – building	200,000
Depreciation X1 – X6 (200,000 × 5/50)	(20,000)
	180,000
Revaluation 1.1.X6	100,000
	280,000

Depreciation (280,000 / 44*) = $6,222   *45 years remaining

5   A

	$'000	$'000
Proceeds		1,500
Less unimpaired goodwill		(76)
Less group share of carrying amount at date of disposal		
Share capital	1,000	
Retained earnings	460	
	1,460	
Less NCI (1,460 × 20%)	(292)	
		(1,168)
Profit on disposal		256

6   A

	$
Fair value less disposal cost (800,000 – 20,000)	780,000
Value in use	950,000

So recoverable amount (higher) is $950,000, giving an impairment loss of $250,000.

7   A   The discontinued operation should be shown as a one-line entry representing the post-tax profit or loss of the operation and the post-tax gain or loss on disposal.

8   C

	$	$
Consideration – cash		300,000
– shares (40,000 × 2.50)		100,000
		400,000
Non-controlling interest (20,000 × 1.75)		35,000
		435,000
Fair value of net assets:		
Shares	100,000	
Retained earnings	85,000	
Revaluation surplus	100,000	
Fair value adjustment	60,000	
		(345,000)
Goodwill		90,000

9	B	$75,000 × 60% × 25/125 × 75% = $6,750

10　D

	$
Frog Co	280,000
Tadpole Co (190,000 × 9/12)	142,500
Intragroup	(40,000)
	382,500

11　A

	$
Cost of investment	700,000
Share of post-acquisition retained earnings	
(650,000 × 30%)	195,000
	895,000

Note. The unrealised profit will be credited to group inventory, not investment in associate.

12　D　Distribution, storage and wastage costs will all be treated as expenses and not subsumed into inventory.

13　B

	$
Costs to date	1,400,000
Expected loss (2.5 – 1.4 – 1.3)	(200,000)
Amounts invoiced	(300,000)
Contract asset	900,000

14　A

	$
Depreciation (1.2 m / 5)	240,000
Unwinding of discount (1.2m × 1.08) × 8%	103,680
	343,680

Note that this is the second year of unwinding the discount.

15　B　Financial assets are initially recognised at fair value plus transaction costs.

16　C　As this is a repurchase option with a repurchase price above the original price, it will be accounted for as a financing arrangement.

17　A　$24,000 × 9/10 = $21,600

$21,600 × 3 = $64,800

Being under 12 months, this is a short-term lease and so does not need to be recognised in the statement of financial position and amortised.

18　A　TERP

4 × 1.8

	7.2
1 × 1.2	
	1.2
	8.4　　/ 5 = 1.68

Shares

200,000 × 1.8/1.68 × 3/12	53,571
250,000 × 9/12	187,500
	241,071

EPS = $560,000 / 241,071 = $2.32

19   C   Cash flow accounting does not apply the accruals concept. It deals with items at the point when they are received or paid.

20   B

	$	$
Consideration received		200,000
Net assets (100,000 + 140,000)	240,000	
Goodwill (50,000 × 60%)	30,000	
Less NCI	(58,000)	
		(212,000)
Loss on disposal		(12,000)

Section B answers

21   A   (i) is an onerous contract and should be provided for.

In the case of (ii) the overhauls should be capitalised as part of the cost of the machine and amortised over the period to the next overhaul.

IAS 37 does not allow provisions to be made for expected future losses, so (iii) would not be a valid provision.

22   B   Provisions are liabilities of uncertain timing or amount.

23   C $((50,000 \times 16\%) + (120,000 \times 5\%))$

24   D   This would be a valid provision.

A is not valid as the law has not yet been enacted. B is not valid as the restructuring has not yet been announced to those affected by it. In the case of C, Figaro Co has avoided the constructive obligation, so no provision is needed.

25   B   A contingent liability is normally simply disclosed but IAS 37 makes an exception for contingent liabilities assumed as part of a business combination.

26   B   This indicates that the lessee does not have control of the right-of-use asset during the lease term.

27   D

	$
Initial measurement of liability	25,000
Interest 6%	1,500
Paid 30 June 20X6	(6,000)
Balance 30 June 20X6	20,500
Interest 6%	1,230
Paid 30 June 20X7	(6,000)
Liability due after one year	15,730

28   A

	$
Initial measurement of liability	25,000
Payment 1.7.X5	(6,000)
	19,000
Interest to 30.6.X6	1,140
Balance 30.6.X5	20,140
Current liability	(6,000)
Non-current liability	14,140

29   C

	$
20,000 / 1.08	18,519
20,000 / 1.08^2	17,147
Initial measurement of lease liability	35,666
Initial payment	20,000
Incentive received	(5,000)
Measurement of right-of-use asset	50,666

30   D   Gain on rights retained = $60,000 \times 175,234/200,000 = 52,570$

Gain on rights transferred = $60,000 - 52,570 = \$7,430$

31 D

	$	$
Original cost 1.1.X0	1,000,000	
Depreciation to 31.12.X6 (1,000,000 × 7/50)	(140,000)	
	860,000	
Depreciation to 30.6.X7 ((1,000,000/50) × 6/12)	(10,000)	10,000
	850,000	
Revaluation surplus	100,000	
	950,000	
Depreciation to 31.12.X7 (950,000 × 0.5/42.5)	(11,176)	11,176
Total depreciation year to 31.12.X7		21,176

32 B   As the revaluation surplus goes directly to equity, the same treatment is applied to the deferred tax.

33 A   Higher of fair value less costs of disposal and value in use.

34 D

	Original amount	*Impairment*	*Post-impairment*
Goodwill	20,000	(20,000)	–
Building	440,000	(54,000)	386,000
Plant and machinery	160,000	(30,000 + 16,000)	114,000
Net current assets	100,000	–	
	720,000	120,000	

The goodwill and the damaged machine are written off in full and the balance is allocated between the building and the rest of the plant and machinery.

35 C

	€	£	*Gain/(loss)*
Contract 10 Nov	150,000	132,743	
Payment 10 Dec	(75,000)	(63,559)	2,813
At closing rate 31 Dec	75,000	66,964	(592)
Net gain for year			2,221

Practice question answers

1 Conceptual framework

(a) The **going concern assumption** is that an entity will continue in operational existence for the foreseeable future. This means that the financial statements of an entity are prepared on the assumption that the entity will **continue** trading. If this were not the case, various adjustments would have to be made to the accounts: provisions for losses; revaluation of assets to their possible market value; all non-current assets and liabilities would be reclassified as current; and so forth.

Unless it can be assumed that the business is a going concern, other accounting assumptions cannot apply.

For example, it is meaningless to speak of consistency from one accounting period to the next when this is the final accounting period.

The **accruals basis** of accounting states that items are recognised as assets, liabilities, equity, income and expenses when they satisfy the definitions and recognition criteria in the *Conceptual Framework*. The effect of this is that revenue and expenses which are related to each other are matched, so as to be dealt with in the same accounting period, without regard to when the cash is actually paid or received. This is particularly relevant to the purchase of non-current assets. The cost of a non-current asset is spread over the accounting periods expected to benefit from it, thus matching costs and revenues. In the absence of the going concern convention, this cannot happen, as an example will illustrate.

Suppose a company has a machine which cost $10,000 two years ago and now has a carrying amount of $6,000. The machine can be used for another three years, but as it is highly specialised, there is no possibility of selling it, and so it has no market value.

If the going concern assumption applies, the machine will be shown at **cost less depreciation** in the accounts (ie $6,000), as it still has a part to play in the continued life of the entity. However, if the assumption cannot be applied, the machine will be given a nil value and other assets and liabilities will be similarly revalued on the basis of winding down the company's operations.

(b) One of the ideas behind the *Conceptual Framework* is to **avoid the fire-fighting approach**, which has characterised the development of accounting standards in the past, and instead develop an underlying philosophy as a basis for consistent accounting principles so that each standard fits into the whole framework. Research began from an analysis of the fundamental objectives of accounting and their relationship to the information needs of accounts users. The *Conceptual Framework* has gone behind the requirements of existing accounting standards, which define accounting treatments for particular assets, liabilities, income and expenditure, to define the nature of assets, liabilities, income and expenditure.

2 Regulators

> **Tutorial note**. It is best to use headings to divide up your answer, as we do here.

Stock Exchange

A quoted company is a company whose shares are bought and sold on a stock exchange. This involves the signing of an agreement which requires compliance with the rules of that stock exchange. This would normally contain amongst other things the stock exchange's detailed rules on the information to be disclosed in quoted companies' accounts. This, then, is one regulatory influence on a quoted company's accounts. The stock exchange may enforce compliance by monitoring accounts and reserving the right to withdraw a company's shares from the stock exchange: ie the company's shares would no longer be traded through the stock exchange. In many countries there is, however, no statutory requirement to obey these rules.

Local legislation

In most countries, companies have to comply with the local companies legislation, which lays down detailed requirements on the preparation of accounts. Company law is often quite detailed, partly because of external influences such as EU Directives. Another reason to increase statutory regulation is that quoted companies are under great pressure to show profit growth and an obvious way to achieve this is to manipulate accounting policies. If this involves breaking the law, as opposed to ignoring professional guidance, company directors may think twice before bending the rules – or, at least, this is often a government's hope.

Standard-setters

Professional guidance is given by the national and international standard-setters. Prescriptive guidance is given in accounting standards which must be applied in all accounts intended to show a 'true and fair view' or 'present fairly in all material respects'. International Financial Reporting Standards and national standards are issued after extensive consultation and are revised as required to reflect economic or legal changes. In some countries, legislation requires details of non-compliance to be disclosed in the accounts. 'Defective' accounts can be revised under court order if necessary and directors signing such accounts can be prosecuted and fined (or even imprisoned).

The potential for the IASB's influence in this area is substantial. It must pursue excellence in standards with absolute rigour to fulfil that potential.

3 Standard setters

(a) The users of financial information – creditors, management, employees, business contacts, financial specialists, government and the general public – are entitled to information about a business entity to a greater or lesser degree. However, the needs and expectations of these groups will vary.

The preparers of the financial information often find themselves in the position of having to reconcile the interests of different groups in the best way for the business entity. For example whilst shareholders are looking for increased profits to support higher dividends, employees will expect higher wage increases; and yet higher profits without corresponding higher tax allowances (increased capital allowances for example) will result in a larger tax bill.

Without accounting standards to prescribe how certain transactions should be treated, preparers would be tempted to produce financial information which meets the expectations of the favoured user group. For example creative accounting methods, such as off balance sheet finance could be used to enhance a company's statement of financial position to make it more attractive to investors/lenders.

The aim of accounting standards is that they should regulate financial information in order that it is relevant and a faithful representation. It should also exhibit the following enhancing characteristics.

(i)   Comparability
(ii)   Verifiability
(iii) Timeliness
(iv)   Understandability

Comparability is a good example of why accounting standards are necessary. In the absence of regulation, entities would be able to present items in the financial statements in whatever form would produce the most favourable result for that reporting period. Different entities would therefore be using different accounting policies and could change them from one period to the next. Analysts and investors would be unable to meaningfully compare the performance of an entity over time or to compare the performance and results of one entity against the performance and results of another entity.

(b)   A number of reasons could be advanced why the financial statements of not-for-profit entities should not be subject to regulation:

- They do not have shares that are being traded, so their financial statements are not produced with a share price in mind.

- They do not have chief executives with share options seeking to present favourable figures to the market.

- They are not seeking to make a profit, so whether they have or not is perhaps irrelevant.

- They are perceived to be on slightly higher moral ground than profit-making entities, so are less in need of regulation.

However a closer look at this brings up the following points.

- Public sector bodies, such as local government organisations, are spending taxpayers' money and should be required to account for it.

- The chief executives of public sector bodies are often highly rewarded and their performance should be verified.

- Charities may not be invested in by the general public, but they are funded by the public, often through direct debits.

- Charities are big business. In addition to regular public donations they receive large donations from high-profile backers.

- They employ staff and executives at market rates and have heavy administrative costs. Supporters are entitled to know how much of their donation has gone on administration.

- Any misappropriation of funds is serious in two ways. It is taking money from the donating public, who thought they were donating to a good cause, and it is diverting resources from the people who should have been helped.

- Not all charities are *bona fide*. For instance, some are thought to be connected to terrorism.

For these reasons, it is important that the financial statements of not-for-profit entities are subject to regulation.

4 Polymer Co

POLYMER CO: STATEMENT OF PROFIT OR LOSS FOR THE YEAR ENDED 31 MAY 20X8

	$
Revenue	1,526,750
Cost of sales (W3)	(1,048,000)
Gross profit	478,750
Distribution costs (W4)	(124,300)
Administrative expenses (W5)	(216,200)
Finance costs (W6)	(18,400)
Profit before tax	119,850
Income tax expense	(40,000)
PROFIT FOR THE YEAR	79,850

POLYMER CO: STATEMENT OF FINANCIAL POSITION AS AT 31 MAY 20X8

	$
ASSETS	
Non-current assets	
Property, plant and equipment (W7)	452,250
Intangible assets	215,500
	667,750
Current assets	
Inventories (W8)	425,750
Trade Receivables (W9)	171,880
Cash and cash equivalents	5,120
	602,750
Total assets	1,270,500
EQUITY AND LIABILITIES	
Equity	
Share capital	300,000
Share premium reserve	100,000
Retained earnings (283,500 + 79,850)	363,350
General reserve	50,000
Revaluation surplus	50,000
	863,350
Non-current liabilities	
10% debentures	100,000
8.4% cumulative redeemable preference shares*	100,000
	200,000
Current liabilities	
Trade and other payables (W10)	115,900
Short-term borrowings	51,250
Current tax payable	40,000
	207,150
Total equity and liabilities	1,270,500

*****Tutorial note.** Redeemable preference shares are presented under IAS 32 *Financial Instruments: Presentation* as a loan payable, and dividends on them as interest payable. This point is covered in Chapter 14.

Workings

			$
1	*Depreciation*		
	Cost of sales:	8% × 150,000	12,000
	Administration:	10% × 50,000	5,000
		1/4 × 20% × 50,000	2,500
			7,500
	Distribution:	3/4 × 20% × 50,000	7,500
2	*Depreciation (amortisation) of lease*		
	$75,000 × 1/50		1,500

3 Cost of sales

	$
Opening inventories (108,400 + 32,750 + 184,500)	325,650
Purchases	750,600
Carriage inwards	10,500
Manufacturing wages	250,000
Manufacturing overheads	125,000
Depreciation of plant (W1)	12,000
Closing inventories (W9)	(425,750)
	1,048,000

4 Distribution costs

	$
Per question	116,800
Depreciation (W1)	7,500
	124,300

5 Administrative expenses

		$
Per question		158,100
Legal expenses	54,100	
less: solicitors' fees capitalised	(5,000)	
		49,100
Depreciation (W1)		7,500
Amortisation of lease (W2)		1,500
		216,200

6 Finance costs

	$
Interest expense on loan notes ($100,000 × 10%)	10,000
Dividend on redeemable preference shares ($100,000 × 8.4%)	8,400
	18,400

7 Property, plant and equipment

	Freehold land $	Leasehold property $	Plant & equipment $	Furniture & fixtures $	Motor vehicles $	Total $
Carrying amount per TB						
Cost or valuation	250,000	75,000	150,000	50,000	75,000	
Accumulated dep'n	–	(15,000)	(68,500)	(15,750)	(25,000)	
Carrying amount	250,000	60,000	81,500	34,250	50,000	
Solicitor's fees	5,000					
Depreciation charge	–	(1,500)	(12,000)	(5,000)	(10,000)	
Carrying amount 31 May 20X8	255,000	58,500	69,500	29,250	40,000	452,250

8 Inventories

	$
Raw materials	112,600
Work in progress	37,800
Finished goods	275,350
	425,750

9 Trade Receivables

	$
Trade receivables (177,630 – 5,750 allowance for receivables)	171,880

10 Trade and other payables

	$
Trade payables	97,500
Loan interest payable	10,000
Preference dividend payable	8,400
	115,900

5 Gains Co

GAINS CO– STATEMENT OF CHANGES IN EQUITY FOR THE YEAR ENDED 31 DECEMBER 20X9

	Share capital $'000	Share premium $'000	Retained earnings $'000	Revaluation surplus $'000	Total $'000
Balance at 1 January 20X9	2,800	1,150	2,120	750	6,820
Change in accounting policy			40	(40)	–
Restated balance	2,800	1,150	2,160	710	6,820
Changes in equity for 20X9					
Issue of share capital	600	(40)	–	–	560
Dividends			(200)		(200)
Total comprehensive income for the year (566 – (W1) 50)	–	–	516	120	636
Transfer to retained earnings (W2)			35	(35)	–
Balance at 31 December 20X9	3,400	1,110	2,511	795	7,816

Workings

1 Loss on investment property (160 – 110)   (50)

2 *Calculation of profit realised on sale of revalued asset*

	$
Revaluation recognised in past	50,000
Less: amounts transferred to retained earnings: (80,000 / 10 – 30,000 / 10) × 3	(15,000)
	35,000

6 Biogenics Co

(a) To be recognised, an intangible asset must first of all meet the definition of an intangible asset in IAS 38. It must be controlled by the entity, it must be separably identifiable and it must be something from which the entity expects future economic benefits to flow. It must then meet the recognition criteria of having a cost that can be measured reliably.

For this reason internally-generated intangibles are not normally recognised as assets. They have not been acquired for a consideration and therefore do not have a cost or value that can be measured reliably. For this reason, a brand name that has been acquired can be capitalised, a brand name that has been internally developed can not be capitalised. The exception to this is development costs which can be capitalised if/when they meet the IAS 38 criteria. They are initially recognised at cost.

After initial recognition development costs are amortised over the life cycle of the product. If at any point it becomes apparent that the development costs no longer meet the capitalisation criteria, they should be written off. Intangible assets with an indefinite useful life are not amortised but tested annually for impairment.

(b) STATEMENT OF FINANCIAL POSITION (extracts)

	$
Non-current assets	
Property, plant and equipment (W1)	187,500
Intangible assets (W2)	6,691,000

COSTS CHARGED TO PROFIT OR LOSS

Depreciation (W1)	12,500
Amortisation (W2)	1,309,000
Staff salaries	400,000

Workings

		$
1	*Computer equipment*	
	Cost	200,000
	Depreciation (200 × 3/48)	(12,500)
	Carrying amount	187,500

why [handwritten]

2 *Intangible assets*

	Patent $'000	*Development costs* $'000	*Customer list* $'000	*Total* $'000
Cost	1,500	6,000	500	8,000
Amortisation:				
(6/36)	(250)	(1,000)	–	–
(4/34)	–	–	(59)	(1,309)
	1,250	5,000	441	6,691

34 months [handwritten]

cust List only has a life of 34 months with this company. [handwritten]

7 Multiplex Co

The impairment losses are allocated as required by IAS 36 *Impairment of assets.*

	Asset @ 1.1.20X0 $'000	*1st loss (W1)* $'000	*Assets @ 1.2.20X0* $'000	*2nd loss (W2)* $'000	*Revised asset* $'000
Goodwill	200	(200)	–	–	–
Operating licence	1,200	(200)	1,000	(100)	900
Property: stations/land	300	(50)	250	(50)	200
Rail track/coaches	300	(50)	250	(50)	200
Steam engines	1,000	(500)	500	–	500
	3,000	(1,000)	2,000	(200)	1,800

Workings

1 *First impairment loss*

$500,000 relates directly to an engine and its recoverable amount can be assessed directly (ie zero) and it is no longer part of the cash-generating unit.

IAS 36 then requires goodwill to be written off. Any further impairment must be written off the remaining assets pro rata, except the engine which must not be reduced below its net selling price of $500,000.

2 *Second impairment loss*

The first $100,000 of the impairment loss is applied to the operating licence to write it down to net selling price.

The remainder is applied pro rata to assets carried at other than their net selling prices, ie $50,000 to both the property and the rail track and coaches.

8 Hewlett Co

HEWLETT CO
STATEMENT OF PROFIT OR LOSS AND OTHER COMPREHENSIVE INCOME FOR THE YEAR ENDED
31 DECEMBER 20X2

	$m
Revenue	2,648
Cost of sales (W1)	(1,765)
Gross profit	883
Distribution costs (W1)	(514)
Administrative expenses (W1)	(360)
Finance costs (150 × 4%)	(6)
Fair value gain on investment properties (588 – 548)	40
Rental income	48
Profit before tax	91
Income tax expense (Note vi) (45 – 17)	(28)
PROFIT FOR THE YEAR	63
Other comprehensive income:	
Gain on property revaluation (W2)	55
Income tax relating to gain on property revaluation	(17)
Other comprehensive income, net of tax	38
TOTAL COMPREHENSIVE INCOME FOR THE YEAR	101

HEWLETT CO
STATEMENT OF FINANCIAL POSITION AS AT 31 DECEMBER 20X2

	$m
ASSETS	
Non-current assets	
Property, plant and equipment (W2)	852
Investment properties (Note ix)	588
	1,440
Current assets	
Inventories (388 – (21 – 14))	381
Trade receivables	541
Cash and cash equivalents	32
	954
	2,394
EQUITY AND LIABILITIES	
Equity	
Share capital	125
Share premium	244
Retained earnings	810
General reserve	545
Revaluation surplus ((W2) 55 – 17)	38
	1,762
Non-current liabilities	
4% loan notes 20X8	150
Deffered tax	17
Current liabilities	
Trade payables	434
Income tax payable (Note vi)	28
Interest payable ((4% × 150) – 3)	3
	465
	2,394

HEWLETT CO
STATEMENT OF CHANGES IN EQUITY FOR THE YEAR ENDED 31 DECEMBER 20X2

	Share capital	Share premium	Retained earnings	General reserve	Revaluation surplus	Total
	$m	$m	$m	$m	$m	$m
Balance at 1 January 20X2	100	244	753	570	–	1,667
Changes in equity for 20X2						
Issue of share capital (W4)	25			(25)		–
Dividends (W5)			(6)			(6)
Total comprehensive income for the year			63		38	101
Balance at 31 December 20X2	125	244	810	545	38	1,762

Workings

1   Expenses

	Cost of sales	Distribution	Admin
	$m	$m	$m
Per TB	1,669	514	345
Opening inventories	444		
Depreciation of buildings (W2)			15
Depreciation of plant and equipment (W2)	24		
Impairment loss on plant (W3)	4		
Loss on sale of equipment ((15 − 3) − 7)	5		
Closing inventories (388 − (21 − 14))	(381)		
	1,765	514	360

2   Property, plant and equipment

	Land	Buildings	Plant & equipment	Total
	$m	$m	$m	$m
Cost	90	750	258	
Accumulated depreciation b/d	–	(120)	(126)	
Carrying amount b/d at 1 January 20X2	90	630	132	
Disposal of equipment (15 − 3)			(12)	
	90	630	120	
Depreciation during year				
Buildings ($750m / 50 years)		(15)		
Plant & equipment ($120m × 20%)			(24)	
Impairment loss on plant (W3)			(4)	
	90	615	92	
Revaluation (balancing figure)	10	45		55
Carrying amount c/d at 31 December 20X2	100	660	92	852
(Buildings 760 − 100)				

3   Impairment loss on plant

	$m
Carrying amount	22
Recoverable amount (Value in use: (3.8m × 3.993) + (4.2m × 0.677))	(18)
	(4)

Recoverable amount is the higher of value in use ($18m) and fair value less costs of disposal ($16m).

4   Bonus issue

    Dr General reserve ($100m /$0.50 × 1/4 = 50m shares × $0.50) $25m

    Cr Share capital $25m

5   Dividends (proof)

                                              $m

    Interim ($100m /$0.50 = 200m shares × $0.03)   6 per trial balance

The final dividend has not been paid and is not a liability of the company at the year end.

9 Barcelona Co and Madrid Co

BARCELONA GROUP
CONSOLIDATED STATEMENT OF FINANCIAL POSITION AS AT 30 SEPTEMBER 20X6

	$m
Non-current assets	
Property, plant & equipment (2,848 + 354 + (W6) 18)	3,220
Patents	45
Goodwill (W2)	26
	3,291
Current assets	
Inventories (895 + 225)	1,120
Trade and other receivables (1,348 + 251)	1,599
Cash and cash equivalents (212 + 34)	246
	2,965
	6,256
Equity attributable to owners of the parent	
Share capital	920
Retained earnings (W3)	2,238
General reserve (W4)	796
	3,954
Non-controlling interests (W5)	202
	4,156
Non-current liabilities	
Long-term borrowings (558 + 168)	726
Current liabilities	
Trade and other payables (1,168 + 183)	1,351
Current portion of long-term borrowings	23
	1,374
	6,256

Workings

1   *Group structure*

                Barcelona Co
                    |
                          60% (1.10.X2)

                Madrid Co

2   *Goodwill*

	$m	$m
Consideration transferred (250m × 60% × $1.06)		159
Non-controlling interests at fair value		86
Net assets at acquisition as represented by:		
Share capital	50	
Retained earnings	104	
General reserve	11	
Fair value adjustments (W6)	34	
		(199)
Goodwill at acquisition		46
Impairment losses to date		(20)
Goodwill at year end		26

3   *Retained earnings*

	Barcelona $m	Madrid $m
Per question	2,086	394
Pre-acquisition		(104)
Movement on fair value adjustment (W6)		(16)
		274
Group share of post acquisition retained earnings:		
Madrid Co (274 × 60%)	164	
Less group impairment losses to date (20 × 60%)	(12)	
	2,238	

4   *General reserve*

	Barcelona $m	Madrid $m
Per question	775	46
Pre-acquisition		(11)
		35
Group share of post acquisition general reserve:		
Madrid Co (35 × 60%)	21	
	796	

5   *Non-controlling interests*

	$m
NCI at acquisition (W2)	86
NCI share of post acquisition:	
Retained earnings ((W3) 274 × 40%)	110
General reserve ((W4) 35 × 40%)	14
Goodwill impairment (20 × 40%)	(8)
	202

6   *Fair value adjustments*

	Acquisition date $m	Movement $m	Year end $m
Inventories	8	(8)	–
Land	6	–	6
Buildings	20	(8)*	12
	34	(16)	18

*20 / 10 years × 4

10 Reprise Group

REPRISE GROUP – CONSOLIDATED STATEMENT OF FINANCIAL POSITION AS AT 31 MARCH 20X4

	$'000
Non-current assets	
Land and buildings	3,350
Plant and equipment (1,010 + 2,210)	3,220
Motor vehicles (510 + 345)	855
Goodwill (W2)	826
	8,251
Current assets	
Inventories (890 + 352 – (W5) 7.2)	1,234.8
Trade receivables (1,372 + 514 – 39 – (W6) 36)	1,811
Cash and cash equivalents (89 + 39 + 51)	179
	3,224.8
	11,475.8
Equity attributable to owners of the parent	
Share capital	1,000
Retained earnings (W3)	5,257.3
Revaluation surplus	2,500
	8,757.3
Non-controlling interests (W4)	896.5
	9,653.8
Non-current liabilities	
10% debentures	500
Current liabilities	
Trade and other payables (996 + 362 – (W6) 36)	1,322
	11,475.8

Workings

1   *Group structure*

Reprise Co
|
75%   ∴ non-controlling interests = 25%

Encore Co

2   *Goodwill*

	$'000	$'000
Consideration transferred		2,000
Non-controlling interests (at 'full' FV) (125k shares × $4.40)		550
Net assets at acquisition as represented by:		
Share capital	500	
Retained earnings	1,044	
		(1,544)
		1,006
Impairment losses to date		(180)
		826

3   Consolidated retained earnings

	Reprise Co	Encore Co
	$'000	$'000
Per question	4,225	2,610
PUP (W5)	(7.2)	
Pre-acquisition retained earnings		(1,044)
		1,566
Group share of post acquisition retained earnings:		
Encore Co (1,566 × 75%)	1,174.5	
Group share of impairment losses (180 × 75%)	(135)	
	5,257.3	

4   Non-controlling interests

	$'000
NCI at acquisition (W2)	550
NCI share of post acquisition retained earnings ((W3) 1,566 × 25%)	391.5
NCI share of impairment losses (180 × 25%)	(45)
	896.5

5   Unrealised profit on inventories

Unrealised profit included in inventories is:

$$\$31,200 \times \frac{30}{130} = \$7,200$$

6   Trade receivables/trade payables

Intragroup balance of $75,000 is reduced to $36,000 once cash-in-transit of $39,000 is followed through to its ultimate destination.

11 Fallowfield Co and Rusholme Co

FALLOWFIELD GROUP
CONSOLIDATED STATEMENT OF PROFIT OR LOSS FOR THE YEAR ENDED 30 JUNE 20X8

	$
Revenue (403,400 + 193,000 – 40,000)	556,400
Cost of sales (201,400 + 92,600 – 40,000 + 4,000)	(258,000)
Gross profit	298,400
Distribution costs (16,000 + 14,600)	(30,600)
Administrative expenses (24,250 + 17,800)	(42,050)
Profit before tax	225,750
Income tax expense (61,750 + 22,000)	(83,750)
Profit for the year	142,000
Profit attributable to:	
Owners of the parent	125,200
Non-controlling interests (W2)	16,800
	142,000

STATEMENT OF CHANGES IN EQUITY (EXTRACT)

	Retained earnings
	$
Balance at 1 July 20X7 (W3)	190,000
Dividends	(40,000)
Profit for the year	125,200
Balance at 30 June 20X8 (W4)	275,200

Workings

1   *Group structure*

Fallowfield Co
|
　　60%　three years ago
　　　Pre-acquisition ret'd earnings: $16,000
Rusholme Co

2   *Non-controlling interests*

	$
Rusholme – profit for the year	46,000
Less PUP (40,000 × ½ × 25/125)	4,000
	42,000
Non-controlling interest share 40%	16,800

3   *Retained earnings brought forward*

	Fallowfield Co	Rusholme Co
	$	$
Per question	163,000	61,000
Pre-acquisition retained earnings		(16,000)
		45,000
Group share of post acquisition retained earnings:		
Rusholme Co(45,000 × 60%)	27,000	
	190,000	

4   *Retained earnings carried forward*

	Fallowfield Co	Rusholme Co
	$	$
Per question	238,000	82,000
PUP	–	(4,000)
Pre-acquisition retained earnings		(16,000)
		62,000
Group share of post acquisition retained earnings:		
Rusholme Co (62,000 × 60%)	37,200	
	275,200	

12 Panther Group

PANTHER GROUP
CONSOLIDATED STATEMENT OF PROFIT OR LOSS AND OTHER COMPREHENSIVE INCOME FOR THE YEAR ENDED 31 DECEMBER 20X4

	$'000
Revenue (22,800 + (4,300 × 6/12) − (640 × 6/12))	24,630
Cost of sales (13,600 + (2,600 × 6/12) − (640 × 6/12) + (W3) 10 + (W5) 5)	(14,595)
Gross profit	10,035
Distribution costs (2,900 + (500 × 6/12))	(3,150)
Administrative expenses (1,800 + (300 × 6/12))	(1,950)
Finance costs (200 + (70 × 6/12) − (W4) 20 cancellation)	(215)
Finance income (50 − (W4) 20 cancellation)	30
Profit before tax	4,750
Income tax expense (1,300 + (220 × 6/12))	(1,410)
7Profit for the year	3,340
Other comprehensive income for the year, net of tax (1,600 + (180 × 6/12))	1,690
Total comprehensive income for the year	5,030

	$'000
Profit attributable to:	
Owners of the parent (3,340 − 124)	3,216
Non-controlling interests (W2)	124
	3,340
Total comprehensive income attributable to:	
Owners of the parent (5,030 − 160)	4,870
Non-controlling interests (W2)	160
	5,030

CONSOLIDATED STATEMENT OF CHANGES IN EQUITY
FOR THE YEAR ENDED 31 DECEMBER 20X4 (EXTRACT)

	$'000
	Reserves
Balance at 1 January 20X4 (Panther only)	12,750
Dividend paid	(900)
Total comprehensive income for the year	4,878
Balance at 31 December 20X4 (W6)	16,728

Workings

1   *Timeline*

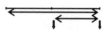

2   *Non-controlling interests*

	PFY	TCI
	$'000	$'000
Profit/TCI for the year (610 × 6/12) / (790 × 6/12)	305	395
Less PUP (W3)	(10)	(10)
Add back intragroup interest		
Additional depreciation on fair value adjustment (W5)	(5)	(5)
	310	400
NCI share (× 40%)	124	160

3   *Unrealised profit on intragroup trading*

Sabre Co to Panther Co = $60,000 × $\frac{20\%}{120\%}$ = $10,000

Adjust cost of sales and non-controlling interests in books of seller (Sabre Co).

4   *Interest on intragroup loan*

The loan is an intragroup item for the last six months of the year (ie only since Sabre Co's acquisition by Panther Co):

$800,000 × 5% × 6/12 = $20,000

Cancel in books of Panther Co and Sabre Co

5   *Fair value adjustments*

	At acq'n 1.7.X4 $'000	Movement $'000	At year end 31.12.X4 $'000
Property	200	(200/20 × 6/12) (5)	195

6 Group reserves carried forward (proof)

	Panther Co $'000	Sabre Co $'000
Reserves per question	16,500	3,270
PUP (W3)		(10)
Fair value movement (W5)		(5)
Pre acquisition reserves [2,480 + ((610 + 180) × 6/12)]		(2,875)
		380
Group share of post acquisition reserves:		
Sabre Co (380 × 60%)	228	
	16,728	

13 Hever Co

CONSOLIDATED STATEMENT OF FINANCIAL POSITION AS AT 31 DECEMBER 20X4

	$'000
Non-current assets	
Property, plant & equipment (370 + 190 + (W7) 45)	605
Goodwill (W2)	8
Investment in associate (W3)	165
	778
Current assets	
Inventories (160 + 100 − (W6) 1.5)	258.5
Trade receivables (170 + 90)	260
Cash and cash equivalents (50 + 40)	90
	608.5
	1,386.5
Equity attributable to owners of the parent	
Share capital	200
Share premium reserve	100
Retained earnings (W4)	758.5
	1,058.5
Non-controlling interests (W5)	168
	1,226.5
Current liabilities	
Trade and other payables (100 + 60)	160
	1,386.5

Workings

1 Group structure

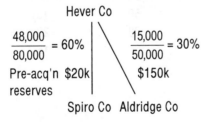

∴ In the absence of information to the contrary, Spiro Co is a subsidiary, and Aldridge Co an associate of Hever Co

2   *Goodwill on consolidation – Spiro Co*

	$'000	$'000
Consideration transferred		128
Non-controlling interests (at 'full' fair value)		90
Net assets at acquisition:		
Share capital	80	
Retained earnings	20	
Share premium	80	
Fair value adjustments (W7)	30	
		(210)
Goodwill arising on consolidation		8

3   *Investment in associate*

	$'000
Cost of associate	90
Share of post-acquisition retained reserves (W4)	75
	165

4   *Retained earnings*

	Hever Co $'000	Spiro Co $'000	Aldridge Co $'000
Per question	568	200	400
PUP (W6)	(1.5)	–	–
Fair value movement (W7)		15	
Pre-acquisition retained earnings		(20)	(150)
		195	250
Group share of post acquisition ret'd earnings:			
Spiro Co (195 × 60%)	117		
Aldridge Co (250 × 30%)	75		
Less group share of impairment losses to date	(0)		
Less impairment losses on associate to date	(0)		
	758.5		

5   *Non-controlling interests*

	$'000
NCI at acquisition (W2)	90
NCI share of post acquisition ret'd earnings ((W4) 195 × 40%)	78
	168

6   *Unrealised profit on inventories*

Mark-up: \$16,000 − \$10,000 = \$6,000 ∴ ¼ × \$6,000 = \$1,500

7   *Fair values – adjustment to net assets*

	At acquisition	Movement	At year end
Property, plant and equipment	50	(5)	45
Inventories	(20)	20	0
	30	15	45

14 Highveldt Co

(a)   *Group Structure as at 31 March 20X5*

```
┌─────────────────────────────┐
│      Highveldt Co           │
│        parent               │
└─────────────────────────────┘
        75% │ Since 1.4.X4
┌─────────────────────────────┐
│       Samson Co             │
│       subsidiary            │
└─────────────────────────────┘
```

(i)   *Goodwill in Samson Co*

	$m	$m
Consideration transferred		
80m shares × 75% × $3.50		210
Contingent consideration		108
		318
Non-controlling interest		74
Fair value of net assets at acquisition:		
Carrying value of net assets at 1.4.20X4:		
Ordinary shares	80	
Share premium	40	
Retained earnings	134	
Fair value adjustments (W)	42	
		(296)
		96
Impairment charge given in question		(22)
Carrying amount at 31 March 20X5		74

Notes (not required in the exam)

The contingent consideration is recognised at fair value. The increase in contingent consideration arose post-acquisition so will not affect the goodwill calculation. The additional amount is added to the liability and charged to group retained earnings.

Only the initial $20m fair value adjustment to land and buildings is relevant at the date of acquisition. The $4m arising post acquisition will be treated as a normal revaluation and credited to the revaluation surplus. (See (a)(iii) below.)

Samson Co was right not to capitalise an internally developed brand name because, without an active market, its value cannot be measured reliably. However the fair value of a brand name can be measured as part of a business combination. Therefore the $40m fair value will be recognised at acquisition and an additional $4m amortisation will be charged in the consolidated statement of profit or loss.

At acquisition Samson Co had capitalised $18m of development expenditure. Highveldt Co does not recognise this as an asset, so the net assets at acquisition are reduced by $18m. A further $32m is capitalised by Samson Co post acquisition; this will be written off in the consolidated statement of profit or loss (net of the $10m amortisation already charged).

(ii)   *Non-controlling interest in Samson Co's net assets*

	$m
NCI at acquisition (per question)	74
NCI share of post acquisition retained earnings ((W(iii)) 48 × 25%)	12
NCI share of post-acquisition revaluation surplus ((W(iii)) 4 × 25%)	1
NCI share of goodwill impairment (22 × 25%)	(6)
	81

(iii)   *Consolidated Reserves*

Share premium

The share premium of a group, like the share capital, is the share premium of the parent only ($80m)

Revaluation surplus

	$m
Parent's own revaluation surplus	45
Group share of Samson Co's post acquisition revaluation; $4m × 75%	3
	48

Retained earnings attributable to owners of the parent

	Highveldt Co	Samson Co
	$m	$m
Per question	350	76
Accrued interest from Samson Co ($60m × 10%)	6	–
Additional contingent consideration (116 – 108)	(8)	–
Amortisation of brand ($40m / 10 years)	–	(4)
Write off development expenditure as incurred ($50m – $18m)	–	(32)
Write back amortisation of development expenditure	–	10
Unrealised profit	–	(2)
	348	48
Group share (75%)	36	
Impairment of goodwill in Samson Co – group share (22 × 75%)	(16)	
	368	

Working	$m
Fair value adjustment:	
Revaluation of land and buildings	20
Recognition of fair value of brands	40
Derecognition of capitalised development expenditure	(18)
	42

(b)   *Usefulness of consolidated financial statements*

The main reason for preparing consolidated accounts is that groups operate as a single economic unit, and it is not possible to understand the affairs of the parent company without taking into account the financial position and performance of all the companies that it controls. The directors of the parent company should be held fully accountable for all the money they have invested on their shareholders behalf, whether that has been done directly by the parent or via a subsidiary.

There are also practical reasons why parent company accounts cannot show the full picture. The parent company's own financial statements only show the original cost of the investment and the dividends received from the subsidiary. As explained below, this hides the true value and nature of the investment in the subsidiary, and, without consolidation, could be used to manipulate the reported results of the parent.

- The cost of the investment will include a premium for goodwill, but this is only quantified and reported if consolidated accounts are prepared.
- A controlling interest in a subsidiary can be achieved with a 51% interest. The full value of the assets controlled by the group is only shown through consolidation when the non-controlling interest is taken into account.

- Without consolidation, the assets and liabilities of the subsidiary are disguised.

  - A subsidiary could be very highly geared, making its liquidity and profitability volatile.

  - A subsidiary's assets might consist of intangible assets, or other assets with highly subjective values.

- The parent company controls the dividend policy of the subsidiary, enabling it to smooth out profit fluctuations with a steady dividend. Consolidation reveals the underlying profits of the group.

- Over time the net assets of the subsidiary should increase, but the cost of the investment will stay fixed and will soon bear no relation to the true value of the subsidiary.

15 Villandry Co

(a)

	Cost less 2½% trade discount $	NRV $	Valuation $
Product Arctic	3,510.00	5,100.00	3,510.00
Product Brassy	2,827.50	2,800.00	2,800.00
Product Chilly	4,095.00	4,100.00	4,095.00
			10,405.00

(b) The weighted average method values items withdrawn from inventory at the average price of all goods held in inventory at the time. Thus, it smooths out any fluctuations due to rising or falling prices.

The FIFO method of inventory valuation assumes that items sold are the oldest ones received from suppliers. Thus, any goods held at the year end will be assumed to have been purchased recently. Thus, changing from weighted average to FIFO (assuming inventory purchase prices are rising over time) is likely to increase the value of closing inventory (from historical to current price levels). This would reduce the cost of sales figure in profit or loss and increase the reported profit figure.

16 Biological assets

(a) A biological asset is a living animal or plant. Agricultural produce is the harvested product obtained from a biological asset.

(b) Agricultural produce is measured at its fair value less estimated point-of-sale costs at the point of harvest.

(c) Examples of biological assets and agricultural produce are:

Biological asset	Agricultural produce
Sheep	Wool
Pigs	Meat
Dairy cattle	Milk
Fruit tree	Oranges etc
Plant	Cotton
Bush	Tea leaves
Vine	Grapes
Chicken	Eggs

(d) Consumable biological assets are those that are to be harvested as agricultural produce or sold as biological assets. Examples include livestock intended for the production of meat, livestock held for sale, fish in farms, crops such as maize and wheat and trees being grown for lumber.

Bearer biological assets are those other than consumable biological assets. Examples include livestock from which milk is produced or livestock held for breeding, vines, fruit trees and trees from which firewood is harvested without felling.

Plant-based bearer biological assets are now accounted for under **IAS 16**. These are assets which are not in themselves consumed, but are used solely to grow produce over several periods. This would apply to grape vines, tea bushes and fruit trees from the list above.

17 Provisions

(a) **Why there was a need for an accounting standard dealing with provisions**

IAS 37 *Provisions, contingent liabilities and contingent assets* was issued to prevent entities from using provisions for creative accounting. It was common for entities to recognise material provisions for items such as future losses, restructuring costs or even expected future expenditure on repairs and maintenance of assets. These could be combined in one large provision (sometimes known as the 'big bath'). Although these provisions reduced profits in the period in which they were recognised (and were often separately disclosed on grounds of materiality), they were then released to enhance profits in subsequent periods. To make matters worse, provisions were often recognised where there was no firm commitment to incur expenditure. For example, an entity might set up a provision for restructuring costs and then withdraw from the plan, leaving the provision available for profit smoothing.

The criteria that need to be satisfied before a provision is recognised

IAS 37 states that a provision should not be recognised unless:

(i)   An entity has a present obligation (legal or constructive) as a result of a past event

(ii) It is probable that an outflow of resources embodying economic benefits will be required to settle the obligation

(iii) A reliable estimate can be made of the amount of the obligation

An obligation can be legal or constructive. An entity has a constructive obligation if:

(i)   It has indicated to other parties that it will accept certain responsibilities (by an established pattern of past practice or published policies)

(ii) As a result, it has created a valid expectation on the part of those other parties that it will discharge those responsibilities

(b)   Extraction Co should recognise a provision for the estimated costs of making good the site because:

(i)   It has a present obligation to incur the expenditure as a result of a past event. In this case the obligating event occurred when it became virtually certain that the legislation would be passed. Therefore the obligation existed at 31 December 20X0

(ii) An outflow of resources embodying economic benefits is probable

(iii) It is possible to make a reliable estimate of the amount

Effect on the financial statements

For the year ended 31 December 20X0:

- A provision of $1,242,000 (2,000,000 × 0.621) is reported as a liability.

- A non-current asset of $1,242,000 is also recognised. The provision results in a corresponding asset because the expenditure gives the company access to an inflow of resources embodying future economic benefits; there is no effect on profit or loss for the year.

For the year ended 31 December 20X1:

- Depreciation of $248,400 (1,242,000 × 20%) is charged to profit or loss. The non-current asset is depreciated over its remaining useful economic life of five years from 31 December 20X0 (the site will cease to produce output on 31 December 20X5).

- Therefore at 31 December 20X1 the carrying amount of the non-current asset will be $993,600 (1,242,000 − 248,400).

- At 31 December 20X1 the provision will be $1,366,000 (2,000,000 × 0.683).

- The increase in the provision of $124,000 (1,366,000 − 1,242,000) is recognised in profit or loss as a finance cost. This arises due to the unwinding of the discount.

18 Financial assets and liabilities

(a)

	$
Issue costs	120,000
Interest $6,000,000 × 3.5% × 7	1,470,000
Premium on redemption	1,100,000
Total finance cost	2,690,000

(b) The premium on redemption of the loan notes represents a finance cost. The effective rate of interest must be applied so that the debt is measured at amortised cost (IFRS 9: para. 4.2.1).

At the time of issue, the loan notes are recognised at their net proceeds of $599,800 (600,000 − 200).

The finance cost for the year ended 31 December 20X4 is calculated as follows.

	$
1.1.20X3 Proceeds of issue (600,000 − 200)	599,800
Interest at 12%	71,976
Balance 31.12.20X3	671,776
Interest at 12%	80,613
Balance at 31.12.210X4	752,389

The finance cost for the year ended 31.12.20X4 is $80,613.

(c)

> **Top tip.** The method to use here is to find the present value of the principal value of the bond, $500,000 (10,000 × $50) and the interest payments of $25,000 annually (5% × $500,000) at the market rate for non-convertible bonds of 6%, using the discount factors. The difference between this total and the principal amount of $500,000 is the equity element.

	$
Present value of principal $500,000 × 0.747	373,500
Present value of interest $25,000 × 4.212	105,300
Liability value	478,800
Principal amount	500,000
Equity element	21,200

19 Alpha

(a) **Creative accounting**, the manipulation of figures for a desired result, takes many forms. Off-balance sheet finance is a major type of creative accounting and it probably has the most serious implications.

It is very rare for a company, its directors or employees to manipulate results for the purpose of fraud. The major consideration is usually the effect the results will have on the share price of the company. If the share price falls, the company becomes vulnerable to takeover. Analysts, brokers and economists, whose opinions affect the stock markets, are often perceived as having an outlook which is both short-term and superficial. Consequently, companies will attempt to produce the results the market expects or wants. The companies will aim for steady progress in a few key numbers and ratios and they will aim to meet the market's stated expectation.

The number of methods available for creative accounting and the determination and imagination of those who wish to perpetrate such acts are endless. It has been seen in the past that, wherever an accounting standard or law closes a loophole, another one is found. This has produced a change of approach in regulators and standard setters, towards general principles rather than detailed rules.

Here are a few examples of creative accounting.

(i) **Income recognition and cut-off**
Manipulation of cut-off is relatively straightforward. For instance a company may delay invoicing in order to move revenue into the following year.

(ii) **Revaluations**
The optional nature of the revaluation of non-current assets leaves such practices open to manipulation. The choice of whether to revalue can have a significant impact on a company's statement of financial position.

(iii) **Window dressing**
This is where transactions are passed through the books at the year end to make figures look better, but in fact they have not taken place and are often reversed after the year end. An example is where cheques are written to creditors, entered in the cash book, but not sent out until well after the year end.

(iv) **Change of accounting policies**
This tends to be a last resort because companies which change accounting policies know they will not be able to do so again for some time. The effect in the year of change can be substantial and prime candidates for such treatment are depreciation, inventory valuation, changes from current cost to historical cost (practised frequently by privatised public utilities) and foreign currency losses.

(v) **Manipulation of accruals, prepayments and contingencies**
These figures can often be very subjective, particularly contingencies. In the case of impending legal action, for example, a contingent liability is difficult to estimate, the case may be far off and the lawyers cannot give any indication of likely success, or failure. In such cases companies will often only disclose the possibility of such a liability, even though the eventual costs may be substantial.

(b) 'Faithful representation' requires that transactions and other events should be accounted for and presented in accordance with their substance and financial reality and not merely with their legal form.

This is a very important concept and it has been used to determine accounting treatment in financial statements through accounting standards and so prevent off balance sheet transactions.

(i) **Group accounting** is perhaps the most important area of off balance sheet finance which has been prevented by the application of this concept.

The most important point is that the definition of a subsidiary (under IAS 27 and IFRS 10) is based upon the **principle of control rather than purely ownership.** Where an entity is controlled by another, the controlling entity can ensure that the benefits accrue to itself and not to other parties. Similarly, one of the circumstances where a subsidiary may be excluded from consolidation is where there are severe long-term restrictions that prevent effective control.

(ii) Finance leases and their accounting treatment under IAS 17 *Leases* are another example.

Operating leases do not really pose an accounting problem. The lessee pays amounts periodically to the lessor and these are charged to profit or loss. The lessor treats the leased asset as a non-current asset and depreciates it in the normal way. Rentals received from the lessee are credited to profit or loss in the lessor's books.

For assets held under **finance leases** this accounting treatment would not disclose the reality of the situation. If a lessor leases out an asset on a finance lease, the asset will probably never be seen on his premises or used in his business again. It would be inappropriate for a lessor to record such an asset as a non-current asset. In reality, what he owns is a stream of cash flows receivable from the lessee. The asset is a receivable rather than a non-current asset.

Similarly, a lessee may use a finance lease to fund the 'acquisition' of a major asset which he will then use in his business perhaps for many years. The substance of the transaction is that he has acquired a non-current asset, and this is reflected in the accounting treatment prescribed by IAS 17, even though in law the lessee may never become the owner of the asset.

(iii) With regard to **measurement or disclosure of current assets**, a common example where the distinction between financial reality and legal form is relevant are sale and repurchase agreements. These are arrangements under which the company sells an asset to another person on terms that allow the company to repurchase the asset in certain circumstances. A common example of such a transaction is the sale and repurchase of maturing whisky inventories. The key question is whether the transaction is a straightforward sale, or whether it is, in effect, a secured loan. It is necessary to look at the arrangement to determine who has the rights to the economic benefits that the asset generates, and the terms on which the asset is to be repurchased.

If the seller has the right to the benefits of the use of the asset, and the repurchase terms are such that the repurchase is likely to take place, the transaction should be accounted for as a loan.

Another example is the factoring of **trade receivables**. Where debts are factored, the original creditor sells the receivables to the factor. The sales price may be fixed at the outset or may be adjusted later. It is also common for the factor to offer a credit facility that allows the seller to draw upon a proportion of the amounts owed.

In order to determine the correct accounting treatment it is necessary to consider whether the benefit of the receivables has been passed on to the factor, or whether the factor is, in effect, providing a loan on the security of the receivables. If the seller has to pay interest on the difference between the amounts advanced to him and the amounts that the factor has received, and if the seller bears the risks of non-payment by the debtor, then the indications would be that the transaction is, in effect, a loan.

(c) (i) The Finance Director may be right in believing that renewing the non-current assets of the company will contribute to generating higher earnings and hence improved earnings per share. However, this will not happen immediately as the assets will need to have been in operation for at least a year for results to be apparent. Earnings will be higher because of the loan being at a commercially unrealistic rate, namely 5% instead of 9%.

As regards gearing, the Finance Director may well wish to classify the convertible loan stock as equity rather than debt; thus gearing will be lower. He may argue that because the loan is very likely to be converted into shares, the finance should be treated as equity rather than as debt.

(ii) IAS 33 *Earnings per share* requires the calculation of **basic earnings per share** (para. 9). The Finance Director believes that the convertible loan he is proposing will not affect EPS and that an interest cost of 5% will not impact heavily on gearing.

However, IAS 32 will require the interest cost to be based on 9% and IAS 33 also requires the calculation and disclosure of **diluted EPS** (IAS 32: paras. 28–32).

The need to disclose diluted earnings per share arose because of the limited value of a basic EPS figure when a company is financed partly by convertible debt. Because the right to convert carries benefits, it is usual that the interest rate on the debt is lower than on straight debt. Calculation of EPS on the assumption that the debt is non-convertible can, therefore, be misleading since:

(1) Current EPS is higher than it would be under straight debt

(2) On conversion, EPS will fall – diluted EPS provides some information about the extent of this future reduction, and warning shareholders of the reduction which will happen in the future

IAS 32 *Financial instruments: presentation* affects the proposed scheme in that IAS 32 requires that convertible loans such as this should be split in the statement of financial position and presented partly as equity and partly as debt. Thus the company's gearing will probably increase as the convertible loan cannot be 'hidden' in equity.

20 Jenson Co

> **Tutorial note.** This is an important subject and it is closely linked with the IASB's *Conceptual Framework*. You need to use your imagination to come up with examples in (b).

(a) IFRS 15 *Revenue from contracts with customers* defines a performance obligation as a promise in a contract with a customer to transfer to the customer goods and/or services (App. A). A performance obligation is satisfied when the customer obtains control of the asset.

Each good or service that is **distinct** is treated as a separate performance obligation and revenue is recognised as performance obligations are satisfied. A contract can include a number of separate performance obligations.

A performance obligation can be satisfied at a point in time, such as a contract for the sale of goods, or satisfied over time, as in a construction contract. When a performance obligation is satisfied over time, an entity must allocate revenue according to the amount of the performance obligation that has been satisfied during a period.

The IASB *Conceptual Framework* defines income and expenses in terms of increases in economic benefits (income) and outflow or depletion of assets (expenses), not in terms of an earnings or matching process (paras. 4.29–4.35). The statement of financial position thus assumes primary importance in the recognition of earnings and profits. Income **can only be recognised** if there is an **increase** in the equity (ie net assets) of an entity not resulting from contributions from owners. Similarly, an expense is recognised if there is a **decrease** in the ownership interest of an entity not resulting from distributions to owners. Thus income arises from recognition of assets and derecognition of liabilities, and expenses arise from derecognition of assets and recognition of liabilities. The IASB explains that it is not possible to reverse this definitional process, ie by defining assets and liabilities in terms of income and expenses, because it has not been possible to formulate robust enough base definitions of income and expenses (partly because the choice of critical event can be subjective). Nevertheless commentators often attempt to link the two approaches by asserting that **sufficient evidence** for recognition or derecognition will be met at the critical event in the operating cycle.

BPP LEARNING MEDIA

(b) (i) This agreement is worded as a **sale**, but it is a repurchase agreement with a call option that is likely to be exercised and a repurchase price that is above the original sale price. It is therefore accounted for as a **financing arrangement**. Jenson Co should continue to recognise the inventory in the statement of financial position and should treat the receipt from Lauda Co as a loan, not revenue. Finance costs will be charged to profit or loss of $35,000 × 12% × 9/12 = $3,150.

(ii) The franchise agreement represents a performance obligation satisfied over time, so the initial fee of $50,000 should be spread evenly over the term of the franchise. This will give revenue of $10,000 in year 1 and $15,000 thereafter. The profit will therefore be 20% for year 1 and approximately 46% for years 2–5.

(iii) Jenson Co has received payment for 24 publications but only six have been despatched. So it has satisfied six out of 24 performance obligations. It can therefore recognise revenue of $60,000 (240,000 × 6/24) and the remaining $180,000 should be presented as a liability.

21 Trontacc

(a) Treatment of construction contracts (contracts where performance obligations are satisfied over time) in the statement of financial position of Trontacc Co at 30 September 20X7.

	Aspire $'000	Bigga $'000	Construct $'000	Total $'000
Contract asset (Note 1)	80	–	–	80
Trade receivables (Note 2)	–	–	–	–
Contract liabilities (Note 1)	–	(25)	(45)	(70)

Notes

1

	Aspire $'000	Bigga $'000	Construct $'000
Contract assets/liabilities			
Contract costs incurred	500	550	320
Recognised profits less losses	120	(100)	35
	620	450	355
Invoices raised to date	(540)	(475)	(400)
	80	(25)	(45)

2

	A $'000	B $'000	C $'000
Trade receivables			
Invoices raised to date	540	475	400
Less cash received	(540)	(475)	(400)
	–	–	–

(b) Treatment of construction contracts in the statement of profit or loss of Trontacc Co for the year ended 30 September 20X7

	Contract			
	Aspire $'000 (W1)	Bigga $'000 (W2)	Construct $'000 (W3)	Total $'000
Revenue	600	500	350	1,450
Expenses	(480)	(550)	(315)	(1,345)
Expected loss	–	(50)	–	(50)
Gross profit/(loss)	120	(100)	35	55

Workings

1   *Contract Aspire*

	$'000
Statement of profit or loss	
Revenue (60% × 1,000)	600
Expenses (60% of 800)	(480)
Gross profit	120

2   *Contract Bigga*

	$'000
Statement of profit or loss	
Revenue (50% × 1,000)	500
Expenses (all costs to date)	(550)
Expected losses	(50)
Gross profit	(100)

3   *Contract Construct*

	$'000
Statement of profit or loss	
Revenue (35% × 1,000)	350
Expenses (35% × 900)	(315)
Gross profit	35

22 Crayzee Co

	Maryhill bypass	*Rottenrow centre*
	$'000	$'000
Revenue	2,800	3,000
Profit/(loss) (W1)	622	(100)
Cost of sales	2,178	3,100
Current liabilities		
Contract liabilities (W2)	578	600

Workings

1   Maryhill: $(9,000 - (1,400 + 5,600)) \times \dfrac{2,800}{9,000} = 622$

Rottenrow: $8,000 - (2,900 + 5,200) = (100)$

2

	Maryhill	*Rottenrow*
	$'000	$'000
Costs incurred to date	1,400	2,900
Recognised profits/(losses)	622	(100)
Amounts invoiced	(2,600)	(3,400)
	(578)	(600)

23 Telenorth Co

(a) (i)   TELENORTH CO
        STATEMENT OF PROFIT OR LOSS FOR THE YEAR ENDED 30 SEPTEMBER 20X1

	$'000
Revenue	283,460
Cost of sales (W1)	(155,170)
Gross profit	128,290
Other income	1,500
Distribution costs	(22,300)
Administrative expenses (W2)	(44,600)
Finance costs: (W10)	(1,560)
Profit before tax	61,330
Income tax expense (W9)	(24,600)
Profit for the year	36,730

    (ii)   TELENORTH CO
         STATEMENT OF FINANCIAL POSITION AS AT 30 SEPTEMBER 20X1

	$'000	$'000
Assets		
Non-current assets		
Property, plant and equipment (W3)		83,440
Investments		34,500
		117,940
Current assets		
Inventories (W4)	16,680	
Trade receivables	35,700	
		52,380
Total assets		170,320
Equity and liabilities		
Equity		
Ordinary shares of $1 each (W7)		30,000
Revaluation surplus 3,400 – 1,000		2,400
Share premium (W7)		16,000
Retained earnings (W8)		48,890
		97,290
Non-current liabilities		
8% preference shares	12,000	
6% loan notes	10,000	
Deferred tax: 5,200 + 2,200	7,400	
		29,400
Current liabilities		
Trade and other payables (W5)	18,070	
Current tax payable	23,400	
Preference dividend payable (W6)	480	
Bank overdraft	1,680	
		43,630
Total equity and liabilities		170,320

Workings

1   *Cost of sales*

	$'000
Opening inventory	12,400
Purchases	147,200
	159,600
Closing inventory (W4)	(16,680)
	142,920
Depreciation of leasehold and plant (W3)	12,250
	155,170

2   *Administrative expenses*

	$'000
Per question	34,440
Depreciation of computer system (W3)	10,160
	44,600

3   *Property, plant and equipment*

	Cost	Depn	Carrying amount
	$'000	$'000	$'000
Leasehold	56,250	20,250*	36,000
Plant and equipment	55,000	22,800*	32,200
Computer system	35,000	19,760*	15,240
			83,440

*Depreciation charge:

Leasehold: 56,250 / 25 years	2,250
Plant: (55,000 – 5,000)/5 years	10,000
Charge cost of sales	12,250

Computer equipment: charged to administration (35m – 9.6m) × 40%	10,160

4   *Closing inventory*

No inventory count took place at the year end. To arrive at the figure for closing inventory, the count needs to be adjusted for the movements between 30 September and 4 October, making appropriate adjustments for mark ups.

	$'000
Balance as at 4 October 20X1	16,000
Normal sales at cost: $1.4m × 100/140	1,000
Sale or return at cost: 650,000 × 100/130	500
Less goods received at cost	(820)
Adjusted inventory value	16,680

5   *Current liabilities*

	$'000
Trade and other payables	
Per question	17,770
Interest on loan note	300
	18,070

6   *Dividend payable*

	$'000
Preference: ($12m × 8%) – 480	480

7 *Share capital and suspense account*

Elimination of suspense account:

	Dr $'000	Cr $'000
Suspense account (per trial balance)	26,000	
Directors' options: share capital (4m at $1)		4,000
share premium (4m at $1)		4,000
Rights issue: $\frac{20m + 4m}{4}$ share capital		6,000
Share premium 6m × (3 − 1)		12,000
	26,000	26,000

Share capital: $20m + $4m + $6m = $30m

Share premium: $4m + $12m = $16m

8 *Retained earnings*

	$'000
As at 1 October 20X0	14,160
Net profit for the year (Part (a)(i))	36,730
Dividend: ordinary	(2,000)
	48,890

9 *Income tax*

	$'000	$'000
Provision for year		23,400
Increase in deferred tax provision	2,200	
Less charged to revaluation surplus	(1,000)	
		1,200
		24,600

10 *Finance costs*

	$'000
8% Preference shares	960
6% Loan notes	600
	1,560

(b) TELENORTH CO
EARNINGS PER SHARE FOR THE YEAR TO 30 SEPTEMBER 20X1

Date	Narrative	Shares '000	Time	Bonus fraction	Weighted average
1.10.X0	Share b/f	20,000			
1.10.X0	Options exercised	4,000			
		24,000	9/12	4/3.80 (W)	18,947
1.7.X1	Rights issue (1/4)	6,000			
		30,000	3/12		7,500
					26,447

Workings

Calculation of theoretical ex-rights price:

	$
4 shares @ $4	16
1 share @ $3	3
	19

∴ Theoretical ex-rights price = $\frac{19}{5}$ = $3.80

$$\therefore \text{Bonus fraction} = \frac{4.00}{3.80}$$

$$\text{EPS} = \frac{36,730}{26,447} = \$1.39$$

24 Bulwell Aggregates Co

STATEMENTS OF PROFIT OR LOSS (EXTRACTS)

	20X1 $	20X2 $	20X3 $	20X4 $
Finance cost	11,250	8,063	4,078	
Depreciation on lorries	13,500	13,500	13,500	13,500

STATEMENTS OF FINANCIAL POSITION AT 31 DECEMBER (EXTRACTS)

	20X1 $	20X2 $	20X3 $	20X4 $
Non-current assets				
Right-of-use assets	54,000	54,000	54,000	54,000
depreciation	12,500	25,000	37,500	50,000
	41,500	29,000	16,500	4,000
Current liabilities				
Lease obligations	15,937*	16,313	–	–
Non-current liabilities				
Lease obligations	16,313	–	–	–

*(24,000 – 8,063)

Working

	$
Lease	
Original measurement of right-of-use asset	54,000
Deposit	(9,000)
Balance 1.1.20X1 (lease liability)	45,000
Interest 25%	11,250
Payment 31.12.20X1	(24,000)
Balance 31.12.20X1	32,250
Interest 25%	8,063
Payment 31.12.20X2	(24,000)
Balance 31.12.20X2	16,313
Interest 25%	4,078
Payment 31.12.20X3	(20,391)
	–

25 Lis

The right-of-use asset should be capitalised in the statement of financial position. The asset should be depreciated over the shorter of its useful life (five years) and the lease term (six years).

A lease liability will be shown in the statement of financial position reduced by lease payments made in advance and increased by interest calculated using the interest rate implicit in the lease, 12.5%.

The lease liability will initially be recognised at $65,586. The right-of-use asset will be measured at $84,006 (the initial measurement of $65,586 + the first payment of $18,420 made at commencement of the lease).

Financial statement extracts

STATEMENT OF PROFIT OR LOSS (extract)	$
Depreciation (W1)	16,801
Finance costs (W2)	8,198

STATEMENT OF FINANCIAL POSITION (extract)	$

Non-current assets
Right-of-use asset (W1)	67,205

Non-current liabilities
Lease liability (W2)	55,364

Current liabilities
Lease liability (W2) (73,784 – 55,364)	18,420

Workings

1   *Carrying amount of right-of-use asset*

	$
Initial measurement of right-of-use asset	65,586
Initial lease liability	18,420
Rental payment at commencement of lease	84,006
Depreciation of asset: $84,006 / 5 years useful life	16,801
Carrying amount at year end ($84,006 – $16,801)	67,205

The asset is depreciated over the shorter of its useful life (five years) and lease term (six years).

2   *Lease liability*

		$
1.1.X3	Initial measurement of lease liability	65,586
1.1.X3 – 31.12.X3	Interest at 12.5% ($65,586 × 12.5%)	8,198
31.12.X3	**Lease liability c/d**	**73,784**
1.1.X4	Payment in advance	(18,420)
1.1.X4	**Lease liability c/d after next instalment**	**55,364**

The interest element ($8,198) of the current liability can also be shown separately as interest payable.

Tutorial note. If the lease payments were in arrears instead of in advance, the calculation of the lease liability would differ to that given above. The initial lease liability would be higher at $74,672, being six payments of $18,420 discounted using a discount rate of 12.5%, as the first lease lease payment, excluded from the answer above because it is paud at commencement of the lease, would be included. The lease liability would then be calculated as follows:

Lease payments are made in arrears:

		$
1.1.X3	Initial measurement of lease liability	74,672
1.1.X3 – 31.12.X3	Interest at 12.5% ($65,586 × 12.5%)	9,334
31.12.X3	Instalment in arrears	(18,420)
31.12.X3	**Lease liability c/d**	**65,586**
1.1.X4-31.12.X4	Interest at 12.5%	8,198
1.1.X4	Installment in arrears	(18,420)
1.1.X4	**Lease liability due in more than 1 year**	**55,364**

26 Carpati Co

Deferred tax liability

	20X6
	$'000
Accelerated tax depreciation (W1)	186
Revaluation (W2)*	252
	438

*The deferred tax on the revaluation gain will be charged to the revaluation surplus as IAS 12 requires deferred tax on gains recognised in other comprehensive income to be charged or credited to other comprehensive income.

Workings

1 Tax depreciation

	$'000	$'000
At 30 September 20X6:		
Carrying amount		1,185
Tax base:		
At 1 October 20X5	405	
Expenditure in year	290	
	695	
Less tax depreciation (25%)	(174)	
		(521)
Cumulative temporary difference		664
@ 28% =		186

2 Revaluation surplus

Temporary difference ($1,500,000 − $600,000) @ 28% = $252,000

> **Tutorial note.** IAS 12 requires the deferred tax liability on revaluations to be recognised **even if** the entity does not intend to dispose of the asset since the value of the asset is recovered through use which generates taxable income in excess of tax depreciation allowable.

27 Pilum Co

(a) **Earnings per share**

	$
Profit before tax	2,530,000
Less income tax expense	(1,127,000)
Profit for the year	1,403,000
Less preference dividends	(276,000)
Earnings	1,127,000
Earnings per share =	1,127,000
	4,120,000
	$0.27

(b) The first step is to calculate the theoretical ex-rights price. Consider the holder of 5 shares.

	No.	$
Before rights issue	5	8.90
Rights issue	1	1.20
After rights issue	6	10.10

The theoretical ex-rights price is therefore $10.10 / 6 = $1.68.

The number of shares in issue before the rights issue must be multiplied by the fraction:

$$\frac{\text{Fair value immediately before exercise of rights}}{\text{theoretical ex-rights price}} = \frac{\$1.78}{\$1.68}$$

Weighted average number of shares in issue during the year:

Date	Narrative	Shares	Time period	Bonus fraction	Total
1.1.X4	b/d	4,120,000	× 9/12	1.78/1.68	3,273,929
1.10.X4	Rights issue	824,000			
		4,944,000	× 3/12		1,236,000
					4,509,929

$$\text{EPS} = \frac{\$1,127,000}{4,509,929}$$

$$= \$0.25$$

(c) The maximum number of shares into which the loan stock could be converted is 90% × 1,500,000 = 1,350,000. The calculation of diluted EPS should be based on the assumption that such a conversion actually took place on 1 January 20X4. Shares in issue during the year would then have numbered (4,120,000 + 1,350,000) = 5,470,000 and revised earnings would be:

	$	$
Earnings from (a) above		1,127,000
Interest saved by conversion (1,500,000 × 10%)	150,000	
Less attributable tax (150,000 × 30%)	(45,000)	
		105,000
		1,232,000

$$\therefore \text{Diluted EPS} = \frac{1,232,000}{5,470,000}$$

$$= \$0.23$$

28 Biggerbuys Co

REPORT

To: The bankers of Biggerbuys Co
From: Consultant management accountant
Subject: Financial performance 20X7 – 20X9
Date: 30 October 20X9

1   Introduction

1.1   In accordance with your instructions, I set out below a review of the entity's financial performance over the last three years.

1.2   The main focus of this report is on the reasons for the increase in the level of bank loans.

1.3   Appropriate accounting ratios are included in the attached appendix.

2   Bank lending

2.1   The main reason for the steep increase in bank lending is due to the entity not generating sufficient cash from its operating activities over the past three years.

2.2   For the year ended 30 June 20X8, the entity had a **net cash deficiency on operating activities** of $18m.

2.3 In addition, for at least the past two years, the cash generated from operating activities has not been sufficient to cover interest payable. Therefore those payments, together with tax and dividends, have had to be covered by borrowings.

2.4 As at 30 June 20X9, bank borrowings were $610m out of a total facility of $630m. Payment of the proposed dividends alone would increase the borrowings to the limit.

3 Operating review

3.1 Although revenue has been rising steadily over the period, operating profit has remained almost static.

3.2 Over this period the profit margin has risen, but not as much as would be expected. The cost of sales have risen in almost the same proportion as sales. This may be due to increased costs of raw materials, as inventories have risen steeply; but the turnover of inventory has been falling or static over the same period.

3.3 There has also been a large increase in trade receivables. Both the increase in inventories and trade receivables have had to be financed out of operating activities leading to the present pressure on borrowings.

3.4 Although the number of days sales in trade receivables has fallen steadily over the period, the trade receivables at the end of June 20X9 still represent nearly a year's credit sales. This is excessive and seems to imply a poor credit control policy, even taking into account the extended credit terms being granted by the company.

4 Recommendations

4.1 The entity needs to undertake an urgent review of its credit terms in order to reduce the levels of trade receivables.

4.2 Inventory levels are also extremely high (representing over four months' sales) and should be reviewed.

4.3 Operating costs also need to be kept under control in order to generate more cash from sales.

Please contact me if you need any further information.

Signed: An Accountant

Appendix: Accounting ratios

		20X7	20X8	20X9
1	Profit margin			
	$\dfrac{\text{Profit before interest}}{\text{Revenue}} \times 100$	$\dfrac{(50+45)}{1,850} \times 100\%$	$\dfrac{(60+60)}{2,200} \times 100\%$	$\dfrac{(50+90)}{2,500} \times 100\%$
		= 5.1%	= 5.5%	= 5.6%
2	Operating costs			
	$\dfrac{\text{Other operating costs}}{\text{Revenue}} \times 100$	$\dfrac{550}{1,850} \times 100\%$	$\dfrac{640}{2,200} \times 100\%$	$\dfrac{700}{2,500} \times 100\%$
		= 29.7%	= 29.1%	= 28.0%
3	Inventory turnover			
	$\dfrac{\text{Cost of sales}}{\text{Inventory}}$	$\dfrac{1,250}{400}$	$\dfrac{1,500}{540}$	$\dfrac{1,750}{620}$
		= 3.1 times	= 2.8 times	= 2.8 times
4	Trade receivables turnover			
	$\dfrac{\text{Trade receivables}}{\text{Credit sales}} \times 365$	$\dfrac{492}{(300+45)} \times 365$	$\dfrac{550}{(400+60)} \times 365$	$\dfrac{633}{(600+90)} \times 365$
		= 523 days	= 436 days	= 334 days

	20X7	20X8	20X9
5 Cash generated from operations			
		20X8	20X9
		$m	$m
Profit before interest		120	140
Depreciation		60	70
Increase in inventory		(140)	(80)
Increase in trade receivables		(58)	(83)
Increase in trade payables		–	10
		(18)	57

6 ROCE

	20X7	20X8	20X9
$\dfrac{\text{Profit before interest}}{\text{Net assets} + \text{borrowings}} \times 100\%$	$\dfrac{95}{(372+520)} \times 100\%$	$\dfrac{120}{(382+720)} \times 100\%$	$\dfrac{140}{(372+930)} \times 100\%$
	= 10.6%	= 10.9%	= 10.7%

7 Interest cover

	20X7	20X8	20X9
$\dfrac{\text{Profit before interest}}{\text{Interest payable}}$	$\dfrac{95}{25}$	$\dfrac{120}{60}$	$\dfrac{140}{110}$
	= 3.8	= 2.0	= 1.3

8 Gearing

	20X7	20X8	20X9
$\dfrac{\text{Borrowings}}{\text{Net assets} + \text{borrowings}}$	$\dfrac{520}{892}$	$\dfrac{720}{1,102}$	$\dfrac{930}{1,302}$
	= 58.3%	= 65.3%	= 71.4%

9 Asset turnover

	20X7	20X8	20X9
$\dfrac{\text{Revenue}}{\text{Net assets} + \text{borrowings}}$	$\dfrac{1,850}{892}$	$\dfrac{2,200}{1,102}$	$\dfrac{2,500}{1,302}$
	= 2.1 times	= 2.0 times	= 1.9 times

29 Webster Co

> **Top tip.** This question is at the upper end of the scale of difficulty which you are likely to encounter, particularly part (a). Study the answer carefully.

(a)   STATEMENTS OF PROFIT OR LOSS (RESTATED)

	Cole Co		Darwin Co	
	$'000	$'000	$'000	$'000
Revenue (3,000 – 125) (Note 1)		2,875		4,400
Opening inventory	450		720	
Purchases (Note 2)	2,055		3,080	
Closing inventory	(540)		(850)	
		1,965		2,950
Gross profit		910		1,450
Operating expenses	480		964	
Depreciation (Note 3)	40		(120)	
Loan interest	80		–	
Overdraft interest (W3)	15		–	
		(615)		(844)
Profit for the year		295		606

STATEMENT OF FINANCIAL POSITION (RESTATED)

	Cole Co		Darwin Co	
	$'000	$'000	$'000	$'000
Assets				
Non-current assets				
Property, plant, equipment (W1)		3,100		2,620
Current assets				
Inventories	540		850	
Trade receivables (W2)	897		750	
Cash and cash equivalents (W3)	–		60	
		1,437		1,660
		4,537		4,280
Equity and liabilities				
Equity shares ($1)		1,000		500
Revaluation surplus (800 – 40)		760		700
Retained earnings to 31 March 20X9				
(684 + 295 + 40) / (1,912 + 606)		1,019		2,518
		2,779		3,718
Non current liabilities				
10% loan note		800		–
Current liabilities				
Trade payables (W4)		163		562
Overdraft (W3)		795		–
		4,537		4,280

Workings

1   *Non-current assets*

		Cost/valuation	Depreciation	Carrying amount
		$'000	$'000	$'000
Cole Co:	property	2,000	100	1,900
	plant	6,000	4,800	1,200
				3,100
Darwin Co:	property	2,000	100	1,900
	plant (3,000 – 600)	2,400	1,680	720
				2,620

2   *Trade receivables*
Cole Co: 522 + 375 (Note 1) = 897

3   *Cash and cash equivalents*

	Cole	Darwin
	$'000	$'000
As stated	20	(550)
Reversal of sale (Note 1)	(500)	
Payment for purchases (Note 2)	(300)	
Payment for plant (Note 3)		600
Payment/saving of interest to statement of financial position	15	10
	(795)	60

4   *Trade payables*
Cole Co 438 – 275 (Note 2) = 163

Tutorial notes

1 Sale to Brander Co is at gross margin 40%, therefore the cost of sale is $500 × 60% = $300.

   Had a normal margin of 20% applied, the cost of this sale would represent 80% of the selling price. The normal selling price would be $\frac{300}{0.8}$ = $375.

   Sales and receivables would reduce by $125 and the proceeds of $500 would not have been received.

2 Purchase of goods from Advent Co on normal terms would have increased purchases by $25. Using the normal credit period would mean these goods would have been paid for by the year end, increasing the overdraft and reducing trade payables.

3 The plant bought in February 20X9 has not yet generated income for Darwin Co, so it is sensible to ignore it in the acquisition comparison.

   The effects are:

   - Cost of plant – $600, overdraft affected
   - Depreciation reduced $600 × 20% = $120

   The depreciation charged changes:

	Cole Co $'000	Darwin Co $'000
As stated for property	(60)	
Depreciation on revaluation	100	
Reduction (above)		(120)
	40 increase	(120) (decrease)

(b)

Ratios	Cole Co		Darwin Co	
Return on capital employed:	(295 + 80) / (2,779+800)	= 10.5%	606/3,718	= 16.3%
Asset turnover	2,875 / (4,537 – 958)	= 0.8 times	4,400/(4,280 – 562)	= 1.2 times
Gross profit %	910/2,875	= 31.7%	(unchanged)	= 33%
Net profit %	295/2,875	= 10.3%	606/4,400	= 13.8%
Receivables collection (days)	897/2,875 × 365	= 114	(unchanged)	= 62
Payables period (days)	163/2,055 × 365	= 29	(unchanged)	= 67

Using the unadjusted figures, Cole Co would be preferred, as its key ratios given are better than those of Darwin Co. Cole Co achieves better profitability due to greater unit margins. Both companies have poor asset turnover implying under-utilisation or inefficient methods.

Both companies manage working capital in a similar fashion. Webster Co should examine liquidity ratios:

Cole Co: 1,082/438 = 2.5
Darwin Co: 1,600/1,112 = 1.4

The acid test ratio of Cole Co is 1.23 whereas Darwin Co's is 0.67.

Using the adjusted accounts, the above position is reversed showing Darwin Co to be more profitable and to manage its assets more efficiently. Cole Co's true liquidity position is not so healthy – Cole Co controls receivables poorly and appears to pay suppliers earlier.

Darwin Co's poor liquidity position is probably due to financing non-current assets from its overdraft. Alternative refinancing would be beneficial.

Cole Co's parent company has produced an initially favourable set of ratios by creating favourable payment terms and trading conditions, and Darwin Co's original ratios were distorted by revaluations and the timing of new plant purchases.

Other factors to consider include:

(i) The asking price
(ii) The future prospects, profits and cash flow forecasts
(iii) The state of forward order books
(iv) The quality of the management and labour force
(v) Other possible acquisitions

30 Xpand Co

This is a recent question and looks at the financial statements from the viewpoint of an acquirer. There are 6 marks for the adjustments and ratios and 9 for the analysis.

(a) Adjusted statement of profit or loss for Hydan Co:

	$'000
Revenue	70,000
Cost of sales (45,000/0.9 (i))	(50,000)
Gross profit	20,000
Operating costs	(7,000)
Directors salaries (ii)	(2,500)
Loan interest (10% × 10,000 (iii))	(1,000)
Profit before tax	9,500
Income tax expense	(3,000)
Profit for the year	6,500

The adjusted ratios, based on the statement of profit or loss as above, the equity of $30m and the replacement of the directors' loan accounts by a commercial loan are as follows:

Return on equity	((6,500/30,000) × 100)	21.7%
Net asset turnover	(70,000/(30,000 + 10,000))	1.75 times
Gross profit margin	((20,000/70,000) × 100)	28.6%
Net profit margin	((6,500/70,000) × 100)	9.3%

(b) The ratios based on the original summarised financial statements of Hydan Co show a very healthy picture, well above the sector average. Hydan Co has high gross and net profit margins and an impressive net asset turnover, giving a return on equity of more than twice the sector average. On the face of it, Hydan Co is trading very profitably and efficiently, keeping costs well under control.

However, when the financial statements are adjusted to show the likely picture post-acquisition, it becomes clear that Hydan Co has been to quite a large degree cushioned by the family and by the other family-owned companies. Removing the 10% discount Hydan enjoys on its purchases reduces the gross profit margin from 35.7% to 28.6%, slightly under the sector average.

If Xpand Co purchases Hydan Co, it will need to appoint a new board of directors and replace the directors' loan accounts with a commercial loan. Both of these expenses have up to now been subsidised by the family.

Adjusting further for the increased directors' remuneration and interest on the loan takes the net profit margin down from 20% to 9.3%, significantly below the sector average of 12%. The value of equity would not change significantly as a result of the acquisition, as the increase to $30m is compensated for by the reclassification of the loan as debt. The fall in the return on equity from 47.1% to 21.7% is therefore driven by the fall in net profit. However it is worth noting that 21.7% return on equity is not much below the sector average of 22%.

Xpand Co should take the view that if it acquires Hydan Co it will be acquiring a business that is performing slightly below the average for its sector. The impressive profitability pictured in the summarised financial statements is obviously not going to survive the acquisition. But Hydan Co will still be trading quite profitably and it could be that there are cost savings which were not considered necessary by the previous management but which could now be made, which will bring its performance into line with the average for its sector.

31 Dundee Co

Statement of cash flows for the year ended 31 March 20X7

	$m	$m
Cash flows from operating activities		
Profit before taxation	1,050	
Adjustments for:		
Depreciation	970	
Interest expense	250	
	2,270	
Decrease in inventories (W4)	100	
Increase in trade receivables (W4)	(400)	
Increase in trade payables (W4)	160	
Cash generated from operations	2,130	
Interest paid	(250)	
Income taxes paid (W3)	(210)	
Net cash from operating activities		1,670
Cash flow from investing activities		
Purchase of property, plant and equipment (W1)		(870)
Cash flows from financing activities		
Payment of lease liabilities (W3)	(450)	
Dividends paid	(300)	
Net cash used in financing activities		(750)
Net increase in cash and cash equivalents		50
Cash and cash equivalents at beginning of year		(205)
Cash and cash equivalents at end of year		(155)

Workings

1 Assets – Property, plant and equipment

	$'000
B/d	3,700
Depreciation	(970)
Right-of-use assets	600
Acquired for cash (β)	**870**
C/d	4,200

2 Equity

	Share capital	Retained earnings
	$'000	$'000
B/d	1,200	1,900
Profit for year		600
Dividend paid (per Q)	–	(300)
C/d	1,200	2,200

3 Liabilities

	Lease	Taxation
	$m	$m
B/d – (1,200 + 450) / (850 + 205)	1,650	1,055
Addition	600	
Charge for year		450
Cash paid (β)	(450)	(210)
C/d – (500 + 1,300) / (225 + 1,070)	1,800	1,295

4   Working capital changes

	Inventories $m	Trade receivables $m	Trade payables $m
b/d	1,600	1,800	1,090
Increase / (decrease)	(100)	400	160
	1,500	2,200	1,250

32 Elmgrove Co

(a)   STATEMENT OF CASH FLOWS FOR THE YEAR ENDED 31 MARCH 20X9

	$m	$m
Cash flows from operating activities		
Profit before taxation	109	
Adjustments for		
Loss on disposal	6	
Depreciation	43	
Interest income	(6)	
Interest expense	17	
	169	
Decrease in inventories (W4)	53	
Increase in trade receivables (W4)	(8)	
Increase in trade payables (W4)	56	
Cash generated from operations	270	
Interest paid (W3)	(13)	
Income taxes paid (W3)	(62)	
Net cash from operating activities		195
Cash flows from investing activities		
Purchase of property, plant and equipment (W1)	(165)	
Proceeds from sale of property, plant and equipment (28 – 6)	22	
Interest received	6	
Net cash used in investing activities		(137)
Cash flows from financing activities		
Proceeds from issuance of share capital (W2)	60	
Dividend paid	(32)	
Net cash from financing activities		28
Net increase in cash and cash equivalents		86
Cash and cash equivalents at beginning of the period		8
Cash and cash equivalents at end of the period		94

Workings

1   Assets – Property, plant and equipment

	$m
B/d	264
Depreciation	(43)
Disposal	(28)
Revaluation surplus	(31)
Cash additions (β)	**165**
C/d	327

2   Equity

	Share capital $m	Share premium $m	Revaluation surplus $m	Retained earnings $m
B/d	120	–	97	41
Debentures converted	50			
Surplus on disposal			(31)	
SPL				62
Cash received/(paid)	30	30	–	(32)
C/d	200	30	66	71

IAS 7 requires that investing and financing activities that do not require the use of cash, such as converting debt to equity, should be excluded from the statement of cash flows.

3   Liabilities

	Interest $m	Income tax $m
B/f	3	54
Finance costs	17	
Tax expense		47
Paid (β)	(13)	(62)
C/f	7	39

4   Working capital changes

	Inventories $m	Trade receivables $m	Trade payables $m
b/d	176	87	70
Increase / (decrease)	(53)	8	56
c/d	123	95	126

(b)   MEMO

To: Memorandum to the directors of Elmgrove Co
From: AN Accountant
Date: 1.4.20X9

Subject: Major benefits to the users of financial statements from the publication of statements of cash flows

The users of financial statements can basically be divided into the following groups.

(i)   Shareholders
(ii)   Management
(iii)   Creditors and lenders
(iv)   Employers

The needs of these groups are not identical and hence not all benefits listed below will be applicable to all users.

Benefits

(i)   Statements of cash flows direct attention to the survival of the entity which depends on its ability to generate cash.

(ii)   Statements of cash flows indicate the ability of an entity to repay its debts.

(iii)   They give information which can be used in the decision making and stewardship process.

(iv)   They are more easily understood than statements of profit or loss that depend on accounting conventions and concepts.

(v)   Statements of cash flows give a better means of comparison between different companies.

33 CPP and CCA

> **Tutorial note.** It is unlikely that a detailed computation will be asked for, but you must have an understanding of the principles of CPP and CCA, the differences between them and the ways in which they try to improve on HCA.

(a)   In accounting, the value of income and capital is measured in terms of money. In simple terms, profit is the difference between the closing and opening statement of financial position values (after adjustment for new sources of funds and applications such as dividend distribution). If, because of inflation, the value of net assets in the closing statement of financial position is shown at a higher monetary amount than net assets in the opening statement of financial position, a profit has been made. In traditional accounting, it is assumed that a monetary unit of $1 is a stable measurement; inflation removes this stability.

CPP accounting attempts to provide a more satisfactory method of valuing profit and capital by establishing a stable unit of monetary measurement, $1 of current purchasing power, as at the end of the accounting period under review.

A distinction is made between monetary items, and non-monetary items. In a period of inflation, keeping a monetary asset (eg trade receivables) results in a loss of purchasing power as the value of money erodes over time. Non-monetary assets, however, are assumed to maintain 'real' value over time, and these are converted into monetary units of current purchasing power as at the year end, by means of a suitable price index. The equity interest in the statement of financial position can be determined as a balancing item.

The profit or deficit for the year in CPP terms is found by converting sales, opening and closing inventory, purchases and other expenses into year-end units of $CPP. In addition, a profit on holding net monetary liabilities (or a loss on holding net monetary assets) is computed in arriving at the profit or deficit figure.

CPP arguably provides a more satisfactory system of accounting since transactions are expressed in terms of 'today's money' and similarly, the statement of financial position values are adjusted for inflation, so as to give users of financial information a set of figures with which they can:

(i)   Decide whether operating profits are satisfactory (profits due to inflation are eliminated)
(ii)   Obtain a better appreciation of the size and 'value' of the entity's assets

(b)   CPP and CCA accounting are different concepts, in that CPP accounting makes adjustments for general inflationary price changes, whereas CCA makes adjustments to allow for specific price movements (changes in the deprival value of assets). Specific price changes (in CCA) enable a company to determine whether the operating capability of a company has been maintained; it is not a restatement of price levels in terms of a common unit of money measurement. The two conventions use different concepts of capital maintenance (namely operating capability with CCA, and general purchasing power with CPP).

In addition CPP is based on the use of a general price index. In contrast, CCA only makes use of a specific price index where it is not possible to obtain the current value of an asset by other means (eg direct valuation).

(c)   In CCA, holding gains represent the difference between the historical cost of an asset and its current cost. If the asset is unsold, and appears in the statement of financial position of a company at current cost, there will be an 'unrealised' holding gain, which must be included in a current cost reserve. When the asset is eventually sold, the profit (equal to the sale price minus the historical cost) may be divided into:

(i)   An operating profit which would have been made if the cost of the asset were its current value

(ii)   A *realised* holding gain which has arisen because of the appreciation in value of the asset between the date of its acquisition and the date of its sale

34 Not-for-profit

There are two main areas in which the Department would be expected to monitor the performance of the school.

Although the school is a not-for-profit organisation, it still has to account for the funding it receives. It is spending taxpayers money so the government has a duty to ensure that it is delivering **value for money**. This is particularly important in the light of the criticisms that have been made.

The accounts kept by the school should be **regularly audited** to ensure that no financial mismanagement has occurred and it will be expected to prepare and implement budgets. The school should be expected to show some excess of **income over expenditure**, which will give it a surplus for emergencies, even if this will be lower than in a profit-making entity, and a number of accounting ratios can be use to monitor its performance.

Investor ratios such as ROCE will not be particularly appropriate but working capital ratios, such as payables days, will be important, as will liquidity ratios. The school may not be expected to make a profit, but it will be expected to remain **solvent**. Additional ratios, such as expenditure per pupil, can be calculated and compared to the same ratio for other schools in the area.

Value for money is composed of three elements – **economy, efficiency and effectiveness**. Financial performance can be monitored to assess economy and efficiency but in the case of a school the government will be most interested in effectiveness. This requires looking at the **non-financial indicators**.

The mission of the school, however it is worded, will be to maximise the educational attainment of its pupils and it will need to demonstrate that it is making progress in this direction. The basic measure of this is the external exam scores of its pupils and this can be directly compared to the performance of other schools, such as percentage of pupils achieving grade A–C in maths, etc. However, these scores need to be weighted to take account of the number of pupils from deprived backgrounds, such as those eligible for free school meals, and the number of pupils with English as a second language. More subjective measures could also be used, such as feedback from pupils and parents.

Bibliography

IFRS Foundation (2017) *IFRS* [Online]. Available at: http://eifrs.ifrs.org [Accessed 2017].

International Accounting Standards Board (1989) *Framework for the Preparation and Presentation of Financial Statements.* [Online]. Available from: http://eifrs.ifrs.org [Accessed 2017].

International Accounting Standards Board (2001) *Statement of Cash Flows IAS 7* [Online] Available from http://eifrs.ifrs.org [Accessed 2017]

International Accounting Standards Board (2001) *Income Taxes IAS 12* [Online] Available from http://eifrs.ifrs.org [Accessed 2017]

International Accounting Standards Board (2001) *Provisions, Contingent Liabilities and Contingent Assets IAS 37* [Online] Available from http://eifrs.ifrs.org [Accessed 2017]

International Accounting Standards Board (2003) *Property, Plant and Equipment IAS 16* [Online] Available from http://eifrs.ifrs.org [Accessed 2017]

International Accounting Standards Board (2003) *The Effects of Changes in Foreign Exchange Rates IAS 21* [Online] Available from http://eifrs.ifrs.org [Accessed 2017]

International Accounting Standards Board (2003) *Earnings per Share IAS 33* [Online] Available from http://eifrs.ifrs.org [Accessed 2017]

International Accounting Standards Board (2003) *Financial Instruments: Presentation IAS 32* [Online] Available from http://eifrs.ifrs.org [Accessed 2017]

International Accounting Standards Board (2003) *Inventories IAS 2* [Online] Available from http://eifrs.ifrs.org [Accessed 2017]

International Accounting Standards Board (2003) *Accounting policies, Changes in Accounting Estimates and Errors IAS 8* [Online] Available from http://eifrs.ifrs.org [Accessed 2017]

International Accounting Standards Board (2003) *Events after the Reporting Period IAS 10* [Online] Available from http://eifrs.ifrs.org [Accessed 2017]

International Accounting Standards Board (2004) *Impairment of Assets IAS 36* [Online] Available from http://eifrs.ifrs.org [Accessed 2017]

International Accounting Standards Board (2004) *Intangible Assets IAS 38* [Online] Available from http://eifrs.ifrs.org [Accessed 2017]

International Accounting Standards Board (2004) *Business Combinations IFRS 3* [Online] Available from http://eifrs.ifrs.org [Accessed 2017]

International Accounting Standards Board (2004) *Non-current Assets Held for Sale and Discontinued Operations IFRS 5* [Online] Available from http://eifrs.ifrs.org [Accessed 2017]

International Accounting Standards Board (2005) *Financial Instruments: Disclosures IFRS 7* [Online] Available from http://eifrs.ifrs.org [Accessed 2017]

International Accounting Standards Board (2007) *Borrowing Costs IAS 23* [Online] Available from http://eifrs.ifrs.org [Accessed 2017]

International Accounting Standards Board (2010) *Presentation of Financial Statements IAS 1* [Online] Available from http://eifrs.ifrs.org [Accessed 2017]

International Accounting Standards Board (2010) *Conceptual Framework for Financial Reporting.* [Online]. Available from: http://eifrs.ifrs.org [Accessed 2017].

International Accounting Standards Board (2010) *Consolidated Financial Statements IFRS 10* [Online] Available from http://eifrs.ifrs.org [Accessed 2017]

International Accounting Standards Board (2014) *Agriculture: Bearer Plants (Amendments to IAS 16 and IAS 41)* [Online]. Available from: http://eifrs.ifrs.org [Accessed 2017].

International Accounting Standards Board (2014) *Revenue from contracts with customers IFRS15* [Online]. Available from: http://eifrs.ifrs.org [Accessed 2017].

International Accounting Standards Board (2014) *Financial Instruments IFRS 9* [Online] Available from http://eifrs.ifrs.org [Accessed 2017]

International Accounting Standards Board (2016) *Due Process Handbook.* [Online]. Available from: http://eifrs.ifrs.org [Accessed 2017].

International Federation of Accountants (IFAC) (2013) *Public Sector Conceptual Framework Phase 1* [Online]. Available from: www.ifac.org/publications-resources [Accessed 2017].

International Public Sector Accounting Standards Board (2013) *Conceptual Framework for General Purpose Financial Reporting by Public Sector Entities.* [Online]. Available from: www.ipsasb.org/publications-resources [Accessed 2017].

International Public Sector Accounting Standards Board (2016) *Handbook of International Public Sector Accounting Pronouncements* [Online]. Available from: www.ipsasb.org/publications-resources [Accessed 2016].

Index

BPP
LEARNING MEDIA

Review Form – Financial Reporting (FR) (02/18)

Please help us to ensure that the ACCA learning materials we produce remain as accurate and user-friendly as possible. We cannot promise to answer every submission we receive, but we do promise that it will be read and taken into account when we update this Study Text.

Name: _____   Address: _____

_____

_____

How have you used this Study Text?
(Tick one box only)

☐ On its own (book only)

☐ On a BPP in-centre course _____

☐ On a BPP online course

☐ On a course with another college

☐ Other _____

Why did you decide to purchase this Study Text? *(Tick one box only)*

☐ Have used BPP Study Texts in the past

☐ Recommendation by friend/colleague

☐ Recommendation by a lecturer at college

☐ Saw information on BPP website

☐ Saw advertising

☐ Other _____

During the past six months do you recall seeing/receiving any of the following?
(Tick as many boxes as are relevant)

☐ Our advertisement in *ACCA Student Accountant*

☐ Our advertisement in *Pass*

☐ Our advertisement in *PQ*

☐ Our brochure with a letter through the post

☐ Our website www.bpp.com

Which (if any) aspects of our advertising do you find useful?
(Tick as many boxes as are relevant)

☐ Prices and publication dates of new editions

☐ Information on Study Text content

☐ Facility to order books

☐ None of the above

Which BPP products have you used?

Study Text	☑	Passcards	☐	Other	☐	
Kit	☐	i-Pass	☐			

Your ratings, comments and suggestions would be appreciated on the following areas.

	Very useful	Useful	Not useful
Introductory section	☐	☐	☐
Chapter introductions	☐	☐	☐
Key terms	☐	☐	☐
Quality of explanations	☐	☐	☐
Examples	☐	☐	☐
Exam focus points	☐	☐	☐
Questions and answers in each chapter	☐	☐	☐
Fast forwards and chapter roundups	☐	☐	☐
Quick quizzes	☐	☐	☐
Question Bank	☐	☐	☐
Answer Bank	☐	☐	☐
Index	☐	☐	☐

Overall opinion of this Study Text.	Excellent ☐	Good ☐	Adequate ☐	Poor ☐

Do you intend to continue using BPP products?   Yes ☐   No ☐

On the reverse of this page is space for you to write your comments about our Study Text. We welcome your feedback.

The BPP Learning Media author of this edition can be emailed at: accaqueries@bpp.com

TELL US WHAT YOU THINK

Please note any further comments and suggestions/errors below. For example, was the text accurate, readable, concise, user-friendly and comprehensive?